THE OXFORD HANDBOOK OF

CAPITALISM

THE OXFORD HANDBOOK OF

CAPITALISM

Edited by

DENNIS C. MUELLER

OXFORD
UNIVERSITY PRESS

OXFORD
UNIVERSITY PRESS

Oxford University Press, Inc., publishes works that further
Oxford University's objective of excellence
in research, scholarship, and education.

Oxford New York
Auckland Cape Town Dar es Salaam Hong Kong Karachi
Kuala Lumpur Madrid Melbourne Mexico City Nairobi
New Delhi Shanghai Taipei Toronto

With offices in
Argentina Austria Brazil Chile Czech Republic France Greece
Guatemala Hungary Italy Japan Poland Portugal Singapore
South Korea Switzerland Thailand Turkey Ukraine Vietnam

Published by Oxford University Press, Inc.
198 Madison Avenue, New York, New York 10016
www.oup.com

Library of Congress Cataloging-in-Publication Data

The Oxford handbook of capitalism/edited by Dennis C. Mueller.
p. cm.
Includes bibliographical references and index.
ISBN 978-0-19-539117-6 (cloth :alk. paper)
1. Capitalism—Handbooks, manuals, etc. I. Mueller, Dennis C.
II. Title: Handbook of capitalism.
HB501.O97 2012
330.12'2—dc23
2011034409

1 3 5 7 9 8 6 4 2

Printed in the United States of America
on acid-free paper

Contents

Preface

This handbook has three objectives: (1) to describe the advantages of capitalist sytems, (2) to discuss some of their disadvantages, and (3) to describe some of the differences in capitalist systems in different countries. In putting this volume together, I have been fortunate in being able to work with a great group of scholars.

The original outline included two additional chapters: one discussing market competition, and a second describing capitalist institutions in Europe. Unfortunately, these chapters did not materialize. Because the first of these would have focused on the positive side of capitalism, its absence makes the volume seem a bit more critical of capitalist institutions than was originally intended. This bias would have been even greater had Thorsten Beck not offered to write a second chapter on financial markets. Despite the two missing chapters, I think the diligent reader will come away with a rather complete picture of capitalism's pluses and minuses.

In putting this volume together, I have been greatly aided by Heide Wurm, who has edited the essays and made sure that they are properly formatted. I thank her for all of her efforts.

Contributors

Dennis C. Mueller is Professor of Economics, Emeritus, at the University of Vienna. Before coming to Vienna, he was at the University of Maryland, College Park. His research interests are industrial economic, public choice, and constitutional political economy.

William J. Baumol is Harold Price Professor of Entrepreneurship and Academic Director of the Berkley Center for Entrepreneurship and Innovation at New York University and Senior Economist and Professor Emeritus at Princeton University.

Thorsten Beck is Professor of Economics at Tilburg University and Chairman of the European Banking Center, as well as a CEPR fellow. Before joining Tilburg University and the CenTER, he worked at the Development Research Group of the World Bank.

John C. Coffee Jr. is Adolf A. Berle Professor at the Columbia University Law School, and Director of its Center on Corporate Governance. He is a Fellow at the American Academy of Arts and Sciences.

Martin J. Conyon is Professor of Corporate Governance and Finance at Lancaster University and Senior Fellow and Lecturer at the Wharton School, University of Pennsylvania.

Keith Cowling is Professor Emeritus at the University of Warwick. His research interests are in industrial economics, especially the deficiencies of monopoly capitalism, economics and democracy, industrial policy, and corporate governance and the public interest.

Jeffry A. Frieden is Professor in the Department of Government at Harvard University. His research focus is on the politics of international monetary and financial relations.

Victor P. Goldberg is Jerome L. Greene Professor of Transactional Law at Columbia Law School. His areas of research are law and economics, antitrust, regulation, and contracts.

Tilman Klumpp is Assistant Professor in the Economics Department at Emory University. His research fields are microeconomics, applied game theory, public economics, political economics, economics of discrimination, and industrial organization.

Robert E. Litan is Vice President of Research and Policy at the Kauffmann Foundation.

Burton G. Malkiel is Chemical Bank Chairman's Professor of Economics Emeritus and Senior Economist at Princeton University.

Randall Morck is Jarislowsky Distinguished Professor of Finance and University Professor at the School of Business at the University of Alberta. His research interests are corporate finance, economic development, and political economy.

Richard R. Nelson is George Blumenthal Professor Emeritus of International and Public Affairs, Business, and Law at Columbia University. His research has concentrated on the processes of long-run economic change, with particular emphasis on technological advances and the evolution of economic institutions.

Hiroyuki Odagiri is Professor at Seijo University and Professor Emeritus at Hitotsubashi University. His research interests are theory of the firm, industrial organization, and economic studies of innovation.

Edmund S. Phelps is McVickar Professor of Political Economy at Columbia University and Director of the Columbia Center on Capitalism and Society. He was the winner of the 2006 Nobel Prize in Economics.

Mark J. Roe is David Berg Professor of Law at Harvard Law School. His research interests are corporate bankruptcy and reorganization, corporate finance, and corporate law. He is a fellow of the American Academy of Arts and Sciences.

Paul H. Rubin is Samuel Candler Dobbs Professor of Economics at Emory University. His main area of research is law and economics.

F. M. Scherer is Aetna Professor Emeritus at the John F. Kennedy School of Government, Harvard University. His research specialties are industrial economics and the economics of technological change.

Carl J. Schramm is President and CEO at the Kauffmann Foundation.

David J. Teece holds the Thomas W. Tusher chair in Global Business and is Director at the Center for Global Strategy and Governance at Haas School of Business, University of California, Berkeley.

Philip R. Tomlinson is Lecturer in Economics in the School of Management at the University of Bath. His research interests and publications lie predominantly in the area of industrial development and political economy. He is a member of the European Union Network for Industrial Policy.

Bernard Yeung is Stephen Riady Distinguished Professor and Dean at NUS Business School, National University of Singapore.

INTRODUCTION: THE GOOD, THE BAD, AND THE UGLY

DENNIS C. MUELLER

I have chosen the title of Sergio Leone's classic spaghetti Western as the subtitle for this introductory essay because it nicely captures the range of views of capitalism contained in this volume. One might expect that a *Handbook of Capitalism* would focus only on its merits—why describe at length a set of institutions that is essentially bad? This volume does contain several chapters that highlight the positive side of capitalism. Most (if not all) contributors to this volume probably believe, as I do, that capitalism's virtues greatly outweigh its faults. The high standards of living observed in Europe, North America, and other highly developed parts of the world would be impossible without exploiting the great potential of capitalistic production. But there is a darker side to capitalism, and this volume contains several contributions that explore some of the negative consequences or, perhaps better, *side effects* of capitalism.

Although it is customary to speak of "capitalism" as if it were a well-defined set of institutions that either exists or does not exist in a given country at a particular point in time, capitalistic institutions actually come in many varieties and have evolved in different ways in different countries. Chapters by Frieden, Beck, Roe, Coffee, and Odagiri describe the great variety of capitalistic systems that exist and how they evolved. I briefly describe the essentials of capitalism in the next section. I then proceed to take up its good, bad, and ugly characteristics. Some conclusions are drawn in the final section.[1]

What Is Capitalism?

The defining feature of capitalism is that the means of production—capitalistic production—are in the hands of private individuals and firms. Implicit in the notion of a capitalist system, however, is also the existence of a market economy—a "free market" economy. A planned, socialist economy could engage in capital-intensive production—as the Soviet Union did—and we would not think of it as a capitalist system. Even if the capital was nominally held by private parties, it would not be a true capitalist system if the state intervened to set prices, restrict the flow of finance, and so on. Indeed, when economists extol the virtues of capitalism, they typically dwell on the efficient allocation of resources that market competition is thought to produce, rather than the benefits from capitalist production as such. If traders are endowed with initial stocks of goods, Walrasian markets can produce Pareto optimal reallocations of these stocks. "Invisible hand" stories can be told without having to invoke capitalistic production.

The vast wealth of the rich countries of the world did not arise, however, because Walrasian markets efficiently reallocated existing stocks of goods. Starting around the time Adam Smith wrote *Wealth of Nations*, the Industrial Revolution began to enfold (see Frieden's chapter). The Industrial Revolution changed both the way goods were produced and the nature of the goods themselves. Production processes became more capital-intensive and this necessitated the development of institutions to accumulate and allocate capital. Building on the advances of the scientific revolution of the seventeenth and eighteenth centuries, entrepreneurs during the Industrial Revolution introduced new products and new production techniques. The innovations creating these new products and production techniques introduced great uncertainty into the capitalist production process and gave rise for the need for contracts and institutions to enforce them.

Contracts exist due to uncertainty. In a spot market transaction, say, the exchange of an apple for an orange, two traders will not bother to write a contract (I promise to give you my orange...), nor does it add insight into the nature of the transaction to say that an *implicit* contract exists. Each trader knows what he is giving up and what he gets in return. There is no uncertainty. However, when a transaction takes place over a longer period of time (I promise to buy a train carload of apples from you in one year), uncertainty enters into the transaction (the spot price of apples in one year), and the traders might well choose to write a contract specifying the terms of the transaction to ensure against unknown contingencies that may arise because of the long-run nature of the exchange, or to ensure against the opportunistic behavior of the other party in the transaction. If they do not write an explicit contract, there will still be some sort of implicit contract underlying the transaction. (I promise to buy a train carload of apples from you in one year at the spot market price at that time.) Thus, the uncertainty inherent in capitalistic production makes contracts an important institution underpinning the system (see chapter by Goldberg).

If an entrepreneur is going to invest time and money to develop a new product, she must know that she can sell it at a sufficiently high price to recoup her investment and earn a profit. In capitalist systems, this assurance is typically afforded through the grant of a patent or trademark—a form of *property right* to the new product. The product or the innovative ideas behind it belong to the entrepreneur, at least for a limited period. Property rights are thus a second, key institution underlying capitalism that help induce entrepreneurs to make the investments and take the risks needed for successful capitalist development (see chapter by Rubin and Klumpp).

As the scale of production expanded over the nineteenth century, the accumulated wealth of rich families no longer sufficed to finance all of the profitable large-scale investments that appeared. Alternative institutions were needed to accumulate savings and transfer them to the entrepreneurs who could profitably invest them. The rise of modern capitalism thus brought with it the rise of large banks, and the development of organized stock and bond markets. The role of financial institutions in capitalist systems is discussed by Thorsten Beck.

As the Industrial Revolution unfolded, the scale of production increased, and new organizational structures had to be created. The large corporation began to emerge. Although not a logical necessity for a capitalist system, large corporations have become a salient feature in virtually every rich, developed capitalist country. Indeed, so great is the role played by large corporations in modern capitalist systems, it is more revealing to refer to them as *corporate capitalism* instead of just *capitalism*.

The modern corporation represents a kind of economy within an economy with its own internal capital market, internal labor market, and system of incentives to induce good performance. To understand how capitalism works today, one must understand the internal workings of the large corporation (see chapter by Teece).

Although large corporations exist in all capitalist economies today, there are important differences in ownership and control structures across countries. In some countries, founding families continue to control companies decades or even centuries after their creation. In other countries, control lies mainly with professional managers, and ownership is in the hands of dispersed individual and institutional shareholders (see discussion in chapters by Coffee and Odagiri). An ongoing debate exists in the profession to try to account for the conspicuous differences in capitalist systems across the world. Are these differences due to differences in the politics and ideologies of different countries, differences in legal institutions, or some other idiosyncratic events specific to a particular country? The chapters by Frieden, Beck, Roe, Coffee, and Odagiri describe and account for these differences.

Thus, the answer to the question posed in the title of this section—what is capitalism?—is that it is not a single institution but a set of institutions—private ownership of the means of production, competitive product and factor markets, large banks and financial markets, contracts, property rights and judicial institutions to enforce them, and large corporations. Although all capitalist systems have these institutions in common, there are also many important differences across countries in the forms these institutions take and how they are combined.

The Good

Since the agricultural revolution during the Neolithic Age some 10,000 years ago, nearly all societies have consisted of small, relatively well-off elites ruling and often exploiting the rest of society, whose members toiled long hours to produce just enough to survive. For the first time in history, today countries in the rich, capitalist countries of the West do not confront the problem of people lacking food and dying too young but of being overweight and living too long.

In the eighteenth century it took several months to cross the Atlantic Ocean on a trip fraught with danger. At the beginning of the twentieth century, it still took the better part of a week to cross the Atlantic with the possibility of a collision with an iceberg still creating some risk. Today, the trip takes a matter of hours and involves almost no risk. Indeed, a trip to the moon takes less time than a transatlantic crossing a century ago, and by the end of the twenty-first century, private citizens are likely to find a trip to the moon about as arduous as a transatlantic flight is today. For those disinclined to fly, the Internet provides instant face-to-face communication between Buffalo and Berlin.

The growth in incomes afforded by capitalism has made it possible for all citizens to acquire an education, not just a small elite. With mass education, rule by the masses becomes possible. The term "the West" today conjures up the image of both capitalism and democracy.

The term "democracy," in turn, carries with it the idea of individual freedom. Individual freedom requires more, however, than just the absence of slavery. An individual who must work twelve hours a day, seven days a week just to earn enough to survive cannot be said to be truly free. The rising incomes produced by capitalism have enabled work weeks to be shortened and vacations lengthened. The automobile, airplane, and mass transit have reduced transportation costs. Home appliances have freed people from the drudgery of housework. Most important for women, the invention of the birth control pill made family planning a practical reality and freed them to acquire educations and pursue careers. Individuals have never had as much freedom to choose their careers and lifestyles as they have today in capitalist countries. If one seeks proof for this, one need only look at the plight of individuals in the many countries of Africa, Asia, and South America where capitalism does not exist or exists in only a rudimentary, state-controlled form. Or one can look at the plight of individuals in former members of the Soviet Union, which are technically no longer communist but also are not truly free and capitalistic.

At the heart of any successful capitalist system are free and competitive markets. If one sought a single explanation for why countries that were once part of the Soviet Union continue to perform poorly after communism's official demise, it is because their authoritarian governments continue to interfere with the workings of market institutions. Much research in the laboratory and real-world markets demonstrates that they do function, for the most part, as our textbooks say they do.

Adam Smith did not exaggerate. The long queues of people waiting to buy shoddy products so often observed in communist countries do not appear when markets are allowed to function freely.

Capitalism's virtues are not restricted to achieving a Pareto optimal allocation of an initial stock of apples and oranges, however. Capitalism's triumph over Soviet-style socialism was not simply because capitalist economies got the prices right. Western capitalism triumphed because it was vastly superior to Soviet-style social planning in producing new and superior products and production techniques. The dramatically higher standards of living achieved in Western capitalist countries arose because of the steady increases in productivity that brought prices down over time and the steady stream of new products reaching the market that expanded consumers' range of choices. The former Soviet Union countries continue to lag the West because they have failed to establish secure property rights and the other institutions of capitalism that give would-be entrepreneurs incentives to innovate.

Once we recognize the importance of innovations for the success of capitalism, we see that it is not Adam Smith's account of the wealth of a nation but Joseph Schumpeter's that explains the great increase in living standards over the last two centuries in the West. Competition remains at the heart of a capitalist system, but it is competition from the new product, the new production technique, and the new organizational structure that drives economic progress and growth (see chapters by Scherer and Baumol, Litan, and Schramm). To understand how capitalism functions, and why it produces the increases in wealth we associate with it, it must be viewed as a dynamic process. Changes in prices can lead to Pareto improvements as consumers and producers move toward the production possibilities' frontier, but shifts in the frontier brought about by innovations have the greatest impacts on individual well-being.

The Bad

The most obvious negative feature of capitalism is that it can produce private monopolies that restrict output and thereby harm consumers. The chapter by Cowling and Tomlinson describes the many possible adverse consequences of "monopoly capitalism." Thus, monopoly in a capitalist system can be seen as a double-edged sword. The lure of monopoly and the rents that accompany it are what drive individuals to become entrepreneurs and introduce the innovations from which we all benefit. Those who succeed to become monopolists, however, have the incentive to prolong their monopolies as long as possible to the detriment of social welfare. Without Schumpeter's perennial gale of creative destruction, capitalism can atrophy into the kind of "oligarchic capitalism" described by Baumol, Litan, and Schramm, where only an oligarchic elite benefits from capitalist production.

In addition to the static welfare losses produced by monopoly in the form of high prices and smaller than optimal outputs, there are the *dynamic* welfare losses that arise from the rent-seeking activities of monopolists and those who aspire to become monopolists. Without economic rents there cannot be rent seekers. The great success of entrepreneurs innovating and creating monopoly rents opens the door for others to attempt to seize those rents. For the individual who seeks to become rich, it is a matter of indifference if she does so by *creating* a large rent through the introduction of a new product or by *acquiring* an existing rent. As Baumol, Litan, and Schramm point out, patents are an important institution for protecting the monopoly rents generated by an innovation, and thereby provide entrepreneurs with incentives to innovate. But once granted, they produce additional incentives for the innovator's competitors to try to break or circumvent the patents. Thus, dominant firms that invest heavily in R&D, like Intel, Microsoft, Pfizer, and Merck, must employ armies of lawyers to protect the rents that their many patents generate, and their competitors match their expenditures with lawyer armies of their own. These rent-seeking outlays—vast as they are—generate little or no benefits for consumers.

A similar observation can be made with respect to advertising. Advertising the introduction of a new product increases social welfare, because the benefits from consuming the new product cannot be obtained if one does not know of its existence. Much advertising is of existing products, however, and is undertaken to protect the rents associated with a particular brand or to capture the rents of a rival's brand. No new consumer surplus is created, no social benefits are generated.

An innovative idea—a formula for a new drug, a blueprint for a new production technique—is essentially a piece of information. Patents give their holders property rights to these pieces of information. The peculiar properties of information give rise to all sorts of rent-seeking activities.

Jack Hirshleifer (1971), in an important and neglected article, pointed out that investments to acquire information had social value only when they lead to individual decisions that improve the allocation of resources. Launching satellites to gather weather information has social value if the information leads to better decisions by farmers as to when to plant and harvest crops. Gathering information about the extent of damage to this year's orange crop caused by an unexpected severe frost might be highly profitable to someone wishing to speculate on orange futures before the extent of damage became widely known, but it would have no impact on the size of this year's harvest and little or no social value.

Some 95 percent of the shares traded on the New York Stock Exchange are not new issues. The funds spent buying them do not flow into new investment, but go to the previous owners of the shares. Large gains from trading can be made from knowing which share prices are likely to rise or fall, and large sums are invested generating and acquiring information to predict price movements. Although this information may make the capital market somewhat more efficient and lower corporate costs of capital a bit, or improve the market for corporate control, the bulk of it simply results in private gains to those who have good information, which are matched by the private losses to those with poor information. Much of the information gathering surrounding financial markets is a form of rent seeking. This fact helps explain the empirical results discussed by Beck in his chapter on financial institutions. In poor or middle-income countries large financial markets facilitate the flow of funds to firms making investments and innovations, thereby promoting economic growth. The link between the size of the financial sector and economic growth weakens—or even reverses—once countries become rich and reach the technological frontier. Now rent seeking in financial markets can lead to great private gains but have little impact on economic growth. Growth is actually harmed to the extent that talented risk takers are drawn into the financial sector to engage in rent transfers, rather than starting businesses and engaging in rent creation.

When Joseph Schumpeter (1934, pp. 93–94) described the goals of the entrepreneur in his classic treatise on economic development, he depicted the entrepreneur as an empire builder first and foremost. At the time when he wrote—the beginning of the twentieth century—the only way that an entrepreneur could command an empire was to build one.[2] This was just as true in the United States, where the Carnegies and Rockefellers were building empires, as it was in Europe, where Schumpeter observed the Krupps and Thyssens building empires. A young man wishing to command an empire today has two options: he can follow the paths of Carnegie and Krupp and build a corporate empire from scratch, or he can try to work his way to the top of one of the many existing corporate empires in the United States, Europe, and the other developed countries of the world. The risks involved in building an empire are far greater than those in trying to mount an existing one—even if one does not make it all the way to the top, one can expect a comfortable income—and thus most people who wish to command an empire today choose to join existing corporate empires rather than to create new ones.

If we define a rent as the difference between a person's income with his present employer and his opportunity costs with a different employer, then LeBron James's $40 million salary with the Cleveland Cavaliers in 2009 probably contained no rents, as many NBA teams would match this figure to acquire his talents. If, however, we define a rent as the difference between a person's income in his present occupation and his opportunity costs in a different occupation, then most of the $40 million salary is an economic rent. Thousands (if not millions) of young boys in the United States spend countless hours playing basketball in the hopes of developing the talents that would make them the next LeBron James. Only a tiny fraction will get to play professional basketball, only one or two will have the success of James. The hours spent playing basketball by those who do not succeed—treated as an investment—go wasted. Society and the boys themselves would be much better off if they had spent the time studying algebra and chemistry.

Something similar happens in the world of business. At the top of the *Forbes* list of CEO incomes in 2009 was Oracle's Lawrence J. Ellison, with a total compensation of $557 million. Although Ellison would no doubt have earned a sizable income if he had chosen another profession—say, law or medicine—much of his more than half billion dollar income must be considered an economic rent from being a business manager. As with basketball, thousands if not millions of young men, and in this case also women, in the United States spend countless hours getting MBAs and trying to work their way up corporate ladders in the hopes of becoming the next Ellison.

If the procedures corporations use to select and promote their personnel function well, the most talented managers will reach the tops of the most important companies. The performance of these companies is no doubt better than it would be if a less competitive process with smaller rewards for success existed, just as the quality of basketball in the NBA is undoubtedly better with top salaries of $40 million than it would be with top salaries of $4 million. But the social gains are unlikely to exceed the rent-seeking costs. The United States would almost certainly be better off if more young people went to work for small, new businesses or started their own businesses, rather than entering large companies in the hopes of rising to the top.

Monopoly and the rents it creates are often referred to as *market imperfections* in economic textbooks. Such market imperfections can be regarded as part of a much wider class of problems in market economies that fall under the heading of *market failures*. Although monopolies are *intended* consequences of individual actions, many other market failures like negative externalities are unintended consequences of the pursuit of profit. Richard Nelson's chapter makes clear that these "side effects" of the market process cannot be ignored when considering the performance of capitalist systems.

The Ugly

Rents are an inevitable part of capitalistic production in a world in which resource movements are not costless and instantaneous, that is to say, in the real world. *Rent seeking*, therefore, is a central feature of every capitalist system, and the more successful the system is at generating rents, the more resources are wasted in rent-seeking activities. Although this seems quite obvious today, some forty years ago the concept of rent seeking was unknown.[3] Even today, although all economists know what rent seeking is, often when they discuss broad issues, like the virtues of capitalism, they ignore rent seeking and the costs that come with it.

The same can be said of the principal agent problem. Principal agent problems abound (see the chapter by Morck and Yeung). We enter into one every time we go to a dentist, have our car repaired, or enter a taxi. The greater the division of labor, the more principal agent problems we confront. Yet despite their ubiquity, the term "principal agent problem," like rent seeking, is a scant forty years old.[4] The "problem," however, was recognized much earlier. The *separation of ownership from control* in U.S. corporations was described and documented by Berle and Means nearly eighty years ago in their classic *Modern Corporation and Private Property* (1932, 1968). In this book, Berle and Means identified the most serious of all principal agent problems—at least in capitalist systems like the United States where shareholdings are widely dispersed—that between the stockholders as principals, who want to have their wealth maximized, and their agent-managers, who have their own goals to pursue.

Despite the attention that the Berle and Means book received, the implications of the existence of this form of principal agent problem in large corporations did not affect the way economists analyzed corporate and market behavior for many years after the book's publication. Indeed, at a conference held at the University of Chicago ostensibly to commemorate the fiftieth anniversary of the book's publication, most participants presented papers claiming that the problem did not exist or was of little importance.[5] How can one explain such neglect of a problem that today seems so obvious and important? Perhaps the answer lies with the fact that Berle and Means were "outsiders" to the economic profession. Indeed, Berle was not even an economist, and Means worked in the Roosevelt administration at first. Means even had the audacity in 1935 to publish a paper that attempted to explain the "stickiness" of prices in the downward direction during the Great Depression by claiming that managers of large corporations did not set prices by equating marginal revenue to marginal cost.

Today, it is difficult to ignore the existence of a major principal agent problem between managers and shareholders in large, dispersed ownership corporations—although a surprising number of economists still do. What is it that managers pursue with the great amount of discretion that the separation of ownership and control gives them? To this question, economists have given many answers. Perhaps the most obvious goal of all, at least to an economist, is money. Managers use their freedom to pursue their own interests by increasing their wealth at the shareholders' expense. Berle and Means were concerned that managers would simply steal or embezzle money from the shareholders. Many examples of this happening came to light during the first few years of the Great Depression, and the recent examples of Enron and WorldCom reveal that some managers still do succumb to this temptation. The more frequent accusation, however, is that managers greatly overpay themselves. Someone who earned the minimum hourly wage of $7.25 in 2009 and worked forty hours a week for fifty-two weeks would have earned $15,080. If Lawrence J. Ellison put in the same number of hours of work, he earned more than this minimum-wage worker in the first three minutes and sixteen seconds that he worked. Is Ellison's marginal product really that much higher than the minimum-wage worker's?

As Conyon describes in his chapter, the literature offers two sets of answers to this question. One group of scholars emphasizes the principal agent problem in large corporations and claims that this effectively allows managers to select their own compensation packages. It is thus unsurprising that these compensation packages seem overly generous.

The other stream of the managerial compensation literature sees the high salaries of managers as a consequence of intense compensation for managerial talent. Although managerial compensation has grown rapidly over the past quarter century, so have the sales and market values of companies. The growth in managerial compensation has simply kept pace with the growth in firm valuations.

These are two, quite divergent views of what has been happening with respect to managerial compensation. Over one fact, both sides agree, however—the single best predictor of managerial compensation is some measure of company size. Company size is a far better predictor of managerial compensation than measures of company performance like profitability and returns to shareholders that one might think should be closely linked to managerial compensation.

The close association between company size and managerial compensation does not dispose of the principal agent problem as far as managerial compensation is concerned, however. Early contributions to the managerial discretion literature by Baumol (1959, 1967) and Marris (1964) claimed that it was size or growth in size that managers maximized, not profits or shareholders' wealth. One justification for this claim was the close association between size and compensation.[6]

A manager who wishes her firm to grow fast has several options. One is to invest heavily in R&D, innovate, and enjoy the rapid growth that innovations often generate. Microsoft might be regarded as a classic example of such a Schumpeterian firm. After twenty years it was the dominant firm in computer software and its founder, Bill Gates, was the richest man in the world. Such growth through innovation takes time, however, and can carry enormous risks. A quicker and surer path to growth is through mergers. General Electric did not attain its current size merely by exploiting the potential in Edison's light bulb invention. Most *Fortune* 500 companies owe a considerable fraction of their size to mergers.

Whether managers choose to grow internally by innovating or through mergers should be a matter of societal indifference, if both strategies generate wealth. On this question the merger literature—like the managerial compensation literature—divides into two streams, and the streams are nearly parallel in their assumptions and conclusions (see my chapter). One stream in the merger literature assumes that managers maximize shareholder wealth, markets work efficiently, including "the market for corporate control," and thus that mergers generate wealth and improve the allocation of resources. The other assumes the existence of agency problems, that managers seek to advance their own personal welfare, and that they may undertake mergers that destroy shareholder wealth.

The assumption that managers maximize shareholder wealth when they undertake mergers is difficult to reconcile with the overwhelming evidence that the average merger generates little or no gains to the acquiring companies' shareholders at the merger announcements and large and significant losses after two to three years. Some mergers definitely do benefit the shareholders of acquiring companies and improve the allocation of resources, but this cannot be said for the average merger.

The preponderance of mergers in the United States and United Kingdom have taken place during stock market booms. This is an empirical fact that researchers on both sides of the merger issue agree on. It is also an empirical regularity that is difficult to reconcile with many theories of mergers that assume wealth-creating motives. Wealth-creating opportunities, like achieving economies of scale and scope, should be attractive even when stock prices are behaving normally. An agency explanation for the link between share prices and merger activity would be that managers prefer to announce mergers that are likely to destroy shareholder wealth at times when optimism in the stock market is high. In such periods of "irrational exuberance," when shareholders are looking for reasons to buy shares, announcements of mergers, with accompanying predictions of economies of scale and scope and undefined synergies, are more likely to be greeted favorably by investors than when made in periods of more sober stock market sentiment. This agency explanation for the link between share prices and merger activity also helps account for the more favorable performance of acquirers' share prices around merger announcements than in the years that follow.

Thus, to understand mergers one must also understand stock market booms. As Malkiel's chapter shows, asset bubbles existed even before the Industrial Revolution. Perennial gales of destruction of asset values are another common feature of the economic landscape, along with Schumpeter's gales produced by innovative activity. Although the assets subject to bubbles have varied widely from tulip bulbs in Holland to condominiums in Japan, the psychology underlying bubbles seems to be remarkably the same. Prices of an asset begin to rise producing an expectation that they will rise further. This expectation proves to be self-fulfilling. The gains made by early speculators feed their optimism and lead them to buy still more of the inflating assets. Prices continue to rise until they are far above their historical values and above any possible calculation of true, underlying economic value. As they rise higher and higher, more and more traders realize that the bubble is unsustainable. Once these traders begin to sell, prices begin to fall and the bubble breaks.

Each of the bubbles in share prices in the United States dating back to the end of the nineteenth century has been accompanied by a merger wave. The stock market boom and merger wave of the late 1920s was followed by a "lost decade"—the Great Depression. The stock market boom and merger wave of the late 1960s was followed by another lost decade, and at the time of this writing (2010), the decade of buoyant share prices and surging merger activity that began in the mid-1990s seems likely to be followed by yet another lost decade. The recurring asset bubbles and merger waves that seem a part of capitalism inflict heavy economic losses on society.

Conclusions

At the end of the Korean War, both North and South Korea were poor countries with devastated economies. South Korea chose to develop a capitalist system, and North Korea followed the path of communism. Today, South Korea has a GDP per capita of over $27,000, comparable to that of New Zealand, and North Korea remains mired in poverty, scarcely able to feed its population.[7] A more vivid example of the advantages of capitalism and freedom extolled by Friedman (1962) is difficult to find.

I have devoted more space in this introduction to problems associated with capitalism than to its virtues because the advantages of capitalism seem so obvious, as the two Koreas demonstrate. Even China, one of the last surviving communist countries, has relied heavily on capitalist institutions to foster its "economic miracle" over the past two decades.

Capitalism is at its best when individual self-interest is channeled into the production of goods and services and innovative activity. To undertake the huge risks that surround the innovation process, entrepreneurs must possess great optimism about their ability to make decisions. Although many entrepreneurs fail, the innovations generated by the few who succeed lead to the great advances in wealth that we associate with the developed, capitalist countries of the world. Once the pioneers show the way, the pursuit of wealth leads imitators to follow, generating Schumpeter's gale of creative destruction, and it in turn leads to falling prices and still more benefits to consumers.

The seamy side of capitalism is largely the reverse of its attractive side. The creation of rents through the introduction of new products and production processes is the driving force behind capitalist development, but once they are created they become the target of rent seekers who devote their efforts to capturing existing rents rather than creating new ones. Asset bubbles are fed by the great optimism of traders in their ability to make decisions. In their pursuit of growth, managers exploit the (over)optimism in equity markets during stock market booms to undertake wealth-destroying acquisitions. Indeed, so contagious is optimism during stock market booms that the managers making acquisitions may overestimate their ability to make decisions and actually believe their acquisitions will create wealth.[8] Thus, the desire to create empires, the pursuit of great wealth, and the optimism needed to fuel entrepreneurship and innovation, when channeled into rent seeking, growth through acquisitions, and asset speculation, can undermine the efficiency of a capitalist system.

The policy implications are obvious—channel the self-interest of potential entrepreneurs, managers, investors, and speculators into creating wealth rather than transferring or destroying it. The exact form such policies should take, however, is far from obvious. Should original patents be better protected from challenges by followers, or should patents be done away with? Should the state intervene in setting managerial salaries? While markets can fail in many ways, the public choice literature is replete with examples of state failures. Some of the essays in this volume offer constructive suggestions for how to improve the functioning of capitalist systems, but there are no silver bullets in this area. Fortunately, the wealth generated by the productive side of capitalism generally is great enough to sustain the wealth destruction that transpires on its seamy side.

Notes

1. Edmund Phelps's chapter arrived after I had completed a first draft of this introduction. There are some similarities in organization and content between our work, but the differences are great enough that I decided to leave this introduction largely as it was.
2. The German edition of *The Theory of Economic Development* first appeared in 1911. The 1934 date in the text is for the English translation.
3. Gordon Tullock (1967) was the first to discuss rent-seeking activities. The term "rent seeking" was first used by Anne Krueger (1974).
4. To my knowledge, Ross (1973) introduced the term.
5. See the special issue of the *Journal of Law and Economics* (vol. 26, June 1983) devoted to the conference. Douglass North's contribution was a notable exception to the pattern described in the text.
6. See evidence surveyed by Marris (1964, chapter 2).
7. The CIA estimates North Korea's GDP per capita to be $1,800. CIA, *The World Factbook,* January 28, 2010.
8. To explain why acquiring shareholders lose as a result of mergers, Roll (1986) advanced the hypothesis that acquiring companies' managers often suffer from hubris. They know that the average merger is unsuccessful but believe that they are better than the average manager. Although Roll did not put forward his hypothesis as an explanation for merger waves, the kind of hubris he describes is particularly likely to grip managers during stock market booms, when their companies' share prices are rising rapidly.

References

Baumol, William J. *Business Behavior, Value and Growth.* 1959; New York: Macmillan, 1967.

Berle, Adolf A., and Gardiner C. Means. *The Modern Corporation and Private Property.* New York: Commerce Clearing House, 1932; rev. ed., New York: Harcourt, Brace, Jovanovich, 1968.

Friedman, Milton. *Capitalism and Freedom.* Chicago: University of Chiago Press, 1962.

Hirshleifer, Jack. "The Private and Social Value of Information and the Reward to Incentive Activity." *American Economic Review* 61 (Sept. 1971): 561–574.

Krueger, Anne O. "The Political Economy of the Rent-Seeking Society." *American Economic Review* 64 (June 1974): 291–303; reprinted in *Toward a Theory of the Rent-Seeking Society,* ed. James M. Buchanan, Robert D. Tollison, and Gordon Tullock, 51–70. College Station: Texas A&M Press, 1980.

Marris, Robin. *The Economic Theory of Managerial Capitalism.* Glencoe, Ill.: Free Press, 1964.

North, Douglass C. "'The Literature of Economics: The Case of Berle and Means.' Comment on Stigler and Friedland." *Journal of Law and Economics* 26 (June 1983): 269–271.

Roll, Richard. "The Hubris Hypothesis of Corporate Takeovers." *Journal of Business* 59 (April 1986): 197–216.

Ross, Stephen A. "The Economic Theory of Agency: The Principal's Problem." *American Economic Review* 63 (May 1973): 134–139.

Schumpeter, Joseph A. *The Theory of Economic Development*. 1911; Cambridge, Mass.: Harvard University Press, 1934.
Tullock, Gordon. "The Welfare Costs of Tariffs, Monopolies and Theft." *Western Economic Journal* 5 (June 1967): 224–32; reprinted in *Toward a Theory of the Rent-Seeking Society*, ed. James M. Buchanan, Robert D. Tollison, and Gordon Tullock, 39–50. College Station: Texas A&M Press, 1980.

PART I

ORIGINS

CHAPTER 1

THE MODERN CAPITALIST WORLD ECONOMY: A HISTORICAL OVERVIEW

JEFFRY A. FRIEDEN

Capitalist economic activities are of very long standing—some would say they were present in proliferation during Roman times.[1] By the late medieval and early modern period, large areas of Western Europe had thriving, relatively free markets for labor and capital, both in the city and in the countryside. We can most fruitfully and confidently speak of the full flowering of modern capitalism once it became a truly international economic order. That epoch evolved over the course of the sixteenth, seventeenth, and eighteenth centuries, as capitalism expanded from a limited Western European base to affect much of the world, from the Americas to East Asia.

A Mercantilist World Economy

Market economies flourished in many parts of Europe during the high and late Middle Ages, most prominently in Italian commercial and manufacturing centers such as Genoa, Venice, and Tuscany. Although they relied heavily on long-distance trade, these islands of capitalism had little structural economic impact on the rest of the world. But after the 1450s, the Ottoman Empire's control of the Eastern Mediterranean drove Europeans out into the Atlantic, and eventually around the world, in search of trade routes. Western Europeans' recognition of the economic potential of the New World and of more consistent interaction with Africa and Asia opened a new era.

For nearly four centuries, from the mid-1400s to the mid-1800s, the rest of the world was drawn into an economic and political order dominated by European capitalism. This order was organized around the overseas colonial empires of the Atlantic powers: first Spain and Portugal, then the Netherlands, England, and France. This was the first true international economy, and it was controlled in a very particular manner by its European founders. The economic system they built has come to be known as mercantilism.

Mercantilist ordering principles defined the international capitalist economy for several hundred years. Although there was variation among the principal mercantilist powers, the system's main features were common to all. First and foremost, mercantilism depended on substantial government involvement in the economy. These were, after all, colonial systems, and military might underpinned the predominance of the colonial powers over their possessions. But that was not all. Mercantilist governments considered their economic policies to be part and parcel of broader national goals, especially in the continuing struggle for diplomatic and military supremacy. Mercantilism enriched the country and the Crown, which then used those riches to build up military force. "Wealth is power," wrote English philosopher Thomas Hobbes, "and power is wealth." One of his fellow mercantilist thinkers drew the connections: "Foreign trade produces riches, riches power, power preserves our trade and religion."[2]

The mercantilist economic order relied on systematic government intervention in the economy, particularly in international economic transactions. Although there was variation among countries and over time, core mercantilist goals and policies were similar. Mercantilist governments tried to stimulate demand for domestic manufactures and for such national commercial and financial services as shipping and trade. They did this, typically, by requiring their colonies to sell certain goods only to the mother country (the "metropole") and buy certain other goods only from the mother country. Restrictions on trade turned the terms of trade against the colonies: prices of colonial exports were depressed, while prices of colonial imports were elevated. This, of course, benefited metropolitan producers, who could purchase their inputs (raw materials, agricultural products) at artificially low prices and sell their output (manufactures) at artificially high prices. Virginia tobacco farmers had to sell their leaf to London, although Amsterdam would have paid more; they had to buy their cigars from London, although Amsterdam would have charged less. The rents created this way went to enrich the manufacturers and "merchant princes," whose alliance with the Crown characterized the mercantilist political economy.

Mercantilist governments also required many international economic transactions to be carried out by their preferred, national agents: shipping, insurance, finance, wholesale trade. In some cases, trade had to be channeled through certain favored ports. Like import and export restrictions, this provided rents to the privileged. The colonial governments also endeavored to discover and exploit precious metals. The Crown usually took (or taxed very heavily) the gold and silver discovered in the colonies. Mercantilist governments typically chartered monopolistic enterprises to which they delegated both economic and administrative functions in the colonies, such as the Hudson's Bay Company and the Dutch East India Company.

Mercantilist policies achieved several interrelated goals. They provided revenue for the government. This might come directly from precious metals and other forms of tribute or indirectly from the revenue provided by those enriched by the policy. This was one sense in which mercantilist economic policies supported the broader diplomatic and military goals of the government: they made available the wherewithal to sustain and increase national power. Mercantilist policies also aimed explicitly at encouraging early manufacturing, seen as central to modern economic and military advance.[3] And the restraints on trade and monopolistic charters cemented ties between the government and its powerful supporters in business.

The political economy of mercantilism was largely based on an implicit or explicit alliance between the government—the Crown, except in the Dutch Republic—on the one hand, and the merchants, manufacturers, and investors that carried out the bulk of economic interactions with the colonies on the other.[4] The character of this alliance varied from country to country. In the Netherlands, the mercantile classes effectively and directly controlled the state; in the other colonial powers, the government had interests of its own, which sometimes conflicted with those of its business allies. The Spanish Crown, for example, was particularly concerned with consolidating its control over the country, which was only fully freed of Muslim rule in 1492, and in which there were powerful regional noblemen. This made the Spanish Crown more insistent on centralizing control and revenue and less willing to encourage the rise of powerful private actors than many other mercantilist rulers.

Mercantilist policies benefited the favored metropolitan businesses, at the expense of the colonies (and consumers). To be sure, some colonial subjects valued membership in a powerful empire, especially inasmuch as the empire protected them from others. While many citizens of Great Britain's North American colonies chafed at mercantilist restrictions on their trade, many others appreciated the security British naval and military power provided.

The mercantilist era's main characteristics highlight enduring features of modern capitalist economies. The first is an ambivalent relationship with the world economy. To be sure, the leading colonial powers were heavily oriented toward engagement in the international economy and eager to take advantage of what the rest of the world economy had to offer. At the same time, mercantilist policies were highly nationalistic and strongly protected the home market and national producers from foreign competition. This tension, between the desire to take advantage of international economic opportunities, on the one hand, and the fear of harm from foreign competition, on the other, is a recurring theme in capitalist attitudes toward the world economy. The mercantilist powers dealt with the issue by aggressively expanding their access to foreign markets, but jealously guarding and protecting the markets they conquered within their colonial empires.

A second feature of the mercantilist experience was the tension between state and markets. In the mercantilist period, as at other times, market actors wanted economic freedom, and governments wanted the prosperity markets could provide. Indeed, markets were almost certainly much better developed and much freer in this era than they had been in the previous medieval centuries. At the same time, mercantilist governments were aggressive in their intervention in the economy. To some extent this reflected real or imagined demands of national security and military power, in an attempt to harness economic dynamism to national goals. To some extent it reflected the interests of powerful economic interest groups, which were enriched by state-enforced monopolies, state controls on trade, and the backing of their governments. The result was a mix of state intervention and market development—not always harmonious.

Indeed, these two dimensions have been at issue throughout the history of capitalism. The first is the international-national dimension: the conflicting desire for integration with and insulation from the world economy. The second is the state-market dimension: the conflicting desire for government involvement in markets and market freedom from government. Over time, both countries and the world in general have oscillated between periods of greater and lesser economic openness and between periods of greater and lesser government intervention in the economy.

Mercantilism reflected the economic and political realities of its era. Western European economies had advanced enough beyond those in the rest of the world, both in technology and in organization, that their predominance was largely unchallenged. Meanwhile, previously unimaginable overseas economic prospects had opened up, a whole world of resources and markets that could be tapped and, in most cases, controlled. This provided the incentive, to rulers and capitalists alike, to assert themselves wherever possible. At the same time as the mercantilist powers were subjugating vast areas to their colonial control, they engaged in continuing conflicts with one another for supremacy. This gave them powerful motivations to use their colonies to enhance their military might and to use their military might to amass more colonies. Domestically and internationally, at home and abroad, the mercantilist systems generally reflected a mutually rewarding partnership between rulers and capitalists, enriching both and drawing most of the world into their orbit.

The End of Mercantilism

A combination of political and economic developments began to erode the mercantilist system. Politically, one of the attractions of mercantilist policies had been their connection to the struggle for diplomatic supremacy: reserving access to colonies to the home country and restricting it to others served to help the government amass resources for military purposes and to deny resources to real or potential enemies. But in 1815, a British-led alliance defeated Napoleon at Waterloo and effectively ended three centuries of warfare among the Atlantic powers. With British maritime supremacy ensured, and the Continent largely stable, the military arguments for mercantile colonialism faded.

Domestic political trends also undermined the mercantilist system. Throughout Western Europe, autocratic dynastic rule came under challenge, largely from the rising business and middle classes. Although political reform was slow, and certainly did not result in anything we would recognize as democratic, it did loosen the exclusive grip on power of some previously favored groups. Among these were the monopolistic enterprises created and favored by mercantilist policy, whose preferential position was increasingly resented by more modern entrepreneurs in industry, trade, and finance. As the foreign policy arguments for mercantilism faded, so did the domestic political alliances underpinning it.

Economic trends also eroded the previous political economy. Most important was the rise of modern industry. Manufacturing in the earlier era, though certainly an advance over the medieval norm, was on a small scale, often based on cottage industry. Over the course of the eighteenth and early nineteenth centuries, manufacturing was fundamentally transformed, especially in Great Britain and some areas of Northern Europe. A flurry of technological innovations revolutionized production. Employers brought dozens, even hundreds of workers together in large factories to use new machinery, new energy sources, and new forms of organization. Power looms and mechanical spinners transformed the textile industry. Improvements in the use of water power, and eventually the development of steam power, made the machinery more powerful still. The Industrial Revolution and the rise of the modern factory system meant that the new industries could undercut competitors in virtually every market, which made mercantilist barriers to trade either irrelevant or harmful.

Great Britain led the way in gradually jettisoning mercantilism. As British military predominance was secured, both Crown and Parliament were less concerned about tight colonial control. Many in Britain had indeed, as far back as the American Revolution, begun to regard the cost of keeping the colonies as outweighing the benefits. As Parliament, increasingly representative of business and middle-class interests, imposed ever greater restrictions on royal prerogatives, it increasingly challenged the royally chartered monopolies.

As the British economy evolved, dissatisfaction with mercantile controls grew. British industrialists wanted to eliminate the country's trade barriers. Removing restrictions on imports would allow British producers access to cheaper inputs and would give British consumers access to cheaper imported food, which would allow factory owners to pay lower wages without reducing workers' standard of living. At the same time, industrialists believed that removing trade restrictions would increase world demand for British goods. For these reasons, Britain's manufacturing classes and regions developed an antipathy to mercantilism and a strong desire for free trade.

As the city of London became the world's financial center, it added its influence to that of other free-trade interests. Britain's international bankers had a powerful reason to open up the British market to foreigners: the foreigners were their customers. American or Argentine access to the thriving British market would make it easier for Americans and Argentines to service their debts to London. The industrial and financial interests mounted a concerted attack on what antimercantilist crusader Adam Smith called "the mean and malignant expedients of the mercantile system."[5] By the 1820s those "malignant" mercantilist expedients were under constant challenge.

The battle over mercantilism was joined especially over the Corn Laws, tariffs imposed during the Napoleonic Wars on imports of grain.[6] Industrialists and financiers opposed the agricultural tariffs, as did the urban middle and working classes, and were opposed by the country's powerful farmers. The free traders won after a protracted struggle. They might not have prevailed had there not been a major reform of British political institutions: a changed electoral system that reduced the power of farm constituencies and increased that of the cities and their middle-class residents. Even with the electoral reforms in place, the final votes in 1846 and 1847 were extremely close and tore the Conservative Party apart. A few years later, Parliament repealed the last vestiges of British mercantile controls on foreign trade.

The Classical Era: Free Trade and the Gold Standard

After Britain, the world's most important economy, discarded mercantilism, most of the other major economic powers followed suit. In 1860, France joined Great Britain in the Cobden-Chevalier Treaty, which freed trade between them and helped draw the rest of Europe in this direction. As the German states moved toward unification in 1871, they created a free trade area among themselves, then opened trade with the rest of the world. Many New World governments also liberalized trade, as did the remaining colonial possessions of the free-trading European powers. Mercantilism was dead, and integration into world markets was the order of the day.[7]

Over the course of the nineteenth century, much of the world opted for general openness to the international economy and for a reduced level of state involvement in the economy. Although mercantilism had been marked by a strong role for the government in both domestic and international economic affairs, the classical order that arose over the course of the 1800s saw a dramatic reduction in government involvement on both dimensions.

Technological change dramatically reduced the cost of international economic exchange, making an open economy that much more attractive. Over the course of the century telegraphs, telephones, steamships, and railroads replaced horses, carrier pigeons, couriers, and sails. The railroad fundamentally changed the speed and cost of carrying cargo over land. The steamship revolutionized ocean-going shipping, reducing the Atlantic crossing from over a month in 1816 to less than a week in 1896.

The new technologies took hold and diffused very rapidly, even in developing regions. In 1870, Latin America, Russia, Canada, Australia, South Africa, and India *combined* had barely as much railroad mileage as Great Britain. By 1913, these regions had ten times Britain's railroad mileage. Argentina alone went from a few hundred miles of rail in 1870 to a system more extensive than Britain's.[8] On the seas, there was a twentyfold increase in the world's shipping capacity during the nineteenth century.[9]

These advances reduced the cost of land transportation by more than four-fifths and of sea-going transport by more than two-thirds. Europe flooded the world with its manufactures and was in turn flooded with farm products and raw materials from the prairies and the pampas, the Amazon and Australia. Over the course of the 1800s, the trade of the advanced countries grew twice to three times as fast as their economies; by the end of the century, trade was seven or eight times as large a share of the world's economy as it had been at the beginning of the century.[10]

International investment also soared. As telegraphy allowed information to be transmitted instantaneously from any reasonably developed area to investment houses and traders in London, Paris, and Berlin, new economic opportunities attracted the interests of European savers like never before. Foreign capital flooded into rapidly growing regions in the New World, Australia, Russia, and elsewhere. By the early 1900s, foreign investments, largely in bonds and stocks, accounted for about one-third of the savings of the United Kingdom, one-quarter of France, and one-tenth of Germany.[11] This was also an era of virtually free international immigration, at least for Europeans. Some fifty million Europeans moved abroad, along with another fifty million Asians. Markets for goods, capital, and labor were more tightly linked than they had ever been.

Perhaps the most striking, and most powerful, organizing principle of global capitalism during the nineteenth century was the gold standard. After centuries of stable bimetallism, in the 1870s governments were faced with a choice. New silver discoveries drove the price of silver down and made the existing rate of exchange between the two metals unstable, so governments had to either change the rate or choose between gold and silver. Meanwhile, as international trade and investment grew, gold—the traditional international medium of exchange—became more attractive than domestic silver. Finally, Great Britain had been on gold since 1717, and its status as the global market leader attracted other countries to use the same system. In the 1870s most major industrial countries joined the gold standard, with more countries joining all the time. By the early 1900s, the only two countries of economic importance not on gold were China and Persia.

When a country's government went "on gold," it promised to exchange its currency for gold at a preestablished rate. This provided an important degree of predictability for world trade, lending, investment, migration, and payments. The impact on trade was substantial; being on gold in this period is variously estimated to have raised trade between two countries by between 30 and 70 percent.[12] The gold standard was even more important for international finance than it was for trade. International financiers regarded being on gold as an obligation of well-behaved members of the classical world economy, a signal of a country's economic reliability.[13] Investors had good reasons to focus on government commitments to the gold standard. The balance of payments adjustment mechanism under the gold standard might require a government whose economy was running a payments deficit to reduce wages and spending to move back toward balance. To stay on gold, governments had to be able to privilege international ties over domestic demands, imposing austerity and wage cuts on unwilling populations if necessary. This made the gold standard a litmus test that international investors used to judge the financial reliability of national governments.[14] Membership in the gold club conferred a sort of blessing on its initiates, and gave participating countries access to an enormous pool of international savings.

Technological and policy change turned a world of closed colonial empires into an integrated global economy. The results were impressive by almost any standard. Transportation and communications improvements, along with policies to further economic integration, led to a significant convergence of prices.[15] This in turn created important opportunities for countries to gain access to world markets for goods and capital. As railroads, steamships, and eventually refrigeration brought grain and beef prices in Omaha and Buenos Aires up toward European levels, rural backwaters quickly became some of the most attractive places in the world to farm and invest.

Economic integration also led to convergence of levels of development, as many of the countries drawn into this new world economy grew very rapidly. Industrialization spread from its Northwestern European homeland to the rest of Europe and much of the world. Great Britain was overtaken: in 1870, British iron and steel production was greater than that of Germany and the United States combined, while by 1913 Germany and the United States combined outproduced the United Kingdom roughly six to one. This was true also of living standards: per capita incomes in the United States, Australia, and New Zealand were higher than in the United Kingdom, and Argentina and Canada were gaining fast.[16] Although there were periodic panics and recessions, the 100 years from 1815 to 1914 were marked by a general macroeconomic stability that matched the general stability of diplomatic affairs—which is why the era is often called the Hundred Years' Peace or the *Pax Britannica*.

Whatever its economic achievements, there were plenty of evils in the classical era. The end of mercantilism was associated with a decline of the early colonial empires, especially in the New World. But in the 1880s, the major powers began accumulating new colonial possessions. Europe's colonialists divided most of Africa, Southeast Asia, and East Asia among themselves (and Japan); the United

States joined the fray in the Pacific and the Caribbean. Many of the new empires were run on lines reminiscent of mercantilism, giving preferential treatment to the colonial power's economic interests, although the monopolistic features were typically more muted. Some colonies were afforded reasonable treatment; but some were mercilessly exploited. The horrific abuses of Belgium's King Leopold in the Congo were particularly egregious (Hochschild 1998). In part as a result, many parts of the world—especially in Africa and Asia—stagnated or declined economically even during the best of times.

The classical economic order was also no political idyll. Leaving colonialism aside, political rights were severely limited even in the industrial world. Most of the developed nations made no pretense of being democratic; those that did had such restricted franchise and limited freedom that today we would not consider them democratic. Indeed, limited political voice by farmers and the middle and working classes may well have been essential to the ability of governments to play by the rules of the classical game: it is hard to imagine truly representative governments being able to impose the austerity measures necessary to sustain economic openness in a world largely without social safety nets.

The economic dislocations created by economic integration were also not trivial. As cheap farm products flooded into Europe from the New World, Australia, Russia, India, and elsewhere, most of the Continent's farmers were made redundant. For decades, much of Europe suffered through a wrenching agrarian crisis. Tens of millions left the land to resettle in the cities or move abroad. Others demanded protection from imports, and sometimes governments provided this. Foreign competition also harmed many traditional producers in the developing world, who could not compete with inexpensive factory products.

Nonetheless, despite problems and challenges, a recognizable economic order prevailed over most of the world in the nineteenth and early twentieth centuries. This order was almost the diametric opposite of mercantilism. Where the mercantilist system was based on aggressive closure of home and colonial markets to foreigners, the norm in the classical period was of openness to international trade, investment, and migration. Where mercantilism presumed extensive government intervention in the economy, both at home and abroad, governments in the classical system tended—with variations—to leave markets largely to their own devices. Both international openness and a market orientation were debated and contested, but both prevailed most of the time and in most countries.

The classical international economic order that reigned in the nineteenth and early twentieth centuries has to be considered generally successful. The world economy as a whole grew more in the 75 years before 1914 than it had in the previous 750. There was a great deal of convergence as many poorer countries grew more rapidly than rich countries. Goods, capital, technologies, information, ideas, and people moved quite freely around the world. Macroeconomic conditions were stable overall, economic relations among the major economic powers were generally cooperative, and there was a broad consensus about the desirability of sustaining an open world economy.

The Interwar Collapse

Despite the achievements of an integrated international economy in the previous century, it came to an end with World War I, and efforts to re-create it failed for the next twenty years. Instead, capitalism turned inward, in some cases toward the most insistently nationalistic policies in modern history. In much of the world, a general trend toward engagement with the world economy and in the direction of minimal government involvement in markets was reversed almost completely.

World War I had two profound and lasting effects. The first was to shift the center of gravity of the world economy definitively away from Europe and toward the United States. The war absorbed the energies of the European belligerents and drew them out of their colonial possessions. The United States rushed into the vacuum this created, supplying the belligerents with everything from food to weapons and supplanting the Europeans as principal traders, lenders, and investors in much of the developing world. By 1919, the United States had gone from being the world's largest debtor to its leading lender, and it was also the arbiter of the economic and political settlement worked out among the warring parties at Versailles.

The second enduring effect of the war was to change the political landscape of Europe. Although political institutions had gradually become more representative over the course of the previous century, on the eve of the war they remained quite limited. The war led to a remarkable increase in the depth and breadth of democratic reform, especially in Europe. In part this was due to the collapse of four autocratic empires—the Russian, Austro-Hungarian, Ottoman, and German—and their replacement by successor states, many of which were democratic. In part, democratization was a direct result of belligerent governments' attempts to garner support for the war effort, in particular from socialist parties and their working-class bases of support. Many European governments rewarded popular backing for the war with some combination of political representation, social reform, and labor rights. By the early 1920s almost every industrialized nation was governed by a civilian democracy with universal male suffrage, and many had universal female suffrage as well. Largely as a result, over the course of the interwar years, Europe's socialist parties—generally anathema, often illegal, before 1914—were parliamentary fixtures and frequent members of ruling coalitions.

The rise to economic predominance of the United States had a number of implications. It symbolized a significant change in the nature of modern capitalism. By the 1920s, the United States had pioneered a path soon followed by other industrial nations,—toward an economy dominated by mass production and mass consumption. Some of this was the result of economic growth. As incomes rose, the demand for consumer goods beyond food, clothing, and shelter grew, especially to include more sophisticated consumer durables—including such recently invented ones as the radio, the phonograph, the telephone, the refrigerator, and the automobile. More and more of what industry produced was aimed at the general public.

The ways industry produced evolved along with its products. Technological advances in production, especially the spread of electricity and electrical machinery, drove increases in the scale of manufacturing, including the use of the assembly line. Organizational developments gave rise to the modern multiplant corporation, integrating many stages of the production process; some of the new industrial corporations became multinational. Corporations grew, and oligopolies came to dominate many markets. At the same time, labor unions organized much larger shares of the labor force.

Where the typical industrial economy of the nineteenth century was characterized by small firms, family farms, and unorganized workers, by the 1920s most major industrial economies were dominated by oligopolistic corporations and organized labor unions. Modern societies were driven by big business and big labor. The automobile industry was both typical of and in the forefront of the change: by the 1920s, motor vehicle production was the largest industry in most developed societies; the sector was dominated by large corporations and, in many instances, large labor unions.

In addition to the more general impact of American-style capitalism, the economic rise of the United States had some more specific effects. The United States largely determined the shape of the postwar settlement, as the Treaty of Versailles that ended the war largely followed the proposals of U.S. President Woodrow Wilson. These included institutionalized cooperation among the major powers, on economic issues as well as others. But almost as soon as the American blueprint was put in place, with the League of Nations and a series of monetary and economic conferences, the United States turned its back on the rest of the world. In 1920, a Republican Party committed to "isolationism" swept the presidency and both houses of Congress. The isolationists were hostile to international cooperation on economic matters that they felt would compromise U.S. autonomy.

The United States remained the most important trading, investing, and financial center in the world, but the government largely withdrew from international economic affairs. The impact of this was compounded by the enduring hostility among the former European belligerents. This made it extremely difficult for the major economic powers to work together on international economic issues.

The difficulties of interwar cooperation, and a more detailed examination of earlier experiences, demonstrated the importance of purposive collaboration to maintain an open international economic order. During the classical era, there had been a widespread belief that an integrated world economy was self-regulating and self-sustaining. Although this may have been true of some markets, and to a limited extent to the operation of the gold standard, it was clearly not the case with the global economic order itself. There had been very substantial cooperation among the major financial and monetary centers, especially in times of crisis. Monetary authorities lent substantial amounts to foreign governments facing financial difficulties and helped organize concerted efforts to stabilize markets.

More generally, the classical international economic order had depended on the willingness and ability of participant governments to adjust their domestic economic activities to international economic conditions. This meant, most important, allowing and reinforcing the austerity measures required to restrain—even reduce—wages and prices as necessary to maintain a national commitment to the gold standard. This in turn was possible due largely to the fact that those principally affected by this austerity—farmers, workers, the middle classes—tended to be underrepresented, or not represented at all, in the political systems of the classical era.

But the spread of democracy after World War I meant that most industrial-country governments faced substantial political opposition to attempts to impose gold standard–style adjustments.[17] Unlike in the nineteenth century, by the 1920s farmers, workers, and the middle classes were well represented in national political systems and strongly resisted adjustment measures that had been imposed with relative ease in an earlier era. The classical system had been based on a consensus among elites in favor of an open international economic order. The national political economies that emerged from World War I largely lacked such a consensus.

The interwar years were marked by almost continual conflict among the major economies. Attempts at monetary cooperation were largely inconclusive or failures. Trade policies tended to become more protectionist over time. Important financial problems—such as war debts owed by the Allies to the United States, or reparations owed by the Germans to the Allies—created continual frictions.

Over the course of the 1920s, as economies recovered rapidly, political difficulties seemed less important. At the start, the immediate postwar years were very difficult in Central and Eastern Europe. The new successor states struggled to put their economies on a sound financial footing, often after suffering through several years of very high and hyperinflation. By the time Germany's hyperinflation was brought to an end in 1923, the price level was one trillion times what it had been in 1919. But by 1924, economic growth had been restored in most of the Continent and in the rest of the world. Over the next few years, countries gradually came back to the gold standard, international investment reached and surpassed the prewar levels, and international trade grew rapidly. Latin America and many of the more advanced colonies increased their primary exports dramatically and regained access to international capital markets—especially to loans from the new U.S. lenders. It appeared that the world economy had been restored in something similar to its former conditions.

However, the underlying weaknesses of the post–World War I settlement became painfully obvious when crisis hit in 1929. What started as a minor recession dragged on and on, exacerbated by growing conflict among the major financial centers. Debtors in Latin America and Central and Eastern Europe defaulted, exacerbating financial distress. Financial and currency crises raced through Europe, eventually driving most of the region's countries off gold. Desperate governments raised trade barriers, imposed capital controls, and restricted currency convertibility in an effort to combat the growing crisis.

From 1929 until 1936, virtually every attempt at a cooperative response to the crisis failed. Meanwhile, insistent government attempts to implement the kind of austerity measures that had worked reasonably well in the classical era ran into economic and political obstacles. Economically, gold standard–style adjustments had been relatively rapid in the nineteenth-century environment of small firms, small farms, and unorganized labor, which made for quite competitive markets and flexible prices and wages. But in the conditions of the 1930s, with industrial economies dominated by large firms in oligopolistic markets and well-organized labor unions, prices and wages were much less flexible. As a result, attempts to bring the economy back into balance by reducing wages and prices largely failed. Even when prototypical adjustment succeeded, in the new conditions it created a vicious circle that Irving Fisher called "debt deflation," in which deflation raised real debt burdens, which caused further bankruptcies and further deflation (Fisher 1933). Attempts to hew to gold standard orthodoxy simply worsened the downward spiral—and often heightened political tensions.

The new political realities of the industrial world also affected responses to the crisis that began in 1929. Governments could no longer ignore the impact of the crisis, or of austerity measures, on farmers, the middle classes, and the working classes, for these groups were now well represented in national politics. Attempts to fit national economies to their international commitments ran into powerful political opposition and often ended with the toppling of the government that tried to do so, whether by democratic or authoritarian means.

The result almost everywhere was a turn inward in trade, finance, and investment. In Southern, Central, and Eastern Europe, Japan, and Latin America, governments imposed high trade barriers, defaulted on their foreign debts, left the gold standard, and slapped on capital controls. Governments in these nations also typically began to play a more directive role in economic affairs, sometimes nationalizing large portions of the economy. The Soviet Union, which had jettisoned capitalism in 1917 but permitted some aspects of a market economy to persist, shut down these vestiges and embarked on a forced march toward industrialization under central planning. The order of the day was autarky—a classical Greek term recoined to mean a purposive economic policy of national self-sufficiency: trade protection, capital controls, an inconvertible currency. This was usually carried out by an authoritarian government—fascist in Central and Eastern Europe, communist in the Soviet Union, nationalist in Latin America—as almost all the preexisting democracies were swept away.

The new autarkic governments changed direction toward heavy-handed intervention in the economy and international economic relations, so much so that the policy was sometimes, and with some justification, called "neomercantilist." Yet developing and semi-industrial countries could hardly be faulted for falling back on their own resources: international trade dropped by two-thirds between 1929 and 1932, international finance was dead in the water, and the gold standard had largely been abandoned by its strongest proponents. The autarkies could, with some reason, argue that their turn inward was driven by the failure of the global capitalist economy.

Most of the principal economic centers had also largely abandoned their international commitments. In 1931, Great Britain left the gold standard, after more than two centuries on it, and so did most of Europe; the United States followed in 1933. Governments everywhere increased trade protection; even formerly free-trade Britain built tariff walls around its empire. Every attempt to cobble together some semblance of cooperation among the major economic powers failed.

It was only late in the 1930s that an alternative to autarky began to emerge in Western Europe and North America. Governments in these areas—which had largely remained democratic amid the flowering of authoritarianism—expanded their social policies, experimented with countercyclical macroeconomic policies, and gradually increased the role of the public sector. The new model, which eventually gave rise to the modern social democratic welfare state, attempted to blend markets with regulation, an open economy with social insurance. The governments involved also, by 1936, were recommitting themselves to international cooperation in commercial and monetary affairs, trying to bring down trade barriers and stabilize currencies. These attempts were halting and preliminary, but they pointed the way toward a new economic policy synthesis. General sympathy for a market economy and international economic integration coexisted with substantial government involvement in the economy, especially in macroeconomic management and social policy.

Second Chance: The Bretton Woods System

Even as World War II raged, the Allies planned the postwar economy, hoping not to repeat the experience of the aftermath of World War I. This time around, the United States was committed to both building and sustaining an open international economy—and although there remained plenty of isolationist Americans, postwar governments stayed this course. The result was the first international economic order whose general contours had largely been planned by governments, in this case the U.S. and British governments. Because the final negotiations over the arrangement were held in July 1944 at a resort in Bretton Woods, New Hampshire, it became know as the Bretton Woods System.

The Bretton Woods System reflected a general commitment by the capitalist allies (not the Soviet Union), and eventually by virtually all of the advanced industrial capitalist nations, to an open international economic order. All developed parties to the agreement shared the goal of generally free trade and investment and stable currency values. As the system evolved, the General Agreement on Tariffs and Trade (GATT, eventually succeeded by the World Trade Organization, WTO) oversaw a process of gradual trade liberalization. The International Monetary Fund (IMF) supervised monetary relations among member nations, providing balance of payments financing and encouraging generally stable exchange rates. The International Bank for Reconstruction and Development (IBRD or World Bank) financed long-term infrastructure projects that would facilitate private investment in developing countries. Together, these three Bretton Woods institutions watched over an integrated capitalist world economy, which would avoid the protectionism, financial disarray, and currency volatility of the interwar years. (The Soviet Union and its allies were not included in this system, as they had opted out of international capitalism.)

The Bretton Woods monetary order was centered on the U.S. dollar, fixed to gold at $35 an ounce. Other currencies were fixed to the dollar but could be varied in the event "fundamental disequilibria" (never clearly defined) dictated a devaluation or revaluation. This was meant to provide both the currency stability that had been lacking in the interwar years and the flexibility that had been lacking in the classical era. In this way, it was something of a compromise. Governments were expected to abide by the rules of the balance of payments adjustment game, but not at the expense of important national economic goals.

The Bretton Woods System was replete with this sort of compromise. The system itself was, in the broadest sense, meant to reconcile a national commitment to economic integration with a parallel national commitment to demand management and the social democratic welfare state. These two sets of commitments had largely been seen as inconsistent under the gold standard and during most of the interwar period, but appeared both economically and politically desirable and obtainable by the 1940s.[18] There were other compromises as well. Although trade was liberalized, this was achieved only gradually. Not only that, but agricultural and services trade were not included, the developing countries were exempt, and there were many escape clauses written into the agreements, which allowed governments to impose trade barriers in certain circumstances. The same spirit of gradualism and compromise was clear in financial affairs: although there was a general belief in the desirability of free capital movements, virtually all governments imposed capital controls of one sort or another to manage international payments.

The Bretton Woods System governed relations among the industrialized capitalist economies from the late 1940s until the mid-1970s. Over these twenty-five years, the capitalist world grew more rapidly that it had at any time in history. Real per capita GDP had risen 1.3 percent a year between 1870 and 1913, a rate vastly higher than anything previous seen; after dropping below 1 percent a year in the troubled interwar period, from 1950 to 1973 GDP per capita grew by more than 2.9 percent a year—more than twice as rapidly as during the classical age. This average was brought down by relatively slow growth in the developing world: Western Europe's GDP per person grew by more than 4 percent a year, Japan's by more than 8 percent a year. Even though the developing and noncapitalist worlds largely withdrew from international commerce, world trade overall grew twice as fast as world output.[19] There is little question that this compromise between national macroeconomic management and international economic integration was extraordinarily successful.

The less developed countries (LDCs) of Asia, Africa, and Latin America did somewhat less well. Latin American nations were hit hard by the Great Depression and spent most of the subsequent twenty years building self-sufficient national markets. To some extent, this was forced on them by the Depression, World War II, and postwar reconstruction, all of which limited their foreign economic opportunities. But even after wartime conditions faded, Latin American governments maintained and increased their barriers to trade with the rest of the world. They did permit foreign direct investment by multinational corporations, but their principal policies were associated with what has been called import substituting industrialization (ISI), a systematic attempt to encourage domestic manufacturing to replace previously imported manufactured goods. Governments imposed high trade barriers, subsidized domestic manufacturing, taxed exports, took over large portions of basic industry, and generally biased economic incentives against exports and toward production for the domestic market.

As they decolonized, most of the former European colonies in Africa and Asia followed the Latin American example and pursued ISI. The result was a world largely divided in three parts: the industrialized capitalist nations, gradually increasing economic ties among themselves; the developing capitalist nations, growing quite separately from the world economy; and the centrally planned economies of the communist nations, which rejected most ties with the capitalist world. Each of these three segments of the world economy represented a different mix of state and market, openness and closure. The centrally planned economies rejected both markets and international economic integration. The capitalist LDCs accepted markets domestically, but their governments were deeply involved in their national economies and also cordoned themselves off from the rest of the world. The industrial capitalist countries pursued a modest compromise between state and market at home, and a general if restrained commitment to international economic integration.

From Bretton Woods to Globalization

These three approaches appeared stable for several decades. But over the course of the 1970s, each ran into difficulties. Over the course of the 1980s, all were fundamentally transformed. The result was a more inclusive—indeed, virtually global—and heightened trend toward international economic integration.

The Bretton Woods monetary order was strained by the late 1960s. This was primarily due to divergence between monetary conditions in the rest of the industrial world, on the one hand, and the United States, on the other. U.S. spending on the Vietnam War and expanded social programs were contributing to a higher rate of inflation in the United States than in Europe, which undermined confidence in the dollar. Austerity measures could have brought down inflation and restored confidence, but the U.S. government was reluctant to sacrifice its domestic macroeconomic policy autonomy to maintain the gold–dollar link, even if this link was the centerpiece of the Bretton Woods monetary system. In August 1971, the United

States broke the link and devalued the dollar, ending the Bretton Woods era of fixed but adjustable exchange rates.

Another source of tension in the Bretton Woods system was, ironically, due to its success in rekindling international financial markets. While foreign direct investment had continued through the postwar period, international financial flows had effectively stopped in 1929 and stayed minimal until the 1960s. As macroeconomic stability and economic growth were restored, financial institutions rediscovered foreign operations. By the early 1970s, international financial markets were large and growing, and the increased level of international financial flows helped undermine the fixed exchange rate regime by heightening speculative pressures on some currencies (including the U.S. dollar).

Once the Bretton Woods exchange rate arrangement ended, most major currencies began floating freely against one another. This loosened the previous monetary straitjacket, and a bout of inflationary pressures ensued. On top of this, in 1973 a cartel of oil producing nations (the Organization of Petroleum Exporting Countries or OPEC) quadrupled the price of petroleum, putting further upward pressure on prices. A deep recession in 1973–75 led to an unaccustomed mixture of high unemployment and high inflation—stagflation, as it was called. Inflation continued to rise, aggravated by another round of OPEC oil price increases in 1979–80.

The rebirth of international finance also made foreign lending newly available to developing countries, which had been frozen out of capital markets for forty years, and a burst of LDC borrowing ensued. By the early 1980s, a dozen or so developing countries had accumulated substantial debts to commercial banks in Europe, North America, and Japan.

Macroeconomic difficulties came to a head after 1979. The developed countries began to adopt more contractionary monetary policies to slow the rate of inflation. This led to extremely high interest rates and several years of recession. The spike in interest rates and global recession threw the LDC debtors into a severe debt crisis, which took many of them the better part of the decade to resolve. Meanwhile, while inflation was brought down in the advanced capitalist countries, unemployment remained at very high levels. The centrally planned economies, too, had been experiencing stagnant growth, and their economic and political systems came under ever greater strain.

In this crisis atmosphere, the developed countries gradually moved to recommit themselves to a market orientation and international economic openness. Governments exercised greater monetary restraint, deregulated many economic activities, and privatized previously public enterprises. The trend was epitomized by the policies of British Prime Minister Margaret Thatcher and U.S. President Ronald Reagan, who made the case for less government involvement in their respective economies. Reagan did so, anomalously, while running up enormous budget deficits in the United States. Nonetheless, and despite such setbacks as a costly banking crisis, by the mid-1980s the developed capitalist countries had made clear their reinforced dedication to an integrated international economy.

The developing countries, for their part, emerged from debt and related crises with a new-found orientation toward international markets. To be sure, some few LDCs, especially in East Asia, had been following an export-led strategy, but until the 1980s ISI had been the almost universal policy choice of developing nations. The debt and oil crises, along with the accumulated problems of relatively closed markets in an increasingly open world economy, led almost every country in Latin America, Africa, and Asia to jettison the prior inward orientation in favor of much more economic openness to the rest of the world. Developed and developing capitalist countries continued to reduce barriers to trade and investment, leading to a characterization of the era as one of "globalization."

The most stunning development on the path to globalization was the collapse of the centrally planned economies. The economic problems of the late 1970s and early 1980s eventually drove these countries away from central planning and toward international markets. China and Vietnam were the first to move, in 1979: while maintaining communist rule, both governments reoriented their economies toward exporting to the capitalist world. After 1985, the Soviet Union embarked on an attempt at gradual reform, which was quickly overtaken by events as the country's social and political system unraveled. After the Soviet Union collapsed in 1991, the entire Soviet bloc quickly gave up central planning and moved toward capitalism at speeds varying from gradual to breakneck.

Along with globalization came a renewed interest in regional economic blocs. The European Union (EU) added a whole host of new members, until it encompassed virtually all of Europe. Meanwhile, by 1992 the EU had put in place a single market that eliminated barriers to the movement of goods, capital, and people and that harmonized the regulation of investment, migration, product and production standards, professional licensing, and many other economic activities. A subset of EU members went a step further in 1999, creating a single currency, the euro, and a common European Central Bank. The United States, Canada, and Mexico formed a free trade area in 1994, as did Brazil, Argentina, Uruguay, and Paraguay. All over the world, countries rushed to open their borders, increase their exports, attract foreign capital, and strengthen their economic ties with each other.

By the beginning of the twenty-first century, the modern world economy looked strikingly similar to the classical order of the beginning of the twentieth century. International trade, investment, and finance were generally free from government restrictions. Most governments limited their intervention in markets and in international economic transactions. Migration was less free than it had been, and there was no overarching monetary standard, but otherwise there were many similarities to conditions a century earlier. Capitalism was global, and the globe was capitalist.

Global capitalism had, however, changed profoundly in the intervening years. Today, there is substantial government involvement in the economy, both in macroeconomic demand management and in the provision of a wide array of social insurance and other social programs. This is true of all developed countries and of many developing countries as well. The social democratic welfare state is now the norm rather than a novelty, and despite periodic objections it seems unchallenged as the standard organizational form of a modern capitalist political economy.

Just as contemporary capitalism incorporates substantial government supervision of national economic activities, it is also characterized by a dense network of international institutions. Some are regional, such as the European Union. Many are global, such as the IMF and the WTO. The informal cooperative arrangements of the gold standard era have given way to a much more complex array of formal international organizations.

However successful the contemporary economic order may be, it has not eliminated problems that have plagued capitalism since its beginnings. Foremost among these is the recurrence of periodic crises. A deep recession that began late in 2007 served as a reminder that financial and commercial ties among countries can transmit crises—even panics—from market to market with lightning speed. The crisis of 2007–10 also highlights the role of international financial flows, as it was in large part the result of a decade of very substantial cross-border lending and borrowing (Chinn and Frieden 2011). Financial and currency crises, it seems, are the price of open financial markets.

Although contemporary capitalism has been associated with rapid economic growth in many parts of the world—most strikingly, in communist-ruled China—there are still many parts of the developing world that remain mired in poverty. Whether this is due to excessive or insufficient reliance on markets or excessive or insufficient integration into the world economy remains a topic of hot debate. This is not surprising. It is almost certainly in the nature of capitalist political economies that there will be enduring conflicts over how and how much government should intervene in markets and how tightly and on what terms national economies should be tied to the world economy.

Over the past five centuries, capitalism has gone from being a novel economic system in a small region in Western Europe to being the prevailing form of economic organization in the whole world. The rise and eventual triumph of capitalism on a global scale has been associated with the most rapid economic growth in world history. It has also been associated with spectacular crises, wrenching conflicts, and a great and growing gap between the world's rich and the world's poor. Global capitalism holds out the hope of extraordinary social and economic advances, but it must address its weaknesses to realize these advances.

Notes

1. Rostovtzeff (1960) is the best-known argument for Rome's capitalism. Temin (2006) presents strong evidence for the operation of markets in the Roman empire but does not explicitly consider whether the society should be considered capitalist.
2. Cited in Viner (1948).
3. On a more arcane but still important note, as Keynes pointed out (1936, chapter 23), the mercantilist emphasis on bullion and on a trade surplus served to increase the

money supply (in a specie-based monetary system) and to reduce borrowing costs. In societies heavily oriented toward entrepreneurial activities and novel endeavors, the "shortage of money" (high interest rates) was seen as a major brake on progress. In fact, some of the protectionist measures associated with mercantilism may have been triggered by the emphasis on increasing the money supply to lower interest rates, which would of course also have raised domestic prices.

4. Classic analyses are Ekelund and Tollison (1981) and Ekelund and Tollison (1997).
5. Smith (1776, Book Four).
6. For the definitive analysis, see Schonhardt-Bailey (2006).
7. The remainder of this essay draws loosely on material in Frieden (2006). See that reference for many more details.
8. Maddison (1995, p. 64).
9. Stamp (1979); Mathias and Pollard (1989, p. 56); Maddison (2001, p. 95).
10. Maddison (1995, p. 38). For an excellent survey of the period, see Marsh (1999).
11. O'Rourke and Williamson (1999, p. 209).
12. See, for example, Estevadeordal et al. (2003) and López-Córdova and Meissner (2003).
13. Bordo and Rockoff (1996, pp. 389–428).
14. Eichengreen (1992); Eichengreen and Flandreau (1997). The presentation here is greatly simplified. Governments generally tried to manage their economies so as to avoid major gold flows. This could involve trying to retain gold by raising interest rates, which would tend to keep money at home to take advantage of the higher rate of return. Or it could involve trying to brake domestic wages, prices, and profits, so as to make exports more competitive. Nonetheless, these policies had their origin in the pressures that being on gold exerted on national economies and national governments.
15. O'Rourke and Williamson (1999, pp. 43–53). See also Capie (1983).
16. The classic summary of the technological aspects of the process is Landes (1969, pp. 231–358).
17. Eichengreen (1992) is the canonical analysis of the period.
18. Ruggie (1982) is the classic statement of the argument.
19. Maddison (2001).

References

Bordo, Michael, and Hugh Rockoff. "The Gold Standard as a 'Good Housekeeping Seal of Approval.'" *Journal of Economic History* 56 (June 1996): 389–428.

Capie, Forrest, H. "Tariff Protection and Economic Performance in the Nineteenth Century." In *Policy and Performance in International Trade*, ed. John Black and L. Alan Winters1-24. London: Macmillan, 1983.

Chinn, Menzie, and Jeffry Frieden. *Lost Decades: The Making of America's Debt Crisis and the Long Recovery*. New York: Norton, 2011.

Eichengreen, Barry. *Golden Fetters: The Gold Standard and the Great Depression, 1919–1939*. New York: Oxford University Press, 1992.

Eichengreen, Barry, and Marc Flandreau, eds. *The Gold Standard in Theory and History*. New York: Routledge, 1997.

Ekelund, Robert B., and Robert D. Tollison. *Mercantilism as a Rent-Seeking Society*. College Station: Texas A&M University Press, 1981.

Ekelund, Robert B., and Robert D. Tollison. *Politicized Economies: Monarchy, Monopoly, and Mercantilism*. College Station: Texas A&M University Press, 1997.

Estevadeordal, Antoni, Brian Frantz, and Alan M. Taylor. "The Rise and Fall of World Trade, 1870–1939." *Quarterly Journal of Economics* 118 (May 2003): 359–407.
Fisher, Irving. "The Debt-Deflation Theory of Great Depressions." *Econometrica* 1 (Oct. 1933): 337–357.
Frieden, Jeffry. *Global Capitalism: Its Fall and Rise in the Twentieth Century.* New York: Norton, 2006.
Hochschild, Adam. *King Leopold's Ghost.* Boston: Houghton Mifflin, 1998.
Keynes, John Maynard. *The General Theory of Employment, Interest and Money.* London: Macmillan, 1936.
Landes, David. *The Unbound Prometheus: Technological Change and Industrial Development in Western Europe from 1750 to the Present.* Cambridge: Cambridge University Press, 1969.
López-Córdova, J. Ernesto, and Christopher M. Meissner, 2003. "Exchange-Rate Regimes and International Trade: Evidence from the Classical Gold Standard Era." *American Economic Review* 93 (March 2003): 344–353.
Maddison, Angus. *Monitoring the World Economy 1820–1992.* Paris: OECD, 1995.
Maddison, Angus. *The World Economy: A Millennial Perspective.* Paris: OECD, 2001.
Marsh, Peter. *Bargaining on Europe: Britain and the First Common Market 1860–1892.* New Haven, Conn.: Yale University Press, 1999.
Mathias, Peter, and Sydney Pollard. "European Trade Policy, 1815–1914." In *The Cambridge Economic History of Europe* (vol. 8): *The Industrial Economies: The Development of Economic and Social Policies*, ed. Peter Mathias and Sidney Pollard, 1–160. Cambridge: Cambridge University Press, 1989.
O'Rourke, Kevin, and Jeffrey Williamson. *Globalization and History: The Evolution of a Nineteenth-Century Atlantic Economy.* Cambridge, Mass.: MIT Press, 1999.
Rostovtzeff, Mikhail. *Rome.* New York: Oxford University Press, 1960.
Ruggie, John G. "International Regimes, Transactions, and Change: Embedded Liberalism in the Postwar Economic Order." *International Organization* 36 (March 1982): 379–415.
Schonhardt-Bailey, Cheryl. *From the Corn Laws to Free Trade: Interests, Ideas and Institutions in Historical Perspective.* Cambridge, Mass.: MIT Press, 2006.
Smith, Adam. *An Inquiry into the Nature and Causes of the Wealth of Nations.* New York: Modern Library, 1937 (1776).
Stamp, A. H. *A Social and Economic History of England from 1700 to 1970.* London: Research Publishing, 1979.
Temin, Peter. "The Economy of the Early Roman Empire." *Journal of Economic Perspectives* 20 (Winter 2006): 133–151.
Viner, Jacob. "Power versus Plenty as Objectives of Foreign Policy in the Seventeenth and Eighteenth Centuries." *World Politics* 1 (Oct. 1948): 1–29.

CHAPTER 2

LEGAL INSTITUTIONS AND ECONOMIC DEVELOPMENT

THORSTEN BECK

STARK cross-country differences in levels of economic development have motivated economists to look for factors that explain these differences. But there is also a historic dimension; only for the past 500 years has Europe gained a dominant socioeconomic position, which has gone hand in hand with the rise of capitalism. What has driven this increasing divergence in the economic fates of societies? This chapter focuses on the efficiency of legal institutions as a major explanation for the rise of capitalism in Europe and other parts of the world, including some—but far from all—areas settled and colonized by Europeans. Specifically, this chapter (1) defines and discusses indicators of legal institutions; (2) surveys the historic, theoretical, and empirical literature on the importance of legal institutions for market-based capitalism and economic development; and (3) presents and compares different theories of why and how legal institutions developed differently across societies.

Until thirty years ago, economists focused mostly on production factors as major drivers of cross-country differences in GDP per capita. Specifically, technological progress, capital accumulation, and population growth have been considered critical factors of growth in the neoclassical growth theory (Solow, 1956). The endogenous growth theory has focused on endogenous human capital accumulation as additional production factor and technological progress and constant returns to scale production functions as additional growth drivers (Romer, 1990; Aghion and Howitt, 1998). However, early on, economists noted the large extent to which cross-country differences in levels of economic development could not be explained by production factors. Solow (1957) pointed to the residual of more than

80 percent of cross-country variation in GDP growth, unexplained by differences in production factors, and attributed it to productivity growth. Economists have therefore looked beyond the production function and focused on the organization of economies. Adam Smith (1776) already stressed the importance of private property right protection for specialization and market exchange and thus ultimately for innovation and growth. Hayek (1960, p. 140) pointed to private property right as "vital for preventing coercion, securing liberty and enhancing personal welfare." Economic historians, such as North and Thomas (1973), have provided first accounts of the critical role of institutions. The Barro-style growth regression model has been used extensively by economists to study the relationship between institutions and growth.

However, it is not only economists that have explored the divergence in economic development and the rise of capitalism in Europe. Historians, sociologists, and anthropologists have studied the importance of institutions for economic development over the past centuries. Going back even further, Jared Diamond (1997) reviews the past 10,000 years of human history and attributes the success of Europe to the east–west geographic extension of Eurasia as opposed to the north–south orientation of Africa and the Americas. The east–west extension along similar climatic conditions allowed an easier spread of plants, domesticated animals, and technology and thus enabled the faster development of Europe and Asia from hunters to settlers to states, implying an earlier build-up of the necessary institutions, ultimately explaining why it was Europeans who colonized the Americas and Africa and not the other way around.

This chapter focuses on the economic approach to institutions, thus focusing on their role of supporting markets and exchange between economic agents, overcoming market frictions. This is somewhat different from the sociological and legal approaches to institutions and their role in society. The sociological view of institutions focuses on interactions between individuals within society and on dimensions such as normative behavior, social codes of conduct and beliefs, social structures and relationships, and tradition (Smelser and Swedberg, 1994; Greif, 2006, chapter 1). In the legal profession, there are different schools of thought, ranging from traditionalists who see law as supra-human to realists who see law as manipulated by humans and interpreting it in the context of public choice theory (McNollgast, 2007). Increasingly, however, economists have been influenced by the work in related disciplines. Social codes and traditions are seen as important determinant of institutions and comparative law study has informed the legal origin view of legal institutions.

Legal institutions comprise a wide array of rules, arrangements, and actual institutions. They support commercial transactions among agents that do not know each other, might not meet again, and can therefore not rely on reputation and repeated interaction. We can categorize legal institutions along several dimensions, whether they are private or public, information- or enforcement-based, and whether they govern relationships between private agents or between private agents and governments. Recent cross-country data collection efforts have allowed researchers to quantify certain legal processes and measure the efficiency of legal systems. Legal system indicators range from very general measures of the institutional framework over indicators of specific institutional arrangements and political structures to measures of specific legal procedures, such as contract enforcement or property registration. These different measures can also be mapped into different concepts of institutions, ranging from specific rules to a broader concept of the institutional framework as encompassing both informal and formal institutions of a society.

Historic accounts, theory, and empirical work have shown that legal institutions have a first-order impact on the structure and development of economies and have supported the rise of capitalism in Europe since medieval times. Critically, a growing literature has shown the importance of property rights for economic development (Acemoglu, Johnson, and Robinson, 2005b). This is confirmed by a large literature showing the importance of legal institutions explaining cross-country and cross-industry variation in entrepreneurship, formality, corporate governance and structure, firm investment, and firm growth. The experience of the transition economies over the past two decades has underscored the importance that effective legal institutions play for the successful transformation into a market economy (Beck and Laeven, 2006). Similarly, a large empirical literature has shown the critical role that legal institutions play in the development and structure of financial systems, corporate structure and governance, and firms' investment decisions and growth (Beck and Levine, 2005).

If legal institutions are so critical to economic development, why do not all countries adopt sound legal institutions? Different hypotheses have been put forward to explain the large cross-country divergence in legal system quality. While the social conflict hypothesis conjectures that the socioeconomic distribution of resources and political power determines formal institutions, including the legal framework, the legal origin view sees today's legal institutions as result of legal tradition, which in most countries was inherited through colonization or imitation. Policy choices made in France, the United Kingdom, and Germany several centuries ago therefore have critical repercussions for legal institutions around the world today. A third hypothesis points to different attitudes of major religions and different approaches of societies toward individualism and risk taking as driving institutional differences across countries.

It is important to point out the limitations of this survey. First, although we review the institution and growth literature to the extent that it is relevant for the role and origin of legal institutions in modern economies, this is not a complete survey of that literature (Acemoglu, Johnson, and Robinson, 2005b). This is also not a complete survey of the influence of historical development on today's economic outcomes (Nunn, 2009). Second, reform issues will not be discussed in depth, only to the extent that they illustrate the importance of specific legal institutions.[1] This chapter is also related to several other recent surveys, including on the role of finance in economic growth (Levine, 2005a and chapter 6) and the importance of corporate governance for economic development (Morck, Wolfenzon, and Yeung, 2005).

The remainder of the chapter is structured as follows. The next section defines legal institutions and presents different attempts at measuring them. Then, the chapter surveys the historic, theoretical, and empirical literature that shows the importance of legal institutions for capitalism and economic development. We present different theories of the divergence of legal institutions across countries and empirical evidence. The final section summarizes and looks forward.

What Are Legal Institutions and How Do We Measure Them?

Discussing the importance of legal institutions requires first defining them. Furthermore, using legal institutions in empirical work requires having appropriate measures for them. This section first defines legal institutions before discussing different indicators and measures.

Defining Legal Institutions

According to North (1990, p.3) institutions are the "rules of the game in a society or, more formally, are the humanly devised constraints that shape human interaction. In consequence, they structure incentives in human exchange, whether political, social or economic."[2] Legal institutions—as subset of the overall institutional framework—can be defined as rules that govern commercial relationships between different agents of the society, that is, firms, households, and government. In the broadest sense, legal institutions thus support market-based transactions by defining property rights and allowing for their transfer and protection. They allow for writing and enforcing contracts between agents that do not know each other, in a cost-effective manner, thus helping avoid hold-up problems. Legal institutions also provide public goods and govern externalities and third-party effects through providing coordination mechanisms and resolving collective action problems (Rubin, 2005).

When defining legal institutions, one can distinguish between several levels, which are also reflected in the measurement of institutions, as I discuss shortly. On the most general level, "legal institutions" refer to the institutional framework that underpins contractual relationships in a society and encompasses not only laws and their enforcement but also norms and values. On a more specific level, we can refer to specific institutions that can be found across the world, such as court systems or property registries. On an even more specific level, "legal institutions" refer to specific legal procedures, such as enforcing contracts or registering property, which can be undertaken in a different manner and by different institutional structures across countries.

One specific set of institutions governs the relationship between agents within corporations. Corporate governance is an important area of legal institutions (Morck, Wolfenzon, and Yeung, 2005) that defines the relationship between investors and managers and among investors with different stakes in the corporations. This relationship can be defined by public rules and laws, but also rules within the corporation as well as norms and traditions developed over time. One important dimension is the distribution of cash-flow rights on a corporation's profits, the control rights over management, and how the two relate to each other. Over time, societies have defined these relationships in different ways and allowed for different corporate forms, such as partnerships, limited liability companies, and publicly traded companies that allow separation of management and ownership. As we will discuss, corporate governance institutions also help define the boundary between intra- and interfirm transactions.

Given the intertemporal character of financial transactions and the high degree of asymmetric information and the resulting agency problems, legal institutions play an especially important role in the financial sector. Among the institutions that financial economists have focused on are those governing agency relationships, such as the rights of secured and unsecured creditors vis-à-vis borrowers in- and outside bankruptcy and the rights of minority shareholders vis-à-vis management and blockholders, as well as institutions that help overcome information asymmetries, including the quality of accounting and auditing frameworks and systems of credit information sharing.

One can classify the large number of legal institutions along different dimensions. Specifically, one can distinguish between (1) organic and designed institutions, (2) information-based and enforcement-based institutions, and (3) private and public institutions.[3] Critically, one can distinguish between contract enforcement and coercion-constraining institutions.

Let's first discuss the difference between information-based and enforcement-based institutions (Dixit, 2009). On the one extreme would be the internal value system, which might be influenced by social preferences and education, and bilateral interactions that govern the behavior of agents and commercial transactions. Information intermediaries, such as social networks, trade organizations, credit bureaus, or credit rating agencies are multilateral institutions that focus on information exchange, either in a decentralized or more centralized manner, and provide a disciplining tool by helping agents build (or destroy) reputation capital. Enforcement institutions, on the other hand, focus on direct, monetary or non-monetary punishment as consequence of violating rules and can be regulatory agencies, courts, and ancillary judicial services, thus mostly public institutions.[4]

Another important distinction, which we use throughout this chapter, is that between institutions governing commercial relationships between two private parties and institutions governing relationships between private parties and the government. These are also referred to as contract enforcement institutions and coercion-constraining institutions (Greif, 2005), respectively. Coercion-constraining institutions prevent governments from expropriating private citizens and defaulting on their commitments. Contract enforcement institutions, on the other hand, help resolve disputes between private parties. Although these two sets of institutions are certainly not independent from each other, there is not a perfect correlation, as we discuss shortly.

Among contract enforcement institutions, one can distinguish between private- and public-order legal institutions as well as between organic and designed institutions (Greif, 2005). Whereas organic institutions arise endogenously out of the repeated exchange of agents, designed institutions are the result of coordinated actions of many individuals or government. The former can also be characterized as informal, the latter as formal institutions. While the development of human societies from bands and tribes to chiefdoms and states has resulted in the development of public legal institutions supporting commercial transactions between agents that do not know each other, multilateral private institutions have also developed, both complementary and as substitute to public legal institutions.

Beyond bilateral organic private-order institutions, which are based on reputation and relationships, multilateral reputation institutions can support market transactions in a wider range of circumstances and in somewhat broader markets, including across geographic distances and borders. Multilateral arrangements rely on punishment by an individual member against another member who cheated a third party, also member of the network, without being directly negatively affected by the cheater (Greif, 2005). The organic character of these institutions implies that in many cases common social, ethnic, or cultural norms provide the conditions for such networks to arise and enable punishment. Greif (1993) provides a detailed discussion of the Jewish Maghribi traders who traded all over the Muslim-dominated Mediterranean in the eleventh century and who used each other as agent for the sale of their goods. Based on merchant law, a multilateral punishment system, and the expectation that only members of the network could be hired as agents, the Maghribi trader network survived for many decades.

Although organic multilateral private institutions can help overcome the problem of asymmetric information, they also have shortcomings. First, they are not inclusive because they are limited to members of certain groups with common backgrounds or common interests and thus exclude others. Today's ethnic networks in Africa are a good example; while helping their members, they exclude the majority of agents in the economy and therefore undermine demand for public institutions. Second, organic multilateral private institutions are built for a specific, static environment but cannot easily adapt to new and changing socioeconomic circumstances. They "are more likely to arise where markets are thin and participants locked into relationships" (Greif, 2005, p. 732). Dixit (2003) shows theoretically how growth in the market beyond a certain threshold can lead to the breakdown of such networks. Finally, the initial fixed costs of setting up organic multilateral private institutions are low, whereas the marginal costs of extending them are high; on the other hand, fixed costs are very high for the set-up of formal legal institutions, and marginal costs are low. This makes the relative benefit of organic private multilateral arrangements decrease as the size of the population widens and the market increases in size and participants.

Unlike organic private institutions, designed private institutions are "intentionally established by economic agents in response to profit opportunities" (Greif, 2005, p. 739). They are similar to organic private institutions because they rely on socioeconomic sanctions by their members, while they share with public institutions the formal rules, the intentional design, and therefore also adaptability. They include business associations and self-regulated stock exchanges, but also private information providers, such as credit rating agencies and hotel franchises. The Internet revolution has given rise to new multilateral private institutions enabling market exchange, such as eBay, an online auction and shopping website, and Craigslist, a centralized network of online classified advertisements. The optimal size of such a private institutions depends positively on the speed with which information can be exchanged; in large networks with slow information sharing, violators might be able to continue in the network before word of their violation spreads. Internet platforms such as eBay and Craigslist can therefore sustain a large number of participants, as information exchange is almost instantaneous.

Another important private multilateral legal institution is arbitration, often an alternative to the public legal system that solves conflicts between contract parties that have precommitted to using the arbitration system. The advantages for the users are greater specialization and thus competence of the arbitrators, the use of customary law, and flexibility in terms of which legal system to choose. Arbitration without the backup by a public court system, however, is often not feasible, unless reputation forces the losing party to comply with the ruling (Rubin, 2005).

Compared to private institutions, public-order institutions use the power of a third party, the state, to enforce rules and laws. They are open as they concern all agents in a political entity or beyond it in case of international legal institutions. As in the case of private contract enforcement institutions, however, incentives for this third party, the courts, police and so on, are important. Judges and enforcement officials can be bribed, and they can abuse their power. Limiting the extent to which this happens is the function of coercion-constraining institutions.

Coercion-constraining institutions govern the relationships between private citizens and the government and are therefore an important basis for public contract enforcement institutions as well as a backdrop for private legal institutions. Effective coercion-constraining institutions protect private citizens against unjustified expropriation from the government. They provide incentives for rulers and enforcement institutions to protect rather than abuse private property rights. There are coercion-constraining institutions based on an administrative structure or on the absence of the state in the commercial area, such as in China during most of the empire (Greif, 2005). The form of coercion-constraining institutions can determine the efficiency of public legal institutions. Coercion-constraining institutions built on the absence of the state are not conducive to building efficient public contract enforcement institutions (Greif, 2005).

Legal institutions are typically very persistent. Public legal institutions are especially difficult to change because this involves large fixed costs. Legal institutions are also self-enforcing, if they reflect the socioeconomic power distribution in a society and help preserve it (see later discussion). In addition, initial private institutions influence the development of public institutions through the value system developed with these initial private institutions (Greif, 2005). The persistence of legal institutions is also reflected in the classification of legal systems into common and civil law systems (see later discussion).

Measuring Legal Institutions

Although the legal and early institutional literature has extensively discussed different legal institutions and their importance, up until recently few quantitative measures of legal institutions and their quality were available.[5] Early indicators were survey-based responses by experts to questions such as: "How strong and impartial is the legal system?" or "what is the risk of expropriation of private foreign investment by government?" compiled by the Political Risk Services (PRS) or Business Environment Risk Intelligence (BERI).[6] Such indicators are typically constructed on a scale of 1 to 6 or 1 to 10, with higher numbers indicating higher levels of institutional development.

There are several concerns with expert survey-based measures of legal institutions. First, they are perception-based and might reflect outcomes, especially levels of economic development, rather than institutional inputs, which would undermine their use in establishing the relationship between institutions and GDP per capita (Glaeser et al., 2004). Second, these measures are very broad, encompassing both formal and informal institutions, and do not allow any statement about institution-specific characteristics. They therefore also allow limited space for linking empirical findings to specific policy recommendations. Third, the scaling can be rather arbitrary; is the difference between a 4 and a 5 in rule of law the same as the difference between a 5 and a 6? Finally, these measures are based on responses by experts often focusing on conditions for foreign investors, thus affecting only a small part of the economy (Pande and Udry, 2006). Institutional development, as perceived by these experts, might therefore not be relevant for economic decisions by large parts of the population in developing countries.

An alternative approach tries to gauge the quality of coercion-constraining political institutions. The Polity IV measure of *constraints on the executive* is one of the most frequently used indicators of coercion-constraining institutions.[7] Although more specific than the PRS or BERI indicators, they are still based on expert opinion and do not refer to specific rules or institutional arrangements.

More detailed measures of political structure and the relative power of different players focus on specific rules. La Porta et al. (2004), for example, measure the tenure of Supreme Court justices and the possibilities of Supreme Courts to judge cases involving government administrations to construct indicators of judicial independence. Beck et al. (2001) construct indicators of checks and balances based on the number of potential veto players in the political decision process, and Keefer and Stasavage (2003) show that political independence of central banks in the conduct of monetary policy is more likely in countries with higher checks and balances. Similarly, voting procedures and average district sizes in parliamentary elections can have an important first-order effect on economic development (Persson and Tabellini, 2003).

A third type of institutional data refers to very specific contract enforcement institutions and their functioning. Since 2000, the Doing Business initiative at the World Bank Group has collected data on very specific legal procedures.[8] These indicators measure the time it takes to register a new company or property claims and the registration costs. They gauge the time and costs of enforcing a standard contract and the recovery rate for creditors in a bankruptcy. Cross-country comparability is ensured by defining standard situations, such as recovering the amount of a bounced check or evicting a nonpaying tenant and standard asset size—for example, relative to GDP per capita—for registration of property. Another and related set of indicators refers to specific laws on the books protecting the rights of secured creditors in and outside bankruptcy and the rights of minority shareholders vis-à-vis majority shareholders and management.[9] These indicators have also been used to rank countries according to the ease of doing business and have provided impetus for reform efforts.

Indicators of the political structure and specific dimensions of the business environment have the advantage that they measure very specific institutional arrangements on a consistent basis, which facilitates cross-country comparisons. However, they also have several shortcomings. First, they measure only public, not private institutions. This is important as Fafchamps (2004) points to the lack of private rather than public legal institutions as characterizing institutional development (or the lack thereof) in Sub-Saharan Africa. Second, they might reflect de jure but not de facto institutions, as illustrated very well by McMillan and Zoido (2004) for Peru under the Fujimoro regime in the 1990s, when the country received a perfect score for judicial independence while corruption was rife in the judicial system.

A fourth category of proxies of the quality of legal institutions is based on firm- or household-level data. Firm-level surveys since the late 1990s have included questions on the perceived quality of the judiciary, the extent to which the legal system constitutes a constraint to operation and growth of the enterprise, and the risk of expropriation by government.[10] Such micro-data can capture not only cross-country variation in legal institutions but also within-country variation in how legal institutions affect firms. Schiffer and Weder (2001) and Beck et al. (2006a) show that these obstacles vary across firms of different sizes, ownership, and corporate form. There are several shortcomings to the use of such micro-data, however. First, they are subjective and might not necessarily represent binding constraints on firms. Second, similar to aggregate survey data, they might be driven by outcomes, such as firm growth, rather than being the driving force behind firm performance. Nevertheless, using appropriate econometric models, firm-level assessments of legal institutions have been widely used to assess the relationship between legal institutions and firm performance (see the next section).

Kaufman, Kraay, and Zoido-Lobaton (1999) and Kaufman, Kraay, and Mastruzzi (2006, 2009) have developed six meta-indicators of institutional development, based on a large array of different institutional indicators, among them an indicator of the rule of law, based on more than forty underlying indicators from over twenty sources. These indicators are estimates from an unobserved components model that assumes that the observed data on institutions are a linear function of the unobserved "true" measure of institutions.[11] Country estimates of institutions therefore come with standard errors, which helps underscore an important point often ignored when using such indicators to compare and rank countries: small differences between countries or changes over time within countries might not be significant.

Using different indicators of legal institutions also provides insights into the persistence of legal institutions. Although few indicators are available for more than ten years, some studies have collected data for one or few countries many years back. Balas et al. (2009) show that judicial formalism was higher in civil code than in common code countries not only in 2000 but also in 1950. On the other hand, Mussachio (2008) shows a reversal in shareholder and creditor rights in Brazil after a left-wing military takeover in 1945 and presents evidence that many French civil code countries had as strong creditor rights as common law countries in the early twentieth century, whereas the opposite holds nowadays.

Does the variation in the efficiency and quality of legal institutions across countries matter? Are informal legal institutions substitutes for formal legal institutions? Or are they the results of the economic development process? The next section discusses historical and empirical evidence that legal institutions—both formal and informal—matter for modern market economies and the economic development process.

Why Are Legal Institutions Important for a Modern Market Economy?

Many commercial transactions are sequential, that is, the quid and the quo are temporally separated. This is especially true for financial transactions where the gap between quid and quo can be years. This provides opportunities for one of the parties to renege on her contractual commitments and can lead to hold-up problems that increase in the specificity of assets and relationships. When deciding to renege, a party will compare the benefit of doing so with the cost, which—in the absence of legal institutions or plain violence—would be the loss of future business with the other party.

Informal, bilateral arrangements are only feasible if there is no information asymmetry, implying geographic proximity and no alternative trading partner. Even today, the limited choice of available partners can lock people into partnerships as McMillan and Woodruff (1999) report for Vietnam. During most of human history (except for the last 5,000 years or so), humans lived without formal private or public legal institutions. Organizations in bands or tribes did not require formal legal institutions because transactions were repeated and among agents who knew each other. Instead, humans could rely on the logic of repeated games and reputation.

Bilateral arrangements break down if markets become thicker, that is, if contract parties have alternative partners for future transactions, thereby reducing the cost of cheating. In addition, information asymmetries increase as markets grow in size and geographic extension. Therefore, as tribes developed into chiefdoms and states, the likelihood of repeated transactions decreased and the need for rules to govern transactions between strangers arose. As shown by Brown, Falk, and Fehr (2004), third-party enforcement enables a society to move away from being "a collection of bilateral trading islands" to a market with public offers and one-shot transactions between anonymous trading partners.

Historic Evidence

Adam Smith (1776) already stressed that private property rights encourage economic agents to develop their property, generate wealth, and efficiently allocate resources based on the operation of markets. The importance of property rights and legal system efficiency in the rise of capitalism in the West has been documented by several economic historians. Among the first, North and Thomas (1973) pointed to the critical role of property right protection for international trade and economic development in Europe and North America. Similarly, Rosenberg and Birdzell (1986) point to institutions favorable to commerce and the emergence of the corporation as critical explanations for the rise of Europe and the West. Engermann and Sokoloff (1997) describe how extractive coercion-constraining institutions helped secure the entrenchment of the ruling elite in large parts of Latin America and undermined the build-up of effective market-supporting legal institutions and public infrastructure, while broad-based coercion-constraining institutions in the northern part of the Americas and the resulting private property right protection helped develop markets and ultimately fostered economic development.

Greif has described the positive effect of multilateral private and public contract enforcement institutions in the medieval ages on international trade and economic development. Merchant guilds, such as those based in several Italian cities and the Hansa in Northern Europe, were important institutions to support international trade expansion in the eleventh to fourteenth centuries, also known as the Commercial Revolution, by overcoming rulers' commitment problem to not expropriate through the threat of a complete boycott if one trader's rights got abused (Greif, 1992). Similarly, the community responsibility system, whereby a community was held responsible for the debts of a single member, was critical not only to the surge of European trade during that time but also to the rise of financial markets, including the use of letters of credit, today a standard instrument of international trade credit (Greif, 2004). But as already discussed, organic private multilateral legal institutions such as the Maghribi trader network also helped expand international trade.

Greif (2006) also argues that the historic absence of public legal institutions in the commercial area explains why China did not manage to develop a functioning market economy. While this gap was filled by private legal institutions, a tradition of coercion-constraining institutions supporting public contract enforcement institutions could not develop, so that the eventual introduction of coercion-constraining institutions in the early twentieth century did not protect private property rights from government abuse and expropriation.

Legal Institutions and the Real Economy

A growing empirical literature has documented the important relationship between efficiency and structure of legal institutions and the process of economic development. By documenting this relationship, this literature has also explored the different channels through which legal institutions help economic development.

First, in environments where property rights are well defined and protected, people focus their entrepreneurial energy on innovative entrepreneurship rather than on predation and other criminal activity (Baumol, 1990). At the same time, people have to spend less time and resources to protect themselves from predation—from other private agents or the government—and can therefore become more productive. One convincing piece of micro-level evidence to support this hypothesis comes from Field (2007), who exploits the staggered issue of land titles to over 1.2 million Peruvian households between 1996 and 2003 and finds a significant and large effect of formal property rights on labor supply. Entry barriers into the formal economy can also have negative repercussions for entrepreneurship by preventing the entry of new firms and thus ultimately undermine innovation and competition. Klapper, Laeven, and Rajan (2006) show that high registration costs impede the entry and growth of new firms, especially in industries that rely more on new firm entry. Along the same lines, Fisman and Sarria-Allende (2010) document how entry restrictions distort industrial competition, and Ciccone and Papaioannou (2007) show that countries with lower entry regulations see more entry in industries that are subject to expanding global demand and technology shifts. Berkowitz and Jackson (2006) compare the experience in Poland and Russia and find that lower entry barriers in Poland led to not only a higher share of small enterprises after the start of transition than in Russia but also a significantly smaller increase in income inequality. Using variation in the implementation of a business registration reform across Mexican municipalities, Bruhn (2008) finds a significant increase in registered enterprises as result of lower registration requirements and the introduction of a one-stop registration process.

Exit barriers can also prevent the reallocation of assets to their most productive use in society. The insolvency regime defines how a society deals with failing corporations—whether to restructure or liquidate them—and the rights of different stakeholders in this process. The goal of the insolvency process should be a speedy, efficient, and impartial resolution that maximizes the value of a firm's assets by liquidating nonviable enterprises and restructuring the liabilities of viable ones. In reality, however, there is a wide variation in duration, efficiency, and recovery rate of insolvency procedures around the world (Djankov et al., 2008a). Gine and Love (2010) show that a reform leading to a streamlined bankruptcy and reorganization procedure in Colombia contributed to a more efficient selection of viable firms into reorganization and nonviable firms into liquidation, thus improving the economy-wide allocation of assets. But it is not only the laws on the books that matter; Claessens and Klapper (2005) find a higher use of insolvency procedures in countries with more efficient judicial systems. The empirical evidence, however, does not always point to strong creditor rights in insolvency as the optimal policy. Acharya and Subramanian (2009) show that countries with more creditor-friendly insolvency regimes see fewer patents in industries that rely more on patents. Industries relying more on innovation grow more slowly in countries with stronger creditor rights.

Second, and related to the first point, the certainty of property rights facilitates investment and ultimately firm growth, as it increases investors' confidence that they will be able to appropriate the returns of their investment. Johnson, McMillan, and Woodruff (2002) show that in transition countries with strong private property rights protection, entrepreneurs are more likely to reinvest their profits. Similarly, Cull and Xu (2005) find for China that both property rights protection and access to credit matter for investment decisions of firms. Beck, Demirgüç-Kunt, and Maksimovic (2005) find that both financial and legal constraints can hold back firm growth, with this effect being stronger for smaller firms and in countries with less developed financial and legal institutions. Through their impact on investment, legal institutions also impact resource allocation by influencing the industry structure of countries. Industries that rely more on intangible assets, such as patents or trademarks, whose returns are harder to appropriate and which are easier to expropriate by competitors, grow faster in countries with better property rights protection (Claessens and Laeven, 2003). Similarly, more efficient legal institutions increase the availability of financing to industries that need them most and foster the creation of new establishments in these industries (Beck and Levine, 2002).

Third, entrepreneurs have higher incentives to work in the formal as opposed to the informal economy, if their property rights are protected and contract enforcement allows them to broaden their market outreach. By participating in the formal economy, enterprises can access broader markets and benefit from public investment, so a higher share of firms in the formal economy has positive repercussions for economic growth (La Porta and Shleifer, 2008). Several cross-country studies provide empirical evidence for this hypothesis. Djankov et al. (2002) show that countries with higher entry barriers in the form of higher registration costs have larger informal economies. Johnson et al. (1997, 1998, 2000) and Friedman et al. (2000) document the importance of the contractual framework in explaining variation in informality across countries.

Fourth, legal institutions can have a critical impact on corporate structure and governance and ultimately firm size. Specifically, better legal institutions allow firms to grow faster by becoming more efficient and expanding their markets. Laeven and Woodruff (2007) show that firms in Mexican states with weaker legal institutions are smaller than in states with strong legal systems. The effect of legal system quality is stronger for proprietorships than for incorporated enterprises, which is consistent with theories predicting that proprietors are relatively more reluctant to invest in their companies than incorporated firms in weak legal environments, given the absence of risk diversification possibilities of such an enterprise. However, legal system efficiency is also important for the rise of the limited liability corporation. One of the reasons for cross-country variation in the likelihood of incorporating is the fact that incorporated firms face lower obstacles to their growth in countries with better developed financial sectors and efficient legal systems, strong shareholder and creditor rights, low regulatory burdens and corporate taxes, and efficient bankruptcy processes; it is thus more attractive to incorporate in countries with more effective legal systems (Demirgüç-Kunt, Love, and Maksimovic, 2006).

The impact of legal institutions on corporate governance structures of shareholding companies is also reflected in the valuations of firms by outside investors. Claessens et al. (2000, 2002), La Porta et al. (2002), and Caprio, Laeven, and Levine (2007) find a positive relationship between the protection of minority shareholder rights and corporate valuation on the stock exchange. Nenova (2003) shows that the control premium stemming from holding a control proportion of a company's shares can be as high as 50 percent of firms' market value and is higher in countries with less efficient legal systems, where expropriation by the majority shareholder is easier, whereas Dyck and Zingales (2004) use data on sales of controlling blocks to show the importance of legal institutions, but also alternative control mechanisms, such as media and tax enforcement, to lower the private benefits of controlling a corporation.

Through its impact on governance structures, legal institutions have a critical impact on the boundary between intrafirm and interfirm transactions. In societies with better property protection and contract enforcement, there will be more market transactions because agents can rely on the enforcement of third-party market exchanges, but also larger hierarchies and thus larger freestanding enterprises possible (Beck, Demirgüç-Kunt, and Maksimovic, 2006b). On the other hand, weak property rights protection will lead to the rise of pyramidal structures (Khanna and Palepu, 2000), with negative repercussions for innovation and growth, for several reasons. First, in societies where most of the transactions takes place within (groups) of enterprises, capital allocation is also limited to intragroup allocation, thus reducing aggregate allocative efficiency (Almeida and Wolfenzon, 2005). Second, a limitation to intragroup transactions goes often hand in hand with barriers to entry and thus competition. Third, there will be less innovation, as the losses for other enterprises and products arising from innovation might not be external to the group, as would be the case for most freestanding enterprises (Morck, Wolfenzon, and Yeung, 2005). Finally, these negative effects are exacerbated by connected lending through banks, especially if they are part of the group.[12]

Fifth, a very rich literature has shown the importance of legal system efficiency for financial sector development, both in general and with respect to specific institutions (Beck and Levine, 2005). The rights of secured creditors and minority shareholders have been found to be positively associated with the size of credit and stock markets across countries;[13] credit information sharing is important for financial sector depth;[14] the effect of legal institutions on financial development can be traced through to economic growth;[15] and more efficient contract enforcement institutions are associated with lower interest margins, thus a higher intermediation efficiency.[16]

The impact of legal institutions on financial sector development has also been explored on the country level. Visaria (2009) exploits subnational variation in the introduction of new tribunals to resolve large claim contract disputes and finds not only lower delinquency rates but also lower ex ante interest rates for borrowers of large amounts. Variation in legal procedures (and thus trial duration) across Indian states can explain variation in farmers' access to credit market and growth of the manufacturing sector (Chemin, 2009b). Recent research has also been able to differentiate between different institutions. In the transition economies of Central and Eastern Europe, bank lending is more sensitive to reforms of collateral regimes than bankruptcy reform.[17] In Pakistan, better judicial training for judges has a significant productivity effect, with the results of a higher case load for courts and new firm entry in the real sector (Chemin, 2009a).

Given the micro-economic evidence for the importance of legal institutions, it is not surprising that researchers have been able to link institutional quality to economic development. Using historical data to extract the exogenous component of countries' legal institutions, and thus mitigate the concerns of reverse causation and simultaneity bias already discussed, recent work has shown the importance of institutions for economic growth. Hall and Jones (1999), Knack and Keefer (1997), and Mauro (1995) were among the first establishing an empirical relationship between institutions and growth across countries using an instrumental variables approach and exogenous country characteristics such as ethnic fractionalization to extract the exogenous component of institutions. However, the most convincing empirical analysis so far is by Acemoglu, Johnson, and Robinson (2001, 2002), who combine historical evidence with new data. They show that former colonies with geographic endowments conducive to the rise of coercion-constraining institutions that protect property rights have significantly higher levels of GDP per capita today than former colonies with geographic endowments conducive to the rise of extractive coercion-constraining institutions. In transition economies, the speed at which market-compatible institutions were built after the start of transition had a critical impact on growth during the first postcommunist decade (Beck and Laeven, 2006).

Legal Institutions and the International Economy

Legal system efficiency also has critical repercussions for the level and structure of real and financial flows across countries. Lucas (1990) was the first to point to the paradox that capital does not flow to capital-scarce countries, where the highest returns should be, but to capital-abundant countries with low returns. Khan (2001) explains this with the lower private appropriation of investment returns in countries with less efficient legal institutions. This is confirmed by empirical work. Alfaro, Kalemli-Ozcan, and Volosovych (2008) show that cross-country differences in institutional development are an important factor in explaining the Lucas paradox. Similarly, Papaioannou (2009) finds a positive relationship between the level of institutional development and international capital flows.

Cross-country variation in legal institutions also has an impact on international trade patterns, as both theoretical and empirical work has shown. This impact comes on top of the overall positive impact that public contract enforcement institutions have on the level of international trade, though the effect is economically smaller than one would expect (Leeson, 2008), which points to the importance of private contract enforcement institutions, as already discussed in the context of the historic evidence.[18] Including differences in the quality of contract enforcement institutions across countries can theoretically reverse predictions about factor price convergence and gains from trade.[19] Countries with more efficient contract enforcement institutions can gain comparative advantage in industries that depend more on legal institutions. Using import data at the four-digit industry level for the United States, Levchenko (2007) shows that countries with better developed institutions are more likely to export goods to the United States in industries that rely on a greater number of inputs. Along similar lines, Nunn (2007) constructs an indicator of the extent to which each industry relies on inputs that are traded on an exchange, reference priced, or neither, with the latter conjectured to be more relationship-specific and thus relying more on legal institutions. He finds that countries with more effective contract enforcement institutions export more in industries that rely more on relationship-specific inputs.

The empirical work cited in this section has addressed endogeneity concerns using different econometric techniques, including instrumental variables, such as historic country traits relating to colonial history. However, what is the reason that historic country traits such as legal origin or colonial experience are related to the quality of legal institutions today? On a more basic level, why do some countries have more effective legal institutions than others? In the next section, we address this question.

Why Do Legal Institutions Vary across Countries?

If legal institutions are critical for the development of economies and for the rise of capitalism, well-informed policy makers around the globe should focus on constructing such institutions. In reality, however, we observe a large variation in the design and efficiency of legal institutions across countries. We can distinguish between three broad hypotheses for such variation—the social conflict, legal origin, and culture views. These theories refer to institutions in the broader sense, both formal and informal, both coercion-constraining and contract-enforcing, although they have different emphases.

A fourth hypothesis that has dominated economic thinking until recently is that of efficient institutions. This hypothesis would imply that each society adopts the institutions that meets its needs best (Coase, 1960; Williamson, 1985). This builds on one of the most important principles in institutional economics and in the field of law and economics—the Coase theorem, which states that as long as property rights are tradable, their initial definition and distribution is irrelevant because parties can trade these rights and thus achieve a Pareto improvement (Coase, 1960). However, such a trade requires a clear definition of rights and a mechanism to trade them. In the face of high transaction costs or the lack of a mechanism to transfer property rights in a certain and final manner to the most efficient owner, the Coase theorem will break down. As we will discuss, the Coase theorem also breaks down on a higher level on the creation of coercion-constraining institutions, as one of the parties involved (the state) is also an interested party in the transfer. The efficient institution hypothesis has therefore lost appeal as an explanation for cross-country differences in the efficiency of legal institutions. Informed by history, comparative legal studies, and sociology, economists have considered alternative explanations for the wide cross-country variation in the efficiency of legal institutions.

Social Conflict Theory

The social conflict view, most clearly and eloquently formulated by Acemoglu, Johnson, and Robinson (2005b), builds on the premise that the institutional framework is endogenous, imposed by the group with the largest political power. De jure political institutions reflect de facto political institutions that in turn are driven by resource distribution in a society. Political institutions are persistent, as the ruling group will fortify its de facto political power with the structure of de jure political power. The institutional framework is therefore not necessarily the most efficient, but the reflection of the economic and political distribution of power, which makes it inflexible when new opportunities or technologies arise. The ruling elite will create coercion-constraining institutions that entrench its powers and dominance, rather than institutions that maximize society's aggregate welfare. Critically, negotiated solutions to improve the institutional framework to increase aggregate welfare are not possible because winners cannot commit to compensate losers, as they will be able to write the rules afterward. This is why the political Coase theorem does not hold for coercion-constraining institutions (Acemoglu, 2003).

Changes in the political and therefore legal institutions are only possible under outside pressure or exogenous shocks, such as new technologies, diseases, or globalization. One historic example, discussed by Acemoglu, Johnson, and Robinson (2005b) is the devastating effect of the Black Death epidemics in the 1340s in Europe. The dramatic reduction in the labor–land ratio increased peasants' bargaining power vis-à-vis landlords and started the decline of feudalism.

Acemoglu, Johnson, and Robinson (2005a) apply the social conflict theory to explain the rapid development of Europe after 1500, a process that can be seen as the First Great Divergence. There was also a divergence within Europe, with some countries or areas developing significantly faster than others. Specifically, Britain and the Netherlands saw more rapid economic development after 1600 than did other countries in Europe. The access to Atlantic trade opportunities after 1500 in interaction with initially better institutions explains the divergence. Specifically, both Britain and the Netherlands had institutions that allowed merchants to benefit from the new trade opportunities in the Atlantic and thus gain economic power. In the case of Britain, the merchants used this newly found economic power to fight for greater political power during the civil war (1642–49) and the Glorious Revolution (1688/89). In the Netherlands, the new wealth was used in the fight for independence from the Hapsburg Empire. In other countries with vast Atlantic trade opportunities (France, Portugal, and Spain), on the other hand, trade was monopolized by the government, with the gains thus flowing to the Crown and further strengthening their economic and political power.

The social conflict hypothesis also finds support in the colonization experience. Acemoglu, Johnson, and Robinson (2001, 2002) show how economic development across the areas colonized by Europeans experienced a great reversal in the eighteenth and nineteenth centuries, with areas that were wealthier at the time and during the initial period of colonization losing their position vis-à-vis areas that were relatively poor during the initial period of colonization. They attribute this reversal to two main factors. First, in areas with disease environments friendly for colonizers, settler colonies were established with the necessary institutional framework for commercial transactions. In areas with hostile disease environments, on the other hand, extractive colonies were established with little if any institutions. Second, the population density of the colonized areas was critical in determining the nature of colonization. Where areas were densely populated, little new European immigration took place; rather, the native population was used for forced labor. The institutional development during the colonial period persisted even after independence as the new incumbents used the existing institutional arrangements for their own purposes. Critically, the reversal and divergence in economic development among colonies started after the Industrial Revolution, as institutions became more important with new technologies requiring broad and long-term investment.

The evidence presented by Acemoglu, Johnson, and Robinson is complemented by historic accounts. Engerman and Sokoloff conjecture that climatic conditions across the Americas provided different conditions for different crops and therefore agricultural organization and production.[20] While the climatic conditions in the northern parts of North America were conducive to crops such as wheat and corn that were best produced by small-hold farmers, the conditions in the southern United States and the Caribbean were conducive to crops that were best grown on large plantations, such as tobacco or cotton. Similarly, large parts of Spanish America had higher levels of natural resources and an abundant population that could be used for forced labor. These differences had repercussions for the choice of agricultural production and immigration policies. While the United States and Canada (as well as Argentina and Chile) encouraged open immigration from across Europe, immigration was restricted in other areas, and the focus was on importing slaves rather than attracting free labor. This went hand in hand with colonial governments granting monopolies to the ruling elite. These different policies had implications for the political structure and the coercion-constraining institutions built across different parts of the Americas. While the large middle class arising in the north of the United States and Canada led to institutions that protected individual property rights, the enormous inequality in socioeconomic conditions in other parts of the Americas led to building extractive institutions that protected and entrenched the interests of the elite. This had implications not only for public investment, including in education, but also the process of economic development and inequality over the following 200 years.[21] Easterly and Levine (2003) confirm this hypothesis for a large cross-section of countries, linking different crops that are conducive to different agricultural organizations to institution building.

A related strand of literature relates to the existence and/or dominance of natural resources in an economy as explaining the lack of institution building (Sachs and Warner, 2001). It is generally easier to materialize short-term profits from natural resources, such as oil, than from fixed assets, such as manufacturing plants, equipment, and machinery, because proceeds from natural resources depend less on the creation of a market, human capital, and R&D investments. This in turn reduces incentives to invest in institutions (Besley and Persson, 2010). Higher natural resource abundance can thus increase the share of entrepreneurs engaged in rent-seeking rather than productive activities, with negative repercussions for economic growth (Torvik, 2002). The surplus nature of natural resources allows elites to extract rents and perpetuate their sociopolitical power. Beck and Laeven (2006) show that variation in the extent of natural resources across transition economies can partly explain variation in institution building after 1990, when all these countries faced the same challenge of building market-compatible institutions. Cross-country regressions have confirmed this negative relationship between natural resource abundance and the rule of law (Norman, 2009), control of corruption (Papyrakis and Gerlagh, 2004), and overall institutional capacity (Isham et al., 2005).

Related to the social conflict view is the hypothesis that ethnically fractionalized societies are more likely to develop extractive institutions as the ruling ethnic group tries to cement its dominance over the other group(s) (ab)using coercion-constraining institutions. Easterly and Levine (1997) show that the ethnic fractionalization can explain a large share of today's underdevelopment in Africa, and Coffee (2001) posits that the ethnic and societal homogeneity in Scandinavia can explain the socioeconomic success of these countries.

Although institutions are persistent, they can also be endogenously unstable, as with the community responsibility system in the medieval ages already discussed (Greif, 1992). This contract enforcement system was supported by coercion-constraining institutions reflecting the interests of those benefiting most from international trade. As the size of the network as well as the heterogeneity within the communities and across communities in terms of wealth and size increased, the benefits became less and less equally distributed within and across communities, and the costs of verification of community affiliation increased. Ultimately, the system became a victim of its own success.

Social conflict theory also makes predictions about the relationship between the corporate sector and the political elite. In societies with more concentrated ownership in the corporate sector, entrepreneurs will be more likely to invest in political connections to preserve their privileged position and erect entry barriers against potential competitors, a phenomenon that Morck, Wolfenzon, and Yeung (2005) refer to as economic entrenchment.[22] Through political connections, the corporate elite is able to influence the development of legal institutions, ultimately leading to something that Hellman et al. (2000) referred to as "state capture" in the context of the transition economies.[23]

Critically, the social conflict view holds that coercion-constraining institutions have a first-order effect on economic development and attributes less importance to contract enforcement institutions. Greif (2005, p. 728) posits that "the ability to effectively supply designed... contract-enforcement institutions, depends on the prevailing coercion constraining institutions."

This is confirmed by the historical accounts by Malmendier (2009) that the Roman form of the shareholding company developed in the early—legally less developed—days of the Roman Republic, when it was supported by the political environment, while it disappeared during the Roman Empire, when the coercion-constraining environment was not favorable toward such an institution, in spite of increasing legal sophistication. Acemoglu and Johnson (2005) show that coercion-constraining institutions can explain cross-country variation in GDP per capita, whereas contract enforcement institutions cannot. As discussed by Woodruff (2006), however, these results might reflect the accuracy with which these two kinds of institutions are measured, rather than their importance.

In summary, social conflict theory posits that the efficiency of legal institutions, especially coercion-constraining institutions, is the result of the distribution of socioeconomic resources and power. It also posits that institutions are persistent and can most easily be affected and changed by influences outside the "system," including technological innovations, trade, or war. The work by Acemoglu, Johnson, and Robinson has started a large and still growing literature that relates historical events to patterns of institutional and ultimately socioeconomic development today. Some of the work is on the cross-country or regional level, and other work exploits historic and institutional variation within large countries, such as India or the United States.[24]

Though there is considerable historical and empirical evidence in support of social conflict theory, it has also been criticized.[25] Specifically, geographic endowments, such as the disease environment or distance from the equator, might have a direct impact on economic development rather than through institution building. This geography view posits that temperate climates, such as in Europe, North America, and Australia have the advantage of higher crop yields, fewer fatal diseases, and more conducive temperatures for economic activity.[26] Similarly, being landlocked can have negative repercussions for accessing other markets and thus exploit scale economies. Several studies, however, show that the effect of geographic endowments goes through institution building rather than having a direct impact on economic development.[27] Perhaps most convincingly, Acemoglu, Johnson, and Robinson (2002) show that the growth divergence between settler and extractive colonies started with the Industrial Revolution rather than before, underscoring the importance of institutions for sectors that rely heavily on specialization and division of labor.

Legal Origin View

A second view is that the legal tradition adopted by countries has a critical impact on the nature of legal institutions and ultimately economic and societal organization.[28] This view has been informed by the comparative law literature that categorizes legal systems into several families or traditions as, most importantly, common and civil law code systems.[29] Whereas common law can be described as decentralized or bottom-up law, code or statute law is centralized or top-down law. Djankov et al. (2003b) argue that in constructing their legal institutions, societies face the trade-off between addressing disorder stemming from market failure and avoiding government failure and abuse. Any government strong enough to impose effective public contract enforcement on institutions is strong enough to abuse them unless restrained by effective coercion-constraining institutions. Different legal traditions have chosen different points along the line of this trade-off. Specifically, European history has determined the relative trade-off for a few countries and enshrined them in legal tradition, with repercussions for the rest of the world that received these legal traditions through colonization or imitation.

But let us step even further back. Different approaches to legal system development can be observed during Roman history. Although Roman law had developed over centuries on a case-by-case basis, adjusting from the needs of a small farmer community to the needs of a world empire with only a minor role left for formal legislation, Emperor Justinian changed this process by codifying existing law into the Codex Justinian in A.D. 529. This was part of an attempt to not only eliminate jurisprudence and gain control by the chief executive over the law- and rule-making process but also a political attempt at power concentration. This "Justinian deviation," however, did not succeed; rather, jurisprudence continued to shape the law. Over the next centuries, European law developed in a piecemeal manner, with several legal frameworks, such as canonical and merchant law, competing with each other.

The medieval ages saw a critical difference in political structure between England and France that shaped the development of their legal systems.[30] The French Crown wanted to use the judiciary to unify a politically divided and strife-ridden country and therefore adopted a centralized and inquisitor judicial system, whereas the English Crown could afford a relatively decentralized judiciary as England was relatively more peaceful but also politically more unified during this period. Therefore, England developed jury trials as early as the twelfth century and adopted the Magna Carta with habeas corpus rights in 1215. The legal development in England in the following centuries was dominated by competition between several court systems, including ecclesiastical, royal, feudal, and mercantile law courts (Zywicki, 2003). As parties could choose their court, the outcome—the adoption of the merchant law into common law—can be considered the most efficient one.

The seventeenth and eighteenth centuries deepened the differences between the legal traditions in England and the European Continent. English common law asserted its independence from the state during the great conflict between Parliament and the English kings in the sixteenth and seventeenth centuries. While the Crown attempted to reassert feudal prerogatives and sell monopoly rights to cope with budgetary shortfalls, Parliament (composed mostly of landowners and wealthy merchants), along with the courts, took the side of the property owners against the Crown. This political struggle culminated in 1688, when the Stuarts were thrown out and James I lost his head. Being on the winning side, the English judiciary gained considerable independence from the Crown, including lifetime tenure in the Act of Settlement (1701). Important consequences of this independence were the respect for private property in English law, especially against possible encroachments by the sovereign, and for freedom of contracting.

On the other extreme, Napoleon made a similar attempt as Justinian at codifying law, exploiting the fact that the French judiciary had been on the losing side of the revolution. Like Justinian, Napoleon sought a code that was so clear, complete, and coherent that there would be no need for judges to deliberate publicly about which laws, customs, and past experiences apply to new, evolving situations. As in the case of Justinian, the French deviation did not hold for long. Nevertheless, critical differences between both legal traditions survived and were widened in their export to other countries. Specifically, jurisprudence and precedence have a limited role in the French civil code system, and procedural rigidity is more important. Similarly, the judicial approach of the civil code system is inquisitor as opposed to the adversary approach of the common law system that requires open arguments. Finally, the role of the judge is quite different in the two legal traditions, with the judge being independent from government in the common law tradition and being seen as an executor of law in the civil law tradition.

The German and Scandinavian legal systems developed somewhat separately, but were informed by the common law and French civil code approach. In the case of the German legal tradition, simultaneously developed in Germany, Austria, and Switzerland, the development and adaptability of legal systems is a critical element in the respective codes. In the German civil code, for example, several articles refer to "good faith" (Art. 157 and 242) and emphasize that the "underlying intention and not the literal meaning of the word should prevail" (Art. 133), which allows judges to adapt to new circumstances and go beyond formal rules.

The British common law tradition was transplanted around the globe via colonization, while Napoleon spread his code throughout continental Europe, and the French legal tradition was in turn spread by the French, Belgians, Dutch, Spanish, and Portuguese to their respective colonies. The German civil code spread through imitation to Japan and from there to Korea and China. Critically, not only the codes but the legal culture was transplanted, with important repercussions for legal system efficiency in the receiving countries. As shown by La Porta el al. (1997, 1998) and Beck, Demirgüç-Kunt, and Levine (2003a), the different development of the legal families had important implications for the legal institutions. Although there are arguments that legal systems within the industrialized world have started to converge recently, the differences across legal families have been exacerbated in their export outside Europe.

There are several reasons that transplantation of the Napoleonic code to colonies outside Europe had more detrimental consequences than within Europe. First, the Europeans rigidly imposed the civil code in their colonies even though there were—and remain—serious tensions between the code and indigenous laws, which impeded the efficient development of legal institutions.[31] Second, while the European nations overcame the rigidities of the Napoleonic code, they exported its antagonism toward jurisprudence and its reliance on judicial formalism to minimize the role of judges. They also exported the French tradition of avoiding open disputes about legal interpretation and the Napoleonic doctrine to formally inhibit open disputations by judges on how to weigh competing statutes, ambiguous laws, and past court decisions in deciding new cases hindered the development of efficient legal systems around the world. Third, given the Napoleonic doctrine, judges frequently "are at the bottom of the scale of prestige among the legal professions in France and in many nations that adopted the French Revolutionary reforms, and the best people in those nations accordingly seek other legal careers" (Merryman, 1996, p. 116). As a consequence, the legislature will have a tendency to write "bright line laws" to limit the role of the courts. Once a country adopts the "bright line" approach to law making, it is very difficult to change, as courts will not be challenged to develop legal procedures and methods to deal with new circumstances, thus retarding the development of efficiently adaptive legal systems (Pistor et al., 2002, 2003).

Legal traditions in Europe have repercussions for both coercion-constraining and contract-enforcement institutions. The political structure implied by the civil code tradition foresees a strong executive vis-à-vis a purely executing and not-independent judiciary, whereas the common law tradition foresees a strong and independent judiciary. This is confirmed when comparing indicators of judicial independence across legal families (La Porta et al., 2004). Similarly, Berkowitz and Clay (2005, 2006, 2007) use the fact that parts of the United States were originally colonized by civil code countries, such as Mexico, France, or Spain to show the persistence of legal tradition, as states with civil law tradition were less likely to grant independence to their judiciary in the twentieth century, provide them with fewer resources, and have lower quality courts at the beginning of the twenty-first century. The flexibility and adaptability of contract enforcement institutions also vary across legal traditions. While the French civil code systems rely more on formalistic procedures and judgments based narrowly on statutory law, the common law tradition embraces case law and judicial discretion (Djankov et al., 2003a). Furthermore, litigation against existing rules and laws helps find the most efficient outcome (Posner, 1973). Beck, Demirgüç-Kunt, and Levine (2003b, 2005) demonstrate that this difference in adaptability of legal systems, rather than judicial independence, can explain differences in financial sector development and financial constraints reported by firms.

The effect of legal origin is not limited to legal institutions, but has had a much broader impact on the societal organization of economies.[32] The approach of the civil law system is policy implementing and socially conditioned private contracting, whereas common law can be considered dispute resolving and unconditioned private contracting.[33] This difference can even be traced back to different schools of philosophy. Jean-Jacques Rousseau's social contract (1762) built on the idea of the state securing freedom, equality and justice for all, even if against the will of the majority, whereas John Locke (1689) started from the individual and his right to defend his "life, health, liberty of possessions." These different approaches toward society and policy making can be observed across a large set of policy areas. Entry into the formal economy is subject to more cumbersome regulation in civil than in common law countries (Djankov et al., 2002); labor market regulation is less employer friendly in civil code countries (Botero et al., 2004); media freedom is lower in civil code countries (Djankov et al., 2003c); military conscription is more likely in civil code countries (Mulligan and Shleifer, 2005a, 2005b); and individual liberties and private property rights are more strongly protected in common law countries.[34] Mahoney (2001) finds a higher growth rate of common law countries over the period 1960–92 than in civil code countries.

Common law and civil law also have different approaches to enterprises, with repercussions for corporate governance (Ahlering and Deakin, 2007). While the common law tradition sees an enterprise as a purely private initiative with workers being contractual claimants on its revenues, the civil code tradition of continental Europe sees workers as stakeholders with rights beyond their contractual claims and employers with obligations beyond contractual relationships. On an even broader level, Pistor (2005) links the legal origin of the Organisation for Economic Co-operation and Development countries with two different models of market economies: liberal market economies where the control rights are on the individual level and transactions are undertaken in competitive markets and at arm's length and coordinated market economies where control rights are vested to a larger extent in groups and the government and nonmarket exchanges have an important role. She links the difference between liberal and coordinated market economies to the respective legal tradition: common law in the case of liberal and civil code in the case of coordinated market economies.

The legal tradition view has been criticized for several different reasons. First, categorization into a few legal families is seen as too crude. For instance, Franks and Sussman (2005) describe differences in the adaptability of two common law countries: the United Kingdom and the United States, where in the U.K. freedom of contracting predominates the rights of judges, whereas the reverse holds in the United States. Berkowitz, Pistor, and Richard (2002) stress that the transplant process—not just whether countries are classified as having British, French, German, or Scandinavian legal origins—is important for establishing well-functioning legal systems. Pistor et al. (2002) describe the significant differences in the transplant process in Colombia and Chile, which resulted in the latter adopting more appropriate and efficient legal institutions than the former. Second, several authors have focused on the time variation in legal institutions, which is not compatible with time-invariant legal traditions and have suggested that changing political conditions determine institutions (e.g., Pagano and Volpin, 2005). Brunt (2007) analyzes the transition of South Africa from a Dutch to an English colony and shows that the definition of property rights and thus coercion-constraining institutions (rather than changes in contract enforcement institutions) resulted in improvements in agricultural productivity and output in the early nineteenth century.

Beck, Demirgüç-Kunt, and Levine (2003a) and Levine (2005b) conduct a horse race between the social conflict and the legal origin view and show that among former colonies, both proxies for the social conflict view and legal origin dummies can explain cross-country variation in property rights protection and financial development.

Culture and Religion

A third strand of the literature focuses on cultural and religious differences across nations driving differences in legal institutions. Weber (1958) attributes the success of Great Britain and other European countries to the Calvinistic Reformation and its emphasis on individual accountability, thus fostering entrepreneurship and competition. The more hierarchical religions, such as Catholicism and Islam, on the other hand, are more hostile to free competition and market exchanges (La Porta et al., 1999). In the nineteenth century this became obvious, when the Catholic Church embraced corporatism as an alternative economic model to socialism and capitalism that featured an economy's organization into vertical corporations and cartel-like structures that prevented competition from new entrants as well as wage and price controls (Morck and Yeung, 2009). This model was happily adopted by several south European dictators in the twentieth century, including Benito Mussolini and Francisco Franco, as well as later by several Latin American countries. This should be therefore also reflected in the legal institutions developed in countries dominated by different religions or denominations. La Porta et al. (1999) show that the quality of government is indeed higher in Protestant countries than in countries dominated by Catholics or Muslims. The difference in legal institutions across major religions can also be observed in the legal institutions underpinning the financial sector (Stulz and Williamson, 2003). In particular, the Catholic Church has historically taken a negative stance toward the charging of interest and creditor rights, and the Quran prohibits the charging of interest. In contrast, the Protestant Reformation advanced a different religious attitude toward finance, whereby the payment of interest was considered a normal part of commerce, so that the rights of creditors were more naturally emphasized in countries dominated by Protestant religions. As shown by Stulz and Williamson (2003), countries with a predominantly Catholic religious heritage tend to have less developed credit markets and more poorly developed financial institutions.

Another critical difference across nations is the attitude toward individualism and risk taking. Licht, Goldschmidt, and Schwartz (2005) show that the variation in the quality of legal institutions across countries can be partly explained by variation in societal attitudes toward assertiveness, venturing and active determination, and individualism, as opposed to risk avoidance and collectivism. Greif (1994) applies the distinction between communalist/collectivist and individualist societies to discuss the different development of China and Europe and explains why it was Europe that gave rise to capitalism, not China. The absence of the Chinese state in the commercial area and the rise of organic communalist contract-enforcement institutions, influenced by the Confucian ideology that focuses on informal conflict resolution, ultimately resulted in an institutional development that did not provide for the necessary public contract-enforcement institutions as in Europe.[35] This is different from the individualistic tradition in Europe, going back to ancient Greece and early Christianity, which allowed the establishment of economically motivated (rather than kin-based) private institutions. Similarly, the ethnic fractionalization in many African countries gives rise to segregated organic communalist private legal systems that prevent the rise of designed private and public legal institutions. The ultimate consequence is that the absence of designed private multilateral legal institutions, and not necessarily the lack of public legal institutions, explains the low quality of legal institutions in many developing countries (Fafchamps, 2004). More than in the other two views, the culture and religion view sees private institutions, both organic and designed, as critical because they impact the subsequent development of public institutions.

Finally, specific historic events might turn into a traumatic experience for nations, with long-ranging implications for institutions. Murphy (2005) sees the 1720s Mississippi Bubble, with its subsequent banking crisis and hyperinflation, as critical for the negative French attitude toward the financial sector. Similarly, the hyperinflationary experience in Germany has resulted in a hawkish approach toward monetary policy deeply entrenched for the following 80 years. Malmendier and Nagel (2010) show that "Depression babies," that is, individuals growing up during the Depression era in the United States, are less likely to invest in equity and have overall more risk-averse investment strategies.

From the Origin of Institutions to Their Impact on Economic Development

The three explanations just discussed are competing but not exclusive; however, they have different implications for policy reforms, focusing either on coercion-constraining institutions, public contract-enforcement institutions, or the underlying informal institutions. All three hypotheses posit the persistence of institutions, though for different reasons. However, increasing globalization together with the recent IT revolution has reduced communication costs to almost zero and might have an additional impact (Morck and Yeung, 2009). Specifically, suppressive coercion-constraining institutions might be easier to challenge in times of globalization and rapid information flows, as suggested by political revolutions in Eastern Europe, Central Asia, and North Africa in the early years of the twenty-first century.

The systematic variation of legal institutions with historic country characteristics allows the use of these characteristics as instrumental variables in regressions of real sector outcomes on indicators of (legal) institutions. They are exogenous to today's real sector outcome, including economic development, and can explain cross-country variation in today's (legal) institutions. At first look, these variables therefore seem to be good instruments, and their use will allow us to answer several questions on the origin of institutions and the channels through which institutions affect real sector outcomes. Recently, however, doubts have been raised.

First, as already discussed, measurement issues have been raised. Albouy (2004) has shed doubts on the Acemoglu, Johnson, and Robinson data on settler mortality. Legal origin dummies have been seen as too rough and simplistic. Measuring religion is complicated by the fact that the dominance of a religion or denomination might not necessarily be captured by the percentage of population being nominally registered but the intensity of religious practice. In addition, there might be a high correlation between French legal origin and the dominance of the Catholic denomination, as becomes obvious in the discussion of corporatism, originally championed by the Catholic Church but propagated in countries both dominated by the Catholic denomination and political structures fostered by the Napoleonic legal tradition.

Second, the exclusion condition, that is, the condition that the exogenous characteristics influence the dependent variable only through the endogenous variable, is hard to test. As shown by the prolific La Porta et al. group, legal origin can explain an array of institutional arrangements. However, this also disqualifies legal origin as instrument for one specific institution, because using it as an instrument for one institution might lead to an upward coefficient estimate in the second stage if the instrument is correlated in the same direction with another omitted institution. This problem is exacerbated by the fact that the number of exogenous country traits is limited.

Relating exogenous country traits to the development of legal institutions has therefore helped us understand the origins of legal system development. However, there is a limit to which using these country traits as instruments can help us understand the relationship between legal institutions and real sector outcomes and help us even less unbundling institutions. Other methodologies might be more helpful, an issue I pick up next.

Implications for Policy Reform and Future Research

This chapter surveyed the literature on legal institutions and their importance for market-based capitalism and economic development. This section discusses what we have learned and where there are still gaps. I also point to some policy conclusions from this research program.

A large body of literature has shown the importance of legal institutions for the real economy. Coercion-constraining institutions that guarantee private property rights and effective contract enforcement institutions that resolve conflicts in a swift, predictable, and fair manner foster entrepreneurship and investment in the formal economy, enhance market exchange and trade within and between countries, and ultimately help economies grow faster. Less is known, however, about which institutions matter. Although Acemoglu and Johnson (2005) have undertaken a first attempt in disentangling the effect of coercion-constraining and public contract-enforcement institutions, more work remains to be done. More promising than cross-country work seems to be in this context, country-level studies allow the study of the functioning of specific institutions within a country and are best to do when these institutions are introduced in a staggered manner.[36] The shortcoming of such a country-specific approach is the lack of external validity beyond the country being studied. One can hope that through accumulation of studies the profession will get to consistent results. Furthermore, most of the empirical literature has focused so far on public institutions, whereas private contract-enforcement institutions and their interaction with public institutions have been significantly less explored. A recent but growing literature has linked social capital to real sector outcomes;[37] bridging the gap between that literature and the literature on public legal institutions will bring us closer in understanding the relative importance and complementarities of public and private institutions. New private institutions arising on the Internet, such as eBay and Craigslist, are important to understand in this context. On a more general level, the faster speed and lower costs of information transfer and dissemination might have important repercussions for the emergence and importance of private legal institutions, an area that will certainly be the focus of intensive research in the coming years.

While a large body of literature has helped us understand the historic origins of legal institutions, including colonial ties, less is known about the cultural origins of legal institutions. This debate has obtained new attention as China has recently been cited as counterexample for the law and development and—more specifically—the law and finance literature, as it has economically thrived without the public legal institutions of the West.[38] Understanding the interaction between private and public legal institutions over time and across countries is thus important not only for assessing their relative importance for economic development but also for understanding the origins of legal institutions.

As already discussed, a lot of progress has been made in constructing indicators of public legal institutions, but there is still a significant gap on measures of private institutions. Promising in this context seem to be enterprise and household data. Although firm-level surveys regularly include questions on the functioning of legal systems from firms' viewpoint, these questions focus on public institutions only; expanding the questionnaire to private legal institutions is important to understand the use of both public and private contract enforcement. Similarly, designing household surveys on the use of public institutions and private arrangements for conflict resolution can help make progress in this area.[39]

The research discussed in this survey also has critical repercussions for policy reform in developing countries. The finding that legal institutions have a critical impact on the development and structure of economies calls for attaching a high priority to reforms in this area. This certainly has been heeded by international organization and donors. However, the experience in transition and developing countries as well as the literature also provides important insights into how to reform legal institutions. First, legal institutions have to be seen in the context of the legal tradition of a country. Trying to impose institutions out of a different legal tradition is not helpful, as Russia found out the hard way—the short flirtation with the common law tradition did not bear fruit. A different focus might be called for. Consider the example of court reform. In spite of their shortcomings and deficiencies, court systems in the former British colonies still have a reasonable reputation. They can rely on a large body of case law and precedents, from London and other parts of the former British Empire. What courts in many common law countries in Africa are lacking are capacity and specific skills. The introduction of commercial courts might be helpful in this context. The situation in most civil code countries in Africa is different, as courts in these countries have deficiencies along many dimensions and suffer from very low reputation. In these countries, establishing alternative dispute resolution systems might be more helpful. Second, in the absence of external pressures, legal system reform cannot happen against the interests of the ruling elite. Again, the experience of the transition economies has clearly shown this. In countries with more entrenched communist elite and where these elites had higher surplus stakes in the form of natural resource rents, there was a slower or no development of the necessary legal institutions for a functioning market economy (Beck and Laeven, 2006). A third important insight from the literature is that contract enforcement institutions cannot be separated from coercion-constraining institutions. Although the legal and economic literature has made a distinction between these two types of institutions (Acemoglu and Johnson, 2005), there is a high correlation and interaction between them, even if this is not always documented in the data. The state cannot really function as neutral arbiter in disputes between private agents if it cannot be held accountable through coercion-constraining institutions (Greif, 2005).

NOTES

1. As one example, see Black and Tarassova (2002) for the challenges of legal system reform in Russia.
2. An alternative concept refers to "economic governance," defined as "structure and functioning of the legal and social institutions that support economic activity and economic transactions by protecting property rights, enforcing contracts, and taking collective action to provide physical and organizational infrastructure" (Dixit, 2009).
3. See Dixit (2009) and Greif (2005).
4. Dixit (2009) refers to these different institutions as first-party (values), second-party (bi- and multilateral private institutions), and third-party (public institutions).
5. For a similar discussion on measuring institutions more generally, see Woodruff (2006).
6. For a good description of indicators measuring different aspects of the institutional framework, see Kaufman, Kraay, and Zoido-Lobatón (1999) and subsequent papers by Kaufman, Kraay, and Mastruzzi (2006, 2009).
7. Specifically, this indicator "refers to the extent of institutionalized constraints on the decision-making powers of chief executives, whether individuals or collectivities," ranging from unlimited authority (1) to executive parity or subordination (7). See Marshall and Jaggers (2009).
8. For details and data, see http://www.doingbusiness.org.
9. La Porta et al. (1997, 1998) and Djankov et al. (2008b).
10. For details and data, see http://www.enterprisesurveys.org.
11. See Kaufman, Kraay, and Zoido-Lobaton (1999) and Kaufman, Kraay, and Mastruzzi (2006, 2009) for detailed discussions.
12. See Caprio, Laeven, and Levine (2007) and La Porta, Lopez-de-Silanes, and Zamarripa (2003).
13. La Porta et al. (1997, 1998).
14. Djankov, McLiesh, and Shleifer (2007).
15. Levine (1998, 1999) and Beck, Levine, and Loayza (2000).
16. Demirgüç-Kunt, Laeven, and Levine (2004) and Laeven and Majnoni (2005).
17. Haselmann, Pistor, and Vig (2010). Not surprisingly, given their heavier reliance on secured lending, foreign bank lending increases by even more.
18. See Rauch (2001) for an overview.

19. Costinot (2009); Acemoglu, Antras, and Helpman (2007); and Levchenko (2007).
20. Engerman and Sokoloff (1997) and Sokoloff and Engerman (2000).
21. See Engerman, Mariscal, and Sokoloff (2009) and Nunn (2008).
22. See Faccio (2006) and Braun and Raddatz (2009) for the financial sector.
23. The role of the oligarchs in Russia is probably one of the most illustrative examples of how the new corporate elite entrenched their position through political connections, culminating in the dominance of politics by oligarchs toward the end of the Yeltsin government and maybe beyond.
24. See Nunn (2009) for an overview.
25. Given the high profile nature of the Acemoglu, Johnson, and Robinson work, it is not surprising that their work has been especially closely scrutinized. Albouy (2004) sheds doubt on their settler mortality measure, and Glaeser et al. (2004) claim that human capital accumulation, rather than institutions, can explain cross-country variation in economic growth.
26. Landes (1998), Bloom and Sachs (1998), and Diamond (1997).
27. Acemoglu, Johnson, and Robinson (2002); Easterly and Levine (2003); and Rodrik, Subramanian, and Trebbi (2004).
28. See La Porta, Lopez-de-Silanes, and Shleifer (2008) for a recent overview.
29. Zweigert and Kötz (1998); Reynolds and Flores (1989); Glendon, Gordon, and Osakwe (1982); and David and Brierley (1985).
30. Dawson (1960), Berman (1983), and Glaeser and Shleifer (2002).
31. Zweigert and Kötz (1998) and Berkowitz, Pistor, and Richard (2002).
32. See La Porta, Lopez-de-Silanes, and Shleifer (2008) for an overview.
33. Damaska (1986) and Pistor (2005).
34. Scully (1992); Beck, Demirgüç-Kunt, and Levine (2003a); and Levine (2005b).
35. See also Hamilton (1990).
36. See, for example, Chemin (2009a, 2009b), Visaria (2009), and Bruhn (2008).
37. See Guiso, Sapienza, and Zingales (2006) for a survey.
38. See, for example, Allen and Qian (2009).
39. See, for example, Gramatikov et al. (2010).

References

Acemoglu, Daron. "Why Not a Political Coase Theorem? Social Conflict, Commitment and Politics." *Journal of Comparative Economics* 31 (Dec. 2003): 620–652.

Acemoglu, Daron, Pol Antràs, and Elhanan Helpman. "Contracts and Technology Adoption." *American Economic Review* 97 (June 2007): 916–943.

Acemoglu, Daron, and Simon Johnson. "Unbundling Institutions." *Journal of Political Economy* 113 (Oct. 2005): 949–995.

Acemoglu, Daron, Simon Johnson, and James A. Robinson. "The Colonial Origins of Comparative Development: An Empirical Investigation." *American Economic Review* 91 (Dec. 2001): 1369–1401.

Acemoglu, Daron, Simon Johnson, and James A. Robinson. "Reversal of Fortunes: Geography and Institutions in the Making of the Modern World Income Distribution." *Quarterly Journal of Economics* 117 (Aug. 2002): 1231–1294.

Acemoglu, Daron, Simon Johnson, and James A. Robinson. "The Rise of Europe: Atlantic Trade, Institutional Change, and Economic Growth." *American Economic Review* 95 (June 2005a): 546–579.

Acemoglu, Daron, Simon Johnson, and James A. Robinson. "Institutions as a Fundamental Cause of Long-Run Growth." In *Handbook of Economic Growth*, ed. Philippe Aghion and Steven Durlauf, 385–472. Amsterdam: Elsevier, 2005b.

Acharya, Viral V., and Krishnamurthy V. Subramanian. "Bankruptcy Codes and Innovation." *Review of Financial Studies* 22 (Dec. 2009): 4949–4988.

Aghion, Philippe, and Peter Howitt. *Endogenous Growth Theory*. Cambridge, Mass.: MIT Press, 1998.

Ahlering, Beth, and Simon Deakin. "Labor Regulation, Corporate Governance, and Legal Origin: A Case of Institutional Complementarity?" *Law & Society Review* 41 (Dec. 2007): 865–908.

Albouy, David. "The Colonial Origins of Comparative Development: A Reexamination Based on Improved Settler Mortality Data." University of California, Berkeley, September 2004.

Alfaro, Laura, Sebnem Kalemli-Ozcan, and Vadym Volosovych. "Why Doesn't Capital Flow from Rich to Poor Countries? An Empirical Investigation." *Review of Economics and Statistics* 90 (May 2008): 347–368.

Allen, Franklin, and Jun Qian. "Comparing Legal and Alternative Institutions in Finance and Commerce." In *Global Perspectives on the Rule of Law*, ed. James J. Heckman, Robert L. Nelson, and Lee Cabatingan, 118–144. London: Routledge, 2009.

Almeida, Heitor, and Daniel Wolfenzon. "Should Business Groups Be Dismantled? The Equilibrium Costs of Efficient Internal Capital Markets." *Journal of Financial Economics* 79 (June 2005): 99–144.

Balas, Aron, Rafael La Porta, Florencio Lopez-de-Silanes, and Andrei Shleifer. "The Divergence of Legal Procedures." *American Economic Journal: Economic Policy* 1 (Aug. 2009): 138–162.

Baumol, William. "Entrepreneurship: Productive, Unproductive and Destructive." *Journal of Political Economy* 98 (Oct. 1990): 893–921.

Beck, Thorsten, George Clarke, Alberto Groff, Philip Keefer, and Patrick Walsh. "New Tools in Comparative Political Economy: The Database of Political Institutions." *World Bank Economic Review* 15 (2001): 165–176.

Beck, Thorsten, Asli Demirgüç-Kunt, and Ross Levine. "Law, Endowments, and Finance." *Journal of Financial Economics* 70 (Nov. 2003a): 137–181.

Beck, Thorsten, Asli Demirgüç-Kunt, and Ross Levine. "Law and Finance. Why Does Legal Origin Matter?" *Journal of Comparative Economics* 31 (Dec. 2003b): 653–675.

Beck, Thorsten, Asli Demirgüç-Kunt, and Ross Levine. "Law and Firms' Access to Finance." *American Law and Economics Review* 7 (Spring 2005): 211–252.

Beck, Thorsten, Asli Demirgüç-Kunt, Luc Laeven, and Vojislav Maksimovic. "The Determinants of Financing Obstacles." *Journal of International Money and Finance* 25 (Oct. 2006a): 932–952.

Beck, Thorsten, Asli Demirgüç-Kunt, and Vojislav Maksimovic. "Financial and Legal Constraints to Firm Growth: Does Firm Size Matter?" *Journal of Finance* 60 (Feb. 2005): 137–177.

Beck, Thorsten, Asli Demirgüç-Kunt, and Vojislav Maksimovic. "The Influence of Financial and Legal Institutions on Firm Size." *Journal of Banking and Finance* 30 (Nov. 2006b): 2995–3015.

Beck, Thorsten, and Luc Laeven. "Institution Building and Growth in Transition Economies." *Journal of Economic Growth* 11 (June 2006): 157–186.

Beck, Thorsten, and Ross Levine. "Industry Growth and Capital Allocation: Does Having a Market- or Bank-Based System Matter?" *Journal of Financial Economics* 64 (May 2002): 147–180.

Beck, Thorsten, and Ross Levine. "Legal Institutions and Financial Development." In *Handbook of New Institutional Economics*, ed. Claude Ménard and Mary Shirley, 251–278. Dordrecht: Springer, 2005.
Beck, Thorsten, Ross Levine, and Norman Loayza. "Finance and the Sources of Growth." *Journal of Financial Economics* 58 (2000): 261–300.
Berkowitz, Daniel, and Karen Clay. "American Civil Law Origins: Implications for State Constitutions." *American Law and Economics Review* 7 (Spring 2005): 62–84.
Berkowitz, Daniel, and Karen Clay. "The Effect of Judicial Independence on Courts: Evidence from the American States." *Journal of Legal Studies* 35 (June 2006): 399–440.
Berkowitz, Daniel, and Karen Clay. "Legal Origins and the Evolution of Institutions: Evidence from American State Courts." Mimeo, 2007.
Berkowitz, Daniel, and John Jackson. "Entrepreneurship and the Evolution of Income Distributions in Poland and Russia." *Journal of Comparative Economics* 34 (June 2006): 338–356.
Berkowitz, Daniel, Katharina Pistor, and Jean-Francois Richard. "Economic Development, Legality, and the Transplant Effect." *European Economic Review* 47 (Feb. 2002): 165–195.
Berman, Harold J. *Law and Revolution. The Formation of the Western Legal Tradition*. Cambridge, Mass.: Harvard University Press, 1983.
Besley, Timothy, and Torsten Persson. "State Capacity, Conflict, and Development." *Econometrica* 78 (Jan. 2010): 1–34.
Black, Bernard S., and Anna Tarassova. "Institutional Reform in Transition: A Case Study of Russia." *Supreme Court Economic Review* 10 (2002): 211–278.
Bloom, David E., and Jeffrey D. Sachs. "Geography, Demography and Economic Growth in Africa." *Brookings Papers on Economic Activity* 2 (1998): 207–295.
Botero, Juan C., Simeon Djankov, Rafael La Porta, Florencio Lopez-de-Silanes, and Andrei Shleifer. "The Regulation of Labor." *Quarterly Journal of Economics* 119 (Nov. 2004): 1339–1382.
Braun, Matias, and Claudio Raddatz. "Banking on Politics." World Bank Policy Research Working Paper no. 4902. Washington, D.C.: World Bank, 2009.
Brown, Martin, Armin Falk, and Ernst Fehr. "Relational Contracts and the Nature of Market Interactions." *Econometrica* 72 (May 2004): 747–780.
Bruhn, Miriam. "License to Sell: The Effect of Business Registration Reform on Entrepreneurial Activity in Mexico." World Bank Policy Research Working Paper no. 4538. Washington D.C.: World Bank, 2008.
Brunt, Liam. "Property Rights and Economic Growth: Evidence from a Natural Experiment." CEPR Discussion Paper 6404, September 2007.
Caprio, Gerard, Luc Laeven, and Ross Levine. "Governance and Bank Valuation." *Journal of Financial Intermediation* 16 (Oct. 2007): 584–617.
Chemin, Matthieu. "The Impact of the Judiciary on Entrepreneurship: Evaluation of Pakistan's 'Access to Justice Program.'" *Journal of Public Economics* 93 (Feb. 2009a): 114–125.
Chemin, Matthieu. "Do Judiciaries Matter for Development? Evidence from India." *Journal of Comparative Economics* 37 (June 2009b): 230–250.
Ciccone, Antonio, and Elias Papaioannou. "Red Tape and Delayed Entry." *Journal of European Economic Association* 5 (April/May 2007): 444–458.
Claessens, Stijn, Simeon Djankov, Joseph P. H. Fan, and Larry H. P. Lang. "Disentangling the Incentive and Entrenchment Effects of Large Shareholdings." *Journal of Finance* 57 (Dec. 2002): 2741–2771.

Claessens, Stijn, Simeon Djankov, and Larry H. P. Lang. "The Separation of Ownership and Control in East Asian Corporations." *Journal of Financial Economics* 58 (2000): 81–112.
Claessens, Stijn, and Leora Klapper. "Bankruptcy around the World: Explanations of Its Relative Use." *American Law and Economics Review* 7 (Spring 2005): 253–283.
Claessens, Stijn, and Luc Laeven. "Financial Development, Property Rights, and Growth." *Journal of Finance* 58 (Dec. 2003): 2401–2436.
Coase, Ronald. "The Problem of Social Cost." *Journal of Law and Economics* 3 (Oct. 1960): 1–44.
Coffee, John C. "Do Norms Matter? A Cross-Country Evaluation." *University of Pennsylvania Law Review* 149 (June 2001): 2151–2177.
Costinot, Arnaud. "On the Origins of Comparative Advantage." *Journal of International Economics* 77 (April 2009): 255–264.
Cull, Robert, and Lixin C. Xu. "Institutions, Ownership, and Finance: The Determinants of Profit Reinvestment among Chinese Firms." *Journal of Financial Economics* 77 (July 2005): 117–146.
Damaska, Mirjan R. *The Faces of Justice and State Authority: A Comparative Approach to the Legal Process*. New Haven, Conn.: Yale University Press, 1986.
David, Rene, and John E. C. Brierley. *Major Legal Systems in the World Today*. London: Stevens and Sons, 1985.
Dawson, John P. *A History of Lay Judges*. Cambridge, Mass.: Harvard University Press, 1960.
Demirgüç-Kunt, Asli, Luc Laeven, and Ross Levine. "Regulations, Market Structure, Institutions, and the Cost of Financial Intermediation." *Journal of Money, Credit, and Banking* 36 (June 2004): 593–622.
Demirgüç-Kunt, Asli, Inessa Love, and Vojislav Maksimovic. "Business Environment and the Incorporation Decision." *Journal of Banking and Finance* 30 (Nov. 2006): 2967–2993.
Diamond, Jared. *Guns, Germs, and Steel: The Fates of Human Societies*. New York: Norton, 1997.
Dixit, Avinash. "Trade Expansion and Contract Enforcement." *Journal of Political Economy* 111 (Dec. 2003): 1293–1317.
Dixit, Avinash. "Governance Institutions and Economic Activity." *American Economic Review* 99 (March 2009): 5–24.
Djankov, Simeon, Edward Glaeser, Rafael La Porta, Florencio Lopez-de-Silanes, and Andrei Shleifer. "The New Comparative Economics." *Journal of Comparative Economics* 31 (Dec. 2003b): 595–619.
Djankov, Simeon, Oliver Hart, Caralee McLiesh, and Andrei Shleifer. "Debt Enforcement around the World." *Journal of Political Economy* 116 (Dec. 2008a): 1105–1149.
Djankov, Simeon, Rafael La Porta, Florencio Lopez-de-Silanes, and Andrei Shleifer. "The Regulation of Entry." *Quarterly Journal of Economics* 117 (Feb. 2002): 1–37.
Djankov, Simeon, Rafael La Porta, Florencio Lopez-de-Silanes, and Andrei Shleifer. "Courts." *Quarterly Journal of Economics* 118 (May 2003a): 453–517.
Djankov, Simeon, Rafael La Porta, Florencio Lopez-de-Silanes, and Andrei Shleifer. "The Law and Economics of Self-dealing." *Journal of Financial Economics* 88 (June 2008b): 430–465.
Djankov, Simeon, Caralee McLiesh, Tatiana Nenova, and Andrei Shleifer. "Who Owns the Media?" *Journal of Law and Economics* 46 (Oct. 2003c): 341–381.
Djankov, Simeon, Caralee McLiesh, and Andrei Shleifer. "Private Credit in 129 Countries." *Journal of Financial Economics* 84 (May 2007): 299–329.

Dyck, Alexander, and Luigi Zingales. "Private Benefits of Control: An International Comparison." *Journal of Finance* 59 (April 2004): 537–600.
Easterly, William, and Ross Levine. "Africa's Growth Tragedy: Policies and Ethnic Divisions." *Quarterly Journal of Economics* 112 (Nov. 1997): 1203–1250.
Easterly, William, and Ross Levine. "Tropics, Germs, and Crops: How Endowments Influence Economic Development." *Journal of Monetary Economics* 50 (Jan. 2003): 3–39.
Engerman, Stanley L., Elisa V. Mariscal, and Kenneth L. Sokoloff. "The Evolution of Schooling in the Americas, 1800–1925." In *Human Capital and Institutions: A Long Run View*, ed. David Eltis, Frank Lewis, and Kenneth Sokoloff, 93–142. Cambridge: Cambridge University Press, 2009.
Engerman, Stanley L., and Kenneth L. Sokoloff. "Factor Endowments, Institutions, and Differential Paths of Growth among New World Economies." In *How Latin America Fell Behind*, ed. Stephen Haber, 260–304. Stanford, Calif.: Stanford University Press, 1997.
Faccio, Mara. "Politically Connected Firms." *American Economic Review* 96 (March 2006): 369–386.
Fafchamps, Marcel. *Market Institutions in Sub-Saharan Africa: Theory and Evidence.* Cambridge, Mass.: MIT Press, 2004.
Field, Erica. "Entitled to Work: Urban Property Rights and Labor Supply in Peru." *Quarterly Journal of Economics* 122 (Nov. 2007): 1561–1602.
Fisman, Raymond, and Virginia Saria-Allende. "Regulation of Entry and the Distortion of Industrial Organization." *Journal of Applied Economics* 13 (May 2010): 91–111.
Franks, Julian, and Oren Sussman. "Financial Innovations and Corporate Bankruptcy." *Journal of Financial Intermediation* 14 (July 2005): 283–317.
Friedman, Eric, Simon Johnson, Daniel Kaufmann, and Pablo Zoido-Lobaton. "Dodging the Grabbing Hand: The Determinants of Unofficial Activity in 69 Countries." *Journal of Public Economics* 76 (June 2000): 459–493.
Gine, Xavi, and Inessa Love. "Do Reorganization Costs Matter for Efficiency? Evidence from a Bankruptcy Reform in Colombia." *Journal of Law and Economics* 53 (2010): 833–864.
Glaeser, Edward L., Rafael La Porta, Florencio Lopez-de-Silanes, and Andrei Shleifer. "Do Institutions Cause Growth?" *Journal of Economic Growth* 9 (Sept. 2004): 271–303.
Glaeser, Edward L., and Andrei Shleifer. "Legal Origins." *Quarterly Journal of Economics* 117 (Nov. 2002): 1193–1229.
Glendon, Mary Ann, Michael W. Gordon, and Christopher Osakwe. *Comparative Legal Traditions in a Nutshell.* St. Paul, Minn.: West, 1982.
Gramatikov, M., M. Barendrecht, M. Laxminarayan, J. H. Verdonschot, L. Klaming, and C. van Zeeland. *A Handbook for Measuring the Costs and Quality of Access to Justice.* Apeldoorn: Maklu, 2010.
Greif, Avner. "Institutions and International Trade: Lessons from the Commercial Revolution." *American Economic Review* 82 (May 1992): 128–133.
Greif, Avner. "Contract Enforceability and Economic Institutions in Early Trade: The Maghribi Traders' Coalition." *American Economic Review* 83 (June 1993): 525–548.
Greif, Avner. "Cultural Beliefs and the Organization of Society: A Historical and Theoretical Reflection on Collectivist and Individualist Societies." *Journal of Political Economy* 102 (Oct. 1994): 912–950.
Greif, Avner. "Impersonal Exchange without Impartial Law: The Community Responsibility System." *Chicago Journal of International Law* 5 (Summer 2004): 109–138.

Greif, Avner. "Commitment, Coercion and Markets: The Nature and Dynamics of Institutions Supporting Exchange." In *Handbook of New Institutional Economics*, ed. Claude Ménard and Mary M. Shirley, 727–788. Dordrecht: Springer, 2005.

Greif, Avner. *Institutions and the Path to the Modern Economy: Lessons from Medieval Trade*. Cambridge: Cambridge University Press, 2006.

Guiso, Luigi, Paola Sapienza, and Luigi Zingales. "Does Culture Affect Economic Outcomes?" *Journal of Economic Perspectives* 20 (Spring 2006): 23–48.

Hall, Robert E., and Charles I. Jones. "Why Do Some Countries Produce so Much More Output per Worker than Others?" *Quarterly Journal of Economics* 114 (Feb. 1999): 83–116.

Hamilton, Gary G. "Patriarchy, Patrimonialism and Filial Piety: A Comparison of China and Western Europe." *British Journal of Sociology* 41 (March 1990): 77–104.

Haselmann, Rainer, Katharina Pistor, and Vikrant Vig. "How Law Affects Lending." *Review of Financial Studies* 23 (Feb. 2010): 549–580.

Hayek, Friedrich A. *The Constitution of Liberty*. Chicago: University of Chicago Press, 1960.

Hellman, Joel S., Geraint Jones, Daniel Kaufmann, and Mark Schankerman. "Measuring Governance and State Capture: The Role of Bureaucrats and Firms in Shaping the Business Environment." Working Paper no. 51, London: European Bank for Reconstruction and Development, June 2000.

Isham, Jonathan, Michael Woolcock, Lant Pritchett, and Gwen Busby. "The Varieties of Resource Experience: Natural Resource Export Structures and the Political Economy of Economic Growth." *World Bank Economic Review* 19 (2005): 141–174.

Johnson, Simon, Daniel Kaufmann, and Andrei Shleifer. "The Unofficial Economy in Transition." *Brookings Papers on Economic Activity* 2 (1997): 159–239.

Johnson, Simon, Daniel Kaufmann, and Pablo Zoido-Lobaton. "Regulatory Discretion and the Unofficial Economy." *American Economic Review* 88 (May 1998): 387–392.

Johnson, Simon, Daniel Kaufmann, John McMillan, and Christopher Woodruff. "Why Do Firms Hide? Bribes and Unofficial Activity after Communism." *Journal of Public Economics* 76 (June 2000): 495–520.

Johnson, Simon, John McMillan, and Christopher Woodruff. "Property Rights and Finance." *American Economic Review* 92 (Dec. 2002): 1335–1356.

Kaufman, Daniel, Aart Kraay, and Massimo Mastruzzi. "Measuring Governance Using Cross-Country Perceptions Data." In *International Handbook on the Economics of Corruption*, ed. Susan Rose-Ackerman, 52–104. Cheltenham: Edward Elgar, 2006.

Kaufman, Daniel, Aart Kraay, and Massimo Mastruzzi. "Governance Matters VIII: Aggretate and Individual Governance Indicators 1996–2008." World Bank Policy Research Working Paper no. 4978. Washington, D.C.: World Bank, June 2009.

Kaufman, Daniel, Aart Kraay, and Pablo Zoido-Lobatón. "Governance Matters." World Bank Policy Research Working Paper 2196; Washington, D.C.: World Bank, Oct. 1999.

Keefer, Philip, and David Stasavage. "The Limits of Delegation: Veto Players, Central Bank Independence, and the Credibility of Monetary Policy." *American Political Science Review* 97 (Aug. 2003): 407–423.

Khan, Aubhik. "Financial Development and Economic Growth." *Macroeconomic Dynamics* 5 (June 2001): 413–433.

Khanna, Tarun, and Krishna Palepu. "Is Group Affiliation Profitable in Emerging Markets? An Analysis of Diversified Indian Business Groups." *Journal of Finance* 55 (April 2000): 867–891.

Klapper, Leora, Luc Laeven, and Raghuram Rajan. "Entry Regulation as a Barrier to Entrepreneurship." *Journal of Financial Economics* 82 (Dec. 2006): 591–629.

Knack, Stephen, and Philip Keefer. "Does Social Capital Have an Economic Payoff? A Cross-Country Investigation." *Quarterly Journal of Economics* 112 (Nov. 1997): 1251–1288.

Laeven, Luc, and Giovann Majnoni. "Does Judicial Efficiency Lower the Cost of Credit?" *Journal of Banking and Finance* 29 (July 2005): 1791–1812.

Laeven, Luc, and Chris Woodruff. "The Quality of the Legal System, Firm Ownership, and Firm Size." *Review of Economics and Statistics* 89 (Nov. 2007): 601–614.

Landes, David. 1998. *The Wealth and Poverty of Nations*. New York: Norton, 1998.

La Porta, Rafael, Florencio Lopez-de-Silanes, Christian Pop-Eleches, and Andrei Shleifer. "Judicial Checks and Balances." *Journal of Political Economy* 112 (April 2004): 445–470.

La Porta, Rafael, Florencio Lopez-de-Silanes, and Andrei Shleifer. "The Economic Consequences of Legal Origins." *Journal of Economic Literature* 46 (June 2008): 285–332.

La Porta, Rafael, Florencio Lopez-de-Silanes, Andrei Shleifer, and Robert W. Vishny. "Legal Determinants of External Finance." *Journal of Finance* 52 (July 1997): 1131–1150.

La Porta, Rafael, Florencio Lopez-de-Silanes, Andrei Shleifer, and Robert W. Vishny. "Law and Finance." *Journal of Political Economics* 106 (Dec. 1998): 1113–1155.

La Porta, Rafael, Florencio Lopez-de-Silanes, Andrei Shleifer, and Robert W. Vishny. "The Quality of Government." *Journal of Law, Economics and Organization* 15 (March 1999): 222–279.

La Porta, Rafael, Florencio Lopez-de-Silanes, Andrei Shleifer, and Robert W. Vishny. "Investor Protection and Corporate Valuation." *Journal of Finance* 57 (June 2002): 1147–1170.

La Porta, Rafael, Florencio Lopez-de-Silanes, and Guillermo Zamarripa. "Related Lending." *Quarterly Journal of Economics* 118 (Feb. 2003): 231–268.

La Porta, Rafael, and Andrei Shleifer. "The Unofficial Economy and Economic Development." *Brookings Papers on Economic Activity* (Fall 2008): 275–352.

Leeson, Peter T. "How Important Is State Enforcement for Trade?" *American Law and Economics Review* 10 (Spring 2008): 61–89.

Levchenko, Andrei A. "Institutional Quality and International Trade." *Review of Economic Studies* 74 (July 2007): 791–819.

Levine, Ross. "The Legal Environment, Banks, and Long-Run Economic Growth." *Journal of Money, Credit, and Banking* 30 (Aug. 1998): 596–613.

Levine, Ross. "Law, Finance, and Economic Growth." *Journal of Financial Intermediation* 8 (Jan. 1999): 8–35.

Levine, Ross. "Finance and Growth: Theory, Evidence." In *Handbook of Economic Growth*, ed. Philippe Aghion and Steven Durlauf, 865–934. Amsterdam: Elsevier, 2005a.

Levine, Ross. "Law, Endowments and Property Rights." *Journal of Economic Perspectives* 19 (Summer 2005b): 61–88.

Licht, Amir N., Chanan Goldschmidt, and Shalom H. Schwartz. "Culture, Law and Corporate Governance." *International Review of Law and Economics* 25 (June 2005): 229–255.

Locke, John. *Two Treatises of Government* (1689).

Lucas, Robert E. Jr. "Why Doesn't Capital Flow from Rich to Poor Countries?" *American Economic Review* 80 (May 1990): 92–96.

Mahoney, Paul G. "The Common Law and Economic Growth: Hayek Might Be Right." *Journal of Legal Studies* 30 (June 2001): 503–525.

Malmendier, Ulrike. "Law and Finance 'at the Origin.'" *Journal of Economic Literature* 47 (Dec. 2009): 1076–1108.

Malmendier, Ulrike, and Stefan Nagel. "Depression Babies: Do Macroeconomic Experiences Affect Risk-Taking?" *Quarterly Journal of Economics* 126 (2011): 373–416.
Marshall, Monty G., and Keith Jaggers. *Polity IV Project. Political Regime Characteristics and Transitions, 1800–2008*. Severn, Md.: Center for Systemic Peace, 2009.
Mauro, Paolo. "Corruption and Growth." *Quarterly Journal of Economics* 110 (Aug. 1995): 681–712.
McMillan, John, and Christopher Woodruff. "Dispute Prevention without Courts in Vietnam." *Journal of Law, Economics and Organization* 15 (Oct. 1999): 637–658.
McMillan, John, and Pablo Zoido. "How to Subvert Democracy: Montesinos in Peru." *Journal of Economic Perspectives* 18 (Fall 2004): 69–92.
McNollgast. "The Political Economy of Law." In *Handbook of Law and Economics*, vol. 2, ed. A. Mitchell Polinsky and Steven Shavell, 1651–1738. Amsterdam: North Holland, 2007.
Merryman, John Henry. "The French Deviation." *American Journal of Comparative Law* 44 (Winter 1996): 109–119.
Morck, Randall, Daniel Wolfenzon, and Bernard Yeung. "Corporate Governance, Economic Entrenchment and Growth." *Journal of Economic Literature* 43 (Sept. 2005): 655–720.
Morck, Randall, and Bernard Yeung. "Never Waste a Good Crisis. An Historical Perspective on Comparative Corporate Governance." *Annual Review of Financial Economics* 1 (Dec. 2009): 145–179.
Mulligan, Casey B., and Andrei Shleifer. "Conscription as Regulation." *American Law and Economics Review* 7 (Spring 2005a): 85–111.
Mulligan, Casey B., and Andrei Shleifer. "The Extent of the Market and the Supply of Regulation." *Quarterly Journal of Economics* 120 (Nov. 2005b): 1445–1473.
Murphy, Antoin. "Corporate Ownership in France: The Importance of History." In *A History of Corporate Governance around the World*, ed. Randall Morck, 185–219. Chicago: University of Chicago Press, 2005.
Musacchio, Aldo. "Can Civil Law Countries Get Good Institutions? Lessons from the History of Creditor Rights and Bond Markets in Brazil." *Journal of Economic History* 68 (March 2008): 80–108.
Nenova, Tatiana. "The Value of Corporate Voting Rights and Control: A Cross-Country Analysis." *Journal of Financial Economics* 68 (June 2003): 325–351.
Norman, Catherine S. "Rule of Law and the Resource Curse: Abundance versus Intensity." *Environmental and Resource Economics* 43 (June 2009): 183–207.
North, Douglass. *Institutions, Institutional Change, and Economic Performance*. Cambridge: Cambridge University Press, 1990.
North, Douglass C., and Robert P. Thomas. *The Rise of the Western World*. Cambridge: Cambridge University Press, 1973.
Nunn, Nathan. "Relationship-Specificity, Incomplete Contracts, and the Pattern of Trade." *Quarterly Journal of Economics* 122 (May 2007): 569–600.
Nunn, Nathan. "Slavery, Inequality, and Economic Development in the Americas: An Examination of the Engerman-Sokoloff Hypothesis." In *Institutions and Economic Performance*, ed. Elhanan Helpman, 148–180. Cambridge, Mass.: Harvard University Press, 2008.
Nunn, Nathan. "The Importance of History for Economic Development." *Annual Review of Economics* 1 (Sept. 2009): 65–92.
Pagano, Marco, and Paolo F. Volpin. "The Political Economy of Corporate Governance." *American Economic Review* 95 (Sept. 2005): 1005–1030.

Pande, Rohini, and Christopher Udry. "Institutions and Development: A View from Below." In *Advances in Economics and Econometrics*, vol. 2, ed. Richard Blundell, Whitney K. Newey, and Torsten Persson, 349–412. Cambridge: Cambridge University Press, 2006.

Papaioannou, Elias. "What Drives International Financial Flows? Politics, Institutions and Other Determinants." *Journal of Development Economics* 88 (March 2009): 269–281.

Papyrakis, Elissaios, and Reyer Gerlagh. "The Resource Curse Hypothesis and its Transmission Channels." *Journal of Comparative Economics* 32 (March 2004): 181–193.

Persson, Torsten, and Guido Tabellini. *The Economic Effects of Constitutions*. Cambridge, Mass.: MIT Press, 2003.

Pistor, Katharina. "Legal Ground Rules in Coordinated and Liberal Market Economies." In *Corporate Governance in Context: Corporations, States, and Markets in Europe, Japan, and the US*, ed. Klaus J. Hopt et al., 249–280. Oxford: Oxford University Press, 2005.

Pistor, Katharina, Yoram Keinan, Jan Kleinheisterkamp, and Mark D. West. "The Evolution of Corporate Law: A Cross-Country Comparison." *University of Pennsylvania Journal of International Economic Law* 23, 4 (2002): 791–871.

Pistor, Katharina, Yoram Keinan, Jan Kleinheisterkamp, and Mark D. West. "Innovation in Corporate Law." *Journal of Comparative Economics* 31 (Dec. 2003): 676–694.

Posner, Richard A. *Economic Analysis of the Law*. Boston: Little, Brown, 1973.

Rauch, James E. "Business and Social Networks in International Trade." *Journal of Economic Literature* 39 (Dec. 2001): 1177–1203.

Reynolds, Thomas H., and Arturo A. Flores. *Foreign Law: Current Sources of Codes and Basic Legislation in Jurisdictions of the World*. Littleton, Colo.: Rothman, 1989.

Rodrik, Dani, Arvind Subramanian, and Francesco Trebbi. "Institutions Rule: The Primacy of Institutions over Geography and Integration in Economic Development." *Journal of Economic Growth* 9 (June 2004): 131–165.

Romer, Paul M. "Endogenous Technical Change." *Journal of Political Economy* 98 (Oct. 1990): S71–S102.

Rosenberg, Nathan, and L. E. Birdzell. *How the West Grew Rich: The Economic Transformation of the Western World*. New York: Basic Books, 1986.

Rousseau, Jean Jacques. *Du contrat social* (1762).

Rubin, Paul H. "Legal Systems as Frameworks for Market Exchanges." In *Handbook of New Institutional Economics*, ed. Claude Ménard, and Mary M. Shirley, 205–228. Berlin: Springer, 2005.

Sachs, Jeffrey, and Andrew M. Warner. "The Curse of Natural Resources." *European Economic Review* 45 (May 2001): 827–838.

Schiffer, Mirjam, and Beatrice Weder. "Firm Size and the Business Environment: Worldwide Survey Results." Discussion Paper no. 43. Washington, D.C.: International Finance Corporation, 2001.

Scully, Gerald W. *Constitutional Environments and Economic Growth*. Princeton, N.J.: Princeton University Press, 1992.

Smelser, Neil J., and Richard Swedberg. *Handbook of Economic Sociology*. Princeton, N.J.: Princeton University Press, 1994.

Smith, Adam. *The Wealth of Nations*. 1776; New York: Random House, 2000.

Sokoloff, Kenneth L., and Stanley L. Engerman. "Institutions, Factor Endowments, and Paths of Development in the New World." *Journal of Economic Perspectives* 14 (Summer 2000): 217–232.

Solow, Robert. "A Contribution to the Theory of Economic Growth." *Quarterly Journal of Economics* 70 (Feb. 1956): 65–94.

Solow, Robert. "Technical Change and the Aggregate Production Function." *Review of Economics and Statistics* 39 (Aug. 1957): 312–320.

Stulz, René M., and Rohan Williamson. "Culture, Openness, and Finance." *Journal of Financial Economics* 70 (Dec. 2003): 313–349.

Torvik, Ragnar. "Natural Resources Rent Seeking and Welfare." *Journal of Development Economics* 67 (April 2002): 455–470.

Visaria, Sujata. "Legal Reform and Loan Repayment: The Microeconomic Impact of Debt Recovery Tribunals in India." *American Economic Journal: Applied Economics* 1 (July 2009): 59–81.

Weber, Max. *The Protestant Ethic and the Spirit of Capitalism*. New York: Scribner's, 1958.

Williamson, Oliver. *The Economic Institutions of Capitalism: Firms, Markets, Relational Contracting*. New York: Free Press, 1985.

Woodruff, Christopher. "Measuring Institutions." In *International Handbook on the Economics of Corruption*, ed. Susan Rose-Ackerman, 105–125. Cheltenham: Edward Elgar, 2006.

Zweigert, Konrad, and Hein Kötz. *An Introduction to Comparative Law*. New York: Oxford University Press, 1998.

Zywicki, Todd J. "The Rise and Fall of Efficiency in the Common Law: A Supply-Side Analysis." *Northwestern University Law Review* 97, 4 (2003): 1551–1633.

CHAPTER 3

CAPITAL MARKETS AND FINANCIAL POLITICS: PREFERENCES AND INSTITUTIONS

MARK J. ROE

FOR capital markets to function, political institutions must support capitalism in general and the capitalism of financial markets in particular. Yet the shape, support, and extent of capital markets are often contested in the polity. Powerful elements—from politicians to mass popular movements—have reason to change, co-opt, and remove value from capital markets. The competing capital markets' players themselves have reason to seek rules that favor their own capital channels over those of others. How these contests are settled deeply affects the form, extent, and effectiveness of capital markets. Investigation of the primary political economy forces shaping capital markets can lead us to better understand economic, political, and legal institutions overall.

Much important work has been done in recent decades on the vitality of institutions. Less well emphasized, however, is that widely shared, deeply held preferences, often arising from the interests and opinions that prevail at any given time, sometimes can sweep away prior institutions, establish new ones, or, less dramatically but more often, sharply alter or replace them. At crucial times, preferences can trump institutions, and how the two interact is well illustrated by the political economy of capital markets. Since North's (1990) famous essay, academic work has focused on the importance of institutions for economic development. Here, I emphasize the channels by which immediate preferences can trump institutional structure in determining the shape and extent of capital markets.

• • •

It's not fully obvious how and why political institutions come to support a deep, wide, well-functioning capital market, because it's focused capital owners who benefit most directly from a strong capital market, and many widespread interests have reason to undermine the capital market and the capital owners. The polity in a functioning democracy must come to see capital markets as benefiting the majority, despite the fact that the benefit is indirect and not always vivid.

In this chapter, I outline the main weaknesses in the interaction between political institutions and capitalism in both developed and developing nations, illustrate this interplay with historical capital markets examples, and show how the interaction between capital markets and politics has been seen in the academic literature. I focus not on the standard and important channel of how institutions affect preferences and outcomes, but on how and when immediate preferences can trump, restructure, and even displace established institutions.

Two core afflictions affect the interaction between politics and financial markets, both emanating from capitalism's propensity to generate large pools of financial assets whose disposition and use the polity can contest. The first is that those who do not control or benefit directly from the assets, the have-nots, can use the political arena to grab financial assets that they could not obtain in the economic arena, thereby creating a pernicious contest between the haves and the have-nots, burning resources and needing to be settled or accommodated for the economy to progress. How that contest is resolved deeply affects both the shape and the extent of the capital market.

The second recurring problem is that the haves—typically the capital owners themselves, and sometimes those who control capital but do not directly own it—often have considerable political influence. They often fight among themselves in the political arena for rights to those assets. Much of the political economy of capital markets arises from varieties of these two fundamental conflicts—one between the haves and the have-nots, the other among the haves themselves.

Although it is tempting to explain the survival of long-standing financial and corporate structures as resulting from rational optimization of private goals, these structures are often just as much reactions to conflicts among capital owners or mandates from the winners. I give some examples of how conflicts among capitalists and their managers largely explain core features of the capital market for the large public firm in the United States. Other examples can be seen in Western Europe. Private rational optimization explanations alone cannot fully explain these fundamental events that construct capital markets institutions.

When we academics see weak capital markets in a nation, or when we ask why a nation's capital market takes on a particular configuration, there's a tendency to look to explanations based on efficiency considerations and institutional capabilities. Less well highlighted, even today, are the political economy explanations that are also core to any full explanation. Look to the dominant political interests and decision makers in the society. If we do not see strong capital markets, it's often because it's not in the interest of politically decisive players to allow them to be strong. If their interests change, or their power declines, we should expect that the nation's capital markets' characteristics will change as well.

This political explanation is especially compelling in nations that have had little difficulty in building other resilient institutions, because for such nations, political support for capital markets is particularly likely to be a policy choice rather than an issue of institutional capabilities.

Complications abound. Causation is bidirectional; several economic, institutional, and political features are determined simultaneously. Few political features are fully discrete. These political, economic, and institutional determinants interact, with coalitions and multiple political forces in play. I sketch the simple stories first, then show several of the interactions, complications, and causation reversals.

• • •

Financial markets can be seen as primarily a function of a nation's governing institutions. Considerable progress has been made in economics since North (1990) demonstrated institutions' importance. But institutions interact with preferences, and indeed, widespread deeply held preferences (emanating from immediate interests and, at times, overall ideologies) can bend, destroy, and build institutions. Here I give more emphasis than is typical to the role of preferences in constructing the institutions of financial markets.

I divide the inquiry along two major dimensions. First, what is the political economy of capitalism's financial channels for the nation's haves versus the have-nots? Who prefers what financial outcome, and who dominates political decision making? Second, what is the political economy of capitalist finance that divides the nation's haves? Subsidiary to each dimension, I ask how these questions play out in the world's richer nations and in the world's developing nations. Are there enough commonalities across nations so that patterns can be discerned?

I also show how this inquiry highlights the importance of attending to the interaction between institutions and immediate preferences. The former has been central in scholarship of the past few decades. Institutions are important, but they do not always fully shape preferences and interests. Immediate preferences, often emanating from immediate interests, when sufficiently powerful and sufficiently widely held, can wash institutions away as easily as hurricanes blow away institutional shacks in their path. That does not happen often outside of severe crisis, but during those severe economic and political crises, preferences' and immediate interests' impact on institutions and finance can be, and have been, especially strong. Immediate, powerful, widespread preferences can then induce politicians to build the institutions that can withstand (some of) the future's fickleness. Today's institutions developed out of the preferences that dominated in the past. Tomorrow's institutions may well be as much a function of today's preferences as they are of today's institutions.

• • •

A roadmap for this chapter: in the first part, I describe the concepts of how capital markets depend on political institutions and preferences. In the second part, I describe how political divisions can lead to differing capital markets outcomes in the developed world, describing conflicts between haves and have-nots and fissures among the haves. In the third part, I develop these concepts for the developing world, looking at elites' interests, nonelites' interests, political stability, and the impact of economic inequality. In the fourth part, I examine several contemporary and historical examples in the developed world, including the power of labor in Europe, managers in modern America, populists in American history, and the forces for codetermination in mid-twentieth-century Germany. In the fifth part I extend and deepen the argument, showing the impact of left-to-right shifts over time and how these can be better analyzed in the academic literature. I describe overall limits to a political economy approach in the sixth section. Last, I conclude.

Concepts

Capital Markets' Dependence on Political Institutions

Simply put, if a nation's polity does not support a strong capital market, that nation will not have a strong capital market. Ask whether strong capital markets are in the interest of the decisive political actors—or what shape of capital markets best implements their interests—and one is likely to have a primary explanation for the shape and extent of that nation's capital market. The concept is simple, but powerful.

The Interests that Support or Denigrate Capital Markets

Capital owners typically have an interest in promoting capital markets and their supporting institutions, but other interests may not. Local interests may oppose centralized financial institutions that transfer capital in the economy. Those with strong human capital could fear that strong capital markets would erode that human capital's value if strong, liquid capital markets are more likely than other configurations to force workplace changes that would threaten their human capital. Those without financial capital today and with poor prospects of acquiring capital in the future could prefer that the polity take capital from those who have it and use it to benefit those who do not.

Capital is usually unevenly distributed in a nation, facilitating conflict between haves and have-nots. Even when income and property are more evenly distributed than is typical, economic rationality demands aggregation institutions, like banks and securities markets, to achieve operational economies of scale. These aggregations can become vivid in the polity and attract negative attention.

Capital markets are not generic. Banks have an interest in preserving bank financing channels and in weakening securities market channels. Securities dealers and investment bankers have an interest in preserving and expanding securities markets. Dominant owners, such as wealthy families traditionally or private equity firms more recently, have interests in preserving their privileges. Owners of existing firms want access to cheap capital but prefer that their competitors not have the same easy access.

Government bureaucracies can be wary of rival power centers in capital markets or, sometimes, wish to promote them as counterweights to other power centers in their society.

Capital Markets and Financial Politics in the Developed World

Two basic political splits organize the inquiry for developed nations: (1) the contest between those who control capital and those who do not, and (2) contests among those who control capital.

Haves versus Have-Nots

Private Power versus Governmental Power

A basic political economy type of "have versus have-not" conflict is between governmental authorities and private sector players who command capital. Though not usually seen as a conflict between haves and have-nots, it is indeed such a conflict—as government often seeks to obtain capital for its own spending needs or seeks to command its private sector use. In extreme form, a nondemocratic, dictatorial government could prefer to directly allocate capital itself, stifling the development of a private sector in general and capital markets in particular, to thwart such markets from becoming a rival power center.

Governmental authorities can build, shape, or destroy capital markets, for their own reasons and not as tools of other interests or ideologies. Governmental authorities may wish to denigrate a rival power center, one that could seek to control the government. Governmental authorities could also be susceptible to ideologies and unstructured beliefs that capital markets just will not produce social welfare and that the government needs to direct and control capital flows to better produce wealth or justice. Finally, governmental authorities may see government action as the vanguard of economic and social development; in pursuing policies to implement their goals, they can crowd out private capital markets and thereby impede them from developing.

More standard accounts, which I address shortly, examine how interests lobby, capture government decision making, and then use captured governmental institutions for their own ends. One account does not exclude the other, but the concept in this section differs from the more standard ones. Government authorities are themselves an interest, one that's separate from those outside, in the civil society. Their own direct interests and beliefs can motivate their actions vis-à-vis capital markets.[1]

Power versus Populism; Business Elites versus Masses

Populism can affect financial markets and institutions, often in reaction to financial crises and poor economic results. Popular opinion may seek as much to punish financiers and their institutions as to improve the financial system's functioning, as the two—punishment and improvement—could be conflated in the popular mind. When this feature is powerful in politics, it can induce an institutionalization of anticapital rules and reaction. Then, once institutionalized, interests arise with reason to perpetuate the new rules and the resultant arrangements. Thus, even when the popular animus against finance dissipates in more normal political times, the created interests can stymie a return to the previous arrangements.

Analogously, workers could dislike capital and capital markets. Farmers may blame financial markets for their misfortunes as much as bad weather. Each group may have simple redistributional goals, or their thinking and voting may be influenced by envy.

Capital Markets versus Social Democracy

Social democracy played a central role in how capital markets developed in Western Europe after World War II. "Social democracy," as I use it here, means a nation committed to private property but where distributional considerations are vital, labor is typically powerful, and government action to foster economic equality is central on the political agenda.

Social democratic pressures can pressure managers to stray from capital owners' interests. For diffuse stock markets to persist, the diffuse capital owners must see their firms as managed by agents who are sufficiently loyal to shareholders to provide shareholder value. For dominant shareholders to turn their firm over to ownership in liquid stock markets and, hence, to turn the owners' operational control over to managers, they must expect that the net value of turning the firm over to managers and markets benefits them, the original owners. But if the benefits of liquidity and professional management are offset by managerial disloyalty, fewer dominant stockholders will turn their firms over to managers. For shareholders to count on this managerial loyalty, they need institutions and norms that induce loyalty to shareholders. But if a polity does not provide those institutions, or if it denigrates such norms, shareholders can obtain more value if dominant stockholders keep control of the firm. Managerial control will not ordinarily appear and will be unstable if it does. Stock markets will not be strong in such nations, because managerial agency costs will be too high and too hard to bring down to levels acceptable to the original owners.

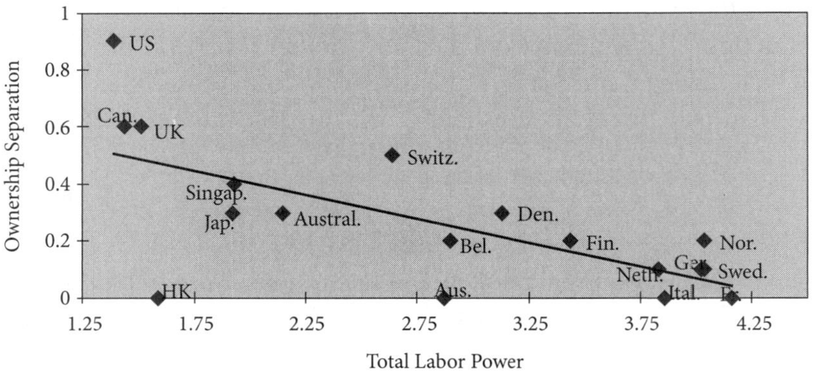

Figure 3.1. Relationship between Labor Power and Ownership Separation

Figure 3.1 illustrates the relationship between labor power (quantified by union and job security rules) and the degree to which large firms have large blockholders. Greater labor power is associated with greater ownership concentration; weaker labor power is associated with more diffuse ownership. Details, sources, and background to the graphic can be found in Roe (2000, 2003).

Visible incentive compensation that ties managers to owners may be denigrated in a social democracy more than it is in a more conservative polity. Any resulting wealth disparity could especially demoralize lower level employees and lead them to demand further compensation for themselves. As already noted, governmental players can be less willing to provide capital market–supporting institutions, such as disclosure rules and enforcement, insider trading sanctions, and commercial courts. The social democratic authorities may see these difficulties as merely disputes among the well-to-do—disputes that the public authorities need not attend to. These private costs to owners of controlling managerial agency problems can accordingly be particularly severe in social democratic polities.

A considerable literature has developed on the primacy of institutions in property rights protection, which has obvious relevance to protection of capital market investors. Although institutions are surely important, the possibility exists that the academic literature is oversold on institutions now, while underestimating simple, basic political power. Politicians and public opinion can mold institutions.

Even in the United States, where property rights institutions are typically seen as being as strong as they can be, a Congress that wanted to attack capital markets could do so effectively. Legal institutions—constitutional, judicial, and otherwise—may not explain why that kind of an attack is unlikely to succeed as well as is commonly thought.

What may well count as much as institutions for the United States is that there is no political will for a frontal assault on U.S. capital markets, even when capital institutions are seen as not serving the public interest, as was widely thought to be the case in the recent financial crisis. Outside of the United States, recent evidence indicates that right-leaning governments are perceived by property owners to protect their property better than left-leaning ones, and this partisanship dimension dominates institutional characteristics in explaining the degree of perceived property protection (Weymouth and Broz, 2008).

• • •

Those, then, are the major "have versus have-not" breaks affecting capital markets in developed nations.

Haves versus Haves

Vertical conflict—between the capital markets' haves and the nation's have-nots—is not the only political economy array here. There is a horizontal dimension as well, of conflict among the haves, with that conflict coming in three major varieties: conflicts between capital owners, conflicts between large firm managers and capital markets, and conflicts between controlling shareholders and capital markets.

Capital Markets' Internal Fissures: Banks versus Stock Markets

Different capital markets owners and capital markets players compete to maintain and expand their control over capital. They compete both in the market economy and in the political arena.

If securities markets are weak, more capital will flow through the banking system, thereby benefiting bankers. Deposit banks have an interest in keeping securities markets weak, unless they can control securities flows themselves. The interests seek to protect themselves using the political realm. Macey and Miller (1991) showed that in the United States, deposit banks often lobbied for state-based securities laws ("blue sky" laws in the trade) that raised the costs of stock sales.

Small banks have an interest in weakening the competitive strength of big banks. In the United States, this historically took the primary form of small banks inducing political decision makers to bar the large, money-center banks from entering the small banks' local market. The result was that the small banks had local monopolies or oligopolies, and large banks lacked a nationwide deposit base. Roe (1994) emphasizes this feature of nineteenth-century (and most of twentieth-century) American financial history, particularly when the power of local bankers combined with populist opinion that militated against large, centralized financial institutions. With even the largest banks relatively small in relation to the economy, banks could not readily provide the financing for continent-spanning industries at the end of the nineteenth century. The consequence was that the demand and need for securities markets grew.

Intra-capital market tactical conflict can have unexpected but profound outcomes, as Langevoort (1987) shows. During the 1933 banking crisis, larger money-center banks sought to dissuade Congress from enacting deposit insurance, because they thought they would end up paying disproportionately for the insurance but not benefit much from it. Without deposit insurance, deposits would run off from smaller, country banks to the larger, more stable money-center banks. (Yes, there was a time when such large, money-center banks were seen as the most stable in the American economy.) Because they knew that Congress would insist on doing something visible during the crisis, and because they hoped to dissuade it from mandating deposit insurance, the large banks suggested and supported splitting investment from commercial banking (as they were not making much money in the securities business anyway). Congress did sever investment from commercial banking via the famous Glass-Steagall Act of 1933, as the large banks suggested. But Congress also decided nevertheless to insure banks deposits, which the large money-center banks had opposed but which the more politically powerful small banks wanted.

Managers versus Capital Markets

Managers of large, diffusely owned firms have reason to disrupt their shareholders' capacity to aggregate their stock ownership, as aggregations will reduce managerial autonomy. Although they do not necessarily own capital themselves, managers effectively control capital in large diffusely owned firms and they seek to maintain their control over the capital in their own firm. They seek laws that impede or bar hostile takeovers, rules that make it costly for shareholders to take large, active positions, and proxy contest rules that make it hard for shareholders to elect directors other than those that incumbent managers support. (Corporate election contests are costly. Stockholder votes need to be solicited, corporate election contest rules have to be complied with, and publicity needs to be sought. The firm pays for the incumbents' nominees, while insurgents generally pay their own costs but must split any corporate gains they induce with all other shareholders. Free rider problems abound, deterring otherwise valuable contests.) These conflicts could be characterized alternatively as politically powerful haves (the managers) moving value into their hands (or keeping it there, if it has already moved) and away from economically well-to-do haves (capital owners) who are less politically powerful.

These managerial efforts have been significant in the United States historically and continue to be central today. Managers have successfully opposed the strongest proposals in this past decade to allow shareholders to elect directors not supported by incumbent managers. Prior outbreaks of these shareholder-power proposals in the United States, starting in the 1940s, also died after managers successfully opposed the proposals. There's a considerable literature on managerial-shareholder conflict in the United States, see, for example, Berle and Means (1933), and Jensen and Meckling (1976). The literature on the spillover of managerial preferences and authority into the political sphere is thinner, although efforts can be found in Roe (1990, 1993), Grundfest (1990), and Bebchuk and Neeman (2010).

Managers of fully stockholder-controlled firms could not readily turn to the polity to seek such rules initially, as their controlling shareholders would be unhappy with such managerial lobbying to stymie shareholder power. But once ownership became diffuse, perhaps because of the combined impact of American populism and the interests of small-town bankers in the nineteenth century, managers could more readily engage in such political action, free from shareholder veto.

Controlling Shareholders versus Capital Markets

Controlling shareholders have reason to maintain rules that allow them to shift value to themselves. Corporate rules affect the private benefits of control—such as the ease with which small shareholders can reverse related-party transactions between the firm and the controlling insiders, and the ease with which controlling shareholders can squeeze out minority stockholders at an unfair price. Once a player controls a public firm, it has an interest in maintaining (or expanding) its capacity to shift value to itself (Bebchuk and Roe, 1999). This feature has been important in several Western European nations in recent decades.[2]

Capital Markets and Financial Politics in the Developing World

Rudiments without Government Institutions

Before we focus on the "have versus have-not" issues in the developing world—the setting to which we now switch—consider the developmental authorities' capital markets' programs and the basic academic understandings of what must be done. Development authorities often focus on bolstering institutions that promote financial markets, in the belief that better financial markets will lead to economic development. They seek to develop superior corporate laws, better securities laws, and better courts and other institutions to enforce financial and other contracts. Although these efforts are appropriate, the initial conditions needed historically for financial markets have been simple, with political economy conditions central. If the developing nation is sufficiently stable politically and socially, the first steps for financial markets institutions can be taken, and often have been taken, with limited government action. Thereafter, as the financial markets develop, there will be interests that seek to institutionalize that development and push it to the next level—and who have the know-how to do so. This alternative view implicates core have versus have-not issues, as we shall see.

First, though, let's understand that this sequence—first social and political stability, then financial market development, and then legal consolidation—is illustrated in studies of the initial development of the world's strongest securities markets. They all show a rather weak corporate institutional environment initially, but one embedded in a sufficiently stable environment so that reputational forces could propel initial, extralegal financial market development. Related concepts of repeated games, with expectations of long time lines for repeated interaction, which generates mild but real institutional self-enforcement, are relevant here. See Greif (2006, ch. 3 and pp. 441–443) and Scott (1987).

Consider Bradford DeLong's (1991) famous piece on J.P. Morgan's directors. In an environment of weak corporate law (see Rock, 2001), the Morgan firm put their partners on firms' boards to offer their own reputation to protect shareholders from scurrilous or incompetent management. (And, it must be added, perhaps facilitating cartelization, through the Morgan partners sitting on boards of competitors.) Pernicious insider dealings, or undiscovered managerial incompetence, would have cost the Morgan firm dearly, so they warranted (albeit weakly) that such nefarious or incompetent results would be unlikely to occur in the firms on whose boards they sat. Outside investors might not trust the firm, but they had more reason to trust the Morgan directors. Other investment banking firms presumably acted similarly.

Miwa and Ramseyer (2002) find an analogous reputational market at work in the nascent Japanese stock market of post–Meiji Restoration, late nineteenth-century Japan. Firms sought directors with sterling reputations to warrant to smaller stockholders that the firm had and would continue to have fair and competent management. The reputational directors had a lot to lose socially and perhaps psychologically, so they cared what happened inside the firm. Franks, Mayer, and Rossi (2009) and Mayer (2008) demonstrate a similar process at work in Britain at the end of the nineteenth and early twentieth centuries. Reputations and repeat dealings supported a nascent stock market. Hard-edged, government-facilitated legal institutions came later.

The point here is not that reputational structures are a panacea, obviating the need to build supportive institutions. Rather, the point is twofold: a capital market can start developing without preexisting strong institutional support, but it needs a stable political and social environment that makes the reputational markets valuable (and possible) to build. Once a rudimentary capital market is in place, a constituency in the nation that would support more rigorous institutions to regulate and promote capital markets begins developing.

The steps toward more rigorous institutions do not need to lead immediately to "hard" law. Stock markets' enforcement, for example, can initially be built, again albeit weakly, by the financial players (Coffee, 2001; Mahoney, 1997). They can punish miscreants by exclusion (such as by delisting in stock market terms or breaking the miscreants' trading bench at medieval trading fairs; North and Weingast, 1989).

These private, exclusionary mechanisms were important in the development of U.S. stock markets.[3] But such private ordering is imperfect, as the punishments the private players can invoke—typically exclusion or a besmirched reputation—cannot reach the severity that public punishments can via criminal penalties and fines. Still, the point persists that some sanctions can start before the public authorities act, as long as the political and social setting is sufficiently stable. Gilson, Hansmann, and Pargendler (2011) show this bottom-up process, starting in the market itself, has been in motion in Brazil in recent years.

Presumably such private ordering mechanisms could come forth and be effective in other nations, including developing nations today. But for many nations without sufficient political stability, such reputational and private ordering institutions are difficult or impossible to start up. Hence, those seeking to promote capital markets should have reason to inquire into the sources of political stability, a subject I look at next and which we see depends in important part on have versus have-not considerations.

Elites' Interests

The interests of a developing nation's elites are often key in pushing for or preventing capital market development.

A nation's elites may oppose capital market development. Two self-interested reasons could be in play. First, the elites may have satisfactory access to capital through, say, family banks or informal channels. Their grip on the polity may also allow them to stifle entry into banking, thereby keeping capital in the channels they already control. But a strong capital market could challenge the elite's monopoly status by facilitating upstart competitors' access to capital and, hence, increasing the upstarts' capacity to compete with the elites.

Rajan and Zingales (2003a) analyze this channel in several contexts, in both developing and developed nations, and show how trade openness affects a nation's elites' calculations. If the nation is open to trade, then the elites' underlying businesses must compete, simultaneously making efficient allocation of capital vitally important to them and making any suppression of competition with local upstarts less valuable (because international, cross-border competition will be intense anyway). Thus, Rajan and Zingales (2003b) conclude that in open-trade countries, elites would be less likely to oppose capital market development. Elites in closed countries would have greater incentives to suppress capital market development.

For developing nations, Acemoglu, Johnson, and Robinson (2001), Engerman and Sokoloff (2002, 2005), and Engerman, Haber, and Sokoloff (2000) each indicate how land and agricultural conditions, settlement conditions, and factor endowments could affect early colonial structures so as to strengthen (or weaken) elites with repressive interests and capacities. Particularly where settlement conditions were difficult due to terrain or climate, or where plantation-style agriculture was most efficient, colonial conditions induced powerful, concentrated elites who had little need for either broad-based property rights or open opportunity societies. Those original conditions persist, or they induced equality-impeding institutions that persist to today. In other colonial settings, particularly where land, climate, and agriculture made European settlement easy and favored smaller, more widely distributed and often individually owned farms, colonization induced broad-based property rights, with weaker elites. These contrasting original settlement conditions then set the stage for equality-enhancing or equality-impeding institutions, which in turn affected property rights and capital markets over the long run. Analyses of the same general genre can be found in Boix (2003, pp. 45–46, 93) and Rodrik (1999); see also Olson (1984). Land, agricultural conditions, and local economic strengths and weaknesses gave more power or less power to elites and nonelites, and these have versus have-not differences shaped subsequent capital market and institutional development.

For Russia, Sonin (2003) and Hoff and Stiglitz (2008) analogously evaluate the political economy of the elites—there, the "oligarchs." Property protection can be provided privately or publicly. The oligarchs were well positioned to protect their property from other less powerful private players, and accordingly opposed strong public protection of property rights. Adequately protected already, they judged that publicly provided property protection would mostly facilitate competition from the less powerful, which could only hurt their own secure position. Hence, strong protection of property, financial and otherwise, did not arise, and financial markets did not develop.[4]

This elite suppression of competition explanation is important, although incomplete, because the elites that can shut down local financial markets can presumably *also* shut down open border trading markets. The explanation works well when trade barriers decline for an exogenous reason, such as European political goals of fostering a continent-wide economy in recent decades, in ways that overrode local interests. But these explanations work less well in other nations at other times, where exogenous shocks do not reduce trade barriers.

Moreover, in a democracy, one must explain why the democratic polity accedes to the elites' interests. A plausible starting point is that the elites' interests coincide with those of others, making a politically dominant coalition possible. A common example is that labor in the elites' industries also have reason to stifle product competition. The two may ally, with labor providing the democratic voting muscle, as Roe (2001, 2003) indicates. (Consideration of more complex coalitions comes later in this chapter.) For now, let us observe that movement to democracy, all else equal, should foster deeper capital markets, as elites have less weight in the nation's decision making, and hence, their goal of suppressing competitive upstarts will be harder to attain. However, all else will not be equal when an oligarchy becomes a democracy, as the elites would then have reason to form coalitions with broader voting groups, like labor. Corporatism and varieties of capitalism concepts (see Hall and Soskice, 2001) contain this kind of coalition of elites with similarly interested nonelites embedded in the conceptualization.

Nonelites' Interests

Nonelites in developing nations can affect property protection and capital markets. If they are living a subsistence life, then they can improve their immediate well-being by appropriating capital. If they have weak prospects or are currently calorie-deprived, their immediate survival considerations should trump long-run development goals. Their long run may be capital markets' short run.

The have-nots can see property rights, such as investor protection, as protecting the haves. They could conclude that weaker investor protection would enable them to become the equivalent of squatters on the elites' financial assets.

Elites may want government protection against financial squatters, but their offsetting desire to suppress new competition may weaken their interest in greater property protection overall. The have-nots may want to protect their meager property, and a few of the upwardly mobile may think they could enter the elite. But most conclude that investor protection protects the elites' capital from the have-nots' incursions and hence oppose strong property rights for capital.

Political Stability

Roe and Siegel (2011) advance a complementary idea—that financial markets cannot develop easily in severely unstable political environments. As Huntington (1968, p. 8) observes, "authority has to exist before it can be limited, and it is authority that is in scarce supply in those modernizing countries where government is at the mercy of alienated intellectuals [and] rambunctious colonels." Roe and Siegel find that political instability robustly explains differing levels of financial development, even after controlling for trade openness and the level of economic development—and does so in both country fixed effects and instrumental variable regressions, and across multiple measures of instability and financial development. In an unstable society, investors' basic property rights cannot be secure, because they cannot be sure what the polity will look like over the life of their investments.

Moreover, a political economy literature plants instability's roots in inequality-perpetuating institutions and ethnic fractionalization.[5] The first factor, economic inequality, fits tightly with explaining why investor protection doesn't develop in unstable environments: for the unstable polity to protect investors, it would have to protect the most favored elements in that polity. Haves versus have-nots again. Yet that unstable polity is riven by contention over the division of wealth and income—that is, whether the favored can keep their wealth. Roe and Siegel use proxies for inequality-perpetuating institutions and social fractionalization of the type that Engerman and Sokoloff (2002) brought forward and that Easterly (2007) validated, as further evidence of the old idea that inequality induces instability. A developing nation needs to break the negative causal chain of inequality to instability to weak financial development in order to position itself to develop its capital market.

Inequality

It bears separate emphasis that inequality—haves and have-nots—is at the base of several of these theories. Severe inequality undermines political stability, and political stability is foundational for financial market development. Yet it may not be easy to reduce that inequality, not just for the obvious reason that those who lose from reducing inequality do not always support its reduction. Inequality may be due to the production technologies available in the economy; it may be endogenous to the polity itself.

Yet several of the world's most developed financial markets are in nations, like the United States, that have quite high Gini coefficients for the distribution of wealth and property. This characteristic deserves further inquiry.

Original Conditions

Path dependence could explain this outcome. The nation's income and wealth distribution may have been substantially equal when financial markets first developed, and then the nation accepted the inequality later. For the United States, such path dependence is plausible, as U.S. income and property distribution until the end of the nineteenth century was relatively flat (Lindert, 2006). Financial markets started to develop during that era and persisted, without a major political upheaval pushing the country off that path. Preferences were not always pro–capital market, but they sought to channel and confine that market, not destroy it. Conversely, in countries that suffered a major political upheaval, the distribution of income and wealth during the period in which the capital market was reconstructed could have profoundly influenced its subsequent shape.

A similar sequential process holds true for England. England was the locus of the first Industrial Revolution. Its severe labor shortage at the time and its energy abundance pushed forward the technological development needed for the first Industrial Revolution (Allen, 2009). Less well noted is that the higher wage rate that accompanies scarce labor also mitigated inequality, thereby reducing potential political instability, and hence, creating a favorable environment for capital market development.

Engerman and Sokoloff (2002, pp. 44–46, 63–83), as noted previously, offer a general structure of the political economy of property rights in the developing world, in which we can place rights in the capital market as a subset. If a colonizing power came to land areas best used for plantation-style crops or, say, mining activities using mass unskilled labor, then the original political institutions would reflect the underlying land use characteristics. The colonizers then had little reason to foster broad-based property rights, as they could protect themselves well enough. They had little reason to foster developing broad-based education and skills for their plantation workers, because the elites only needed unskilled labor.[6] The consequence is that the nation early on, while still a colony, lacked widely distributed property and had weak property protection institutions. Oppressive institutions persisted and capital markets had little role in future development.[7]

Conceptualizing Economic Inequality

A second characteristic is related but not identical. Politically destabilizing inequality may not be a function of the raw ratio of wealth and income of the richest to that of the poorest. Rather, it might be based on something more complex, which we can call a severity ratio. To construct the ratio, we look at the number of people unable to obtain, say, their 2,000 calories per day. That is the denominator. The numerator counts those who have no difficulty obtaining the minimal calories for a comfortable existence (Williamson, 2009).

In these terms, the United States is less severely unequal than the conventional Gini concept indicates—even the bottom fifth can usually get their 2,000 calories per day. In another polity, where the bottom fifth struggles to obtain only 1,500 calories per day, the reconceptualized severity ratio could be quite high, even though the usual Gini calculation would consider the nation to be more equal than the United States.

Mapping Inequality and Equality onto Race

Race, ethnicity, and religion can be central in a polity, particularly when wealth and income disparities cleave along racial or ethnic lines. If race and economic class map onto one another, it becomes easier for groups to demonize and dehumanize opposing groups and make a stable polity harder to achieve. Several studies have found such ethnic conflicts to be central to political instability.[8]

Race and ethnicity can have other effects that complicate analysis of their impact. They can make it easier for capital markets to flourish by diverting political conflict from economic to noneconomic issues, thereby pushing conflict between haves and have-nots lower on the political agenda. If the polity cleaves along cultural or multiple identity lines that do not map onto distributional differences, those distributional differences can recede in political contentiousness. Dahl (1971), Benson (1961), Sombart (1906), and Schattsneider (1960) speak to this kind of issue.

Overall, though, instability increases if class and property-owning fault lines are also race and ethnicity fault lines. When they are, capital market–debilitating conflict intensifies.

Contemporary and Historical Examples in the Developed World

In this part, I expand on several of the have versus have-not categories, with an eye on political economy configurations around the developed world in recent decades and further reference to the existing political economy of finance literature. For several of these examples, rational systemic optimization in a system of preexisting institutions does not well explain the capital markets outcomes. Powerful preferences and compelling interests seem as important, or more important, as preexisting institutions.

Contemporary

Labor in Europe

After World War II, labor was particularly powerful in Europe in ways that profoundly affected postwar capital market development. Capital market institutions were poorly supported, even decades after the war, in terms of budgets and personnel for the capital markets' regulatory apparatus (Jackson and Roe, 2009). Strong owners had two reasons to stay close to the firm, one to better ensure that the firm's cash flowed to them, the owners, and the other to be sure that the polity supported policies that would protect the firm's profitability.

On the first, with labor able to make strong claims on firms' cash flows, owners had more reason to stay in place and run the firm themselves, or keep a controlling block of stock to facilitate keeping close watch on the managers. Owners had reason to stay involved to better ensure that managers resist powerful labor's strong claims on the firm's cash flow. On the second, strong owners had reason to influence the polity to keep the firm's market position dominant; in the weakened international trading markets after the war, labor and owners had reason to unite in this dimension to preserve their firm's market position, to keep out competition, and then to bargain to divide the spoils (Roe, 2000, 2001, 2003).

Managers in the United States

Managers in the United States—major American "haves"—are a powerful interest group in making the rules governing corporate finance and capital markets. In the 1980s, for example, capital markets created the hostile takeover to facilitate capital markets' control over managers. (As is well known, American diffuse ownership facilitated high levels of managerial agency costs, because managers lacked a day-to-day boss and often drifted from shareholders' interests with higher compensation, unnecessary expansion, and mistaken operating policies.) This technique had the outside firm or entrepreneur buying up enough stock of the target firm such that the new owner could direct managerial policy or replace the target firm's managers.

But the American "haves"—the managers and directors of large companies—successfully disrupted those hostile takeovers both transactionally and by using their political muscle. Transactionally, managers and directors developed poison pills and staggered boards that made it costly for the outsider to buy up the target company's stock. Politically, managers, through their lobbying organizations such as the Chamber of Commerce, the Business Roundtable, and often enough the business section of the American Bar Association, obtained favorable laws through the political process—laws that validated and often added to these disruptions of the hostile takeover.

Historical

American Populism: Have-Nots versus the Powerful

Populism can affect financial markets and institutions. Andrew Jackson's destruction of the Second Bank of the United States in the 1830s is the most famous example in U.S. history. It was a seminal event in American financial political history, leaving the United States without a truly national banking system until the latter part of the twentieth century. The effect of the bank's demise was to make securities markets more vital for the United States and to deny the nation even the rudiments of a central bank until the beginning of the twentieth century (perhaps not until 1935). American capital markets could not develop via a nationwide banking system in the nineteenth and most of the twentieth centuries. Roe (1994) attributes a significant fraction of the differences between American and many other nations' capital markets to the U.S.-specific aftermath of Jackson's veto, fueled by populist interests and thinking. Thereafter, institutions and new interests developed to accommodate and perpetuate the resulting weak national banking system.

It could have gone the other way, as two early Congresses and two U.S. presidents chartered the First and Second Banks, making the decision to have a quasi-central bank a closer one than basic history books usually have it. The happenstance of political maneuvering derailed the American incipient central bank, as an ambitious Henry Clay mistakenly thought that early passage of a rechartering bill would put Jackson on the defensive, forcing him to approve it, while at the same time, the incumbent head of the Second Bank of the United States, Nicholas Biddle, proved to be politically clumsy. Clay underestimated both Jackson's resolve and the influence of smaller, weaker banks that preferred not to be challenged by the Second Bank's regulatory impulses. Jackson's veto and destruction of the Second Bank left the United States without a strong, national banking system and created the interests—small banks, scattered throughout the country—that deeply influenced financial market development in the country for the next century and a half.

Political economy and populist political impulses persisted, and institutions created by earlier preferences had staying power. After Jackson's destruction of the Second Bank, there were multiple efforts to facilitate a truly national banking system. However, these failed on the twin shoals of smaller banks' influence in Congress and populist resistance to a truly national banking system.

During the Civil War, for example, the United States built institutions called national banks, which substantively received their governing charter from Washington. But these banks were national in name only and not in their operation, as they were restricted to a single physical location. This limit was challenged in the 1890s, as the Treasury proposed to allow nationwide branching, but the proposal failed in Congress. It was challenged again in the 1920s and 1930s, but it was only mildly tweaked: branching of banks was still limited to a single state at most and, for many states, a smaller geographic profile.

Popular animus continued to play a role in major banking and insurance legislation. Glass-Steagall's separation of investment and commercial banking, the Bank Holding Company Act of 1956's limits on bank activities (recall, for those familiar with the politicians of the time, Wright Patman's influence), and the major life insurance companies' lack of power to own common stock (due to the Armstrong investigation of 1906) can all be traced in major part to this popular animus. This left the United States with severe limits on national financial operations: a lack of a national banking system, banks without power to engage in commerce, and insurance companies without authority to own common stock. Although other nations have had some of these limits, few have had them all. Britain, for example, has had powerful insurers. Germany has had universal banks with substantial stock ownership and even more powerful control of their customers' votes. Japan has had nation-spanning banks with significant stock ownership.

German Codetermination

German codetermination is a formal institution reflecting this shareholder–social democratic balance of power, vividly illustrating the political economy effects on core corporate institutions. To settle raw political conflict at several moments in the twentieth century, German social democracy led to the Bundestag enacting laws mandating that labor be represented in firms' boardrooms, culminating in the 1976 law requiring near-parity representation for labor in the boardrooms of the nation's largest firms. Because unconstrained managers have tended to have an agenda favoring firm continuance, size, and risk avoidance (see Jensen, 1986) and that agenda maps onto employees' own agenda for the same, an implicit coalition can easily form between managers and employees. When it does, shareholders will want to have a cohesive countercoalition in the boardroom. Concentrated ownership is a primary way to build that countercoalition.

Preference Aggregation and Combinatorics

Thus far I have generally examined discrete interests and their preferences for and against various capital markets forms. But, as the German codetermination experience shows, discrete interests can overlap and coalitions can arise. In this part, through a series of historical examples, I examine, first, how coalitions form, persist, and morph. Second, I examine the political institutions resulting from preference aggregation and how they shape political results and institutional formation, which in turn affect capital market results.

Shifting Coalitions

Banks and Labor in Europe

One of the more interesting instances of the formation of a capital market–affecting coalition can be seen in post–World War II Western Europe. Perotti and von Thadden (2006) provide compelling argumentation and significant data to support the idea that Western European polities in the post–World War II era had the equivalent of a banker-labor coalition that impeded capital market development.

Their argument begins with the median voter theorem: In postwar Western Europe, they posit that the median voter had strong human capital but little financial capital. As such, the median voter had little interest in promoting financial markets, for fear that powerful financial markets would more readily erode his or her human capital than weak financial markets. Stronger capital markets punish slow-moving firms. They demand that firms more quickly adopt new technologies, if profitable, and those new technologies could readily erode the value of labor's human capital, tied as it is to experience with the old technologies. Lacking financial capital and dependent on human capital, the median voter was risk-averse to policies that could erode the voter's human capital.[9]

At the same time, banks—to the extent that their creditors' interest dominated their other financial interests—were moderately risk-averse (because the downside disproportionately affected their loans, whereas the upside benefited stockholders). Accordingly, banks that became primary corporate governance players had a risk-averse profile that fit well with the median voter's preferences. Labor with limited capital preferred banks to stock markets—and that is what they sought from the polity and, powerful as they were, that is what they got from it. The median voter voted for bank-oriented capitalism.[10]

Managers, Labor, and Populism in the United States

A similar, albeit indirect alignment of interests existed between American managers and American populism at several times. A plausible view of the sequential development of U.S. capital markets history is the following. In the 1890s, national enterprises became viable: railroads had by then spanned the North American continent, turning the nation into a single market, and engineering economies of scale made large-scale production especially valuable, inducing local firms to merge to form nation-spanning enterprises. With American populism having facilitated a weak national banking system, mergers needed stock market financing. With stock market financing in place, ownership started separating from control and managers increasingly gained control over the firm, with the stockholder-owners becoming geographically distant, poorly informed, and not motivated to control or even influence the firm's operations. Once ownership separated from control in the large American public firm, managers then became political actors in their own right, via their lobbying organizations such as the Business Roundtable, the National Association of Manufacturers, and Chambers of Commerce. Their interest was to preserve and enhance managerial authority, which they have accomplished.

A similar American coalition formed in the 1980s. Hostile takeovers made managers' lives considerably more difficult during that decade. These takeovers also disrupted workers' expectations of their future in the firm by putting their jobs at risk. Even if a potential takeover would not leave the workers unemployed, the employees would find themselves in a disrupted work environment. Thus, they shared managers' opposition to hostile takeovers.

This kind of managerial-labor coalition was often enough decisive in pressing states to pass antitakeover laws. When a Pennsylvania corporation was targeted for a hostile takeover, it sought strong antitakeover law from the state legislature. For many Pennsylvania lawmakers, voting for the legislation was an easy political decision, as both the Chamber of Commerce and the AFL-CIO supported the legislation. Roe (1993, p. 339), quotes a contemporary comment: "[The] lobbying effort is the product of teamwork between... Pennsylvania labor unions and a coalition of over two dozen corporations working for the passage of the bill under the well-organized direction of the Pennsylvania Chamber of Business and Industry."

Constituency statutes, which allowed boards to consider labor interests when deciding whether to support or oppose a takeover, are also manifestations of this coalition.

Dominant Stockholders and Labor

Dominant stockholders could ally with labor. As we've seen, business elites often have an interest in suppressing financial markets, as upstarts need access to capital to compete with incumbent elites, which they cannot get without strong financial markets. But this begs the question of why, in a democracy, the polity would accede to the elites' interests.

Mistake is one possibility. Ideology is another. A tactical coalition is a third: Labor at the incumbent firms may get a slice of the incumbent firms' profits, motivating labor at the business elites' firms to support the elites' interests in suppressing new competitors because the elites' interests here coincide with their own. If labor obtains such a rent, it wants to suppress product market competition with their employer, suppress upstarts' access to new finance, and suppress open trade with foreign competitors.

• • •

A sophisticated rendition of the multiple possible coalitions can be found in Gourevitch and Shinn (2005), who show how there are almost as many permutations in play between and among labor, owners, and managers as there are rich nations. Labor power can dominate owners and managers, as in Sweden. Or owners and managers can coalesce to dominate workers, as in Korea. Or owners can dominate both, as in oligarchic nations. Or workers and owners can coalesce to dominate managers. Or workers and managers can dominate owners, as in corporatist states, such as Germany, Japan, and the Netherlands.

Western European nations have been analyzed as corporatist systems for some time, with analysts viewing the economy as being largely governed by tripartite decision makers: the government, peak labor associations, and employer representatives. The varieties of capitalism literature (Hall and Soskice, 2001) integrated this thinking into production characteristics. That literature argues that economies that depend on skilled labor tend not to have liquid stock markets, which would disrupt labor skills. Conversely, economies that depend less on labor with firm-specific skills could handle capital markets' disruptions. These analyses look at the informal institutions of coalition formation. Business leaders would want to be represented at the centralized decision-making institutions, thereby putting a thumb on the scale for close ownership and weaker capital markets as well.

Political Institutions and Preference Aggregation

Here I shift focus from how raw preferences and interests can shape institutions and financial markets to how the political economy of institutions shapes financial outcomes. Conceptually more traditional than the former, the political economy of institutional structure deserves to be applied to capital markets formation and deserves summary and development here.

Since Arrow's impossibility theorem, political scientists have examined mechanisms of preference aggregation in a polity, because these profoundly affect policy outcomes. As is well known, the impossibility theorem's conceptual power comes from voters having differently ordered preferences. When a choice between two of three viable options is presented, the voting result may differ from what would result if the ordering of the choices had been otherwise.

Parliamentary versus Presidential Systems: Proportional Representation and Party Lists

Pagano and Volpin (2005) apply Persson and Tabellini's (2000, 2005) general inquiry into parliamentary systems, proportional representation, and presidential systems to the specifics of corporate and capital markets. Party-list and proportional representation enable a coalition among business owners and labor to enact rules that poorly protect capital providers (so that incumbent business owners benefit at the expense of outside investors) and protect incumbent labor well. Decisions are driven not by the median voter but by the way a dominant coalition is formed.

Iversen and Soskice (2006) argue that proportional representation structures facilitate center-left redistributive coalitions, whereas majoritarian, presidential, first-past-the-post systems facilitate center-right, low-redistribution outcomes. In majoritarian systems, they indicate, the decisive middle-class vote will side with the well-to-do for fear of being taxed by the poor; but in proportional representation systems, the middle class can ally with the poor to redistribute from the well-to-do while still maintaining enough influence in the middle-poor coalition to ensure that the middle class are not themselves the target for redistribution.

Mueller (2006) shows further how first-past-the-post electoral systems, such as those in the United States, can affect corporate governance outcomes. In such political systems, a national interest group, such as labor, needs to persistently recapture a working majority in the legislature, working district by district, legislator by legislator. This is hard to accomplish. But in a party-list system, the identity of the particular legislator is not vital to the interest group getting that legislator's vote: the legislator follows party discipline, thereby facilitating national deal making in which national labor institutions could be quite influential. In systems with first-past-the-post territorial elections, such national coalitions (and their concomitant influence) are harder to create and maintain. It's thus no accident that Tip O'Neill's famous aphorism—that all politics is local—came from a U.S. national politician, the locally elected leader of the House of Representatives, a legislative body that is a collection of locally elected representatives who make national policy.

Mechanisms for preference aggregation can have a profound impact on the ability of players to form coalitions and, consequently, on the influence they can exert on the development of capital markets.

American Federalism I

The organization of the U.S. Congress is relevant here in another dimension as well. If all politics (in the United States) is local, then local interests can determine national outcomes. One reason all politics is local is that the House of Representatives is organized and elected by local geographic districts. With representatives dependent on local interests for their election, the House was responsive historically to local bankers who wished to be shielded from out-of-district competition. When technology only allowed for localized bricks-and-mortar banking (i.e., before the era of automated teller machines, online banking, and cheap telecommunications), bankers had the means and motivation to influence their local representatives' voting on whether to facilitate nationwide bank branching, a result that we've seen deeply affected U.S. capital markets. The state-by-state organization of the Senate presumably has had a similar albeit weaker impact.

Hence, one can see a structure-driven process: U.S. political structure promoted local interests. When local banking was technologically possible, this local power *overly* emphasized local banking, making national banking markets impossible during the formative years of national industry. This meant that large industrial firms had to raise their capital from disparate sources that could not readily concentrate their stock holdings, facilitating a shift in authority inside the firm to managers.

American Federalism II: Delaware

U.S. corporate and capital markets law is made in two principal jurisdictions: Delaware (via the laws of corporate organization) and Washington, D.C. (via the laws covering securities regulation). Unlike other polities, the United States effectively allows the corporation to choose its own state of incorporation, regardless of where it does business in the nation; the corporation thus chooses its own governing law. Most major American public firms choose to incorporate in Delaware.[11]

The federal organization of U.S. corporate lawmaking has long been a focus of corporate law academics, who have seen competition among states for corporate charters (and their resulting revenues) as a core driver in making corporate law, thereby applying Tiebout's (1956) insights on political jurisdictional mobility to the specifics of corporate lawmaking. Some thought the competition was "to the top" in making corporate law more efficient,[12] whereas others saw the competition as one "to the bottom," by favoring the corporate players most central to the incorporation decision—managers, controlling shareholders, and their lawyers.[13]

This federal organization of the polity can affect capital markets, as interests dominant on the state level can get rules that a busy Congress might not provide. During the hostile takeover era, many states passed strong antitakeover laws, making it transactionally more expensive for an outsider to buy up stock of a public firm. In the political balance were the managerial, labor, and capital interests. Local managers did not want the hostile takeover to proceed. Local labor employed by the target company did not want the offer to proceed. While shareholders in the capital market presumably wanted the takeover to proceed, many of them were not local, because capital markets were national or international. Hence, the balance favored in-state managerial and labor interests over capital market interests.[14] Again, all politics is local.

American Federalism III: Delaware and Washington

The simultaneous state-federal structure of U.S. corporate lawmaking can affect capital markets in another dimension. The interests that prevail in Delaware, the dominant state corporate lawmaker, are not the same as those making corporate and securities law in Washington. Particularly during times of financial crisis or scandal, the populist input to weaken shareholder and financial strength in the corporation, or to punish managers who are seen to be overcompensated, is strong in Washington and weaker in Delaware, where the interests of managers and shareholders dominate.

In areas that are of overlapping concern to national and Delaware lawmakers, the national and local polities interact in two major ways. First, Delaware may preemptively pass financial and corporate law to reduce the chance of federal action. It may do so out of self-preservation: If Delaware is far out of line with national sentiment, corporate lawmaking could move from Delaware to Washington and become, like securities law, national, congressionally made law. Second, Delaware may act to protect its local interests: with first-mover advantages, Delaware may pass rules that go some but not all of the way to satisfying the national appetite. Doing so would allow it to preserve as much autonomy for managers (or value for shareholders) as possible, by persuading Washington decision makers that enough had been done, so that nothing more is needed from Washington. This is analogous to the process Spiller and Gely (2008) posited for the Supreme Court, by which the Court often decides cases in ways that diminish the chance of congressional action (by coming closer to congressional preferences than they would have otherwise).

Weak Capital after World War II

Earlier in the chapter, I indicated that a defining feature of the political economy of U.S. capital markets can be found in the destruction of the Second Bank of the United States, which left the country without a nationwide banking system during the nineteenth century, when a continent-wide, nationwide industrial economy arose. The interests, ideologies, and institutions that resulted tended to reinforce themselves during times of crisis, because no subsequent American crisis was so severe as to leave the economy flat, destroyed, and needing a fully new set of institutions. Even the 1930s New Deal tended to strengthen preexisting interests, not destroy them.

Could there be a similar foundational political economy event for Western European and East Asian capital markets? I think there is, but as of now that possibility must be seen as a hypothesis, needing further theoretical and factual development.

The concept would be that after World War II enough political and economic institutions had been destroyed that a substantial new construction of those institutions took place. In those years, capital owners and labor interests sought to establish the new rules of the game that would then govern markets and finance from that time on. The twist arises from the following difficulty: we know that the continental European rules of the game had a prolabor and not a procapital tilt in the subsequent decades. But with capital scarce after World War II—the physical capital was, after all, largely destroyed—and with labor (especially skilled labor) relatively abundant, the bargaining process in the economic arena should have *favored* the scarce resource's preferences in rules and returns. Yet at least as far as the rules were concerned, the results went the other way. Labor markets, including wage rates and other benefits, were favored in the decades after World War II.

When the bargaining began for a new postwar understanding as to how to organize capital and labor markets, the pro–capital markets players were relatively weak in the political arena—relative both to labor at the time and to their own more usual strength in influencing results. Their physical capital had largely been destroyed during the war; they had limited capacity to affect the politics of the time with campaign contributions, lobbying, or otherwise when the foundational deals were made. Only later could they afford the time, money, and personnel for such efforts; then they made sure that they were represented at the peak bargaining of the corporatist model. By that later time, however, labor had acquired its postwar favored status. For now, the original conditions idea—that the preferences and weak institutional structure in continental Europe right after World War II set the institutional framework for subsequent, relatively weak capital market development—is a hypothesis for further development. During the immediate postwar period, strongly held popular preferences and politically weak ownership interests could well have established the new institutional arrangements that would endure, affecting capital markets structure for decades.

Geopolitics

Geography and national political power influence political preferences and the strength and nature of internal political economy institutions. Geopolitical features of the last half of the twentieth century are relevant and can be quickly sketched out. Geopolitical features over time are more subtle, but can also be seen.

Countering the Soviet Union

The central geopolitical fact in continental Europe in the second half of the twentieth century was the looming presence of the Soviet Union. In the initial postwar elections, communist parties did quite well in France and Italy, making it important for centrist and conservative parties to coopt the communist program, which they did. The result was policy that favored incumbent labor and that disfavored capital markets.

One can think of the geopolitics as lying along a continuum: in Eastern Europe, communists gained power and capital markets ended. In Western Europe, to stave off communist power, the political center had to adopt some of the left's program. For Japan, South Korea, and Taiwan, the relationship with China in the immediate postwar decades could well have brought similar domestic sensibilities into play.

European Geography over the Centuries

The state has been seen as stronger in Europe than in the United States. This view maps onto the view of state actors as their own interest group that seeks to diminish the power of private capital markets, as outlined in the initial section of this chapter. The strength of the European states could have first originated in European geography: the open east–west plains of Europe meant that local security from invasion was always at issue, and that vulnerability induced national militaries and strong states (Roe, 2007). Postwar geopolitics reproduced the incentives for a strong state.

This geographic history contrasted with that of the United States and Britain historically, and with that of Europe today. The United States and Britain were both separated from invaders by bodies of water—narrow but real in Britain's case and wide for the United States. That geographic separation meant that centralized, standing armies were not needed for national security, and the state could be weaker than otherwise, thereby leaving space for private capital markets to develop. Today, after the fall of the Berlin Wall and a safer European geopolitical reality—one including European economic integration—the geopolitics of a centralized state for smaller European nations is historical, not current.

Political Change: Rightward and Leftward Shifts over Time

The postwar European setting leads to another consideration. One might examine the postwar left–right shifts for their impact on financial markets (see Perotti and von Thadden, 2006; Roe, 2003). Left–right splits and the impact of shifts can be tested over time, but tests done thus far are not dispositive. That is, financial markets in the developed nations, especially in Europe, strengthened in the 1990s, even in nations with locally left-of-center governments. Several commentators have made much of this (see Botero et al., 2004).

This is an understandable misconception.[15] The problem and its misconception can easily be conceptualized (and diagrammed, see figure 3.2). Over time, the center of gravity in a polity can change, sometimes sharply. As an example, Tony Blair's election as U.K. prime minister in 1997 marked not the ascendancy of the hard left that long dominated the Labour Party, but the ascendancy of the *moderating* of the left as it tacked toward the center. Yet it would be coded as the ascent

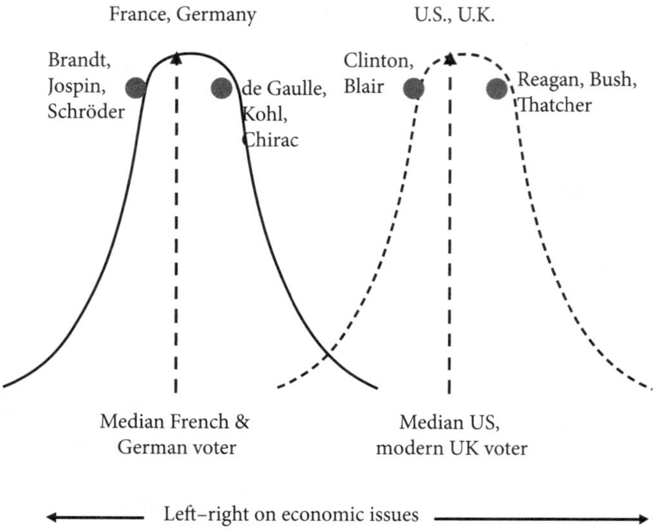

Figure 3.2. Local versus Absolute

of a left-of-center government in the usual academic studies thus far. But capital markets may draw comfort from a tame left and flourish not because the left was in power but because the left had moved rightward. Brazil's experience with a market-friendly former union leader in the past decade also illustrates the phenomenon and potential for a left–right attribution error. Similarly, Bill Clinton's presidency represented the U.S. left-of-center, but that administration was as market-oriented as a right-tilting government in Western Europe in many eras.

Indeed, in a pure median voter theory, the *identity* of the party in power makes no difference: it's the *left–right location* of the median voter that determines the polity's policies. Because some of the most substantial empirical work done thus far on left–right influence on capital markets suffers from this misconception, more work needs to be done here.

Eichengreen (2007, p. 333) explains why a left-of-center government can enact reforms that, in a prior decade, only a right-of-center government would have considered: "The German chancellor Gerhard Schröder's Agenda 2010 of labor-market reforms was motivated, in part, by the specter of German manufacturing moving east if steps were not taken to reduce labor costs."[16]

Indeterminacy, Overgeneralization, and Local Variation

Two characteristics can undermine the influence of the political economy academic agenda for understanding capital markets. First, although politics may well be decisive in determining capital markets' shape and extent, too many political explanations are local: a particular coalition in this nation, the happenstance of deal making in that nation. A narrative of national financial legislation may reveal the likely political economy story for that piece of legislation, but the explanation may not test well, because a testable characteristic may not repeat in a sufficient number of nations to yield significant regression results. Consequently, only the most general of political economy theories may be susceptible to strong empirical analysis. National case studies could be how we see what explains capital markets' depth (or lack of it).

A second problem afflicts a political economy approach. Often underlying our analysis is the goal of finding out what works for policy and recommending that policy's adoption. If we can find a simple rule or two that helps capital markets, or can find an existing rule that hinders them without ancillary benefit, then we can recommend which rules should be adopted and which should not. But a political economy analysis does not yield such strong, precise normative results for us. National politics is hard enough to understand, much less to influence with academic work.

But understanding the political economy inputs is still vital to normative analysis. If there's a menu of improvements for financial markets, but some choices on that menu will run into political economy problems and others will not, then policy makers should order their preferences accordingly, picking perhaps a less efficient but politically viable policy. International aid agencies may be particularly susceptible to ignoring political economy influences because they see it as illegitimate for them to seek political influence. But if the earlier focus on the centrality of political instability is correct, the development agencies can use the resulting insights to better decide how to allocate their aid and advice. Highly unstable polities are unlikely to benefit from even good rules; attempts to graft institutions for finance into such polities will be unlikely to "take." Hence, the development agencies can channel their efforts into nations that already have sufficient stability to allow for success. They can also select from among the different capital markets' development policies, choosing those that are more likely to stabilize than destabilize the polity, presumably keeping distributional outcomes in mind.

Conclusion

Two fundamental fractures can cripple the politics of capitalism. One is the contest between the haves and the have-nots. Have-nots can conclude that they gain too little from capitalism, so they may expropriate capital from the haves. Capitalism may persist in form, but its productivity would be demolished, as savers will not save—that is, will not create capital—because in such polities, owners of physical and financial capital do not see their capital as safe. Instead, they will consume it, for if they do not, the have-nots will appropriate it. Alternatively, the haves may capture political institutions themselves and seek to put in place institutions that redistribute value to themselves. Due to that tension, capitalist institutions may not survive or, even if they do survive, would fail to provide prosperity.

The second problem cuts the polity along another dimension. The capitalist haves may split and contest the polity among themselves. Those haves who have captured political institutions may seek to redistribute value away from other haves. The winners obtain rules that further their wealth and their preferred capital market channel. With enhanced wealth, they have both the strength and the motivation to preserve their position and suppress competitive upstarts. If the institutions are roughly democratic, the haves will find it valuable to form alliances with have-not voting masses, presumably starting with labor from their own industry.

These two problems arise in multiple dimensions in the economy, affecting welfare and social payments, antitrust policy, taxation, corporate law, income distribution, and financial markets. Many seemingly smaller problems in implementation of rules and laws are local manifestations of one of these two problems. For the most part I have analyzed these two basic problems in the politics of capitalism in terms of how they specifically affect financial markets and corporate structures. The issues may be more general.

The political problem of capitalism is to find institutions and preference distributions that keep the extent of such fissures and their costs low. No country succeeds in getting them to zero. Much that seems superficially inefficient to an economics-oriented analyst is a polity's effort to keep these fissures from rupturing the terrain.

• • •

We have made much headway in the past few decades, since North's (1990) focus on institutions, in understanding how institutions persist through time. Institutions, though, are created at some point in time. Similarly, institutions are also sometimes torn down, radically reconstructed, or even replaced. People and polities with preferences and interests create them, change them, and at times destroy them. Sometimes long-standing institutions can withstand a tidal wave from current preferences; at other times they cannot, and new, widespread, powerful preferences create new institutions that endure thereafter. Sometimes today's result can be predicted from the preexisting institutional framework; at other times current preferences that emerge during an economic or political crisis determine today's result. The political economy of capital markets well illustrates this interaction between preferences and institutions. Only when we understand how preferences for and against capital markets interact with institutions in the political economy will we understand the shape and extent of the capital market. Today's preferences, when effective and dominant in the political arena, can become tomorrow's governing institutions. In this chapter, I focused on how preferences can overwhelm preexisting institutions and establish new ones that support, channel, or determine the strength, nature, and quality of capital markets.

NOTES

1. See Douglas (1940, pp. 11, 14) (statement from chair of the Securities and Exchange Commission: people who dominate financial markets have "tremendous power.... Such [people] become virtual governments in the power at their disposal. [Sometimes it is] the dut[y] of government to police them, at times to break them up"); compare with Skocpol (1979).
2. Morck (2000) (concentrated ownership).
3. Mahoney (1997), Coffee (2001), Roe (2001).
4. The oligarchs' opposition to both stronger property rights and strong financial market development may have been short-sighted: the private oligarchs were advantaged in property protection vis-à-vis less well-placed private actors, but they did less well when pitted against emboldened public players when Putin came to power. Had stronger property protection and financial market depth been in place when the stronger state emerged, the government might have had more difficulty in suppressing the oligarchs in as many dimensions as it did.
5. For example, Alesina and Perotti (1996); see also Ayyagari, Demirgüç-Kunt, and Maksimovic (2008).
6. See Bobonis (2008).
7. See also Acemoglu, Johnson, and Robinson (2001) and Engerman, Haber, and Sokoloff (2000). See also Glaeser (2006).
8. See Alesina et al. (2003), Easterly and Levine (1997).
9. It's also possible to recast the argument in property-owning terms. The relevant question would be whether the median voter owns property, not simply whether he or she owns financial property. If the median voter owns significant property—a house, a car—then he or she may support property rights generally, which include rights to financial property.
10. Or, analogously, their political parties made appropriate deals to support bank-oriented capitalism. Pagano and Volpin (2005). Moreover, if a decisive, median-voter middle class had seen its savings and wealth destroyed by the interwar inflation, it would plausibly put a premium on pension obligations guaranteed by the government. Then, as the government became the principal provider of pension and retirement funding, private pension funds, a major conduit for capital in the United States but not in Europe, would play a smaller role in that economy. See Perotti and Schwienbacher (2009).
11. European integration may induce a similar structure, as recent EU Court of Justice decisions have facilitated corporations using the corporate law of a nation that is not its main place of business.
12. Romano (1993), Winter (1977).
13. Cary (1974), Bebchuk (1992). Kahan and Kamar (2002) question how intense that state competition really is.
14. For example, Romano (1988), Roe (1993), Miller (1998).
15. See Pinto, Weymouth, and Gourevitch (2010), Culpepper (2011).
16. The rents-oriented version of the social democratic theory helps explain Eichengreen's observation. Let's posit, again, that rents to labor and owners in key industries help fuel the social democratic conventions that demean capital markets, whose corrosive effects would erode rents to elites (see Rajan and Zingales, 2003a) and to the favored labor sectors that induce social democratic governments to oppose capital market development (see Roe, 2001, 2003). As the rents erode, labor and its

allies have fewer reasons to be wary of capital market development. Hence, their preferred policies would change.

Preferences and institutions interact. For example, many British corporate institutions developed early in the twentieth century (Franks, Mayer, and Rossi 2009) when Britain was a conservative polity. These institutions could have persisted, even when the polity moved leftward. The polity might not have allowed those institutions to arise in that era, but the extant interests (and institutions) could have been strong enough to resist severe destruction.

References

Acemoglu, Daron, Simon Johnson, and James A. Robinson. "The Colonial Origins of Comparative Development: An Empirical Investigation." *American Economic Review* 91 (Dec. 2001): 1369–1401.

Alesina, Alberto, Arnaud Devleeschauwer, William Easterly, Sergio Kurlat, and Romain Wacziarg. "Fractionalization." *Journal of Economic Growth* 8 (June 2003): 155–194.

Alesina, Alberto, and Roberto Perotti. "Income Distribution, Political Instability, and Investment." *European Economic Review* 40 (June 1996): 1203–1228.

Allen, Robert. *The British Industrial Revolution in Global Perspective.* Cambridge: Cambridge University Press, 2009.

Ayyagari, Meghana, Asli Demirgüç-Kunt, and Vojislawv Maksimovic. "How Well Do Institutional Theories Explain Firms' Perceptions of Property Rights?" *Review of Financial Studies* 21 (July 2008): 1833–1871.

Bebchuk, Lucian. "Federalism and the Corporation: The Desirable Limits on State Competition in Corporate Law." *Harvard Law Review* 105 (1992): 1435–1510.

Bebchuk, Lucian, and Zvika Neeman. "Investor Protection and Interest Group Politics." *Review of Financial Studies* 23 (March 2010): 1089–1119.

Bebchuk, Lucian, and Mark J. Roe. "A Theory of Path Dependence in Corporate Ownership and Governance." *Stanford Law Review* 52 (Nov. 1999): 127–170.

Benson, Lee. *The Concept of Jacksonian Democracy: New York as a Test Case.* Princeton, N.J.: Princeton University Press, 1961.

Berle, Adolf, and Gardiner Means. *The Modern Corporation and Private Property.* New York: Macmillan, 1933.

Bobonis, Gustavo J. "Political Institutions, Labor Coercion, and Emergence of Public Schooling: Evidence from the 19th Century Coffee Boom." Working Paper, University of Toronto, 2008.

Boix, Carles. *Democracy and Redistribution.* New York: Cambridge University Press, 2003.

Botero, Juan, Simeon Djankov, Rafael La Porta, Florencio Lopez-de-Silanes, and Andrei Shleifer. "The Regulation of Labor." *Quarterly Journal of Economics* 119 (Nov. 2004): 1339–1382.

Cary, William L. "Federalism and Corporate Law: Reflections upon Delaware." *Yale Law Journal* 83 (March 1974): 663–705.

Coffee, John C. "The Rise of Dispersed Ownership: The Roles of Law and the State in the Separation of Ownership and Control." *Yale Law Journal* 111 (Oct. 2001): 1–82.

Culpepper, Pepper. *Quiet Politics and Business Power: Corporate Control in Europe and Japan.* New York: Cambridge University Press, 2011.

Dahl, Robert. *Polyarchy: Participation and Opposition.* New Haven, Conn.: Yale University Press, 1971.

DeLong, J. Bradford. "Did J.P. Morgan's Men Add Value? An Economist's Perspective on Financial Capitalism." In *Inside the Business Enterprise*, ed. Peter Temin. Chicago: University of Chicago Press, 1991.

Douglas, William O. *Democracy and Finance*. New Haven, Conn.: Yale University Press, 1940.

Easterly, William. "Inequality Does Cause Underdevelopment: Insights from a New Instrument." *Journal of Development Economics* 84 (Nov. 2007): 755–776.

Easterly, William, and Ross Levine. "Africa's Growth Tragedy: Policies and Ethnic Divisions." *Quarterly Journal of Economics* 112 (Nov. 1997): 1203–1250.

Eichengreen, Barry. *The European Economy since 1945: Coordinated Capitalism and Beyond*. Princeton, N.J.: Princeton University Press, 2007.

Engerman, Stanley L., Stephen H. Haber, and Kenneth L. Sokoloff. "Inequality, Institutions and Differential Paths of Growth among New World Economies." In *Institutions, Contracts and Organizations: Perspectives from New Institutional Economics*, ed. Claude Ménard, 108–134. Northampton: Edward Elgar, 2000.

Engerman, Stanley L., and Kenneth L. Sokoloff. "Factor Endowments, Inequality, and Paths of Development among New World Economies." Comments by Miguel Urquiola and Daron Acemoglu. *Economia* 3 (Fall 2002): 41–109.

Engerman, Stanley L., and Kenneth L. Sokoloff. "Institutional and Non-Institutional Explanations of Economic Differences." In *Handbook of New Institutional Economics*, eds. Claude Ménard and Mary M. Shirley, 639–665. New York: Springer, 2005.

Franks, Julian, Colin Mayer, and Stefano Rossi. "Ownership: Evolution and Regulation." *Review of Financial Studies* 22 (Oct. 2009): 4009–4056.

Gilson, Ronald J., Henry Hansmann, and Mariana Pargendler. "Regulatory Dualism as a Development Strategy: Corporate Reform in Brazil, the United States, and the European Union." *Stanford Law Review* 63 (March 2011): 475–537.

Glaeser, Edward. "Inequality." In *Oxford Handbook of Political Economy*, ed. Barry Weingast and Donald Wittman, 624–641. New York: Oxford University Press, 2006.

Gourevitch, Peter, and James Shinn. *Political Power and Corporate Control: The New Global Politics of Corporate Governance*. Princeton, N.J.: Princeton University Press, 2005.

Greif, Avner. *Institutions and the Path to the Modern Economy: Lessons from Medieval Trade*. New York: Cambridge University Press, 2006.

Grundfest, Joseph. "Subordination of American Capital." *Journal of Financial Economics* 27 (Sept. 1990): 89–114.

Hall, Peter A., and David Soskice, eds. *Varieties of Capitalism: The Institutional Foundations of Comparative Advantage*. New York: Oxford University Press, 2001.

Hoff, Karla, and Joseph E. Stiglitz. "Exiting a Lawless State." *Economic Journal* 118 (Aug. 2008): 1474–1497.

Huntington, Samuel P. *Political Order in Changing Societies*. New Haven, Conn.: Yale University Press, 1968.

Iversen, Torben, and David Soskice. "Electoral Institutions and the Politics of Coalitions: Why Some Democracies Redistribute More than Others." *American Political Science Review* 100 (May 2006): 165–181.

Jackson, Howell E., and Mark J. Roe. "Public and Private Enforcement of Securities Laws: Resource-Based Evidence." *Journal of Financial Economics* 93 (Aug. 2009): 207–238.

Jensen, Michael. "Agency Costs of Free Cash Flow, Corporate Finance, and Takeovers." *American Economic Review* 76 (May 1986): 323–329.

Jensen, Michael, and William Meckling. "Theory of the Firm: Managerial Behavior, Agency Costs and Ownership Structure." *Journal of Financial Economics* 3 (Oct. 1976): 305–360.

Kahan, Marcel, and Ehud Kamar. "The Myth of State Competition in Corporate Law." *Stanford Law Review* 55 (Dec. 2002): 679–749.

Langevoort, Donald. "Statutory Obsolescence and the Judicial Process: The Revisionist Role of the Courts in Federal Banking Regulation." *Michigan Law Review* 85 (Feb. 1987): 672–733.

Lindert, Peter. "Economic Inequality and Poverty." In *Historical Statistics of the United States*, ed. Susan B. Carter et al. Cambridge: Cambridge University Press, 2006.

Macey, Jonathan, and Geoffrey Miller. "Origin of the Blue Sky Laws." *Texas Law Review* 70 (1991): 347–397.

Mahoney, Paul. "The Exchange as Regulator." *Virginia Law Review* 83 (Oct. 1997): 1453–1500.

Mayer, Colin. "Trust in Financial Markets." *European Financial Management* 14 (Sept. 2008): 617–632.

Miller, Geoffrey. "Political Structure and Corporate Governance: Some Points of Contrast between the United States and England." *Columbia Business Law Review* 1 (1998): 51–78.

Miwa, Yoshiro, and Mark Ramseyer. "The Value of Prominent Directors: Corporate Governance and Bank Access in Transitional Japan." *Journal of Legal Studies* 31 (June 2002): 273–301.

Morck, Randall, ed. *Concentrated Corporate Ownership*. Chicago: University of Chicago Press, 2000.

Mueller, Dennis C. "The Economics and Politics of Corporate Governance in the European Union." In *Investor Protection in Europe: Corporate Law Making, the MiFID and Beyond*, ed. Guido Ferrarini and Eddy Wymeersch, 3–29. Oxford: Oxford University Press, 2006.

North, Douglass C. *Institutions, Institutional Change, and Economic Performance*. Cambridge: Cambridge University Press, 1990.

North, Douglass C., and Barry R. Weingast. "Constitutions and Commitment: The Evolution of Institutions Governing Public Choice in Seventeenth-Century England." *Journal of Economic History* 49 (Dec. 1989): 803–832.

Olson, Mancur. *The Rise and Decline of Nations: Economic Growth, Stagflation, and Social Rigidities*. New Haven, Conn.: Yale University Press, 1984.

Pagano, Marco, and Paolo F. Volpin. "The Political Economy of Corporate Governance." *American Economic Review* 95 (Sept. 2005): 1005–1030.

Perotti, Enrico C., and Armin Schwienbacher. "The Political Origin of Pension Funding." Tinbergen Institute Discussion Paper 2007–004/2; published in *Journal of Financial Intermediation* 18 (July 2009): 384–404.

Perotti, Enrico C., and Ernst-Ludwig von Thadden. "The Political Economy of Corporate Control and Labor Rents." *Journal of Political Economy* 114 (Feb. 2006): 145–174.

Persson, Torsten, and Guido Tabellini. *Political Economics*. Cambridge, Mass.: MIT Press, 2000.

Persson, Torsten, and Guido Tabellini. *The Economic Effect of Constitutions*. Cambridge, Mass.: MIT Press, 2005.

Pinto, Pablo M., Stephen Weymouth, and Peter Gourevitch. "The Politics of Stock Market Development." *Review of International Political Economy* 17 (May 2010): 378–409.

Rajan, Raghuram G., and Luigi Zingales. "The Great Reversals: The Politics of Financial Development in the Twentieth Century." *Journal of Financial Economics* 69 (July 2003a): 5–50.

Rajan, Raghuram G., and Luigi Zingales. *Saving Capitalism from the Capitalists*. New York: Crown, 2003b.
Rock, Edward B. "Encountering the Scarlet Woman of Wall Street: Speculative Comments at the End of the Century." *Theoretical Inquiries in Law* 2 (2001): 237–264.
Rodrik, Dani. "Where Did All the Growth Go? External Shocks, Social Conflict, and Growth Collapses." *Journal of Economic Growth* 4 (Dec. 1999): 385–412.
Roe, Mark J. "Political and Legal Restraints on Corporate Control of Public Companies." *Journal of Financial Economics* 27 (Sept. 1990): 7–41.
Roe, Mark J. "Takeover Politics." In *The Deal Decade*, ed. Margaret Blair, 321–352. Washington: Brookings, 1993.
Roe, Mark J. *Strong Managers, Weak Owners: The Political Roots of American Corporate Finance*. Princeton, N.J.: Princeton University Press, 1994.
Roe, Mark J. "Political Preconditions to Separating Ownership from Corporate Control." *Stanford Law Review* 53 (Dec. 2000): 539–606.
Roe, Mark J. "Rents and Their Corporate Consequences." *Stanford Law Review* 53 (July 2001): 1463–1494.
Roe, Mark J. *Political Determinants of Corporate Governance*. Oxford: Oxford University Press, 2003.
Roe, Mark J. "Delaware's Politics." *Harvard Law Review* 118 (June 2005): 2491–2543.
Roe, Mark J. "Juries and the Political Economy of Legal Origin." *Journal of Comparative Economics* 35 (June 2007): 294–308.
Roe, Mark J., and Jordan I. Siegel. "Political Instability: Effects on Financial Development, Roots in the Severity of Economic Inequality." *Journal of Comparative Economics* 39 (Sept. 2011): 279–309.
Romano, Roberta. "The Future of Hostile Takeovers: Legislation and Public Opinion." *University of Cincinnati Law Review* 57 (1988): 457–506.
Romano, Roberta. *The Genius of American Corporate Law*. Washington: AEI Press, 1993.
Schattsneider, Elmer Eric. *The Semisovereign People: A Realist's View of Democracy in America*. New York: Holt, Rinehart and Winston, 1960.
Scott, Robert E. "Conflict and Cooperation in Long-Term Contracts." *California Law Review* 75 (Dec. 1987): 2005–2054.
Skocpol, Theda. *States and Social Revolutions: A Comparative Analysis of France, Russia and China*. New York: Cambridge University Press, 1979.
Sombart, Werner. *Why Is There No Socialism in the United States?* Trans. Patricia Hocking, and C.T. Husbands. 1906; New York: International Arts and Sciences Press, 1976.
Sonin, Konstantin. "Why the Rich May Favor Poor Protection of Property Rights." *Journal of Comparative Economics* 31 (Dec. 2003): 715–731.
Spiller, Pablo, and Rafael Gely. "Strategic Judicial Decision-Making." In *The Oxford Handbook of Law and Politics*, ed. Keith Whittington, Daniel Kelemen, and Gregory Caldeira, 34–45. New York: Oxford University Press, 2008.
Tiebout, Charles. "A Pure Theory of Local Expenditures." *Journal of Political Economy* 64 (Oct. 1956): 416–424.
Weymouth, Stephen, and J. Lawrence Broz. *Partisanship versus Institutions as Determinants of Property Rights: Firm-Level Evidence*. SSRN Working Paper, Jan. 3, 2008. http://ssrn.com/abstract=1080259.
Williamson, Jeffrey. *History without Evidence: Latin American Inequality since 1491*. NBER Working Paper no. 14766, March 2009. http://www.nber.org/papers/w14766.
Winter, Ralph K. "State Law, Shareholder Protection, and the Theory of the Corporation." *Journal of Legal Studies* 6 (June 1977): 251–292.

PART II

THE NATURE OF CAPITALISM

CHAPTER 4

THE FOUR TYPES OF CAPITALISM, INNOVATION, AND ECONOMIC GROWTH

WILLIAM J. BAUMOL, ROBERT E. LITAN, AND CARL J. SCHRAMM

"O for a muse of fire, that would ascend / The brightest heaven of invention."

—Shakespeare, *Henry V*, Act I, Prologue

Capitalism and the Unequaled Power of Its Innovation, the Supply–Demand Mechanism

Capitalism is neither unalloyed vice nor perfectly uncontaminated virtue. It is characterized by periods of inflation and eras of unemployment; it is not immune to corruption and may pose threats to the environment. One can easily add to this list of its shortcomings—particularly in the short run, though it must be emphasized that other forms of economic organization are hardly immune from criticism.

Here, however, we focus on the role played by entrepreneurs in the *long-term* consequences of capitalism. The one enormous benefit that a well-designed capitalist regime offers, which no other economic system has yet matched, is long-term economic growth unprecedented in its speed. In turn, growth is the driving force behind enduring improvements in standards of living and the accompanying reduction of poverty.

These exceptional accomplishments can be attributed primarily to the outpouring of innovations, which are systematically put to effective use, thereby providing society with constantly improving living standards. Societies with other economic systems have been remarkably inventive, and some have been comparatively wealthy—but none have experienced rates of wealth increase anywhere near those of the world's successful capitalist regimes.

But not all forms of capitalism produce economic success. Among those societies with economies organized as forms of capitalism are a substantial number that have continually failed to achieve remarkable growth. As such, we believe the distinction between successful and unsuccessful capitalist systems—as well as the reasons underlying capitalist countries' divergent growth performances—urgently require exploration. The well-being of future generations may be at stake.

More specifically, we argue that an essential part of this explanation can be found by examining the special supply–demand mechanism of the capitalist market for innovation. Special features of both the demand and the supply sides of the market for novelties go far in explaining what underlies the extraordinary growth of the successful economies. On the demand side, for instance, we analyze what we have labeled the *Red Queen game* setup (see later discussion). Meanwhile, on the supply side, there is the unprecedented reward arrangement—the *Willie Sutton mechanism*—that drives the entrepreneur to work tirelessly to adapt inventions to the preferences and needs of prospective users and promote their effective utilization.

The Demand Side of the Innovation Market: A Red Queen Game

Under the Red Queen's regime in Lewis Carroll's *Through the Looking Glass*, "it takes all the running you can do, to keep in the same place. If you want to get somewhere else, you must run at least twice as fast as that!" That is precisely the key feature of the arrangement that prevails in today's high-tech industries, especially in a highly competitive global economy. Such a feature has no precedent in history; it arose by itself, out of the workings of the market mechanism in which no firm, or at least no substantial enterprise, dares to lag in its provision of new products or its adoption of new processes. If a firm does not run as quickly as it can in these activities, it will be condemned to fall behind its competitors and lose its position in the market.

This Red Queen game dynamic, as we call it, produces an insatiable demand for innovation. As such, high-tech firms must unceasingly engage in financing and carrying out R&D, rather than surviving on successful past innovations. This arrangement has not been replicated or even approximated in any type of past society. It ensures that the demand curve for innovation shifts unceasingly upward—for whenever one firm in a market happens to enhance its innovative efforts, its rivals have no choice but to follow.

On the Supply Side of the Innovation Market

Simultaneously, the supply side of the innovation market is driven by an incentive mechanism with novel features that entice enterprising individuals to seek out promising innovations, promote their adaptation to the preferences and needs of the market, and ensure that the suppliers of the novel products and processes carry out their side of the activity. The incentives that induce such entrepreneurial behavior are provided by newly adopted laws. In recent centuries, these have been exemplified by institutions such as the patent system, the enforceability of contracts, the banking system, the corporate form of business organization, and the rule of law, more generally. Moreover, because invention can make subsequent invention less difficult by contributing new insights, the supply curve will likely continue to shift rightward with the passage of time—and ever more inventions will emerge, given the types of financial reward awards that are available.

In all of this, the entrepreneur plays an indispensable role. As J-B Say pointed out two centuries ago (1803, p. 11), without the activities of entrepreneurs, novel ideas would be in danger of going nowhere, remembered only by those few individuals who participated in their creation, or they may end up recorded only in some obscure volume.

The Bottom Line

Together, these two attributes of a prosperous capitalist regime—the unrelenting demand for innovation and the institutional arrangements that induce entrepreneurs to devote themselves to the supply side—explain much of the unprecedented growth performance by capitalist societies. Although the activities of entrepreneurs are insufficient by themselves to achieve the capitalist growth miracle, we argue that their presence and their efforts play an indispensable role in this achievement.

However we also argue that "capitalisms" are not all equal—some are designed to yield far greater accomplishments than others. In particular, we believe it is useful to distinguish among four types, which we discuss later. Some of these are characterized by little growth, whereas others show strong initial growth performance that soon peters out. Still others benefit from the substantial role played by entrepreneurs, whose accomplishments secure a place for the economy at the frontier of growth.

Entrepreneurs: Their Meaning and Their Interactions

The reader will probably have heard too many times the joke about the two economists who, while walking, see a $20 bill lying on the sidewalk and pass it by without picking it up. The reason, as one of the economists notes in the punch line: "It can't be real; if it were, someone would have picked it up already." The opposite attitude defines the innovative entrepreneur. She is the individual who got there before the two economists, who believes the opportunity is no illusion, and undertakes the necessary steps to make the promise of a $20 bill a reality. Entrepreneurs are the individuals who recognize opportunities that others overlook and do what is necessary to benefit from them. As such, the entrepreneur not only finds the opportunity, she often creates it.

However, not all entrepreneurs are created equal. Most such individuals follow well-trodden paths, replicating organizations that have been created many times before. In pursuing an avenue that is one of the most promising ways out of poverty, such individuals, as a group, make an important contribution to the welfare of society. More than one family of impoverished background has attained a comfortable existence, sometimes even great wealth, via successful entrepreneurship.

In this analysis, however, we focus on those we have elsewhere labeled "innovative entrepreneurs": individuals who search out and put into practice ideas that are significantly *different* from those previously offered. Innovative entrepreneurs are important because they are a prime source of the innovations that spur much of the growth of the world's prosperous economies.

Here it is necessary to make an important distinction regarding our definition of *entrepreneur*. Like the practitioners of any other occupations, entrepreneurs are human beings who display the full range of virtues and vices associated with our species. Consequently, some entrepreneurs (those whom we call "productive entrepreneurs") contribute to an economy's productivity and, by relation, to the general economic well-being of the members of society. However, the activities of other entrepreneurs provide no such benefits—some even damage the general welfare. Those who organize a criminal gang and find a new way to extract money from the population, for instance, are engaged in entrepreneurial activity in the sense that they have introduced an innovative way to pursue wealth, power, and prestige—not unlike the entrepreneur who brings a novel communication device to market. Even corrupt bureaucrats surely can be very enterprising in finding new ways to stimulate the volume of bribes that constitute the prime goal of their activities. The crucial difference is that these "unproductive entrepreneurs" add no wealth to society as a whole. Instead, to the extent that they discourage or inhibit productive entrepreneurs from carrying on their activities, unproductive entrepreneurs detract from social welfare.

We provide this distinction between productive and unproductive entrepreneurs because this way of looking at the matter opens the way to designing policy that encourages innovative entrepreneurial activity that benefits the greater good, while discouraging its unproductive counterpart. If it is true that the activities of many entrepreneurs are driven in pursuit of self-interest—by the generalized profit motive—this means that many entrepreneurs can be induced to redirect their activities from unproductive to productive efforts by changes in laws or other institutions that increase the payoff to beneficial entrepreneurship and curtail the likely gains from unproductive or destructive entrepreneurship.

Capitalism and Its Meanings

Our use of the term *capitalism* may be fairly conventional, but our breakdown of this economic state of affairs into four categories that differ profoundly in their promise for the general welfare is certainly novel. As is common, we define an economy as capitalistic *if a substantial proportion of its means of production is owned and operated by private individuals in pursuit of profit.* Obviously, no economy is perfectly capitalistic, in this sense. There are always some means of production that are owned and operated by government, and some of those means of production may be used for purposes other than profit.

There are, however, some economies that approximate the pure state of capitalism, as we define it. In this analysis, we focus on these, with the central goal of providing an analysis that best facilitates the design of *growth policy* in such regimes. Moreover, because growth performance by capitalist economies in the four categories we outline varies widely, we argue that one effective—perhaps indispensable—way of stimulating economic growth involves transforming capitalist societies with little or no growth into a form of capitalism inherently associated with rapid economic expansion. But first, we provide descriptions of the four forms of capitalistic economies that constitute the framework of our discussion.[1]

Oligarchic Capitalism

There have been and continue to be some places in which a substantial portion of the plant and equipment that constitute the means of production—that is, the "real capital" of the economy—is in private hands. In these cases, the proprietors of that capital are exceedingly few, characteristically composed of a few prosperous families who retain effective control of the bulk of the activities of their economy. These families are the oligarchs who determine a country's economic policy and in whose hands the bulk of control of the economic activity resides. Countries in Latin America, Africa, the Middle East, and, of course, Russia provide the most noteworthy examples of oligarchic capitalism.

Typically, most of the population of such an economy is kept in poverty, with few opportunities available for the betterment of an individual's position. There are also a number of people of intermediate status who serve the oligarchs and ensure that their wishes and decisions are carried out. The oligarchs themselves sometimes choose to take positions in the government, or they may delegate the bulk of governmental activity to their minions. As we will see presently, societies that fall into the category of oligarchic capitalism tend to be characterized by extremely modest or even negative economic growth—in large part because the oligarchs tend to resist change, lest it threaten their supremacy.

State-Guided Capitalism

In some cases where a substantial proportion of the stock of real capital is in private hands, the government still plays a powerful role in guiding the economy. In South Korea, following World War II, this was the state of affairs, and it remains true in China, where the government (at national, regional, and local levels) continues to exercise a substantial controlling influence over the economy—mainly through its role in the banking system and determination of banking policy. On the one hand, state guidance can contribute to economic growth—particularly during a period of take-off in an economy that previously had been essentially stagnant. However, observation of past examples indicates that the intervention of government, which can be a powerful stimulus at an economy's inception, is apt to hold back long-term growth through the distortions government creates when allocating or guiding capital. This latter problem becomes increasingly important as an economy moves toward the technological frontier, and government officials must figure out how to develop and commercialize entirely new products, services, and processes.

Big-Firm Capitalism

In some societies, government policy is characterized by restraint and the bulk of the economy's productive capital stock is in private hands. Meanwhile, a substantial part of the country's economic activity is carried out by oligopolistic industries in which a small number of very large firms have a dominant share of production. Today the oligopoly firm can be very large indeed, with outputs whose magnitude is comparable to the GDP of a small but prosperous country. These companies typically were not formed recently, and their methods tend to be well established. Despite this, it is important to note that these firms' size and extended history do not guarantee them continued success, as the recent collapse and disappearance of a number of such firms illustrates dramatically.

The experience of economies that are dominated by large companies indicates that this arrangement does not preclude growth, but prevents that society from attaining a position at the forefront of productive innovation. Our analysis leads us to conclude that such giant enterprises play a valuable role in stimulating productivity and growth—as they did for a considerable portion of the post–World War II period in Japan, for instance. We conclude, however, that this process is most effective in a hybrid economic arrangement, in which oligopolistic firms are present, along with entrepreneurial capitalists, who also play an important role.

Entrepreneurial Capitalism

This last type of capitalism may well be the oldest. Within economies characterized by entrepreneurial capitalism, small firms predominate, and most innovations are introduced by such organizations—not via the government or an oligopolistic organization. Indeed, such firms often begin by introducing a new invention into an economy. Entrepreneurs, through their alertness, are the first to recognize promising inventions and organize new companies to bring such inventions to market, as was first emphasized by Schumpeter (1911) and analyzed further by Kirzner (1979). With luck, these types of companies prosper and, in doing so, enhance a country's economic growth.

The Mixed Entrepreneurial-Oligopolistic Economy

These days, no economy is entirely entrepreneurial in structure. Since the latter part of the nineteenth century, entrepreneurial firms in the United States, Germany, and elsewhere have coexisted with large oligopolistic enterprises. There is some competition between the two, but there is substantial (though not undisputed) evidence that market forces have induced these two types of firms to specialize and, in doing so, undertake different parts of the innovation process.

For instance, radical inventions and substantial breakthroughs tend to come from smaller and younger entrepreneurial companies. In contrast, large corporations often acquire such new innovations by purchase or by obtaining intellectual property rights. Both of these somewhat specialized activities have made important contributions to the economy's growth. Without the breakthrough ideas contributed by entrepreneurial organizations, the rate of overall technological progress, and thus economic growth, would be much slower. But without the incremental refinements and improvements of entrepreneurial innovations, which are typically provided by larger, established companies—such as those that led to the evolution of aircraft from the Wright brothers' model to the Boeing 777—most innovative products and services could not be successfully commercialized, nor would their broad economic benefits be realized.

Unproductive Entrepreneurship and the Role of Perverse Incentives

Our prior discussion provides much evidence in support of our contention that innovative entrepreneurs play an indispensable role in the evolution of technology and other forms of innovation. Although there is no reason to believe that the entrepreneurs themselves are an invention of the Industrial Revolution, it is evident that at some point in that era, entrepreneurs and the productive fruits of their innovative activities emerged for the first time. We believe the largely unprecedented advent of innovative entrepreneurship can offer insights into policies that the world's impoverished countries might adopt to stimulate their productive entrepreneurial activities and enhance their rate of economic growth.

Economic historians have already plowed some of this ground. Max Weber (1904), Douglass North (1991), and David Landes (1991) are appropriately noted leaders in this literature. Their explorations have focused on the role of the institutions that determine the relative payoff a particular economy offers to different economic activities and occupations. In particular, these scholars have drawn attention to the structure of earnings offered by the different activities to which individuals can devote themselves. North and Landes concluded that the emergence of capitalism entailed the appearance of institutions that induced individuals to forge careers as innovative entrepreneurs. This conclusion is surely valid, but our analysis indicates that it is a truncated portion of the full story.

"Entrepreneurial activity" encompasses a range of innovative activities—not all of them technological and, in the case of unproductive entrepreneurship, not all beneficial to society. The same individuals who have the capability to organize a new type of firm can also create an innovatively organized private army or a crime syndicate. Throughout history, for instance, there has been a profusion of innovative entrepreneurs, whose activity has not contributed to economic productivity or enhancement of the general welfare. The warlord with his private army, the aggressive nobles of medieval Europe, and the modern gangster all have used their entrepreneurial talents to pursue wealth, power, and often prestige—but the means they adopted to do so was through redistributing wealth, rather than creating it. Grabbing the land or other possessions of a neighbor is a direct, fail-proof method of increasing one's wealth. In comparison, contributing to the economy's productivity, particularly in societies lacking institutions that ensure a reward to the contributor of such benefits—namely, patents or enforceability of contracts, offers uncertain economic rewards.

Moreover, unproductive entrepreneurship need not always entail the use of force or violence. Heron of Alexandria, a mathematician and engineer who lived in the Roman Empire during the first century A.D., is a noteworthy example. Heron was one of the most prolific inventors of the era, creating a variety of gadgets ranging from the slot machine to a working (albeit rather feeble) steam engine. There is good reason to believe Heron was compensated for these efforts, even though his inventions were not used to enhance productivity. This is perhaps because productive activity in Rome—aside from gentlemanly agriculture—was regarded as a disgraceful occupation and left largely to manumitted former slaves and their offspring. Instead, Heron seems to have taken advantage of the profusion of religious sects and the desire of their priests to enhance their flocks. The priests paid Heron to acquire his technology, which was unknown to the public, and used it to demonstrate their "magic powers." Heron's early steam engine, for example, was used to open and close the temple door, supposedly by magic—that is, without the use of human or animal power that any spectator of that time would have expected to carry out such a task. Heron of Alexandria's exploits are only one of many illustrations of pre-capitalist era institutional arrangements that employed perverse incentive systems to entice entrepreneurs to apply their ideas to activities that redistributed the wealth of society into the hands of a select few, rather than adding to the flow of productive output benefiting all of society.

Incentives for Productive Entrepreneurship

We have briefly mentioned the importance of incentives for promoting productive entrepreneurship—that is, enterprising activity that adds to the production of goods and services. Here we discuss two such incentive schemes in detail.

Patents

The capitalist institution that offers the most direct incentive for innovative activity and its contribution to production is the patent system, which awards temporary government-sanctioned monopolies for novel inventions. Today the patent system has, with good reason, become the focus of much complaint and criticism (see, e.g., Jaffe and Lerner 2004 and Bessen and Meurer 2008). More recently, two eminent economists have even advocated abolishing the system entirely (Boldrin and Levine 2008).[2]

In suggesting how economic analysis can help to improve the patent system, we focus here on what are arguably two central goals of the system, their apparent conflict, and how their conflict resolves itself, at least to some degree. The two goals are 1) to stimulate R&D and other forms of inventive effort that create novel products and from which productive methods emerge, while 2) eliminating obsolete products and processes, which must be replaced quickly by improved versions. The appearance of a conflict arises because rapid dissemination of an inventors' property, though clearly desirable for society as a whole, also reduces the inventor's reward from the patent monopoly and, along with it, the incentive for innovative effort. On closer examination, however, this apparent conflict is revealed to be a mirage. When properly designed and enforced, patents not only protect and enhance the rewards of inventive activity but also simultaneously increase incentives for dissemination (see Ordover 1991).

In recent decades, voluntary dissemination of patented material has become a major economic activity. To understand fully the capacity of the patent to encourage and facilitate dissemination, consider the ways the creator or the proprietor of some intellectual property (IP) can use it to obtain revenues. For such a monetary reward to be a realistic possibility, the IP must be protected legally somehow.

Without such protection, it can be copied by others—often with far less time and effort than was required for its initial creation.

There are only two devices clearly capable of providing such protection: secrecy and legal usage constraints—namely, the patent or copyright. If secrecy is the only effective means to protect some IP, then its proprietor has no choice but to use the IP *by itself* in the creation of final products. This method also requires that the IP owner be capable of manufacturing those final products because releasing the IP for use by others would undermine its protective secrecy. As such, the owner cannot even sell the IP to others, who inevitably would want to know what it does and *how it works* before paying for it.

This scenario is changed completely by a patent, which transforms the IP into a readily saleable or rentable item by allowing a buyer to use it legally as the owner permits for the duration of the patent. Since at least the latter half of the nineteenth century, the sale or rental of IP has become so attractive that markets dedicated to such transactions, and aided by professionals who specialize in such activities, have been created.[3]

The widespread and voluntary transfer of technology may contradict the common impression that firms with intellectual property generally do whatever they can to prevent others—particularly competitors—from getting access to the innovations that contribute to their competitive advantage. After all, aren't patents intended to prevent others from using inventions without the patent holder's permission? Although this is usually true, if the price offered by a would-be user is right, it will actually be profitable for a patent holder to permit its use. A market operated with this motivation is made possible only by a patent system or some close substitute. Without patent rights, the owner of some intellectual property would have no IP to sell on remunerative terms and could profit only by *withholding the pertinent information* from others.

It is easy to illustrate how the profit opportunity provided by intellectual property arises. Suppose Firm A invents a new widget component and expects to make a net profit of X dollars per widget from the resulting new product. But if rival Firm B, which may be an inferior inventor, offers Firm A license fees in the amount of Y dollars ($Y > X$) per unit of the new widget it is able to sell, Firm A obviously can be better off letting Firm B do so—even if every widget sold by Firm B means one less sale for Firm A. Of course, Firm B will be able to afford such a high fee only if it is a more efficient *producer* of widgets than Firm A. In this way, the price mechanism not only encourages licensing, but also encourages efficient specialization, with inventive activity undertaken primarily by the more effective inventor and production of the resulting products undertaken predominantly by the more efficient producer.

Despite this logic, it still seems to be widely believed that the firm that owns valuable IP, such as a patented invention, is better off keeping it to itself. One reason for this seems to be the absence of any clear and rational criterion for setting license fees. The common standard requires fees to be "reasonable and nondiscriminatory," a criterion widely cited but with no widely accepted specifications or testing procedures. As such, the licensing process can entail difficult negotiation and a marked risk of litigation. We suggest that the competitive model provides a workable and promising method of determining patent-licensing fees, as described next.[4]

The previous example suggests that if a patent holder expects to make a net profit of *X* dollars per unit of the final product created or manufactured with the aid of its patented property, then it would not offer a license for use of this property at any price lower than *X*. However, in a hypothetical competitive market where perfectly substitutable inventions are available, the licensing firm could not charge any price higher than *X*. Moreover, suppose a rival firm that acquires a license at that price takes some sales away from the owner of the IP by undercutting the latter's price and, thus, sells more final product than the licensing firm forgoes. Even in this instance, the licensor's earnings will still increase, as more of the final product will be sold at the given license fee per unit sold.

On Other Improvement Opportunities

The preceding discussion illustrates just one of the many ways the patent system can be improved to enhance the incentives for innovative entrepreneurship. Another idea that would advance the same objective is to modify the tax rules relevant to grants of employee stock options to top corporate management. As they are presently constituted, these rules permit a company to award a huge compensation package—in the form of stock options—to a CEO and other top-level executives, regardless of the firm's performance. Such generous compensation packages undermine any incentives for management to protect the interests of stockholders and employees. This shortcoming could be corrected by either limiting the deductibility or increasing taxes on compensation that is not tied to the *relative performance* of a company, rather than its absolute performance. Such a change in the tax rules would provide much stronger motivation for entrepreneurial behavior, particularly by large companies, than exists now.

We have provided only two ideas—relating to the patent and tax systems—for enhancing incentives for entrepreneurial activity. Surely other proposals also could realize this objective. We invite our readers and policy makers to continue the search.

Government and the Market: Useful Rules of the Game versus Irrational Intervention

All too often, governments have been unable to resist the temptation to use the most obvious method of encouraging growth—that is, for public officials to act as "entrepreneurs" and provide funds from public coffers to support chosen entrepreneurial endeavors. This process, often referred to as "picking winners," has two inherent flaws. First, it can be counted on to elicit political pressures from firms and industries that are in trouble and whose prospects are, therefore, likely to be questionable at best. Second, government agencies typically are not staffed by the individuals who are most qualified to make entrepreneurial decisions.

However, this does not mean that governments in capitalist economic systems can play no legitimate and useful role in encouraging innovation. Certainly, government must set the rules that regulate how entrepreneurs in capitalist economies compete, rewarding productive activities with incentives and penalizing unproductive and socially undesirable activities. Only government, for instance, can punish criminal activities, protect consumers from dangerous products when markets fail to do so, set rules regulating corporate behavior, and protect property rights. In short, society relies on the public sector to design institutions that yield incentives for productive and innovative entrepreneurial activity. In turn, entrepreneurship is most effectively carried out by members of the private sector, but only when guided and encouraged by appropriate "rules of the game" established by government.

Concluding Comments

We have emphasized capitalist economies' main contribution to the general welfare: economic growth far exceeding that achieved by any other economic system throughout history. In emphasizing this, however, we have not argued that capitalism is without warts and blemishes. Instead, we have sought to demonstrate that capitalism includes a variety of arrangements that differ widely in their success in stimulating the growth that has done so much to increase living standards and reduce poverty worldwide.

In our analysis, we found it useful to classify capitalist economies into four categories: oligarchic capitalism, state-guided capitalism, big-firm capitalism, and entrepreneurial capitalism. Moreover, we have concluded that all but the first category play a significant role in the growth process. State guidance has been successful in releasing economies initially mired in stagnancy and in a number of dramatic cases has managed to inaugurate a process of substantial growth. We also note that in several instances, economies dominated by large and actively innovative firms have stimulated remarkable economic performances by the countries in which they are based. The same can be said of economies in which entrepreneurial activity plays a key role.

After assessing the merits of each of these regimes, we concluded that the most effective, in terms of the growth objective, is a combination of the latter two variants. Under such a hybrid regime, the bulk of the more revolutionary innovation would be contributed by small entrepreneurial firms, and the process of making cumulative incremental improvements would be taken over by large enterprises with organized, internal R&D establishments.

In examining a variety of the world's economies, we find much evidence to support these conclusions, but there remains room for further investigation of these issues. We encourage others to continue working in this area, in the hope that continued research will point the way toward eliminating poverty and enhancing general welfare worldwide.

Notes

1. For extended discussion of these four categories and the inferences that can be drawn from this method of categorization, see Baumol, Litan, and Schramm (2007).
2. Although we agree that the patent system clearly can be improved, the case for its abolition has not been made. To the contrary, we believe that well-crafted patents for truly novel inventions remain socially useful.
3. For more on this, see the fascinating work of Lamoreaux and Sokoloff (1996).
4. For more details, see Swanson and Baumol (2005).

References

Baumol, William J., Robert E. Litan, and Carl J. Schramm. *Good Capitalism, Bad Capitalism, and the Economics of Growth and Prosperity*. New Haven, Conn.: Yale University Press, 2007.

Bessen, James, and Michael J. Meurer. *Patent Failure: How Judges, Bureaucrats and Lawyers Put Innovation at Risk*. Princeton, N.J.: Princeton University Press, 2008.

Boldrin, Michele, and David K. Levine. *Against Intellectual Monopoly*. New York: Cambridge University Press, 2008.

Jaffe, Adam B., and Josh Lerner. *Innovation and Its Discontents: How Our Broken Patent System Is Endangering Innovation and Progress and What to Do about It*. Princeton, N.J.: Princeton University Press, 2004.

Kirzner, Israel M. *Perception, Opportunity and Profit*. Chicago: University of Chicago Press, 1979.

Lamoreaux, Naomi R., and Kenneth L. Sokoloff. "Long-Term Change in the Organization of Inventive Activity." *Proceedings of the National Academy of Sciences* 93 (Nov. 1996): 12686–12692.

Landes, David. *The Wealth and Poverty of Nations: Why Some Are so Rich and Some so Poor*. New York: Norton, 1991.

North, Douglass C. "Institutions." *Journal of Economic Perspectives* 5 (Winter 1991): 97–112.

Ordover, Janusz A. "A Patent System Both for Diffusion and Exclusion." *Journal of Economic Perspectives* 5 (Winter 1991): 43–60.

Say, Jean-Baptiste. *Traitê d'Ĕconomie Politique*. Paris, 1803, p. 11.
Schumpeter, Joseph A. *The Theory of Economic Development*. 1911; Cambridge, Mass.: Harvard University Press, 1936.
Swanson, Daniel, and William J. Baumol. "Reasonable and Nondiscriminatory (RAND) Royalties, Standards Selection, and Control of Market Power." *Antitrust Law Journal* 73 (2005): 1–58.
Weber, Max. *The Protestant Ethic and the Spirit of Capitalism*. New York: Routledge, 1904.

CHAPTER 5

THE DYNAMICS OF CAPITALISM

F. M. SCHERER

In this chapter, capitalism is viewed as the set of economic relationships that emerged with the rise of the industrial or factory system during the eighteenth century. To be sure, there were earlier precedents—for example, the commercial ventures, local and international, of Venetian and Florentine businessmen during the Renaissance.[1] Here I focus on production in privately owned, often capital-intensive facilities embodying ever more advanced technologies during and following the Industrial Revolution.

The Industrial Revolution set in motion dynamic forces that will be our primary concern here. Most important among them are technological advances that propelled accelerated economic growth, changes in the structure of enterprise ownership and in the distribution of income among workers and owners, and a tendency toward more or less cyclical fluctuations in economic activity. These are the "dynamics" on which this chapter focuses.

Capitalism and Technological Progress

The most striking feature of industrial capitalism, seen either in its early periods or in historical hindsight, is its enormous success in implementing technological changes that expanded the supply of goods and services available for consumption. No one said it better than Karl Marx and Friedrich Engels in their *Communist Manifesto* of 1848:

> [The bourgeoisie] [Marx's term for the capitalist class] has been the first to show what man's activity can bring about. It has accomplished wonders far surpassing Egyptian pyramids, Roman aqueducts and Gothic cathedrals; it has conducted expeditions that put in the shade all former Exoduses of nations and crusades.
>
> The bourgeoisie cannot exist without constantly revolutionizing the instruments of production. . . . The bourgeoisie, during its rule of scarce one hundred years, has created more massive and more colossal productive forces than have all preceding generations together. Subjection of Nature's forces to man, machinery, application of chemistry to industry and agriculture, steam-navigation, railways, electric telegraphs, clearing of whole continents for cultivation, canalization of rivers, whole populations conjured out of the ground—what earlier century had even a presentiment that such productive forces slumbered in the lap of social labor? (Eastman 1932, p. 324, 326)

A Quantitative Overview

What happened through the capitalistic Industrial Revolution and its successors is compactly shown using estimates of real gross domestic product (GDP) per capita over several centuries. Angus Maddison (2006, appendix tables) has estimated GDP per capita covering numerous nations for three years preceding the onset of the Industrial Revolution—1500, 1600, and 1700—plus more continuous series beginning (with some exceptions) in 1820. The data have been adjusted to hold underlying price levels constant at dollar value purchasing power parities prevailing in 1990. The statistics are almost surely less reliable, the earlier the time interval to which they pertain, and there is reason to suspect that the consequences of the first stages of the Industrial Revolution—from about 1750 to 1820—are underestimated.

Throwing caution to the wind, I begin with the nation commonly viewed as the font of the Industrial Revolution: the United Kingdom. Figure 5.1 summarizes the Maddison time series. A logarithmic scale implies constant exponential growth as a straight-line trajectory, the growth rate being higher, the steeper the line. For the early years, growth is palpably modest, from a value of roughly $714 per capita in 1500 to $1,706 in 1820, implying a growth rate averaging 0.27 percent per annum. From 1820 on, the growth rate increases dramatically and perhaps even accelerates slightly in the latter half of the twentieth century. The average growth rate between 1820 and 2000 is calculated at 1.36 percent per year.

Figure 5.2 adds France, the United States, and Japan, beginning only with the relatively more reliable data for 1820. The United Kingdom started with the highest GDP per capita but was surpassed by the United States following World War I. France followed a lower trajectory at first, but pulled ahead of the United Kingdom after its entry into the European Common Market. Japan lagged as a less developed nation throughout the nineteenth century and was devastated by the consequences of World War II, but recovered after the war and took off on an extraordinarily rapid growth trajectory until virtually catching up with other world leaders. Its annual growth rate from 1950 to 1990—before stagnation set in—averaged 5.17

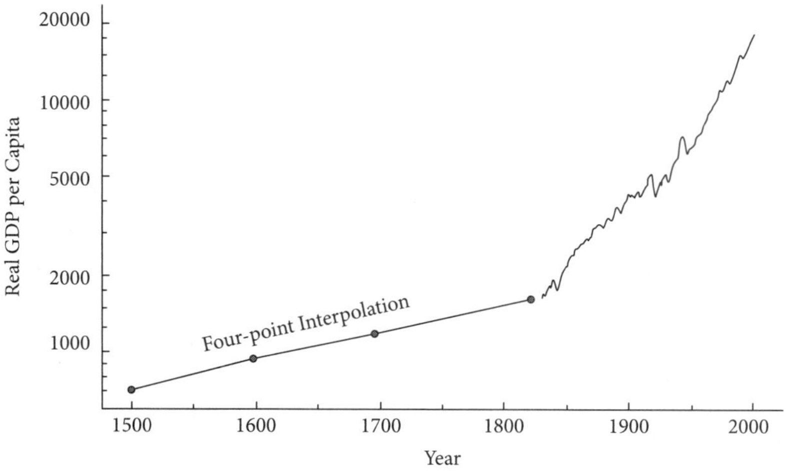

Figure 5.1. GDP per Capita of United Kingdom, 1500–2000 (U.S. Dollars of 1990 Purchasing Power)

percent. Overall, the average growth rates between 1820 and 2000 for these four nations were as follows:

- United Kingdom: 1.36 percent
- United States: 1.73 percent
- France: 1.62 percent
- Japan: 1.92 percent

These numbers may seem modest in comparison with the Japanese growth experience following World War II and the more recent Chinese record (i.e., 5.8 percent between 1980 and 2000), but let us consider them in the context of a

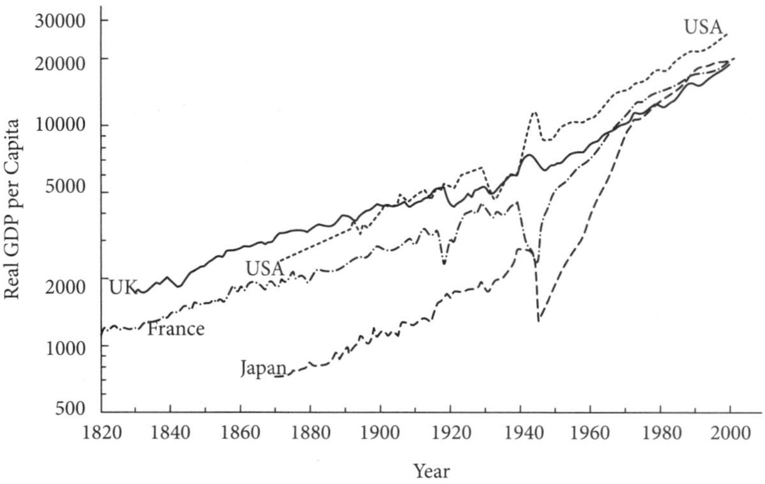

Figure 5.2. GDP per Capita of Four Prominent Capitalist Nations (U.S. Dollars of 1990 Purchasing Power)

Gedankenexperiment. We revert to A.D. 800, when Charles the Great was crowned Holy Roman Emperor in Rome. Obviously, we have no reliable GDP or population figures for that era. Let us assume the relevant benchmark to be $200 in dollars of 1990 purchasing power, or *one-fifth* the average GDP per capita of the 35 nations identified as *least* developed among the 174 on which the United Nations (2000) presented estimates for 1998. Assume then that from $200 per capita in 800, growth began and continued until 2000 at the average annual 1.36 percent rate attained between 1820 and 2000 by the United Kingdom—the slowest growing of our four demonstration countries. What would GDP per capita be in 2000? The answer is $2.45 billion! In 1990 purchasing power, the average man, the average woman, the average child is a billionaire.

Of course, this is inconceivable on a variety of grounds—resource availability, environmental, technological, and perhaps even human perversity. But that is precisely the point. The economic growth experienced during the two centuries since the Industrial Revolution borders on the miraculous. It truly was a revolution in productive power and standards of human welfare.

Economists Puzzle on How it Happened

Contemporary economists were not unaware that something miraculous was happening in the leading capitalistic economies. We have seen already that, writing a century after what arguably dates the onset of the Industrial Revolution, Marx and Engels observed that the capitalist system "has created more massive and more colossal productive forces than have all preceding generations together." Details of the Marxist explanation follow shortly.

First, however, we consider the views of Adam Smith seven decades before Marx and Engels issued their *Manifesto*. Old Adam was acutely aware that a "great multiplication of the productions of all the different arts" conferring "universal opulence" extending to "the lowest ranks of the people" was under way (Smith 1937, p. 11, Book I, chapter 1). Smith attributed these dynamic changes primarily to increases in the division of labor, carrying with them increasing dexterity on the part of workers, time savings when workers focused on a particular activity, and "the invention of a great number of machines which facilitate and abridge labour, and enable one man to do the work of many." This third change agent operated through capitalists' combination of increased capital, embodied in machines, with labor. But Smith's vision was not simply one of increased capital intensity and hence mechanization, emphasized by most economists for nearly two centuries after *The Wealth of Nations* appeared. Smith recognized (1937, Book I, chapter 1) that the division of labor and the improvements flowing from them extended to what today we would call engineering and research and development (R&D) functions:

> Many improvements [in machinery] have been made by the ingenuity of the makers of the machines, when to make them became the business of a peculiar trade; and some by that of those who are called philosophers or men of speculation, whose

> trade it is to observe every thing; and who upon that account, are often quite capable of combining together the powers of the most distant and dissimilar objects.

Despite this seminal insight, Smith had little to say about how the processes of invention and development occurred in the framework of capitalistic enterprises. He could scarcely have dreamed what powers his "men of speculation" would unleash. Smith marveled at the division of labor in a pin factory, where each worker specialized in a particular facet of pin making so that overall plant productivity was 4,800 pins per worker per day. Two centuries after Smith's opus appeared, Clifford Pratten (1980) revisited a modern English pin factory and found that productivity had increased to 800,000 pins per worker per day—an average productivity growth rate of 2.6 percent per year. This rate is not much different from the experience of modern manufacturing industries generally and much less than what one observes in electronic component manufacturing.

Marx was even less forthcoming than Smith on the details as to how technological advances came into being. But in addition to recognizing what enormous gains industrial technology achieved, Marx made the incentive dynamics of technological advance in capitalistic enterprises a centerpiece of his analysis. The motivating principle of Marx's capitalists is to accumulate the capital they command. Capital is invested in plant and equipment with the expectation of surplus value that can be extracted from workers cooperating with the capital. Additional capital and, equally important, technologically improved capital reduce labor cost and, all else equal, increase the capitalist's surplus value. But when all capitalists strive for lower labor costs in this way, their competition drives product prices down, reducing surplus value. As more capital is used with a given quantity of labor to produce more output, the *rate* of profit or surplus value falls. Both of these phenomena conflict with capitalists' desire to maximize the profits or surplus value derived from their capital, forcing them all the more vigorously to seek and implement new labor-saving technologies and also enter new markets in an incessant effort to increase accumulation (see Marx 1967, pp. 222–226 and 230–231). "Development of the social productivity of labor becomes the most powerful lever of accumulation" (Marx 1967, p. 1:621. In the quest for higher labor productivity, the most successful capitalists also build enterprises of ever larger scale, both at the expense of competitors and (through what later became known as imperialism) internationally.[2] As Marx wrote (1967, p. 1:763):[3]

> One capitalist always kills many. Hand in hand with this centralisation, or this expropriation of many capitalists by few, develop, on an ever-extending scale, the cooperative form of the labour-process, the conscious technical application of science, the methodical cultivation of the soil, the transformation of the instruments of labour into instruments of labour usable only in common, the economising of all means of production by their use as the means of production of combined, socialised labour, the entanglement of all peoples in the net of the world-market, and with this, the international character of the capitalistic regime.

Although strong on incentive mechanisms, Marx was vague on exactly how labor-saving and market-expanding technological changes were actually accomplished. Here Joseph A. Schumpeter added important insights. In a pioneering book (1912, 1934), Schumpeter began by postulating an economy typical of what was depicted in the newest theories of equilibrium economics—an economy whose firms make at most only routine technological changes and hence depart minimally from what he called "the circular flow." Into this he introduced entrepreneurs who disrupted the circular flow equilibrium by introducing "innovations"—that is, new products or product qualities, new methods of production, the opening of new markets, the conquest of new sources of supply, and/or new methods of business organization. Indeed, Schumpeter emphasized, once an economy had settled down into the kind of general competitive equilibrium postulated in the most advanced contemporary economic theories, innovating was one of the few ways that supranormal profits could be gleaned. Thus, innovation was a principal means of introducing dynamism to the competitive system. The innovations might well displace existing technologies and firms, obliterating their profits, but in the process, they added to the total value of the goods and services available to consumers—a phenomenon to which Schumpeter (1942) gave the now popular characterization "creative destruction." As other firms fought back to defend their positions with their own imitative changes, the innovation process evolved increasingly to benefit consumers as well as, or even instead of, sustaining profits for the original innovators.

Schumpeter emphatically distinguished (1934, pp. 88–89) his notion of innovation from that of invention:

> Economic leadership in particular must be distinguished from "invention." As long as they are not carried into practice, inventions are economically irrelevant. And to carry any improvement into effect is a task entirely different from the inventing of it, and a task, moreover, requiring entirely different kinds of aptitudes. Although entrepreneurs of course *may* be inventors much as they may be capitalists, they are inventors not by nature of their function but by coincidence and vice versa. . . . It is, therefore, not advisable, and it may be downright misleading, to stress the element of invention as much as many writers do.

In Schumpeter's early vision, the innovating entrepreneur was a person of vision and action who boldly implemented changes where other business firms had defaulted or feared to tread.

This distinction became blurred in later work. In his conception (1912, 1934, p. 66), Schumpeter saw as the most likely innovator candidates outsiders, that is, "new men"—from "new firms which generally do not arise out of the old ones but start producing beside them." By the late 1930s, he recognized that innovations were taking place in new ways, in part because modern research and development activities had become so costly and interwoven with the innovative process that large, well-staffed, generously financed enterprises had an advantage over newcomers in carrying out technological innovations. "There are superior methods available to the monopolist which either are not available at all to a crowd of competitors or are not available to them so readily," he wrote (1942, p. 101). Therefore, he continued (1942, p. 106),

"The large-scale establishment or unit of control must be accepted as a necessary evil inseparable from the economic progress which it is prevented from sabotaging by the [creative destruction] forces inherent in its productive apparatus." This radical change of view became the fodder for many subsequent academic controversies, theoretical and empirical. It, too, has at least partly been overtaken by changes in the world, for only four years after Schumpeter articulated his revised vision, the American Research and Development Corporation—the first modern entity specializing in the provision of capital and business guidance to small, high-technology start-up ventures—was established. Similar venture capital firms proliferated. Since then, it has become widely recognized that small new ventures often prove to be at least as proficient at the game of Schumpeterian innovation as established giant corporations.

In the wake of Schumpeter's 1942 book, a virtual industry—encompassing sociologists, technologists, and management gurus as well as economists—emerged to work out the details, qualitative and quantitative, on how technological change affects economic life. Indeed, so many scholars had a hand in this enterprise that one risks unfairness in singling out particular contributions.[4] The essence of what has been learned can be summarized briefly. First, as Schumpeter came to recognize, modern technological innovations are often built on advances in basic science and knowledge of technological phenomena. Second, partly because patents often cannot be obtained on basic scientific phenomena and partly because sometimes lengthy intervals of time separate a scientific breakthrough from its commercial applications, it is difficult to "appropriate" economic benefits from investment in pure science. Therefore, conventional market incentives for supporting scientific research are deficient, and to sustain progress, science—Smith's "speculation"—must be financed by government or philanthropic donors. Third, industrial R&D laboratories commonly enjoy comparative advantage in identifying scientific possibilities with the best profit-making prospects and carrying them through to the stage of practical application. Fourth, there are rich linkages between academic science institutions and industrial research establishments. Fifth, the profit motive can be a powerful motivator and allocator of resources into activities that yield commercializable innovations. This point was recognized poetically by the eminent economist Kenneth Boulding at a 1962 conference:[5]

> In modern industry, research
> Has come to be a kind of Church
> Where rubber-aproned acolytes
> Perform their Scientific Rites,
> And firms spend funds they do not hafter
> In hope of benefits Hereafter.

A Schematic View of Modern Innovation Theory

From the hundreds of economic models analyzing how technological progress occurs, we present in figure 5.3 one that strips the issues to their essentials.[6] It

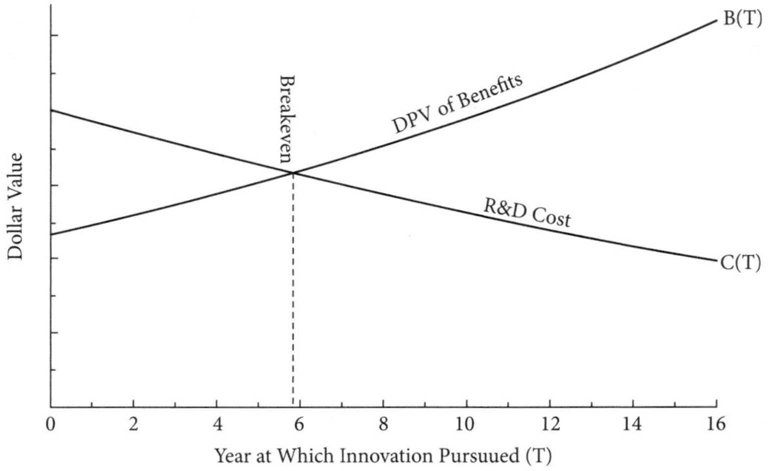

Figure 5.3. How Technology and Demand Influence Incentives for Innovation

assumes that firms attempt to maximize the surplus of the expected benefits from innovation minus expected costs.

The expected costs are the R&D costs required to carry out an innovation, including the costs of process R&D, which in turn determines how much it costs to produce the eventual product. R&D costs are affected by the general state of scientific and technological knowledge. If knowledge advances continuously and smoothly, the cost of carrying out an innovation project is shown by the line C(T), which has R&D cost declining at an exponential rate as one waits until year T to carry out one's innovation. The longer one waits, the more easily one can solve the requisite technical problems. This is not the only possible scenario. Knowledge often advances in fits and starts, in which case C(T) will have abrupt downward displacements at the time relevant new knowledge becomes available.

The benefits from an innovation (i.e., the surplus of expected revenues from product sales minus production costs, discounted to present value at the year of innovation T) depend on the state of demand. If demand is gradually rising, the discounted present value of innovation benefits will be larger, assuming the same duration of sales on the market (e.g., due to finite patent length, or in a mathematically simpler version, out to infinity) when the innovation is made at time T + n than at time T. Thus, reflecting the rising power of "demand-pull,"[7] the benefits function B(T) rises over time. Smoothness of B(T) is not essential, however, for example, when demand increases suddenly for some reason, such as an energy shock or the outbreak of a new disease.

From the vantage point in time of T = 0, as the cost and demand functions are drawn in figure 5.3, the innovation is not economically attractive. Costs exceed benefits. The project reaches the zero profit breakeven point when R&D costs fall into equality with (rising) benefits—that is, just before the onset of year 6. The more time passing *after* the breakeven point, the more attractive innovation becomes, and hence the higher the likelihood that some entrepreneur will seize the opportunity—perhaps precipitating what appear to be multiple but independent innovations. In a situation of secure monopoly, the firm would wait until a much later date—possibly as late as year 15—to maximize the discounted surplus of benefits minus costs. But fear of being competitively preempted—a variant of Schumpeter's creative destruction—forces would-be entrepreneurs to advance their R&D project dates, perhaps all the way to year 6, where breakeven occurs. Competitive advancement of the innovation date to breakeven year 6 is the analogue in the theory of R&D resource allocation to the zero-profit equilibrium of supply and demand in the traditional price-setting Marshallian theory.

Structural Changes Due to Innovation and Rising Prosperity

Adam Smith recognized that the structure of national economies depended in part on the choices made in capital investments, embodying among other things the latest technological improvements, across alternative fields of endeavor. "According to the natural course of things," he suggested in Book II, chapter 2 of *The Wealth of Nations*, "the greater part of the capital of every growing society is, first, directed to agriculture, afterwards to manufactures, and last of all, to foreign commerce." For the American colonies, he observed (1937, p. 347), wealth and greatness stemmed from the fact that "almost their whole capitals have hitherto been employed in agriculture." He continued with what was at the time conventional wisdom in Great Britain:

> Were the Americans, either by combination or by any other source of violence, to stop the introduction of European manufactures, and, by thus giving a monopoly to such of their own countrymen as could manufacture the like goods, divert any considerable part of their capital into this employment, they would retard instead of accelerating the further increase in the value of their annual produce, and would obstruct instead of promoting the progress of their country towards real wealth and greatness.

Soon after Smith's first edition appeared, the colonies became the United States of America, and in a 1791 monograph, Alexander Hamilton vigorously challenged this thesis.[8] Hamilton expected that augmenting manufacturing activity would create a more extensive demand for the U.S. agricultural surplus at home; develop machinery enhancing agricultural productivity; encourage reciprocal trade with other nations; provide diversification against foreign and domestic demand and supply shocks; shorten transportation links; ensure the national supply of essentials such as subsistence, habitation, clothing, and defense; and not least, succeed because early manufacturing efforts in the colonies had already shown considerable success. The United States adopted Hamiltonian policies favoring the development of manufactures. Indeed, groups of British industrialists visiting the United States during the 1850s were surprised to see that U.S. factories were using more advanced labor-saving machinery than their U.K. counterparts (see Habakkuk 1962).

The broad historical trends are revealed by figure 5.4. From 9.5 percent of national totals in 1820, employment in manufacturing and mining grew (after being interrupted by the Great Depression) to a peak of 33.6 percent during World War II. Then, as Hamilton foresaw, manufacturing industries provided a decisive element in U.S. military power. Meanwhile employment in agriculture declined steadily from 72 percent in 1820 (and no doubt even higher in Hamilton's time) to 2.5 percent in 1999. Each of these trends warrants further comment.

The declining share of agriculture was attributable primarily to vigorous productivity growth. In 1820, 1 farm family fed (and helped clothe) 1.4 families. By 2000, the comparable figure was 40 families, not counting the export surplus consistently contributed by American farmers. Between 1950 and 1990, U.S. agricultural output per unit of labor input grew at an average rate of 4.8 percent per year—a rate considerably higher than in other sectors of the economy. This impressive productivity growth is attributable to countless technological innovations in the use of fertilizers and pesticides, better seed hybrids, and a host of labor-saving agricultural machines, complemented by the education and training of farmers in land grant universities and agricultural extension service facilities.

Nor was the United States alone. It appears to be a law of capitalistic development that advances in productivity lessen the share of the workforce in agriculture.[9] Many other technologically advanced nations exhibit agricultural employment shares in the same 1–3 percent range prevailing for the United States. Others, especially those whose economic development is retarded, are more like America in the early nineteenth century. For example, among the sixty-one nations for which The Economist's *Pocket World in Figures*, 2010 edition, reports total agricultural employment shares, the largest four shares were for Cameroon (70 percent),

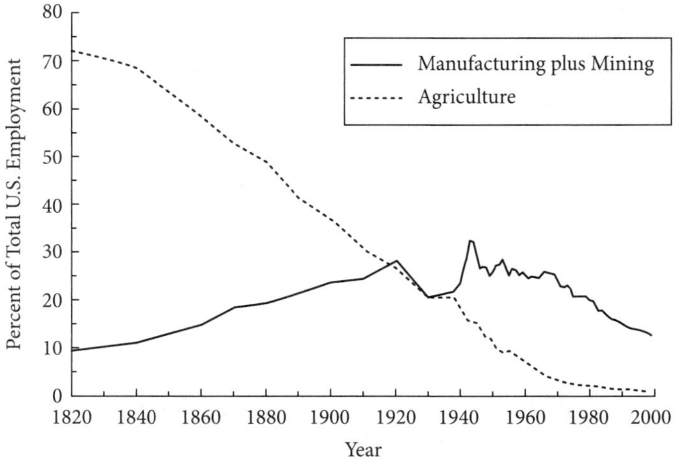

Figure 5.4. Share of U.S. Employment Devoted to Agriculture and to Manufacturing plus Mining, 1820–1999

Vietnam (58 percent), Bangladesh (52 percent), and Morocco (45 percent). China was tied for fifth at 43 percent.[10]

A simple explanation for agriculture's declining employment share as productivity grows is that people's need for food is physically constrained. An economic explanation is rooted in Ernst Engel's (1857) law, which states that the income elasticity of demand for food is less than unity. Therefore, as real incomes rise, the demand for food rises less than proportionately, and so other commodities command an increasing share. For the prosperous United States, the income elasticity of demand for food is estimated to be on the order of 0.2, that is, as income rises by 100 percent, food demand rises 20 percent.

For manufacturing, a more complex explanation is required. As consumers become more prosperous owing to technological change and productivity growth, their consumption shifts from agricultural products to manufactured goods with higher income elasticities. With further growth, income elasticities for manufactured goods also decline, so consumers' demand moves toward services fulfilling needs for health, enlightenment (e.g., education), amusement, mobility, safety (e.g., police and fire services at the local level, defense at the national level), and community (e.g., telecommunications and churches). This could explain the surprising drop in the share of U.S. employment devoted to manufacturing and mining from 29.6 percent in 1953 to 14.3 percent in 1999. It seems improbable that superior productivity growth and hence declining relative prices explain the shift in demand toward services, because productivity growth has tended to be less rapid in the service sectors than in agriculture and manufacturing.[11] Some of the relative decline in manufacturing employment is attributable to the growth of international trade and a shift of comparative advantage toward rapidly developing but still low-wage nations. Supporting this shift is the fact that manufactured goods (and minerals) are more easily transported long distances to the consumer than most services (although this is also changing with reductions in communication costs). The role of international trade, however, must be subordinate to an explanation focusing on relative income elasticities of demand for services as compared to manufactured goods, because the surplus of U.S. manufactured goods imports over exports in 2000 was only about 13 percent of the sales value of domestic manufactured goods. The balance of trade component seems too small to account for the halving of the manufacturing sector employment share between 1953 and 1999.

Who Benefits from Capitalist Economic Progress?

Marx is best known for his argument that despite its ability to expand economic output phenomenally, capitalism would exploit and impoverish workers (the proletariat) so severely that they would revolt and overthrow the capitalist system, substituting a socialist "dictatorship of the proletariat." History reveals that he was wrong. But it is useful to analyze the sources of his error.

Marx's Error

Marx argued that capitalists' drive to accumulate would lead them to embrace labor-saving machinery, displacing workers in the production of any given quantity of output and relegating them into a growing "reserve army of the unemployed." The reserve army would impose pressure on wages, allowing capitalists increasingly to exploit the workers still employed—that is, to extract surplus value, adding to the capitalists' wealth. The net tendency of rising unemployment plus depressed wages would be the immiserization (in German, *Verelendung*) of the working class. Concentration of workers into larger scale enterprises would facilitate their organization and foment eventual revolution. The climax is characterized in one of Marx's most colorful passages (1967, Book I, chapter 32, p. 763):

> Along with the constantly diminishing number of the magnates of capital, who usurp and monopolise all advantages of this process of transformation, grows the mass of misery, oppression, slavery, degradation, exploitation; but with this too grows the revolt of the working-class, a class always increasing in numbers, and disciplined, united, organised by the very mechanism of the process of capitalist production itself. The monopoly of capital becomes a fetter upon the mode of production, which has sprung up and flourished along with, and under it. Centralisation of the means of production and socialisation of labor at last reach a point where they become incompatible with their capitalist integument. Thus integument is burst asunder. The knell of capitalist private property sounds. The expropriators are expropriated.

Marx went astray most fundamentally because he relied on a misguided theory of price and wage determination—the labor theory of value—that was overtaken by advances in economic theory known as the neoclassical synthesis. The latter was beginning to emerge by 1867, when Marx finished his German-language draft of *Das Kapital*, and had triumphed by 1886, when Friedrich Engels completed his English translation.

Developed most thoroughly by eminent English economist David Ricardo (1772–1823), the labor theory of value held that commodities' prices were determined by the amount of labor—both direct labor and labor congealed in capital equipment—that went into their production. But what determined the price or value of labor? According to Marx, it was the amount of labor need to produce that labor, that is, to keep the worker's body and soul together and permit reproduction of the workforce for future generations. Marx was aware that this "socially necessary quantity of labor" would vary with circumstances. More skilled workers required more costly training and therefore needed to receive higher wages. In an aside that might be used to rescue some Marxian predictions, Marx admitted that wages might depend on "the degree of civilisation of a country... and on the habits and degree of comfort in which the class of free laborers has been formed" (Book I, chapter 6, p. 171). "Exploitation" was measured by the difference between the value of the products created by labor, delineated by their socially necessary labor content, and the cost of maintaining and reproducing workers. Technological innovations permitted more output and hence more value to be produced with a given labor input, widening the wedge between what the laborer had to be paid (his reproduction cost) and what he produced. Competitive pressure from the reserve army of the unemployed might also allow capitalists to increase the length of the workday and hence widen the value wedge, although Marx recognized that maximum work hours were limited by legal regulations in some nations. The combination of technological progress and a growing reserve army meant for Marx an increase in the rate to which workers were exploited and constrained workers to lives of constant or ever more grinding poverty.

Although Marx recognized that wages might temporarily be raised by unusually strong demand for labor, he lacked a valid theory of how both labor markets and product markets reached equilibrium—a theory that emerged only with the neoclassical synthesis. He also lacked an appreciation for Say's law, articulated in 1803 by Jean-Baptiste Say but incorporated fully into economic theory only with the contributions of John Maynard Keynes in the 1930s. Specifically, a reduction in the amount of labor required to produce output, all else equal, led to product price reductions, increased quantities sold, and, in the aggregate, an increase in the real wealth of the economy's participants. More real output meant more compensation in the aggregate to producers. Competition among producers experiencing lower costs through technological change ensured sooner or later that the benefits from higher productivity were not simply captured as additional profit (or surplus value) by the capitalists. Despite various slippages, increases in output under Say's law led to more demand for output—in simple terms, supply created its own demand. And—again with possible slippages—more demand averted the tendency for the reserve army of the unemployed to grow and instead flowed back into increased demand for labor, which, for a labor supply determined by considerations more complex than Marx's simple reproduction theory, by no means mandated increasing immiserization of the work force and more likely led to increased real wages per worker.

The Pure Microeconomic Theory

Things can go wrong in this rosy scenario, in part for reasons anticipated imperfectly by Marx. We return to one aspect of the problem later. Here, however, it may be useful to illustrate what happens to economic values when technological innovations are made. Two cases—process or cost-saving innovation and product innovation—can be distinguished, although in practice, they overlap because one firm's product innovation can become another firm's process innovation (see Scherer 1984, chapters 3 and 15).

Figure 5.5 illustrates the process innovation case. We assume a competitive industry in equilibrium with (constant) unit costs OC_1. The competitive price

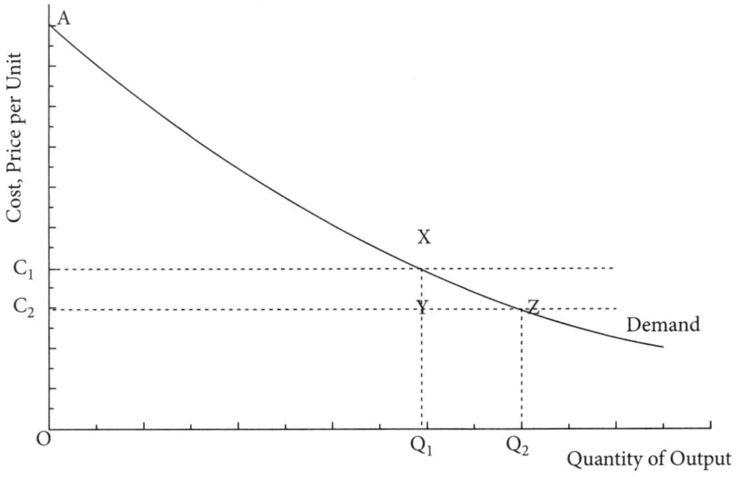

Figure 5.5. Illustration of Process Innovation in Competitive Market

equals cost at OC_1 and output is OQ_1. Now let an innovation reduce costs to OC_2. At first the cost saving may be monopolized, so price remains at OC_1. If so, the benefits of the cost saving, measured by rectangular area C_1XYC_2 are retained entirely by the producing firm(s), that is, the capitalists. This implies increased income for the capitalists, which, under Say's law, is spent somewhere else in the economy, possibly for additional capital goods but perhaps also for new luxuries. Sooner or later, however, competition will force the price down to the new lower cost level, OC_2. Then output is increased to OQ_2, what was the capitalist's gain C_1XYC_2 is redistributed as gain to consumers (including workers, who will have more money to spend on other goods), and in addition, consumers gain a surplus delineated by triangle XYZ. Once the product price falls, the impact of the innovation on the quantity of labor used in producing the product in question depends on the elasticity of product demand. If demand for the product is relatively price-inelastic, output after the competitive price reduction expands only modestly and labor continues to be displaced—possibly into the ranks of the unemployed, but in long-run equilibrium abiding inter alia by Say's law, to make other products. If demand is quite price-elastic, the increase in the quantity demanded at reduced prices may be so great that despite the reduction in labor required to produce any given unit of output, the total amount of labor demanded in producing the relevant product rises.

The product innovation case is illustrated in figure 5.6. We assume that a completely new product is created, giving rise to a new demand curve AD along with a cost function (horizontal at level OC_1). Assume that initially the new product is sold under monopoly conditions. The monopolist maximizes its profits by setting price OP_M, leading to consumption of quantity OQ_M. Fresh labor is hired to produce the new product. In addition, the monopolist gains profits measured by the rectangle $P_MBE\ C_1$, which under Say's law will be spent on other commodities. Furthermore, consumers enjoy a consumers' surplus—that is, a surplus of intrinsic product value over the price they must pay—measured by triangle ABP_M. There is no reason to

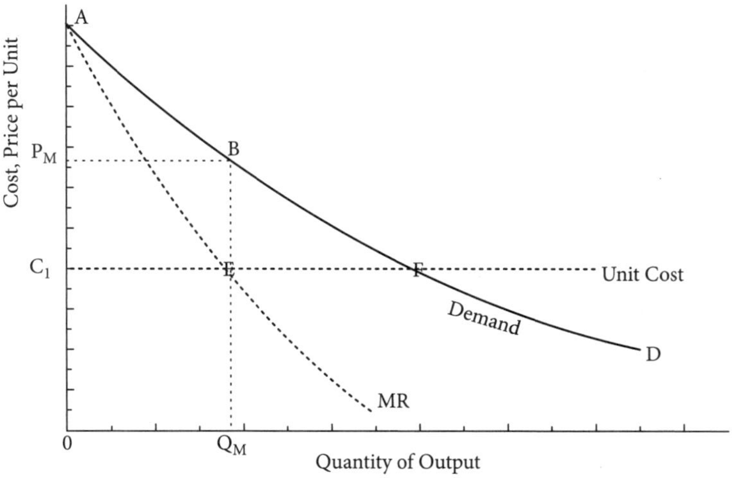

Figure 5.6. Illustration of New Product Monopoly

believe this surplus should lead to still more employment. However, sooner or later competition will emerge in the supply of the new product. Eventually the price falls to OC_1. What was monopoly profit (rectangle P_MBEC_1) now redounds to consumers as consumers' surplus, freeing more funds for the purchase of other commodities. In addition, output increases to C_1F, leading to more labor being hired and the realization of additional consumers' surplus measured by triangle BFE.

How Are the Gains Shared?

Sooner or later, consumers (who are also workers) benefit from product and process innovations, although the timing and magnitudes of the gains can vary. It is therefore useful to turn from pure theory to actual evidence as to how workers have fared as a result of the incessant technological innovations introduced since the onset of the Industrial Revolution.

The richest early data come from Phelps Brown and Hopkins (1955, 1956) on the wages of building trades craftsmen and unskilled workers in southeastern England and the prices of products those workers might consume. Given our concern with the fate of Marx's proletariat, we focus in figure 5.7 on the real wages—that is, money wages deflated by price indices—of ordinary building laborers during an interval spanning the onset of the Industrial Revolution. For ordinary laborers, wages were more likely to parallel those in alternative occupations such as the proliferating factories, about which Friedrich Engels wrote a seminal tract (1845, 1999). During the earliest decades of the Industrial Revolution, real wages of building workers trended downward, not upward. The explanation probably stems from extensive displacement of farm workers, outstripping demand from both the emerging factories and alternative unskilled trades. The Napoleonic Wars had a sharp negative impact. After that, there was a distinct upward trend as the Industrial Revolution gained traction. Between 1804 and 1883, real wages increased at an average rate of 0.85

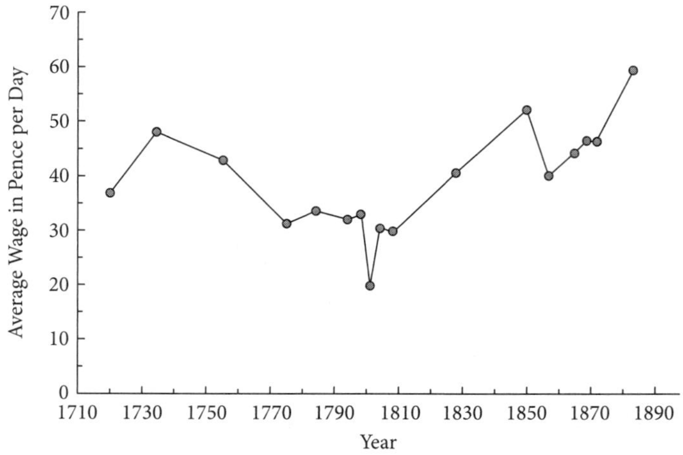

Figure 5.7. Estimated Real Wages of English Building Laborers, 1710–1892, Pence per Day's Work (1800 Price Levels = 100)

percent per year. The annual gain for skilled workers was similar. Immiserization during the period surrounding Marx's writing is not evident.

We pick up the thread with figure 5.8, tracking the cost of living-adjusted wages of manufacturing production workers in the United States from 1890 to 2005.[12] From 1890 to the 1970s, there was a fairly steady increase in manufacturing workers' hourly real wages, perceptibly accelerating despite the Great Depression and temporarily severe unemployment.[13] The average annual rates of growth for extended periods were as follows:

- 1890–1930: 1.40 percent
- 1930–1970: 2.41 percent

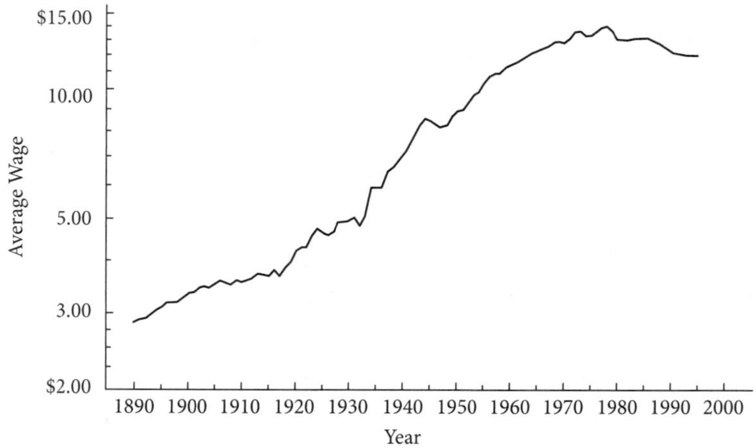

Figure 5.8. Real Wages of U.S. Manufacturing Production Workers, 1890–1995 (Expressed in Constant 1995 Dollars)

- 1970–2005: 0.18 percent
- 1890–2005: 1.90 percent

Clearly, there is no evidence of immiserization. The average U.S. manufacturing worker in 2005 enjoyed a real wage 4.3 times that of his 1890 counterpart. Nor did a reserve army of the unemployed allow employers to extract longer working hours from their workers. Between 1890 and 2005, the average work week in manufacturing dropped from 54 to 40.7 hours.[14]

The remarkable and seemingly persistent stagnation that set in during the 1970s, however, cries out for explanation. We advance toward that goal following a brief detour.

The Factor Shares Paradox

Consistent with the predictions of both Smith and Marx, production has become more capital-intensive over time; that is, capital inputs have increased more rapidly than labor inputs.[15] Yet the relative shares of payments to productive inputs have tended to be remarkably stable. Using data disclosed by Simon Kuznets and William Fellner, Binswanger and Ruttan (1978, chapter 2) report that the share of labor relative to combined payments to labor and capital in the United States varied narrowly between 1920 and 1966, between 61 and 66 percent. If capital inputs were rising more rapidly than labor inputs, this means that labor wages—which we know were rising steadily until at least the 1970s—were increasing more rapidly than the returns on capital.

Support for this conjecture is provided by figure 5.9, which traces the shares of total U.S. national income absorbed by employees and corporate profits from 1929 to 2000. Except during the Great Depression, the profits share varies between 7.73 percent (in the trough of the 1982 recession) to 14.69 percent (at the peak of a post–World War II boom), with no statistically significant trend following 1945.

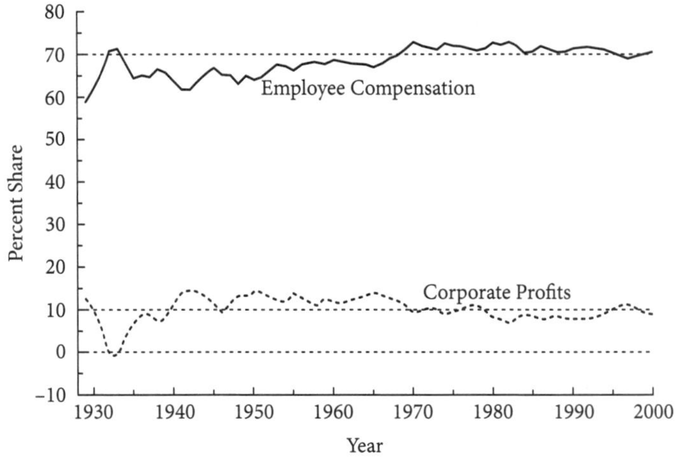

Figure 5.9. Shares of U.S. National Income for Employee Compensation and Profits, 1929–2000

Employee compensation trended upward gradually, with a post-Depression minimum of 62 percent in 1942 (when the government imposed pervasive wage controls) to 74 percent in 1982 (when corporate profits were unusually depressed).

Economic theory applied at an heroic level of abstraction can shed light on why labor's share of the national income remained relatively steady despite labor-saving technological change and rising capital intensity. We assume that the average industry (or in an even more heroic version, industry in the aggregate) operates on a production function characterizing how output responds to changes in labor and capital inputs. A standard textbook example is illustrated in figure 5.10. There is a curved "isoquant" showing varying combinations of capital and labor inputs that can yield an output of 100 units. The production function shown happens to conform to Cobb-Douglas assumptions, with an equation $Q = K^{0.33} L^{0.67} = 100$. With labor costing $1,000 per working month and capital $2 per unit, shown by a dashed "isocost" line marked A, the cost-minimizing production strategy is to use 16.25 months of labor and (rounded) 4,000 units of capital, with labor sharing 67 percent in the combined outlay of $24,250. But a rise in the price of labor relative to the cost of capital, indicated by isocost lines B and C in figure 5.10, creates an incentive to substitute away from the higher priced labor and toward the now lower priced capital. Production becomes more capital-intensive. From 16.25 units of labor and 4,000 units of capital in the original equilibrium, the new equilibrium entails (approximately) 12.44 months of labor and 6,885 units of capital. Total expenditures on inputs are reduced as a result of this substitution to $1,225 × 12.44 + $1.09 × 6,885 = $22,744. Labor's share of total outlays is 67 percent—despite the substitution, the same as labor's share was before the relative increase in wages!

This is a rigged example, but it illustrates a hypothesis that economists have proposed to explain the relative constancy of labor's national income share despite rising wages and rising capital intensity. Specifically, with the Cobb-Douglas

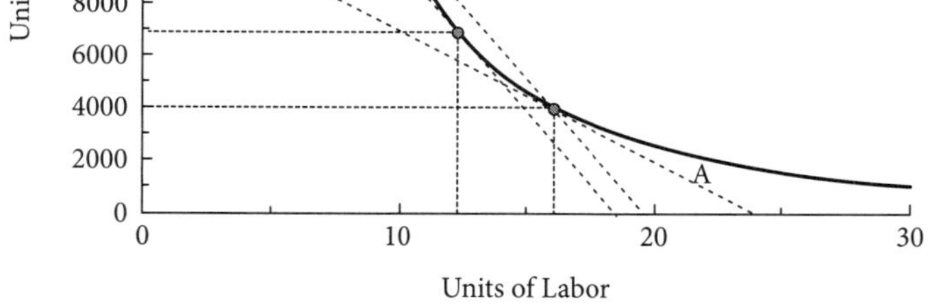

Figure 5.10. Production Optima with Cobb-Douglas Production Function

production function and constant returns to scale, the total output (and hence income) shares of capital and labor are equal to the values of the exponents on K and L in the production function equation, if production costs are minimized and each input is competitively paid the value of its marginal product. It is, of course, a special case, but there is statistical evidence that real-world production functions often approximate the Cobb-Douglas form.

The Stagnation of U.S. Workers' Real Wages

We return now to another anomaly: the pronounced break from the long-run trend in rising U.S. manufacturing worker wages, which in effect shattered the American dream, that is, the expectation that each new generation would be much better off materially on average than its parents.

To begin, a tension between the worker wage stagnation shown in figure 5.8, emerging in the mid-1970s, and the absence of clear downtrends in the compensation shares revealed by figure 5.9 needs to be clarified. There are two explanations.

First, figure 5.8 focuses on straight wages without fringe benefits. "Employee Compensation" in figure 5.9 covers all compensation, including fringe benefits. Other slightly incompatible sources show significant increases in the fraction of U.S. national income associated with "supplements to wages and salaries"—notably, mandatory federal Social Security, Medicare, and unemployment compensation fund payments levied on employers and voluntary employer set-asides for health care and retirement pay. The health care fraction has risen especially rapidly as total U.S. health care expenditures have expanded to absorb 17 percent of GDP—offset, to be sure, by some employers' cancellation of their health insurance programs. The fractions of all national income flowing into compensation supplements in recent time periods is as follows:

- 1965–1970: 6.5 percent
- 1971–1980: 9.8 percent
- 1981–1990: 11.5 percent
- 1991–1999: 11.5 percent

Because these contributions clearly confer standard-of-living benefits, compensation data that exclude them underestimate the welfare conferred on the recipients.

Second, the plot in figure 5.8 covers only the (inflation-adjusted) wages of manufacturing production workers. It excludes the pay of manufacturing supervisors, which, at least for top executives, has increased much more rapidly than the wages of production workers. It also excludes nonmanufacturing industries, some of which (such as retailing) pay lower wages than in manufacturing but others (e.g., law, medicine, accounting, finance, and the like) that pay much higher wages. One redeeming value of the figure 5.8 data is that the sample approximates Marx's notion of the proletariat.

Despite these caveats, there is widespread consensus that the average U.S. worker fared badly from the mid-1970s onward and that the previous trend toward steadily rising real incomes had been bent, even if not totally broken. Several things appear to have gone wrong.

That the changes materialized during the 1970s suggests one causal element. The growth of productivity—real output per hour of labor input in the nonfarm sector of the U.S. economy—slumped during the 1970s. Average growth rates over decades were 2.39 percent for the 1960s, 1.69 percent in the 1970s, and 1.59 percent in the 1980s, with a rebound to 2.33 percent between 1990 and 2005. It must be noted that the productivity rebound did not yield a wage rebound for manufacturing workers.

The initially perplexing difficulties in the 1970s did, however, contribute to changes in the political climate that in turn affected compensation patterns. Levy and Temin (2007) argue that the 1970s precipitated a transition from what has been called the golden age for labor and the "Detroit consensus" to a "Washington consensus" less favorable to the interests of workers. The Depression of the 1930s led in the United States to legislation establishing minimum hourly wages and encouraging the formation of labor unions and supporting workers in their collective bargaining. These were followed after World War II by agreements between the Big Three automobile companies and the strong United Auto Workers union indexing wages for inflation, guaranteeing additional annual pay increments to reward anticipated future productivity growth, and extending health care and pension programs. This Detroit consensus then spread to other strongly unionized industries. An initial setback to these worker-friendly developments was the Taft-Hartley Act of 1947, which limited unions' ability to picket outlets for the goods of producers with whom disputes were pending. The 1970s brought more significant changes in the political climate. Deregulation of key industries such as railroads, airlines, trucking, and telecommunications undermined seller monopoly power out of which generous wages had been paid. Laws to increase the minimum hourly wage lagged price inflation. Officials hostile to labor were appointed to mediating bodies such as the National Labor Relations Board. In 1981, President Ronald Reagan broke a strike of air traffic controllers by threatening to fire persisting strikers within forty-eight hours. For these and other reasons, the fraction of the U.S. workforce unionized fell from 24.4 percent in 1955 to 10.5 percent in 2000, and the incidence of strikes declined sharply.[16]

Macroeconomic measures taken to combat the stagflation of the 1970s raised interest rates sharply, attracting huge inflows of foreign capital and (at least until the late 1980s) raising the value of the U.S. dollar. This gave rapidly industrializing nations an opportunity to gain footholds in the U.S. market, which were not relinquished later. Although most academic studies attribute only a small role to import competition generally in depressing U.S. workers' wages,[17] there was undoubtedly a subtle interaction effect as increasing foreign competition weakened the position of U.S. import-sensitive industries' unions.

Averages conceal as much as they reveal. Although U.S. production workers' (and indeed most middle-class workers') wages stagnated, some employees—especially those whose skills meshed with changing industry demands—fared exceptionally well. The proliferation of computers displaced middle-class employees who had performed data processing and similar tasks mechanically, but it increased the demand and pay for skills in more creative and abstraction-based occupations, for which computers were a complementary input best used by those with high skills. Among the set of all employees, therefore, the distribution of wages became more unequal, with high-skill workers benefiting and medium-skill workers losing out.[18] Growing inequality in employee compensation was encouraged by competition to hire high-skill individuals; winner-take-all competitions to garner the skills best-suited for corporate leadership, law, medicine, professional athletics, the performing arts, and the like;[19] and failures in corporate governance permitting boards of directors routinely to approve salaries and bonuses for top managers dramatically higher and rising sharply relative to those of ordinary workers. Earnings of the top 0.1 percent of income recipients rose relative to averages for the base of the employment compensation pyramid—the bottom 90 percent—from roughly twenty times the base average during the 1960s and 1970s to seventy times in the early years of the twenty-first century.[20]

Tracing U.S. income distribution patterns over the course of a century, Piketty and Saez (2003) show that the share of total U.S. wage and capital income gained by the most affluent 1 percent of tax return filers (usually families) fell from a peak in 1929, stabilized in the range of 8–11 percent between the 1950s and the 1980s, and then rose briskly to 14.6 percent in 1998 and an even higher value in 2007.[21] See the solid line in figure 5.11. When wage shares alone are tallied, a doubling of the top 1 percent's share is seen between 1970 and 1998 (dashed line in figure 5.11). Although the rich were becoming richer relative to the middle class in income before taxes, rates of income taxation for the top income brackets were reduced—for example, in the United States from 91 percent in the 1950s to 50 percent in the 1970s, 40 percent in the 1990s, and 35 percent in the early years of the twenty-first century.

For the United Kingdom and France, top-tier income shares declined until the early 1980s and then rose, but more gradually than in the United States (Piketty and

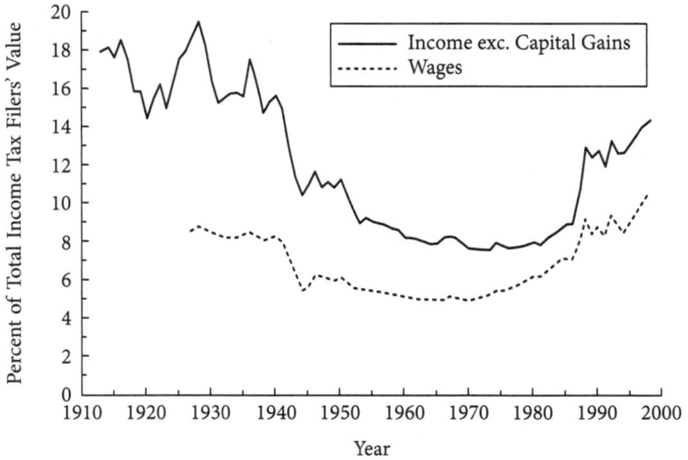

Figure 5.11. Shares of U.S. Income and Wages Gained by the Top 1 Percent

Saez 2003, figure XII). The extent to which income is concentrated in the hands of the most affluent varies from nation to nation, depending on public policies as well as national levels of economic development. During the 1990s, for example, the share of income received by the richest 20 percent of income earners is reported by United Nations sources to have varied as follows among a cross-section of highly developed nations (United Nations Development Programme 2000, p. 172):

- New Zealand: 46.9 percent
- United States: 46.4 percent
- United Kingdom: 43.0 percent
- France: 40.2 percent
- Germany: 38.5 percent
- Italy: 36.3 percent
- Japan: 35.7 percent
- Denmark: 34.5 percent
- Sweden: 34.5 percent

Certainly, in the leading capitalist nations, nothing like the immiserization predicted by Marx can be found for all but small minorities of the population. Nevertheless, trends toward increasing inequality and stagnation of middle-class incomes during recent decades provide grounds to fear a rising tide of discontent among the average citizens of classically capitalist nations.

Capitalism and Economic Fluctuations

Another characteristic of capitalism—recognized already by Marx and emphasized by Schumpeter[22]—is the tendency toward fluctuations in economic activity or, more pejoratively, crises.[23] Abstracting from the Great Depression of the early 1930s, seen in figure 5.2 to be especially severe for the United States and the United Kingdom, and the major slump of 2008–2010, figure 5.12 provides perspective on the phenomenon for the more normal times following World War II up to 1999. The dominant picture remains one of growth in GDP per capita. But that growth is marred by occasional interruptions and downturns—notably, in mild recessions centered on 1954, 1958, 1970, and 1991 and in the somewhat sharper recessions following from an abrupt oil price surge and shift of purchasing power to OPEC in 1974–1975 and the inflation-fighting "double-dip" recession of 1980–1982.

The control of capital by private individuals or groups is the essence of capitalism. Capital is accumulated through investment, and changes over time in investment activity are the leading cause of economic fluctuations. An oversimplified notion of how fluctuations emerge is provided by the so-called accelerator model.[24] It is assumed that businesses are operated most efficiently when they maintain a more or less fixed ratio k of capital to their output. That is, $K^* = kQ^*$. If the growth

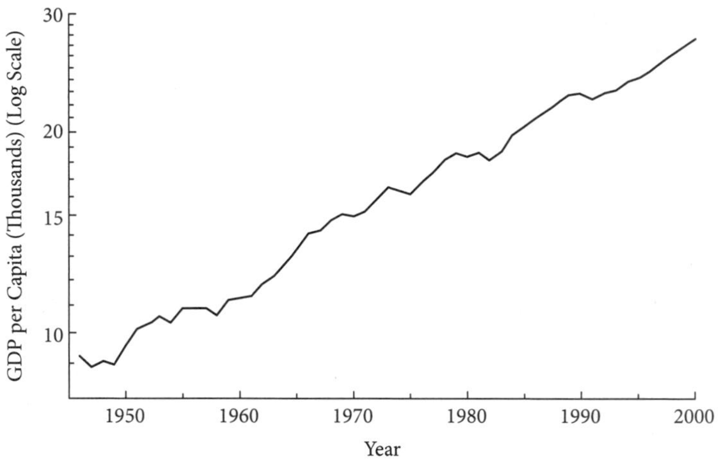

Figure 5.12. Magnitude of Postwar U.S. Recessions: 1946–2000 (Meausred in Constant 1990 Dollars)

of output dQ/dt is steady, investment I is approximately equal to dK/dt and can be adjusted to increase the capital stock at a relatively smooth rate over time.[25] But if for any reason—a technological change, events related to war, harvest conditions, or a sudden increase in the monetary supply from the central bank or foreign sources—Q rises by twice the expected growth increment, and if the increase is expected to be more than temporary, investment must be increased disproportionately (e.g., with a doubling of the Q increment, by twice the normal investment flow rate I) to maintain the desired proportionality of capital to output. The jump in investment, if correlated with many similar shocks throughout the economy, increases aggregate economic activity and income, and added spending generates multiplier effects that intensify the upward pressure on aggregate output. At some point, however, the unexpected growth of output reaches limits and slows, putting the cyclical movement of investment and ultimately output into reverse. The cutback in investment is likely to be sharper for quickly adjusted inventories than for longer lived capital, giving rise to fluctuations that may vary in duration.

This is only a beginning, however. The unanticipated rise in aggregate output and the accompanying increases in investment may in themselves make businesspeople more optimistic about future profit prospects. Their optimism may be heightened if prices and profits rise because of capacity constraints and/or increased money supply. Investment, John Maynard Keynes famously observed (1936, p. 161), is driven by expectations, and the favorable expectations generated by an upswing may excite businessmen's "animal spirits," inducing more of an investment increase than the objective facts warrant. The upward movement or boom is amplified. But as limits to output growth are approached and a downward adjustment of investment is signaled, negative accelerator and multiplier effects are compounded by excess capacity, price reductions, and a sharp decline in profits, turning the animal spirits negative and reducing investment incentives all the more. The fall in profits may be so sharp that borrowers—both business firms and home mortgage holders—default on their loans. If there is widespread and synchronized default on loans, banks may become insolvent, the more so the more highly they have leveraged their lending in the hope of higher returns on equity. Banks' difficulties in turn impair the flow of credit and turn what might have been a run-of-the-mill recession into a downward spiraling panic.

With his emphasis on the role of innovation as a key source of economic growth, Schumpeter (1939) viewed fluctuations in innovative activity as a prime cause of macroeconomic fluctuations. He recognized that innovations come in all sizes and shapes. Only a few innovations are economy-transforming. The transformative innovations induce major increases in investment but also trigger waves of improvement inventions that call for further investments. Increases in output stemming from the technological improvements themselves and the facilitating investments stimulate further innovating efforts across a wider variety of fields.

Schumpeter stressed interaction effects among innovation, investment, and further innovation as propelling forces giving rise to a fairly regular oscillation of long upturns and downturns. An alternative hypothesis was advanced by Nordhaus (1989). He assumed that the distribution of economic effects associated with a random sample of inventions is not only skew but conforms to the so-called Pareto-Levy distribution with an extremely long—indeed, asymptotically infinite—high-value tail. Embedding this assumption in a large Monte Carlo simulation experiment, he shows that what is in fact a random walk of diverse economic impacts from inventions distributed plausibly over time gives rise to economic fluctuations that appear cyclical. It is questionable whether the true underlying value distribution is indeed Pareto-Levy rather than a somewhat less skew log normal form, but even with the latter, cyclical fluctuations resembling those observed in real-world business cycles are generated by Monte Carlo experiments.[26]

With his emphasis on the clustering of innovations as a key stimulus to business upswings, Schumpeter (1939, p. 119) saw recessions as a necessary element in "harvesting" the fruits of creative destruction. Widespread imitation of successful innovations makes the fruits of innovation more broadly available and, through intensified competition, reduces prices and raises average real (i.e., price-deflated) standards of living. Obsolete technologies are at the same time vanquished from the economy. Schumpeter distinguished, however, between "recession," in which this working-out process occurs, and "depression," in which bankers and industrialists panic, choking off useful investment and aggravating unemployment. Depression, he wrote (1939, p. 131), unlike recession, "is a pathological process to which no organic functions can be attributed."

From his birth and educational origins, Schumpeter might be considered an iconoclastic member of the Austrian school of business fluctuations analysis. A more conventional Austrian was Ludwig von Mises, who, in place of technological innovation, emphasized the role of excessive credit expansion as the genesis of booms. "The essence of the credit-expansion boom is not overinvestment, but investment in the wrong lines, i.e., malinvestment."[27] He continues (pp. 562–565):

> As soon as the afflux of additional fiduciary media comes to an end, the airy castle of the boom collapses.... Factories are closed, the continuation of construction projects in progress is halted, workers are discharged.... Accidental institutional and psychological circumstances generally turn the outbreak of the crisis into a panic... [A] credit expansion boom must unavoidably lead to a process which everyday speech calls the depression. [One] must realize that the depression is in fact the process of readjustment, of putting production activities anew in agreement with the given state of market data.... Consumers... must for the time being renounce certain amenities which they could have enjoyed if the boom had not encouraged malinvestment. But, on the other hand, they can find partial compensation in the fact that some enjoyments are now available to them which would have been beyond their reach if the smooth course of economic activities had not been disturbed by the orgies of the boom. It is slight compensation only... [but] it is the only choice left to them as conditions and data are now.

An extreme version of this view appears to have been held by former banker Andrew Mellon, U.S. Treasury Secretary between 1921 and 1932. In President Herbert Hoover's (unauthorized) characterization of Mellon's philosophy, the recession "will purge the rottenness out of the system. High costs of living and high living will come down. People will work harder, live a moral life. Values will be adjusted, and enterprising people will pickup the wrecks from less competent people."[28] In Hoover's synopsis, Mellon's formula was to "Liquidate labor, liquidate stocks, liquidate the farmers, liquidate real estate."

Obviously, there are alternative perspectives that see depressions as sources of unwarranted and widespread pain, to be avoided by appropriate public policy measures. Paramount among these was Keynes (1936), who stressed (pp. 315–320) business investors' "animal spirits" as the cause of overinvestment and the eventual emergence of corrections:

> The basis for [investors' expectations] is very precarious. Being based on shifting and unreliable evidence, they are subject to sudden and violent changes.... It is not so easy to revive the marginal efficiency of capital, determined, as it is, by the uncontrollable and disobedient psychology of the business world.... In conditions of *laissez-faire* the avoidance of wide fluctuations may, therefore, prove impossible without a far-reaching change in the psychology of investment markets such as there is no reason to expect. I conclude that the duty of ordering the current volume of investment cannot safely be left in private hands.

Keynes proposed (1936, p. 327) as one corrective to exaggerated business fluctuations "a banking policy which always nipped in the bud an incipient boom by a rate of interest high enough to deter even the most misguided optimists." As William McChesney Martin, chairman of the U.S. Federal Reserve system between 1951 and 1970, observed memorably, "The job of the Federal Reserve is to take away the punch bowl just when the party starts getting interesting."[29] If preemptive action fails, Keynes visualized monetary policy easing as a means of encouraging depressed investment. But that, too, could fail if business expectations are so bleak that a monetary supply surge sufficient to induce zero interest rates could not restore investment—a condition described as a liquidity trap. In that instance, Keynes urged, only government stimulatory spending or government-induced changes in the distribution of income that enhanced individuals' propensity to consume, for example, through tax remissions and minimum wage laws, could save the economy from unwarranted suffering.

Conclusion

"Capitalism," a witticism prevalent in the Soviet Union during the 1960s observed, "is the exploitation of man by man. Communism is the opposite." Indeed, capitalism is not without problems—at times low wages, which might be viewed as exploitation, or even worse, a tendency toward occasionally violent fluctuations and involuntary unemployment. But it is hard to conceive of a practical economic system exhibiting superior dynamic performance, notably in the opportunity and incentive free markets provide to capitalistic entrepreneurs for technological innovation—more efficient production processes, new products conferring superior consumer utility, and better methods of business organization—which in turn has raised living standards by astonishing amounts. The problem for public policy is to secure the dynamic benefits of capitalism while minimizing its negative side effects.

Notes

1. See, for example, Shylock's assessment of Antonio's business in Shakespeare's *Merchant of Venice*, Act I, Scene III: "He hath an argosy bound to Tripolis, another to the Indies,... he hath a third at Mexico, a fourth for England, and other ventures he hath, squandered abroad.... The man is, notwithstanding, sufficient. Three thousand ducats; I think I may take his bond."
2. See Lenin (1917). For a seminal contribution with a more benign explanation, see Vernon (1966).
3. See also (Marx 1967, 1:627) recognition but not a prediction that an extreme limit to the centralization process was to have all capital united under a single enterprise. More than a century later, centralization had not proceeded to anywhere near Marx's limits. For a review of the evidence, see Scherer and Ross (1990), pp. 59–65. The year 1997, the last year for which census data were available, the largest 100 U.S. manufacturing corporations accounted for 32 percent of total manufacturing sector value added. On *Fortune* magazine's May 4, 2009, list of the largest U.S. corporations in all fields (not only manufacturing), the top 20 accounted for 32 percent of the top 500 corporations' assets—a universe smaller than all corporate assets. Given their emphasis on the power of financial capital, Marx and Engels would have been impressed that a merger wave brought the share of all U.S. financial institution assets

controlled by the largest twenty entities from 15 percent in 1990 to 62 percent in 2002. Kaufman (2009, p. 100). The result was implementation of a "too big to fail" policy by the U.S. government in 2008.

4. But see Hall and Rosenberg (2010).
5. The poem is not included in Boulding's conference paper (1965), but was published in Boulding (1980), p. 96.
6. It is derived from Barzel (1968) and Scherer (1967, 2007).
7. The concept is attributable to Schmookler (1966).
8. Reproduced in Hamilton (2001).
9. This was foreseen by Marx (1967, Book I, chapter 25): "As soon as capitalist production takes possession of agriculture, and in proportion to the extent to which it does, demand for an agricultural labouring population falls absolutely, while the accumulation of capital employed in agriculture advances.... Part of the agricultural population is therefore constantly on the point of passing over into an urban or manufacturing proletariat."
10. Employment data for India were not reported. The fraction of GDP originating in agriculture was 56 percent higher in India than in China.
11. See Baumol et al. (1989), chapters 6 and 7.
12. The data are spliced from Carter et al. (2006), vol. 2, Tables Ba4361–4366, and Table Cc1–2; and U.S. Executive Office of the President (2009), Tables B-47 and B-62.
13. During the 1930s, new government policies were introduced favorable to unionization and the wages of employed workers, even though arguably they may temporarily have displaced workers not tracked by figure 5.8 into the ranks of the unemployed.
14. U.S. Bureau of the Census (1960), p. 92; and U.S. Executive Office of the President (2009), p. 340 (Table B-47). The figure for 2005 includes 4.6 hours of overtime. Overtime was not generally paid at premium rates in the United States until 1938.
15. See also Cain and Patterson (1981).
16. Source: *Statistical Abstract of the United States*, various years.
17. See, for example, Burtless (1998), Rodrik (1997), and Lawrence (2008).
18. See, for example, Autor et al. (2006) and more generally Goldin and Katz (2008).
19. See Frank and Cook (1995).
20. See "Spare a Dime? A Special Report on the Rich," *The Economist* (April 4, 2009), p. 4.
21. Drawn from tables II and IV in Piketty and Saez (2003). Because high-income earners are better able to accumulate wealth than low earners, the distribution of wealth is even more concentrated than the distribution of income. For the Piketty-Saez sample in 1998, the top *10 percent* of income earners reported 41.4 percent of total U.S. income, whereas the same group had 65.9 percent of U.S. families' net worth, compared to 2.0 percent of net worth for the bottom 20 percent of income earners. The net worth share of the top 10 percent rose to 70 percent in 2007. See Bucks et al. (2009), p. A11.
22. See Schumpeter (1939). I adopt here the more agnostic "fluctuations" descriptor of Gordon (1951) rather than agreeing that the movements are of cyclic regularity.
23. A definitive history is Kindleberger and Aliber (2005).
24. The most seminal contribution was Harrod (1936).
25. I ignore the complications introduced by depreciation.
26. See Scherer and Harhoff (2000).
27. Mises (1949, 1996), p. 559. See also Ebeling (1996).
28. Kindleberger and Aliber (2005), p. 205, quoting from *The Memoirs of Herbert Hoover.*
29. See http://www.cbsnews.com/2316-100_162-975818-9.html

References

Autor, David H., Lawrence Katz, and Melissa Kearney. "The Polarization of the U.S. Labor Market." *American Economic Review* 96 (May 2006): 189–194.

Barzel, Yoram. "Optimal Timing of Innovations." *Review of Economics and Statistics* 50 (August 1968): 348–355.

Baumol, William J., Sue Anne Batey Blackman, and Edward Wolff. *Productivity and American Leadership*. Cambridge, Mass.: MIT Press, 1989.

Binswanger, Hans, and Vernon Ruttan. *Induced Innovation: Technology, Institutions, and Development.* Baltimore, Md.: Johns Hopkins University Press, 1978.

Boulding, Kenneth. "Research and Development for the Emerging Nations." In *Economics of Research and Development*, ed. Richard Tybout, 422–457. Columbus: Ohio State University Press, 1965.

Boulding, Kenneth. *Beasts, Ballads, and Bouldingisms.* Ed. Richard P. Beilock. New Brunswick, N.J.: Transaction Books, 1980.

Bucks, Brian K., Arthur B. Kennickell, Traci L. Mach, and Kevin B. Moore. "Changes in U.S. Family Finances from 2004 to 2007." *Federal Reserve Bulletin* 95 (February 2009): A1–A55.

Burtless, Gary. "Technological Change and International Trade: How Well Do They Explain the Rise in U.S. Income Inequality?" In *The Inequality Paradox: Growth of Income Disparity*, ed. James Auerbach and Richard Belous, 60–91. Washington: National Planning Association, 1998.

Cain, Louis P., and Donald Patterson. "Factor Biases and Technical Change in Manufacturing." *Journal of Economic History* 41 (June 1981): 341–360.

Carter, Susan B., et al., eds. *The Historical Statistics of the United States: Millennial Edition.* New York: Cambridge University Press, 2006.

Eastman, Max, ed. *Capital, The Communist Manifesto and Other Writings by Karl Marx.* New York: Modern Library, 1932.

Ebeling, Richard, ed. *The Austrian Theory of the Trade Cycle.* Auburn, Ala.: Ludwig von Mises Institute, 1996.

The Economist. *Pocket World in Figures*, 2010 edition. London: 2009.

Engel, Ernst. *Die Productions- und Consumptionsverhaeltnisse des Koenigsreiches Sachsen* (1857). Reprinted in *International Statistical Institute Bulletin* 9 (1895): Anlage 1–54.

Engels, Friedrich. *The Condition of the Working Class in England.* London, 1845. Reproduced in *The Condition of the Working Class in England,* ed. David McLellan. Oxford: Oxford University Press, 1999.

Frank, Robert, and Phillip J. Cook. *The Winner-Take-All Society.* New York: Free Press, 1995.

Goldin, Claudia, and Lawrence Katz. *The Race between Education and Technology.* Cambridge, Mass.: Harvard University Press, 2008.

Gordon, Robert Aaron. *Business Fluctuations.* New York: Harper, 1951.

Habakkuk, H. J. *American and British Technology in the 19th Century.* Cambridge: Cambridge University Press, 1962.

Hall, Bronwyn, and Nathan Rosenberg, eds. *Handbook of the Economics of Innovation.* Amsterdam: Elsevier, 2010.

Hamilton, Alexander. "Report on the Subject of Manufactures, 1791." In *Alexander Hamilton: Writings*, ed. Joanne Freeman, 647–734. New York: Library of America, 2001.

Harrod, Roy F. *The Trade Cycle.* Oxford: Oxford University Press, 1936.

Kaufman, Henry. *The Road to Financial Reformation.* Hoboken, N.J.: Wiley, 2009.

Keynes, John Maynard. *The General Theory of Employment, Interest, and Money*. London: Macmillan, 1936.
Kindleberger, Charles P., and Robert Aliber. *Manias, Panics, and Crashes*, 5th ed. Hoboken, N.J.: Wiley, 2005.
Lawrence, Robert. *Blue Collar Blues: Is Trade to Blame for Rising US Income Inequality?* Washington: Peterson Institute for International Economics, 2008.
Lenin, V. I. *Imperialism: The Highest Stage of Capitalism*. Petrograd, 1917. English translation from New York: International Publishers, 1939.
Levy, Frank, and Peter Temin. "Inequality and Institutions in 20th Century America." National Bureau of Economic Research Working Paper 13106 (May 2007).
Maddison, Angus. *The World Economy: Historical Statistics*. Paris: OECD, 2006.
Marx, Karl. *Capital*. Trans. Samuel Moore and Edward Aveling. New York: International Publishers, 1967.
Mises, Ludwig von. *Human Action: A Treatise on Economics*. 1949; Irvington-on-Hudson: Foundation for Economic Education, 1996.
Nordhaus, William D. "Comment." In *Brookings Papers on Economic Activity: Microeconomics*, 320–325. Washington, D.C.: Brookings Institution, 1989.
Phelps Brown, E. H., and Sheila V. Hopkins. "Seven Centuries of Building Wages." *Economica* 22 (Aug. 1955): 195–206.
Phelps Brown, E. H., and Sheila V. Hopkins. "Seven Centuries of the Prices of Consumables, Compared with Builders' Wage-Rates." *Economica* 23 (Nov. 1956): 296–314.
Piketty, Thomas, and Emmanuel Saez. "Income Inequality in the United States." *Quarterly Journal of Economics* 118 (Feb. 2003): 1–39.
Pratten, Clifford F. "The Manufacture of Pins." *Journal of Economic Literature* 18 (March 1980): 93–96.
Rodrik, Dani. *Has Globalization Gone Too Far?* Washington: Institute for International Economics, 1997.
Scherer, F. M. "Research and Development Resource Allocation under Rivalry." *Quarterly Journal of Economics* 81 (August 1967): 359–394.
Scherer, F. M. *Innovation and Growth: Schumpeterian Perspectives*. Cambridge, Mass.: MIT Press, 1984.
Scherer, F. M. "Schumpeter and the Micro-Foundations of Economic Growth." In *Edward Elgar Companion to Neo-Schumpeterian Economics*, ed. Horst Hanusch and Andreas Pyka, 671–687. Cheltenham: Elgar, 2007.
Scherer, F. M., and Dietmar Harhoff. "Technology Policy for a World of Skew-Distributed Outcomes." *Research Policy* 29 (April 2000): 559–566.
Scherer, F. M., and David Ross. *Industrial Market Structure and Economic Performance*, 3rd ed. Boston: Houghton Mifflin, 1990.
Schmookler, Jacob. *Invention and Economic Growth*. Cambridge, Mass.: Harvard University Press, 1966.
Schumpeter, Joseph A. *Theorie der wirtschaftlichen Entwicklung*. Leipzig: Duncker & Humblot, 1912. Translated by Redvers Opie, *The Theory of Economic Development*. Cambridge, Mass.: Harvard University Press, 1934.
Schumpeter, Joseph A. *Business Cycles*. New York: McGraw-Hill, 1939.
Schumpeter, Joseph A. *Capitalism Socialism and Democracy*. New York: Harper, 1942.
Smith, Adam. *An Inquiry into the Nature and Causes of the Wealth of Nations* (1776). Ed. Edward Cannan. New York: Modern Library, 1937, reproducing with annotations the fifth (1789) edition.

United Nations Development Programme. *Human Development Report: 2000*. Oxford: Oxford University Press, 2000.

U.S. Bureau of the Census. *Historical Statistics of the United States: Colonial Times to 1957*. Washington: U.S. Bureau of the Census, 1960.

U.S. Executive Office of the President, *Economic Report of the President*. Washington, 2009.

Vernon, Raymond. "International Investment and International Trade in the Product Cycle." *Quarterly Journal of Economics* 80 (May 1966): 190–207.

PART III

THE INSTITUTIONS OF CAPITALISM

CHAPTER 6

THE ROLE OF FINANCE IN ECONOMIC DEVELOPMENT: BENEFITS, RISKS, AND POLITICS

THORSTEN BECK

WHAT role does finance have in the development of market-based economies? Early on, politicians and economists alike emphasized the importance of the financial system for the rise of capitalism, industrialization, and economic development. Smith (1776) pointed to the role of money in lowering transaction costs, thus permitting greater specialization, and fostering technological innovation. Alexander Hamilton (1781), one of the founding fathers of the United States, argued that "banks were the happiest engines that ever were invented" for spurring economic growth. Joseph Schumpeter argued in 1911 that financial intermediaries play a pivotal role in economic development because they choose which firms get to use society's savings.[1] On the other hand, development economists for many decades have ignored the financial system and focused on other policy areas. Lucas (1988) described the role of finance in the growth process as overstated, and Robinson (1952) argued that financial development primarily follows economic growth. Following the seminal works by Goldsmith (1969), McKinnon (1973), and Shaw (1973), however, a large and still active theoretical and empirical literature has related financial development to the economic growth process. Empirical studies have found a positive impact of financial deepening on economic growth, statistically and economically significant.

More recently, studies have related the development of the financial sector to other real sector outcomes, including the pattern of countries' trade balance and changes in income distribution and poverty levels.

The same mechanisms that underpin the positive role of finance, however, are also a source of risk and fragility. The history of finance is full of boom-and-bust cycles, bank failures, and systemic bank and currency crises (Reinhart and Rogoff, 2009). Just as there is a comprehensive literature on the impact of finance on growth, there is an equally important literature that has explored the causes and socioeconomic costs of financial fragility, including systemic banking crises. Historic analyses and case studies have given way to more systemic cross-country explorations of idiosyncratic and systemic banking distress and their determinants.

Given the importance of finance for growth, its inherent risks, and the large socioeconomic costs of banking crises, it is not surprising that the financial sector is often at the top of the policy agenda. However, the importance of access to credit as entry barrier into the real sector and the relative ease with which owners and creditors of financial institutions can be expropriated also makes financial sector policies an important tool in the political process. Subsidized credit programs and credit guarantees are often an easy and cheap tool of fiscal policy as they create contingent rather than real liabilities. The dependence of most real sector enterprises on access to external finance makes the financial sector critical in the attempt of ruling elites to entrench their socioeconomic dominance and prevent entry of competitors. The reliance of financial institutions and markets on contractual institutions makes them dependent on the political sphere.

The recent crisis has brought these issues to the forefront of the academic and also political debate. The crisis has also shed doubt on the previous findings of a positive impact of finance on growth. How much finance is good for growth? Are financial crises too high a price for having a thriving financial system? Are credit boom-and-bust cycles behind economic cycles? What is the politics behind financial development and fragility?

This chapter explores the role of the financial sector for economic growth, the causes and consequences of financial fragility, and the politics behind financial deepening and fragility. In doing so, I identify the critical role of the financial sector within capitalist economies, a role with bright and dark sides. Specifically, I survey the large theoretical and empirical literature that links a sound financial system to the process of economic development. I discuss the theoretical and empirical literature on bank fragility and banking crises and survey the literature on the political economy of financial deepening. Importantly, I relate these three strands of the literature to each other and to the current crisis.

Financial institutions and markets depend critically on contractual institutions, and this survey is thus closely related to the institutions and development literature (Acemgolu, Johnson, and Robinson, 2005; see chapter 2 in this volume). Specifically, given the intertemporal nature of financial contracts, the financial system is one of the most institution-sensitive sectors of the economy. The financial sector depends as much as contractual institutions on property rights protection and thus the political structures of societies.

This chapter is related to other recent surveys. Levine (2005) surveys the theoretical and empirical literature on finance and growth, and Beck (2009) surveys the econometric methodologies behind the empirical finance and growth literature. Demirgüç-Kunt and Detragiache (2005) discuss the literature on banking crises, and Haber and Perrotti (2008) offer a critical survey of the finance and politics literature. This survey is also related to recent surveys on the political economy of the financial and legal system (Beck and Levine, 2005). Compared to these previous surveys, this chapter tries to bring these three literatures together and relate them to the first global financial crisis of the twenty-first century.

The remainder of this chapter is organized as follows. The next section surveys the theoretical and empirical finance and growth literature. Then I discuss the theoretical and empirical literature on financial fragility. Following that is a survey of the political economy literature of finance, and a final section brings these three literatures together and concludes.

Finance and Economic Development

What role does the financial sector play in market economies? How important is the financial sector in the growth process of countries? Over the past thirty years, a flourishing theoretical literature has explained the endogenous emergence of financial institutions and markets and has explored their impact on real sector outcomes, including economic growth and income inequality. Over the past twenty years, a still growing empirical literature has explored the effect of financial systems and their different segments on economic growth and other real sector variables. This literature has also explored the relative importance of banks and markets and the impact of financial sector development on other real sector outcomes. More recently, this literature has explored the distributional repercussions of financial deepening and the effect of broadening. I discuss each in turn.

Finance and Growth: Theory

The theoretical literature on financial intermediation has focused on two important dimensions. Why do financial markets and institutions exist? And what is their impact on savings, investment, and economic growth? I discuss each question in turn.

At the core of the existence of financial institutions and markets are market frictions, which financial institutions and markets can help alleviate, such as asymmetric information between contractual partners resulting in agency problems and risks of illiquidity and default. Building on the insights by Stiglitz and Weiss (1983) on the importance of agency problems, several articles have shown how financial institutions and markets can economize on screening and monitoring costs of many individual lenders and, by diversifying risk across many different projects, improve on a world without them.[2] By pooling savings across a large number of savers with differently timed liquidity needs, financial institutions can help overcome liquidity risks and ultimately provide savers with a higher return. Similarly, more liquid financial markets increase incentives for investors to relinquish control over their savings, as they are able to access them through financial markets on an immediate basis, while at the same time earning higher returns. The emergence of financial institutions and markets can thus be explained by the gains for economic agents, a theoretical argument that is consistent with the historical observance that financial institutions and markets have arisen at an early stage of human history and especially as exchange of goods and services across larger geographical distances and within larger societies or between societies has become more prominent.[3]

The endogenous emergence of financial institutions and markets does not in itself imply a positive impact on economic growth. A large theoretical literature, however, has explored several channels through which financial systems can help increase economic growth rates, both through improved capital accumulation as through higher productivity growth. On a broader level, these theories have shown how financial markets can help overcome the market frictions of indivisible projects and inability to diversify risks that have held back development in many developing economies (Acemoglu and Zilibotti, 1997). I discuss these different channels in turn.

First, and on a very basic level, financial systems can support the efficient exchange of goods and services by providing payment services and thus reducing transaction costs. Financial services can foster specialization by enabling more transactions, thus fostering productivity growth.[4]

Second, by pooling savings from many individual savers, financial institutions and markets can help overcome investment indivisibilities and allow exploiting scale economies.[5] This does not necessarily have to be national financial institutions but can be local coalitions of investors, as was the case in the early days of the Industrial Revolution for infrastructure projects.[6]

Third, by economizing on screening and monitoring costs and thus allowing more investment projects to be financed and, ex ante, increasing the aggregate success probability, financial institutions and markets can ultimately have a positive impact on investment and resource allocation. Similarly, by identifying the entrepreneurs with the most promising technologies, financial intermediaries can also boost the rate of technological innovation and ultimately growth.[7] A similar argument holds for financial markets: in larger and more liquid markets, agents have greater incentives to invest in research on enterprises and projects, which produces information that can be turned into trading gains, ultimately improving resource allocation.[8]

Fourth, both financial institutions and markets can help monitor enterprises and reduce agency problems within firms between management and majority and minority shareholders, again improving resource allocation. Debt instruments can reduce the amount of free cash available to firms and thus managerial slack (Aghion, Dewatripont, and Rey, 1999), while liquid stock exchanges can allow investors to monitor and discipline enterprises through the threat of takeovers and subsequent dismissal of management.[9] Linking stock performance to manager compensation can help align the interests of managers with those of owners,[10] although it is important to define a proper benchmark. Similarly, as in the case of screening, financial institutions can economize on the costs of monitoring by functioning as "delegated monitor."[11] By building long-term relationships, financial institutions can further reduce monitoring costs. Both financial markets and institutions can thus improve resource allocation and productivity growth. By reducing control problems of investors vis-à-vis owners and managers of enterprises, improved corporate governance can also increase savings and capital accumulation.

Fifth, banks can also help reduce liquidity risk and thus enable long-term investment, as shown by Diamond and Dybvig (1983). By pooling savings of patient and impatient agents, financial institutions can transform short-term liabilities into long-term assets, enabling long-term investment and ultimately economic growth. Similarly, liquid markets can enable investment in long-term investment projects while at the same time allowing investors to have access to their savings at short-term notice (Levine, 1991). Financial institutions can also ease liquidity needs of enterprises, enabling long-term investment and R&D activities.[12]

Sixth, financial institutions and markets allow cross-sectional diversification across projects, allowing risky innovative activity while guaranteeing an ex ante contracted interest rate to savers (King and Levine, 1993b). Furthermore, aggregate risk that cannot be diversified away at a specific point in time can be diversified by long-living financial intermediaries over time (Allen and Gale, 1997).

Beyond theoretical models, economists have explained the take-off of the Industrial Revolution in some countries earlier than others by the availability of finance. Hicks (1969) argued that the Industrial Revolution in the United Kingdom was possible due to the relatively developed British financial system. Although many inventions were made before the Industrial Revolution, liquid capital markets enabled investment into long-term projects that could use these inventions. Similarly, the Netherlands and the United States experienced financial deepening before their economic and political rise in the seventeenth and twentieth centuries, respectively.

The relationship between finance and growth is not a one-way street; rather, higher growth induced by financial deepening increases demand for financial services, ultimately resulting in a virtuous circle of economic and financial development (Greenwood and Jovanovic, 1990). This theoretical insight has also resulted in additional challenges for the empirical finance and growth literature, as a positive relationship between financial and economic development might reflect causation from economic to financial development.

Theory, however, is not unambiguous in predicting a positive impact of financial deepening on economic growth. Better resource allocation may depress saving rates enough such that overall growth rates actually drop with enhanced financial development.[13] This can happen if the income effect of higher interest rates is larger than the substitution effect. The financial sector might also attract too many resources relative to the real sector, with negative repercussions for growth.[14] Critically, the impact of finance on growth might vary across different levels of income per capita, with the positive relationship being strongest among low- and middle-income countries that are catching up to high-income countries in their productivity levels and fading away as countries approach the global productivity frontier (Aghion, Howitt, and Mayer-Foulkes, 2005). A somewhat separate but related discussion is that about the importance of financial sector development compared to other sectors and policies in explaining growth. This ambiguity has motivated a large empirical literature over the past twenty years, to which I turn now.

Finance and Growth: From Correlation to Causality

The empirical literature on finance and growth has made enormous progress over the past two decades. To the same extent that the challenge of causality has been addressed, researchers have moved from aggregate macro-level data to more micro-level data, in the process also disentangling the mechanisms and channels through which financial development is associated with economic growth.

Goldsmith (1969) was the first to show empirically the positive correlation between financial development and GDP per capita, using data on the assets of financial intermediaries relative to GNP and data on the sum of net issues of bonds and securities plus changes in loans relative to GNP for thirty-five countries over the period 1860 to 1963. Such a correlation, however, does not control for other factors associated with economic growth and might thus be driven by other country characteristics correlated with both finance and growth. Second, such a correlation does not provide any information on the direction of causality between finance and growth. The early finance and growth literature has used standard cross-country ordinary least squares (OLS) regressions to control for other country characteristics associated with growth differences across countries (King and Levine, 1993a, 1993b). This literature has shown that both banking sector as well as equity market development are robust predictors of GDP per capita growth (Levine and Zervos, 1998).

In a second step, researchers have addressed the issue of reverse causation and omitted variables using instrumental variable techniques. Using external instruments, such as historic country characteristics that can explain cross-country variation in financial sector development, or internal instruments such as lagged values of financial sector indicators, several papers have shown that the relationship between financial sector development and economic growth is not due to reverse causation or omitted variable bias. Specifically, Levine, Loayza, and Beck (2000) and Beck, Levine, and Loayza (2000) show that instrumenting financial development with the legal traditions of countries and applying dynamic panel techniques with lagged values as instruments confirm the positive relationship between finance and growth.[15]

An alternative approach has been to explore the relationship between financial development and GDP per capita for a specific country over time. Compared to cross-country research, the time-series approach relies on higher frequency data (mostly yearly) to gain econometric power. The causality approach of the time-series approach, however, is different; specifically, the Granger causality tests are tests of forecast capacity—that is, to what extent does one series contain information about the other series? Unlike the cross-country panel regressions discussed earlier, this concept therefore does not control for omitted variable bias by directly including other variables or by controlling with instrumental variables. Rather, by including a rich lag structure, which is lacking in the cross-sectional approach, the time-series approach hopes to capture omitted variables. Numerous papers have found evidence for Granger causality from finance to economic development, though the evidence has been not unambiguous.[16] There is also evidence for bidirectional causality, consistent with theory.[17]

An alternative to the instrumental variable and time-series approaches is to explore the mechanisms or channels through which financial development affects economic growth, which can also be seen as "smoking gun" approach. This implies testing for a differential impact of financial development on different sectors or industries. In a seminal paper, Rajan and Zingales (1998) show that industries that depend more on external financing grow faster in countries with higher levels of financial development. It is important to note that this is a relative effect, because it is gauged by differences-in-differences—the difference between a high-dependence and low-dependence industry in a well-developed financial system compared to a less developed financial system. Critical for their methodology is that their measure of external dependence captures purely demand-side effects; the authors claim to achieve this by focusing on a sample of large listed U.S. enterprises that should face a perfectly price-elastic supply curve. Following Rajan and Zingales, this differences-in-differences technique has been used widely in the literature, showing that financial development is conducive to the growth of industries with larger growth opportunities, more dependent on intangible assets, and with a larger share of small enterprises.[18]

An alternative differences-in-differences approach is similar to an event study that focuses on a financial sector policy change. Most prominent in this context is the branch deregulation episode in the United States in the 1970s and '80s when states liberalized intra- and interstate branching. Using this almost identical policy reform implemented at different points in time, Jayaratne and Strahan (1996) show that deregulation led to lower loan losses and higher economic growth. Subsequent work has shown that this deregulation was also associated with an increase in entrepreneurship[19] and lower economic volatility.[20]

The finance and growth literature has also explored the channels through which financial deepening fosters economic growth. There is robust evidence that the impact is more through improved resource allocation, accumulation of knowledge, and productivity growth rather than through capital accumulation.[21] There is also evidence that financial deepening affects the corporate structure of the private sector; firms are more likely to incorporate in countries with better developed financial and legal systems (Demirgüç-Kunt, Love, and Maksimovic, 2006).

One of the critical functions of the financial system, as already described, is maturity transformation. By enabling long-term investment projects, finance can help foster economic growth. Through this channel, financial systems can also help reduce volatility. Financial systems can alleviate firms' liquidity constraints and facilitate long-term investment, which ultimately reduces the volatility of both investment and growth.[22] Similarly, well-developed financial markets and institutions can help dampen the negative impact that exchange rate volatility has on firms' liquidity and thus investment capacity.[23]

Recent publications have tested for the cross-country heterogeneity of the finance and growth relationship. There is evidence that the effect of financial development is strongest among middle-income countries, whereas other work finds a declining effect of finance and growth as countries grow richer, explaining this effect with finance helping countries catch up to the productivity frontier but not having any effect beyond this.[24] More recently, Arcand, Berkes, and Panizza (2011) find that the finance and growth relationship turns negative for high-income countries, identifying a value of 110 percent private credit to GDP as approximate turning point, with the negative relationship between finance and growth turning significant at around 150 percent private credit to GDP, levels reached by some high-income countries in the 2000s.

It is important to note that there have also been a number of empirical studies criticizing the finance and growth relationship. A series of articles have shed doubt on the robustness of the finance and growth relationship.[25] Other authors have focused on a direct relationship between the contractual framework that underpins financial sector development and economic growth. Using the Rajan and Zingales (1998) methodologies of matching industry with country characteristics, Claessens and Laeven (2003) find that industries more reliant on intangible assets, such as patents and trademarks, grow faster in countries with stronger contractual institutions. Evidence for a sample of four East European transition economies shows that trust in property rights, rather than access to credit, encourages entrepreneurs to reinvest their profits (Johnson, McMillan, and Woodruff, 2002), whereas evidence for China shows that both the quality of contractual institutions and access to finance explains profit reinvestment (Cull and Xu, 2005). Acemoglu and Johnson (2005) undertake a horse race on the aggregate level between contractual institutions that underpin financial development and protection of private property rights from expropriation by government and find that the latter (rather than the former) matters for long-term economic development. There is evidence, however, that this finding is due to the selection of the proxies for both contractual institutions and property rights protection and can be reinterpreted as the relative importance of the overall institutional framework (including informal institutions and norms) vis-à-vis formal institutions (such as courts) (Woodruff, 2006).

Overall, the overwhelming empirical evidence so far points to a positive relationship between financial deepening and economic growth beyond a pure correlation, a relationship that might vary over time and country conditions, however. In addition, there are important nonlinearities. This evidence also gives a first hint at the fragility that can arise from rapidly expanding financial systems, a topic I return to .later.

Banks versus Markets: Does Financial Structure Matter?

Until now, I have treated the financial system as a homogeneous sector. However, financial institutions, most prominently banks, and financial markets overcome the agency problem in different ways. Financial institutions create private information, which helps them reduce information asymmetries. Financial markets, on the other hand, create public information, aggregated into prices. Similarly, there are differences in the mechanisms through which financial institutions and markets exercise corporate governance. Banks can help improve corporate governance directly through loan covenants and direct influence on firm policy and indirectly through reducing the amount of free cash flows senior management has available. Financial markets can help improve corporate governance by linking payment of senior management to performance, through voting structures and the threat of takeover if the stock price falls below a value that is seen as being below fair value. Finally, there are different ways financial institutions and markets help diversify risks. Banks offer better intertemporal risk diversification tools, whereas markets are better in diversifying risk cross-sectionally. Markets are better in offering standardized products, and banks are better in offering customized solutions. However, banks and markets can also be complementary through instruments such as securitization, allowing exit strategies for venture capitalists, and by providing competition to each other.[26]

However, there are also important arguments of why banks are better than markets and vice versa. In liquid markets, investors can inexpensively and quickly sell their shares and consequently have fewer incentives to expend resources monitoring managers.[27] Bank-based systems mitigate this problem because banks reveal less information in public markets.[28] Also, efficient markets can reduce the effectiveness of takeovers as a disciplining tool. Atomistic shareholders have incentives to capture the benefits from a takeover by holding their shares instead of selling them, thus making takeover attempts less profitable (Grossman and Hart, 1980). On the other hand, proponents of the market-based view emphasize that powerful banks frequently stymie innovation by extracting informational rents and protecting established firms (Hellwig, 1991). The banks' market power then reduces firms' incentives to undertake profitable projects because banks extract a large share of the profits (Rajan, 1992). Also, banks—as debt issuers—have an inherent bias toward conservative investments, so that bank-based systems might stymie innovation and growth.[29]

Cross-country comparisons have not provided evidence for either view. Empirical work on the aggregate cross-country level, on the cross-country cross-industry level, and on the cross-country firm level has not found any evidence that countries, industries, or firms grow faster with either more bank-based or more market-based financial systems.[30] Rather, the overall level of financial development, not structure, explains cross-country variation in economic growth. This is consistent with the financial services view, which focuses on the delivery of financial services and less on who delivers them. However, it is also consistent with the view that the optimal financial structure changes as financial systems develop, consistent with theoretical models to this effect (Boyd and Smith, 1998). It is also consistent with findings on different income elasticities of different segments of the financial system. The development of contractual savings institutions and capital markets is much more income-elastic than the development of the banking system (Beck et al., 2008). This finding is consistent with the observation that most low-income countries have more bank-based financial systems. As more detailed data on different segments of the financial system and on the users of financial services, including firms and households, become available, more research can be undertaken in this area.

International Dimension: Finance and Trade Patterns

The efficiency with which the financial system intermediates society's savings has a significant effect on resource allocation and thus economic structure. It is therefore not surprising that financial sector development also has a significant effect on the structure of a country's trade balance. Because financial development can steer resource allocation toward specific sectors and industries, it can also turn into a comparative advantage in certain sectors and industries.

Theoretical models have shown that financial development turns into a comparative advantage for countries in sectors and industries with higher needs for external finance.[31] Ju and Wei (2005) show that if the external finance constraint is binding in the economy, then further financial deepening will increase the output of industries more dependent on external finance. On a micro-level, Manova (2010) shows that productivity cutoffs for enterprises to become exporters vary across sectors with different needs for external finance and decrease with financial development. In addition to traditional endowments, such as land, labor, and human and physical capital, the degree to which financial systems can ease financing constraints of enterprises can thus also turn into a comparative advantage.

There is quite a bit of empirical support for these theoretical models. Countries with higher levels of financial development have higher shares of manufacturing exports and higher export shares in industries with higher financing needs (Beck, 2002, 2003). Countries with higher levels of financial development have higher export shares and trade balance in industries with more intangible assets (Hur, Raj, and Riyanto, 2006). Equity market liberalization increases exports disproportionately more in financially vulnerable sectors that require more outside finance or employ fewer collateralizable assets (Manova, 2008). In addition, total exports in financially more developed countries are more sensitive to exchange rate movements than in countries at lower levels of financial development (Becker and Greenberg, 2007). These cross-country findings are further confirmed by more disaggregate data. Using state-level data for the United States, Michalski and Örs (2011) find that interstate branch deregulation led to a significant increase in exports relative to domestic shipments. On the firm level, several papers have found a significant relationship between credit constraints and the decision to become an exporter.[32]

Access to Financial Services

Until now, I have discussed the relationship between financial development and aggregate economic welfare or aggregate real sector outcomes. However, financial development can have distributional effects because it benefits different groups of households or firms to a different extent. Transaction costs and risk profiles vary across the firm and household population and can be binding constraints for certain groups, especially small enterprises and the poor, when trying to access financial services. Small firms consistently report higher financing obstacles than medium and large enterprises, and they are also more adversely affected in their operation and growth by these obstacles.[33] This can have an impact on firm size distribution across economies. For example, survey analysis has shown that smaller firms grow relatively faster in Germany than in Côte d'Ivoire, whereas the opposite holds for large firms (Sleuwaegen and Goedhuys, 2002).

Financial sector development can help reduce information asymmetries for small enterprises. The growth-constraining effect of financing obstacles has been found to be smaller in countries with better developed financial systems, and industries that have naturally more small enterprises grow faster in countries with higher levels of financial development.[34] The positive effect of financial and institutional development can also be observed in the use of external finance. Better protection of property rights increases external financing of small firms significantly more than it does for large firms, particularly due to the differential impact it has on bank and supplier finance (Beck, Demirgüç-Kunt, and Maksimovic, 2008). Easier physical access to banking outlets is also associated with lower financing obstacles (Beck, Demirgüç-Kunt, and Martinez Peria, 2007). Finally, evidence for a sample of European countries shows that financial development enhances new firm entry in sectors that depend more heavily on external finance and that the smallest size firms benefit the most from higher financial development in terms of higher entry rates. The same analysis also shows that financial development promotes the postentry growth of firms in sectors that depend more on external finance (Aghion, Fally and Scarpetta, 2007).

Quasi-natural experimental evidence confirms the importance of credit constraints for firm growth. Banerjee and Duflo (2004) analyzed detailed loan information on 253 Indian small and medium enterprises before and after they became eligible for a directed subsidized lending program and found that the additional credit resulted in a proportional increase in sales rather than a substitution for other nonsubsidized credit, indicating that these firms were credit-constrained before receiving subsidized credit. Similarly, Zia (2008) finds that small nonlisted and nongroup firms in Pakistan reduce their sales after they become ineligible for subsidized export credit, indicating the existence of credit constraints; in contrast, large, listed, and group firms do not reduce their sales after losing access to subsidized credit.

The evidence on the effects of access to financial services at the household level is more nuanced. Access to credit is not unambiguously associated with higher welfare; different estimation methods and different samples provide contradictory evidence.[35] More recent evidence, however, has shown a differential impact of improved access to financial services on different household groups (Banerjee et al., 2010), with households that are inclined to become entrepreneurs more likely to do so with improved access to credit or savings services, while others spend more on consumption.[36]

Related to the debate on access to finance by different groups is the question on enterprise versus household credit. Although the theoretical and empirical literature has clearly shown the positive impact of enterprise credit for firm and aggregate growth, theory has made ambiguous predictions on the role of household credit. Although Jappelli and Pagano (1994) argue that alleviating credit constraints on households reduces the savings rate, with negative repercussions for economic growth, Galor and Zeira (1993) and De Gregorio (1996) argue that household credit can foster economic development if it increases human capital accumulation. Tentative cross-country evidence has shown that the positive effect of financial deepening comes mostly through enterprise credit, and there is no significant relationship between the importance of household credit and economic growth (Beck et al., 2009). This finding, together with the observation of an increasing share of household credit in total bank lending in many developed economies over the past decades, mostly for mortgages, can go some way toward explaining the diminishing growth benefits from financial deepening in high-income countries.

The Distributional Effects of Financial Development: Theory and Evidence

Given that financial sector development helps reduce access problems, the question arises about distributional effects of financial sector deepening. Although the cross-country literature has focused mainly on average income growth, researchers have recently turned their attention to distributional implications of financial sector deepening.

Theory makes ambiguous predictions about the distributional repercussions of finance. On the one hand, financial imperfections, such as information and transactions costs, are especially binding on the poor, who lack collateral and credit histories, as already discussed. Thus, any relaxation of these credit constraints will disproportionately benefit the poor. Furthermore, these credit constraints reduce the efficiency of capital allocation and intensify income inequality by impeding the flow of capital to poor individuals with high expected return investments.[37] From this perspective, financial development helps the poor both by improving the efficiency of capital allocation, which accelerates aggregate growth, and by relaxing credit constraints that more extensively restrain the poor, which reduces income inequality.

In contrast, some theories predict that financial development primarily helps the rich. According to this view, the poor rely on informal, family connections for capital, so that improvements in the formal financial sector inordinately benefit the rich. The model by Greenwood and Jovanovic (1990), previously discussed, predicts a nonlinear relationship between financial development, income inequality, and economic development. At all stages of economic development, financial development improves capital allocation, boosts aggregate growth, and helps the poor through this channel. However, the distributional effect of financial development, and hence the net impact on the poor, depends on the level of economic development. At early stages of development, only the rich can afford to access and directly profit from better financial markets. At higher levels of economic development, many people access financial markets so that financial development directly helps a larger proportion of society.

First empirical cross-country evidence points to a pro-poor effect of financial sector deepening. Beck, Demirgüç-Kunt, and Levine (2007) show that countries with higher levels of financial development experience faster reductions in income inequality and poverty levels. Clarke, Xu, and Zou (2006) show a negative relationship between financial sector development and the level of inequality. This suggests that financial sector development is not only pro-growth but also pro-poor. Unlike other policy areas, which might have opposing effects on growth and equity, financial sector development does not present such concerns.

The theoretical models discussed here also give insights into the possible channels through which financial development can help reduce income inequality and poverty. On the one hand, providing access to credit to the poor might help them overcome financing constraints and allow them to invest in microenterprises and human capital accumulation.[38] On the other hand, there might be indirect effects through enterprise credit. By expanding credit to existing and new enterprises and allocating society's savings more efficiently, financial systems can expand the formal economy and pull larger segments of the population into the formal labor market. First explorations of the channels through which finance affects income inequality and poverty levels point to an important role of such indirect effects. Specifically, evidence from both the United States and Thailand suggests that an important effect of financial sector deepening on income inequality and poverty is indirect. By changing the structure of the economy and allowing more entry into the labor market of previously un- or underemployed segments of the population, finance helps reduce income inequality and poverty, but not by giving access to credit to everyone.[39] This is also consistent with cross-country evidence that financial deepening is positively associated with employment growth in developing countries (Pagano and Pica, 2012). It is important to stress that this is preliminary evidence to be confirmed or refuted by future research, but it has focused the debate on an important question: should policy makers focus on deepening or broadening financial sectors? It has also helped broaden the debate on financial services for the poor beyond microcredit to other financial services, such as savings services, payment services (especially in the context of receiving remittances from family members that emigrated to other parts of the country or the world), and insurance services.[40]

Finance and Economic Development: Conclusions and Looking Forward

There is strong historical, theoretical, and empirical evidence for a positive role of financial deepening in the economic development process. Evidence for cross-country heterogeneity and nonlinearity in this relationship, however, has posed new challenges for researchers and establishes a direct link to the theme of the next section—financial fragility resulting from rapid financial deepening. There have been attempts to reconcile the long-term positive effects of finance with the negative short-term effects of rapid credit growth (Loayza and Rancière, 2006). More research along these lines is certainly needed. Furthermore, recent evidence that financial sector deepening might actually have a negative effect on growth beyond a certain threshold has raised additional questions on the optimal size and resource allocation to the financial sector.

The increasing availability of micro-data has broadened the research agenda to exploring the effect of broadening access to financial services by enterprises and households, which will give additional insights into the channels through which finance fosters growth and helps reduce poverty. The literature on finance, income inequality and poverty, is still in its early years; more research can be expected in this area. This will also help bring empirical work closer to theoretical explorations of the finance and growth link.

Financial Fragility: Causes and Policies

The same mechanism that makes finance growth-enhancing also contains the seed of destruction, as illustrated by the Diamond and Dybvig (1983) model. By transforming short-term liabilities into long-term assets, banks can foster economic growth but can also become susceptible to bank runs, be they informed or uninformed. Agency problems between banks and their depositors and creditors can lead to excessive risk taking and fragility.

In the following, I focus mostly on fragility of banks, although boom-and-bust cycles are very common to financial markets in general and are often related to banking distress. However, due to the maturity mismatch and promissory intensity, the contagion risk is highest in the banking sector. After covering the sources of banking fragility, I discuss the empirical literature on idiosyncratic and systemic bank fragility, before turning to regulatory issues.

Financial Fragility: Bank Runs and Moral Hazard

Theoretical models focus on two different sources of fragility related to liability and asset risk. As already discussed, liability risk arises from the maturity mismatch between assets and liabilities. When some depositors withdraw their funds prematurely and unexpectedly, this can lead to bank runs and collapses. Such runs can be either based on fundamentals, and thus be information-based, or irrational. If the return on banks' long-term assets is stochastic, new information about future negative shocks on these investments can lead to the expectation by depositors that banks will not be able to meet future commitments and will therefore lead to runs (Jacklin and Bhattacharya, 1988). Irrational bank runs, on the other hand, arise from the simple fear of some depositors that others might withdraw before them. Irrational bank runs might also be based on the inability of uninformed depositors to distinguish between liquidity and solvency shocks of banks, that is, the inability to distinguish between regular withdrawal behavior of depositors and the reaction of informed depositors to negative information about the future solvency of the bank (Chari and Jagannathan, 1988).

A bank run is not only disruptive for the bank in question, as it might imply costly divestment or liquidation of assets and/or liquidation of assets, it can also have contagion effects throughout the banking and financial system through the domino effect. Such effects can happen either through bank runs on other banks or through the payment system or the interbank market. Observation by depositors of runs on one bank can lead to panic runs on other banks to not be the last one to withdraw money or due to information updates about the underlying solvency position of other banks. Domino effects can also happen through linkages in interbank market, with failure of one bank to satisfy commitments leading to negative solvency shocks at other banks. Similarly, a payment system based on netting out of positions between banks can lead to contagion effects throughout the banking system, unlike the real-time gross payment system, where each transaction is settled separately and immediately.[41]

A second important risk is on the asset side, related to the principal agent problem between the bank and depositors and other creditors. Previously I discussed the principal agent problems between banks and borrowers, but there is a similar agency problem, based on asymmetric information, between banks and their depositors and creditors. As can be easily shown, banks' incentives to properly screen and monitor borrowers and thus ensure repayment decrease in their leverage ratio. This has been also described as the put option character of banking; given limited liability, bank owners have the option to sell the bank with the strike price being the value of liabilities. Whereas depositors bear only the downside risk of banks' risk decisions, owners and managers (acting in the interest of owners) participate in both the up and down side of these risk decisions. Although this is a common problem throughout corporate finance, the situation is exacerbated in the case of banks by the fact that debtholders are disperse (there are many depositors with small deposits), often uninformed, and always have the incentive to free-ride on the efforts of others, and the opacity of banks' assets, most of which are not market-priced or priceable.

The fragility of banking and the negative repercussions of bank failure for the financial system and the economy at large has made it one of the most regulated sectors in human history, with the exception of few episodes in modern history, such as free banking in Scotland between 1695 and 1845 and the experience of some U.S. states in the nineteenth century. Deposit insurance has been considered a policy to reduce the likelihood of bank runs because it insures depositors for their savings (Diamond and Dybvig, 1983). Alternatively, liquidity support by a lender-of-last-resort can help address banks' short-term liquidity problems (Bagehot, 1873). Capital requirements and lending restrictions have been advocated to address the potential for asset fragility, as well as strong supervisors that can replace weak or missing monitoring and discipline from depositors. I return to the regulatory approach toward banking and the financial sector in general later, but first discuss the link between idiosyncratic bank fragility and systemic banking distress.

From Idiosyncratic to Systemic Distress

Financial history is full of bank failures and financial boom-and-bust cycles, linked to a variety of factors, often with similar features (Reinhart and Rogoff, 2009). To the same extent that well-developed financial systems can foster economic growth, banking crises are often associated with deep economic recessions and long-term negative growth repercussions. Recent comparisons of economic crises have shown that economic recessions related to banking distress tend to be deeper and longer than other recessions.[42] Specifically, output losses of recessions with credit crunches are two or three times as high as in other recessions. Many of these banking crises are related to the failure of several (rather than single) financial institutions or even systemic distress throughout the banking system. In the following, I discuss the link between idiosyncratic bank failures, due to incentive misalignments and inherent fragility, and systemic banking distress.

Due to the agency problems between lenders and borrowers and lenders and depositors, already described, bank credit is inherently cyclical and typically more volatile than the economic cycle. As agency costs on both sides of banks' balance sheets fluctuate with the business cycle, so do cost of credit and credit flows. Credit booms typically feed on themselves and are often linked with asset price booms. As asset prices rise and thus collateral values, more credit is granted. The reverse can happen during a downturn, where asset prices fall, borrowers' balance sheets deteriorate, and bank lending is typically reduced at a faster pace than GDP and can in turn dampen real sector activity further. Credit and asset price movements feed on each other, which can lead to upward and downward spirals.[43]

Beyond credit cycles related to agency costs, financial systems are subject to recurrent systemic fragility, often related to financial liberalization. In the 1970s and '80s, the search for growth benefits led many countries to liberalize financial systems, privatize government-owned banks, and open capital accounts. These liberalizations often led to credit and asset booms and aggressive risk taking by banks. Though fiscal profligacy, exchange rate policy, and external shocks have also contributed to crises, problems in the financial systems were often at the core of the fragility, and these systemic banking crises put in doubt the overall positive contribution of financial development to economic development. Careful analysis of these crises, however, has shown that often the absence of the necessary regulatory reforms that should accompany liberalization can explain the fragility (Demirgüç-Kunt and Detragiache, 1999). Systemic banking distress is often also related to currency crises. Rapid real exchange rate movements can undermine banks' solvency position, and the need to support failing banks can undermine exchange rate stability. Common causes, such as macroeconomic policies, might drive both. Theoretical and empirical work has confirmed the close interlinkages of banking distress and currency crises.[44]

Banking crises, however, have not been limited to developing and emerging economies. Even before the current crisis, the 1980s and 90s saw the savings and loan crisis in the United States, the Japanese banking crisis, and several banking crises in Scandinavia. Many of the systemic banking crises in developing and developed countries involved large amounts of nonperforming assets and bank insolvencies, the need for nationalization and recapitalization, bank holidays, and government guarantees for deposits and assets. In many cases, frameworks for systematic work-out of nonperforming assets were created, either by banks on a decentralized basis or by creation of asset management companies.

Statistical analyses of systemic banking crises have pointed to several macroeconomic signals, including real exchange rate appreciation (often linked to rapid capital inflows), low growth, high real interest rates and inflation, as well as rapid credit growth.[45] Other studies have linked the exchange rate regime, the degree of dollarization, and banking market structure to the likelihood of systemic banking distress.[46]

The costs of systemic banking distress can be substantial, as reported by Laeven and Valencia (2008), reaching over 50 percent of GDP in some cases in fiscal costs and over 100 percent in output loss. Fiscal costs arise typically from recapitalization of failing banks or deposit insurance losses, whereas output costs can arise through several channels, most importantly through firms losing access to external finance. Several studies have shown the negative economic repercussions of bank failures in the 1920s and '30s in the United States and the consequent loss of lending relationships,[47] and documented the decline in lending and local GDP following the closure of a large (solvent) affiliate in a regional bank holding company in Texas in the 1990s (Ashcraft, 2005). Other studies have shown the importance of lending relationships across a sample of Korean firms that worked with either failed or surviving banks after the crisis and the negative effect of bank insolvency announcement during the East Asian crisis on market values of the banks' borrowers.[48] On a more aggregate level, cross-country comparisons have shown that during banking crises, industries that depend more on external finance are hurt disproportionately more, an effect that is stronger in countries with better developed financial systems.[49]

The trade-off between the positive growth effects of financial deepening following liberalization and the costs of systemic banking distress that also often comes after liberalization has raised the question of relative benefits and costs of liberalization. A cross-country comparison of the growth benefits of liberalization and growth costs of subsequent crises, however, has shown that the benefits outweigh the costs significantly, that is, the positive growth effect of financial liberalization is larger than the negative growth effect from a crisis that follows liberalization (Rancière, Tornell, and Westermann, 2006).

Directly related to the transmission of idiosyncratic shocks to systemic distress is the debate on the relationship between competition and banking distress. Some models predict that more concentrated and less competitive banking systems are more stable, as profits provide a buffer against fragility and provide incentives against excessive risk taking. This "charter value" view of banking sees banks as choosing the risk of their asset portfolio.[50] In a more competitive environment with more pressures on profits, banks have higher incentives to take more excessive risks, resulting in higher fragility. In systems with restricted entry and therefore limited competition, on the other hand, banks have better profit opportunities, capital cushions, and therefore fewer incentives to take aggressive risks, with positive repercussions for financial stability. In addition, in more competitive environment, banks earn fewer informational rents from their relationship with borrowers, reducing their incentives to properly screen borrowers, again increasing the risk of fragility.[51] These models thus predict that deregulation resulting in more entry and competition, such as in the United States in the 1970s and 1980s and in many emerging markets, would lead to more fragility.

An opposing view is that a more concentrated banking structure results in more bank fragility. Boyd and De Nicoló (2005) argue lower interest following from higher competition incentivizes borrowers to choose less risky investment projects. Thus, in many parameterizations of the model, Boyd and De Nicoló (2005) find a positive relationship between concentration and bank fragility and thus the probability of systemic distress.[52]

The empirical evidence on the relationship between competition and stability has not been conclusive, partly due to measurement challenges on both competition and stability. Empirical studies for specific countries—many if not most for the United States—have not come to conclusive evidence for an either stability-enhancing or stability-undermining role of competition. However, two conclusions can be drawn. First, a higher degree of market concentration does not necessarily imply less competition. Specifically, testing for the relationship between market structure and stability and for the relationship between competition and stability does not necessarily yield the same results. Second, as predicted by several theoretical studies, there is an important interaction effect between the regulatory and supervisory framework, on the one hand, and market structure and competitiveness, on the other hand, in their effect on banking system stability, a topic I return to later.

The cross-country literature has found that more concentrated banking systems are less likely to suffer a systemic banking crisis as are more competitive banking systems.[53] There also seems to be evidence that banks in more competitive banking systems hold more capital, thus compensating for the potentially higher risk they are taking.[54] This debate is certainly still ongoing and has received additional impetus with the recent crisis.

Market Discipline or Regulation?

The functions and structure of financial institutions make their failures especially damaging for other financial institutions and the economy at large. The provision of payment services is only feasible if banks belong to a network, the maturity transformation results in the risk of maturity mismatch and liquidity shortages in the case of shocks such as bank runs, and the screening and monitoring function of financial institutions implies the creation of private information. The consequence of these functions is that the failure of a financial institution results in negative externalities beyond the private costs of failure; it imposes external costs on other financial institutions and the economy at large. As already discussed, these external costs materialize especially in systemic banking crises, though also with idiosyncratic bank failures, increasing in the size and importance of financial institutions.

The external costs that bank failure imposes on the rest of the financial system at large has made banking one of the most regulated sectors. The question, however, is what kind of regulations reduce the risk of bank runs and contagion and of excessive risk taking. Diamond and Rajan (2001) show that the combination of short-term liabilities and long-term assets provides for the necessary incentives of depositors to monitor and discipline banks and thus reduces principal agent problems. Regulations that reduce incentives of depositors to monitor and discipline banks, on the other hand, can exacerbate the principal agent problem and are thus counterproductive. Combining the analysis of fragility risks on asset and liability sides thus provides different insights than when focusing only on the liability side.

This matches with empirical evidence that has pointed to the risks of regulations and mechanisms protecting depositors and reducing possibilities and incentives for them to monitor and discipline banks. Specifically, while deposit insurance schemes have been conceived to protect depositors (especially those with no means to monitor and discipline banks) and to avoid contagion effects, explicit deposit insurance schemes also have perverse incentive effects, as they send the signal that authorities stand ready to bail out banks, and thus provide incentives for banks to take excessive risks. This has been confirmed by empirical evidence, at least for developing countries.[55]

Hand in hand with the skepticism about the role of deposit insurance goes an emphasis on mechanisms that encourage and enable depositors and creditors to monitor and discipline banks. This private monitoring view thus focuses on transparency of financial statements, liability of auditors and senior management for financial statements, and the availability of marketable securities, such as subordinated debt, whose holders have an incentive to closely monitor and discipline banks. This view does not minimize the role of supervisors, but emphasizes that supervisors have an important role in enabling the private sector to play an appropriate role in the supervision process.[56]

This view stands in contrast to the official supervision view that takes the failure of markets, including depositors, to appropriately monitor and discipline banks as a starting point and therefore posits a strong and active if not interventionist role for supervisors. This implies the right to intervene in good and bad times, screen and replace management, and restrict activities. The two approaches are not exclusive, a country like the United States has both powerful supervisors and the necessary conditions for market discipline, with an important caveat, as will be discussed. In many developing countries, the emphasis has been on building up powerful supervisory authorities, again on the premises that market discipline cannot work in small markets with few sophisticated investors.

The recent crisis seems prima facie a rejection of the private monitoring view, as the market did not price risk accurately. One might also argue that discipline cannot be provided by markets that provide incentives for financial institutions to engage in herding (Boot, 2011). On the other hand, the period up to the crisis can be seen as a period where authorities across the developed world systematically undermined market discipline by signaling ex ante that systemically important financial institutions would be bailed out.[57] The repercussions of the Lehman Brothers insolvency—seen by authorities as a signal to reestablish market discipline—can be seen as the nail in the coffin to market discipline, as authorities in the future will avoid the messy failure of an institution so central to the global financial system and consequent freeze of global financial markets.

Even where supervisors were powerful—as in the United States—they failed to detain excessive risk taking in time. Levine (2010) argues convincingly that regulatory policies created incentives to aim for short-term profit, while at the same time allowing increased long-term fragility. Regulatory capital arbitrage was allowed whereby risky assets were shifted off the balance sheet, securitized in the form of special investment vehicles, and then put back on the balance sheet in the form of triple A–rated securities that did not need any capital. The crisis thus "represents the unwillingness of the policy apparatus to adapt to a dynamic, innovating financial system" (Levine, 2011).[58] The assessment that the inability of supervisors to detect and reduce fragility at early stages with traditional means contributed to the crisis is also consistent with evidence that the quality of bank supervisory standards, as measured by the Basel Core Principles is not significantly associated with bank stability, with the notable exception of transparency standards (Demirgüç-Kunt, Detragiache, and Tressel, 2008).

The skepticism against supervisory and regulatory standards goes hand in hand with a differentiated view on capital regulation (Barth, Caprio, and Levine, 2006). Although designed as cushion against unexpected losses and to reduce incentives to "bet the bank," bank governance and ownership structure critically influence the impact of capital regulations on risk taking, as shown by several empirical studies. Specifically, Laeven and Levine (2009) find that banks with more powerful owners, as measured by the size of their shareholdings, tend to take greater risks, even more so in countries with more stringent capital requirements, whereas capital regulations have the opposite effects on widely held banks dominated by managers.

Although their effect in preventing systemic banking distress is doubtful, powerful supervisors can have a negative effect on the efficiency and fairness of lending, as shown by Beck, Demirgüç-Kunt, and Levine (2006b). Specifically, self-reported obstacles on corruption in loan officers' lending decisions are higher in countries with more powerful supervisors, and they are lower in countries where supervisory entities rely more on market power.

There is similar and consistent evidence for financial markets (La Porta, Lopez-de-Silanes, and Shleifer, 2006). Specifically, there is limited evidence for a positive role of public enforcement benefiting stock market development, while disclosure and liability rules enabling private monitoring foster larger and more liquid stock markets.

Financial Fragility: A New Research Agenda

The first global financial crisis of the twenty-first century has provided new challenges and new opportunities for exploring the causes of financial fragility and policy implications. It has reignited interest in the competition-stability debate. It has shed doubts on risk measures. It has shown that runs can not only happen on the retail level; new forms of contagion, such as through common asset exposure, have occurred.[59] The crisis has also shown the urgent need for bridging the gap between macro- and financial economists, where the former focus on macroeconomic models without a properly modeled financial system and the latter ignore macroeconomic repercussions of financial sector fragility. The interest in bridging the gap has become obvious in recent work incorporating the two literatures and also in the debate on macroprudential regulation that looks beyond idiosyncratic risks toward the interaction between financial institutions and between different segments of the financial system and feedback loops between banking, financial markets, and the real economy. This also includes recent papers that empirically explore the relationship between monetary policy, securitization through financial markets, and banks' risk taking.[60]

The recent crisis has also reignited the debate on the appropriate regulation of the financial system. Stronger capital requirements and more powerful supervisors are called for. One important area, often ignored, that calls for intensive reform is the resolution of failing banks. A similar trade-off as for deposit insurance exists: on the one hand, imminent failure of a large, too-important-to-fail bank provokes an immediate bail-out decision to protect depositors, other financial institutions, and the financial system at large as well as the real economy that—as shown—will suffer from bank failure. On the other hand, the expectation of a bail-out creates perverse incentives on the side of banks to take excessive risks, knowing that the downside part of these risks will be covered by taxpayers. Enforcing market discipline, however, by forcing financial institutions into regular insolvency proceedings, as with any regular corporation, can lead to the effects already described and observed in the case of Lehman Brothers. A solution that minimizes these external effects of bank insolvency while at the same time enforcing market discipline is thus necessary, especially for systemically important financial institutions. Recent suggestions include ex ante planned winding-down plans (living wills) and the issue of debt instruments that are automatically converted into equity claims when the value of existing equity nears zero.

Financial crises offer opportunities and challenges for researchers; they force them to rethink existing paradigms, develop new models, and reassess empirical relations. Similarly to the Great Depression of the twentieth century, the first global crisis of the twenty-first century will have an important impact on how researchers, analysts, and policy makers view financial fragility and the regulatory framework necessary to reduce this fragility and its impact.

The Politics of Financial Development

Given the importance of the financial system for economic growth and fragility, it is not surprising that financial sector policies often top the agenda of policy makers, though more so during crisis periods. As I discuss, however, there are different views on where this interest stems from—to maximize the growth benefits for the economy or to protect the interests of the incumbent elite.[61]

Finance and Politics

There are different hypotheses of why financial institutions and markets are so high on policy makers' list. The public interest view argues that policy makers act in the best interest of society, ultimately maximizing the social planner's problem, though possibly with less information available. This view also argues that the market failures inherent in financial markets and already discussed require a strong government involvement in the financial system beyond regulation and supervision. The private interest view, on the other hand, argues that policy makers, including regulators, act in their own interest, maximizing private rather than public welfare. Politicians thus do not intervene into the financial system to further public welfare but to divert the flow of credit to politically connected firms.[62]

The importance of access to external finance for entrepreneurs makes it an important tool in the struggle for real market shares. Access to finance can be used as barrier to entry into the real economy; empirical analysis has shown that exit rates during banking crises—especially for finance-dependent young firms—are abnormally high in countries with more corrupt political institutions (Feijen and Perrotti, 2005). Access to external finance can also be used by incumbent political and economic elites to protect rents and entrench their dominant position. The use of financial as opposed to other resources is facilitated by the contingent nature of the liabilities as well as the authority of governments to create money.

The U.S. financial history is plenty of examples for political influence on the banking system. Benmelech and Moskowitz (2010) show a strong relationship between voter suffrage and financial regulation. In times of low suffrage, the ruling elite used interest rate ceilings and entry barriers into banking to prevent competitors from gaining strength. Granting banking licenses was used to gain access to preferable loans for states and for the ruling elites. As voting suffrage expanded, there was a trend toward free banking where licensing was no longer controlled by the state legislature.

One of the striking elements of the U.S. banking history is the predominance of branching restrictions throughout long periods, results of a compromise between populists and local bankers who wanted to protect their rents. Not until the 1970s and under the impact of technology were these restrictions loosened. As shown by Kroszner and Strahan (1999), the decision to deregulate branching on the state level was a function of both political structure and the lobbying strength of the banking sector.

Recent theoretical and empirical work has modeled and estimated the relative power and coalitions between labor and firm insiders, including management and majority shareholders, against minority shareholders to explain cross-country differences in contractual institutions underpinning financial institutions and markets.[63] An alternative explanation is the experience of the middle class losing their financial assets due to inflation in the period between the wars and subsequent political resistance against vibrant financial markets. This went hand in hand with a decision in these countries toward state-funded and -managed pension funds, with lower need and demand for private pension funds and thus lower demand for protection of individual investor rights (Perotti and Schwienbacher, 2009).

Finance and Politics: From Government Banking to Activist Policies

Government intervention in the financial sector has been strong throughout history. Some countries initially only allowed government-owned banks or at a minimum made bank licensing subject to parliamentary approval. Many developing countries nationalized their banking system after independence to gain direct control over this critical part of the economy. Across the globe, government ownership has been widespread throughout the twentieth century and today is still dominant in some developing countries.[64] In this context, it is important to distinguish between government ownership as long-term policy and as crisis resolution tool, as applied after the 2008 global financial crisis in many European countries. Government-owned banks have often been seen as critical in helping overcome market failures and funnel domestic savings to strategically important projects (Gerschenkron, 1962). On the other hand, government ownership can lead to inefficient allocation of scarce resources and political capture. These different views of government ownership relate directly to the public and private interest view on government's involvement in the financial sector, as already discussed.

A large empirical literature has shown that government ownership is inefficient. Government-owned and -managed banks run the risk of being captured by the ruling elite or special interest and have—on average—a miserable record in expanding access. Firms with political connections have easier access to state banks and receive larger loans but are less likely to repay.[65] On an aggregate level, government ownership of banks is associated with lower levels of financial development and lower rates of economic growth (La Porta, Lopez-de-Silanes, and Shleifer, 2002).

Privatization, however, is not a panacea, especially if undertaken in an institutionally weak environment, and can lead to capture by socioeconomic elites linked to political elites. Poorly designed and executed privatization processes can lead to fragility and banking crises, as numerous examples have shown over the past thirty years. Studies of privatization processes have shown the benefits of privatizing government-owned banks but also the pitfalls.[66] One interesting case is Mexico, where privatization in 1988 was restricted to domestic shareholders, most of whom had no banking experience and borrowed money from their own banks to acquire the banks from the government. A subsequent boom-and-bust cycle led to a new nationalization and recapitalization episode in the mid-1990s, after which most of the banks were sold to multinational banks.

Beyond ownership, government intervention into the financial system can take many forms. Excessive reserve requirements, interest rate ceilings and floors, and credit quotas are some of the policies that collectively are referred to as financial repression (Fry, 1988). As shown mostly by country-level studies, some of them of qualitative rather than quantitative nature, most of these policies have benefited the incumbent elite and enterprises connected to it, rather than marginal groups. Credit quotas and interest caps and floors have impeded the efficient allocation of society's savings to its most productive uses and have especially hurt "smaller" depositors and borrowers. In case of binding ceilings, banks are prevented from charging adequate risk premiums for riskier and more opaque borrowers or from recovering fixed transaction costs through a mark-up on smaller loan amounts. Furthermore, competition between credit institutions and for more deposits is hampered as financial institutions have no incentives to become more efficient or to attract more deposits if they cannot finance more marginal customers. Similarly, given fixed transaction costs in financial intermediation, floors on deposit interest rates make savers with small transaction amounts unattractive for financial institutions. Credit quotas have resulted in fragmentation of credit markets and higher costs for nonpriority sectors. In many cases, financial institutions have found ways around these restrictions, but at high costs and with consequent efficiency losses. Such policies focus especially on sectors that are considered marginalized or as politically critical, such as rural areas.

The failure of many of these interventionist policies have led to a move toward more market-based financial systems over the past two decades, often associated with the Washington Consensus. Many developing countries have moved toward more stable banking systems, and some have experienced financial deepening. Expectations of more inclusive financial systems and more significant financial deepening have often not been achieved, however. Although this raises questions on the proper sequencing and implementation of reform policies to deepen and broaden financial systems, it has also led to a renewed debate on the role of government in the financial system, beyond institution building and providing the macroeconomic framework. Activist or market-enabling policies that try to overcome coordination and first mover problems in small financial systems with incomplete markets have been suggested, such as attempts to provide the necessary infrastructure to launch new financial products, such as factoring, or credit guarantee programs.[67]

One region where market-based financial sector reform has been successful is the transition economies of Central Europe. The challenge for these countries was to make banks independent from government and from their past links with state-owned enterprises, as the continuing relationships between banks and incumbent enterprises and the resulting fragility had severe macroeconomic repercussions. The need for recapitalization of banks resulted in rising fiscal deficits, monetary overhang, and thus inflation. The solution to this continuous cycle of repayment problems, accumulation of nonperforming assets, recapitalization, and inflation was the adoption of a disciplining tool to impose a hard budget constraint on enterprises and banks alike. Credibly committing to monetary stability in turn forced the necessary reforms in the financial sector to avoid future recapitalization. In many countries, banks were therefore not only privatized but sold to foreign banks, which helped sever the links between state-owned enterprises and banks.[68] What essentially was needed was a straightjacket that tied policy makers' hands and prevented them from bailing out financial and nonfinancial institutions.

Political Structure as Basic Factor for Financial Development

How do some countries develop the necessary legal and regulatory structures to support market-based financial systems and others do not? Why do some countries have political structures that are conducive to financial development and property rights protection, more broadly, and others do not? Here the literature on the historic roots of financial sector development overlaps with the literature on institutions and growth (see also chapter 2 in this volume).

The government's position as party to (financial) contracts and arbiter of the same contracts creates a conflict of interest and makes the Coase Theorem that distribution and efficiency can be determined independently break down (Acemoglu, 2003). A basic condition for thriving financial markets is thus constraints on political power and the protection of individual property rights from expropriation through both other private parties and the government. It is important to stress in that context that property rights must be for everyone, not just the elite. Autocratic regimes dislike independent and competitive financial systems because they are afraid they might finance opponents. On the other hand, the financial system can serve as source of rents for the ruling elite, as especially the case of resource-based economies has shown. Evidence from broad cross-country samples shows that countries with autocratic political regimes are more likely to have restrictive regulation and entry barriers into the banking systems (Barth, Caprio, and Levine, 2006), whereas the most robust predictor of long-term financial development (as opposed to short-term boosts) is political accountability (Quintyn and Verdier, 2010), evidence that is consistent with historic analysis that shows for a panel of countries over the period 1880–1997 that more restrictions on political power and stable political regimes are more conducive to financial development (Bordo and Rousseau, 2006). Countries with captive political institutions also suffer more from financial instability (Acemoglu et al., 2003). The political environment is also important for the effectiveness of financial liberalization, which is more likely to produce instability in countries with captive political institutions (Bekaert, Harvey, and Lundblad, 2006).

Historically, the financial centers of modern history in Europe developed in independent cities in northern Italy and, later in sixteenth century, the Netherlands, both areas where government was supported by broad parts of the population and with systems of checks and balances. The Glorious Revolution in seventeenth-century England secured property rights from government expropriation and reinforced the status of an independent judiciary. This enabled the British Crown to borrow at much lower interest rates in the international markets, as these institutions reassured investors of a low default risk (North and Weingast, 1989).

There are two sets of theories—not necessarily exclusive—that explain the development of the necessary property rights and contractual institutions for financial development across the world. One set of theories sees historical events in Europe more than 200 years ago as shaping the legal and regulatory frameworks across the globe today through their influence on political structures in these countries. Specifically, the legal origin theory sees political conflicts in England and France in the medieval age and during the Glorious and French Revolutions shaping the role and independence of judiciaries in these countries. Different points on the trade-off between centralized power to avoid civil unrest and freedom to allow economic activity in England and France during medieval times shaped the government's approach to the judiciary, with France taking a much more centralized approach than England (Glaeser and Shleifer, 2002). Alternatively, one can consider the role of the judiciary during the Glorious Revolution, where the judges sided with the winning Parliament, and the French Revolution, where the judges were on the losing side. This resulted in a strengthening of the judiciary's independence but also their role in lawmaking in England, while it reduced the judiciary to an executing role in France, with law- and rule-making concentrated in legislature and executive. However, this also resulted in a different degree of flexibility and adaptability of the legal systems in England and France. England's legal system was more adaptable due to a stronger role for jurisprudence and past decisions and the ability of judges to base decisions on principles of fairness and justice, whereas France's legal system was more rigid, based on bright-line rules and little if any role for jurisprudence and previous decisions.[69]

Through the Napoleonic Wars in the early nineteenth century, the Napoleonic legal tradition was spread throughout continental Europe. Subsequently, legal traditions were spread throughout the rest of the world, mostly in the form of colonization, with the British common law tradition adopted in all British colonies and the Napoleonic civil code tradition transplanted to Belgian, Dutch, Portuguese, Spanish, and French colonies. The legal structures originating in these different traditions have proven to be very persistent, especially in developing countries. Take the example of the Napoleonic legal tradition. First, while the European nations overcame the rigidities of the Napoleonic code, they exported its antagonism toward jurisprudence and its reliance on judicial formalism to minimize the role of judges. This comes with the tradition of avoiding open disputes about legal interpretation and the aversion against jurisprudence. Second, as the Napoleonic doctrine sees judges as purely executing civil servants, judges frequently "are at the bottom of the scale of prestige among the legal professions in France and in many nations that adopted the French Revolutionary reforms, and the best people in those nations accordingly seek other legal careers" (Merryman, 1996, p. 116). Third, and as a consequence of the previous point, there is a stronger reliance on bright-line laws to limit the role of the courts. Once a country adopts the bright-line approach to lawmaking, this can lead into a trap, as courts will not be challenged to develop legal procedures and methods to deal with new circumstances, thus retarding the development of efficiently adaptive legal systems (Pistor et al., 2002, 2003).

Empirical evidence has indeed shown that countries with a Napoleonic legal tradition have less independent judiciaries and less adaptable legal systems.[70] Important in the context of this chapter, countries with a Napoleonic legal tradition have—on average—weaker property rights protection and contractual institutions that are less conducive to external finance, including weaker protection for minority shareholders and secured and unsecured creditors. Enforcement of contracts is more costly and slower in civil code countries as is the registration of property and collateral. This has the overall effect of smaller and less effective financial markets in civil code countries (Beck, Demirgüç-Kunt, and Levine, 2003a).

An alternative explanation refers not to the identity of the colonizing power but the mode of colonization. Distinguishing between settler and extractive colonies, Acemoglu, Johnson, and Robinson (2001, 2002) show that the former developed stronger property rights protection than the latter, given the political and societal structures that natural resource extraction in the latter implied. The initial colonization mode, in turn, was determined by the disease environment that European colonizers encountered as well as the incidence of native population in the colonized areas. Areas with more hostile disease environments and/or large native population concentrations were more likely to be settled in an extractive mode. The political structures developed during the colonization period endured after independence, therefore also making the weak property rights and contract enforcement institutions persistently weak beyond independence.

Empirical evidence shows the importance of the colonization mode for the development of financial markets today (Beck, Demirgüç-Kunt, and Levine, 2003a). Countries that were initially colonized in an extractive mode have less developed financial markets today. This effect is in addition to the effect of the legal tradition already discussed.

Beyond the colonization experience, the legal tradition and endowment views show the importance of political structures and persistence in financial system development. These hypotheses suggest that changes in the legal institutions that underpin thriving financial markets are only possible under outside pressure or exogenous shocks, such as new technologies, diseases, or globalization. Similarly, changes in financial sector policies are more likely under exogenous pressure. I already discussed the example of the Central European transition economies where banking crises and pressure to establish macroeconomic stability forced privatization of banks to foreign banks. Similarly, in Brazil the introduction of the Real Plan in 1994 that terminated the long-running inflationary tradition prevented the government from bailing out banks owned by individual states, as it had done several times earlier, and thus forced a complete restructuring of these institutions (Beck, Crivelli, and Summerhill, 2005). In Argentina, the establishment of a currency board in 1991 started the restructuring process of provincial banks (Clarke and Cull, 2002). Technological innovation was critical in driving branch deregulation in the United States in the 1970s and 1980s. As shown by Kroszner and Strahan (1999), the invention of automatic teller machines (ATMs), in conjunction with court rulings that ATMs are not bank branches, weakened the geographical bond between customers and banks, and improvements in communications technology lowered the costs of using distant banks. These innovations reduced the monopoly power of local banks, weakening their ability and desire to fight against deregulation, ultimately leading to branch deregulation. The timing of this deregulation across states, in turn, was very much a function of initial conditions, ranging from party politics to the importance and independence of insurance companies.

Conclusions

This chapter surveyed three related strands of the literature—finance and growth, financial fragility, and finance and politics. The three literatures are closely linked to each other. The growth benefits of financial sector deepening and the fragility of banking are two sides of the same mechanism—maturity transformation. While overcoming agency problems between investors and entrepreneurs is an important growth-enhancing role of financial institutions and markets, agency problems between financial institutions and their depositors are the basis for possible financial fragility. Empirically, long-term financial deepening is related to faster economic growth, and short-term credit booms are related to a higher probability of systemic banking distress. Underlying both growth and fragility are political constraints, often related to historic conditions, that prevent the necessary property rights and contractual institutions to develop and might foster connected and politicized lending.

Throughout the chapter I discussed the linkages between the three strands of literature. One example—already referred to—are the transition economies of Central and Eastern Europe, which experienced rapid financial deepening over the past twenty years, in line with the transition to market-based economies. The deepening was stronger where the underlying political institutions allowed for checks and balances, property rights protection, and conducive contractual institutions. However, in some countries financial deepening turned into a household and mortgage credit boom, ultimately increasing fragility and ending in a bust during the recent global financial crisis.

The current crisis, especially the development of financial markets in the United States, also offers an interesting background on which to bring together the three themes of this chapter. First, as discussed, financial liberalization in the 1970s and '80s has helped deepen the financial system, with positive repercussions for growth and smoothing volatility. Financial liberalization, however, has also created the basis for a boom-and-bust cycle, with banks taking increasing risks. There has also been evidence for a herding effect with financial institutions taking increasingly risks in the same sectoral and geographical portfolios. Behind the rapid growth of the subprime mortgage segment, there was a political focus on home ownership for low-income Americans. As laid out convincingly by Rajan (2010), in the absence of easy solutions to reduce income inequality, there was a political focus on reducing consumption inequality, which included boosting access to credit. Government policies such as the Community Reinvestment Act and guarantees provided by government-sponsored financial institutions, such as Fannie Mae and Freddie Mac, created incentives to look beyond the usual risk-return trade-off. However, there were also important regulatory distortions, as described by Levine (2010, 2011). But maybe one of the decisive incentives was provided by the Bernanke-Greenspan put—the expectation of financial market participants to be bailed out by the U.S. authorities in case of distress, be it through monetary policy or more direct intervention.

What effect does the current crisis have on our thinking about the financial sector and its role in the economy? The picture of the financial system as an unconditionally growth-enhancing sector has been tarnished. Excesses have become clear, as also obvious from wage trends in the financial sector, documented by

Phillipon and Reshef (2009). In the United States, wages in the financial sector relative to general wage levels have increased substantially during the recent boom period, to a comparable extent as in the 1920s in the period leading up to the Great Depression. Most critically, the current crisis should return the debate on financial sector development to the benefits of financial services and, more specifically, financial intermediation.

Although academics refer mostly to the intermediation functions of financial systems and thus to a facilitating role of the financial sector, practitioners and policy makers often view financial services as a growth sector in itself. This view toward the financial sector sees it more or less as an export sector, that is, one that seeks to build an often nationally centered financial stronghold by building on relative comparative advantages, such as skill base, favorable regulatory policies, subsidies, and so on. Economic benefits discussed often point at important spin-offs coming from professional services (legal, accounting, consulting, etc.) that typically cluster around a financial center. Reconciling these different views will be a challenge going forward.

For better or worse, the financial sector is an integral part of modern market economies. Well-functioning and sound financial institutions and markets underpin the smooth exchange of services and goods and foster long-term investment and thus growth. Aggressive risk taking and distortions can lead to systemic distress and economic crises. It is important, however, to not throw out the baby with the very dirty bathwater, but to focus on the necessary regulatory and supervisory frameworks for sound and effective financial systems. Similarly, a better understanding of the political economy of financial sector policies is important. An increasing governance focus is important—not only for central banks and regulatory authorities but also for financial institutions and their relationships with political and regulatory authorities.

Notes

1. See Schumpeter (1934). The author is grateful to Ross Levine for sharing many of the historic references.
2. See Diamond (1984) and Boyd and Prescott (1986), among many others.
3. For a discussion of the role of the shareholding company in Rome, see Malmendier (2009). For a discussion on the role of different financial contracts to finance trade across the Mediterranean, see, for example, Williamson (2010) and the literature quoted therein.
4. See, for example, Greenwood and Smith (1997).
5. See, for example, McKinnon (1973), Sirri and Tufano (1995), and Acemoglu and Zilibotti (1997).
6. See, for example,Trew (2010).
7. See, for example, King and Levine (1993b) and Blackburn and Huang (1998).
8. See Grossmann and Stiglitz (1980), among others.
9. Scharfstein (1988) and Stein (1988).

10. Diamond and Verrecchia (1982) and Jensen and Murphy (1990).
11. Diamond (1984) and Bencivenga and Smith (1993).
12. See Holmström and Tirole (1998) and Aghion et al. (2010).
13. See, for example, Bencivenga and Smith (1991) and King and Levine (1993b).
14. Philippon (2010) models the trade-off between the financial sector helping overcome agency problems, while at the same time competing for human resources with the real sector. In a situation where the social value of entrepreneurship is larger than the private value, the financial sector can be too large compared to the entrepreneurial sector. Similarly, Bolton, Santos, and Scheinkman (2011) model how individuals can choose to work in the real sector or as dealers in the financial sector. While dealers can provide entrepreneurs incentives to originate good assets, they might extract excessively high informational rents and thus attract too much young talent toward the financial industry, thus leading to lower GDP per capita growth.
15. A related literature has explored the relationship between financial liberalization and economic growth. See, for example, Bekaert, Harvey, and Lundblad (2005) and Henry (2003).
16. See, for example, Rousseau and Sylla (2005) for the United States, Bell and Rousseau (2001) for India, and Neusser and Kugler (1998) and Xu (2000) for cross-country samples.
17. See, for example, Demetriades and Hussein (1996).
18. For an application of the differences-in-differences estimation, see, for example, Beck and Levine (2002), Beck (2003), Beck et al. (2008), Braun and Larrain (2005), Fisman and Love (2003), and Raddatz (2006).
19. Black and Strahan (2002) and Kerr and Nanda (2009).
20. Morgan, Rime, and Strahan (2004), Acharya, Imbs, and Sturgess (2011), and Demyanyk, Ostergaard, and Sørensen (2007). Similar work has been undertaken across different regions of Italy; see Guiso, Sapienza, and Zingales (2004).
21. See Ang (2011), Beck, Levine, and Loayza (2000), and Wurgler (2000).
22. See Aghion et al. (2010).
23. See Aghion et al. (2009).
24. Rioja and Valev (2004a, 2004b) and Aghion, Howitt, and Mayer-Foulkes (2005).
25. Favara (2003) criticizes the lack of robustness of the findings of Beck, Levine, and Loayza (2000) to changes in the sample. Rousseau and Wachtel (2011) question the robustness of the cross-country relationship between finance and growth in a sample extended to the period of the Great Moderation of the early twenty-first century.
26. See Stulz (2001) for an overview.
27. See Bhide (1993) and Stiglitz (1985).
28. See Boot, Greenbaum, and Thakor (1993).
29. See Weinstein and Yafeh (1998) and Morck and Nakamura (1999).
30. See Levine (2002), Beck and Levine (2002), and Demirgüç-Kunt and Maksimovic (2002), respectively.
31. See Kletzer and Bardhan (1987), Beck (2002), and Matsuyama (2005).
32. See, for example, Berman and Héricourt (2008) and Muûls (2008).
33. See Beck et al. (2006) and Beck, Demirgüç-Kunt, Laeven, and Levine (2008), respectively.
34. See, for example, Beck, Demirgüç-Kunt, and Maksimovic (2005) and Beck, Demirgüç-Kunt, and Maksimovic (2008).
35. See, for example, Pitt and Khandker (1998), Morduch (1998), Coleman (1999), Karlan and Zinman (2010); see Karlan and Morduch (2010) for a recent overview.

36. See also Dupas and Robinson (2009) for an assessment of improved access to savings services in Kenya.
37. See Galor and Zeira (1993), Aghion and Bolton (1997), and Galor and Moav (2004).
38. See Galor and Zeira (1993) and Galor and Moav (2004).
39. See Beck, Levine, and Levkov (2010) and Giné and Townsend (2004).
40. For a more in-depth discussion of these issues and the relevant literature, see World Bank (2007).
41. For other work on contagion through the payment system and interbank market, see Rochet and Tirole (1996), Allen and Gale (2000b), and Freixas, Parigi, and Rochet (2000).
42. See Claessens, Kose, and Terrones (2008).
43. See Bernanke and Gertler (1989), Kiyotaki and Moore (1997), and Fisher (1933).
44. See Chang and Velasco (2001) and Kaminsky and Reinhart (1999).
45. See Kaminsky and Reinhart (1999) and Demirgüç-Kunt and Detragiache (1998).
46. See Demirgüç-Kunt and Detragiache (2005) for a survey.
47. Bernanke (1983), Calomiris and Mason (2003), and Kupiec and Ramirez (2009).
48. Ferri, Kang, and Kim (2001), and Djankov, Jindra, and Klapper (2005), respectively.
49. Dell'Ariccia, Detragiache, and Rajan (2008), Braun and Larrain (2005), and Kroszner, Laeven, and Klingebiel (2007).
50. For theoretical models, see Marcus (1984), Chan, Greenbaum, and Thakor (1986), and Keeley (1990).
51. Boot, Greenbaum, and Thakor (1993) and Allen and Gale (2000a, 2004).
52. Martinez-Miera and Repullo (2010), however, show that higher interest rates also imply higher interest revenues for banks, which might result in a U-shaped relationship between competition and bank fragility. Similarly, Caminal and Matutes (2002) show that less competition can lead to less credit rationing, larger loans, and higher probability of failure if loans are subject to multiplicative uncertainty.
53. Beck, Demirgüç-Kunt, and Levine (2006a) and Schaeck, Cihak, and Wolfe (2009).
54. Schaeck and Cihák (2007) and Berger, Klapper, and Turk-Ariss (2009).
55. See Demirgüç-Kunt and Kane (2002) for an overview.
56. For a broader discussion, see Barth, Caprio, and Levine (2006).
57. On a macroeconomic level, this is often referred to as the Bernanke-Greenspan put, in reference to the two chairmen of Federal Reserve in office during the boom period of the early 2000s.
58. For a more in-depth discussion, see also Barth, Caprio, and Levine (2012).
59. Allen, Babus, and Carletti (2010) and Wagner (2010).
60. See, for example, Jiménez et al. (2012) and Mian and Sufi (2009).
61. For a recent more complete survey, see Haber and Perotti (2008).
62. Becker and Stigler (1974), Stigler (1975), Haber, Razo, and Maurer (2003).
63. Pagano and Volpin (2005) and Perrotti and von Thadden (2006).
64. See La Porta, Lopez-de-Silanes, and Shleifer (2002).
65. Faccio (2006), Khwaja and Mian (2005), and Claessens, Feijen, and Laeven (2008).
66. Compare Clarke, Cull, and Shirley (2005) and other articles in the same issue.
67. For a more detailed discussion, see De la Torre, Gozzi, and Schmukler (2007).
68. See Giannetti and Ongena (2009).
69. Other important groups constitute the German and the Scandinavian legal systems, which are based on similar political structures as the French civil code tradition but have a more flexible and adaptable structure.
70. La Porta et al. (2004) and Beck, Demirgüç-Kunt, and Levine (2003b).

References

Acemoglu, Daron. "Why Not a Political Coase Theorem? Social Conflict, Commitment and Politics." *Journal of Comparative Economics* 31 (Dec. 2003): 620–652.

Acemoglu, Daron, and Simon Johnson. "Unbundling Institutions." *Journal of Political Economy* 113 (Oct. 2005): 949–995.

Acemoglu, Daron, Simon Johnson, and James A. Robinson. "The Colonial Origins of Comparative Development: An Empirical Investigation." *American Economic Review* 91 (Dec. 2001): 1369–1401.

Acemoglu, Daron, Simon Johnson, and James A. Robinson. "Reversal of Fortunes: Geography and Institutions in the Making of the Modern World Income Distribution." *Quarterly Journal of Economics* 117 (Aug. 2002): 1231–1294.

Acemoglu, Daron, Simon Johnson, and James A. Robinson. "Institutions as a Fundamental Cause of Long-Run Growth." In *Handbook of Economic Growth*, ed. Philippe Aghion and Steven Durlauf, 385–472. Amsterdam: Elsevier, 2005.

Acemoglu, Daron, Simon Johnson, James A. Robinson, and Yunyong Thaicharoen. "Institutional Causes, Macroeconomic Symptoms: Volatility, Crises and Growth." *Journal of Monetary Economics* 50 (Jan. 2003). 49–123.

Acemoglu, Daron, and Fabrizio Zilibotti. "Was Prometheus Unbound by Chance? Risk, Diversification, and Growth." *Journal of Political Economy* 105 (Aug. 1997): 709–751.

Acharya, Viral V., Jean Imbs, and Jason Sturgess. "Finance and Efficiency: Do Bank Branching Regulations Matter?" *Review of Finance* 15 (Jan. 2011): 135–172.

Aghion, Philippe, George-Marios Angeletos, Abhijit Banerjee, and Kalina Manova. "Volatility and Growth: Credit Constraints and the Composition of Growth." *Journal of Monetary Economics* 57 (April 2010): 246–265.

Aghion, Philippe, Philippe Bacchetta, Romain Rancière, and Kenneth Rogoff. "Exchange Rate Volatility and Productivity Growth: The Role of Financial Development." *Journal of Monetary Economics* 56 (May 2009): 494–513.

Aghion, Philippe, and Patrick Bolton. "A Trickle-Down Theory of Growth and Development with Debt Overhang." *Review of Economic Studies* 64 (April 1997): 151–172.

Aghion, Philippe, Mathias Dewatripont, and Patrick Rey. "Competition, Financial Discipline and Growth." *Review of Economic Studies* 66 (Oct. 1999): 825–852.

Aghion, Philippe, Thibault Fally, and Stefano Scarpetta. "Credit Constraints as a Barrier to the Entry and Post-Entry Growth of Firms." *Economic Policy* 22 (Oct. 2007): 731–779.

Aghion, Philippe, Peter Howitt, and David Mayer-Foulkes. "The Effect of Financial Development on Convergence: Theory and Evidence." *Quarterly Journal of Economics* 120 (Feb. 2005): 173–222.

Allen, Franklin, and Douglas Gale. "Financial Markets, Intermediaries, and Intertemporal Smoothing." *Journal of Political Economy* 105 (June 1997): 523–546.

Allen, Franklin, and Douglas Gale. *Comparing Financial Systems*. Cambridge, Mass.: MIT Press, 2000a.

Allen, Franklin, and Douglas Gale. "Financial Contagion." *Journal of Political Economy* 108 (Feb. 2000b): 1–33.

Allen, Franklin, and Douglas Gale. "Competition and Financial Stability." *Journal of Money, Credit and Banking* 36 (June 2004): 453–480.

Allen, Franklin, Ana Babus, and Elena Carletti. "Financial Connections and Systemic Risk." Working Paper 10-20, Wharton Financial Institutions Center, July 2010.

Ang, James B. "Financial Development, Liberalization and Technological Deepening." *European Economic Review* 55 (June 2011): 688–701

Arcand, Jean Louis, Enrico Berkes, and Ugo Panizza. "Too Much Finance?" Mimeo, 2011.

Ashcraft, Adam B. "Are Banks Really Special? New Evidence from the FDIC-Induced Failure of Healthy Banks." *American Economic Review* 95 (Dec. 2005): 1712–1730.

Bagehot, Walter. *Lombard Street.* 1873; Homewood, Ill.: Richard D. Irwin, 1962.

Banerjee, Abhijit V., and Esther Duflo. "Do Firms Want to Borrow More? Testing Credit Constraints Using a Directed Lending Program." CEPR Discussion Paper 4681, Oct. 2004.

Banerjee, Abhijit, Esther Duflo, Rachel Glennerster, and Cynthia Kinan. "The Miracle of Microfinance? Evidence from a Randomized Experiment." MIT paper, June 2010.

Barth, James R., Gerard Caprio Jr., and Ross Levine. *Rethinking Bank Regulation: Until Angels Govern.* Cambridge: Cambridge University Press, 2006.

Barth, James R., Gerard Caprio Jr., and Ross Levine. *The Guardians of Finance: Making Regulators Work for Us. Cambridge, Mass.: MIT Press, 2012.*

Beck, Thorsten. "Financial Development and International Trade: Is There a Link?" *Journal of International Economics* 57 (June 2002): 107–131.

Beck, Thorsten. "Financial Dependence and International Trade." *Review of International Economics* 11 (May 2003): 296–316.

Beck, Thorsten. "The Econometrics of Finance and Growth." In *Palgrave Handbook of Econometrics*, vol. 2, ed. Terence Mills and Kerry Patterson, 1180–1211. Houndsmill: Palgrave Macmillan, 2009.

Beck, Thorsten, Berrak Büyükkarabacak, Felix K. Rioja, and Neven T. Valev. "Who Gets the Credit? And Does it Matter? Household vs. Firm Lending across Countries." European Banking Center Discussion Paper no. 2009-2012, May 24, 2009. http://ssrn.com/abstract=1411029.

Beck, Thorsten, Juan Miguel Crivelli, and William Summerhill. "State Bank Transformation in Brazil—Choices and Consequence." *Journal of Banking and Finance* 29 (Aug./Sept. 2005): 2223–2257.

Beck, Thorsten, Asli Demirgüç-Kunt, Luc Laeven, and Ross Levine. "Finance, Firm Size, and Growth." *Journal of Money, Banking and Credit* 40 (Oct. 2008): 1379–1405.

Beck, Thorsten, Asli Demirgüç-Kunt, Luc Laeven, and Vojislav Maksimovic. "The Determinants of Financing Obstacles." *Journal of International Money and Finance* 25 (Oct. 2006): 932–952.

Beck, Thorsten, Asli Demirgüç-Kunt, and Ross Levine. "Law, Endowments, and Finance." *Journal of Financial Economics* 70 (Nov. 2003a): 137–181.

Beck, Thorsten, Asli Demirgüç-Kunt, and Ross Levine. "Law and Finance: Why Does Legal Origin Matter?" *Journal of Comparative Economics* 31 (Dec. 2003b): 653–675.

Beck, Thorsten, Asli Demirgüç-Kunt, and Ross Levine. "Bank Concentration, Competition, and Crises: First Results." *Journal of Banking and Finance* 30 (May 2006a): 1581–1603.

Beck, Thorsten, Asli Demirgüç-Kunt, and Ross Levine. "Bank Supervision and Corruption in Lending." *Journal of Monetary Economics* 53 (Nov. 2006b): 2131–2163.

Beck, Thorsten, Asli Demirgüç-Kunt, and Ross Levine. "Finance, Inequality and the Poor." *Journal of Economic Growth* 12 (March 2007): 27–49.

Beck, Thorsten, Asli Demirgüç-Kunt, and Vojislav Maksimovic. "Financial and Legal Constraints to Firm Growth: Does Size Matter?" *Journal of Finance* 60 (Feb. 2005): 137–177.

Beck, Thorsten, Asli Demirgüç-Kunt, and Vojislav Maksimovic. "Financing Patterns around the World: Are Small Firms Different?" *Journal of Financial Economics* 89 (Sept. 2008): 467–487.

Beck, Thorsten, Asli Demirgüç-Kunt, and Maria Soledad Martinez Peria. "Reaching Out: Access to and Use of Banking Services across Countries." *Journal of Financial Economics* 85 (July 2007): 234–266.

Beck, Thorsten, Erik Feijen, Alain Ize, and Florencia Moizeszowicz. "Benchmarking Financial Development." World Bank Policy Research Working Paper 4638, Washington, D.C., June 2008.

Beck, Thorsten, and Ross Levine. "Industry Growth and Capital Allocation: Does Having a Market- or Bank-Based System Matter?" *Journal of Financial Economics* 64 (May 2002): 147–180.

Beck, Thorsten, and Ross Levine, "Legal Institutions and Financial Development." In *Handbook of New Institutional Economics*, ed. Claude Menard and Mary Shirley, 251–278. Dordrecht: Kluwer, 2005.

Beck, Thorsten, Ross Levine, and Alexey Levkov. "Big Bad Banks? The Winners and Losers from Bank Deregulation in the United States." *Journal of Finance* 65 (Oct. 2010): 1637–1667.

Beck, Thorsten, Ross Levine, and Norman Loayza. "Finance and the Sources of Growth." *Journal of Financial Economics* 58 (2000): 261–300.

Becker, Bo, and David Greenberg. "Financial Development, Fixed Costs and International Trade." Harvard Business School Working Paper, 2007.

Becker, Gary, and George Stigler. "Law Enforcement, Malfeasance, and Compensation of Enforcers." *Journal of Legal Studies* 3 (Jan. 1974): 1–18.

Bekaert, Geert, Campbell R. Harvey, and Christian Lundblad. "Does Financial Liberalization Spur Growth?" *Journal of Financial Economics* 77 (July 2005): 3–55.

Bekaert, Geert, Campbell R. Harvey, and Christian Lundblad. "Growth Volatility and Financial Liberalization." *Journal of International Money and Finance* 25 (April 2006): 370–403.

Bell, Clive, and Peter L. Rousseau. "Post-Independence India: A Case of Finance-Led Industrialization?" *Journal of Development Economics* 65 (June 2001): 153–175.

Bencivenga, Valerie R., and Bruce D. Smith. "Financial Intermediation and Endogenous Growth." *Review of Economics Studies* 58 (April 1991): 195–209.

Bencivenga, Valerie R., and Bruce D. Smith. "Some Consequences of Credit Rationing in an Endogenous Growth Model." *Journal of Economic Dynamics and Control* 17 (Jan.–March 1993): 97–122.

Benmelech, Efraim, and Tobias Moskowitz. "The Political Economy of Financial Regulation: Evidence from U.S. State Usury Laws in the 19th Century." *Journal of Finance* 65 (June 2010): 1029–1073.

Berger, Allen N., Leora F. Klapper, and Rima Turk-Ariss. "Bank Competition and Financial Stability." *Journal of Financial Service Research* 35 (April 2009): 99–118.

Berman, Nicolas, and Jerome Hericourt. "Financial Factors and the Margins of Trade: Evidence from Cross-Country Firm-Level Data." CES Working Paper 2008.50, Centre d'Economie de la Sorbonne; published in *Journal of Development Economics* 93 (Nov. 2010): 206–217.

Bernanke, Ben S. "Nonmonetary Effects of the Financial Crisis in the Propagation of the Great Depression." *American Economic Review* 73 (June 1983): 257–276.

Bernanke, Ben, and Mark Gertler. "Agency Costs, Net Worth, and Business Fluctuations." *American Economic Review* 79 (March 1989): 14–31.

Bhide, Amar. "The Hidden Costs of Stock Market Liquidity." *Journal of Financial Economics* 34 (Aug. 1993): 31–51.

Black, Sandra E., and Philip E. Strahan. "Entrepreneurship and Bank Credit Availability." *Journal of Finance* 57 (Dec. 2002): 2807–2833.

Blackburn Keith, and Victor T. Y. Huang. "A Theory of Growth, Financial Development and Trade." *Economica* 65 (Feb. 1998): 107–124.

Bolton, Patrick, Tano Santos, and Jose A. Scheinkman. "Cream Skimming in Financial Markets." NBER Working Paper no. 16804, Cambridge, Mass., Feb. 2011.

Boot, Arnoud W. A. "Destabilising Market Forces and the Structure of Banks Going Forward." In *The Future of Banking*, ed. Thorsten Beck, 29–34. CEPR, 2011.

Boot, Arnoud W. A., Stuart I. Greenbaum, and Anjan V. Thakor. "Reputation and Discretion in Financial Contracting." *American Economic Review* 83 (Dec. 1993): 1165–1183.

Bordo, Michael D., and Peter L. Rousseau. "Legal-Political Factors and the Historical Evolution of the Finance-Growth Link." *European Review of Economic History* 10 (Dec. 2006): 421–444.

Boyd, John H., and Edward C. Prescott. "Financial Intermediary-Coalitions." *Journal of Economic Theory* 38 (April 1986): 211–232.

Boyd, John H., and Gianni De Nicoló. "The Theory of Bank Risk Taking and Competition Revisited." *Journal of Finance* 60 (June 2005): 1329–1343.

Boyd, John H., and Bruce D. Smith. "The Evolution of Debt and Equity Markets in Economic Development." *Economic Theory* 12 (Oct. 1998): 519–560.

Braun, Matias, and Borja Larrain. "Finance and the Business Cycle: International, Inter-Industry Evidence." *Journal of Finance* 60 (June 2005): 1097–1128.

Calomiris, Charles W., and Joseph R. Mason. "Consequences of Bank Distress during the Great Depression." *American Economic Review* 93 (June 2003): 937–947.

Caminal, Ramon, and Carmen Matutes. "Market Power and Banking Failures." *International Journal of Industrial Organization* 20 (Nov. 2002): 1341–1361.

Chan, Yuk-Shee, Stuart I. Greenbaum, and Anjan V. Thakor. "Information Reusability, Competition and Bank Asset Quality." *Journal of Banking and Finance* 10 (June 1986): 243–253.

Chang, Roberto, and Andres Velasco. "A Model of Financial Crises in Emerging Markets." *Quarterly Journal of Economics* 116 (May 2001): 489–517.

Chari, V. V., and Ravi Jagannathan. "Banking Panics, Information, and Rational Expectations Equilibrium." *Journal of Finance* 43 (July 1988): 749–760.

Claessens, Stijn, Erik Feijen, and Luc Laeven. "Political Connections and Preferential Access to Finance: The Role of Campaign Contributions." *Journal of Financial Economics* 88 (June 2008): 554–580.

Claessens, Stijn, M. Ayhan Kose, and Marco Terrones. "What Happens during Recessions, Crunches and Busts?" IMF Working Paper 08/274, Washington, D.C., Dec. 2008.

Claessens, Stijn, and Luc Laeven. "Financial Development, Property Rights, and Growth." *Journal of Finance* 58 (Dec. 2003): 2401–2436.

Clarke, George R. G., Lixin Colin Xu, and Heng-fu Zou. "Finance and Income Inequality: What Do the Data Tell Us?" *Southern Economic Journal* 72 (Jan. 2006): 578–596.

Clarke, George R. G., and Robert Cull. "Political and Economic Determinants of the Likelihood of Privatizing Argentine Public Banks." *Journal of Law and Economics* 45 (April 2002): 165–197.

Clarke, George R. G., Robert Cull, and Mary M. Shirley. "Bank Privatization in Developing Countries: A Summary of Lessons and Findings." *Journal of Banking and Finance* 29 (Aug.–Sept. 2005): 1905–1930.

Coleman, Brett E. "The Impact of Group Lending in Northeast Thailand." *Journal of Development Economics* 60 (Oct. 1999): 105–141.

Cull, Robert, and Lixin Colin Xu. "Institutions, Ownership, and Finance: The Determinants of Profit Reinvestment among Chinese Firms." *Journal of Financial Economics* 77 (July 2005): 117–146.

De Gregorio, José. "Borrowing Constraints, Human Capital Accumulation, and Growth." *Journal of Monetary Economics* 37 (Feb. 1996): 49–71.

De la Torre, Augusto, Juan Carlos Gozzi, and Sergio L. Schmukler. "Innovative Experiences in Access to Finance: Market Friendly Roles for the Visible Hand?" World Bank Policy Research Working Paper 4326, Washington, D.C., Aug. 2007.

Dell'Ariccia, Giovanni, Enrica Detragiache, and Raghuram Rajan. "The Real Effect of Banking Crises." *Journal of Financial Intermediation* 17 (Jan. 2008): 89–112.

Demetriades, Panicos O., and Khaled A. Hussein. "Does Financial Development Cause Economic Growth? Time-Series Evidence from 16 Countries." *Journal of Development Economics* 51 (Dec. 1996): 387–411.

Demirgüç-Kunt, Asli, and Enrica Detragiache. "The Determinants of Banking Crises in Developing and Developed Countries." IMF Staff Papers 45(1), Washington, D.C., March 1998, 81–109.

Demirgüç-Kunt, Asli, and Enrica Detragiache. "Financial Liberalization and Financial Fragility." In *Proceedings of the 1998 World Bank Conference on Development Economics*, ed. Boris Pleskovic and Joseph E. Stiglitz. Washington, D.C.: World Bank, 1999.

Demirgüç-Kunt, Asli, and Enrica Detragiache. "Cross-Country Empirical Studies of Systemic Banking Distress: A Survey." *National Institute Economic Review* 192 (April 2005): 68–83

Demirgüç-Kunt, Asli, Enrica Detragiache, and Thierry Tressel. "Banking on the Principles: Compliance with Basel Core Principles and Bank Soundness." *Journal of Financial Intermediation* 17 (Oct. 2008): 511–542.

Demirgüç-Kunt, Asli, and Edward Kane. "Deposit Insurance around the Globe? Where Does it Work?" *Journal of Economic Perspectives* 16 (Spring 2002): 175–195.

Demirgüç-Kunt, Asli, Inessa Love, and Vojislav Maksimovic. "Business Environment and the Incorporation Decision." *Journal of Banking and Finance* 30 (Nov. 2006): 2967–2993.

Demirgüç-Kunt, Asli, and Vojislav Maksimovic. "Funding Growth in Bank-Based and Market-Based Financial Systems: Evidence from Firm-Level Data." *Journal of Financial Economics* 65 (Sept. 2002): 337–363.

Demyanyk, Yuliya, Charlotte Ostergaard, and Bent E. Sørensen. "U.S. Banking Deregulation, Small Businesses, and Interstate Insurance of Personal Income." *Journal of Finance* 62 (Dec. 2007): 2763–2801.

Diamond, Douglas W. "Financial Intermediation and Delegated Monitoring." *Review of Economic Studies* 51 (July 1984): 393–414.

Diamond, Douglas W., and Philip H. Dybvig. "Bank Runs, Deposit Insurance and Liquidity." *Journal of Political Economy* 91 (June 1983): 401–419.

Diamond, Douglas W., and Raghuram G. Rajan. "Liquidity Risk, Liquidity Creation, and Financial Fragility: A Theory of Banking." *Journal of Political Economy* 109 (April 2001): 287–327.

Diamond, Douglas W., and Robert E. Verrecchia. "Optimal Managerial Contracts and Equilibrium Security Prices." *Journal of Finance* 37 (May 1982): 275–287.

Djankov, Simeon, Jan Jindra, and Leora F. Klapper. "Corporate Valuation and the Resolution of Bank Insolvency in East Asia." *Journal of Banking and Finance* 29 (Aug.-Sept. 2005): 2095–2118.

Dupas, Pascaline, and Jonathan Robinson. "Savings Constraints and Microenterprise Development: Experience from a Field Experiment in Kenya." NBER Working Paper no. 14693, Cambridge, Mass., Jan. 2009.

Faccio, Mara. "Politically Connected Firms." *American Economic Review* 96 (March 2006): 369–386.

Favara, Giovanni. "An Empirical Reassessment of the Relationship between Finance and Growth." IMF Working Paper 03/123, Washington, D.C., June 2003.

Feijen, Erik, and Enrico C. Perotti. "The Political Economy of Financial Fragility." CEPR Discussion Paper 5317, London, Oct. 2005.

Ferri, Giovanni, Tae Soo Kang, and In-June Kim. "The Value of Relationship Banking during Financial Crises: Evidence from the Republic of Korea." World Bank Policy Research Working Paper no. 2553, Washington, D.C., 2001.

Fisher, Irving. "The Debt-Deflation Theory of Great Depressions." *Econometrica* 4 (1933): 337–357.

Fisman, Raymond, and Inessa Love. "Trade Credit, Financial Intermediary Development, and Industry Growth." *Journal of Finance* 58 (Feb. 2003): 353–374.

Freixas, Xavier, Bruno M. Parigi, and Jean-Charles Rochet. "Systemic Risk, Interbank Relations and Liquidity Provision by the Central Bank." *Journal of Money, Credit and Banking* 32 (Aug. 2000): 611–638.

Fry, Maxwell. *Money, Interest, and Banking in Economic Development.* Baltimore, Md.: Johns Hopkins University Press, 1988.

Galor, Oded, and Omer Moav. "From Physical to Human Capital Accumulation: Inequality and the Process of Development." *Review of Economic Studies* 71 (Oct. 2004): 1001–1026.

Galor, Oded, and Joseph Zeira. "Income Distribution and Macroeconomics." *Review of Economic Studies* 60 (Jan. 1993): 35–52.

Gerschenkron, Alexander. *Economic Backwardness in Historical Perspective—A Book of Essays.* Cambridge, Mass.: Harvard University Press, 1962.

Gianneti, Mariassunta, and Steven Ongena. "Financial Integration and Firm Performance: Evidence from Foreign Bank Entry in Emerging Markets." *Review of Finance* 13 (April 2009): 181–223.

Giné, Xavier, and Robert M. Townsend. "Evaluation of Financial Liberalization: A General Equilibrium Model with Constrained Occupation Choice." *Journal of Development Economics* 74 (Aug. 2004): 269–307.

Glaeser, Edward L., and Andrei Shleifer. "Legal Origins." *Quarterly Journal of Economics* 117 (Nov. 2002): 1193–1229.

Goldsmith, Raymond W. *Financial Structure and Development.* New Haven, Conn.: Yale University Press, 1969.

Greenwood, Jeremy, and Boyan Jovanovic. "Financial Development, Growth, and the Distribution of Income." *Journal of Political Economy* 98 (Oct. 1990): 1076–1107.

Greenwood, Jeremy, and Bruce D. Smith. "Financial Markets in Development, and the Development of Financial Markets." *Journal of Economic Dynamics and Control* 21 (Jan. 1997): 145–181.

Grossman, Sanford J., and Oliver D. Hart. "Takeover Bids, the Free-Rider Problem, and the Theory of the Corporation." *Bell Journal of Economics* 11 (Spring 1980): 42–64.

Grossman, Sanford J., and Joseph E. Stiglitz. "On the Impossibility of Informationally Efficient Markets." *American Economic Review* 70 (June 1980): 393–408.

Guiso, Luigi, Paola Sapienza, and Luigi Zingales. "Does Local Financial Development Matter?" *Quarterly Journal of Economics* 119 (Aug. 2004): 929–969.

Haber, Stephen, Armando Razo, and Noel Maurer. *The Politics of Property Rights: Political Instability, Credible Commitments, and Economic Growth in Mexico 1876–1929.* Cambridge: Cambridge University Press, 2003.

Haber, Stephen, and Enrico Perotti. "The Political Economy of Financial Systems." Tinbergen Institute Discussion Paper 2008-045/2, Amsterdam, 2008.

Hamilton, Alexander. 1781; quoted in Bray Hammond, *Banks and Politics in America: From the Revolution to the Civil War*. Princeton, N.J.: Princeton University Press, 1991, p. 36.

Hellwig, Martin. "Banking, Financial Intermediation, and Corporate Finance." In *European Financial Integration*, ed. Alberto Giovanni and Colin Mayer, 35–63. Cambridge: Cambridge University Press, 1991.

Henry, B. Peter. "Capital-Account Liberalization, the Cost of Capital and Economic Growth." *American Economic Review* 93 (May 2003): 91–96.

Hicks, John. *A Theory of Economic History*. Oxford: Clarendon Press, 1969.

Holmström, Bengt, and Jean Tirole. "Private and Public Supply of Liquidity." *Journal of Political Economy* 106 (Feb. 1998): 1–40.

Hur, Jung, Manoj Raj, and Yohanes E. Riyanto. "Finance and Trade: A Cross-Country Empirical Analysis on the Impact of Financial Development and Asset Tangibility on International Trade." *World Development* 34 (Oct. 2006): 1728–1741.

Jacklin, Charles J., and Sudipto Bhattacharya. "Distinguishing Panics and Information-Based Bank Runs: Welfare and Policy Implications." *Journal of Political Economy* 96 (June 1988): 568–592.

Jappelli, Tullio, and Marco Pagano. "Saving, Growth, and Liquidity Constraints." *Quarterly Journal of Economics* 109 (Feb. 1994): 83–109.

Jayaratne, Jith, and Philip E. Strahan. "The Finance-Growth Nexus: Evidence from Bank Branch Deregulation." *Quarterly Journal of Economics* 111 (Aug. 1996): 639–670.

Jensen, Michael C., and Kevin J. Murphy. "Performance Pay and Top Management Incentives." *Journal of Political Economy* 98 (April 1990): 225–264.

Jiménez, Gabriel, Steven Ongena, José-Luis Peydró, and Jesús Saurina. "Credit Supply and Monetary Policy: Identifying the Bank Balance-Sheet Channel with Loan Applications," *American Economic Review*, forthcoming.

Johnson, Simon, John McMillan, and Christopher Woodruff. "Property Rights and Finance." *American Economic Review* 92 (Dec. 2002): 1335–1356.

Ju, Jiandong, and Shang-JinWei. "Endowment versus Finance: A Wooden Barrel Theory of International Trade." IMF Working Paper 05/123, Washington, D.C., June 2005.

Kaminsky, Garciela L., and Carmen M. Reinhart. "The Twin Crises: The Causes of Banking and Balance-of-Payments Problems." *American Economic Review* 89 (June 1999): 473–500.

Karlan, Dean, and Jonathan Morduch. "Access to Finance." In *Handbook of Development Economics*, vol. 5, ed. Dani Rodrik and Mark Rosenzweig, 4703–4784. Amsterdam: Elsevier, 2010.

Karlan, Dean, and Jonathan Zinman. "Expanding Credit Access: Using Randomized Supply Decisions to Estimate the Impacts." *Review of Financial Studies* 23 (Jan. 2010): 433–464.

Keeley, Michael C. "Deposit Insurance, Risk and Market Power in Banking." *American Economic Review* 80 (Dec. 1990): 1183–1200.

Kerr, William R., and Ramana Nanda. "Democratizing Entry: Banking Deregulations, Financing Constraints, and Entrepreneurship." *Journal of Financial Economics* 94 (Oct. 2009): 124–149.

Khwaja, Asim Ijaz, and Atif Mian. "Do Lenders Favor Politically Connected Firms? Rent Provision in an Emerging Financial Market." *Quarterly Journal of Economics* 120 (Nov. 2005): 1371–411.

King, Robert G., and Ross Levine. "Finance and Growth: Schumpeter Might Be Right." *Quarterly Journal of Economics* 108 (Aug. 1993a): 717–738.

King, Robert G., and Ross Levine. "Finance, Entrepreneurship, and Growth: Theory and Evidence." *Journal of Monetary Economics* 32 (Dec. 1993b): 513–542.
Kiyotaki, Nobuhiro, and John Moore. "Credit Cycles." *Journal of Political Economy* 105 (April 1997): 211–248.
Kletzer, Kenneth, and Pranab Bardhan. "Credit Markets and Patterns of International Trade." *Journal of Development Economics* 27 (Oct. 1987): 57–70.
Kroszner, Randall S., Luc Laeven, and Daniela Klingebiel. "Banking Crises, Financial Dependence, and Growth." *Journal of Financial Economics* 84 (April 2007): 187–228.
Kroszner, Randall S., and Philip E. Strahan. "What Drives Deregulation? Economics and Politics of the Relaxation of Bank Branching Deregulation." *Quarterly Journal of Economics* 114 (Nov. 1999): 1437–1467.
Kupiec, Paul, and Carlos Ramirez. "Bank Failures and the Cost of Systemic Risk: Evidence from 1900–1930." FDIC Center for Financial Research Working Paper 2009-2006, April 2009.
Laeven, Luc, and Ross Levine. "Bank Governance, Regulation and Risk Taking." *Journal of Financial Economics* 93 (Aug. 2009): 259–275.
Laeven, Luc, and Fabian Valencia. "Systemic Banking Crises: A New Database." IMF Working Paper 08/224, Washington, D.C., Sept. 2008.
La Porta, Rafael, Florencio Lopez-de-Silanes, Christian Pop-Eleches, and Andrei Shleifer. "Judicial Checks and Balances." *Journal of Political Economy* 112 (April 2004): 445–470.
La Porta, Rafael, Florencio Lopez-de-Silanes, and Andrei Shleifer. "Government Ownership of Commercial Banks." *Journal of Finance* 57 (Feb. 2002): 265–301.
La Porta, Rafael, Florencio Lopez-de-Silanes, and Andrei Shleifer. "What Works in Securities Laws?" *Journal of Finance* 61 (Feb. 2006): 1–32.
Levine, Ross. "Stock Markets, Growth, and Tax Policy." *Journal of Finance* 46 (Sept. 1991): 1445–1465.
Levine, Ross. "Bank-Based or Market-Based Financial Systems: Which Is Better?" *Journal of Financial Intermediation* 11 (Oct. 2002): 398–428.
Levine, Ross. "Finance and Growth: Theory and Evidence." In *Handbook of Economic Growth*, ed. Philippe Aghion and Steven N. Durlauf, 865–934. Amsterdam: Elsevier, 2005.
Levine, Ross. "An Autopsy of the U.S. Financial System: Accident, Suicide or Negligent Homocide?" *Journal of Financial Economic Policy* 2 (2010): 196–213.
Levine, Ross. "The Governance of Financial Regulation: Reform Lessons from the Recent Crisis." *International Review of Finance*, forthcoming.
Levine, Ross, Norman Loayza, and Thorsten Beck. "Financial Intermediation and Growth: Causality and Causes." *Journal of Monetary Economics* 46 (Aug. 2000): 31–77.
Levine, Ross, and Sara Zervos. "Stock Markets, Banks, and Economic Growth." *American Economic Review* 88 (June 1998): 537–558.
Loayza, Norman V., and Romain Rancière. "Financial Development, Financial Fragility, and Growth." *Journal of Money, Credit and Banking* 28 (June 2006): 1051–1076.
Lucas, Robert E. Jr. "On the Mechanics of Economic Development." *Journal of Monetary Economics* 22 (July 1988): 3–42.
Malmendier, Ulrike. "Law and Finance 'at the Origin.'" *Journal of Economic Literature* 47 (Dec. 2009): 1076–1108.
Manova, Kalina. "Credit Constraints, Equity Market Liberalizations and International Trade." *Journal of International Economics* 76 (Sept. 2008): 33–47.
Manova, Kalina. "Credit Constraints and the Adjustment to Trade Reform." In *Trade Adjustment Costs in Developing Countries: Impacts, Determinants, and Policy*

Responses, ed. Guido Porto and Bernard M. Hoekman, 315–329. Washington, D.C.: World Bank, 2010.
Marcus, Alan J. "Deregulation and Bank Financial Policy." *Journal of Banking and Finance* 8 (Dec. 1984): 557–565.
Martinez-Miera, David, and Rafael Repullo. "Does Competition Reduce the Risk of Bank Failure?" *Review of Financial Studies* 23 (Oct. 2010): 3638–3664.
Matsuyama, Kiminori. "Credit Market Imperfections and Patterns of International Trade and Capital Flows." *Journal of the European Economic Association* 3 (April–May 2005): 714–723.
McKinnon, Ronald I. *Money and Capital in Economic Development*. Washington, D.C.: Brookings Institution, 1973.
Merryman, John Henry. "The French Deviation." *American Journal of Comparative Law* 44 (1996): 109–119.
Mian, Atif, and Amir Sufi. "The Consequences of Mortgage Credit Expansion: Evidence from the U.S. Mortgage Default Crisis." *Quarterly Journal of Economics* 124 (Nov. 2009): 1449–1496.
Michalski, Tomasz, and Evren Örs. "U.S. Banking Integration and State-Level Exports." Mimeo, Paris, HEC, 2011.
Morck, Randall, and Masao Nakamura. "Banks and Corporate Control in Japan." *Journal of Finance* 54 (Feb. 1999): 319–339.
Morduch, Jonathan. "Does Microfinance Really Help the Poor? New Evidence from Flagship Programs in Bangladesh." Princeton University, mimeo, June 1998.
Morgan, Donald P., Bertrand Rime, and Philip E. Strahan. "Bank Integration and State Business Cycles." *Quarterly Journal of Economics* 119 (Nov. 2004): 1555–1584.
Muûls, Mirabelle. "Exporters and Credit Constraints. A Firm-Level Approach." Working Paper no. 139, National Bank of Belgium, Sept. 2008.
Neusser, Klaus, and Maurice Kugler. "Manufacturing Growth and Financial Development: Evidence from OECD Countries." *Review of Economics and Statistics* 80 (Nov. 1998): 638–646.
North, Douglass C., and Barry R. Weingast. "Constitutions and Commitment: The Evolution of Institutions Governing Public Choice in Seventeenth-Century England." *Journal of Economic History* 49 (Dec. 1989): 803–832.
Pagano, Marco, and Giovanni Pica. "Finance and Employment." *Economic Policy* (2012), forthcoming.
Pagano, Marco, and Paolo F. Volpin. "The Political Economy of Corporate Governance." *American Economic Review* 95 (Sept. 2005): 1005–1030.
Perotti, Enrico C., and Armin Schwienbacher. "The Political Origin of Pension Funding." *Journal of Financial Intermediation* 18 (July 2009): 384–404.
Perotti, Enrico C., and Ernst-Ludwig von Thadden. "The Political Economy of Corporate Control and Labor Rents." *Journal of Political Economy* (Feb. 2006): 145–175.
Philippon, Thomas. "Financiers versus. Engineers: Should the Financial Sector Be Taxed or Subsidized?" *American Economic Journal: Macroeconomics* 2 (July 2010): 158–182.
Philippon, Thomas, and Ariell Reshef. "Wages and Human Capital in the U.S. Financial Industry: 1909–2006." NBER Working Paper 14644, Cambridge, Mass., Jan. 2009.
Pistor, Katharina, Yoram Keinan, Jan Kleinheisterkamp, and Mark D. West. "The Evolution of Corporate Law: A Cross-Country Comparison." *University of Pennsylvania Journal of International Economic Law* 23 (Winter 2002): 791–871.
Pistor, Katharina, Yoram Keinan, Jan Kleinheisterkamp, and Mark D. West. "Innovation in Corporate Law." *Journal of Comparative Economics* 31 (Dec. 2003): 676–694.

Pitt, Mark M., and Shahidur R. Khandker. "The Impact of Group-Based Credit Programs on Poor Households in Bangladesh: Does the Gender of Participants Matter?" *Journal of Political Economy* 106 (Oct. 1998): 958–996.
Quintyn, Marc, and Geneviève Verdier. "Mother, Can I Trust the Government? Sustained Financial Deepening—A Political Institutions View." IMF Working Paper 10/210, Washington, D.C., Sept. 2010.
Raddatz, Claudio. "Liquidity Needs and Vulnerability to Financial Underdevelopment." *Journal of Financial Economics* 80 (June 2006): 677–722.
Rajan, Raghuram. "Insiders and Outsiders: The Choice between Informed and Arm's-Length Debt." *Journal of Finance* 47 (Sept. 1992): 1367–1400.
Rajan, Raghuram. *Fault Lines: How Hidden Fracture Still Threaten the World Economy.* Princeton, N.J.: Princeton University Press, 2010.
Rajan, Raghuram G., and Luigi Zingales. "Financial Dependence and Growth." *American Economic Review* 88 (June 1998): 559–586.
Rancière, Romain, Aaron Tornell, and Frank Westermann. "Decomposing the Effects of Financial Liberalization: Crises vs. Growth." *Journal of Banking and Finance* 30 (Dec. 2006): 3331–3348.
Reinhart, Carmen M., and Kenneth S. Rogoff. *This Time Is Different: Eight Centuries of Financial Folly.* Princeton, N.J.: Princeton University Press, 2009.
Rioja, Felix, and Neven Valev. "Finance and the Sources of Growth at Various Stages of Economic Development." *Economic Inquiry* 42 (Jan. 2004a): 127–140.
Rioja, Felix, and Neven Valev. "Does One Size Fit All? A Reexamination of the Finance and Growth Relationship." *Journal of Development Economics* 74 (Aug. 2004b): 429–447.
Robinson, Joan. "The Generalization of the General Theory." In *The Rate of Interest and Other Essays.* London: Macmillan, 1952.
Rochet, Jean-Charles, and Jean Tirole. "Interbank Lending and Systemic Risk." *Journal of Money, Credit and Banking* 28 (Nov. 1996): 733–762.
Rousseau, Peter L., and Richard Sylla. "Emerging Financial Markets and Early U.S. Growth." *Explorations in Economic History* 42 (Jan. 2005): 1–16.
Rousseau, Peter L., and Paul Wachtel. "What Is Happening to the Impact of Financial Deepening on Economic Growth?" *Economic Inquiry* 49 (Jan. 2011): 276–288.
Schaeck, Klaus, and Martin Cihák. "Banking Competition and Capital Ratios." IMF Working Paper 07/216, Washington, D.C., Sept. 2007.
Schaeck, Klaus, Martin Cihák, and Simon Wolfe. "Are Competitive Banking Systems More Stable?" *Journal of Money, Credit and Banking* 41 (June 2009): 711–734.
Scharfstein, David. "The Disciplinary Role of Takeovers." *Review of Economic Studies* 55 (April 1988): 185–199.
Schumpeter, Joseph A. *The Theory of Economic Development.* 1911; translated by Redvers Opie, Cambridge, Mass.: Harvard University Press, 1934.
Shaw, Edward. *Financial Deepening in Economic Development.* New York: Oxford University Press, 1973.
Sirri, Erik R., and Peter Tufano. "The Economics of Pooling." In *The Global Financial System: A Functional Approach*, ed. Dwight B. Crane et al., 81–128. Boston: Harvard Business School Press, 1995.
Sleuwaegen, Leo, and Micheline Goedhuys. "Growth of Firms in Developing Countries, Evidence from Côte d'Ivoire." *Journal of Development Economics* 68 (June 2002): 117–135.
Smith, Adam. *An Inquiry into the Nature and Causes of the Wealth of Nations.* 1776; New York: Modern Library, 1937.

Stein, Jeremy C. "Takeover Threats and Managerial Myopia." *Journal of Political Economy* 96 (Feb. 1988): 61–80.
Stigler, George. *The Citizen and the State: Essays on Regulation*. Chicago: University of Chicago Press, 1975.
Stiglitz, Joseph E. "Credit Markets and the Control of Capital." *Journal of Money, Credit and Banking* 17 (May 1985): 133–152.
Stiglitz, Joseph E., and Andrew Weiss. "Incentive Effects of Terminations: Applications to the Credit and Labor Markets." *American Economic Review* 73 (Dec. 1983): 912–927.
Stulz, René M. "Does Financial Structure Matter for Economic Growth? A Corporate Finance Perspective." In *Financial Structure and Economic Growth: A Cross-Country Comparison of Banks, Markets, and Development*, ed. Asli Demirgüç-Kunt and Ross Levine, 143–188. Cambridge, Mass.: MIT Press, 2001.
Trew, Alex. "Infrastructure Finance and Industrial Takeoff in England." *Journal of Money, Credit and Banking* 42 (Sept. 2010): 985–1010.
Wagner, Wolf. "Diversification at Financial Institutions and Systemic Crises." *Journal of Financial Intermediation* 19 (July 2010): 373–386.
Weinstein, David E., and Yishay Yafeh. "On the Costs of a Bank-Centered Financial System: Evidence from the Changing Main Bank Relations in Japan." *Journal of Finance* 53 (April 1998): 635–672.
Williamson, Dean. "The Financial Structure of Commercial Revolution: Financing Long-Distance Trade in Venice 1190–1220 and Venetian Crete 1278–1400." Tilburg University, mimeo, 2010.
Woodruff, Christopher. "Measuring Institutions." In *International Handbook on the Economics of Corruption*, ed. Susan Rose-Ackerman, 105–125. Cheltenham: Edward Elgar, 2006.
World Bank. "Finance for All? Policies and Pitfalls in Expanding Access." Policy Report, Washington, D.C., Nov. 2007.
Wurgler, Jeffrey. "Financial Markets and the Allocation of Capital." *Journal of Financial Economics* 58 (2000): 187–214.
Xu, Zhenhui. "Financial Development, Investment and Economic Growth." *Economic Inquiry* 38 (April 2000): 331–344.
Zia, Bilal H. "Export Incentives, Financial Constraints, and the (Mis)allocation of Credit: Micro-Level Evidence from Subsidized Export Loans." *Journal of Financial Economics* 87 (Feb. 2008): 498–527.

CHAPTER 7

PROPERTY RIGHTS AND CAPITALISM

PAUL H. RUBIN AND TILMAN KLUMPP

Property rights are a necessary but not sufficient condition for capitalism. This is because all humans have some form of property rights; even our prehuman ancestors seem to have had property rights, although forms of property were quite basic (Rubin, 2002). Moreover, as Bailey (1992) has shown, even relatively primitive tribes studied by anthropologists have reasonably efficient property rights systems. For example, property rights are defined in agricultural land when crops are being grown, but the land is available for hunting in the fallow season. Nonetheless, these societies cannot in any sense be said to be capitalistic. Thus, more is needed for capitalism than property rights. On the other hand, capitalism cannot exist without property rights.

Other institutions that are needed for capitalism, in addition to property rights, are free markets (including capital markets) and competition to organize exchange; the presence of (profit-maximizing) firms and entrepreneurs to organize production; and the enforcement of contracts. This chapter explores why private property is essential for the working of capitalist economies. It does not attempt to illuminate all aspects of property rights but focuses on the relationship between property rights and capitalism.

The essay is organized as follows. We begin with a definition of property rights as a bundle of rights, noting its various practical limitations. Then we briefly describe the historical and philosophical development of private property rights. We discuss the functions of property rights in capitalist systems, in particular the creation of wealth by facilitating efficient resource use and development, trade, capital accumulation, and the peaceful resolution of conflict. We discuss the creation of property rights to intellectual resources. Then we take the reverse perspective from previously and focus on the role of capitalism for the creation and continued evolution of property rights.

A Definition of Property

What is property? In its idealized form, a property right entitles its holder to a strong form of authority over an asset, called ownership. Ownership can be viewed as a "bundle of sticks," composed of the following rights:

C: The right to *control* the asset and decide on its use.
V: A claim to the *value* the asset generates.
E: The right to *exclude* others from using the asset.
T: The right to *transfer* the bundle *C*, *V*, *E*, *T* to another holder.

It is important to understand that property rights do not regulate the relationship between the owner and his or her property but the relationship between the owner and other persons, with respect to the property. Unlike contract, which regulates the relationship between *specific* parties, property rights are rights against the world. Owners of property can be individuals, groups of individuals, organizations, or the state, and property owned can be tangible, such as personal property or real property (land), or intangible, such as corporate stock or intellectual property. Furthermore, property rights may or may not be formally recorded and may be granted perpetually or over a limited duration (e.g., patents, copyrights).

The Limits of Property

Rarely, if ever, does one encounter the bundle of sticks *C*, *V*, *E*, *T* in its entirety. A good example is the question of whether a person truly owns his or her body. Efforts by states to prevent suicide and controls over drug use (both legal and illegal) interfere with *C*, income taxation and laws against prostitution interfere with *V*, and laws prohibiting slavery or the sale of human organs interfere with *T*.

In general, property rights can be limited by the following factors: where they interfere with other rights, such as another person's property (e.g., noise and pollution ordinances), by law (e.g., owners of pets or livestock must abide by laws against animal cruelty), by public policy (e.g., regulation of industries, use of eminent domain, regulation of controlled substances or firearms), by community standards (e.g., real estate ownership may require that the property is kept according to aesthetic standards set by neighborhood associations), and by economic constraints (e.g., fencing or policing of land may cost more than the damages inflicted by occasional trespassers).

One could make an argument that property rights cannot be practically distinguished from bundles that contain some but not all of the rights just discussed and thus fall short of "true" ownership. In fact, it is possible to define ownership via the bundle of (unspecified) *residual rights* that are left over after any specific rights have been contractually assigned (Grossman and Hart, 1986). For the purpose of this chapter, however, we simply speak of a property right when significant degrees of the rights *C*, *V*, *E*, *T* are present.[1] Furthermore, we focus on private property rights (meaning property owned by individuals or firms), as opposed to communal property or state property. Moreover, the greater the set of rights *C*, *V*, *E*, and *T* associated with some system, the more that system is "capitalist" (everything else equal).

History of Thought on Property Rights

Scholastic inquiry into the nature of property has a long history and can be traced back to the ancient Greek philosophers, at least. In *The Republic* (1955), Plato (428–348 B.C.) endorses a concept of common ownership on the basis that common ownership is best suited to promote what he calls the common interest. Aristotle (384–322 B.C.) rejects Plato's ideal of common ownership in *Politics* (1981), noting the ills associated with common property and advocating private property instead, for reasons we discuss later. In the rest of this section, we focus on the philosophical arguments starting with the British philosophers of the seventeenth century.

Political Liberalism

With the British philosophers of the seventeenth and eighteenth centuries, the inquiry into the nature of property becomes at the same time an inquiry into the nature and justification of government. One might frame this question as a debate over whether property is a function of government or government a function of property. The first view has its origins in the writings of Thomas Hobbes (1588–1670). In *Leviathan* (1651), Hobbes identifies the right to property solely with the power to take possession over things and protect them from being taken by others. David Hume (1711–1776), in *Enquiry Concerning the Principles of Morals* (1748), views private property as an organizing principle for the use of resources, justified by their scarcity. Like Hobbes, however, Hume regards property rights as stable only to the extent that the social customs that (implicitly) assign such rights are protected souvereign power. Thus, Hobbes and Hume advance positive theories of property, according to which a right to property is derived from power because it is created and protected through the exercise of power, ergo by government.

Natural Rights Doctrine

The second view originates in John Locke's (1632–1704) *Two Treatises of Government* (1689). Locke argues that property rights are natural rights that exist absent of any form of government. The normative basis of Locke's theory is the notion that every man holds a quintessential property right to his own body and labor. Because physical things are created by mixing privately owned labor with unclaimed resources of nature, man acquires private property over what he produces. The significance of the Lockean paradigm is that it fundamentally redefines the relation of government and property-owning citizens. For Locke, government cannot create property rights or assign such rights to citizens, but instead exists solely to preserve man's natural, preexisting right to property. Adam Smith (1723–1719) continues the Lockean tradition in *The Wealth of Nations* (1776) and *Lecture on Justice* (1896), where he asserts the existence of natural rights, though to liberty, not property. Importantly, the right to liberty includes the right to prosper through trade, to which secure property rights are a precondition. Smith therefore arrives at a similar justification for government as Locke: to guarantee and defend property rights, as a necessary condition for exchange and hence man's natural right to liberty.

Utilitarianism

A decidely different viewpoint is adopted by writers of the utilitarian school. In *Theory of Legislation* (1914), Jeremy Bentham (1748–1832) advances a role for government that goes beyond merely exercising power because it can, or securing the natural rights of citizens through the exercise of power. Instead, government must act to maximize the welfare of its citizens. For Bentham, this meant the provision of those government goods and services whose benefits, measured as the sum of utilities, exceed their costs. The implication of the Benthamite perspective for property rights is profound, as it endows government with the power to tax citizens' property for the greater good. This conclusion, however, is not arrived at through an investigation of property rights but through an investigation of the purpose of government. John Stuart Mill (1806–1863) further expands the envisioned role of utilitarian government in *Principles of Political Economy* (1848), to include the redistribution of income and resources. Again, this is not without implications for property rights. For example, Mill rejects Locke's notion that a property right to land derives solely from human use of land. He argues instead that the distribution of land and other resources to productive uses must maximize the social value generated by them. To the extent that existing ownership rights maximize this value, such rights are endorsed. Thus, for utilitarians, private property is a means to the end of value maximization, but not an end in itself.

Socialism and Communism

Toward the middle nineteenth century, socialist writers Karl Marx (1818–1883) and Friedrich Engels (1820–1895) continued the utilitarian tradition but began to see private property as a major impediment to welfare maximization. Interestingly, Marx and Engels generally seem to agree with the Lockean view that every man holds a claim to the value of his labor. Private ownership of land and accumulated factors, however, deprives workers of part of this value, especially if land and capital are owned by relatively few—a viewpoint according to which the human struggle for well-being can be understood essentially as a conflict among the working-class proletariat and the property-owning classes. The classless utopia envisioned by Marx and Engels hence had to be a society free of private property.

Modern Evolutionary Theory

The theory of evolution as applied to humans is most consistent with the Lockean natural rights theory (Ridley, 1998; Rubin, 2002). This is because institutions of property evolved with humans. That is, there was never a time when humans existed without property. Therefore, it is not useful to think of governments as creating property rights, although governments can assist in enforcing property rights and can also interfere with property rights.

The Role of Private Property for Capitalism

Societies that respect private property have prospered, and societies that tried to abolish private property have failed. The institution of private property is strongly correlated with the prosperity of nations because private property is, indeed, a necessary condition for prosperity. Moreover, capitalism is also a necessary condition for prosperity.

In this section, we review the theoretical arguments in support of this hypothesis. Some of the arguments apply to societies in general, not just capitalist ones. Specifically, we discuss the role of property rights for the efficient use and development of resources, for trade and specialization, for capital accumulation and growth, and for the resolution of conflict. We also highlight what advantages the institution of private property may have compared to other institutions that try to achieve the same goals.

Property Rights Encourage the Efficient Use and Development of Resources

It is well known that resources that are rivalrous but nonexcludable—so-called common pool resources, or commons—face the dual threat of overuse (a demand-side failure) and underinvestment (a supply-side failure). Social scientists have examined various kinds of solutions to this problem, which one might call the "modes of governance" of resources. Arranged by the degree to which authority is centralized, these range from state regulation, to local governance and community ownership,[2] to full privatization. Each of these modes comes at a cost, of course.

Governance costs can include the costs of asymmetric information, agency costs, the costs of enforcing rules, and transaction costs, and the ideal form of governance is determined to a large part by its relative cost advantage over other forms.[3] In the following, we focus on the role of private property rights as a form of governing access to rivalrous resources.

Through the right to exclude, private property rights transform common pool resources into private goods. Excludability, together with the right to control and claim to value, eliminates both problems. To see how private property facilitates efficient use, consider an example. Imagine an area of grassland to be used for cattle grazing. We make the realistic assumption that the value of this resource for each herder decreases with the total amount of cattle on the range, as his herd must compete with other cattle over a fixed amount of grass. As long as a positive value is received by herders, however, the range will attract additional users, and may continue to do so even if the arrival of an additional animal results in a loss of value to others that is in excess of the value generated to the new user. Hardin (1968) calls this effect the "tragedy of the commons." One mechanism to turn the tragedy around is private ownership of the resource. As long as the owner's exclusion right can be enforced at a reasonable cost, the owner will have an incentive to set the size of the herd to a level that maximizes the overall value of the resource. In case the landowner does not also own cattle, he could sell or rent access to the range to other cattlemen at a price that induces optimal use. In either case, there would be no overuse of the property, as all value generated by the property is received by the owner either directly through his own use or indirectly by selling use rights to others.

For similar reasons, nonexcludable resources may be underdeveloped. Consider again a piece of land, to be used for farming instead of grazing. Assume that the farming yield can be increased through irrigation and that the value of the additional harvest exceeds the cost of irrigation. If the land is privately owned, the owner would clearly want to irrigate the land. On the other hand, if the land is not privately owned or otherwise made excludable, irrigation may not occur. The reason is that a potential entrepreneur, who contemplates whether to invest in irrigation technology, will anticipate that the potential profits from the additional yield would likely be dissipated by users who free-ride on the investment. Without a property right on what they create, entrepreneurs may not receive adequate compensation for their investment, and therefore may choose not to invest even if this activity is socially desirable. To the extent that the owner's exclusion rights can be enforced at reasonable costs, however, private ownership promotes enterprise and the efficient development of resources.

Property Rights Facilitate Trade and Foster Growth and Long-Term Prosperity

Specialization is central to the wealth of societies, and exchange is necessary to realize the gains from specialization. In capitalist economies, exchange typically takes place in markets, and the price signals these markets generate are effective in coordinating the production, consumption, and investment decisions made by individuals and firms. Recognition and enforcement of property rights is indispensable for individuals to voluntarily engage in the activity of exchanging one thing for another. Note that the recognition and enforcement of property rights is complementary to, but not the same as, the recognition and enforcement of contracts, that is, a way to make individuals keep their promises.

To be willing to give up things in their possession, individuals need assurance that what is received in return actually becomes their property and is respected by others as such. A system of stable, secure private property rights provides this assurance in two ways: the receiver gains confidence in the legitimacy of the title he is about to receive, and he anticipates immunity from the interference of others with his acquired property. Only if these conditions are met is he willing to part with things in his possession. It should be clear that the outlined mechanism relies not simply on the existence of property rights but on the public's trust in their recognition. A government's declaration to respect and enforce private property rights, for example, is not sufficient to facilitate exchange unless it is believed to be true.

For similar reasons, stable property rights are necessary for the accumulation of resources in the form of capital by private citizens, and thus for economic growth. There is little incentive to save resources for later use if it is anticipated that these savings will be appropriated by others. This aspect is particularly significant for the development of the modern, capitalist firm, because investment is a particular type of intertemporal exchange. The entrepreneur supplies resources to the firm, in exchange for a claim to the (risky) returns generated by these resources. The right to property of the firm secures this claim for the investor. The risk the investor is taking is therefore the risk associated with the business itself, but not the risk of appropriation if the business is successful. Private property rights can hence be viewed in parallel to the contracts that secure (certain) payments promised to those who supply labor or debt capital to the firm.

Property Rights Can Resolve Conflicts

Many conflicts arise out of conflicting uses of a scarce resource to which multiple parties lay claim. Others arise out of negative externalities that one individual's actions impose on others. The resolution of such conflicts may involve considerable costs on the parties involved and on others. These costs range from the cost of protecting one's possessions from appropriation, to the cost of protecting oneself from externalities, to the cost of litigation, to outright violence. From an aggregate economic perspective, these costs constitute a welfare loss. A system of clearly defined private property rights, as long as it is enforced, and believed to be enforced, can reduce conflict resolution costs considerably.

A celebrated result in economics, the Coase theorem, states that if property rights—or, more generally, entitlements—are clearly defined and there are no transaction costs (such as the costs of writing and enforcing contracts), then the allocation of externalities in an economy must be Pareto-efficient regardless of the initial allocation of entitlements (Coase, 1960). Consider an example where residents in a certain neighborhood are harmed by the air pollution of a nearby factory. Assume the damage to the residents (e.g., a reduced quality of life or the cost of treating respiratory illnesses) is larger than what it would cost the factory to stop polluting (e.g., the lost profit of ceasing production or the cost of installing air filters). It is then efficient for pollution to cease, and this state can be reached in several ways. If the residents are entitled to clean air, they can simply demand that the factory stop polluting and have the courts enforce this demand if necessary. If, on the other hand, the factory is entitled to pollute the air, the parties can agree that the factory will stop the pollution in exchange for a payment by the residents. Because the residents are willing to pay more to be free from pollution than it costs the factory to install filters, such a payment can be found. In either case, the final outcome is efficient. The initial allocation of entitlements has distributional consequences, of course: in our example, the residents are clearly better off in the first case than in the second; the reverse is true for the firm.

Reality is different from the ideal state envisioned by the Coase theorem in two important aspects. First, transaction costs are typically not equal to zero: enforcing one's rights, or reaching agreements with others, is expensive. Simply notice the number of parties involved in the example—a possibly very large number of residents plus the polluting factory, which itself might be controlled by more than a single owner or manager. Thus, the transaction costs do not only contain the costs of reaching an agreement between "the residents" and "the factory" but also among the residents and within the firm. Practical complications like these mean that some theoretically efficient outcomes will not be reached in reality, as the actual process of reaching the outcome is more expensive than the additional welfare generated by it.

The second difference is that entitlements are often *not* well defined. This is especially important in situations where economic progress or technological change necessitate the establishment of new rights that hitherto have not existed.[4] The consequence of such a (temporary) lack of entitlements for economic welfare is subtle but important. In the absence of clearly defined property rights, conflicts are bound to arise both over ownership of assets and over externalities. The resolution of these conflicts induces costs, including possibly the cost of violence.[5] In the presence of property rights, and in transitional phases during which new rights are being created (by customs, policy, and the courts), conflicts arise over the *definition* of property rights rather than over ownership. Because the definition of rights has long-lasting distributional consequences, much is at stake in these conflicts. Thus, resolution often comes at considerable costs (think of patent litigation). Our point is that the second type of conflict is much less costly in the long run than the first kind: conflicts over the definition of rights are temporary until the rights are established and recognized, whereas conflicts over ownership can be perpetual and are in principle solvable without violence. One can make the argument that the success of peaceful capitalist economies has much to do with the development of legal systems, most notably the Anglo-American common law system, which (a) enforce existing property rights efficiently, and (b) offer an effective environment in which new property rights are being defined.

Intellectual Property and Innovation

Intellectual property concerns the rights to patents, trade secrets, copyrights, and trademarks. Loosely speaking, a patent or a trade secret is the right to exclude others from using an invention, such as a machine, an algorithm, or a particular production process. A copyright is the right to exclude others from using original works of authorship, such as literary or musical works. A trademark is a signifier such as a name, symbol, or slogan that can distinguish the source of a seller's goods and from others; a trademark is thus the right of a seller to exclude others from using the seller's reputation. In addition to these exclusion rights (*E*), the other dimensions of property (*C*, *V*, and *T*) are typically included as well in patents, copyrights, and trademarks.[6] Thus, we may talk of intellectual *property* rights.

Intellectual property is extremely important for capitalism. Whereas static markets lead to efficient use of existing resources, for economic growth innovation and technical change is necessary (Schumpeter, 1942). The success of capitalism is in large part due to the growth it fosters; people would not accept some of the negatives of capitalism (such as substantial economic inequality and cyclical activity) without the prospect of growth. Jones (2001) has shown that the most important factor leading to modern increases in income is the share of created wealth going to creators of innovations, and these innovations are facilitated by the existence of intellectual property.

Historical Development of Intellectual Property

The idea that property rights might extend to intellectual goods has a long history. Trademarks, for example, have been used since ancient times in almost all cultures to identify the creator of artistic and craft items. Intellectual property laws usually emerged as a means of economic policy by the state. The first trademark law was passed in 1266 in England, protecting bakers' stamps placed on bread loaves. The first patent law emerged in 1474 in Venice to encourage innovation, and the first copyright law appeared in 1709 in England. The French adopted a patent system in 1791. Patent and copyright laws of the United States were first passed in 1790, and U.S. trademark legislation dates to 1870. These laws have undergone various major revisions since their first inception, each time refining their definitions of what constitutes intellectual property. Modern U.S. patent law dates to 1952, and modern U.S. copyright law dates to 1976.

The degree to which intellectual property rights are recognized and protected has varied over time and across countries, and has always been subject to the pressures of advocates for and against intellectual property.[7] This is in part because once intellectual property has been created, the marginal cost of additional users is often close to zero, so that there is a short-run deadweight loss from protecting rights to existing intellectual property. However, the overall trend in intellectual property protection is broadly correlated with the rise of capitalism. In fact, some institutional features associated with capitalism had to exist prior to the full development of intellectual property rights, as we discuss later.

Economic Benefits of Intellectual Property

In the following, it is sometimes convenient to draw a distinction between patents and copyrights, on the one hand, and trademarks, on the other, as the former differ from the latter in important economic aspects.

Patents and copyrights are rights to the "products of the mind," and such rights are different from physical property rights in very elementary ways. If one subscribes to the natural rights theory of Locke, it is unclear whether it would support a right to intellectual property. On one hand, ideas, novels, or musical compositions are products of the mind, and if a man owns his mind as much he owns his body then it seems that, indeed, he would acquire property over what he conceives in his mind. On the other hand, ideas are vague and often conceived in similar form by many people. Because two persons cannot, independently of each other, have ownership over the same good, how can property be acquired over an idea that one conceives the day after it was conceived by somebody else? If one subscribes to utilitarian reasoning, then the justification of patents and copyrights as a means to welfare maximization faces a different challenge. Unlike most physical items, the goods protected by patents and copyrights are nonrivalrous: once used, they remain intact for further beneficial use. Protecting an idea as intellectual property therefore does not transform a commons into a private good (which is desirable, as we have argued) but a public good into a club good. Why, then, should utilitarian society create an institution that excludes individuals from the use of goods that can be produced in arbitrary quantities at no incremental cost?

The answer, quite obviously, is that it is not costless to create the first copy of an idea—even if additional copies can be produced at zero cost. The costs of creating intellectual goods include both tangible costs of research and development activities, as well as intangible effort and opportunity costs. The benefits include both their value as consumption goods and their value as inputs in production. Because the cost of creating intellectual goods is borne privately, the intellectual entrepreneur must be able to appropriate a sufficiently large fraction of the benefits created by his idea, otherwise he would be unwilling to incur the cost. Thus, patents and copyrights rights enable innovators to receive rewards for their efforts and thereby create innovation incentives. Granting ownership rights, including exclusive use rights, over "products of the mind" therefore serves a utilitarian role similar to ownership over physical resources: to encourage the efficient development of (intellectual) resources.

The story for trademarks is different and somewhat more subtle. Similar to patents and copyrights, trademarks facilitate the development of socially valuable intellectual resources. The intellectual resource in this case is the trademark owner's reputation, typically concerning a seller's reputation for the quality of his goods. Good reputations, which can be viewed as a form of informational capital, are costly to establish but privately and socially beneficial because they facilitate trade when sellers are privately informed about the quality of their goods (reputations can help overcome adverse selection). An important aspect of reputations is that a unique, distinguishable trademark can serve as a "sufficient statistic" for it, even if buyers have not observed the seller's past transaction history (see Tadelis, 1999). Thus, being able to exclude others from using one's trademark is essential to protect one's reputation from appropriation by others (i.e., imitators). Trademark protection thereby provides incentives to establish reputations in the first place.

Trade secrets are an additional form of intellectual property. These are useful when a product cannot be reverse-engineered, so that competitors cannot easily duplicate the idea. The advantage of a trade secret is that it does not expire, as does a patent. The disadvantage is that if a rival can determine the method of production, the originator of the item has no protection. Courts will recognize rights to trade secrets if owners take steps to protect them, as by having workers or others (e.g., potential acquirers of the firm) sign nondisclosure and noncompete contracts.[8]

Economic Policy toward Intellectual Property

Unlike property rights over physical goods (and also unlike trademarks), patents and copyrights have considerable social costs: the inefficiency that arises from granting the owner monopoly power over his property. Monopoly power arises because intellectual goods often cannot be perfectly substituted for one another.[9] Although monopoly creates rents that compensate the owner for his innovation costs, it also induces a deadweight loss. Thus, unlike physical property rights, patents and copyrights generally lead to an inefficient use of the intellectual resources they protect. Economists speak of a trade-off between static efficiency (the welfare loss) and dynamic efficiency (the innovation incentives), and patent/copyright policy can best be understood as an attempt to maximize welfare by achieving an optimal balance in this trade-off.

States have various tools available to fine-tune intellectual property rights to achieve this balance, for example, by limiting the lifespan of an intellectual property right, or regulating the owner's exercise of market power. The first economic analysis of optimal patent life span in Nordhaus (1969) and Scherer (1972), who show that patents should have a finite lifespan after which the owner's monopoly power ceases. In fact, intellectual property rights are typically not granted forever: in the United States, for example, patents are granted for twenty years while copyrights expire seventy years after the author's death.[10] The analysis by Nordhaus and

Scherer is extended in Klemperer (1990), Gilbert and Shapiro (1990), Tandon (1982), and others, who investigate what they call "patent breadth," that is, the degree to which owners can benefit from the patent during its life span. The result is that if it is possible to regulate the flow of profits the patent holder receives during the life span of his patent, then reducing this flow while increasing the life span (perhaps to infinity) is preferable.

Finally, there is some evidence that actual patent and copyright protection might offer too large rewards for the innovator and hence be suboptimal. Scherer (2006) summarizes a number of studies and reports that compulsory licensing, used as an antitrust instrument in the United States and Great Britain from the 1930s to 1960s, has had no negative impact on innovative activity in U.S. and British corporations, with the exception of the pharmaceutical sector. Burt and Lemley (2003) indicate that the "one-size-fits-all" approach to patents (the existence of one set of patent laws for all industries) is inefficient because different industries would benefit from different forms of patent protection.

Some Recent Developments

The institution of intellectual property continues to evolve, often driven by technological advances and frequently changing business practices and aspects of capitalism along the way. We briefly discuss two examples here.

The first is the issue of digital media, such as music and video files. In the late 1990s, the advent of the MP3 file format and the spread of fast Internet connections made it considerably less costly to obtain and distribute copies of copyrighted content. At the same time, it raised new legal issues, such as the question whether sharers or downloaders of illegally distributed content should be the ones prosecuted for intellectual property rights violations. In response to these challenges, the entertainment industry has responded with a mix of aggressive enforcement tactics (lawsuits against file-sharing college students), technological innovations to prevent unauthorized copying (Digital Rights Management), and new product offerings (unbundled content and a variety of subscription services).

The second issue is that of genetically modified plants, which the courts have considered intellectual property since the 1930 U.S. Plant Patent Act. Traditionally, genetic modification was performed through selective breeding, but it increasingly is done by directly manipulating an organism's DNA, a practice that requires considerable investments in research and technology. Growing crops from seed amounts to making copies of the seed material's genetic information, giving seed companies the right to interfere with the disposition of the harvest, as it embodies copies of their intellectual property. "Buying" seed material of genetically modified plants increasingly does not mean acquiring ownership of the seeds, but licensing intellectual property from seed companies. The licensing agreements of large seed companies, such as the Monsanto Corporation, include the provision to not save any fraction of the harvest, thereby changing traditional farming practices that have existed since the beginning of agriculture.[11]

Capitalism Creates Property

So far we have discussed the effect of property rights on capitalism. However, there is another dimension of the relationship between these constructs. That is, as capitalism advances, new types of property are created by capitalism itself.

Financial Instruments

The creation of new types of property by capitalism is most obvious with respect to financial instruments. We might view stocks and bonds as the essence of capitalism. But these financial instruments are novel forms of capital with novel sets of rights. While bonds are a form of debt instruments, an old form of wealth, stocks represent a new innovation associated with capitalism itself. Fundamentally, stocks enabled an individual to invest in an enterprise with limited risk and separate investments from management.

As capitalism has advanced, new and innovative forms of financial instruments have been created. For example, in his discussion of property rights, Rapaczynski (1996) identifies forms of property owned by wealthy individuals: "When one looks at the more 'propertied classes' of modern America, the intangibles become ever more prevalent and ever more esoteric: patents, futures, financial derivatives, tax shelters, mortgage-backed securities, junk bonds and instruments that only a few wizards understand."[12] These forms of property serve important economic functions (such as efficient allocation of risk), although as we have recently seen, they can be abused.

Intellectual Property

We already discussed intellectual property and its importance for innovation, entrepreneurial vitality, and growth in capitalist systems. Like various modern forms of capital and financial instruments, capitalism not only benefited from intellectual property rights but created these rights in the first place. This is not to say that intellectual achievements have not been made before capitalism, or that precapitalist societies have not used the intellectual outputs of their members, just that there was little need to protect this output from the appropriation of others. There are several reasons for this coevolution of capitalism and intellectual property, and we discuss two here.

First, the idea of exchanging goods for economic profit is important to understanding why and when intellectual property rights emerged. If goods are not produced and sold by profit-maximizing firms, then the reasons to undertake scientific inquiry could not have included the motive of deriving a monetary profit. Hence there seems to be little need for a patent system in this situation. Similarly, the need for copyright protection for works of art and literature depends on whether such works are routinely bought and sold on markets for profit. Throughout most of history, these goods flourished as religious or spiritual artifacts, as part of common folklore, or were the leisurely realm of the feudal classes, but they were not produced by an entertainment industry. Thus, the concept of a copyright did not develop until a commercial need for it arose.

A second reason is that the enforcement of intellectual property rights requires a more sophisticated legal system than what is needed to protect physical property rights, as well as greater effort on the part of the state to police these rights. Although physical property can, in principle, be defended by the owner (or a group of owners) against being taken, the same is not true for intellectual property. Intellectual property requires more elaborate systems for registering these rights, as well as a sophisticated judicial framework to deal with disputes. The act of "stealing" someone else's intellectual property is not easily observable, and proving that it happened requires, among other things, proving that the "owner" either created the property or otherwise legally procured it from its previous owner. Again, it is unlikely that societies would develop this kind of sophistication unless capitalist institutions existed in which intellectual property would be valuable.

From these examples, we can see that capitalism does not merely use existing property rights efficiently. An equally (if not more) important function is the actual creation of property rights of all sorts. These rights—some of them beyond imagination only a few decades ago—are not created by government but by markets themselves, and more particularly by capitalistic markets. The relationship between capitalism and its institutions is therefore an organic relationship, characterized by the coevolution of capitalist economies and the institutions of capitalism, such as property.

Notes

1. An exception will be in the section Property Rights Can Resolve Conflicts, where we include more general entitlements in our discussion.
2. For empirical studies of community governance, see, for example, Ostrom (1990) and De Alessi (2003).
3. If governance costs are too high across forms of governance, it may well be efficient to *not* govern a resource. See, for example, Eggertsson (2003).
4. See the section Some Recent Developments and the conclusion.
5. In the extreme opposite to Coase's ideal (a Hobbesian world), conflicts are over the *possession* of assets, but possession is the same as ownership in this case. These conflicts are resolved by strength alone, which means by violence or at least the threat of violence. Though conflicts need not necessarily arise (Skaperdas, 1992), the closer the environment is to the Hobbesian world, the more likely is it that conflicts are resolved violently.
6. There are certain qualifications. For example, a trademark cannot be sold under U.S. law without at the same time selling the production process to which the trademark applies (that is, empty trademark sales are not allowed). For a discussion of U.S. and international law in this regard, and an economic analysis of empty trademark sales, see Marvel and Ye (2008).

7. See Machlup (1958), Scherer (2006).
8. Noncompete agreements (sometimes called covenants not to compete) with workers serve an additional function. These exist when an employee obtains some "general human capital" (Becker, 1975) that is too valuable to be paid for by accepting reduced wages (Rubin and Shedd, 1981). Then a contract not to use the human capital for another firm is an important way of protecting this capital and therefore providing incentives to create it.
9. For example, if a person owns a car we do not consider him a monopolist owner, as there are many other persons owning similar cars. A pharmaceutical company owning the patent to a certain drug, on the other hand, derives considerable market power from this property right if competitors' drugs are only imperfect substitutes of the one in question.
10. There are exceptions. Copyrights to pseudonymous or commissioned works expire 95 years after publication or 120 years after creation, whichever comes first; design patents expire after 14 years instead of 20 years. In any case, as Machlup (1958, pp. 9–10) notes, patent and copyright life spans are usually not derived from economic analysis, but from political considerations.
11. A recent technological advance, the so-called terminator genes, circumvent enforcement problems of seed licensing by making the patented traits unavailable in all copies.
12. This was written in 1996, before many more modern forms of "instruments that only a few wizards understand" were created, and before this lack of understanding caused our current severe problems.

References

Aristotle. *The Politics*. London: Penguin Books, 1981.

Bailey, Martin J. "Approximate Optimality of Aboriginal Property Rights." *Journal of Law and Economics* 35 (April 1992): 183–198.

Becker, Gary S. *Human Capital: A Theoretical and Empirical Analysis, with Special Reference to Education*, 2nd ed. Cambridge, Mass.: National Bureau of Economic Research, 1975.

Bentham, Jeremy. *The Theory of Legislation*. London: Oxford University Press, 1914.

Burt, Dan L., and Mark A. Lemley. "Policy Levers in Patent Law." *Virginia Law Review* 89 (2003): 1575–1630.

Coase, Ronald H. "The Problem of Social Cost." *Journal of Law and Economics* 3 (Oct. 1960): 1–44.

De Alessi, Louis. "Gains from Private Property: The Empirical Evidence." In *Property Rights: Cooperation, Conflict, and Law*, ed. Terry Anderson and Fred McChesney, 90–112. Princeton, N.J.: Princeton University Press, 2003.

Eggertsson, Thráinn. "Open Access versus Common Property." In *Property Rights: Cooperation, Conflict, and Law*, ed. Terry Anderson and Fred McChesney, 73–89. Princeton, N.J.: Princeton University Press, 2003.

Gilbert, Richard, and Carl Shapiro. "Optimal Patent Length and Breadth." *RAND Journal of Economics* 21 (Spring 1990): 106–112.

Grossman, Sanford, and Oliver Hart. "The Costs and Benefits of Ownership: A Theory of Vertical and Lateral Integration." *Journal of Political Economy* 94 (Aug. 1986): 691–719.

Hardin, Garrett. "The Tragedy of the Commons." *Science* 162, 3859 (Dec. 1968): 1243–1248.

Hobbes, Thomas. *Leviathan.* 1651; London: Penguin Books, 1968.
Hume, David. *An Enquiry Concerning the Principles of Morals.* 1748; Oxford: Oxford University Press, 1902.
Jones, Charles I. "Was an Industrial Revolution Inevitable? Economic Growth over the Very Long Run." *Advances in Macroeconomics* 1 (2) (2001): article 1.
Klemperer, Paul. "How Broad Should the Scope of Patent Protection Be?" *RAND Journal of Economics* 21 (Spring 1990): 113–130.
Locke, John. *Two Treatises of Government.* 1689; Cambridge: Cambridge University Press, 1960.
Machlup, Fritz. *An Economic Review of the Patent System. Study of the Subcommittee on Patents, Trademarks, and Copyrights.* 85th Congress of the United States, Senate Committee on the Judiciary, Study no. 15, 1958.
Marvel, Howard, and Lixin Ye. "Trademark Sales, Entry, and the Value of Reputation." *International Economic Review* 49 (May 2008): 547–576.
Mill, John Stewart. *Principles of Political Economy.* London: Longmans, Green, 1848.
Nordhaus, William. *Invention, Growth, and Welfare: A Theoretical Treatment of Technological Change.* Cambridge, Mass.: MIT Press, 1969.
Ostrom, Elinor. *Governing the Commons: The Evolution of Institutions for Collective Action.* Cambridge: Cambridge University Press, 1990.
Plato. *The Republic.* Translated by H. D. P. Lee. London: Penguin Books, 1955.
Rapaczynski, Andrzej. "The Roles of the State and the Market in Establishing Property Rights." *Journal of Economic Perspectives* 10 (Spring 1996): 87–103.
Ridley, Matt. *The Origins of Virtue: Human Instincts and the Evolution of Cooperation.* New York: Penguin Books, 1998.
Rubin, Paul. *Darwinian Politics: The Evolutionary Origin of Freedom.* New Brunswick, N.J.: Rutgers University Press, 2002.
Rubin, Paul, and Peter Shedd. "Human Capital and Covenants Not to Compete." *Journal of Legal Studies* 10 (Jan. 1981): 93–110.
Scherer, Frederic. "Nordhaus' Theory of Optimal Patent Life: A Geometric Reinterpretation." *American Economic Review* 62 (June 1972): 422–427.
Scherer, Frederic. "The Political Economy of Patent Reform in the United States." Working Paper, Harvard University, 2006; revised version RWP07-042, 2007.
Schumpeter, Joseph A. *Capitalism, Socialism and Democracy.* 1942; New York: Harper, 1975.
Skaperdas, Stergios. "Cooperation, Conflict, and Power in the Absence of Property Rights." *American Economic Review* 82 (Sept. 1992): 720–739.
Smith, Adam. *The Wealth of Nations.* 1776; London: Penguin Books, 1970.
Smith, Adam. *Lectures on Justice, Police, Revenue and Arms.* Oxford: Clarendon Press, 1896.
Tadelis, Steven. "What's in a Name? Reputation as a Tradeable Asset." *American Economic Review* 89 (June 1999): 548–563.
Tandon, Pankaj. "Optimal Patents with Compulsory Licensing." *Journal of Political Economy* 90 (June 1982): 470–486.

CHAPTER 8

MANAGEMENT AND GOVERNANCE OF THE BUSINESS ENTERPRISE: AGENCY, CONTRACTING, AND CAPABILITIES PERSPECTIVES

DAVID J. TEECE

THE modern business enterprise, by which I mean, for purposes of this chapter, the modern corporation (see appendix), is both praised and criticized in contemporary Western society. To some, it is the means by which value- and productivity-enhancing innovations are made available to the general public. To others, it seeks only profits, engages in financial shenanigans, pollutes the environment, and denies workers their proper wages. There is also every shade in between, and some observers maintain both positions simultaneously.

Disparate views of the corporation and its management stem in part from political beliefs; they also arise from the absence of a deep understanding by the public and policy makers of what managers do. The economics profession is partially to blame; academic economists often assume away the key functions of top management when crafting theories of the firm and theories of market organization. Not surprisingly, this leads to misunderstandings and misapprehensions about the corporation and its managers.

The purpose here is to contrast three views or paradigms of the business enterprise and of critical management issues regarding governance. The first two are the agency and contracting paradigms.[1] These dominate most discussion of the governance of corporate activities (see Shleifer and Vishny, 1997, for a review). The third is the capabilities perspective, which is starting to gain attention in the literature (e.g., Sautet, 2000). The differences between these paradigms have important public policy ramifications. Juxtaposing them can help illuminate the befuddling debates about the role of management and the business enterprise in society and about the appropriate degree of regulation and oversight that should be imposed on managers and the corporation.

For the purpose at hand, it is important to have a theory of the business enterprise that is not so abstract that it assumes away a role for management. Any theory crafted so abstractly will fail to enlighten public policy issues involving business behavior, the role of management, and the corporation. How one characterizes the fundamental nature of the enterprise, and the economic function of management, is likely to have a significant impact on how one interprets and assesses business behavior.

In the agency and contracting perspectives, the enterprise is little more than a web of (in some cases implicit) contracts in which the key choice variables are the incentives for and monitoring of performance by management as required by shareholders. In these perspectives, firms are in the business of providing ordinary goods and services. These approaches to economic activity downplay or ignore the central economic function of firms and managers, namely, the entrepreneurial development of new products and services.

Another view, the capabilities perspective, sees the enterprise as clusters of specific complementary—often cospecialized—assets that must be orchestrated to achieve efficiencies and turn knowledge into value for shareholders, customers, and society. The asset creation and orchestration skills of management are vital in this perspective because organizational assets are idiosyncratic and must be built over time. Such assets, many of which are embedded in the routines and culture of the enterprise, must also constantly be renewed if the enterprise is to remain competitive. Moreover, the firm's (organizational) assets must be used in conjunction with a wide range of external assets owned and operated by complementors and, in some cases, competitors. This is a gigantic coordination task in which both managers and markets play key roles.

The coordinating role of markets is now well understood. Hayek (1944) extolled the almost miraculous functioning of the price system, as did Adam Smith before him. However, the market's "invisible hand," as Smith (1776, Book IV, chapter 2) called it, turns out, under closer scrutiny, to also involve the hands of many managers performing indispensable entrepreneurial and operational roles. This latter perspective is often ignored.

The agency, contracting, and capabilities perspectives clearly differ deeply with respect to the societal role the top management team plays in the private enterprise system.

In the closely affiliated agency and contracting perspectives (which are treated as separate for most of this chapter), the management team is viewed as self-seeking, self-aggrandizing, and opportunistic on behalf of both themselves and the enterprise. According to this school of thought, earning a profit is quite incidental to management's true goals. Baser managerial instincts can only be kept in check by good governance and plenty of competition. To offset the frailties and self-interest of professional managers, the scope for managerial discretion should be limited and decisions carefully reviewed. Debt is seen as good because it clips management's wings by committing cash to the servicing of debt, thereby limiting reinvestment flexibility. The effect of a high debt-to-equity ratio is to foil the natural proclivity of managers to grow the enterprise merely to enhance their own power and pay.

The capabilities perspective, in contrast, views the management team as not without self-interest, but the team nonetheless performs critical functions that markets are unable to perform. In particular, management has an essential role in building and maintaining organizational capabilities and achieving continuous renewal. Management also makes critical investment decisions and sets strategic goals. The quality of these decisions shapes enterprise performance.

In the capabilities perspective, the primary governance challenges are not about solving moral hazard problems and guarding against opportunism, although these are important. Rather, management's critical role involves sensing opportunities, seizing them, and protecting profit streams (against appropriation by competitors). Management must also be able to transform the company as technology, consumer desires, and competitors change. The role of good governance by the board of directors is to make sure that capable CEOs are selected carefully and perform well. Agency issues are of second-order importance.

These three schools of thought rarely join each other in the scholarly literature. Jensen and Meckling (1976) and Williamson (1975, 1985a) are representative of the agency and contracting perspectives, respectively. Agency and contracting theories have both been developed extensively in the economics and finance literatures. The capabilities perspective is sometimes only implicit and resides primarily in the business history and strategic management literatures. It is most clearly articulated in Chandler (1990b), Teece et al. (1990, 1997), and Teece (2007).

This chapter endeavors to assess and, to the extent possible, reconcile these paradigms. Insights from all three need to be employed to develop an adequate understanding of corporate governance issues. Corporate governance, as defined here, embraces not just issues around how managers are held in check by internal and external constraints; in the broadest sense, it also involves how economic activity is organized, including whether activities are governed by market processes (such as competition) or by internal controls and management. This is admittedly a broader (economic) definition of governance than might be suggested by legal texts. A broader approach is necessary because an understanding of the fundamental problems of organizing economic activity is necessary before the design of corporate board-level structures can be discussed.

The Agency Perspective on Management and Governance

The widely employed agency approach to governance is an application of principal-agent theory (Ross, 1973), which focuses on monitoring and performance issues in an environment of information asymmetry and uncertainty. It has currency in the economics literature as well as in finance.

The agency approach views the firm as "a nexus for a set of contracting relationships among individuals" (Jensen and Meckling, 1976, p. 311) but focuses narrowly on conflicts of interest. Relevant principal-agent pairs include shareholders and managers, debtholders and shareholders, and managers and employees. Agency theory has also been applied in marketing, organizational behavior, and other settings (Eisenhardt, 1989), but its dominance of the finance literature is of primary concern here.

Jensen and Meckling (1976) set the tone for their financial approach to the enterprise by arguing that the ownership structure of the corporation (insider shareholders, external shareholders, and bondholders) was determined by optimizing among the related agency costs, which include monitoring, bonding, and the loss that is assumed to result from the separation of ownership and management control. Jensen (1989) has taken the argument further by suggesting that public ownership will give way over time to the lower agency costs of private equity.

Jensen claims that "many problems associated with the inadequacy of the current theory of the firm can also be viewed as special cases of the theory of agency relationships" (2000, p. 85). Agency costs are about shirking and the monitoring of team production (as in Alchian and Demsetz, 1972) as well as problems associated with the separation of ownership from control.

Much of Jensen's analysis is centered around how agency issues impact the capital structure (debt versus equity, as well as the fraction of equity held by managers) of the business enterprise. Agency costs reflect not only monitoring costs but also statutory and common law issues, plus human ingenuity in devising contracts (2000, p. 135). Jensen and Meckling define agency costs as the sum of out-of-pocket costs (for both owner and manager) of structuring, administering, guaranteeing, and enforcing contracts plus the "residual loss" (1976, p. 308). The residual loss is the dollar equivalent of the reduction in welfare experienced by the "principal" (owner) as a result of the divergence of interests with the "agent" (manager).

The underlying theme in Jensen's view is that the main problem for organizing and governance is one of agency. Managers undertake negative-value projects, fail to downsize, and spend too much on wasteful R&D. His implicit assumption is that lackluster performance could be remedied if it weren't for bad governance and the "failure of control" (2000, chapter 2).

Though there is some truth to these propositions, Jensen largely ignores the roles of entrepreneurship, innovation, and capabilities. The agency literature completely fails to provide any understanding of how firms first generate the cash flows that wayward managers and boards then supposedly dissipate.

An implication of agency theory is that firm performance will vary positively with the degree of management ownership of the firm. Empirical research on this point using cross-sectional data has failed to find a robust relationship, linear or otherwise (Demsetz and Villalonga, 2001). Agency theory has received somewhat better support from a study comparing firm performance to the presence of governance measures that favor either management or shareholders. This study (Core et al., 2006) found evidence that management-friendly governance leads to lower operating performance.

Transaction Costs and the Contracting View on Management and Governance

A substantial literature that is both competing with, and in part complementary to, agency theory has emerged since Ronald Coase's classic (1937) article, "The Nature of the Firm." It stresses the relative efficiencies of firms and markets. Factors that amplify transaction costs and other frictions associated with relying on markets to organize economic activity (as compared to organizing activities inside the firm) are of central concern. This literature, significantly energized by Nobel Prize Laureate Oliver Williamson (1975, 1985a) and others, has come to be known as transaction cost economics (TCE). It analyzes the relative efficiencies of governance modes: markets and internal organization, as well as intermediate forms of organization such as strategic alliances. Agency problems are not at the core of the organization's issues, as they tend to be with the Jensen-Meckling paradigm discussed in the previous section.[2] Rather, problems associated with incomplete contracts and "lock-in" are given center stage.

The TCE approach views the firm as a collection of bilateral contracts between the firm and each of its constituent parts (Williamson, 1975, 1985b). From this contracting perspective, the chief objective of the firm and its managers is to minimize the combined total of production and transaction costs (Williamson, 1991). Agency costs are decidedly secondary. Firm boundary issues in particular are best understood through the lens of transaction costs (Williamson, 1975, 1985a; Teece, 1986).

As noted, the contracting approach to organizations has its roots in Coase. Coase hypothesized that the boundaries of the firm are determined by bringing transactions inside the firm up to the point where the cost of internally organizing the marginal transaction (assumed to rise with the number of transactions) is equilibrated with the cost of conducting the transaction in the market. The relative costs of organizing transactions across a market (if one exists) or inside a firm explain why some transactions are handled via the price mechanism and others are handled within a managerial hierarchy. The key insight is that there are costs associated with performing market-based transactions including "discovering what the relevant prices are" and "the costs of negotiating" (1937, pp. 390–391).

Williamson took Coase's insights and expanded them into the TCE framework. Two key behavioral assumptions underlie TCE: (1) bounded rationality (economic actors, including managers, are assumed limited to some extent in both access to information and their ability to analyze it fully) and (2) opportunism (economic actors are assumed willing to pursue their own interests to the point of taking advantage of others, particularly when circumstances change and contractual ambiguities arise).

The key characteristics of economic activity that yield managerial/organizational implications in the TCE framework are not agency costs but the transaction costs associated with the asset specificity of investments. "Specificity" is the extent to which capital that must be deployed to fulfill a contract is specialized to the transaction such that some or all of its value is lost when business partners/suppliers are switched. Asset specificity concerns do not exist when the value of physical, human, or locational assets would not decline if they were redeployed to their next best uses.

The presence of high asset specificity on either or both sides of a transaction, when combined with the assumption of opportunism, opens up exposed parties to unfavorable ex post recontracting hazards because options become more limited once transaction-specific capital is deployed and before it is fully amortized. Considerable loss of value (expropriation) by one or more parties to the transaction is possible and must be guarded against when managerial choices with respect to organizational design are made. The focal problem is not managers taking advantage of shareholders; it is that one group of shareholders (enterprise A) can take advantage of another (say, enterprise B) when transaction-specific (nonredeployable) assets have to be put in place (or emerge over time) to support efficient production.

In short, the potential for contractual hazards associated with asset specificity and the resultant transactional difficulties lie at the heart of the relative efficiency calculus in TCE. When investment in specific assets is needed to support efficient production, then the preferred organizational mode is internal organization (e.g., vertical integration). Internal organization minimizes exposure to the hazards of opportunistic recontracting and allows more flexible adaptation (Williamson, 1975, 1985a). Empirical work (e.g., Monteverde and Teece, 1982; Masten, 1984) shows that TCE has statistically significant validity.

The contracting perspective carries implications for corporate governance, too. Boards of directors shouldn't be populated by independents but by stakeholders who are making specific coinvestments to support the enterprise and who might not otherwise have the prospect of adequate safeguards (Williamson, 1985a, chapter 12). Besides shareholders, these stakeholders might include important suppliers or even groups of employees who would lose value if the firm does not fully honor (or might endeavor to wriggle out of) its contractual (and other) commitments. Board composition is discussed more later.

Williamson (1988) provides a detailed account of the commonalities and differences of TCE and agency theory. The behavioral assumptions (bounded rationality, opportunism, and risk neutrality) are similar, but agency theory places greater emphasis on the need to control against opportunism. Whereas agency theory emphasizes incentive design to minimize agency costs, TCE is focused on governance structures that minimize transactions costs. Agency theory also tends to ignore dispute resolution mechanisms and internal organizational design issues that TCE encompasses.

The Capabilities View on Management and Governance

A very different approach to the firm is known as the capabilities perspective. Although it has its roots in industrial economics and, to some degree, in evolutionary economics (Penrose, 1959; Nelson and Winter, 1982; Teece, 1982), it was advanced with vigor within the management field beginning in the 1980s (Teece 1980b, 1982, 1984). The core concept is that companies derive unique advantages from the possession and coordination of resources/assets that are difficult to imitate (and difficult to trade and transfer). These resources/assets accumulate and evolve over time (Dierickx and Cool, 1989), and analyses of the management of this process gave rise to a theory of dynamic capabilities (Teece et al., 1990, 1997; Teece and Pisano, 1994; Teece, 2007).

Somewhat in parallel, a resource-based theory of the firm evolved from the work of Wernerfelt (1984) and Barney (1986). Implicitly using efficient market theory, Barney argued that firms will not be able to achieve competitive advantage in product markets if they must bid against each other in perfect factor markets because they will drive up the factor prices to levels that eliminate product market profits.

Building on transaction cost theory, Teece et al. (1990, 1997) pointed out that (factor) markets for knowhow and other intangibles are anything but perfect so that the ownership of intangible factors can serve as a basis for competitive advantage. In fact, factor markets for intangible assets are generally riddled with "imperfections." This is the kernel around which the capabilities framework developed. The fundamental problem of organization is then a problem of managing intangible assets, which require appropriate governance structures (and management) for the facilitation of their creation, protection, and orchestration.

One market imperfection that complicates organization is that property rights over intangible assets are likely to have fuzzy boundaries, whereas markets work best with clear property rights. Another complication is that the value of intangible assets is highly context-dependent (Teece, 2000). As a result, there is unlikely to be a well-developed market for intangible assets; in fact, trade secrets and the like are typically not traded at all. Internal organization and associated managerial processes are needed to compensate for these "deficiencies" in the market. This is a critical raison d'être for management.

Put another way, specific assets (resources), the most interesting and important of which are intangible, are difficult to transact in because their alternative uses are limited (or nonexistent). Competitive advantage built on such assets is therefore likely to be more sustainable. Management is essential for guiding the development and orchestration of such intangibles.

Asset specificity arises for a variety of reasons, one of which is what Williamson calls "the fundamental transformation" (1985a, p. 61). This occurs when irreversibilities exist after specialized assets have been deployed and cannot be repurposed at low cost.

Another, and potentially more important, category is that of organizational capabilities.[3] These are usually underpinned by both organizational processes/routines and various types of equipment. Routines represent distinct bundles of formal and informal problem-solving approaches and skills. Capabilities cannot generally be bought because there is no marketplace where they are traded. This fact accounts for heterogeneity among firms. As a result, firms develop along path-dependent trajectories.

Because markets and opportunities don't always evolve smoothly or predictably, it is necessary for management to continuously analyze shifting opportunities and reconfigure the firm's assets and activities. Dynamic capabilities reflect the firm's ability to orchestrate, build, and reconfigure internal and external competences and other assets/resources to address and shape changing business environments (Teece et al., 1990, 1997; Teece, 2009). The orchestration of nontradable intangible assets so as to first generate and then capture value is the fundamental economic problem that management confronts. Absent successfully meeting this challenge, there are no profits to worry about protecting and no agency or transaction costs that matter.

Clearly, the dynamic capabilities view of the enterprise sees the economic and governance challenges quite differently from agency theory and TCE. The agency and TCE approaches both assume implicitly that capabilities exist, are operationalized, and are already generating income. The dynamic capabilities approach recognizes that the economic challenge for corporate decision makers is, in part, to discern what customers want and how technology can be developed and/or harnessed to satisfy those wants; to devise a means of profiting from doing so; and to create or build assets that cannot be bought. As noted, Barney (1986) pointed out that resorting to "factor markets" alone to buy what's needed is not generally a good basis for building value. It is a fool's errand in the sense that one ends up with only competitive returns; competitive differentiation cannot be based solely on factors obtained in a market. The problems of (profitably) organizing activity inside the firm are thus considerable. Enormous value can be created by management if this task is done well.

The governance implications of this view of the world are, not surprisingly, quite different from the other approaches. Agency issues and the abuse of "management discretion" are second-order problems in the dynamic capabilities framework. Indeed, management "discretion," if defined as the freedom to orchestrate, act, and operate within board mandates, is the distinctive (and beneficial) feature of the enterprise. Investment in promising projects, reinvestment in existing profitable activities, and building enterprise capabilities—if achieved in a timely fashion—can enable an enterprise to outdistance its rivals even in the face of modest agency and transaction costs.

The Boundaries of the Firm: Reconciling the Transaction Costs and Capabilities Perspectives

The transaction cost and capabilities views of the firm, both of which were developed to correct gaps in mainstream economic theory, address different aspects of organization and different levels of analysis (Williamson, 1999). As such, they can serve a complementary purpose for analyzing one of the fundamental theoretical questions in the study of the business enterprise: what determines the division between activities that are managed internally and those that are arranged via the market? This is both an organizational and a "governance" question.[4] Each is explored in terms of how they inform firm boundary choice (i.e., insourcing and outsourcing) decisions.

The growing range of potential suppliers in the global economy both expands and complicates management's location and outsourcing choices—where and by whom activities from R&D to after-sales service are to be performed. The commoditization of numerous services such as back office operations (e.g., testing, telemarketing, benefits management, record keeping, and IT management) has greatly enlarged the menu of make-or-buy options facing a firm and heightens the need to have a theory that can predict the boundaries of firms (i.e., what they accomplish internally rather than through contracts or alliances).

The agency perspective has little to say about the factors that determine the specific boundaries of the firm; it is also silent on vertical integration. But issues of organizational design, including which activities to outsource and which to perform inside the firm, are among the more significant business model choices facing management. These decisions affect the architecture of the firm and the "governance" of activities in the TCE sense, that is, whether each activity is "governed" by market processes or from within a managerial hierarchy. These firm boundary issues are the focus of this section.

TCE and Firm Boundaries

The vertical integration of activities (i.e., sourcing in-house) can bring advantages. It has long been recognized that technological interdependence of the stages of production (e.g., thermal efficiencies between iron and steel production) can make a functionally integrated structure more cost-effective than separate organizations. However, many such savings can be captured by contract. The question is when a purely contractual relationship is inadequate, especially since choosing vertical integration entails many potential drawbacks, including commitment to internal supplies that may turn out to be relatively high-cost, bureaucratized decision making, weak alignment of employee incentives with firm performance, weak alignment of manager incentives with owner interests (i.e., agency costs), and organizational myopia (Williamson, 1985a, chapter 6; Teece, 1996).

Williamson (1975) showed that it wasn't technological interdependence per se that explained vertical integration; rather, it was the reduction of transaction (contracting) costs. Vertical integration can also bring informational advantages that the economic theory of the firm has not yet fully appreciated (Teece, 2007). One example is the ability to promote a "convergence of expectations" (Malmgren, 1961) with respect to investment decisions upstream and downstream.[5]

Convergence of expectations, and coordination more generally, are of greatest concern when a product's architecture is systemic (Teece, 1988). Systemic architectures require harmonized action among many development groups (e.g., a next-generation communications standard requires, at a minimum, coordinated development of network infrastructure, terminal devices, and applications). Perhaps underestimating the importance of such interdependencies, Boeing discovered hidden costs when it decided to rely on a global array of suppliers to develop parts and subsystems for its new 787 Dreamliner. Unfortunately, some suppliers lacked the experience to develop parts of the necessary quality; and Boeing, having also cut back its monitoring capability, discovered this too late, resulting in years of delay (Michaels and Sanders, 2009). It is not clear, from the perspective of theory, whether this is best viewed as a contracting problem or a capabilities issue.

From a contracting perspective, the insourcing/outsourcing choice is a matter of making sure that internal governance costs are lower/higher than (asset specificity-driven) transaction costs—other things equal. But other things are often not equal. Internal production costs (which are typically not considered in the contracting framework) and "appropriability" conditions may depend endogenously on the "governance" mode, as the Boeing example suggests. Such factors receive more attention in the dynamic capabilities framework.

Capabilities, Appropriability, and Firm Boundaries

It is often the case that Contracting and Capabilities considerations work together in explaining economic decisions, including business model and organization design questions. Integration of the two perspectives in this way occurs in the profiting from innovation (PFI) framework (Teece, 1986). This framework helps explain how imperfections in knowledge markets and the specificity of complementary assets work together to indicate when internal governance (vertical integration) may be preferred over market transactions (such as outward technology licensing) to profitably bring new products and services to market.

The PFI framework combines insights not only from the contracting and capabilities perspectives but also from the appropriability literature (see, e.g., Jacobides et al., 2006).[6] Although it is not in itself a full-fledged theory of firm boundaries, it provides a comprehensive framework that addresses the make-or-buy question prescriptively from the viewpoint of an innovating firm preparing to enter a market.[7] It also helps explain how firms overcome the "public goods" nature of innovation and associated appropriability problems.

An innovation that a firm is bringing to market will invariably require a range of complementary goods to provide value to customers. If these complements are to be produced internally, the firm must have (or build, if there's enough time) the necessary underlying capabilities.

Taking the hypothetical case of the design for a new handheld wireless device, the complements for the design of the device (the focal innovation) include the components needed for manufacture, the existing technologies for which licenses are required, manufacturing services, one or more networks on which the device will function, distribution, and retail facilities. Depending on the type of device, it might also need software applications and/or accessories such as carrying cases.

The owner of the focal innovation must choose between internal and external provision of these complementary products and services, and the PFI framework provides guidance in this. The PFI framework highlights strategic considerations around appropriability, that is, figuring out where to position the firm in the value chain to capture the most profits. The general rule is to figure out which parts of the value chain will become bottlenecks, own those, and forget about the rest.

From the contracting perspective, PFI considers the degree of asset specificity and risk of hold-up from a potential complementor. If the complement is cospecialized with the focal innovation (i.e., there is bilateral asset specificity), then there is a risk of value leakage if the good or service is procured externally. A similar logic applies when the market for the supply of the complement is not highly competitive. In other cases, where there is no bottleneck, procuring the complement through arm's-length or relational contracting is indicated.

Of course these theoretical concerns are not always followed in practice. A case in point was the choice of an operating system for the original IBM personal computer (PC). From a contracting perspective, the PC hardware and its operating system would be cospecialized and therefore should be integrated. From the capabilities perspective, the capabilities required to write an operating system for a new microprocessor like the sixteen-bit Intel 8088 were scarce in 1980, and IBM had world-class software capabilities, which again would have suggested an integration strategy. In reality, however, IBM was in too great a hurry for its first PC to reach the market to develop a new operating system internally. It contracted with Microsoft instead, perhaps counting on its own brand assets to offset the influence of its complementor. The IBM PC was a huge success in volume terms, but Microsoft ultimately ended up capturing more value from it than IBM.

Dynamic Capability Considerations and Firm Boundaries

As the IBM-Microsoft example suggests, there are also important dynamic considerations in choosing the boundaries of the firm. Without drifting too far into strategic considerations, a few are worth mentioning. The contracting perspective presents "the fundamental transformation" in which one among a number of bidders for a contract can become an exclusive supplier with greater bargaining power once the contract is awarded (Williamson, 1985a, chapter 2).

The capabilities perspective recognizes a broader set of hazards relating to a potential loss of control over future developments. A monopolistic supplier who is integrated downstream (i.e., potentially competing with the focal firm) can, for example, exclude others from immediate access to new knowledge that will create future possibilities for technological progress. The supplier's ability to pace, direct, control, and guard the development of new capabilities is a hazard to the buyer that arises in this context.

The software industry provides an illustration of how an integrated firm can pace technological development downstream. Microsoft develops its operating systems in house. It develops some applications while also looking to others to provide additional applications that will enhance the value of the operating system. The independent application designers rely on Microsoft's Windows to run their applications, and Windows acts as a constraint on some of the technological features of the downstream application (e.g., through protocols for data exchange). Microsoft's ability to pace the evolution of the operating system and its ability to use this upstream technology in its own application software helped it become one of the dominant players in applications.

TCE would posit that such hazards can best be understood as contracting issues. However, one can question whether transaction costs and recontracting hazards are always the core issues; rather, it is often the case that outsourcing leads to the denial of opportunities to learn and accumulate critical capabilities important to the firm's future product development. Theoretically, contracts might be written that would require royalty-free grantbacks of any trade secrets accumulated, which would capture external learning. However, such arrangements are rare, in part because they are difficult to negotiate and hard to enforce.

Selected Internal Governance and Control Issues

Governance issues are also implicated in the selection of internal processes, structures, and controls employed inside the business organization. The agency, contracting, and capabilities perspectives each have something to say.

Multidivisional Management and Managerial Discretion

Most large businesses today are managed as multidivisional operations in which product-centered business units have profit-and-loss responsibility for the complete value chain from suppliers to the customer, usually for a specific market or cluster of markets. These business units are overseen by a central office that monitors the business units, selects divisional top management, provides general administrative functions, allocates resources, and sets the overall direction of the enterprise and its divisions.

Prior to the multidivisional structure, which began to appear in the United States during the 1920s (Chandler, 1977), large corporations were managed entirely from a central office that bore responsibility for all operational details. This centralized structure became unwieldy in large firms because top management was too bogged down with operational issues to develop longer term plans.

By separating the central office from operations, the multidivisional form of management allows top management to focus on the overall performance of the organization, rather than becoming absorbed in the affairs of the functional parts. Empirical tests verified that adoption of the multidivisional form was associated with improved enterprise performance, at least temporarily (Armour and Teece, 1978; Steer and Cable, 1978; Teece, 1981). Nevertheless, it took decades for the multidivisional form to become widely adopted (Teece, 1980a).

This is an area in which the contracting and capabilities perspectives lead to similar conclusions. Williamson (1975, 1991) has described the multidivisional form of corporate organization as a means of better allocating corporate capital relative to a unitary, functionally divided organization because it allows market information to receive timely attention from management. This can lead to greater organizational agility and responsiveness. Divisional managers then compete for resources in what Williamson (1975) called a "miniature capital market," with potential gains in efficiency (relative to market-based transactions) deriving from the superior depth of management's knowledge of the firm's opportunities compared to the knowledge of investors and bankers.[8]

From the capabilities perspective, the multidivisional structure permits a more efficient allocation of capital resources. Chandler (1962, chapter 6) showed that diversification into new product lines was facilitated by the multidivisional structure because it eliminated the added operational burden that would have fallen to general managers in a unitary structure. More generally, the separation of central and divisional management facilitates the periodic reconfiguration of the firm's resources. This is a key element of dynamic capabilities (Teece et al., 1990, 1997; Teece, 2007).

Capabilities-based analyses allow room to ascribe positive motives to management. Managers are seen as having the potential to build enterprise value and stockholder wealth through the creation and orchestration of intangible assets. Disappointingly, the agency perspective, introduced earlier, emphasizes managerial opportunism and little else. This arguably promotes a cynical view with respect to management motives. It denies any (positive) role for entrepreneurship, leadership, or building corporate cultures and internal structures. In that regard, the agency perspective is quite deficient. It is also rather tired.

Indeed, it was nearly a century ago that Berle and Means (1932) voiced concerns about the potential for misallocation of resources by nonowner managers stemming from the gap between ownership and control. As a result, many accounts of industrial management (prior to Alfred Chandler's business histories) have been dominated by debate over the moral character of business leaders as "robber barons" or "industrial statesmen" (John, 1997). Berle and Means focused the debate less on the role of the corporation vis-à-vis society and more on the role of managers vis-à-vis shareholders.

However, Chandler's carefully documented accounts (1962, 1977) of how large industrial business firms helped make the benefits of technology available to consumers everywhere somewhat blunted the earlier obsession in the literature with agency issues. Still, Chandler's view of management as responding "to the needs and opportunities of changing technologies and markets" (1969, p. 279), was far from universally embraced. This is an unfortunate consequence of the neglect of history in contemporary business and economic studies.

Indeed, a number of analyses during the 1960s, including Williamson (1964), Marris (1964), Monsen and Downs (1965), and Baumol (1967), expanded, and to some extent obsessed, on the Berle and Means theme of managerial conflicts with respect to shareholders. This literature stressed managerial goals, such as revenue growth, that managers might prefer to pursue at the possible expense of profits.

During the 1980s boom in leveraged buyouts, Michael Jensen (1986, 1989) reignited agency scholarship with his claim that managers in established companies facing limited growth prospects were not to be trusted to invest the company's cash efficiently. Jensen asserted that management had a penchant to reinvest corporate profits internally, even if the new projects had low net present value. He argued that high debt burdens, natural corollaries of leveraged buyouts by private equity investors, were a necessary way to reduce the free cash flow at the disposal of managers, forcing them to be more parsimonious with corporate cash.[9] Moreover, he proposed (1989) that private equity owners would be better, leaner stewards of corporate resources.[10] The corporate "raiders" whose virtues he extolled claimed that companies spent too much on corporate R&D and other long-term investments.

Chandler (1990a) maintained, on the contrary, that the multidivisional form of organization, with its independent profit centers, blunted inefficiencies and helped strike the right balance between discretionary control of resources and access to the capital needed for growth. Moreover, he argued that excessive debt would tend to choke investment in new product and process development, thereby sapping the company's innovation and growth. Chandler's view is consistent with the capabilities perspective outlined earlier. Rappaport (1990) added that, while the credible threat of hostile takeovers of underperforming firms provided a potentially salutary check on managerial misbehavior, leveraged buyouts are at best a transitional device to shake up a company before a new equity offering.

After the excesses of the buyout wave led to some large-scale failures (e.g., the 1990 bankruptcy of Federated Department Stores) and potential target companies became better at warding off private equity interest, the buyout craze waned. However, issues surrounding control, governance, and managerial discretion remain. Capabilities perspectives on firm performance and buyouts are still frequently overlooked, despite the historical and managerial research indicating their importance.

Internal Governance and Control

Chandler (1977) labeled the dynamism he chronicled in his study of the long-run development of the industrial business enterprise as a period of "managerial capitalism." In the first half of the twentieth century, corporations, guided primarily by professional managers, pursued growth strategies that exploited scale and scope economies made possible by technological and organizational innovations.

In the 1980s, the rise of large institutional and private investors ushered in an era of "shareholder value capitalism" (Rappaport, 1990, p. 99). The case law on governance and shareholder rights evolved in a way that made it difficult for boards to reject any takeover offer that provided current benefits to shareholders. This reflected a shift toward a single-minded focus on maximizing stockholder returns, which, in turn, favored short-term strategies, because many shareholders of publicly traded enterprises are active traders with short-term interests potentially at odds with the long-term strategies required to generate future success in large, multidivisional corporations. It is often difficult for managers to convince investors to support a major investment today that will pay off eventually. On the other hand, cutting costs and capital outlays will invariably produce short-term improvement in bottom line performance and please investors, at least for a while.

One result of the contemporary ownership structure of large enterprises is a vigorous debate among investors, managers, boards, and regulators over how companies should be run. An important battleground is the board room.

In the United States, shareholders have become more active in demanding that boards exercise greater authority; the 1990s saw boards at major corporations, including GM and IBM, oust their underperforming CEOs (Monks and Minow, 1996, p. 142). Boards in the United States also seem to oust CEOs for what appear to be minor infractions, as was the case in 2010 when Hewlett-Packard ousted Mark Hurd. This and other board-level blunders raised serious questions in the United States about whether boards with independent directors were in fact exercising too much power and influence and destroying, rather than protecting, shareholder value.[11]

Evidence suggests that the cohesiveness and collaboration of top management teams contributes to firm performance (Carmeli and Schaubroeck, 2006; Lubatkin et al., 2006). A board risks undermining effective management decision making if it recklessly removes a key member of the team and impairs cohesiveness. Apple Computer's famous ouster of founder Steve Jobs in 1985 is a case in point.

An emerging literature looks at the relationship between governance measures and shareholder value, but evidence supporting a positive causal linkages is scarce. Gompers et al. (2003) synthesized a governance index representing twenty-four separate "rules" and calculated it for hundreds of firms during the 1990s. They found that firms with stronger shareholder rights generated larger capital gains for shareholders over the period. However, a subsequent study by Core et al. (2006) found that the relationship was unlikely to be causal and did not hold during a later period, which suggests the possibility of an unidentified factor (perhaps related to the Internet bubble) causing the correlation.

In addition to shareholders, there are several additional constituencies that have been proposed for representation on corporate boards, including employees, suppliers, and society at large. This is an area where international differences loom large. In Germany, for example, workers unions are represented on supervisory boards, whereas in Japan, managers have relatively free rein with limited oversight by shareholders (Monks and Minow, 1996, p. 309).

There may be some movement toward international convergence around the idea of shareholder value because of the international mobility of (and competition for) investment capital. However, vestiges of national differences will likely persist indefinitely because corporations are embedded in a specific local context. For example, Williamson (1991) describes how the distinct Japanese institutions of employment, subcontracting, and banking would bring contracting hazards if they were introduced individually in a different setting such as the United States, but together they support each other.

International differences reinforce the idea that the traditional corporate structures and management methods are far from being the only possible mode of organization. Even in the United States, firms such as Lincoln Electric, which combine guaranteed employment with a strong employee say in running the company, underscore the existence of alternatives.

Such "stakeholder" approaches (Kay, 1997), which add a voice for normally excluded elements to board-level decision making, have their roots in issues of community responsibility that were also debated between A. A. Berle and E. Merrick Dodd in the 1930s (Weiner, 1964). In the wake of the takeovers of the 1980s, which led to plant closures and other economic dislocations, more than half the states in the United States enacted statutes that authorized directors to explicitly consider the interests of employees, customers, suppliers, and others when making decisions (O'Connor, 1991). Nonshareholder interests are often addressed even without legislative permission. For example, corporations often engage in corporate philanthropy that benefits the local community.

The handling of stakeholder interests has been somewhat different in other major economies. In Japan, the welfare of employees is an important consideration for corporations, but there is no legislative requirement to that effect. Stewardship for the long run is an accepted responsibility of the firm's leadership. Other economies have been more explicit. Germany's tradition of corporate social responsibility was first enshrined in law in 1937, and the United Kingdom introduced a legal requirement for boards to consider "employee interests" in 1980 (Conard, 1991).

Stakeholder-based governance, at least in theory, can be reconciled with longer term shareholder perspectives. When shareholder interests are defined in an enlightened fashion, that is, by pursuing profits as part of a long-term strategy (as opposed to, for example, reducing costs to try and drive up the stock price temporarily), then nonshareholding stakeholders such as suppliers, customers, and employees who have contributed to the strategy implementation are likely to benefit. An alignment of goals between the enterprise and key stakeholders is warranted, but there is no evidence that creating formal governance mechanisms for these relationships improves performance.

In the contracting tradition, Williamson (1985a, chapter 12) concludes that only shareholders merit a formal voice on the board. He eliminates other constituencies in part through the assumptions he employs. For example, he assumes that workers, to the extent they face hazards from developing firm-specific skills that aren't readily transferable to other employers, will be granted some form of safeguard by the employer because "it can be presumed that workers and firms will recognize the benefits" of such safeguards (p. 303). There is no empirical evidence on this point that is fully dispositive.

The capabilities perspective does not lead to a specific conclusion regarding the composition of the board of directors. From the capabilities perspective, what matters most is the board's role in verifying that top management is pursuing a coherent strategic vision. In addition to the standard financial monitoring function, the board should also be responsible for responding to evidence of strategic malfeasance by management, that is, identifying situations where top management is making poor decisions with respect to the firm's changing environment (Teece, 2007).

Recent regulatory changes in the United States, such as the Sarbanes-Oxley Act of 2002, have endeavored to create greater financial transparency. Compliance requires implementing tight financial controls and employing rigorous—some might say pedantic—accounting rules. However, this type of accounting rigor and oversight provides little protection against strategic blunders by managers and boards of industrial companies. Indeed, it might indirectly enhance strategic risks by sapping the board's attention with accounting minutiae. Also, with respect to banks and other financial entities, Sarbanes-Oxley provided little in the way of additional transparency with respect to risk. It may even have had the unfortunate unintended consequence of giving some naive investors a false sense of security.

Many of the technical requirements of good governance may in fact be of only second- or third-order importance relative to the larger issues of the enterprise's longer term strategy. The appropriate definition of "good governance" may be context-dependent. For example, in some circumstances, the separation of the CEO and chairman roles may be counterproductive to the rapid transformation required to meet a competitive threat or to develop and commercialize a new technology that is meeting resistance from certain parts of the company.

Many boards may have insufficient strength to help management properly evaluate strategic alternatives. The boards in most large U.S.-based corporations number about a dozen individuals, and the average size has declined even as boards are called on to do more (Green, 2005, p. 32). Board members typically lack staff to conduct their own analyses, which leaves them reliant on themselves and management for their understanding of the industry. Greater weight has been put on the need for board members who are independent of management, but not on members who understand the industry environment in which the company must compete. In fact, the New York Stock Exchange's mandate that boards have more independent members than management members—which goes beyond the Sarbanes-Oxley independence requirement that applies only to the audit committee—may have weakened governance in the areas where it matters most.

Fama and Jensen, in an influential paper from the agency theory perspective, hypothesized that independent directors "have incentives to develop reputations as experts in decision control" (1983, p. 315), where decision control refers to the ratification of proposals from among a range of options and the monitoring of implementation of the chosen alternative. Williamson addressed this hypothesis by writing, "I do not disagree, but would argue that outside directors often have stronger incentives to 'go along'" (1988, p. 571, n. 9). But they also have enough power to mess things up, particularly in situations where they are in the majority. In crafting good public policy, ignorance should be as much of a concern as poor incentive design. Indeed, the capabilities perspective would suggest that independent boards need enough good judgment to sniff out malfeasance and also the ability to assess risk and support management, when necessary, with sensing and seizing opportunities and transforming the company.

In the capabilities perspective, what matters most for board composition is getting highly competent people. Rigid rules such as those imposed by the stock exchanges are a reaction to the Enron debacle, but arguably hurt more than they help in the provision of good governance.

The 2007–2008 Financial Crisis and Corporate Governance

Though the focus of this chapter has been mainly on the industrial enterprise, it does not seem possible to ignore the specialized governance issues surrounding financial institutions. Agency, contracting, and capabilities perspectives all have relevancy.

The recent financial crisis has raised anew fundamental questions about governance in the financial sector. In particular, there was little evidence that boards of directors were willing or able to correct misaligned incentives that, in the United States, led some Wall Street managers to take actions that negatively impacted shareholders and society. Reflecting on the crisis during congressional hearings in 2008, former Federal Reserve chairman Alan Greenspan admitted that "Those of us who have looked to the self-interest of lending institutions to protect shareholders' equity, myself included, are in a state of shocked disbelief" (Andrews, 2008).

There appear to have been major agency issues in the financial sector. There were capabilities deficits, too, because some investment and commercial banks did not have good risk-management systems. Managements and boards were blindsided, along with many other investors.

The agency problems and the moral hazard surrounding banks' investment decisions were further aggravated for several of the largest institutions (e.g., Fannie Mae and Freddie Mac) because regulators in the United States and Europe were known to believe in a policy that some financial actors are "too big to fail" (Ennis and Malek, 2005). This permitted managers to play "heads I win, tails you lose," where the costs of success were private but the costs of failure would be borne partially—or even primarily—by society and/or investors. It was little comfort that they might have thought that the risk of systemic failure was low. Whether it was high or low, there was some expectation that any downside would be absorbed by society.

A similar circumstance exists in Europe, where banks took on too much sovereign debt. They failed to properly assess the risks of sovereign default, or write-down, in light of the European Union's limited mechanisms for addressing imbalances across Eurozone economies.

According to Charles Calomiris (2009), a noted expert in banking and corporate finance, an agency problem of a different kind was a root cause of the crisis, namely, the conflicts of interest between asset managers and their clients—even when the "client" was another part of the same financial institution. Asset managers received income from investing money in the class of assets their investors wanted, not for refusing the investments they might have thought were too risky.

Agency problems also surrounded the ratings agencies that certified the quality of subprime investments. Perhaps some individuals in the ratings agencies understated the risk of potential large losses from subprime (or sovereign debt) issues; most did not. This was a matter of capabilities.

Moreover, a plethora of collateralization and mortgage insurance instruments gave grounds for confidence. The ratings agencies had reasonable (or at least defensible) standards, but there were "hidden" risks from unprecedented complexity and opaqueness that blinded not just the ratings agencies but also regulators and investors. In addition, there were certain fee-based incentives to encourage investment-grade ratings. This has been emphasized in the popular press, but it was probably less of a factor than "capability" considerations. In other words, the ratings agencies themselves did not fully understand the risk. The lack of deep transparency (primarily because of complexity) trapped them as much as did the misaligned incentives.

According to Calomiris (2009), sophisticated institutional users of these ratings were generally more aware than the ratings agencies of the risks, but purposely ignored them. Calomiris suggests (and provides some circumstantial evidence) that institutional investors in the United States fought hard to ensure that the subprime-related securities they wanted to own received investment-grade ratings to comply with regulations. Otherwise these investments would have been off-limits. In fact, financial firms with the largest shareholdings by institutional investors took the greatest risks, which suggests that shareholder/investor "greed" can in some instances be a greater threat to a company than opportunism by management (Erkens et al., 2010). Of course, the two together can be especially toxic.

Board composition also played a role. According to a study by Erkens et al. (2010), board composition, in terms of the number of independents, was tied to performance during the crash, but in a manner quite inconsistent with conventional wisdom. Looking at 296 large financial firms from 30 countries, the authors found that the presence of more outside board members was associated with lower stock returns during the crisis. The more-independent boards were more likely to insist on rapid loss recognition. They were, perhaps, protecting their own interests because the rapid recognition would reduce their own exposure to liability, even if it cost shareholders dearly. The costs were indeed high as the recognized losses forced the affected firms to shore up their capital adequacy ratios by raising more capital in a difficult capital-raising environment. Because much of this new capital was in the form of equity, wealth was effectively transferred from shareholders to debtholders. Beltratti and Stultz (2009) also found that banks with seemingly shareholder-friendly boards performed worse during the crisis.

Put differently, it appears that governance in tune with the conventional wisdom (greater independence, stricter auditing) may have proved harmful to shareholder interests. The agency problem here appears to be that managers were the better stewards of shareholder interests than were independent board members! The traditional agency theory thinking didn't work—or perhaps it works very well in the sense that independent board members (with extremely low or nonexistent equity positions) can be trusted even less than managers (who typically have at least small equity positions) to guard the shareholders' interests.

In the financial sector, regulation is an important component in the overall system of governance and can serve as a complement to or, less satisfactorily, a substitute for internal governance measures. Differences in regulation seem to be a factor in determining outcomes since the crisis, as shown by cross-national research. In a study of ninety-eight large deposit-taking banks in twenty countries over the 2007–2008 crisis period, Beltratti and Stultz (2009) found that those in countries with stricter capital requirement regulations had higher stock market returns.

Some countries (e.g., Canada, Australia, and New Zealand) did not experience excesses in the banking sector in part because of superior structural factors, including regulatory controls and oversight and smaller markets. Thus, agency issues, though present, did need not lead to performance failure in those countries. This demonstrates the complex interplay between governance and regulatory issues.

Canada, for example is dominated by a handful of big banks and experienced low interest rates similar to those in the United States during the run-up to the crisis; yet its mortgage default rate in the years after the crisis set in has been less than 1 percent versus more than 5 percent in the United States at the mid-2009 peak. Total returns to shareholders of Canadian banks have also remained positive in contrast to the losses incurred by shareholders at large U.S. and British banks. And this was done without any government bailout—the only such case in the G7.

Stricter regulations seem to have made the difference between Canada and the worst-affected countries (Freeland, 2010). Canadian regulators resisted the competition with New York and London to attract business by offering looser restrictions. They maintained relatively high capital requirements and required insurance for all mortgages with less than a 20 percent down payment. In addition, adjustable-rate and interest-only mortgages were very rare.

Furthermore, Canadian bank regulation seems to draw more on the holistic, qualitative approach of the capabilities perspective than on the rigid formulations of agency theory. According to the head of Canada's Office of the Superintendent of Financial Institutions, Canadian regulation is based on principles, rather than legalistic rules: "we want to be told everything that is going on. We don't want to have a list of boxes that we tick because that's not very effective."[12]

The circumstances surrounding the crisis seem to provide support for both the agency and capability perspectives, although careful empirical analysis of these issues remains to be done. However, the agency issues most researched and modeled in the past do not appear to be the ones that matter most.

Transaction cost considerations appear to have been less relevant for explaining performance with one possible, but very large exception. I refer here to earlier versions of the transaction cost framework that stressed the importance of vertical integration in facilitating the flow of information inside the enterprise (Malmgren, 1961; Arrow, 1975; Williamson, 1975; Teece, 1976, 1990).

The vertical disintegration of the mortgage market, that is, the advent of securitization and the dramatic diminution in the percentage of loans originated that stayed on the originating bank's balance sheet, naturally amplified agency issues. The invention of mortgage securities and their associated markets meant that the banks that typically originated mortgages no longer had to hold them. As mortgage securitization expanded, the percentage of banks' profits from the performance of portfolio loans declined; banks made more money from securitizing and then selling off the loans they originated. Careless underwriting and poor loan performance could be obscured by packaging up the loans and selling the resulting securities before any observable increase in late payments and defaults.

Yet the transformation of the mortgage industry through the creation of markets for mortgage-backed securities did not seem to trigger sufficient oversight (by regulators, top management, or boards of directors) of the loan origination/securitization process. A better understanding of the informational properties of vertical integration—and the greater visibility across activities that is usually associated with it—might have led to greater concern. It should have been apparent that breaking up vertical structures via "securitization" and handing off mortgages, while bringing short-term efficiencies from specialization (Jacobides, 2005) could lead to opaqueness and poorer risk assessment by the market at large. In fact, there is little doubt now that the disintermediation of the residential mortgage banking business led to structural opaqueness and a corresponding informational inefficiency. Holders of mortgage-backed securities either did not properly understand the (systemic) risk in their portfolios or took comfort that the lack of transparency in the market allowed them plausible deniability (Calomiris, 2009).

Conclusion

The business enterprise is the engine of the capitalist system. It is the locus of innovation. Innovation, in turn, is what drives capitalism forward and allows it to outperform planned economies. Accordingly, the essence of the free market system itself lies as much in how the business enterprise fuels innovation and develops capabilities as in how markets work. The two are closely connected, of course.

Our understanding of the enterprise as an economic organization is still rather primitive. The scholarly work that tries to deepen our understanding of it, from an economics perspective, has developed explicitly or implicitly under the rubric of the nature (or the theory) of the firm. However, despite important progress, the theory of the firm is still in a primitive state. This is perhaps even more true if one is looking for a theory of the firm that can explain banks and their behavior. Even for industrial enterprises, the theory is quite inadequate.

In this chapter, three perspectives have been put forward: agency, transaction costs, and capabilities. Each has something to offer.

Agency theory highlights how incentives should be crafted and governance activities focused to bring about better performance for shareholders when ownership and control are separated. While agency issues are ubiquitous, this approach by itself leads to a fixation on incentive design to the exclusion of other concerns. Moreover, most of the principal-agent issues have been couched in terms of the dissonance between the interests of shareholders and managers. The recent financial crisis reminds us that a broader perspective on stakeholders is needed because bad management decisions (and weak board oversight) can have spillover effects to other groups and to society more generally.

Transaction cost economics highlights, as does agency theory, the importance of opportunism. But it adds asset specificity considerations that are also relevant to organizational design choices, including governance mechanisms.

Finally, this chapter outlined the capabilities perspective, which emerged outside economics, primarily in the strategic management literature. It focuses less on managing *opportunism* and more on harnessing and managing *opportunity*. In that sense, it is closer to the essence of capitalism.

Opportunism plagues both socialist and capitalist systems. Both have difficulty dealing with it. However, the distinctive positive attribute of capitalism (which socialism cannot replicate) is that it allows and requires technological and market opportunities to be embraced. It also allows and requires competition. The sensing, seizing, and transforming capabilities of firms are uniquely brought to life under competitive capitalism.

The capabilities framework has been largely ignored by economic theorists, who have a penchant for taking the existence of new opportunities for granted. In many ways, a good deal of modern economic theory is more like socialist economic theory than one might think in the sense that it ignores the development and exploitation of new opportunities. There is greater attention in modern economic theory to the appropriation of rents through recontracting (in TCE) or the abuse of managerial discretion (in agency theory)—rather than the creation of new value. Ironically, the creative and transformative aspects of capitalism were recognized by Marx (Schumpeter, 1949) far earlier, and perhaps even better, than they have been recognized in a good deal of modern economic theory!

Put differently, the study of organizational capabilities, technological innovation, business models, and managerial entrepreneurship is essential for a deeper understanding of capitalism and related governance issues. If pursued, it offers the hope of providing fresh and profound insights into economic organization, wealth creation, and national competitiveness.

Appendix: The Rise of the Modern Corporation

The corporation is the organizational form in which most economic activity takes place in modern economies.[13] It is the engine of the capitalist system.[14] It spurs and manages innovation, which in turn propels economic growth.

Although "corporations" have existed for centuries, the bundle of characteristics that we think of as the modern corporation has fully taken shape only in the twentieth century in response to changes in how corporations are structured internally and how capital markets and ownership have evolved.

Mass production and large-scale distribution appeared in the United States in the nineteenth century in response to technological and market opportunities. These large corporations required very large investments of capital raised through investment banks and financial markets. Their complex operations necessitated professional management. These factors gradually sidelined owner-managers and gave rise to the professionally managed organizations that dominate the global economy (Chandler, 1990b).

The corporate form, as it currently exists in most countries, has several key features (Monks and Minow, 1996).[15] First, the liability of investors is limited to the size of their investment in the corporation (as opposed to the unlimited personal liability of partners in a partnership). Second, those investors are often able to liquidate their ownership interest in an established (public) market. Third, the corporation is an infinitely lived legal "person," which can be held collectively liable for its actions even when its managers and investors are not held individually responsible. Fourth, the authority to manage the company is devolved to an executive team with oversight provided by a board of directors that has little or no input from individual investors, unless they happen to be major shareholders.

Despite its central role in the economy, the position of the business enterprise in mainstream economic theory is tenuous because the theoretical efficiency of the market system rests on a set of assumptions that are never satisfied in reality. Moreover, in the Arrow-Debreu (1954) general equilibrium theory of the economy, the institutional trappings of the modern corporation are treated as unnecessary noise. Production functions and production sets are supposed to adequately characterize the supply side of the economy. It is no wonder that in this set-up, capitalism and socialism are able to solve an economy's fundamental resource allocation problems equally well.

To better explain the role of private enterprise in economic theory, Richard Nelson (1981), in a much-overlooked article, outlined a neo-Schumpeterian analysis of the business enterprise. He focused on three fundamental functions of the business enterprise operating in a market-oriented economy.

First, firms are a potentially efficient means of organizing activity because they can provide clear lines of responsibility, facilitate flows of information between stages of production, and permit coordination of diverse activities in the execution of a specific plan. Firms are units of planning and control that exchange with each other through market arrangements.

Second, private enterprise generally responds rapidly to market signals (especially in comparison to a central planning mechanism). This is particularly vital in real-world contexts, which are moving toward a seldom-reached equilibrium state, which helps explain Hayekian notions about market responsiveness.

Third, private enterprise excels at innovation, especially of the what-to-make-and-how-to-make-it variety (as opposed to basic research). More important, when there are several competitors, "differences in perception as to what are the best bets will have a greater chance to surface and be made effective in terms of diversity of R&D projects" (1981, p. 108). This makes a competitive regime better than a planned economy despite a certain amount of "waste and duplication" (ibid.). Nelson could have (but did not) couched this third function in terms of building and maintaining (dynamic) capabilities (Teece et al., 1990, 1997; Teece, 2007). Managers do it better than central planners, relying in part (and only in part) on the market to achieve the necessary coordination.

Since Nelson wrote his article, the role of the business enterprise in innovation has become even more amplified. Whereas firms once derived (and in some industries still do) advantage over rivals primarily from devising, implementing, and managing large, vertically structured manufacturing operations that yielded scale and scope advantages (Chandler, 1990b), firms operating in the developed world increasingly build competitive advantage and hence long-term profitability mainly through the creation, ownership, transfer, orchestration, and protection of nontradable (intangible) assets. Knowledge itself is, of course, the prime example of an intangible asset.

The shift in the competitive importance of innovation was brought on by radical changes in the global economy, including the decreased cost (and increased speed) of information flow, decreased cost and increased speed of transportation, greater labor mobility, widespread availability of many components and subassemblies at competitive prices, and easier access to many complementary assets and services (Teece, 2000).

The expansion of trade, especially in intermediate goods, has enabled and requires collaboration across a system in which firms around the globe specialize in narrow parts of the value chain. To make the global system of vertical specialization and cospecialization (bilateral dependence) work, there is an enhanced need for the modern corporation to develop and align assets for combining with other, externally owned elements of the global value chain so as to develop and deliver a joint "solution" that customers value.

Acknowledgment

I thank Greg Linden for helpful assistance and contributions.

Notes

1. The Morck and Yeung chapter in this volume provides a more complete review of the agency perspective on governance. The agency approach is arguably the dominant strand in the literature. This chapter implicitly suggests that the transactions costs and dynamic capabilities approaches are also insightful.
2. Agency problems were already at the core of Williamson's work before he developed the TCE paradigm. See, for example, Williamson (1964).
3. An organization's capabilities are embedded in competences and shaped by the implicit norms and rules of the organization. A competence denotes sufficiency in the performance of a delineated collective task. It's about doing things well enough, or possibly very well, without attention to whether the economic activity is the best thing to do in the context at hand.
4. The term *governance* is used in this section to refer to the question of whether economic activity is organized primarily by market processes or by internal management.
5. Although Williamson analyzed the inability of the market to promote information convergence in contract terms (1971, p. 120–121), it could equally be framed in terms of resource alignment. Eventually, the informational characteristics of the firm will be treated as their own category.
6. The intellectual origins of the framework can also be traced to Abernathy and Utterback (for their work on the innovation life cycle), to economic historians like Nathan Rosenberg and Alfred Chandler (for their work on complementary technologies), to Nelson and Winter (for their work on the nature of knowledge), and to Schumpeter (for his focus on the need for value capture). See Winter (2006) for a review of PFI's intellectual origins.

7. See Conner (1991) for an analysis that claims that that the resource-based view provides a theory of the firm.
8. See Bardolet et al. (2010) for evidence that internal capital markets may be inefficient.
9. This was a variant of the idea perhaps first put forth by Marris (1963) that managers are constrained by the threat of takeover. Marris, however, went on to note that "In real life, take-over raiders are scarce, command high rents and are often themselves managerial organizations. They may impose some degree of conformity between the behavior of managements, but this is not the same as imposing conformity with whatever would be the preferences of investors" (p. 205).
10. The discipline provided by the ever-present threat of takeover for underperforming firms is itself a core underpinning of market (agency) philosophy. The idea is that corporate takeovers allow new owners to replace poor managers with better ones. This is, however, a rather blunt tool for fine-tuning the economic system and addressing governance issues, particularly governance failure at the board level.
11. Oracle CEO Larry Ellison wrote in a public e-mail to the *New York Times* that "the HP board…voted 6 to 4 to go public with this sexual harassment claim against Mark because six of the directors believed that full disclosure was good corporate governance. Publishing known false sexual harassment claims is not good corporate governance; it's cowardly corporate political correctness…their decision has already cost HP shareholders over $10 billion…and my guess (is) it's going to cost them a lot more" (Reuters, 2010). HP's share price fell from $46.35 on August 5, 2010, the day before Hurd's resignation, to $40.14 on August 12, a 13.4 percent drop versus the 3.7 percent drop in the S&P 500 index during the same period. Although HP's shares eventually recovered to a peak of $48.99 on February 16, 2011, missteps by Hurd's replacement, Leo Apotheker (and, arguably, by the board) led to another CEO ousting and another collapse in the stock price, which fell as low as $22.20 on October 3, 2011, before starting to recover.
12. The quotation appears in Freeland (2010).
13. In the United States, the 2007 business receipts of corporations were $24.2 trillion, versus $3.8 trillion for partnerships and $1.3 trillion for nonfarm sole proprietorships (Internal Revenue Service Statistics on Income, Integrated Business Data, table 3). The difference was less exaggerated in net income terms: $1.9 trillion versus $0.7 trillion for partnerships and $0.3 for nonfarm proprietorships (ibid.). Globally, the UN estimates that more than two thirds of world trade in the 1990s took place within and between the international networks of multinational corporations (UNCTAD, 1999).
14. Using a different metaphor, the corporation is the musculature of capitalism. The banking sector is its circulatory system, and the central bank is the heart. If the heart is unable to adjust the movement in the circulatory system as needed, the body weakens and may fail.
15. A U.S. variant that has no equivalent in some countries is the limited liability company, which offers the liability protection of the corporate form but is more flexible as to taxation and governance, which are typically closer to those of a partnership (income passes through to owners, and there is no board of directors).

References

Alchian, Armen A., and Harold Demsetz. "Production, Information Costs and Economic Organization." *American Economic Review* 62 (Dec. 1972): 777–795.

Andrews, Edmund L. "Greenspan Concedes Error on Regulation." *New York Times*, Oct. 23, 2008. http://www.nytimes.com/2008/10/24/business/economy/24panel.html.
Armour, Henry O., and David J. Teece. "Organizational Structure and Economic Performance: A Test of the Multidivisional Hypothesis." *Bell Journal of Economics*, 9 (Spring 1978): 106–122.
Arrow, Kenneth J. "Vertical Integration and Communication." *Bell Journal of Economics* 6 (Spring 1975): 173–183.
Arrow, Kenneth J., and Gerard Debreu. "Existence of an Equilibrium for a Competitive Economy." *Econometrica* 22 (July 1954): 265–290.
Bardolet, David, Dan Lovallo, and Richard Rumelt. "The Hand of Corporate Management in Capital Allocations: Patterns of Investment in Multi- and Single-Business Firms." *Industrial and Corporate Change* 19 (April 2010): 591–612.
Barney, Jay B. "Strategic Factor Markets: Expectations, Luck, and Business Strategy." *Management Science* 32 (Oct. 1986): 1231–1241.
Baumol, William J. *Business Behavior: Value and Growth*, rev. ed. New York: Harcourt, Brace & World, 1967.
Beltratti, Andrea, and Rene M. Stulz. *Why Did Some Banks Perform Better during the Credit Crisis? A Cross-Country Study of the Impact of Governance and Regulation*. Fisher College of Business Working Paper No. 2009–03–012, July 13, 2009. http://ssrn.com/abstract=1433502.
Berle, Adolf A., and Gardiner C. Means. *The Modern Corporation and Private Property*. New York: Commerce Clearing House, 1932.
Calomiris, Charles W. "The Subprime Turmoil: What's Old, What's New, and What's Next." In *Maintaining Stability in a Changing Financial System*. Federal Reserve Bank of Kansas City, Mo., 2009, 19–110. http://www.kansascityfed.org/publicat/sympos/2008/Calomiris.03.12.09.pdf.
Carmeli, Abraham, and John Schaubroeck. "Top Management Team Behavioral Integration, Decision Quality, and Organizational Decline." *Leadership Quarterly* 17 (Oct. 2006): 441–453.
Chandler, Alfred D. Jr. *Strategy and Structure: Chapters in the History of the Industrial Enterprise*. Cambridge, Mass.: MIT Press, 1962.
Chandler, Alfred, D. Jr. "The Structure of American Industry in the Twentieth Century: A Historical Overview." *Business History Review* 43 (Autumn 1969): 255–298.
Chandler, Alfred, D. Jr. *The Visible Hand*. Cambridge, Mass.: Harvard University Press, 1977.
Chandler, Alfred, D. Jr. "The Enduring Logic of Industrial Success." *Harvard Business Review* 68 (March–April 1990a): 130–140.
Chandler, Alfred, D. *Scale and Scope: The Dynamics of Industrial Capitalism*. Cambridge, Mass.: Belknap Press, 1990b.
Coase, R. A. "The Nature of the Firm." *Economica* 16 (Nov. 1937): 386–405.
Conard, Alfred F. "Corporate Constituencies in Western Europe." *Stetson Law Review* 21 (Fall 1991): 73–95.
Conner, Kathleen R. "A Historical Comparison of Resource-Based Theory and Five Schools of Thought within Industrial Organization Economics: Do We Have a New Theory of the Firm?" *Journal of Management* 17 (March 1991): 121–154.
Core, John E., Wayne R. Guay, and Tjomme O. Rusticus. "Does Weak Governance Cause Weak Stock Returns? An Examination of Firm Operating Performance and Investors' Expectations." *Journal of Finance* 61 (April 2006): 655–687.
Demsetz, Harold, and Belén Villalonga. "Ownership Structure and Corporate Performance." *Journal of Corporate Finance* 7 (Sept. 2001): 209–233.

Dierickx, Ingemar, and Karel Cool. "Asset Stock Accumulation and Sustainability of Competitive Advantage." *Management Science* 35 (Dec. 1989): 1504–1511.

Eisenhardt, Kathleen M. "Agency Theory: An Assessment and Review." *Academy of Management Review* 14 (Jan. 1989): 57–74.

Ennis, Huberto M., and H. S. Malek. "Bank Risk of Failure and the Too-Big-to-Fail Policy." *Federal Reserve Bank of Richmond Economic Quarterly* 91 (Spring 2005): 21–44.

Erkens, David, Mingyi Hung, and Pedro P. Matos. "Corporate Governance in the 2007–2008 Financial Crisis: Evidence from Financial Institutions Worldwide." Working paper, Sept. 2010. http://ssrn.com/abstract=1397685.

Fama, Eugene F., and Michael C. Jensen. "Separation of Ownership and Control." *Journal of Law and Economics* 26 (June 1983): 301–326.

Freeland, Chrystia. "What Toronto Can Teach New York and London." *Financial Times Magazine*, Jan. 29, 2010. http://www.ft.com/cms/s/2/db2b340a-0a1b-11df-8b23-00144feabdc0.html.

Gompers, Paul, Joy Ishii, and Andrew Metrick. "Corporate Governance and Equity Prices." *Quarterly Journal of Economics* 118 (Feb. 2003): 107–155.

Green, Scott. *Sarbanes-Oxley and the Board of Directors*. Hoboken, N.J.: Wiley, 2005.

Hayek, Friedrich A. von. *The Road to Serfdom*. Chicago: University of Chicago Press, 1944.

Jacobides, Michael G. "Industry Change through Vertical Disintegration: How and Why Markets Emerged in Mortgage Banking." *Academy of Management Journal* 48 (June 2005): 465–498.

Jacobides, Michael G., Torbjorn Knudsen, and Mie Augier. "Benefiting from Innovation: Value Creation, Value Appropriation and the Role of Industry Architectures." *Research Policy* 35 (Oct. 2006): 1200–1221.

Jensen, Michael C. "Agency Costs of Free Cash Flow, Corporate Finance, and Takeovers." *American Economic Review* 76 (May 1986): 323–329.

Jensen, Michael C. "Eclipse of the Public Corporation." *Harvard Business Review* 67 (Sept./Oct. 1989): 61–74.

Jensen, Michael C. *A Theory of the Firm: Governance, Residual Claims, and Organizational Forms*. Cambridge, Mass.: Harvard University Press, 2000.

Jensen, Michael C., and William H. Meckling. "Theory of the Firm: Managerial Behavior, Agency Costs and Ownership Structure." *Journal of Financial Economics* 3 (Oct. 1976): 305–360.

John, Richard R. "Elaborations, Revisions, Dissents: Alfred D. Chandler, Jr.'s 'The Visible Hand' after Twenty Years." *Business History Review* 71 (June 1997): 151–200.

Kay, John. "The Stakeholder Corporation." In *Stakeholder Capitalism*, ed. Gavin Kelly, Dominic Kelly, and Andrew Gamble, 125–141. London: Macmillan, 1997.

Lubatkin, Michael H., Zeki Simsek, Yan Ling, and John F. Veiga. "Ambidexterity and Performance in Small- to Medium-Sized Firms: The Pivotal Role of Top Management Team Behavioral Integration." *Journal of Management* 32 (Oct. 2006): 646–672.

Malmgren, H. B. "Information, Expectations and the Theory of the Firm." *Quarterly Journal of Economics* 75 (Aug. 1961): 399–421.

Marris, Robin. "A Model of the 'Managerial' Enterprise." *Quarterly Journal of Economics* 77 (May 1963): 185–209.

Marris, Robin. *The Economic Theory of "Managerial" Capitalism*. London: Macmillan, 1964.

Masten, Scott E. "The Organization of Production: Evidence from the Aerospace Industry." *Journal of Law and Economics* 27 (Oct. 1984): 403–417.

Michaels, Daniel, and Peter Sanders. "Dreamliner Production Gets Closer Monitoring." WSJ.com, October 8, 2009.

Monks, Robert A. G., and Nell Minow. *Watching the Watchers: Corporate Governance for the 21st Century*. Cambridge, Mass.: Blackwell Business, 1996.
Monsen, R. Joseph Jr., and Anthony Downs. "A Theory of Large Managerial Firms." *Journal of Political Economy* 73 (June 1965): 221–236.
Monteverde, Kirk, and David J. Teece. "Supplier Switching Costs and Vertical Integration in the Automobile Industry." *Bell Journal of Economics* 13 (Spring 1982): 206–213.
Nelson, Richard R. "Assessing Private Enterprise: An Exegesis of Tangled Doctrine." *Bell Journal of Economics* 12 (Spring 1981): 93–111.
Nelson, Richard R., and Sidney G. Winter. *An Evolutionary Theory of Economic Change*. Cambridge, Mass.: Belknap Press, 1982.
O'Connor, Marleen A. "Introduction: Corporate Malaise-Stakeholder Statutes: Cause or Cure." *Stetson Law Review* 21 (1991): 3–22.
Penrose, Edith T. *The Theory of the Growth of the Firm*, 3rd ed. 1959; Oxford: Oxford University Press, 1995.
Rappaport, Alfred. "The Staying Power of the Public Corporation." *Harvard Business Review* 68 (Jan./Feb. 1990): 96–104.
Reuters. "TEXT-Oracle CEO Ellison's comments on exit of HP's Hurd." August 9, 2010. http://www.reuters.com/article/idUSN0999239201008I0.
Ross, Stephen A. "The Economic Theory of Agency: The Principal's Problem." *American Economic Review* 63 (May 1973): 134–139.
Sautet, Frédéric E. *An Entrepreneurial Theory of the Firm*. London: Routledge, 2000.
Schumpeter, Joseph A. "The Communist Manifesto in Sociology and Economics." *Journal of Political Economy* 57 (June 1949): 199–212.
Shleifer, Andrei, and Robert W. Vishny. "A Survey of Corporate Governance." *Journal of Finance* 52 (June 1997): 737–783.
Smith, Adam. *An Inquiry into the Nature and Causes of the Wealth of Nations*. 2 vols. London: W. Strahan & T. Cadell, 1776.
Steer, Peter, and John Cable. "Internal Organization and Profit: An Empirical Analysis of Large U.K. Companies." *Journal of Industrial Economics* 27 (Sept. 1978): 13–30.
Teece, David J. *Vertical Integration and Vertical Divestiture in the U.S. Oil Industry*. Stanford, Calif.: Stanford University Institute for Energy Studies, 1976.
Teece, David J. "The Diffusion of an Administrative Innovation." *Management Science* 26 (May 1980a): 464–470.
Teece, David J. "Economies of Scope and the Scope of the Enterprise." *Journal of Economic Behavior and Organization* 1 (Sept. 1980b): 223–247.
Teece, David J. "Internal Organization and Economic Performance: An Empirical Analysis of the Profitability of Principal Firms." *Journal of Industrial Economics* 30 (Dec. 1981): 173–199.
Teece, David J. "Towards an Economic Theory of the Multiproduct Firm." *Journal of Economic Behavior and Organization* 3 (March 1982): 39–63.
Teece, David J. "Economic Analysis and Strategic Management." *California Management Review* 26 (Spring 1984): 87–110.
Teece, David J. "Profiting from Technological Innovation." *Research Policy* 15 (Dec. 1986): 285–305.
Teece, David J. "Technological Change and the Nature of the Firm." In *Technical Change and Economic Theory*, ed. G. Dosi, C. Freeman, R. Nelson, G. Silverberg, and L. Soete. London: Pinter, 1988.
Teece, David J. "Structure and Organization of the Natural Gas Industry: Differences Between the United States and the Federal Republic of Germany and Implications for the Carrier Status of Pipelines." *Energy Journal* 11 (July 1990): 1–35.

Teece, David J. "Firm Organization, Industrial Structure, and Technological Innovation." *Journal of Economic Behavior and Organization* 31 (November 1996): 193–224.
Teece, David J. *Managing Intellectual Capital: Organizational, Strategic, and Policy Dimensions*. New York: Oxford University Press, 2000.
Teece, David J. "Explicating Dynamic Capabilities: The Nature and Microfoundations of (Sustainable) Enterprise Performance." *Strategic Management Journal* 28 (Dec. 2007): 1319–1350.
Teece, David J. *Dynamic Capabilities and Strategic Management: Organizing for Innovation and Growth*. New York: Oxford University Press, 2009.
Teece, David J., and Gary Pisano. "The Dynamic Capabilities of Firms: An Introduction." *Industrial and Corporate Change* 3 (1994): 537–556.
Teece, David J., Gary Pisano, and Amy Shuen. "Firm Capabilities, Resources, and the Concept of Strategy." Center for Research in Management. University of California, Berkeley, CCC Working Paper 90–8, 1990.
Teece, David J., Gary Pisano, and Amy Shuen. "Dynamic Capabilities and Strategic Management." *Strategic Management Journal* 18 (Aug. 1997): 509–533.
UNCTAD. *World Investment Report 1999: Foreign Direct Investment and the Challenge of Development*. New York: United Nations Conference on Trade and Development, 1999.
Weiner, Joseph L. "The Berle-Dodd Dialogue on the Concept of the Corporation." *Columbia Law Review* 64 (Dec. 1964): 1458–1467.
Wernerfelt, Birger. "A Resource-Based View of the Firm." *Strategic Management Journal* 5 (April–June 1984): 171–180.
Williamson, Oliver E. *The Economics of Discretionary Behavior: Managerial Objectives in a Theory of the Firm*. Englewood Cliffs, N.J.: Prentice Hall, 1964.
Williamson, Oliver E. "The Vertical Integration of Production: Market Failure Considerations." *American Economic Review* 61 (May 1971): 112–123.
Williamson, Oliver E. *Markets and Hierarchies*. New York: Free Press, 1975.
Williamson, Oliver E. *The Economic Institutions of Capitalism*. New York: Free Press, 1985a.
Williamson, Oliver E. "Assessing Contract." *Journal of Law, Economics, and Organization* 1 (Spring 1985b): 177–208.
Williamson, Oliver E. "Corporate Finance and Corporate Governance." *Journal of Finance*, 43 (July 1988): 567–591.
Williamson, Oliver E. "Strategizing, Economizing, and Economic Organization." *Strategic Management Journal* 12 (Winter 1991, special issue): 75–94.
Williamson, Oliver E. "Strategy Research: Governance and Competence Perspectives." *Strategic Management Journal* 20 (Dec. 1999):1087–1108.
Winter, Sidney G. "The Logic of Appropriability: From Schumpeter to Arrow to Teece." *Research Policy* 35 (Oct. 2006): 1100–1106.

CHAPTER 9

CONTRACTS

VICTOR P. GOLDBERG

In his classic paper, Ronald Coase (1937) asked: why are there firms? If markets worked as perfectly as they did in economists' models, then institutions that interfered with the price system could expect to do no better in allocating resources and would probably do worse. His answer was that markets weren't so darn perfect. Transactions costs—his label for the imperfections—meant that some activities could best be performed within the firm. The organizational problem was to economize with regard to the organization structure given the costs and benefits of using the market (contracts) versus the command-and-control mechanism of the firm. Businessmen face a transactional engineering problem. Which activities should be performed within the firm, and which should be outsourced? If the latter, how should that relationship be structured?

Much has been written attempting to define the boundaries of the firm. What determines whether particular activities are performed inside the firm? That literature is exemplified by the spirited debate over the rationale for General Motors' acquisition of Fisher Body.[1] In this chapter I want to steer clear of that literature and focus entirely on transactions across organizational boundaries.

Voluntary exchange is a positive-sum game, at least ex ante. Contract design entails both value creation and value division. The division does not merely split the gains from producing a larger pie; it can influence the size (and nature) of the pie itself. A particular structure might appear optimal if the parties were concerned only with joint maximization, but it might be quite ineffective once the private interests of the parties are taken into account.[2] Contract law (at least that part of the law that deals with transactions between business firms)[3] should be designed to facilitate those mutually advantageous transactions. I confine my attention to U.S. law, although other bodies of law would be consistent with a capitalist regime.[4]

"Freedom of contract" is at the core of capitalism. Parties must be able to enter into exchanges and coordinate their future interactions with reasonable confidence. The law has to afford them with some protection of property rights and some assurance of the enforceability of their agreements. Starting at least with the work of Douglass North (1990), much of the economic literature on economic growth and development in capitalist systems has emphasized the importance of legal institutions for economic development. It is, however, easy to overstate the importance of contract doctrine in making capitalism work. Legal scholars and economists might agonize over the ideal content of the law. But the system can work reasonably well even with law that is pretty bad. This is partly because extra-legal constraints—notably reputation and repeat dealings—can be very effective, and partly because parties can often contract around bad rules or into better legal systems. Still, the law—both the content and the ease of enforcement (including cost)—does matter.

I begin by suppressing concerns about doctrine and focus on the general problems confronting parties designing a contractual relationship. Contracts concern the future, which is both uncertain and influenced by the behavior of the parties. This presents the parties with a number of problems, the solutions for which are imperfect. Contract doctrine, the focus of the next section, can facilitate their efforts, but it can also be an impediment.

Designing the Contract

The simplest transactions involve the instantaneous exchange of goods for cash. The more interesting ones involve some projection over the future. These can range from straightforward promises to deliver some well-defined commodity at a future date to elaborate governance arrangements for the future interactions of the parties (for example, a joint venture or a long-term shopping center lease). Analytically, these diverse transactions raise many of the same issues, albeit with different weights. I confine my attention to four.

Costly Information

Information is the classic public good. It is costly to produce, and once produced it is nonrivalrous; that is, the use of it by one person will not affect its availability to others. If one party contemplated producing information, but it was immediately available to all so that the value to that party was effectively zero, then it is unlikely that the expenditure would be made. Contracting parties have to determine how to produce information, who should produce it, and how to protect it. Suppose, for example, that one party owns an asset, but both it and a potential buyer are uncertain of its value. A person might, for example, own the mineral rights under his farmland. The counterparty, say, an oil company, would be the superior producer of information, but that poses a problem for the landowner. If it allows the buyer to test drill before a sale, the buyer could then use its superior information to low-ball. Or, if the oil company could not keep the information confidential, the owner could use the information in negotiating with a third party. Even if the owner barred the test drilling, the oil company's superior knowledge of the general contours of the oil field would give it an advantage. A common solution to the problem is to lease the mineral rights to the oil company and make part of the compensation payable as a royalty. That is not without problems. The royalty will distort the oil company's decisions because it gets less than 100 percent of the revenue. Moreover, it might behave strategically, for example, by taking the oil from an adjacent property or holding this oil as in-ground inventory.

A somewhat different information problem arises in multiyear manufacturing contracts in which the product itself has not yet been defined. Examples would be a contract for the future delivery of a computer model that has not yet been designed or parts for a complex product (a car, tractor, or airplane) where the specifications are expected to evolve as the production date gets closer. Rather than setting a firm price for a product not yet defined, the parties often postpone the pricing decision until more information becomes available. One technique is to use a form of cost-plus pricing, perhaps buttressed with benchmarking with other suppliers. Despite the well-chronicled flaws with cost-plus pricing (gold plating, ineffective cost controls), it is often used in such situations, usually with extensive (and costly) monitoring.

Another information problem arises for all forward transactions, including even the future sale of a well-defined commodity. Because future market conditions are unknown, parties have an incentive to expend resources to improve their knowledge. A wheat buyer, for example, might seek information on future weather conditions in certain growing areas. Or a coal mine owner might seek energy demand projections or information on the politics of the construction of nuclear power plants. If an informational advantage would give one party a larger share of the surplus, the parties have an incentive to engage in a rent-seeking game, overspending on the production of private information. Giving the parties "property in the price" by making forward contracts enforceable allows them to contract in advance and jointly economize on these costs. In long-term contracts, price adjustment mechanisms (indexing, for example) can fulfill the same function (Goldberg, 2006, chapters 10 and 18).

Information Asymmetry

For more than a generation, the "lemons problem" has been a staple of economic analysis. If sellers know the quality of what they are selling and do not credibly reveal that quality, rational buyers could reasonably infer that the quality is low and either refuse to buy or only offer to buy at a price reflecting the presumed low quality. The seller needs to convince the potential buyer of the high quality of whatever it is selling, and there are lots of ways it could do so. For a repeat player seller, the need to protect its reputation provides some assurance to buyers. Building and maintaining a reputation is costly, so the seller might choose instead to rent reputation from a third party (for example, the banks are reputational intermediaries in international letter of credit sales). The seller could post a bond, promising to pay if the quality fails to meet the promised standard. The seller could include representations and warranties in the agreement, providing the buyer with some assurance that it will perform as promised. Or the seller could make some of its compensation contingent on quality. If the transaction had a substantial temporal component (a long-term supply contract or a corporate acquisition with a significant gap between execution and closing), the right to renegotiate or terminate provides some assurance to the buyer.

All of these mechanisms have problems. If the buyer were unhappy with the transaction, perhaps because market conditions had changed, it could claim that the supplier had failed to achieve the promised quality or had breached its representation. If the truth were not easily verifiable, the seller would have to take this sort of opportunistic behavior into account. If some of the compensation was contingent, the buyer could influence outcomes to reduce its obligation. For example, suppose that a corporation sold a division with an "earnout," which makes part of the purchase price contingent on future performance. If the earnout was based on, say, the level of sales in the three years following the sale, the buyer could make decisions that time-shifted the revenue stream, reducing sales in the early years and increasing them in the postearnout period. If a buyer of goods had the right to threaten to terminate the contract, it could use that right to renegotiate a more favorable outcome than it could have achieved before the seller had committed to the transaction. And of course, sellers can anticipate that possibility and provide partial protection by, for example, deploying a more expensive production process or producing less buyer-specific customized goods to make it less vulnerable to such opportunistic behavior.

Moral Hazard

In an era of bailouts, the term *moral hazard* has become a staple of political/economic commentary. It arises when actors do not bear the full consequences of their actions. There is a mismatch between incentives and desired outcomes. For example, if a corporation has substantial leverage, the owners have an incentive to make risky, negative expected value investments. Heads we win, tails the lenders lose. Anticipating that, the loan agreement would constrain the firm's behavior with conditions and covenants. Of course, there are trade-offs. If the constraints are too tight, the owners will not be able to take on some desirable projects as well.

If a building is insured against fire damage, the owner's incentive to take care is reduced. The insurance contract will take this into account in two very different ways. First, if, indeed, the incidence of fires increases, the price would reflect the higher expected damages. Second, the incidence might not increase—indeed, it might decrease. The insurer's incentive (if it is a private, profit-oriented firm) is to limit the amount it pays out. Some folks insist that insurers do so by hardball tactics, refusing to pay legitimate claims. Perhaps. However, the insurer can also reduce the expected costs by, for example, providing inspection services ex ante or rehabilitation services ex post.[5]

Moral hazard is endemic in compensation systems for services because the service itself cannot be priced directly. If a lawyer charges for billable hours, the incentive to economize on time is reduced. Commission pricing reduces the agent's incentive to search for the lowest price. A fixed fee bears no relation to effort. A fee contingent on success gives the agent an incentive to conclude a deal, even if it is not the most favorable for the client. The perverse incentives in all these schemes can be partially offset by monitoring of the service provider, as well as the impact of reputation in general and future dealings between the two parties in particular.

Suppose that a firm using a complex piece of machinery sells it to another for delivery three months hence. Its incentive to maintain the machine properly in the interim is reduced. Conversely, if it were to sell the machine with a warranty, the purchaser's incentive to take care is compromised. If a firm were selling a division, these same moral hazard problems arise, taking a somewhat different form. To protect itself against the seller's actions that might reduce the value of the division in the months between execution of the transaction and closing the deal, the contract would include a covenant stating that the representations of the seller were correct at the time they were made and continue to be true at the time of the closing. Typically, they would include a "material adverse change" (MAC) clause that would allow the buyer to back out of the deal if there had been a MAC.[6] Analogous to the warranty, the buyer's incentives will be altered if the seller maintained a stake in the subsequent performance of the division (an earnout). If, for example, the compensation is a function of profits over the next n years, the buyer has an incentive to make investments that will pay off after $n + 1$. The greater the rewards to time shifting, the more the seller would have to do to protect itself.[7]

Moral hazard is at the core of principal-agent models in which a principal has to cope with the divergent incentives of the agent, whose behavior will affect the outcome.[8] In many instances, the outcome can be influenced by both parties—double-sided moral hazard. The sales of a franchisee, for example, will be affected both by the franchisee's effort and the promotional work and product quality of the franchisor. Likewise, unless one of the parties is completely passive, outcomes in a joint venture are determined by the efforts of both parties. The structure of the agreement will have to take into account the need for coordination (be it simultaneous or sequential) and for appropriate incentives. A biotech-pharmaceutical joint venture provides an example of sequential coordination. The biotech company researches a molecule in the first years, with some input from Big Pharma. If it produces a promising product, Big Pharma takes over the development, testing, and marketing of the product. The biotech's compensation involves a number of pieces: cost-based compensation on the initial development work, milestone payments as the product moves toward commercialization, and royalties if the product actually makes it to market.

Adaptation to Change

The Obligation

Because the future is uncertain, there is value in maintaining the ability to adapt as new information becomes available. That flexibility sometimes comes at a cost. Since one party, or both, might want to rely on the continued performance of the other, contracts often reflect a trade-off between flexibility and reliance. For commodities traded in thick markets, the reliance interest typically would be minimal. Parties enter into contracts based on current needs and price projections. These contracts need not have any adjustment mechanism at all. The most effective way to adapt to changing circumstances would be to enter into one-shot deals that would leave the party the freedom to enter into subsequent transactions or not, depending on the then-current circumstances. There would be no reason for the subsequent transaction to be with the same trading partner.

One-shot sales in which there is a temporal gap between execution and closing—for example, a corporate acquisition—present different problems. In the intervening months much can happen. Many of the possible changes are exogenous, for example, a recession, changes in the market for the target's product, and so on. Some of the changes, however, might be under the control of the target. It might attempt to distribute profits, raise the pay of executives, or engage in other activities that would adversely affect the value to the buyer. To prevent this, the contract would include covenants and a MAC clause that would allow the seller to back out if the covenants are breached or a MAC occurs. If the value of the target were to fall, through no fault of the target, the buyer would have an incentive to act opportunistically, invoking the MAC clause to either back out of the deal or force a renegotiation of the price. Contracts anticipate this, to some extent, by including exceptions that hold that particular negative factors do not constitute a MAC. The greater the potential negative impact of a MAC's invocation on the value of the target as a stand-alone, the more protection the target would insist on. The target might, for example, have lost much of its management team; ties with customers, bankers, and suppliers might have been severed; investments might have been postponed; and the invocation of the MAC clause might convey to the market that the target is "damaged goods." The greater the target's reliance on consummation of the deal, the greater the protection it would bargain for, either in the form of more stringent MAC exceptions or a greater termination fee.[9]

The making of a movie or the production of a television series provide good examples of the significance of adaptation as new information becomes available. As an extreme example, production of the *Lord of the Rings* film trilogy began three decades after acquisition of the movie rights.[10] Movie studios take options on the projects and, in effect, take options on the talent in the form of "pay-or-play" clauses. With these clauses the talent promises to set aside a time period to make a particular film; the studio, however, maintains flexibility by reserving the right not to make the film at all or to make the film without using the talent. The flexibility comes at a price, the price depending on the significance of the talent and, implicitly, the talent's reliance (the opportunity cost of the time set aside). For significant talent, this would typically take the form of the fixed fee (which for major artists could be in the range of $20 million).[11] That is, the compensation of a star would typically include a percentage of the gross receipts, which is offset against a fixed fee (to be paid even if the studio decides not to use the star). The making of a TV series adds two wrinkles to this. First, it involves a much longer chain of options—a pilot, initial production, and, if successful, renewals. As the series evolves, the importance of a character can change, and in some cases the character might simply be dropped. Second, if a show is successful, the talent has an incentive to renegotiate the deal, threatening to walk away if better terms are not agreed to.[12] Studios are not defenseless in the face of such threats. They can threaten to eliminate the actor from the show by, for example, killing off the character.

The contracts for development of a new drug by a biotech company and a venture capital deal both involve great uncertainty, and that uncertainty is reduced over time as the project unfolds.[13] In each case, the project is staged so that the financing party (the venture capitalist or the pharmaceutical company—Big Pharma) can evaluate the information produced (including its judgment about the competence and reliability of the party it is funding), to determine whether it should go forward or exercise its option to abandon. In both instances, the performing party is vulnerable to the financing party's threat to abandon the project, to force a revision of the agreement that would give it the larger share of the pie. The biotech company is less vulnerable to this threat in part because it would not need more financing for this project; the biotech company would not have additional costs to incur when the threat would be credible. Two other factors increase its protection. First, the contracts generally call for the intellectual property to revert to the biotech company if Big Pharma terminates. It could then search for an alternative pharma company to commercialize the product; second, Big Pharma's leverage is fairly weak because any delay, given the limited patent life, is costly to it.

The entrepreneur is more vulnerable to the venture capitalist's (VC) threat to abandon. This is especially so if the contract gives the VC a right of first refusal, as is often the case. The VC's decision not to go forward sends a powerful message to third parties—the party with the most intimate knowledge does not think the project worth pursuing. Furthermore, the third party must recognize that the right of first refusal would mean it only wins if the original VC thought the project unpromising. Heads, VC1 wins, tails VC2 loses. The entrepreneur's protection comes from two factors. First, the VC is a repeat player and has to be concerned with its reputation. Second, if its machinations were to delay bringing the entrepreneur's product to market, the value of the firm and the VC's stake in it could be adversely affected. Although the VC might value the option to abandon both for its strategic value and to defer spending decisions until further information became available, the cost of waiting can be great—a competing firm could get to market first.

To produce some products efficiently, one party, or both, might have to provide relation-specific capital. That is, the value of the capital would be contingent on continuation of its relationship with the other firm. An aluminum fabricator might, for example, build a plant adjacent to a smelter to avoid the costs of remelting the ingot. If it were to do so, it would be vulnerable to being held up by the firm owning the smelter. Entering into a long-term contract provides some protection from hold-up and provides some assurance that the costs of the specific capital could be amortized over time. So, too, would integration by ownership. That has its own problems, but for analytical purposes it is convenient to ask how a firm owning both would decide on what sort of plant to build and how to adapt the production schedule as circumstances change.

Suppose the firm had a choice between two technologies. One required construction of a plant that had no value if it could not be used with the adjacent smelter. The other had a higher incremental cost, but the plant could be used equally well in producing other products. Which should it choose? The answer depends on expectations regarding the future changes in the market. If the likelihood that the final product would be obsolescent were high, or if future technological improvements were likely, the less relation-specific investment would be preferred. The integrated firm has the incentives to engage in this balancing act. If the coordination had to be done across organizational boundaries, the same logic applies. The only difference is that it would be necessary to provide a mechanism for conveying to the decision maker the concerns of the other firm. Governance arrangements would form one possible class of mechanisms. A joint board might, for example, have the authority to make certain decisions. Alternatively, more decentralized mechanisms—prices—could be used. Thus, the contract might include a standby fee (we will pay $1 million per year in addition to a price per unit) or a take-or-pay clause (we agree to pay the contract price for 40 percent of the contract quantity regardless of whether we take anything). These and other variations, which I discuss shortly, in effect confront the firm with a price for varying levels of relation-specific investment.

Regardless of the precise level of relation-specific investment the firm chooses, if the contract were to last for any length of time, the firm would want the flexibility to adapt its production as market conditions change. The party that valued flexibility more would be responsible for the quantity decision, and the counterparty would "sell" flexibility, most likely indirectly. The "price" would settle somewhere between the value to the former and the cost to the latter. In some instances, the pricing is explicit. For example, in its agreement with a contract manufacturer, a computer manufacturer like Apple could increase or decrease the quantity without penalty if it were to give satisfactory advance notice (sixty days). With only thirty days notice it could adjust the quantity by 25 percent, still with no premium. If Apple required even greater flexibility, then it would be responsible for any overtime charges and vendor premiums. Apple could cancel any purchase order with thirty days notice provided that it reimburses the manufacturer for costs reasonably incurred.[14]

The pricing can also take more indirect forms, such as the aforementioned take-or-pay. If a buyer had ample storage space, it could provide great flexibility to a seller at a low or zero price. Great Lakes Carbon (with storage capacity for three years' worth of output) was able to offer oil companies a full output contract ("we promise to remove immediately any petroleum coke you choose to produce at a particular site").[15] Conversely, if the buyer needed the flexibility and the seller had a number of customers, a requirements contract would be used. Typically, such a contract would include some limit on the requirements, perhaps by linking the requirements to those of a particular plant. The greater the seller's ability to handle expected fluctuations in this buyer's needs, the lower the "price" for providing this flexibility.

The Price

If parties do enter into a long-term contractual relationship, they have to say something about price. Contracts for the sale of defined goods over a long time period usually include some price adjustment mechanism. One rationale for adjusting price is that if the market price deviates substantially from the contract price, the price signal could lead to an inefficient allocation of resources. This could be a significant problem if the market price was much higher than the contract price and the contract precluded resale. If the parties had a requirements contract, for example, the buyer's incentives would be skewed—it would take advantage of the favorable contract price by using more than it would if confronted with the actual market price. If, however, the contract was for a defined quantity, the inefficiency goes away—the buyer could resell at the market price. There would, of course, be distributional consequences—the windfall would belong to the buyer.

That potential "windfall" motivates two other rationales for including a price adjustment mechanism in the agreement. First, as already noted, a price adjustment mechanism could reduce the wasteful excessive searching for private information. If prices would be adjusted mechanically in subsequent years, there would be less incentive to produce information of future market conditions. Second, if there was a substantial gap between the contract and market prices, the disadvantaged party need not take it lying down. It can attempt to renegotiate the contract, perhaps by engaging in value-reducing acts (for example, "working to the rules" or putting forth a strained interpretation of the contract language). If the probability of wasteful behavior increases as the contract–market gap widens, price adjustment rules that are expected to narrow that gap become increasingly attractive.

There are a lot of mechanisms available for adjusting price within a long-term contract. All are imperfect. Their relative costs and benefits will determine which, if any, the parties should choose. The easiest way to adjust the price is to index. Indexing has the advantage of being mechanical and generally nonmanipulable. The disadvantage of indexing is that the index might track market conditions poorly. One way to allow the contract to track market conditions is to permit the buyer to solicit outside offers with the seller having the right of first refusal (or to meet competition). The buyer could solicit bids from outside sources and if it were to receive a bona fide bid below the contract price, the supplier would be given the option to match. The likelihood that parties to a long-term contract would use some variation on a meeting competition clause for price adjustment would depend on the availability of alternative suppliers; it would not make sense if there were significant relation-specific investments.

Negotiation is, of course, always an option. Even if the contract explicitly uses one of the methods mentioned in the previous paragraphs or unambiguously states that the contract is a fixed price agreement, one party could propose that the price be renegotiated. The contract could explicitly establish the conditions under which renegotiation is to take place. It could require renegotiation at fixed intervals or have it triggered by specific events (for example, a rise in a price index of more than 20 percent). "Gross inequity" clauses call for renegotiation if the contract price is too far out of line, but typically do not spell out the criteria for determining when a gross inequity exists, or what to do if it does exist. The parties could agree to renegotiate in good faith and determine what would happen if the negotiations break down. The failure to negotiate a new price could result in continued performance at the current price, termination, mediation or arbitration, and so forth. The downside of renegotiation, of course, is that one party could behave opportunistically, taking advantage of the counterparty's vulnerability.

Cost-based pricing, as already noted, is often used, despite its well-known flaws. If the subject matter is poorly defined, the likelihood that the parties would opt for some variant of cost-plus pricing increases. So if the contract is for the construction of a factory, the contract might specify a price and a mechanism for pricing "change orders." Because the parties cannot rely on the external market to price the change order, they typically resort to a cost-based solution. As the expected share of the change orders in the final cost of the project increases, the contract becomes more cost-based. If the features of the output are not known at the time of contracting, cost-based pricing is also likely. A supplier might, for example, promise to make parts for future models of a car even though that car has not yet been designed. The General Motors–Fisher Body contract is a venerable example of such an arrangement in which the price was set at cost plus a fixed percentage.[16] Cost-based pricing is common in collaborative agreements when substantial technological change is anticipated; see Gilson, Sabel, and Scott (2009) for illustrations.

Summing Up

Parties face a number of problems when designing (or living with) their contractual relationships. Information on the future is imperfect and improvable at a cost; moreover, information on some aspects is distributed asymmetrically. The incentives of the parties are imperfectly aligned. Circumstances change, and the parties would like to adapt to the new circumstances. The contract design problem is further complicated by the fact that the interests of the parties are not completely compatible. The design has to take into account the possibility that one of the parties will attempt to take advantage of the other party, perhaps by misrepresenting facts in the precontract negotiations or opportunistically taking advantage of the other party's vulnerability to rewriting the contract. The design does not take place in an institutional vacuum. It will reflect the possibility of future dealings between the parties or the availability of reputational constraints. And it will reflect the content of the contract law and the quality and cost of its administration. If the costs of litigating a complex commercial dispute are substantial and the likelihood that a lay jury would be able to make sense of the dispute is low, parties might attempt to design their relationship to avoid litigation regardless of the content of the contract law.[17]

The Law

Parties design their contractual relationships within a legal framework. Much of U.S. contract law is facilitative of private ordering—if parties don't like a particular rule, they can change it. The formal contract law provides only a set of default rules, although not everything is negotiable. At the extreme, some rules are mandatory. More generally, default rules can be sticky either because the law imposes hurdles of varying heights to drafting around the defaults or because of nonlegal factors (for example, the costs of negotiating). A capitalist system can flourish because of a general belief in the enforceability of commercial promises, not because contract law gets it exactly right. Indeed, the following discussion of U.S. contract law should make clear that it falls short of the ideal.

In this section, the discussion is organized around four central issues in contract law. The first question seems simple enough—is there an enforceable agreement? That turns out to be more problematic and controversial than it would appear. The primary determinant of whether a promise would be legally enforceable is whether there is "consideration." Because conditions are likely to change after parties enter into an agreement that is expected to last for a period of time, contract doctrine will establish a set of default rules for adapting to the changed circumstances. One aspect of the consideration problem is the enforceability of a modification. The second and third issues also deal with the modification problem—adjusting to changed circumstances. One adjustment option is termination. That option can be explicit in the agreement, or, if the contract is silent, the option to abandon or terminate would be implicit. The option price would be defined by the second issue I discuss, the default remedies of contract law. Third, one possible adjustment to changed conditions is to excuse performance. Again, the grounds can be explicit (e.g., force majeure clauses or conditions).[18] In the absence of explicit language, the doctrinal bases for excusing performance come under a variety of headings—impossibility, impracticability, frustration, and mistake. Fourth, when contracts are litigated, the issue often comes down to interpretation. Should extrinsic evidence be admitted to determine the contract's meaning (the parol evidence and plain meaning rules)?

Enforceability

"Consideration" is the primary doctrinal tool that determines whether a commercial contract would be enforced. If a promise were "bargained for," then it would be enforceable, otherwise not. That bald statement requires some qualification. First, "bargained for," like "consideration," is a term of art—placing an item on a supermarket checkout counter doesn't seem much like bargaining, but it probably would suffice. Second, enforcement might be denied on other grounds (for example, fraud or "against public policy"). Third, reliance on a promise might be sufficient to make it enforceable even if there were no consideration—promissory estoppel.[19] The doctrine allows the courts to ask an on/off question: did a party give something up? It would not have to ask whether the transaction was fair; there would be no attempt to find the "just price." As long as a party promised to give up something, however little, the consideration requirement would be satisfied. Even a mere "peppercorn" would do.[20]

The Illusory Promise

If a promisor said, in effect, "I will do X if I want to," the promise would be illusory. Since the promisor had not promised to do anything, a court could conclude that there was no consideration and, therefore, no contract. Some agreements that seemed on their face to be legitimate deals—requirements contracts, full output contracts, and exclusive contracts—were held to be unenforceable in the early twentieth century. The courts (and later, the Uniform Commercial Code) responded by implying two doctrinal Band-Aids: (a) good faith and (b) reasonable or best efforts. This, I suggest, was a mistake.

The seminal decision is *Wood v. Lucy, Lady Duff Gordon.*[21] Lucy was a famous fashion designer in the first decades of the twentieth century. She entered into a one-year "evergreen" contract[22] with Otis Wood, who had the exclusive right to place endorsements for her. Revenues would be shared equally. The first year went fine, but in the second year Lucy entered into promotional deals bypassing Wood. He sued. Her defense was that he had only promised to share revenues if he happened to drum up some business, but he did not actually promise to drum up the business. The agreement, therefore, was illusory, she claimed, and a unanimous appellate court agreed. However, in a 4–3 decision, the Court of Appeals reversed. Justice Benjamin Cardozo found that despite the fact that Wood had not overtly promised to do anything, a promise could be implied to use "reasonable efforts." And that would be enough to provide consideration. Cardozo's solution has since been embodied in the Uniform Commercial Code: "A lawful agreement by either the seller or the buyer for exclusive dealing in the kind of goods concerned imposes unless otherwise agreed an obligation by the seller to use best efforts to supply the goods and by the buyer to use best efforts to promote their sale."[23]

Ironically, unbeknownst to Justice Cardozo, in a contract entered into shortly before his contract with Lucy, Otis Wood had entered into an agreement with Rose O'Neill, the originator of the Kewpie doll, and that contract included an *explicit* best efforts clause. That promise would have been sufficient to provide consideration. Cardozo's doctrinal ploy was unnecessary. His solution to the lack-of-consideration problem (which the parties could easily have resolved on their own) was not harmless. It altered the definition of what is to be enforced. The implied reasonable/best efforts standard, however fuzzy that might be, would define the promisor's obligation. As the law has evolved, the reasonable efforts standard would be implied, even if there were a separate source of consideration.

As long as consideration doctrine provides a fairly sharp boundary as to what is enforceable, it shouldn't matter very much to serious commercial firms.[24] The parties could take the rule into account and choose whether they should make their arrangement enforceable by providing explicit consideration. The *Wood* doctrine made this harder. Firms often attempt to arrange their affairs so that there is *not* an enforceable promise going forward. For example, early automobile franchise agreements were held unenforceable because the agreements merely spelled out terms that would be incorporated into a sale if the auto manufacturer accepted an order from the dealer. The auto manufacturers could have redrafted to resolve the technical problem but chose not to do so, because they preferred that their arrangements be terminable at will. Kessler (1957, p. 1149) noted, with disapproval, that the contracts were not enforceable:

> An initial block confronting dealers lay in the argument that a franchise, marked by the absence or indefiniteness of obligations, was not a valid and enforceable contract. Until recently, the validity issue was continuously raised in franchise litigation, the defendant manufacturer almost invariably arguing that the agreement lacked mutuality....
>
> For many decades, the invalidity argument may have been the most powerful weapon available to manufacturers in defending damage suits by dealers. It was honored by most courts, provided the manufacturer engaged in careful draftsmanship.

It should not have required "careful draftsmanship" to achieve a simple result. Nor should it have been necessary to use an oblique doctrinal tool to do so. Clearly, the automobile manufacturers desired that their agreements not be enforceable, their dealers knew (or should have known) it, and the dealers were not willing to give up enough to make an enforceable agreement acceptable to the manufacturers.

In the literature on the economics of vertical integration by ownership versus contract, much has been made of General Motors' decision to end its long-term contractual relationship with Fisher Body by acquiring the company. Implicit in that literature is an assumption that the contract was legally enforceable. It wasn't. To summarize the contract, General Motors promised to order and purchase substantially all its car bodies from Fisher, and it promised to provide schedules of its needs to Fisher in a timely fashion. What did Fisher promise? After receipt of the schedules, Fisher promised to tell General Motors whether it would accept the orders. If it did so, then Fisher would have an obligation to use its best efforts to fill the orders. Fisher did not promise to accept any orders from GM, and that is the crucial point—it did not promise to do anything. It could choose to fill orders or not, and the contract placed no limits on its discretion. Fisher's promise was "I will do it if I want to." That would not be enough to make the contract enforceable in the 1920s. The law has liberalized since then, and it is possible that some courts would now find it enforceable.[25]

Whether the drafters knew the contract would not be enforceable is unclear, although given the uncontroversial state of the law at the time, it is hard to imagine that counsel would be so ignorant. The GM executives, although unhappy with the terms of the deal, acted as if the contract was enforceable. Despite their discontent, they never asked counsel to determine whether they were in fact bound by the contract's terms. So, while we do not know whether the nonenforceability was intentional ex ante, we do know that the legal nonenforceability did not matter ex post.

If GM was unhappy with the deal, why did management not care enough to ask their counsel whether GM was indeed bound by the manufacturing contract? The start of an answer is that they were not that unhappy. Things never got so bad that they were willing to risk rupturing the entire relationship. GM did not want to alienate the Fisher brothers, since its long-term interest was to integrate them into the firm.[26] Regardless of whether the agreement was legally enforceable, it provided a yardstick or reference point against which either party's behavior could be judged. Furthermore, if either party simply walked away, both would have suffered significantly. While the contract language suggested that GM had an option to use other suppliers if the price was not competitive, that wasn't realistic, because there was not enough capacity available to replace Fisher. Similarly, if Fisher lost GM as a customer, it would have taken a huge hit. Over time, the performance of the parties raised the switching costs of both. That might explain why the parties avoided the business equivalent of nuclear war.

The illusory contract problem could be easily solved by the parties if they so chose. As the Fisher Body story suggests, the legal nonenforceability need not be a problem. The doctrinal Band-Aids have probably made things worse by imposing an ill-defined standard on an ill-defined set of promisors.

Contract Modification

As noted, the ability to adapt as circumstances change can be valuable. The world has changed, and the deal can be rearranged to accommodate that change. Some modifications, however, will not be enforced because of a failure of consideration. The seller, to use a simple example, says, "I will sell you 1,000 widgets at $20 a piece." When the time for delivery arrives, costs have risen and he says, "I will deliver those widgets, but only at $30 a piece," and the buyer says, "Yes." The widgets are delivered and the buyer refuses to pay the additional $10,000. Because there was no new consideration for the second promise, there was no deal and the buyer would prevail.

If the seller said that he would do something different—that is, promised to do something in addition to what had previously been promised—then there would be consideration, and the modification might well survive a legal challenge. It would seem that the doctrinal trick would be as easy to pull off as the solution to the illusory promise problem. There is, however, an additional problem. The illusory promise problem can be dealt with ex ante, before the parties have entered into a relationship. The modification issue arises ex post, and the party proposing the modification might be attempting to take advantage of the counterparty's vulnerability. And that is precisely what the rule is supposed to prevent.

The classic illustration of this problem is *Alaska Packers Assn. v. Domenico.*[27] A cannery hired men in San Francisco to go to Alaska and fish for salmon. Once in Alaska the workers balked, and said they would only work if the owners doubled their payment. Rather than lose the entire catch for the season, the owner's agent agreed to the modification, under protest. When the ship returned to San Francisco, the workers asked for the enhanced payment and the owner refused. The court, invoking the so-called preexisting duty rule, held that there was no new consideration for the second contract, and therefore that contract was unenforceable. The general presumption is that this was a pure hold-up case, although the workers attempted to justify the second contract as an appropriate response to changed circumstances. They claimed that the nets were of such poor quality that the original contract arrangement would have been inadequate because part of their compensation was a flat rate of two cents a fish. Even in this case, distinguishing a good faith modification from an opportunistic one is not a simple matter; the workers could present a rationale that at least some would find convincing[28]—although the courts, in this instance, did not.

The modern treatment of modification is to downplay the consideration issue and to allow "good faith" modifications (see UCC 2–209). The exemplar of this standard is *Austin Instrument v. Loral.*[29] Loral, a defense contractor, had a contract with the U.S. Navy to build radar sets in the 1960s. Austin was a subcontractor for twenty-three of the forty parts. In a follow-on contract, Austin insisted that it be the contractor for all forty parts and that Loral raise the price on the original contract; otherwise, it would delay production. After failing to find an alternative supplier, Loral agreed. However, its fingers were crossed; when all the parts were delivered, Loral refused to pay, saying that the second agreement was a result of duress. A closely divided court found in favor of Loral; it would have been subject to substantial liquidated damage payments to the Navy for late delivery and it made a good-faith, albeit futile, search for alternative suppliers. Although many academics agree with this outcome, I am skeptical. Austin was a small subcontractor whose future business required that it maintain a decent reputation with the large defense contractors. It is implausible that it would sacrifice its reputation and its future defense business for a mere $20,000. Most likely, it won the first contract by bidding low, common in defense contracting, with the expectation that it would make it up in future contracts, and Loral shopping for the second round disappointed its expectations.

Ultimately, the question of whether a modification is in good faith is a fact question, and counsel for the firm requesting (demanding?) modification should be clever enough to survive summary judgment. The problem is further complicated by the fact that a party might have the right to take advantage of its counterparty's vulnerability, if that vulnerability is the fault of the "victim." If, for example, *X* is having financial difficulties and desperately needs cash to avoid bankruptcy, *Y* could use that vulnerability to exact a concession.[30]

Remedies and Termination

One way of adapting to changed conditions is to terminate the agreement. The mechanism for termination can be explicit; or, if the contract is silent, the party could breach and be liable for the default contract remedy. One remedy—common in European law, less so in the common law countries—is specific performance. One party will have a "property entitlement" (see Calabresi and Melamed, 1972) and can insist that the other perform or buy itself out of the obligation. Money damages are far more common in U.S. law (and probably in European practice). Remedies are typically classified as expectation damages, reliance damages, and restitution—with the major emphasis on the expectation damages. The victim of the breach, so the story goes, should be as well off as if the contract had been performed. In the simplest case, a sale of a commodity in a thick market, the remedy is simply the contract-market differential. In more complex transactions, application gets more complicated. Indeed, rational parties would often prefer lesser remedies. For example, a seller's breach might subject the buyer to "consequential damages"—that is, damages that arise because of the breach (UCC 2-715(2)). If a transportation company fails to deliver goods, for example, the buyer might find that its factory must shut down, resulting in large lost sales. If sellers are routinely held liable for these damages, in the long run sellers as a class will include the costs of these damages in their price. There are doctrinal limits to the liability (e.g., foreseeability), but there has been a trend in most U.S. jurisdictions to give increased recognition to consequential damages. In effect, if the law liberally awarded consequential damages and placed high barriers to contracting out, it would amount to sellers providing mandatory insurance without the benefit of the insurer's tools for controlling adverse selection and moral hazard. Indeed, it is very common for sellers to disclaim consequential damages. The disclaimer often fails, especially if it is in a seller's standard form. If the buyer's form says otherwise, the majority rule in the United States (UCC §2-207) is that the disclaimer is "knocked out" and it is replaced by the default rule from the Uniform Commercial Code, which allows for the recovery of consequential damages (UCC §2-715).

The contract remedy, whether explicit or the default rule, should, I believe, be treated as just another term of the deal. But it's not. "Compared with the extensive power that contracting parties have to bargain over their substantive contract rights and duties, their power to bargain over their remedial rights is surprisingly limited"[31] (Farnsworth, 1998, §12.18). This mindset manifests itself most in the doctrinal treatment of penalty clauses. The legal standard is that penalty clauses are unenforceable, but liquidated damages clauses are enforceable. Unfortunately, that doesn't tell us anything because a liquidated damages clause can be a penalty and vice versa. Farnsworth notes that the rationale for the refusal to enforce penalties is that a high penalty might "deter breach by compelling performance. Enforcement of such a provision would allow parties to depart from the fundamental principle that the law's goal on breach of contract is not to deter breach by compelling the promisor to perform, but rather to redress breach by compensating the promisee" (1998, §12.18). My own position is that there is no sound basis for making compensation the "fundamental principle." Allowing sophisticated parties to design their relationships in their perceived best interest seems to me the appropriate fundamental principle.[32]

True, there is some basis for not enforcing some penalty clauses. Shylock's pound of flesh could be denied on public policy grounds and a large penalty hidden in the middle of a ten-page consumer contract could also be rejected. But when two sophisticated parties draw up an agreement, there should be a strong presumption that they have a good reason for doing it this way. If, for example, an electric utility promises to pay a coal mine for 30 percent of its annual potential output even if it were to take none (take-or-pay), or a movie studio promises to pay an actor $20 million even if the studio decides not to use the actor in a film (pay-or-play), these promises have a perfectly sensible economic rationale. Their purpose is not compensation of the promisee; it is to provide some protection of the promisee's reliance by confronting the promisor with a price. The promisee, as noted, is in effect selling flexibility to the promisor. The price of that flexibility will be bounded by the promisee's cost of providing it and its value to the promisor. There is no more reason for a court to question this price than there is for questioning the contract's explicit price terms or any other terms, for that matter.

Excuse

Oliver Wendell Holmes (1897, p. 462) observed that "The duty to keep a contract at common law means a prediction that you must pay damages if you do not keep it, and nothing else...If you commit a contract, you are liable to pay a compensatory sum unless the promised event comes to pass." That aphorism has to be qualified by recognizing that in the face of changed circumstances, the performance might be modified or excused and that parties often do include such qualifications in their agreements. Contract law adds some default rules to these qualifications under the rubric of impossibility, impracticability, frustration, and mistake.[33]

The UCC §2–615 has liberalized the rules for excusing performance. The seller would be excused if performance "has been made impracticable by the occurrence of a contingency the non-occurrence of which was a basic assumption on which the contract was made." Large market fluctuations, particularly in the energy sector, have generated a substantial amount of litigation. Despite the relatively generous language of the Code, courts, with some exceptions, have been unsympathetic to aggrieved parties. Some academics argue that courts should excuse promisors (or judicially revise the contract) if market-wide cost changes have resulted in a large increase in the market price.[34] Although courts do excuse in some instances when large cost changes make performance impractical, they rarely do so for market-wide changes. In most instances, the cost change is not market-wide but is transaction-specific. A farmer can't deliver, for example, because a flood destroyed his entire crop. Or a manufacturer's failure to deliver results from his factory being destroyed by fire. Even though the supplier could not perform in either of these cases, it need not be excused—it could still pay money damages. In these cases, unlike the market-wide cost change, the default rule is to excuse.[35] Usually, the default rule excusing performance would not be necessary because such an event would be covered by the force majeure clause.

The rationale for excusing performance in such cases is that, ex ante, the expected market price change from such an event is uncorrelated with the intervening event. On average, the market price will be unaffected by the event and, therefore, the parties' ex ante allocation of market risks will be preserved. The expected cost to the buyer of allowing the excuse would therefore be low; it typically would not be willing to pay for insurance against this risk. (If sellers were held liable, this would be a cost of doing business that would have to be covered.) If the product was perfectly fungible, say, a wallet with $1,000 in it lost in a fire, the litigation costs of determining damages would be zero and the benefits of excusing performance would be trivial. Force majeure clauses typically do not excuse in such situations and in practice, I believe, courts would not use the UCC to imply such an excuse. However, if the product were not so perfectly defined, the measurement of damages would be more costly and more subject to error. These costs could be avoided by excusing performance and, given the low expected cost of excusing performance, we should expect to see force majeure clauses excusing parties (as long as the intervening event was not caused by the promisor).

The UCC and the common law have muddled things a bit by putting weight on the parties' perceptions. The trigger is an intervening event, the "nonoccurrence of which was a basic assumption."[36] This seems to suggest that the concern is remote risks—low-probability events—that rational parties would not have thought about. It focuses the inquiry on whether the parties could possibly have imagined the event taking place. Given the limited imagination of many analysts, their answer is often in the negative.

The problems with this approach can best be seen by considering two of the fundamental excuse cases, both from England and both over a century old: *Taylor v. Caldwell*[37] and *Krell v. Henry*.[38] In the former, generally considered to be the fount of the impossibility doctrine, the plaintiff agreed to pay £100 each for the privilege of producing four concerts at a particular venue. In return it was to get 100 percent of the gate. One week prior to the first concert, the venue was destroyed by a fire. The plaintiff sued for damages; the court ruled that since the fire rendered performance impossible, both parties were excused from any further performance. Was the *particular* circumstance unexpected? Yes. Was the possibility of a fire or any other event that would render the venue unusable so remote that reasonable people should not have even considered it? Hardly. Fire insurance had been available in England since the Great London Fire of 1666 (the *Taylor* fire was two centuries later). Nowadays it would be common for contracts for a live performance to take into account two contingencies: that the artist or the venue would not be available through no fault of the parties. These are predictable risks, and parties can contract to determine how the risks should be allocated. *Taylor v. Caldwell* merely establishes a default rule that would govern if the parties neglected to provide for the possibility in their agreement. The *Taylor* result—leave the parties where they were at the time of the intervening event—is one possibility.[39]

Just before Edward VII's coronation procession, the king came down with appendicitis and the event was postponed. Viewing spots had been sold at exorbitant prices, and many buyers argued that they should not be required to pay following the postponement. A number of cases made their way through the courts with *Krell v. Henry* being the one making most of the casebooks. Henry had agreed to pay £75 for the privilege of using Krell's rooms overlooking the parade route for two days and no nights (per capita income at the time was £45). The contract was silent on the purpose, although it was obvious from the context. Henry had already paid one-third when the postponement was announced, and he refused to pay the remainder. The Law Lords held that the basic purpose of the contract had been frustrated and excused Henry from paying the rest (Henry had dropped his demand that the original payment be refunded): "I think it cannot reasonably be supposed to have been in the contemplation of the contracting parties when the contract was made, that the coronation would not be held on the proclaimed days . . . or along the proclaimed route."[40] The specific event—appendicitis—might not have been contemplated. But is it hard to believe that a sixty-year-old man who was grossly overweight, a heavy smoker, and the target of at least one assassination attempt might be unavailable? In fact, many did believe it. There was a very active insurance market; at least some of the hundreds of thousands of viewing contracts included language dealing with the possibility that the event would not take place on schedule. This is not to say that the outcome was wrong, only that the rationale was. The parties were perfectly capable to protect themselves from this and other remote risks. Had the Lords simply implied a term—for the purpose of viewing the processions—they could have held that the object of the contract no longer existed and simply used the *Taylor* default rule.

The moral of this story is twofold. First, there exist a lot of low-probability events which, were they to occur, would cause one party to very much regret having entered into the agreement. Parties can contract ex ante as to how to deal with classes of such events, and in addition, the law provides a set of default rules. Neither the parties nor the default rules typically excuse further performance if the intervening event is a market-wide shift in costs or prices. Second, doctrine misleadingly emphasizes the limited cognitive ability of parties as the trigger for invoking excuse—the risks, it is claimed, are too remote for rational folks to take into account. Two anecdotes cannot prove otherwise, even if they go to the core cases of the doctrine. But they do illustrate that parties can, and do, take into account classes of remote risks and assign responsibility for them. The doctrinal choices are limited—excuse, don't excuse, reform (the latter rarely used in the United States).[41] They do provide the backdrop for more complex responses, either as incorporated in the initial agreements or as voluntary modifications.

Interpretation

It is common to say that contract interpretation should reflect the parties' intent. The legal meaning of party intentions is not, however, the same as the intentions of some human being. Contracts are written for an organization with those intentions filtered through a lawyer. Moreover, contracts are assignable, so the intentions underlying today's contract might be those of organizations with no current stake in the outcome. To give a somewhat extreme example, in 2008 a suit was filed by plaintiffs complaining that their contract entitled them to a larger share of the earnings of the *Lord of the Rings* film trilogy.[42] The contracts forming the basis of the suit were entered into nearly forty years earlier in 1969. The original buyer of the rights was United Artists, which subsequently transferred its rights to the Saul Zaentz Production Company, which transferred the rights to Miramax, which in turn transferred the rights to New Line Cinema. The seller of the rights was George Allen & Unwin, which in turn transferred its rights to HarperCollins.[43] Whose intent should count? In another context, disputes sometimes arise regarding form contracts, the so-called battle of the forms. The fine print on the back of a seller's invoice says X and the fine print on the buyer's purchase order says Y. The individuals doing the transaction have nothing to do with that language; it is the product of some lawyer, produced years earlier for a class of transactions that might or might not have some common features with the transaction at hand. The "intent" in these cases is not the subjective intent of the litigating parties but the "objective" intent—what intent could an outsider infer from the words of the agreement and perhaps the context.

The interplay between the written contract and the context is controversial. Some, like Schwartz and Scott (2010), argue for a "textualist" approach. That is, the adjudicator (judge, arbitrator, jury) will focus on the document, only turning to the context if the language is vague or ambiguous. Others, including the drafters of the Uniform Commercial Code, opt for a more contextualist approach in which the course of dealing between the parties and trade usage are incorporated into the contract. The textualists prefer a hard parol evidence rule which excludes evidence of precontractual language that might alter the meaning of the final written agreement; the contextualists are more willing to allow such evidence. The same sort of distinction arises with regard to the interpretation of specific contract language, the textualists preferring the so-called plain meaning rule. Part of the battle reflects implicit assumptions about the relative skills of the contracting parties. The contextualist position is more attractive if the contract at issue is between a large corporation on the one hand and a consumer, employee, or franchisee on the other. The textualist position, conversely, is more attractive when both parties are sophisticated firms with access to legal counsel. While both the UCC and the

Restatement 2d both lean toward the contextualist side, the majority of U.S. courts take a more formalist approach.

The key insights of the textualists are, first, that the rules of interpretation themselves should be viewed as default rules subject to modification by the parties, and, second, that they want to balance the virtues of accuracy against the costs of achieving it. Litigation is expensive, time-consuming, and, especially if the transaction was complicated, error-prone. Complex contracts routinely include so-called integration clauses, which say, in effect, that the written document supersedes all prior agreements, understandings, and negotiations whether written or oral. What you see is what you get. Even if the parties really agreed that the promisor should do X, if that obligation did not make it into the final document, the textualists would not hold the promisor to it. Contextualists have a number of doctrinal tricks to undermine the integration clause.[44]

To be sure, the textualists will admit that many contractual obligations cannot be interpreted without the aid of context. Complex agreements are full of fuzzy language—good faith, material, best efforts, reasonable effort, and so forth. Some understanding of the context is essential for interpreting terms of this sort.[45] Scott and Triantis (2006) have suggested that parties engage in a second trade-off—balancing the ex ante costs of additional precision against the ex post expected costs of litigation. Despite the fact that such litigation would be expensive, parties do often opt for the latter. The fuzzy terms are acceptable, not because of the adjudicator's (judge, arbitrator, jury) ability to accurately resolve the dispute but because the probability of a dispute arising over these terms is low.

Concluding Remarks

The economics literature, which emphasizes the importance of institutions for economic development, places great weight on the role of contracts in facilitating exchange, when exchange cannot take place in spot markets. In this chapter I have pried open the black box of contract a bit, focusing on both the problems parties must cope with (sometimes lumped under the heading of "transactions costs") and particular features of the legal regime constraining them. The theme of this volume is the present and future of the capitalist form of social organization. It is fair to ask what the foregoing has to say about that; the answer is: not much. For that question, the specific content of any body of contract law is irrelevant. Other than a few basics—the existence of some third-party enforcement and some ability to modify the default rules—a vibrant capitalism does not depend on contract law "getting it right." To be sure, getting it right can mean making things better. In my discussion of contract law, I have indicated some instances in which the substance could be improved.

Notes

1. See Klein, Crawford, and Alchian (1978); Klein (2000, 2007); Coase (2000, 2006); Cassadesus-Masanell and Spulber (2000); Freeland (2000); and Goldberg (2008).
2. I am reminded of a student a number of years ago who proudly informed me that his new bike weighed only twelve pounds and then reluctantly added that the new lock weighed fifteen.
3. I exclude noncommercial contracts and consumer contracts from the discussion.
4. I gloss over the fact that U.S. contract law is not monolithic. Most contracts are governed by state law, so there are really more than fifty varieties. The general contours are close enough that it is reasonable to generalize about U.S. law.
5. A legal peculiarity might obscure this. If an insurance contract promised inspection services, then the insurer might be found negligent and held liable for damages above the policy ceiling if an accident occurs. To avoid this, the contract would explicitly deny that the insurer is providing such services, even though it is. See Goldberg (1980). For more on the possible benefits of liability insurance, see Goldberg (2009).
6. The buyer has an incentive to invoke the MAC opportunistically if the value of the target falls through no fault of the seller. The typical MAC clause would have some exceptions that would rule out changes beyond the control of the seller. This is especially likely if it appears that reneging by the buyer would cause the value of the target as a stand-alone firm to fall; see Gilson and Schwartz (2005).
7. The seller's incentives to game the earnout often result in the parties abandoning the earnout in their negotiating the deal.
8. See Milgrom and Roberts (1992, chapter 7).
9. Most MAC litigation takes place in Delaware. As of this writing, no buyer has been successful in invoking a MAC clause.
10. See *Tolkien v. New Line Cinema Corp.*, 2008 WL5531078 (Cal. Superior).
11. For more on pay-or-play clauses, see Goldberg (2006, chapter 15).
12. This can happen in movies as well; to avoid this risk, the *Lord of the Rings* trilogy was all shot at the same time. By avoiding the renegotiation risk, the studio gave up the option to abandon if the first film had been a failure.
13. The pharmaceutical company (Big Pharma) sponsoring the research is, in effect, a form of venture capitalist. A venture capitalist prepares the financed company for sale to others. Because it is in the business of commercialization of drugs, Big Pharma would take the next steps itself.
14. Fountain Manufacturing Agreement between Apple Computer and Sci Systems (May 31, 1996). http://contracts.onecle.com/apple/scis.mfg.1996.05.31.shtml.
15. See Goldberg and Erickson (1987). "It is expressly understood that *Seller reserves the sole right to determine when and in what quantity coke shall be produced,* and that seller shall be obligated hereunder to sell and deliver coke to Purchaser *only as, when, and to the extent it is produced*" (emphasis added).
16. See Goldberg (2008, p. 1077). As will be noted, that contract was not legally enforceable, but that is irrelevant.
17. The United States is the only major country in which lay juries would adjudicate contract disputes (and civil cases, generally).
18. A force majeure clause, also known as an "act of God" clause, lists events that will either suspend or excuse performance of the contract.

19. Historically, a seal would make a contract enforceable; "moral obligation" is recognized by some courts as a basis for finding a valid contract, but it is irrelevant for commercial transactions.
20. The peppercorn has long been used to illustrate the point that almost anything would suffice to make the promise enforceable.
21. 118 N.E. 214 (N.Y. 1917).
22. An evergreen contract is renewable on the same terms unless notice is given.
23. UCC §2–306(2). To ensure consideration for variable quantity contracts, the courts, and subsequently the UCC, invoked an implied duty of good faith. UCC §2–306(1). This, too, is problematic.
24. This statement has to be qualified; the "modification" cases, discussed shortly, are not so easily handled.
25. For more on the GM-Fisher contract, see Goldberg (2008). The terms of the contract were incorporated into any orders Fisher Body had accepted. The enforceability issue only concerns the future obligations.
26. By 1925, three of the Fisher brothers were on GM's board of directors and two were officers. Source: material collected by Richard Brooks from General Motors Annual Reports.
27. 117 F. 99 (9th Cir. 1902).
28. See Threedy (2000).
29. 324 N.Y.S. 2d 22 (N.Y. 1971).
30. See *Selmer Co. v. Blakeslee-Midwest Co.*, 704 F.2d 924 (C.A. Wis., 1983). For a decision going the other way, see *Totem Marine Tug & Barge, Inc. v. Alyeska Pipeline Service Co.*, 584 P.2d 15 (Alaska, 1978).
31. "This hostile attitude toward penalties is peculiar to common law countries and is not generally shared by other legal systems." Farnsworth (1998, §12.18).
32. See Goldberg (2006, part IV); this is not an idiosyncratic position, see, for example, Scott and Triantis (2004).
33. For more on this topic see Goldberg (2006, chapter 19) and Goldberg (2010).
34. See Eisenberg (2009).
35. The farmer would not be excused if he only promised to deliver crops but did not specify that the crops come from his land. If the promise was only for a quantity of, say, wheat, he could buy it on the open market, and there would therefore be no excuse.
36. See Eisenberg (2009).
37. B. & S. 826, 122 Eng. Rep. 309 (1863).
38. [1903] 2 K.B. 740.
39. The rule that has evolved in England and the United States requires restitution for prepayment and possibly some compensation for reliance expenditures. *Fibrosa Spolka Akcyjna v. Fairbairn Lawson Combe Barbour, Ltd.* [1942] A.C. 32 established the restitution rule in England, and shortly thereafter Parliament passed the Law Reform (Frustrated Contracts) Act, which allowed for compensation for reliance in certain circumstances. The Restatement Second §272 gives the court the power to "grant relief on such terms as justice requires, including protection of the parties' reliance interests [if necessary to] avoid injustice." However, although they typically grant restitution, they usually deny reliance claims; see Farnsworth (1998, §9.9)
40. [1903] 2 K.B. 740.
41. For a critical analysis of one of the rare U.S. cases to reform the contract, *Alcoa v. Essex* (499 F. Supp. 53 W.D. Pa. 1980), see Goldberg (2006, chapter 20).
42. See *Tolkien v. New Line Cinema Corp.*, 2008 WL5531078 (Cal. Superior).

43. The Tolkien heirs also had a contractual claim.
44. For an egregious example, see *Columbia Nitrogen v. Royster*, 451 F.2d 3 (4th Cir. 1971) discussed in Goldberg (2006, chapter 7).
45. For an illustration of a failure to appreciate the context of a disputed best efforts clause, see *Bloor v. Falstaff Brewing Corp.*, 601 F. 2d 609 (2d cir. 1979), discussed in Goldberg (2006, chapter 6).

REFERENCES

Calabresi, Guido, and A. Douglas Melamed. "Property Rules, Liability Rules, and Inalienability: One View of the Cathedral." *Harvard Law Review* 85 (April 1972): 1089–1128.
Cassadesus-Masanell, Ramon, and Daniel F. Spulber. "The Fable of Fisher Body." *Journal of Law and Economics* 43 (April 2000): 67–104.
Coase, Ronald H. "The Nature of the Firm." *Economica* 4 (November 1937): 386–405.
Coase, Ronald H. "The Acquisition of Fisher Body by General Motors." *Journal of Law and Economics* 43 (April 2000): 15–31.
Coase, Ronald H. "The Conduct of Economics: The Example of Fisher Body and General Motors." *Journal of Economics and Management Strategy* 15, (Summer 2006): 255–278.
Eisenberg, Melvin A. "Impossibility, Impracticability, and Frustration." *Journal of Legal Analysis* 1 (Winter 2009): 207–261.
Farnsworth, E. Allan. *Farnsworth on Contracts*. New York: Aspen Law & Business, 1998.
Freeland, Robert F. "Creating Holdup through Vertical Integration: Fisher Body Revisited." *Journal of Law and Economics* 43 (April 2000): 33–66.
Gilson, Ronald J., and Alan Schwartz. "Understanding MACs: Moral Hazard in Acquisitions." *Journal of Law, Economics & Organization* 21 (Oct. 2005): 330–358.
Gilson, Ronald J., Charles Sabel, and Robert E. Scott. "Contracting for Innovation: Vertical Disintegration and Interfirm Collaboration." *Columbia Law Review* 109 (April 2009): 431–502.
Goldberg, Victor P. "Tort Liability for Negligent Inspection by Insurers." *Research in Law and Economics* 2 (1980): 65–8l.
Goldberg, Victor P. *Framing Contract Law: An Economic Perspective*. Cambridge, Mass.: Harvard University Press, 2006.
Goldberg, Victor P. "Lawyers Asleep at the Wheel? The GM-Fisher Body Contract." *Industrial and Corporate Change* 17 (Oct. 2008): 1071–1084.
Goldberg, Victor P. "The Devil Made Me Do It: The Corporate Purchase of Insurance." *Review of Law and Economics* 5 (Oct. 2009): 542–552.
Goldberg, Victor P. "Excuse Doctrine: The Eisenberg Uncertainty Principle." *Journal of Legal Analysis* 2 (Spring 2010): 359–381.
Goldberg, Victor P., and John R. Erickson. "Quantity and Price Adjustment in Long-Term Contracts: A Case Study of Petroleum Coke." *Journal of Law and Economics* 30 (Oct. 1987): 369–398.
Holmes, Oliver Wendell. "The Path of the Law." *Harvard Law Review* 10 (1897): 457–478.
Kessler, Friedrich. "Automobile Dealer Franchises: Vertical Integration by Contract." *Yale Law Journal* 66 (July 1957): 1135–1190.
Klein, Benjamin. "Fisher-General Motors and the Nature of the Firm." *Journal of Law and Economics* 43 (April 2000): 105–141.

Klein, Benjamin. "The Economic Lessons of Fisher Body-General Motors." *International Journal of the Economics of Business* 14 (2007): 1–36.

Klein, Benjamin, Robert G. Crawford, and Armen A. Alchian. "Vertical Integration, Appropriate Rents and the Competitive Contracting Process." *Journal of Law and Economics* 21 (Oct. 1978): 297–326.

Milgrom, Paul, and John Roberts. *Economics, Organization & Management*. Englewood Cliffs, N.J.: Prentice Hall, 1992.

North, Douglass. *Institutions, Institutional Change and Economic Performance*. Cambridge: Cambridge University Press, 1990.

Schwartz, Alan, and Robert E. Scott. "Contract Interpretation Redux." *Yale Law Journal* 119 (March 2010): 926–964.

Scott, Robert E., and George G. Triantis. "Embedded Options and the Case against Compensation in Contract Law." *Columbia Law Review* 104 (Oct. 2004): 1428–1491.

Scott, Robert E., and George G. Triantis. "Anticipating Litigation in Contract Design." *Yale Law Journal* 115 (Jan. 2006): 814–879.

Threedy, Debora L. "A Fish Story: *Alaska Packers Association v. Domenico*." *Utah Law Review* (2000): 185–221.

PART IV

PROBLEMS WITH CAPITALISM

CHAPTER 10

CAPITALISM AS A MIXED ECONOMIC SYSTEM

RICHARD R. NELSON

INTRODUCTION

MANY factors are stimulating discussion and argument about what reforms are necessary if capitalist economies are to work effectively to meet human economic needs in the twenty-first century: concerns about global warming, the recent financial crisis, the continuing rise in the costs of medical care, stubborn pockets of poverty in many nations with high average incomes, and more. However, almost no one is seriously proposing that capitalism, as a kind of economic system, be abandoned and something significantly different put in its place. That kind of argument died out with the end of the cold war. Today, there seems to be broad consensus that there are no real alternatives to capitalism.

But what is "capitalism" anyway? The now extensive literature on comparative capitalisms shows that the economies of countries that generally are considered to be capitalist differ in important ways. (Hollingsworth and Boyer, 1997, provide a good general discussion. See also the chapter by Odagiri in this volume.) Also, individual capitalist countries themselves obviously have changed greatly over the years.

However, there would appear to be two core characteristics broadly shared by all countries that call themselves capitalist. First, these economies make extensive use of market organization, broadly defined, to govern the production and distribution of goods and services. Second, this practice is supported by broad ideological agreement that market organization is the best way to govern economic activity.

A central argument of this chapter is that in countries that consider their economies basically capitalist, the conception that market organization is the best mode of economic governance is much simpler and more coherent than the complex and variegated way that economic activity actually is governed, which involves a wide range of nonmarket elements. This is both a source and a consequence of a continuing political debate about the appropriate governance of various economic activities and sectors.

The Relatively Simple Ideological Conception of Capitalism

Let us consider the ideological conception first. In a capitalist economy, the general presumption is that for-profit business firms ought to be the principal economic agents responsible for the supply of goods and services. Wants are regarded primarily as a matter of individual and household needs and tastes, and it is presumed that potential customers for goods and services ought to decide what they will buy and from whom on the basis of their own preferences, using their own money. Under the norms and expectations of capitalism, firms are assumed to interact and coordinate with customers, and also with suppliers of the inputs they need to operate, including labor, largely through markets. Along with the profit motive, which keeps firms focused on what consumers want and holding costs down, competition among firms is presumed to keep the prices firms charge in line with costs.

The widely held general conception of how capitalism ought to work does not rule out a significant role for government. Far from it. It is recognized that governments need to play an essential role in providing and protecting conditions under which markets can work well, by establishing and enforcing an effective legal structure, encouraging competition, and ensuring the adequacy of needed infrastructure. However, the norms associated with capitalism rule out attempts at central planning, except under emergency conditions like war. Regulation generally is expected to be mild, and attempts by government to control market outcomes presumed to be limited.

It has long been recognized that a major part of the role of government in maintaining conditions under which market organization can work well involves responsible macroeconomic policies, and at least since the time of Keynes it has been understood that from time to time active fiscal and monetary policies are needed to prevent or turn around raging inflation or severe depression. At least since the early years after World War II, modern capitalism generally is seen as being compatible with government policies to keep down the incidence and severity of poverty and to help people in distress.

When the term "mixed economy" is used these days to characterize modern capitalist systems, people often have in mind the essential role of government in maintaining conditions under which markets can operate effectively, including active fiscal and monetary policies where necessary and in providing a safety net.

However, my focus here is on another sense in which modern economies are mixed.

The More Complex Reality: Capitalism as a Mixed Economic System

The actual structure of modern capitalist economies is much more complex and interesting than the ideological picture of capitalism. Although usually ignored in characterizations of the nature of modern capitalism, a wide range of economic activities, goods and services, and even broad economic sectors are not governed through the kinds of markets modeled in the standard economics textbooks but through quite different structures. Modern capitalist economies make extensive use of market governance. But they also make use of other forms of governance.

I use the term "governance" to highlight what is at stake in choosing how economic activity is structured—who gets what and who pays, who has legitimate authority to do what, mechanisms of control—and to call attention to the fact that society has a choice about the matter, a choice that is ultimately political. I note that economists tend to see the structure of an economic sector as involving a demand side and a supply side, and in the discussion that follows I distinguish between the demand and the supply side of governance.

Simple market organization along the lines of the economic textbooks is one form of sectoral governance, and clearly capitalist economies make much use of markets. However, market organization is far from ubiquitous and seldom is employed in pure form. Although repressed in the conception of capitalism as a general economic system, once the focus of attention is brought to the level of meeting particular needs, of governing particular activities and sectors, this point can be immediately recognized.

National security is a canonical example of a broad national need where, on the demand side, society uses collective governmental processes, not market mechanisms, to decide how much to spend on what. A similar example is police services. The fact that demand is determined through governmental process of course does not mean that supply is governmental, too. Industry is the provider of most of the equipment used by the armed forces and the police. However, there also are certain activities or realms where supply is regarded as an innately governmental function. The armed services are organized and led through government. Providing and running the police system and the courts is another obvious example of public governing of the supply side as well as the demand side. The central role of government in ensuring the physical security of its citizens is taken for granted, even in the most self-consciously capitalist countries.

In virtually all countries, the lion's share of provision of primary and secondary education, as well as its finance, is undertaken though public organizations. While in most countries there are private schools as well as public, and a number of families choose to send their children to them even if they have to pay to do so, the central role in education of public finance and public provision is generally accepted.

The provision of medical care is another "mixed" system in most capitalist counties, and one subject to continuing controversy. In virtually all high-income capitalist countries, most medical care is paid for by insurance. In many there is often heated controversy about the appropriate mix of government-run and -funded versus private insurance and the extent of subsidy of the latter. There is also dispute about the supply side, in particular regarding whether doctors and hospitals should be treated as independent economic agents or as part of a more unified system, and the extent to which the "market" for medical care should be under relatively detailed regulatory control. I note here, for elaboration later, that the medical profession tends to insist that the aim of doctors is to help patients and that they should not be regarded as "profit maximizers," and hence there is no need for government regulation.

As the case of doctors serving patients highlights, in many activities and sectors the nature of the relationship between suppliers who earn their money selling goods and services and their customers does not look quite like the textbook model of market governance. Another example of a market-organized set of activities that looks quite different from the textbook model is TV news broadcasting put on by commercial stations and networks, who do not make their money directly from viewers but from advertisers who buy a piece of the broadcast time. At the same time the broadcasting of reliable and complete news is widely understood to be a public service, and hence erosion of advertising revenues that induce reduction in investments in reporting can be viewed as a potential public policy problem. Or consider professional sports, where the owners of franchises often demand subsidies from the communities whose name they carry, in addition to receiving money from both paying fans and TV channels.

More generally, it is important to recognize that many activities and sectors that generally are thought of as market-governed in fact have a mixed governing structure. Thus, both the products and production methods of pharmaceutical companies are regulated, and public monies go into the basic research that pharmaceutical companies draw from in their development work. Many aspects of airline operation are regulated, the government operates the air traffic control system, and airports are largely funded and often owned by public bodies. Most of the old "public utilities" are still quite regulated and sometimes subsidized.

It is a mistake to see the governance issue as strictly about markets versus government. Child care, an activity that absorbs an enormous amount of resources, is largely provided by family members, with market institutions and government both playing subsidiary roles. Not-for-profit organizations principally govern organized religion and Little League baseball (among others).

Market organization is a widely used and useful governing structure. An important reason is that it can operate in a variety of different ways and be supplemented by other mechanisms in a variety of ways. However, just as one size shoe does not fit all feet, a single mode of sectoral governance cannot cope with the great variety of human activity. Modern economies are made up of many very different sectors governed in different ways. There is no way that a single form of organization and governance is going to be appropriate for all of them.

This chapter is concerned with these kinds of issues and debates. A case can be made that a capitalist bias in favor of simple market organization of economic activity is, on net, a plus. It is biased toward a mode of economic organization that, in fact, has served effectively as a central part of the governing structure over a wide range of activities and sectors where there is general agreement that performance has been pretty good. It is associated with a bias against governing structures that rely heavily on central planning and top-down command and control, which often have proved problematic or worse in contexts where they have been employed. However, when pushed dogmatically, a promarket bias can be counterproductive.

The rest of this chapter is organized as follows. The next section reviews the arguments in favor of market organization of economic activity. I argue that they are more subtle and circumscribed than often proposed. Then, I turn to the economists' market failure concepts and suggest that while limited and somewhat biased, they do provide a case for a "mixed" economic system. Another section considers the positive case for nonmarket forms of governance of certain economic activities. In the concluding section in the light of the foregoing, I consider various areas in which the question of economic governance, in particular the appropriate nature and role of market organization and various alternatives, presently is under dispute.

The Case for Market Organization

Since the days of Adam Smith, British and American economists generally have touted the virtues of the "invisible hand" of market organization. The contemporary argument has two different strands. One is that market-governed economic activity tends to be responsive to consumer wants and is relatively efficient. The second is that capitalist organization provides a remarkably powerful engine of progress. The case I develop, not surprisingly, is that the desirability of market organization strongly depends on the kinds of values associated with the goods and services produced by an economic sector and the nature of supply conditions.

Market Organization and Economic Efficiency

Modern economics has embellished Adam Smith's argument in favor of markets with a formal theoretical argument that, under certain assumptions about the behavior of economic agents and certain context conditions, market organization yields economic outcomes that are optimal in some sense. The position I take here is that this theoretical argument is not very helpful in guiding thinking about how market organization actually works or illuminating where market organization is a desirable mode of economic governance and where it is not.

It is not helpful because, on the one hand, no one really believes that the neoclassical model is a close approximation to how a market economy actually works. On the other hand, real market economies are much richer institutionally than the simple model, and thus theoretical arguments (for example, those contained in market failure theory) may not be an indictment against the actual market economies that we have. It is important to recognize, therefore, that analysis of the pluses and minuses of governing structures that make significant use of markets has to rest on a mixture of the rather rough empirical comparisons plus efforts at sensible, if somewhat ad hoc theorizing.

From this perspective, although market organization as it actually is almost surely never achieves outcomes that are optimal, most economists and many laypersons would argue that market organization and competition often does seem to generate results that are moderately efficient. There are strong incentives for firms to produce goods and services that paying customers want, or can be persuaded they want, and to produce at as low financial cost as possible. Also, under many circumstances competitive market-organized economic sectors seem to respond relatively quickly to changes in customer demands, supply conditions, and technological opportunities. Thus to the extent that producing what customers demand is treated as a plus, and as long as factor prices roughly measure real social costs, there is a strong pragmatic case for market organization, broadly defined, on economic efficiency grounds, at least in certain domains of activity.

But whether market governed economic activity generates economic behavior and outcomes that are desirable clearly depends on the context. There is, first of all, the question of whether the important values at stake are adequately represented in what individual customers want and are willing to pay for. The TV news broadcasting case mentioned earlier is highly interesting in this respect. Whether news broadcasting can make money depends on how potential advertisers view alternative media, which in turn is related only loosely to the value TV watchers place in getting news they regard as complete and reliable through that media. On the supply side, the conditions may or may not be right for competition to develop and be sustained. How many airports are needed to serve a metropolitan community effectively? Of course, there also is the question of whether the costs attended by producers adequately reflect social costs.

In some contexts the notion that market organization yields relatively efficient outcomes is quite plausible. In other contexts it is highly problematic.

Why Not Top-Down Planning?

The kind of economic governance needed would certainly seem to depend on the nature of the salient needs. Thus when engaged in a massive war effort (as in World

War I and II) capitalist economies have largely abandoned market governance and adopted centrally coordinated mechanisms of resource allocation, procurement, and rationing. The rationale has been that such economic governance was essential if production was to be allocated to the highest priority needs and conducted effectively. By and large there is agreement that remarkable feats of production have been achieved under these arrangements.

The experience with wartime planning led some analysts to propose that a number of the mechanisms used then would vastly increase economic efficiency during peacetime. However, most knowledgeable analysts have argued strongly against that position. It is one thing to marshal an economy to concentrate on a central set of consensus high-priority demands over a short period of time, as in wartime production or in the early years of the communist economies where the central objective was to build up a few basic industries. It is something else again to have an economy behave reasonably responsively and efficiently in a context of diverse and changing demands, supply conditions, and technological opportunities over a long time period. The problems experienced by central planning regimes in the old communist countries after the era had passed when building up standard infrastructure sufficed as a central goal bears out this argument. (For a classic discussion of these matters see Lindblom, 1977.)

Some of the advantages of market organization show up clearly when the comparison is with central planning. However, I propose that the argument behind the scenes here is much more complex, and in fact different than the standard textbook argument that profit-maximizing behavior of firms in competitive market contexts yields economically efficient results. It hinges on the multiplicity, diversity, and changeability of wants, resources, and technologies in modern economies that experience shows defy the information processing and resource-allocating capabilities of centrally planned and controlled systems. It also involves the argument that the chances of appropriate responses to changed conditions are enhanced when there are a number of competitive actors who can respond without going through a process requiring approval for proposed action by some central authority or gaining the approval of a large number of people before acting. Hayek (1988) and the modern "Austrian" economists (for example, Kirzner, 1979) have stressed the ability of market economies to experiment, to search for unmet needs and unseized opportunities, and argued that centralized systems are very poor at this.

The empirical evidence suggests that this is true. However, central planning is not the only alternative to pure market organization. Modern capitalist economies have developed and operated a wide variety of alternative and mixed forms.

A Schumpeterian Perspective

Many observers have proposed that it is in dynamic long-run performance, rather than in short-run efficiency, that market capitalism reveals its greatest strength.

As Marx and Schumpeter have argued, capitalism has been a remarkably powerful engine of economic progress. And here, too, we can make a rather explicit comparison, at least with central planning. Indeed, a good case can he made that a central reason for the collapse of the old communist economies was their inability to keep up with and take advantage of the rapid technological progress that was going on in market economics.

But the characteristics and capabilities of market organization that contribute to technological progress are very different than those that relate to static efficiency and the textbook normative model. Indeed, Schumpeter made a great deal of those differences. Some commentators on Schumpeter have proposed that he did not believe that in modern capitalism, competition was important. That is not correct. Rather, his argument was that the kind of competition that mattered was not the sort stressed in the economics textbooks but competition through innovation. The capitalism of his *Capitalism, Socialism, and Democracy* (1942) was an effective engine of progress because competition spurred innovation. His theory placed high value on pluralism and multiple rival sources of invention and innovation. However, under Schumpeter's view of what socially valuable competition is all about, the presence of large firms with R&D laboratories as well as some market power was welcomed, despite the fact that such a market structure diverged from the purely competitive one associated with the static theorem about market-induced economic efficiency.

It is now clear that, writing in the 1930s and greatly impressed with the major role played by large corporations in technological advance over the preceding decades, Schumpeter underplayed the continuing role of new firms in the process. However, many contemporary views of the sources of invention and innovation tend to play down the continuing role of large companies in the advance of many technologies and economic sectors.

In any case, although sectoral structures differ, in virtually all of them I find persuasive the argument that the pluralism, flexibility, and competition of modern capitalism are important ingredients of an effective innovation system.

On the other hand, it can be argued that, at least in recent years, the strong performance of market capitalist economies on the industrial innovation front also has a lot to do with features of modern capitalist economies not highlighted in Schumpeter, for example, public support of university research and training. Earlier I noted the importance of publicly funded research to technological progress in pharmaceuticals and medical technologies more generally. Both electronics and aircraft development have received major government R&D support, and for many years the U.S. Department of Defense provided the most aggressive market for new technologies in these fields. (For an extended analysis see Mowery and Nelson, 1999.) Put another way, an important reason that modern capitalism is such an effective engine of progress is that the system is in fact very mixed, with nonmarket elements playing an important role in innovation in almost all fields. A capitalist system that relied solely on market organization would not be nearly as effective, which leads us to the literature on market failures.

The Positive Case for a Mixed Economy: Market Failure Theory

A large portion of high-level argument about where market organization works effectively, and where market organization works poorly, is conducted using the economists' market failure language. (For a fine articulation see Stiglitz, 1986.) Market failure theory takes as its benchmark the theory I mentioned earlier that under the set of assumptions about behavior built into neoclassical economic theory, and given a particular set of context assumptions, market governance of economic activity yields Pareto optimal outcomes. The orientation of market failure theory is to context conditions that upset that result.

The limitations of market organization as a governing structure for an activity or class of goods or services can stem from the nature of the demand. The case of public goods is a canonical example. It can come from characteristics of the supply side, as in the case of natural monopolies. The problem of governing the provision of goods and services that involves the creation of externalities can be a demand-side or a supply-side problem. So, too, the problem of limited or asymmetric information or required specialized expertise.

The Public Goods Bestiary

Economists use the public good concept to flag a class of goods and services where the benefits are collective and communal rather than individual and private. Under this body of conceptualization, a pure public good has two attributes. One is that unlike a standard private good like a peanut butter sandwich, which can benefit only one consumer (although of course it can be split and shared), a public good provides atmospheric benefits that all can enjoy. In the language of economists, public goods are nonrivalrous in use. Your benefiting from a public good in no way diminishes my ability to benefit. The second attribute is that if a public good or service is provided at all, there is no way to deny access to any person or to require direct payment for access. Clean air and national security are standard examples of pure public goods. Scientific knowledge is often used as another example. For a neighborhood, the quality of access roads has some public good attributes.

There are several things to note about how this conceptualization maps onto real goods and services. First, in many cases publicness is a matter of degree, in both dimensions. A defense force may protect some regions but not others, and given a resource constraint, the protection of one group of people therefore may be at the expense of the protection of another group. Thus defense is not completely atmospheric and nonrivalrous in use. On the other hand, if one lives in a protected region, protection cannot be withheld, although a person can be placed in jail for not paying taxes. In contrast, scientific knowledge does seem truly to be nonrivalrous in use; you and I can use the same fact or understanding at the same time. However, the creator of that knowledge may be able to patent it and sue anyone who uses it without paying a license fee. Access roads can become crowded and worn with use, and neighborhoods may try to limit access.

Second, and partially related, many goods and services are partly private and partly public, in the sense that there is identifiable benefit to particular individuals, who can be made to pay for access, and at the same time broad atmospheric benefits from the availability or provision of the good or service. Education is a prominent example. Urban mass transport is another.

The example introduced earlier, of news provided by newspapers and TV networks and developed through investigative reporting, is another interesting case in point. The availability to a community of reasonably complete information clearly is necessary if citizens are to have the knowledge they need to act intelligently as citizens; in this sense, the development and promulgation of news provides an important public good. But newspapers are private organizations, who may not always aim to maximize profit but certainly need to be able to cover costs to survive. As noted earlier, newspapers make their income from two private good aspects of their publications. One is the value of news to individuals who choose to buy the paper rather than obtaining news through other means. The other is the value to advertisers of spreading their message to readers who, in many cases, find the advertisements an annoyance. TV news programs are almost totally dependent on the latter to bring in the money to cover their costs.

Third, in many cases the public benefits are associated with beliefs about what is appropriate for a society or a polity. Economists tend to treat public goods as if the individuals in society benefit from them in roughly the same way that they benefit from the private goods they procure and use. Thus, clean air is viewed as providing better breathing for individuals, a strong national security position as reducing the risks to individuals, new scientific understanding as increasing the chances of a cure for cancer, and so on. There surely is a lot to this point of view.

However, it is apparent that some people care about the quality of air and water, and the security of wildlife, in areas they never intend to visit and are willing for taxes to be somewhat higher if that will help fund a better environment. National security is an integral aspect of foreign policy, and many citizens support a particular foreign policy not because of any direct benefits to them of a conventional sort but because they believe it is right. Many citizens in a democracy support funding for universal education not because they or their children will take advantage of public schools or because they believe it will reduce the incidence of crime that can affect them, but because they believe that universal free education is a necessary condition for equality of opportunity in a society. The values at stake here seem different in kind than the utility that an individual might get from a nice steak.

Whether a good or service has significant public good properties clearly depends on how the benefits it yields are viewed. In the foregoing cases, the benefits that are seen as "public" are not easily analyzed in terms of the standard kinds of benefits that are the focus of standard economics. Rather, their "publicness" resides in values defined in terms of perceptions about what makes a society decent and just. For this reason, for many goods and services the argument is not about whether innate publicness requires public funding to ensure a decent level of provision, but about whether the good or service should be made available to all, on reasonable or nominal terms, with public monies footing the bill. That is, a considerable part of the debate is about what goods and services "ought to be public."

There are significant costs involved in employing public choice machinery instead of or supplementary to market demand-side machinery. There is, first, the question of just how to decide how much is to be provided, in contexts where individuals and groups may value the public provision of the good or service very differently. There is, second, the question of who is to pay. Because of the number of individuals and groups that may try to have a say in these matters, the process of decision making is either going to be very time-consuming and cumbersome or pruned back and simplified in a way that will certainly outrage certain parties. The outcomes of collective demand-generating processes are inevitably going to be considered unfair and inefficient by some. But if a good or service has strong innate public good properties, or is deemed by some as something that ought to be public, this argument is inevitable.

On the other hand, newspapers and public news broadcasting, both of which presently are having difficulties covering their costs, highlights that there are also problems and dangers of leaving the production and promulgation of important public goods to market incentives associated with private good attributes that are tied to them. As suggested, a wide range of goods have some public and some private good attributes. There inevitably is going to be dispute about whether, or to what extent, their provision should be left to the market, and the appropriate role of other forms of financing.

The Problem of Natural Monopoly and the Need for Public Control

The "publicness" of a good or service raises issues of demand-side governance. Natural monopoly poses supply-side governance problems.

American economists are inclined to rationalize the use of antitrust to prevent undue market power from arising and regulation to deal with cases where there is natural monopoly, on the grounds that monopolists tend to charge too high a price. It is clear, however, that much of the force behind the policies to break up or rein in monopolies, regulate them closely, or adopt public sector provision has to do with people's concerns that arise when private bodies gain considerable power over their lives, concerns that may involve but also may transcend being forced to pay monopoly prices. Economists are inclined to rationalize that governments not only fund but directly control activities related to national security and the criminal justice system to the fact that these activities yield "public goods." But it probably is at least as relevant that there is near consensus that it would be highly dangerous to have control over these activities be in private hands.

These propositions may strike some liberals in the Anglo American tradition as somewhat odd. The heart of that position has been that strong government is the dominant danger to individual freedoms and that placing activities under market governance therefore serves to increase freedom. The implicit assumptions here, of course, are first, that concentrations of private power will not in general arise under market governance, and that second, when they do, they are less threatening to individual freedoms than government power. However, I propose that in many areas, that is just what the debate regarding the appropriate roles of market and nonmarket elements in the governance of an activity is all about.

I propose that concern about the lack of accountability to the public of private power over activities and services that many people believe are of vital importance to them lies at the heart of the current debate about how to govern what used to be called public utilities: activities like telephone service, electricity generation and distribution, water supply both for rural and urban users, and urban mass transport. These used to be regarded as "natural monopolies," in the sense that it was believed that service would be provided more efficiently under a unified supply system than under conditions of multiple suppliers and competition. In the United States, traditionally they were left in private hands but tightly regulated, in other countries they often were governed as "public" enterprises. In either case, with the public utility classification went an imperative to provide access to all potential users on terms that were regarded as fair. The public utilities were understood to be publicly accountable for their actions.

I think that to ignore this aspect of the debate about how to govern these sectors is to miss the point. However, as with the issue of regulation to deal with externalities, which I consider next, the key question of regulation of industries where monopoly or a highly concentrated structure is inevitable is where to draw the line.

The Externalities Problem: Bringing in Broader Interests to the Governing Structure

The externalities concept of economists is meant to refer to by-products of economic activity that have negative or positive consequences that are not reflected in the benefits and costs attended to by those who engage in the activity generating the externalities. Environmental contamination is an obvious example of a negative "externality" and a clear case where there is a value at stake in the operations of an activity, with no one to represent and fight for it, at least in the simple model of market governance put forth in economic textbooks. In a famous article written some time ago, Ronald Coase (1960) argued that if property rights are clear and strong and the number of interested parties relatively small, in fact markets can deal with these kinds of problems. Those who value clean air or water simply can "buy" behavior that respects those values from the potential polluter. The problem arises when those who care about the values that could be neglected are dispersed. In this case some kind of collective action machinery is needed to bring them in. A good way to think about regulation or a tax on pollution is to see these measures as the result of governance machinery that has brought in a broader range of interests and values bearing on decision making in an activity or sector than would be there under simple market organization.

However, the costs and the inefficiencies here can be considerable. Government regulation involves collective decision machinery and has all the problems and limitations discussed in the context of collective decision making regarding the provision of public goods. Clearly the general problem here is to delineate the range of interests that should be represented, their appropriate influence, and the mechanisms through which they can operate to make their values felt. The latter can range from public interest advertising or boycotts, which can proceed without direct access to governmental machinery, to lawsuits that involve general governmental apparatus, to particular pieces of special regulation and associated control machinery. Much of the public controversy is about the latter.

It is conventional in economics to think of the costs of an externality as like the costs of deprivation of a private good, or in terms of expenses needed to remedy damage, for example, extra laundry costs or the extra tine it takes to get to a clean lake when the nearest one is polluted. However, I believe that, as with the case with public goods, externalities issues in many cases do not fit this mold.

To a large extent, prohibitions on certain activities, that economists might be inclined to rationalize as attempts to deal with externalities, reflect notions on the part of some people and groups regarding what is appropriate activity and what is not. A large part of the argument in this arena is about what values, and whose values, are to count and through what mechanisms. As I noted earlier, for many people protecting the environment is a matter of moral concern, a belief that certain values ought to be enforced, and very little about cutting down their own laundry costs or protecting the lake they swim in.

It is hard to identify an activity or a sector where there are not some values at stake that go beyond the direct interests of the customers and the suppliers. On the other hand, the greater the number of interests and values that have to come to some collective conclusion before action is taken, or which have a veto power over change, the more cumbersome the governance system. The wider the range of regulation prohibiting or mandating certain things or behaviors, the smaller the range of individual freedoms. The question, of course, is where to draw the line.

Asymmetric Information, Specialized Expertise, and the Problem of Trust

Economists have only recently begun to pay attention to problems of economic organization and governance that come about when those on one side of a transaction possess information, or have expertise, that those on the other side do not have. Clearly this kind of asymmetry is very widespread across the spectrum of economic activities and concern about its potential abuse is the source of much of the regulation one sees in modern economies, and in some prominent instances strong arguments that market organization, even strongly regulated, is not a suitable form of governance.

Thus, the producer or seller of a good often knows much more about its characteristics, including its quality, than the potential buyer and may have incentive not to divulge that information. The market for used cars is an example often used by economists. The result can be disappointed purchasers, the reluctance of potential purchasers who would be glad to buy a reliable used car to enter into transactions for fear of ending up with a lemon, or some of both. While less stressed in the economic literature on this topic, the problem is present, along with the opportunity for abuse, in relationships where one side has professional expertise and the other side does not and in the normal run of things will follow professional advice regarding what to do. Doctor–patient and financial advisor–client relationships are obvious cases in point.

In wrestling with how market organization can cope with this kind of problem, economists have put considerable emphasis on the importance of good long-run customer relationships and reputation for the sustained profitability of firms as an effective discipline on supplier behavior. Where customers tend to have long-term relationships with their suppliers, and reputations for reliable or shoddy work or goods tend to get around to potential new customers or customers who are open to changing suppliers, there is some force in this argument. And there are nongovernmental organizations like the Better Business Bureau that are intended to make business reputations more reliable and accessible, or at least give potential customers more confidence. In capitalist economies there is a clear ideological inclination to let mechanisms like these deal with the problems and avoid detailed regulation. However, particularly where customers can be harmed by products designed and produced in ways that save the seller money, there is also regulation.

Professions, like those involved with medicine, law, and accounting, generally have codes of ethics and good practice that those in the profession are supposed to abide by. Where expertise is associated with a body of knowledge that can be tested, or with professional training, there are often government-sanctioned license requirements. These measures, and the belief that in general professionals adhere to them, do provide support for trust by clients of doctors and lawyers that they will be treated competently and honestly.

As noted earlier, the medical and other professions claim trust in market organization of the services they provide is justified because their members are not aiming to maximize their own incomes or advantage but to serve their clients as best they can. This defense of market organization of medical care here certainly is not the case put forth in the standard economic textbooks where the profit orientation of firms is viewed positively. In any case, the professions generally strongly resist detailed government overview and regulation, and in many cases they control the licensing system that regulates admission to membership on the grounds that they are effective in governing themselves. By and large, they have been successful in preserving much of their autonomy.

However, particularly after a scandal has come to light, there are strong pressures for regulation of the profession involved and the transactions they engage in. And it is common for the legal system to be used by clients who feel they were hurt or cheated. As the anger of the U.S. medical profession about what they consider unreasonable malpractice suits suggests, it may not be in the interest of a profession to avoid some formal government regulation of what it does.

It is apparent that belief that for-profit organizations, or individuals who are believed to be mostly motivated by hope of profit, are not to be trusted to have the customer's or client's interest at heart, is a prominent reason why the supply side of many activities is largely made up of public or not-for-profit organizations. As noted, the public education system of many countries involves not only public financing but also publicly run schools. Most of the "private" schools that are in the system are not-for-profit. In most countries, the lion's share of day care for young children is provided through government or nonprofit organizations. The recent debate in the United States about how far health insurance plans under government auspices ought to be extended involved centrally the question of whether, through regulation, for-profit insurance plans could be relied on not to overcharge or cheat patients. Similarly there is considerable appeal to many people of not-for-profit organizations that provide medical services.

The evidence is not clear that, where for profit organizations operate in sectors of this sort, as they do in education, child care, and hospital care, that these treat their customers any worse, as a general rule, than do organizations that are nominally not-for-profit or public. But although those steeped in the beliefs and norms of capitalism continue to push for more use of markets in these and similar areas of activity, for many people market organization, at least of the sort described in the economic textbooks, is something to be avoided or tightly regulated.

The Peculiar Bias of Market Failure Theory

I conclude this survey of market failure theory by pointing out a bias built into it. By the way it is formulated, market failure theory carries a heavy normative load to the effect that markets are preferred to other forms of governance, unless they are basically flawed in some sense. Thus the only reason government should provide for national security and protect citizens from crime is that markets can't do these jobs very well. Parents need to take care of children because of market failure. As one reflects on it, the argument that we need government because markets sometimes "fail" seems rather strange, or at least incomplete. Can't one make a positive case for government (or families for that matter) as a form that is appropriate, even needed, in its own right?

The State, the Society, and the Economy

The use of terms like "political economy" and "social economy" signal that economic systems are tightly intertwined with the institutions and activities of government and society. My argument here is that an important reason that capitalist economies are mixed economies is that economic institutions do not stand alone but interact with and shade into the institutions of government and community.

Functions of the State

Economists have an inclination to see the role of the state primarily in terms of legal and physical structures that are needed to provide the basis for an effective economic system and deal with various kinds of market failures. This is a very different view of the role of the state than the arguments debated in the long history of philosophical theorizing on the subject.

In much of its early incarnation, and some of its more recent, the state is viewed in this literature as the structure through which values are defined at the level of the community and decisions regarding the community as a whole are made. Reflect on Plato's discussion in *The Republic*, or Hegel's discussion where the good state is defined in terms of the quality of its justice and the character of its citizens. This formulation of the role of the state of course does not resolve the issue of differences in values among individuals who comprise the state. Indeed, disputes about values are likely to be even more heated than disputes involving choices that affect individual or group economic interests differently. The issue of how to decide may be even more contentious. Plato saw the answer in government by philosophers. For better or worse, modern societies are stuck with democratic process.

A liberal position on how to deal with value differences within the population would be to keep the state out of it and to try to avoid forcing the values of one group to be imposed on another. But in many cases, there is no way to do that. Abortion either is legal or is not. A war is declared or it isn't. All citizens have access to medical care or some don't.

The theory that the state is the vehicle through which a nation defines and enforces collective values clearly captures a lot of the flavor of contemporary debates about matters like rights to life and rights to choose, the commitment of a society to ideals of equal opportunity and fairness, and whether there should be universal health insurance regardless of ability to pay. As I proposed in the earlier discussion of public goods, arguments about these matters involve beliefs about appropriate collective values, or values of the collective, that transcend those of particular individuals. Under this theory, the state, which defines the collective, is the natural vehicle of governance in contexts where a collective position on something has to be taken one way or another. In these areas the state may choose to use markets to further some collective values, but the purpose being served is a public purpose, and the responsibility for furthering it ultimately is a state responsibility.

Another, not mutually exclusive body of theorizing about the state focuses not so much on collective values but sees the state as the necessary vehicle to set the context for fruitful private lives and actions. From at least the time of Hobbes and Locke, theories about the need for a strong state have involved, centrally, the proposition that an effective state is needed for individuals to lead secure, decent, and productive lives.

Originally this body of theorizing had little to do with economics, much less the role of the state in market economies. Thus, Hobbes's case for a strong state to establish and enforce a clear body of law is posed in terms of the need to avoid violence and anarchy. Although this case involved security of property, this was not its central orientation. With Locke the orientation is more toward security of property, but his great writings were before capitalism emerged as a recognizable economic system.

By the time of Locke, political philosophy was paying increasing attention to the rights of citizens of a state, rights that on the one hand were concerned with protecting individuals from the state, and on the other hand were rights to be enforced as well as respected by the state. Thus, under the democratic theory that gradually developed, citizens of a state ought to have the right to vote, to equal treatment under the law, and a variety of freedoms of action regarding personal matters. Access to these basic rights of citizenship were seen as something that should not be rationed through markets and for which government had a fundamental responsibility. I note that in seeing the state as responsible for the defining and enforcement of certain universal citizen rights, this branch of political philosophy was merging with the strand seeing the state as the vehicle for defining and enforcing collective values.

During the nineteenth century, government also came to be charged with protecting those who were regarded as too weak to protect themselves from market arrangements that could hurt them: thus, child labor laws were passed as well as laws limiting hours of work for certain classes of labor. A right of all citizens to a free public education was gradually established. The core arguments of modern welfare state theories add to these venerable political and protective rights a set of rights to access to certain kinds of goods and services. This decoupling of access to a considerable range of goods and services from normal market process is the hallmark of the modern welfare state. "Solidarity" is a word often used by advocates of this position. From another (sometimes closely related) tradition, we all are our brother's keepers.

The orientation to these matters in the political philosophy literature is that they are natural basic functions of the state and don't simply fall to the state by default because of some kind of market failure. Where market mechanisms are used as part of the machinery for provision, this perspective sees government as still responsible for overseeing the operation.

Earlier I called attention to significant differences across nations in the range of activities and sectors that are governed largely through market mechanisms. I propose that an important factor behind these differences, as well as one that often is central in the debates going on within a country, is strongly held differences among individuals and groups regarding the appropriate roles of the state. The nations that make most extensive use of only lightly regulated markets tend to be ones (like the United States) where there has been a long tradition of seeing the state as a danger to individual liberties. On the other hand, nations that have the most extensive welfare states tend to be ones where government is more trusted.

Economics and the Community

Several of the theories of the state just referred to rest heavily on the concept of a natural community of individuals and families, with the units linked to each other by community bonds. Under this conception, the state is the vehicle through which the community makes collective decisions and takes coordinated collective action, when that is appropriate. But from another point of view it is clear that much of the decision making and action taking of the community does not involve state-mediated collective action. Indeed, ensuring that the state not interfere too much in the life of the civil community has been a central issue in Anglo American political theory.

Adam Smith is mostly known today, particularly among economists, for his *Wealth of Nations* (1776). There he stressed the value of self-interest in motivating and guiding individual human action in ways that actually benefited the larger community. The orientation of his *Theory of Moral Sentiments* (1853) is quite different in a number of ways. There he stressed the extended empathy that humans in a community have for each other. Extended empathy can be a powerful ingredient in a governing structure. But extended empathy is not what markets are all about.

Clearly, the community, or parts of it, rather than the market, or the government, provides the governing structures for a wide range of activities that use resources to provide desired services and in that sense are economic activities. Thus, to pick up on an earlier theme, the family is the standard governance structure for child care not because of simple "market failure" but because the family can be counted on (mostly) to hold the extended empathy toward its and related children that seems essential to good care. Similarly, there are a wide variety of other activities involving members of the community where neighborhood groups, voluntary associations, clubs, and so on play a central role in the governing structures, rather than formal government or markets. These include organizations like the Boy Scouts and the Girl Scouts. I note that except for inputs they use that are bought on markets, these activities do not show up in the standard economic accounts, like GNP. But they are definitely economic activities in the sense that they use resources, if largely unpaid, to meet needs.

Much of charity is provided by community organization. Where financial resources are required, voluntary contributions generally play a significant role. Formal organizations may be involved, but they will be chartered as not-for profit organizations rather than as for-profit firms. They may obtain some of their funding from the sale of goods and services. In recent times, many such organizations have been the recipients of government funds. But a hallmark of such groups is an explicit rejection of what might be called commercial values, as well as resistance to government control.

Karl Polanyi (1944) was in a long line of social analysts who saw the extension of markets as an enemy of society, a destroyer of communal modes of governance. This is not a "market failure" argument. It is an argument that markets should be fenced off from certain kinds of activities because they are operated much better under communal governance, in one its various forms.

Economic Organization and Governance as a Continuing Challenge

At the start of this chapter I proposed that the conception and norms of capitalism, in particular the faith that market organization is the best way to govern economic activity, are much more unified and coherent than the actual organization of economic activity in countries that consider themselves capitalist. The latter is marked by great variation in the way different activities and sectors are governed. Although in countries regarded as capitalist market organization plays a powerful role in the governance of many economic activities, there also are many activities that are governed largely through nonmarket mechanisms. I have also argued that few activities or sectors are pure market or nonmarket. Most involve a mix of market and nonmarket elements.

Furthermore, governance of an activity or sector, or at least its fine structure, in many cases is not something that is determined once and for all. Rather, at any time there tends to be a number of arguments going on regarding how particular sectors should be organized and governed. The particular foci of these controversies can differ significantly across countries. But in these first years of the twenty-first century, there are several arenas where many countries are struggling with proposals for reform.

One of these stems from growing awareness of and broad agreement that something should be done about global warming. I note that although the particular focus and the strength of this concern are relatively new, much of the current discussion and argument can be seen as having grown out of the more general and variegated concerns that emerged in the 1960s about the adverse environmental impacts of economic activity. The general diagnosis of the problem is and has been that the prices determining the financial costs of certain economic activities and the goods and services with which they are associated do not reflect the environmental costs of that activity. The proposed reforms are and have been a combination of regulation, adjusting prices and costs so that they better reflect those environmental costs, and public support of R&D and other investments to speed the development of more environmentally friendly technologies.

I want to highlight that today's proposed reforms would not eliminate market organization from the set of structures governing the activities in question, or even diminish significantly the role of market processes. The regulatory reforms for the most part would augment a set of regulations that already are there. The proposed public R&D support programs would augment and stimulate rather than replace private R&D. Part of the new proposed policies would be the creation of a new market, one for licenses to pollute. Put another way, the economic activities and sectors to which the new policies are directed were already "mixed." The proposals for reform involve a change in that mix.

Another arena where there is continuing argument about how to reform governance structures is medical care. The argument is most heated and the proposals for reform most significant in the United States, but similar arguments are going on in many other countries. Again, the policy discussion is about a sector that is already very mixed in its governing structure. Despite the arguments of some parties in the dispute in the United States, the reforms recently passed should not be viewed as taking a sector that has been governed largely by the market and turning it into a government-run sector. The organization and governance of medical care in the United States has long involved government-funded and -run programs that pay for a significant fraction of the care for some groups, public support of the research base for efforts to develop new medical treatments and artifacts, and significant elements of regulation. This will continue to be the case after reform.

As I noted earlier, countries that consider their economic systems basically capitalist can differ greatly in the extent to which they rely on market organization for the governance of certain activities. Medical care is a prominent case in point. Unlike the United States, some other capitalist countries largely fund medical care through a government-run central payer system; in some, like the United Kingdom, provision of medical care is under government auspices. However, it is fair to say that in all of these countries, governance of medical care involves a mix of market and nonmarket elements.

I note that financial institutions, another arena where efforts at reform are going on in many countries, also long has been a very mixed sector or collection of sectors. In all countries there is a public or quasi-public central bank. Commercial and investment banks themselves and institutions that provide mortgages are private and for-profit in all capitalist countries but are subject to a complex set of regulations. The focus of reform here is on those regulations, which many believe the recent financial crisis showed to be inadequate. But again, no one is proposing to nationalize the full banking system or remove the market as part of the governing system. The proposals are to change the mix of an already very mixed system.

This is not to argue that, because virtually all economic sectors have a mixed form of governing structure, there are no differences across sectors in the extent to which the market plays a role or in beliefs about the role market governance should play. Though the question of what kind of regulation is needed is very much on the agenda, there are no arguments to eliminate the central role of market organization and competition in governing the commercial banking sector. While governments have bailed out automobile companies when they otherwise were set to fail, no one is arguing that in the normal run of things market competition should not be the principal determinant of which companies thrive and which ones have to go out of business in that industry. On the other hand, although there is considerable lobbying in the United States for vouchers and charter schools, there is hardly any support for the notion that the government should get out of funding and structuring much of education and simply let the market take over. While there is controversy regarding what kind of work defense departments should procure by contract with private companies, no one is arguing for privatization of the armed services per se.

But at the margins, at least the relative balance of market and nonmarket elements in the governing of these different sectors can and has changed over time and is often a matter of contentious dispute.

Devising and implementing structures to govern its key activities and sectors are among society's most difficult and continuing challenges. In countries that consider themselves capitalist, there is a strong presumption that market organization should be used as much as possible. As the cases described here illustrate, in fact, there is a continuing dispute about the role of market and nonmarket elements in the governance of various economic activities, even in countries that consider themselves staunchly capitalist.

Arguments about appropriate governing structures for an activity or a class of goods and services are difficult for many reasons. In the first place, there are often significant conflicts of interest and differences in views regarding the salient values at stake. Because a central aspect of a governing structure involves the mechanisms that determine what and whose interests and values count, it is easy to see why this may be a contentious issue. The question of the governance of key economic sectors and activities is often tightly bound up with issues of the economic well-being of different groups. Thus the recent U.S. debate about health care reform was largely about how to make health care accessible to poor Americans at reasonable cost and who was to pay for this. Not so far behind the scenes, various professional groups—doctors, nurses, managers of hospitals, insurance company executives—made arguments that supported their economic interests.

The problem is difficult not just because of competing interests and values, but also because of real uncertainties—the better term might be "ignorance"—regarding the consequences of adopting one governance scheme or another. The additional costs of extending health insurance are virtually impossible to predict with any precision. Given the analytic limitations of the social sciences, the complexity of the subject matter, or both, it simply is impossible to foresee reliably the consequences of a market for allowances to emit various quantities of greenhouse gases.

It would be nice if experience with prevailing systems and their variants provided sharp, clear feedback of what works and what does not to guide the next round of adjustments. However, even putting aside that the interests and values of different parties might lead them to evaluate the same thing differently, and even where there is agreement that the current regime is unsatisfactory in certain ways, it may be extremely difficult to identify just what aspect of the current regime is causing the problem or how to fix it. Whereas ex post evaluation of a reform may be somewhat easier than ex ante prediction of the effects of that reform, it still is very difficult.

In such a context, a general broad belief in the efficacy of market organization probably is, on net, a plus, given the broad experience societies have had with market organization and the alternatives. However, if that faith is held dogmatically, that can be a problem. An important reason that modern capitalist economies have worked reasonably well is that they have developed economic systems that, in fact, are very mixed. It is important that they not so blind themselves ideologically that they lose the capability to continue to do that.

Notes

This essay draws extensively on my introductory essay in Nelson (2005).

References

Coase, Ronald. "The Problem of Social Cost." *Journal of Law and Economics* 3 (Oct. 1960): 1–44.

Hayek, F. A. *The Fatal Conceit: The Errors of Socialism*. Chicago: University of Chicago Press, 1988.

Hollingsworth, J. Rogers, and Robert Boyer. *Contemporary Capitalism: The Embeddedness of Institutions*. Cambridge: Cambridge University Press, 1997.

Kirzner, Israel M. *Perception, Opportunity, and Profit: Studies in the Theory of Entrepreneurship*. Chicago: University of Chicago Press, 1979.

Lindblom, Charles E. *Politics and Markets*. New York: Basic Books, 1977.

Mowery, David C., and Richard R. Nelson, eds. *The Sources of Industrial Leadership*. Cambridge: Cambridge University Press, 1999.

Nelson, Richard R. "Introduction." In *The Limits of Market Organization*, ed. Richard R. Nelson, 1–24. New York: Russell Sage, 2005.

Polanyi, Karl. *The Great Transformation*. Boston: Beacon Press, 1944.

Schumpeter, Joseph A. *Capitalism, Socialism, and Democracy*. New York: Harper and Row, 1942.

Smith, Adam. *The Wealth of Nations*. 1776; New York: Modern Library, 11937.

Smith, Adam. *The Theory of Moral Sentiments*. London: Henry G. Bohn, 1853.

Stiglitz, Joseph E. *The Economics of the Public Sector*. New York: Norton, 1986.

CHAPTER 11

MONOPOLY CAPITALISM

KEITH COWLING AND PHILIP R. TOMLINSON

This chapter analyzes the nature of monopoly capitalism and traces its wider implications for the nature of the modern capitalist economy and the society that springs from this base. It adopts as its central proposition the not uncontroversial view that the essence of modern capitalism cannot be captured without an explicit recognition of its monopolistic or oligopolistic nature. In this sense, the approach follows that of Baran and Sweezy (1966), Kalecki (1971), and Cowling (1982) and will reflect and extend some of their ideas. In doing so, fairly orthodox, or mainstream, analytical tools will be used within a slightly unorthodox framework.

The theme of this chapter is that monopoly power is both significant and increasing and has a substantial impact on social welfare, in terms of both allocative efficiency (including quite broad issues of waste) and distribution, and wider questions of democracy and freedom. In developing this theme, one of the objectives will be to spell out why much of the contemporary wisdom on this subject, as expressed by both mainstream but also many heterodox analysts, is largely ill-founded. Finally, we turn to the possibility of combining orthodox and more heterodox views and exploring possibilities for achieving the wider public interest in the world we face, while recognizing this as a difficult and lengthy political process.

The chapter is organized as follows. We begin by outlining the extent of monopoly capitalism in the modern economy. We then explore the theoretical implications of rising market concentration for market outcomes, in particular, with regard to price-cost margins, entry conditions, and profitability. Then we discuss the welfare implications of monopoly, and another section considers the distribution of surpluses. Finally, we discuss issues arising from transnational monopoly capitalism, particularly for development.

Monopoly Power in Modern Capitalism

Contemporary capitalism is characterized by giant, usually transnational corporations. Each market in which they operate is characterized by fewness, at least on the seller's side (Fellner, 1949). Each national economy in which they operate is increasingly dominated by a few large (transnational) corporations: as Rothschild (2005, p. 445) puts it: "the big transnational companies have become—nationally and internationally—an especially powerful interest group." It would seem natural, therefore, to expect to find in such a world evidence of the use of monopoly power at the level of the individual markets for goods and services and at the aggregate level, where economic and political power have become inextricably entwined.

In a world of transnationally organized production, standard measures of market concentration are difficult to interpret. Most measures, for instance, have assumed that import penetration reduces domestic industrial concentration, yet such an approach ignores imported goods from affiliates of transnational corporations, who have operations in the domestic economy: in such cases, imports lead to less and not greater competition (Cowling et al., 2000 Pryor, 2001)[1] Moreover, while censuses of production list many firms, the many are typically dominated by the few, with the independence of the many being more apparent than real. This is usually the case where production occurs—as is common today—through extensive subcontracting (either domestic or global): smaller units are often under the ambit of dominant (transnational) corporations, which exercise strategic control over operations, and as such are unable to make the strategic decisions that determine their long-term future (Cowling and Sugden, 1998; see later discussion)[2] Nevertheless, and despite the reservations with regard to standard measures of industrial concentration, recent evidence points toward a significant rise in industrial concentration. In the case of the United States, Pryor (2001) provides evidence of rising industrial concentration since the early 1980s (having adjusted for imports) in manufacturing, which he largely attributes to increased merger activity. With regard to services, there are difficulties in defining activities within the sector due to structural changes over time. However, where the structure of the services sector is held constant, Pryor (2001, p. 314) again points to a "significant upward trend in concentration," which he suggests is closely linked to the emergence and growth in national (service) chains. He also points out that anecdotal evidence during the 1990s suggests that concentration levels rose in transportation, communications, public utilities, as well as finance, insurance, and real estate: again, merger activity appeared the primary reason (pp. 314–315). Moreover, Pryor argues that growth in U.S. concentration has been supplemented by the rising number of strategic alliances and partnerships, which often serve as cartels and lessen market competition.

Perhaps of more recent significance, on the world stage has been a growing concentration in the communications, information technology (IT), and media industries, together with important merger/consortia activity in those public utility industries recently privatized. Many economists believed that these former industries had been opened up to the forces of global competition enabled via the application of new technologies, but perhaps we should not be so sanguine. There is increasing evidence that a few major corporations are emerging as dominant players in these industries at the global level. For instance, the servicing of worldwide IT networks run by global players in a variety of industries appears to have become the exclusive preserve of two or three service providers. Moreover, the dominance of Microsoft in software and computer operating systems has long been a source of contention for both U.S. and EU antitrust authorities, and there have been recent concerns over Google's monopoly position as the global Internet search engine where it is suggested that hits from Internet searches are not neutral (as claimed by Google) but rather geared toward Google's larger clients, thus squeezing out smaller firms. Google's diversification into other online businesses, such as YouTube and Google News, also potentially blocks access to rival online product providers (see *Financial Times*, 2010). In addition, we have also witnessed significant developments in telecommunications with global consortia emerging. During the late 1990s, there were a number of prominent mergers and strategic alliances involving the world's major telecommunication companies (see Jamison, 1998). These developments are particularly significant because many observers considered IT as a means to nullify the effects of monopoly power. Furthermore, in their study of online markets, Daripa and Kapur (2001) conclude that claims that e-commerce will lead to more (price) competitive environments are overstated and that in many online markets, industrial structures are likely to become more concentrated (see also Pryor, 2001). Indeed, recent discussions of the possible monopoly control of the Internet could completely undermine its democratic base (see Sugden et al., 2009).

Despite this evidence, the dominant view—either explicit or implicit—is that contemporary capitalism is better described as competitive rather than monopolistic or oligopolistic (see Rothschild, 1971, 2002). This view has perhaps been most explicit among American economists, where the existence of large, dominant corporations is reconciled with the view that competitive pricing or output policies prevail by appeal to the existence of real or potential entry by new firms or new products. Within Europe the reconciliation has been achieved by reference to growing international competition in the markets for manufactured goods. But this dominant view of the workings of capitalism is not simply at the level of empirical observation and description. Economic theory generally, including macro-theory, trade theory, and theories of distribution, all find it not only convenient but also acceptable to treat the system as essentially competitive.

Although the dominant view is as described, it should not be inferred that there are no dissenters. Galbraith argued persistently in a sequence of books (for example, in *The New Industrial State*, 1967) that the giant corporation has established control over the consumer and the economy, whereas others writing on managerial capitalism, notably Williamson (1964), have based their analyses on the existence of some degree of market power. However, these views have not been integrated into the mainstream of economic thought, and, indeed, much of the managerial literature has tended to point the way back to a more or less competitive world where capitalism responds to managerialism by organizational innovation (see, for instance, Williamson, 1970). This view of managerial discretion being a transient phenomenon is mirrored in the conventional view of monopoly and market power. There is no general questioning of the proposition that monopoly can exist, the question is whether it can persist and whether it is at all significant. In contrast, the view developed in this chapter is that monopoly, or more generally oligopoly, is the general case and competition the transient phenomenon. Outbreaks of competitive pricing should be seen as such, isolated and ephemeral, not really descriptive of the fundamental characteristics of contemporary capitalism (see Kalecki, 1938, 1971; Cowling, 1982). To sustain this view of the world, we first have to consider the nature of collusion and the general question of market entry, whether intranational or international. We turn to these issues in the next section.

Monopoly Power, Collusion, and Potential Entry

The question of the implications of potential entry for the exploitation of monopoly or oligopoly positions is crucial given that much of the economics literature relies on this mechanism for achieving competitive behavior. We take "entry" here in the broadest sense to refer to either new firms entering a specific market, existing firms producing a new product that is a close substitute for rivals' existing product, or a foreign firm entering a new national market. We also take it as essentially self-evident that monopoly or oligopoly positions are ubiquitous. As noted, concentration in the major sectors of the corporate economy is both high and increasing.

If we take as our measure of monopoly power, the Lerner index, $(p - mc)/p$, then it is very plausible to think that the degree of monopoly varies directly with market concentration. It is useful to distinguish a direct and an indirect effect of concentration on the degree of monopoly. If firms independently maximize their profits, ignoring potential gains from coordinating their strategies, the outcome is that the equilibrium degree of monopoly varies directly with the level of concentration. This is the Cournot result, which establishes a lower bound on the degree of monopoly where the number of firms is fixed. Thus, ignoring entry, an industry will *not* tend to competitive equilibrium even when its members do not coordinate their activities in any way, tacitly or overtly.[3] The Cournot result is a lower bound in exactly this sense—with recognition of their interdependence, firms can achieve an outcome closer to the monopoly result.

The indirect effect of concentration works by facilitating collusion. Not only will the degree of monopoly tend to rise more or less automatically via the independent actions of firms, it also rises because firms will find it easier to coordinate their activities as their numbers fall. Theoretical links between concentration and collusion have been isolated by various authors, and perhaps the best known is that of Stigler (1964), who derives the link from a consideration of the cost of effectively policing a collusive arrangement. The probability of the detection of price cutting increases with concentration, and thus adherence to agreed prices is more likely. Lower concentration among buyers also facilitates collusion among sellers: concentrated sellers and atomistic buyers offer the most conducive conditions for effective collusion. This reflects the situation in retailing: Dobson and Waterson (1997) demonstrate rising concentration and rising margins in U.K. retailing, and Claycombe (2000) concludes that concentration has a strong effect on department store prices in the United States. Similarly in the United States, the price of hospital services is closely related to concentration (see Vita and Sacher, 1999), whereas Simpson (2001) detects little consumer switching in response to large price increases following hospital mergers.

Concentration also influences the degree of collusion via its impact on retaliatory lags: the shorter the lag, the more transient the gains from deviance, the less the incentive to deviate. This is likely to be affected by interfirm communication (Williamson, 1965) and multimarket contact with familiarity breeding cooperation (Hughes and Oughton, 1993). The conclusion (paradoxically) is that rivalry and collusion generally coexist in concentrated markets—closer rivalry, combined with short retaliatory lags, serving to maintain collusion. Here, the "tit-for-tat" strategy provides a useful interpretation of rivalry and collusion: it elicits and rewards the cooperation with retaliation a speedy response to noncooperation (see Axelrod, 1984; Cubbin, 1988). "Competitive" behavior is then diverted away from price toward product and advertising competition, where retaliatory lags are longer. Thus, strategic investment enhances corporate power by creating islands of monopoly power—literally so in the case of supermarkets investing in land banks, which, together with limited planning permission, create local monopolies.

The extent to which the monopoly result diverges from the competitive result also depends on consumer behavior. If the industry demand curve is very elastic, the degree of monopoly will be low even if collusion is strong. However, because consumer tastes are malleable, we can expect corporations to adopt activities such as advertising, which intensify and sustain consumer wants. Advertising is an important characteristic of modern capitalism and a contributory factor in the establishment and maintenance of monopoly positions. In the short run, advertising can induce buyer inertia, and thus contribute to the degree of monopoly; in the longer term advertising can make it more difficult for new firms to enter. Direct evidence linking advertising to the price elasticity of demand is rare, but what exists is compelling. Pagoulatos and Sorensen (1986) report an analysis of the variation in the price elasticity of demand across U.S. four-digit industries within food and tobacco and reveal a significant, negative relationship with the intensity of advertising, after controlling for R&D, concentration, percentage of industry sales to final demand, and the effective tariff rate. They conclude "the empirical results are consistent with the hypothesis that demand elasticity is in part determined by the strategic behavior of firms within an industry... rather than being an exogenous element of market structure, demand elasticity is actually molded to some degree by the nature of the conduct of firms" (ibid., p. 247).[4] We return to the role of advertising later in this chapter.

It is possible, however, that the threat of entry keeps prices low even in concentrated markets. We have now assembled a set of ingredients that seem to point to the existence of potential monopoly power if only we can be sure that this will not all be nullified by the entry question. Does the existence of potential entry and the reaction of firms to it mean that monopoly positions are more apparent than real? Much of the literature on the entry question could lead to either such a conclusion or, alternatively, to an assessment of the height of barriers before the degree of monopoly could be determined. We argue that the question of the degree of monopoly and entry can be seen as essentially separable.

The entry-limiting pricing literature going back to Bain (1956) and Sylos-Labini (1969) in its static form and, developing into an array of dynamic variants, basically says that entry conditions determine the degree of monopoly within an industry (see also Baumol et al., 1983).[5] With a competitive fringe and a homogeneous product, the static model implies competitive pricing by the existing group in the absence of barriers to entry. As soon as we introduce large-scale entry and/or time into the analysis, we move from competitive pricing, even in the absence of conventional barriers to entry.[6] Modigliani (1958) showed that entry is conditional on the size of scale economies, the elasticity of demand, and the size of the market. With substantial scale economies, inelastic demand, and a limited market, the price consistent with zero entry can depart substantially from the competitive price. The dynamic entry-limiting pricing literature reveals that the typical optimal price trajectory for the existing group starts near the monopoly level and decays toward the lower bound (see, e.g., Jacquemin and Thisse, 1972). The important point coming out of this literature is that the optimal rate of entry as far as the existing group is concerned (i.e., that rate consistent with the maximum flow of discounted profits) is not generally zero. The trade-off between profits today and profits tomorrow implies a price today above limit price, which means that profits tomorrow will be lower because of entry. Firms "make hay while the sun shines." To always set a limit price would lead to forgone profits.

However, an alternative view of the reaction to potential entry separates the price/output decision of the existing group from the decision about what to do about entry. Spence (1977) argues that a possible response to the entry is to invest in excess capacity.[7] This will deter entry as long as the incumbent group can raise its output faster than the prospective entrant would and as long as the prospective entrant sees it that way. Since some entry lag can be expected, it seems reasonable that excess capacity can be an effective deterrent. But one can go further and argue that the excess capacity response must always dominate the limit-price response. The grounds on which it can be expected to do so represent an extension of the previous argument about making hay while the sun shines. Limit pricing of whatever sort implies that output is higher/price lower than if entry had been ruled out. Excess capacity implies that the potential output diverges from the actual for the same reason. Provided the implications for entry are the same (or price is an inferior signal), the excess capacity strategy always dominates because actual output at that level is consistent with maximum profits (for a sustainable degree of collusion) in the absence of entry. Entry-limiting pricing can now be seen as having capacity above the monopoly level, *and actually using it*, whereas the excess capacity hypothesis implies that the extra investment occurs, but the usual monopoly restrictions on output are maintained. Thus, monopoly pricing, and therefore the degree of monopoly, is separable from the question of entry.

Spence points out that separability can be achieved if marginal cost is invariant to the level of excess capacity. This is obviously not necessarily the case, and excess capacity (induced by entry) could result in lower marginal costs and therefore lower prices. This would not necessarily change the degree of monopoly, which would remain conditional on the elasticity of demand and the degree of collusion. This raises the interesting point of the link between excess capacity and collusion. If the degree of collusion is essentially determined by the speed of reaction by the group to anyone cutting price, then the existence of excess capacity may bolster collusion by making it clear to all participants that rivals can react immediately. It is possible therefore that the degree of monopoly rises with the threat of entry, a result that turns the conventional wisdom on its head.

The existence of excess capacity nevertheless represents a burden for the group. It implies that profit and the rate of return on capital are below what they might have been. In some circumstances it may be possible to set this capacity without incurring the disadvantages previously outlined. The necessary preconditions would be those generally associated with price discrimination, that is, an ability to isolate different markets with different elasticities, but with control over third-party transactions. Probably the most obvious example is the separate treatment of domestic and foreign markets. As long as the foreign market price is greater than marginal cost, profit can be raised by actually using excess capacity for this purpose—provided that the capacity can be switched into domestic production relatively costlessly (Blattner, 1973). Thus, to maintain their monopoly positions, monopolies or collusive oligopolies invest in capacity that is ultimately used for dumping in foreign markets. Such investment would appear unprofitable in the absence of the initial entry threat in the domestic market.

However, the preconditions for such price discrimination will not always be met, and the threat of entry will simply imply waste. Spence focuses on plant and equipment, but the idea can be generalized to include all types of investment that secure a monopoly position. R&D, patenting, and advertising can all form part of excess capacity and comprise social waste. This obviously does not imply that all activity in these areas is wasteful (we talk more about advertising later), but that in attempting to secure their monopoly positions, firms invest in, say, R&D and simply put the inventions on the shelf (see also Scherer and Ross, 1990).

A remarkable piece of research by Smiley (1988), which for a decade was pretty much unique, did what other economists generally choose not to do—asked business managers what they actually do! He surveyed brand managers in U.S. industry and discovered, despite numerous theoretical papers, that limit pricing was unimportant. Excess capacity was, but not in the sense of physical production capacity: rather, advertising, R&D, marketing (brand proliferation), and distribution were the dimensions of *capacity* of strategic interest to management. This finding was more remarkable in that one might expect there would be a response bias against admitting such tactics. Similar results have since been obtained for the United Kingdom (see Singh et al., 1998). Also supportive is a study of Maxwell House Coffee, revealing attempts to secure extensive featuring of their product in grocery outlets as a strategic response to entry (Nelson and Hilke, 1991); a study of U.K. supermarkets revealing firms using store openings to preempt rivals (Smith, 2000); and a study of U.S. ready-to-eat cereals, with incumbents using advertising to limit entry (Thomas, 1999). We thus conclude that potential competition cannot be expected to dominate actual competition (see also Geroski, 1995). Moreover, our earlier analysis suggests that active rivalry in concentrated markets can lead to collusive outcomes. Indeed, the existence of potential entry, stimulating strategic entry deterrence, reinforces the earlier conclusion that rivalrous behavior and apparent collusion coexist in concentrated markets by providing excess capacity, in a variety of dimensions, that helps sustain such a solution: a feedback loop sustaining, rather than undermining, the result for the fixed-numbers oligopoly outcome.[8]

At this point, we want to focus specifically on international competition because this is popularly felt to be a very real constraint on monopoly in markets within a so-called open economy such as the United Kingdom. This view was expressed fairly forcibly by Glyn and Sutcliffe (1972), who argued that the declining profit share during the 1950s and 1960s was due to workers securing increasing wages in an environment where international competition was on the increase and, therefore, such wage increases could not be followed by the required increase in prices. Of course, such analysis relates to the changing average degree of monopoly within the U.K. corporate sector, whereas our focus has been on the degree of monopoly itself. Nevertheless, there is a clear line in Glyn and Sutcliffe's argument that contemporary capitalism has entered into a relatively competitive state with the decline in trade barriers and the emergence of large, transnational corporations. Although the removal of tariff barriers and the growth of international trade could act as a constraint on domestic monopoly behavior, it is argued here that this phenomenon should be seen as a transitory state with monopoly reemerging on an international plane with enhanced power both in a market and political sense. However, even as a transitory state, there is little hard evidence that increased international trade has led to a reduction in the degree of monopoly, and there are a number of reasons this may be so.

Insofar as domestic firms are simply processing imports, then their market power within remains undisturbed. This is not just true of raw materials or intermediate goods, but is also true of consumer goods as long as they are marketed by the existing monopoly or oligopoly group. This has become the general case via (1) domestic firms buying foreign goods for sale through their own channels or outlets, (2) domestic firms entering franchise arrangements with foreign suppliers, and (3) domestic firms being divisions of large transnational corporations. The first case arises when domestic firms possess market power in distribution, whether to industrial or household consumers. Insofar as monopoly power in distribution is the general case, this would be a very general phenomenon. For instance, one possible scenario is where all industrial markets are competitive but the distributive sector is monopolized. As long as we assume fixed proportions (i.e., consumers cannot avoid the distributive sector when buying goods as the price of goods increase), the monopolized sector can extract the maximum monopoly profits. There would be no monopoly rents to be gained by integrating back into the industrial markets, and imported goods entering this system would not disturb the position of monopoly power. This scenario is obviously not descriptive of the world we live in, but examples of domestic monopoly control of imported goods abound (see Cowling et al., 2000).

This leads into the second case of franchise arrangements. In many industrial markets domestic producers act as agents or hold franchises for foreign goods. Insofar as they have some monopoly control in the relevant market, this will be retained even though imports may rise. They will simply get a larger share of their monopoly rents from foreign goods. The initiation of such arrangements becomes increasingly attractive to domestic firms as trade barriers fall (or as workers become more recalcitrant!). A particularly interesting case was documented in the U.K. Monopolies Commission (1968) report on cellulosic fibers. With the advent of the European Free Trade Area (EFTA), Courtaulds, producing about 98 percent of cellulosic fiber in the United Kingdom and protected up until that time by very high tariffs, saw itself threatened by other EFTA producers and rapidly concluded arrangements with them that left Courtaulds the sole EFTA supplier to the U.K. market. Thus, despite the introduction of a free-trade area, Courtaulds's monopoly position within the U.K. market remained unscathed. Courtaulds's actions underscores the earlier analysis in which we concluded that the threat of entry would not affect the degree of monopoly but would simply induce expenditures that otherwise would not have been made. In the Courtaulds case, these expenditures took the form of the acquisition of shares and the negotiation of agency agreements rather than excess capacity. Market power was thus preserved in the face of increased international trade. Given scale economies in production, the lowering of tariff barriers tends to increase intrafirm trade, which either leaves the degree of monopoly in any given country unchanged or possibly raise it.

This illustrates the transient nature of international competition. In the process of adaptation to a higher level of intrafirm trade, such markets generally appear more competitive as large transnationals compete with domestic firms. The outcome is either that all firms become transnationals or, alternatively, that some firms are eliminated. Casual observation suggests that the usual outcome is the elimination of the smaller, domestic firm, which allows for the emergence of a tighter, but internationally based oligopoly. This process of concentration of power associated with increased international trade can also occur in the absence of formalized, international agreements.[9] Thus, in the case of franchising, it is likely that the dominant firms in any economy conclude arrangements with dominant firms in other economies. Smaller, domestic firms are left out of these arrangements, and their position becomes increasingly untenable. The entry of continental lagers into the United Kingdom during the 1980s and early 1990s might be seen as a case in point, where smaller U.K. brewers often lost out to the large, vertically integrated British brewers/retailers and their continental counterparts (see also Cook, 1997).

Monopoly Power and Welfare

The discussion up to now implies that it is unreasonable to rule out the question of monopoly power on a priori grounds. Yet this is exactly what has been done in most estimates of monopoly welfare loss going back to Harberger (1954). This has inevitably led to the conclusion that the social cost of monopoly is trivial. If, instead, we start out with the assumption that monopoly positions will be fully exploited, we come (perhaps not surprisingly) to quite different conclusions. Initially we limit our analysis to the simple framework adopted by Harberger and later introduce advertising and product differentiation and more general issues of waste.

Taking an orthodox, partial-equilibrium view of social welfare, welfare loss (ΔZ) due to monopoly (assuming linearity) can be written as

$$\Delta Z = (1/2)\, \Delta p\, \Delta q, \tag{11.1}$$

with Δp being the change in price from competition to monopoly and Δq the change in quantity.

Assuming constant marginal costs, monopoly profits are

$$\Pi = q_m\, \Delta p, \tag{11.2}$$

where q_m is monopoly output.

Assuming profit-maximizing behavior, linear demand and constant marginal costs, monopoly output is one-half of competitive output and therefore

$$\Delta q = q_m. \tag{11.3}$$

Substituting from (11.2) and (11.3) into (11.1) gives the result

$$\Delta Z = (1/2)\ \Pi. \tag{11.4}$$

Welfare loss from monopoly equals one-half of monopoly profits.

It is interesting to contrast this with the Harberger derivation:

$$\Delta I = (1/2)\ pq\,\eta\, t^2, \tag{11.5}$$

where $t = \Delta p/p$, and η is the price elasticity of demand. He then *assumed* $\eta = 1$ and, because he observed $\Delta p/p$ to be quite small (assuming constant costs, this will be the ratio of profit to revenue, Π/R), the inevitable conclusion is that welfare loss is minimal. The crucial step in generating this result is to assume that the changes in price and quantity are independent of each other. In contrast, if we assume monopoly pricing behavior, then low price-cost margins are inconsistent with a low price elasticity of demand. Harberger and others have therefore assumed the monopoly problem away by observing low mark-ups and *assuming* low elasticities. Using data for the top 102 firms in the United Kingdom for the period 1968/69, Cowling and Mueller (1978) estimated average welfare loss using the Harberger formula (equation 11.5) at about 1 percent of the gross corporate product, whereas using the monopoly pricing formula (equation 11.4) welfare loss was almost 10 percent of gross corporate product.

However, it may be argued that it is unreasonable to assume monopoly price/output behavior since the industrial structure in the United Kingdom is essentially oligopolistic and perfect collusion is unlikely. This view implies that one-half of monopoly profits defines the upper bound on monopoly welfare loss for a specific firm—true welfare loss may be quite different. We can establish a lower bound by assuming that oligopoly output is independent of entry, and replacing equation (11.3) with the Cournot prediction. However, this calculation also depends on the number of firms in the industry or, where firms are of unequal size, on the Herfindahl measure of concentration. The general formula of welfare loss in the Cournot case is simply $\Pi/2N$ where N is the number of equal size firms. In the case of unequal size firms, the formula is $(1/2)\Pi H$, where H is the Herfindahl measure of concentration. A symmetric duopoly would therefore imply welfare loss equal to half the monopoly case, and a symmetric triopoly one-third of the monopoly loss.[10] It is interesting to note that the Herfindahl would have to fall to 0.1 (e.g., ten equal-size firms) for the estimates to approximate the value of the U.K. estimates based on the Harberger methodology. Since Herfindahls as low as this are not descriptive of most U.K. markets,[11] and also recognizing that these are lower-bound estimates, the inference must be that Harberger-type estimates understate the true welfare loss.

However, this is not the end of the story. Π will normally be understated. First, the competition among firms for monopoly rents induces expenditures, which are treated as costs and result in the understatement of profit (see Tullock, 1967; Posner, 1975). Installing excess capacity to deter entry, advertising, and product differentiation are activities that could fall into this category. Profit will also generally be understated because of intrafirm competition for these monopoly rents. Insofar as managers control the firm, we expect some diversion of net revenue away from reported profits and into various activities yielding managerial utility. There is no obvious reason, however, to believe that managerially controlled firms will not exploit any market power they possess. Managerialism does not imply the abandonment of profit-maximizing price/output policies, but the redistribution of the gains from such policies.[12] This redistribution will introduce a disparity between actual and reported profits, the gap widening with the growth of managerial power.

This brief consideration of the competition for monopoly rents, both between and within firms, has revealed the possibility that calculations of monopoly welfare loss based on reported profits have captured only the tip of the iceberg. Cournot estimates, which imply zero collusion among oligopolists, should be seen as the lowest of lower bounds, whereas estimates based on monopoly, or perfect collusion assumptions, should not necessarily be seen as upper bounds (estimates) as long as they rely on reported rather than actual profits.

To this point we have assumed that the welfare impact of monopoly relates simply to the restriction of output below the social optimum. We now turn to other decisions of the monopolist, namely, advertising and product differentiation. Dixit and Norman (1978) have demonstrated that monopolies tend to overadvertise, even in the absence of an entry threat. Within the standard, partial-equilibrium welfare framework, advertising leads to benefits insofar as it raises the output of the monopolist, but these gains are moderated by the price increase resulting from advertising. There is a second-best optimum level of advertising greater than zero, second-best because the first-best solution would involve the elimination of the monopoly and therefore the elimination of advertising.

Of course, if price falls with advertising, advertising in such cases would be unambiguously beneficial within the orthodox welfare framework as long as the benefits exceeded advertising costs. Similarly, if advertising led to an increase in price and a reduction in quantity, there would be no trade-off—advertising would be unambiguously bad. It could be argued that most advertising is not providing information on price and conditions of sale and therefore is unlikely to create a more elastic demand for the product and therefore a lower price, but the question of whether advertising is excessive tends to become empirical, and any suggestion for control can be fairly easily rebutted. This analysis can divert attention from the basic objections to advertising which must be that the flow of "information"/persuasion will always be biased to the extent that the objectives of the corporation and the consumer are in conflict. Neither is it simply a matter of bias in the flow of "information" embedded within advertising itself but also the inevitable bias in communications in general when large areas of the media become dependent on advertising revenue.

Turning to product differentiation, we note that there are conflicting results in the literature. Until recently the prevailing view had been that the introduction of new products has nothing to do with monopoly. The monopoly problem remains in its traditional form as a problem of the restriction of supply in quantitative rather than qualitative terms. If consumers were sufficiently interested in new products,[13] or new versions of old products, then they would be made available under monopoly, but of course subject to the usual monopoly restrictions on the rate of output (see, for example, Swan, 1970).

The crucial assumption however, is the constant cost one. Under such conditions a monopolist will supply an infinite range of products as long as consumers are willing to pay a price at least equal to marginal cost. This assumption, in the case of the introduction of new products, is clearly untenable. We would normally expect that new products would introduce nontrivial set-up costs, and therefore it would be advantageous for the monopolist to restrict the variety of products on offer, especially if there are either zero or very limited revenue consequences. Under these cost assumptions, Lancaster (1975) demonstrated that monopolists tend to restrict the range of products to less than the social optimum because their policy is dictated solely by fringe consumers, not consumers who remain perfectly inelastic in their demand for the firms' products despite the fact that their preferred products (i.e., combinations of characteristics) are unavailable. The beer industry may provide an example of such behavior. Fringe consumers in this case might be women and young people who, being brought up on soft drinks, may prefer a rather light, bland beer. The inveterate beer drinker, usually an adult male, can be relied on to continue to drink beer despite the fact that his favorite variety is suppressed by the monopolist. The same example suffices for the other important Lancaster result—monopolies, as well as restricting the range to below the social optimum, also pick a socially suboptimal specification for the varieties it actually chooses to offer—for the same reason.

To summarize, it is clear that the existence of monopoly power can impose substantial welfare loss on society via the restriction of output of a given array of commodities. Accurate estimates of such welfare loss are difficult to come by because monopoly profits are generally understated. In addition, monopolists tend to overadvertise and fail to produce the socially optimum range of products. But the mechanism by which monopoly profits are dissipated in the process of competition for those very profits has wider implications for welfare. If monopoly profits were simply redistributed by some costless process, then, given that the welfare framework we have been working within is silent on distributional questions, we would be indifferent about this process. However, this is the case because we expect firms to invest real resources in attempts to acquire and maintain monopoly positions. As far as society is concerned (again ignoring distributional questions), this is pure waste (see Tullock, 1967; Posner, 1975). It can obviously take a variety of forms, varying from lobbying to advertising and excess capacity. It includes the possibility of research and development without progress, insofar as new ideas are generated to be suppressed via patents. Managerialism may also imply pure waste insofar as competition for monopoly profits within the organization imposes real resource costs on society. Posner (1975), for instance, took the actual level of monopoly profits as his estimate of waste, based on the assumption of constant costs in the competitive process for the acquisition of monopoly rents. However, very real problems of measurement remain because the process makes it very difficult to observe monopoly profits. Again, we are likely to err on the side of understating the social cost of monopoly.[14]

Monopoly Power and Distribution

We have argued that the degree of monopoly under contemporary capitalism is substantial, but also that there are indications it is increasing over time as, for example, market concentration and advertising both continue to grow in most economies. We have assessed the welfare implications of monopoly power within an orthodox framework in which distributional implications are ignored. But any tendency for the degree of monopoly to increase must have distributional implications. We now consider the link between the degree of monopoly and the functional distribution of income. Kalecki (1938) did exactly this, although his work was widely criticized. Much of the criticism was quite unjustified and seemed to be concerned more with sustaining the assumptions of perfect competition and full employment, under which orthodox analysis may be tenable, rather than with a balanced evaluation of Kalecki's ideas. We briefly review his ideas and integrate them with more recent theories of the determination of the degree of monopoly (see, for example, Cowling, 1981).

Assuming constant marginal costs (i.e., labor and material costs), we can define the degree of monopoly in the kth industry (μ_k) as the ratio of profits (Π^*_k), plus fixed costs (F_k), which include interest, depreciation, and salaries, to total revenue (R_k):

$$\mu_k = \frac{\Pi_k^* + F_k}{R_k}. \tag{11.6}$$

Π^* is defined as the maximum profit given the degree of concentration in the industry, price elasticity of demand, and the degree of collusion. The formal derivation of μ_k in the oligopoly case is described in Cowling (1981).

The assumption of constant marginal costs has long had considerable empirical support (see, for example, Johnston, 1960) and would appear a reasonable assumption, at least up to capacity. Recalling the Spence result, we also have some grounds for saying that industry will tend to operate with some degree of excess capacity, if the probability of entry is greater than zero.

If we now sum through 1,…, N industries and divide by aggregate turnover ($T = \Sigma_k P_k X_k$), then we derive the result that the weighted average degree of monopoly μ_k equals the ratio of gross capitalist income plus salaries ($\Pi^* + F$) to aggregate turnover (T),

$$\frac{\sum_k P_k X_k \mu_k}{\sum_k P_k X_k} = \bar{u} = \frac{\Pi^* + F}{T}. \tag{11.7}$$

The result will carry over to the long-run situation if for each vintage of capital the assumption of constant marginal operating costs is preserved because, although costs may fall, the degree of monopoly is still the sole determinant of $(\Pi^* + F)/T$.[15] The degree of monopoly may of course be determined by technology, but the effect on distribution comes only indirectly, that is, via its impact on H or α. Multiplying through by T/Y where Y = gross national income = $T - M$,[16] and M = expenditure on materials (i.e., $Y = \Sigma$Value Added) we get the share of gross capitalist income plus salaries in gross national income to be linearly related to the ratio of expenditure on materials to gross national income, with the intercept and slope of the relationship being the degree of monopoly.

$$\frac{\Pi^* + F}{Y} = \bar{u}\left(1 + \frac{M}{Y}\right).^{17} \tag{11.8}$$

Thus, for a given technology,[18] the profit share increases as (1) the degree of monopoly increases and (2) material prices increase. Profit share increases with M/Y because of the monopoly mark-up on nonwage costs. This in fact has a rather broad interpretation since all imports, no matter whether raw materials, intermediate goods, or final consumer goods, come under this umbrella as long as they are marketed via firms in the domestic industry (e.g., beer, shoes, oil, and Ford cars).

It should be emphasized that our aggregation procedures ignore interdependencies across industries. It would be possible but complicated to determine the general equilibrium set of prices in the economy, and there is no reason to expect a different outcome if we did. We have also simplified the analysis by ignoring the realization of surplus. If the degree of monopoly increases, we expect the share of profits to rise, but these profits will only be realized at the aggregate level if aggregate demand is sufficiently large. This will obviously depend on capitalist consumption, capitalist investment, and the activities of the state. We can make two points here—first, with excess capacity we would not expect distribution to vary with excess demand, and second, profits in a world of managerial capitalism will increasingly be absorbed within the organization (for example, salaries and bonuses). This provides a suitable point to look more closely at overhead costs to see how they are partly determined by the degree of monopoly under managerial capitalism.

The upper bound on profit, Π^*, is defined by the degree of monopoly but reported profits, Π, will only equal Π^* in cases of zero managerial discretion and, thus, more generally, $\Pi \leq \Pi^*$. Managerial discretion shifts reported profits to overheads. Thus, the share of *reported* profits in national income is determined by the degrees of monopoly and managerial discretion. What determines the level of discretionary expenditure, $D = \Pi^* - \Pi$? D will be determined by the interaction of the degree of monopoly (μ) and the degree of capital market power possessed by management (θ), each being necessary but not sufficient:

$$D = D(\mu,\theta)$$
$$D_{\mu}, D_{\theta} > 0, \; D_{\mu\theta}, D_{\theta\mu} > 0; \; D(0,\theta) = D(\mu,0) = 0. \qquad (11.9)$$

We have already examined the determinants of μ. What of θ? There are at least three elements involved: (1) the ability of stockholders to displace managers, (2) the ability of raiders to achieve control via takeover, and (3) the efficiency of the internal control apparatus. In addition, government regulation and taxation may encourage discretionary expenditure by penalizing high reported profits. This in itself may work through θ by reducing the profits required to forestall a management displacement effort.

Going back to our equation for the share of gross capitalist income, we can see that the distribution between reported profits and overheads will be partly explained by the variables that determine discretionary expenditures. Thus,

$$\Pi^{*} = \Pi + D(\mu,\theta). \qquad (11.10)$$

Hence,

$$\Pi^{*} + F = \Pi + D(\mu,\theta) + F. \qquad (11.11)$$

For any given θ, the proportion of Π^{*} reported as Π remains constant. Thus, as the degree of monopoly increases, a constant share of the increased monopoly profits are actually reported as profits.

As argued earlier, within the advanced capitalist economies in the post–World War II period, there has been a general tendency for the degree of monopoly to increase, but some changes may appear to have been working in the opposite direction. We have already considered international competition and concluded that there is little evidence to suggest that the degree of monopoly has been significantly constrained, but we may also wish to consider the regulation of monopoly by the state. Finally, it might be argued that the degree of monopoly could rise over time in each industry and yet the average degree of monopoly falls because of the changing industrial composition of national output. In a period of rising incomes the share of a particular industry will ceteris paribus rise, fall, or remain constant as the income elasticity of demand (η_y) is greater, less than, or equal to unity. Would any systematic relationship between η_y and μ be expected? Demand analysis suggests that $\mathrm{cov}(\eta_y,\eta) > 0$. This implies an underlying trend toward a falling degree of monopoly at the aggregate level. However, there is also a tendency for income and price elasticities to fall as income increases, which tends to offset this effect. If the general inference from the evidence reported herein is that the degree of monopoly is increasing, is there any evidence that suggests a corresponding increase in discretionary expenditures in favor of management? Within the United States and the United Kingdom, and perhaps in Europe, the evidence points fairly unambiguously in that direction. Firms have been growing in size largely through mergers and acquisitions, which imply a dilution in shareholder concentration. With an increase in size, the hierarchy has grown and internal control weakened. In addition, government attempts to regulate the behavior of firms in dominant positions has increased, which tends to encourage the internal absorption of profits. The interaction of the growth of the degree of monopoly and the growth in managerial discretion implies that $(\Pi^*/Y) > 0$, but $\dot{D}/D \geq \dot{\Pi}^*/\Pi^*(\dot{\Pi}/Y)$ is problematic. It depends on whether $\dot{D}/D \geq \dot{\Pi}^*/\Pi^*$.

Evidence for the United Kingdom suggested that the *share* of pretax profits declined during the 1960s and 1970s. However, after taxes and subsidies, the results suggest the share of profits has been relatively constant (see King, 1975). These results are consistent with our model but put considerable onus on demonstrating that increased discretionary expenditures by management explain the result, that is, we have to conclude not only that managerial discretion has increased but also that such an increase could have a significant impact on reported profits. Let us turn to the evidence, of necessity fragmentary, on the magnitude of managerial discretion.

Williamson (1964) provides two types of empirical evidence relevant to this analysis: First are case studies of firms to situations of adversity. A two-year program of cost reduction at Chemical Products, for example, led "with no change in the rate of output," to an increase in the return on capital of 125 percent, a reduction of salaried employees by 32 percent, and of headquarters employment by 40 percent. He also details rather dramatic reductions in associated staff expenses.

Second are estimates of the relationship between chief executive compensation and the determinants of the opportunities for discretionary behavior. Williamson argued, based on Simon's classical work (1957), that executive compensation will accurately reflect the general level of salaries, and his results then suggest that doubling the concentration ratio will increase salaries by about 50 percent. He also expects the same sort of relationship for perquisites.

The share of the profits is going down, despite the increase in the degree of monopoly, because of the rise of managerial power. However, if surplus is defined more broadly to reflect the growth of managerial capitalism, then we end up with the prediction of rising surplus. Baran and Sweezy (1966) take a broader view of surplus including both government expenditure (excluding transfer payments) and the difference between aggregate potential output and aggregate actual output. In contrast, we are simply focusing on the share of Π^*, potential profits associated with the increasing degree of monopoly, rather than reported profits, which obscure much of the growth of monopoly power. However, we should note there is some evidence at the end of the twentieth and in the early twenty-first century of the rising share of profits associated with an increasing degree of monopoly.[19]

Faced with the conclusion "that, individually and collectively, capital market controls experience weaknesses sufficient to warrant much of the expressed concern over the separation of ownership from control in the large corporation—at least in an environment in which the unitary form structure prevails" (Williamson, 1970, p. 30), it might appear that the capitalist system would respond with a more adequate system of controls. It was Williamson's view that, at least in the United

States, it has done this via the M-form (multidivisional) structure. Williamson regards this as "American capitalism's most important single innovation of the 20th century" (ibid., p. 176). It began in the 1920s with Dupont and GM, but the rate of diffusion only really gained momentum postwar. This development fits in rather well with the U.S. experience relating to the share of reported profits in national income. Glyn and Sutcliffe's (1972) figures show no visible trend for the United States. In Europe, the M-form innovation was much delayed, and Williamson saw this as the real answer to Servan-Schreiber's (1967) concern with the "American challenge." The falling share of reported profit seemed to be the general perception throughout Europe. Since Williamson projected this view, things have changed as European firms have adopted similar structures.[20]

In developing our view of the distribution of income, the possible importance of other factors, such as unions, is not denied. What is suggested is that it is not necessary to invoke increased union power to explain the declining share of profits in the middle of the twentieth century. Glyn and Sutcliffe (1972) held the view that the joint effect of increased union power and increased international competition explained the falling share of profits, but they do not provide any acceptable evidence to support this view. Despite their inability to demonstrate the importance of unions, this does not mean we should dismiss their effects. We might expect that union strength would grow as industry became more concentrated. But so long as $dw/d\Pi < 1$, firms will still prefer the profit-maximizing price and the lag in adjustment of wages to profits will reinforce this view. Rather than hold down $(p - mc)/p$, rising concentration provides an extra incentive to absorb profits, given the existence of managerial discretion. Generally, however, we might expect unions to appropriate part of discretionary expenditures. Concentration influences the discretionary activity of management and provides a source of monopoly wages.

Transnational Monopoly Capitalism, Development, and Strategic Failure

Here we want to consider broader issues raised by monopoly capitalism in relation to the direction of development in the overall economy. While numerous development paths are possible, the one generally chosen, by both modern and also developing and emerging economies, is to base development on an especially prominent role by larger, transnational corporations and the related unprecedented flow of foreign direct investment. Such transnational firms have significant economic power: essentially this involves the ability to take and subsequently implement strategic decisions that determine its broad business orientation (Zeitlin, 1974). A significant element in formulating these strategic decisions is that of economic planning, which for Coase (1937), was the central feature of the firm's internal (strategic) decision-making processes. Indeed, Coase regarded firms as "islands of planning." The ability to plan employment/output levels and undertake activities such as new capital investments or relocating production are strategic decisions and expressions of a corporation's economic power.

Moreover, strategic decision making in large (transnational) corporations is concentrated in corporate hierarchies—not everybody with an interest in the activities of a firm is able to participate in the strategic decision-making process. This is an idea commanding widespread support among economists, even though it contributes to an analysis that is quite different from mainstream approaches. Industrial economists have long discussed the "control" of firms, where the power to control may be simply viewed as the power to make strategic decisions. Who does and who does not control a firm has been the subject of intense debate ever since Berle and Means (1932) published their path-breaking suggestion that U.S. firms were largely subject to managers' control. Some still argue that control lies with senior managers. Others focus on shareholders, especially on a subset of the total mass of shareholders. Yet others suggest that senior managers and the especially important shareholders are essentially the same set of people anyway. But a consensus across all these views is that control rests with a subset of those having an interest in a firm's activities and certainly does not rest with the firm's workforce (see Branston et al., 2006). Consequently, this subset might be expected to use their position to further their own strategic interests, possibly to the detriment of others. Such power asymmetries can have important implications for the economic governance and future development of regional, national, and international economies. Indeed, it raises the specter of "strategic failure," where corporate interests take precedence and the wider public interest is not met (Cowling and Sugden, 1998).

In this regard, the transnational base of the corporation provides it with significant leverage in bargaining situations with nation-states and international labor. In the first instance, transnationals often bargain with governments over measures—such as the introduction and maintenance of favorable investment subsidies, infrastructural support, employment legislation, and tax regimes—that enable them to increase their profits. Because there are often political rewards in attracting and retaining transnational investment, governments are often compelled to accommodate such measures. This allows transnationals to hold the upper hand in such negotiations, since they can credibly threaten to use their inside option and invest/produce elsewhere (i.e., "divide and rule"). There are numerous examples of such occurrences: both Cowling and Sugden (1994, pp. 75–76) and, more recently, Dicken (2003, pp. 304–312) provide details of illustrative case studies. We have also observed increasing "incentive competition" between countries, regions, and localities for transnational investments.[21] Such competitive pressures undoubtedly place a strain on the state's fiscal resources, which are not necessarily replenished through higher corporate tax revenues that are usually anticipated through inward investment: the transnational base of the corporation facilitates transfer pricing practices to minimize global tax liabilities.[22]

Similarly, divide and rule has become an effective tactic for transnationals in bargaining relations with labor: the credible threat of relocation nullifies potential labour militancy, as workers place a positive utility on attaining/retaining employment. Again, there is a substantive mix of evidence from around the globe to suggest that the corporate sector has adopted such a strategy. In an early international survey of multiplant firms, Scherer et al. (1975, pp. 278–279) recognized the important benefits that multiplant operations afforded firms. Significantly, these authors also noted that "firms with only a single plant... were penalised by lessened bargaining power in dealing with unions" (ibid., p. 279), suggesting that multiplant operations provided firms with a useful tool to bargain effectively with workers. In the case of Japan, Coffey and Tomlinson (2003b, pp. 13–14) note that the large Japanese car assemblers have long used domestic subcontracting and more recently global outsourcing to divide and control their labor force and consequently reduce their wage costs. Peoples and Sugden (2000, pp. 181–188) also provide examples of specific case studies and draw on empirical evidence from the United Kingdom, the United States, and Canada to highlight the extent to which divide and rule occurs. They conclude that the strategy is a significant factor in a firm's decision to "produce in more than one country" (ibid., p. 189).

The consequences of transnational production and the divide and rule of labor are considerable. It can contribute to deindustrialization and economic stagnation because footloose transnationals can relocate to alternative sites when faced with rising labor costs or noncompliant government, and thus deprive regions and localities of employment and investment. We have observed numerous examples of the hollowing out of industries as a consequence of transnationals pursuing their own strategic interests and lower labor costs—Sweden and Japan being recent and relevant cases in point (see Blomström and Kokko, 1997; Cowling and Tomlinson, 2000, 2002). Such a process is more likely in integrated markets—such as NAFTA and the EU—and with "freer" trade agreements, since it is easier for transnationals to coordinate a strategic response to any labor militancy.

Moreover, it has been estimated that transnationals are responsible for some 75 percent of the world's exports (UNCTAD, 1996), and that roughly a third of international trade is intrafirm (this itself might be a substantial underestimate, given, for example, that roughly 80 percent of Britain's manufactured exports are within transnationals; see Dicken, 2003). This leads to important questions about the implications of an international free trade system, carried out by firms without any apparent interference from governments. In such a system, government's role is to implement and enforce a set of property rights and accompanying background conditions that allow firms this freedom. But it is the firms themselves that are left to the business of trading internationally, not governments. In an era where trade is dominated by the global giants, what this really means is that free trade is a system where the large transnational corporations are free to undertake the business of trading across international borders. The inherent implication is that it is a system where the strategic decision makers of large transnational corporations are free to pursue their own interests, globally. Following the distinction made by Berlin (1969) the "free" in free trade therefore protects the negative freedom of strategic decision makers by ensuring their freedom from government intervention, but it emasculates the positive freedom of others to determine their own economic development, their right and ability "to be somebody, not nobody; a doer-deciding, not being decided for" (p. 131).

It is our view that founding economic development on such large, transnational firms raises fundamental problems. Related to this is the issue of uneven development around the globe, which itself is a by-product of transnational monopoly capitalism. According to Hymer (1975, p. 38), the law of uneven development is "the tendency of the system to produce poverty as well as wealth, underdevelopment as well as development." He argued that a world dominated by transnationals would be characterized by such a tendency because the structure of the world's economies, the distribution of wealth, and the pattern of development would reflect the hierarchical structure of transnational corporations. As Hymer puts it:

> one would expect to find the highest offices of the [transnational] corporations concentrated in the world's major cities.... These... will be the major centres of high-level strategic planning. Lesser cities throughout the world will deal with the day-to-day operations of specific local problems. These in turn will be arranged in a hierarchical fashion; the larger and more important ones will contain regional corporate headquarters while the smaller ones will be confined to lower level activities.

These "lower level activities"—for example, the supervision of unskilled production—would be spread throughout the world "according to the pull of manpower, markets and raw materials." Thus, in the international economic system,

> income, status, authority and consumption patterns would radiate out from [the major] centres along a declining curve, and the existing patterns of inequality and dependency would be perpetuated. The pattern would be complex, just as the structure of the corporation is complex, but the basic relationship between different countries would be one of superior and subordinate, head office and branch plant. (ibid., p. 38).

It would appear that a fundamental cause of today's uneven development is that the wishes of the transnationals' strategic decision makers are in a sense imposed on societies. The strategic planning within these giant transnational corporations thus remains the prerogative of the *major centers,* and *lower level activities* are spread to *lesser* areas in which labor is especially cheap. Those in the lesser areas are thus excluded from the strategic decision-making process, with limited opportunities to govern their own development path. This raises welfare implications that feed into cultural, social, political, and more narrowly "economic" concerns. In short, large transnational firms are associated with uneven development across the world, the subversion of supposedly free international trade, the use of divide and rule strategies, a curtailed level of innovation, and a general constraining of communities and regions and their ability to participate in the development process and determine the evolution of their economies in the broader public interest.

The systematic consequence of the concentration of economic power leads to "free" markets being plagued by such strategic failures. It would therefore seem essential to explore the possibility of development paths that avoid such failures. Moreover, the obvious possibility is to tackle the source of the failures head-on and look for ways of appropriately widening participation in strategic decision-making processes. To identify the most appropriate ways forward, it is also not sufficient simply to demonstrate the inefficiency of the market as it has evolved, compared with its origins or with abstract models of the market economy. It can also not be presumed that state intervention will improve matters. For example, state intervention may be used by currently powerful corporations to extend their own interests: witness the history of European colonial development while, more recently, some would argue that the Single European Market is the product of the major transnational corporations. The development of the Japanese economy, particularly in the post–World War II era, was also based on close corporate ties with the polity and the promotion of large business interests and "national champions" rather than the wider public interest (see Johnson, 1982; Cowling and Tomlinson, 2000, 2002). A similar case can also be made for the World Bank/IMF policy with respect to the transition in Eastern Europe and the former Soviet Union, and their policy toward the so-called third world, which has been heavily influenced by commercial interests (see Stiglitz, 2002, 2006). It is also not obvious that replacing market capitalism with state socialism is a preferable development path. The history of those countries that have been through such an experience would argue against such a course improving welfare, although there undoubtedly were some areas of progress.

In choosing development paths it is of course possible and advisable to learn from a variety of rich experience (of success and failure) in the world's collective histories and from experiments currently under way. But again, we cannot rely on the market to choose the most efficient path spontaneously: the exercise of power and therefore control will obviously disallow such outcomes. Overcoming strategic failures in practice would be very much a long-term project requiring the initiation of multidimensional changes. In part these would need to be sought within the hierarchical structures of the giant firms to enable a broader involvement within their strategic decision making. A necessary but not sufficient condition would be the broadening of the legal membership of the corporation to include the various parties affected by its decisions. In this respect, Europe's social chapter provided a tentative and limited first step in this direction, although it needs to be built on to allow for wider participation of relevant stakeholders. It might be possible that suitable incentive structure, operated through the tax system, could be devised to encourage the effective implementation of such changes in legislation. This could be reinforced by the provision of appropriate training facilities for employees and communities to allow effective participation in strategic decision making. It would provide a whole new purpose within business education, in which economists, political scientists, and lawyers would need to be active. An important adjunct would be monitoring the activities of large firms so as to provide appropriate information for regions and communities to assess the impact, influence, and the desirability of such organizations within the community (see Bailey et al., 1994).

At a fundamental level, policy should aim toward nurturing an alternative structure of production, characterized by symmetric, horizontal relations, rather than the asymmetric, hierarchical relations seen within the dominant mode of production of modern, monopoly capitalism. In this regard, we have in mind basing economic, social, and political development on more diffuse system of governance, perhaps based on the activities of small firms—more particularly, on certain types of networks or webs of small firms both within and across localities, including "multinational webs" (Cowling and Sugden, 1999).

Initially, such networks might be nurtured at the local and regional levels, which would allow opportunities for a wider set of actors to participate in the development process. In essence, one might envision a system emerging with characteristics that resemble the traditional Italian district, with its propagation of small firms (with no one firm being dominant) and numerous criss-crossing (cooperative) relationships existing, and where economic and social development are closely coordinated between firms and institutions (Beccattini, 1990). Such districts have no distinct head (Brusco, 1982) and have long been regarded as successful in terms of both economic and social development (Piore and Sabel, 1984). Over time, we might visualize such small firm networks taking a multinational dimension through which international (small firm) cooperative production networks might emerge. Unlike the current transnational production networks, which are directed from corporate hierarchies, these webs would be organized along nonhierarchical lines with wider opportunities for small firm participation in international cooperative activities and technological development (see Cowling and Sugden, 1999). Given that many small firms (and regions) across the world face similar problems, such a process could lead not only to wider understanding between societies and cultures but also facilitate a wider cross-fertilization of ideas.

Moving toward such an industrial structure will be difficult and will obviously take considerable time. To imagine that a production system based on small firms organized in locally based networks will emerge and usurp the dominance of the large, vertically integrated corporation on the basis of any innate efficiency advantage is not tenable. Yet to do nothing is to favor the status quo. A purposive economic and industrial strategy aimed at a radical restructuring of economic power within the economy and society can lead to the displacement of the large and inefficient.

Notes

1. To illustrate the situation, in the case of the United States, Pryor (2001, p. 302) notes that in 1997 "about 40% of all imports were accounted for by US multinationals importing from their foreign affiliates and an additional 30% came from imports of US branches of foreign MNEs from their parent company." Pryor also infers that imports from foreign cartels (with informal ties to domestic firms) also make up a proportion of U.S. imports, which lessens competition. Inadequate data make import-adjusted concentration ratios difficult to calculate, although Cowling et al. (2000) provide an appropriate measure of concentration (accounting for imports) in their

analysis of the U.K. motor vehicle and truck industry and show that imports have not reduced concentration since the early 1970s.

2. For examples of control mechanisms exercised by Japanese corporations over their supply chains see Coffey and Tomlinson (2003a, 2003b).
3. Of course, as the number of firms tends to infinity, the Cournot result will approach competitive equilibrium. However, we are not dealing with markets that can reasonably be described as atomistic.
4. Moreover, in her review of the evidence, Koutsoyiannis (1982, p. 133) concludes, "most of the available evidence supports the hypothesis that higher prices result from advertising." Such evidence is indicative of firms' enhanced market power as a result of advertising and is supportive of the thesis advanced here.
5. This led Stigler to the remark that the oligopoly problem was being solved by murder—that is, the question of the interaction among firms within the market is put on one side and the focus is entirely on potential competition. Stigler implied that entry conditions are not sufficient to determine the degree of monopoly.
6. We take the Stigler view here, that economies of scale are not classified as a barrier to entry.
7. This possible approach had been alluded to previously; see, for example, Modigliani (1958).
8. It is also possible to imagine another feedback loop having similar effects: if product differentiation is one of the dimensions of excess capacity, then we may expect that the price elasticity of demand will also be reduced in the process, which, in turn, may favor a high degree of collusion within the incumbent oligopoly group.
9. It is also possible that a foreign firm could replace domestic firms in their dominant positions, leaving the degree of market power unchanged or even enhanced. The motorcycle industry in the United Kingdom may be a case in point (see Cowling et al., 2000).
10. In the case of a symmetric duopoly $\Delta q = (1/2)q$ and in the triopoly case, $\Delta q = 1/3q$. Thus in the two cases ΔZ is, respectively, $(1/4)\ \Pi$ and $\Pi/6$.
11. For the array of markets studied in Cowling et al. (1975) the estimated Herfindahls varied between 0.1 and 0.6.
12. This does not mean that equilibrium price is unaffected by managerial discretion but the inference is that this is a second-order effect. Thus, Oliver Williamson (1964) has suggested that staff expenses will enter the managerial utility function, and as a result staff expenses are taken beyond the profit-maximizing point. However, in his model, staff expenses (interpreted as selling and administrative expenses) enter the inverse demand function with a positive sign. The implication is that the degree of monopoly for managerial firms will be greater, and therefore monopoly welfare loss will be increased given that increased selling expenses will be expected to reduce the price elasticity of demand.
13. "Sufficiently interested," of course, means that their demand function for the new product must intersect with the average cost function for that product.
14. Two recent books survey this field: Congleton et al. (2008) and Just et al. (2008).
15. Baran and Sweezy (1966, p. 80) are not very clear on this point when they argue that profit margins will increase as capitalists cut costs, without being very precise about what is happening to the degree of monopoly.
16. To simplify matters, we assume no domestic intermediate goods.
17. *M* at the aggregate level is in fact imported materials because domestic materials would become someone's value added.

18. Because technology could influence the value of M/Y, that is, reduce the import content of British output, we are assuming no substitution in the short run between materials and labor.
19. See, for instance Gordon's (1998) empirics and discussion on the rise of monopoly in U.S. manufacturing during the late twentieth century and how this has coincided with an increase in corporate profitability. More recently, Russell and Dufour (2007) report on rising profit (and falling wage) shares in Canada, an economy that has similarly experienced a rise in the degree of monopoly power.
20. Indeed, recent history has pointed to the inadequacies of views of so-called alliance capitalism that were often seen as being concomitant within European and Japanese business models (see, for instance, Coffey and Tomlinson, 2003a, 2003b, for a critique of the model of the Japanese firm).
21. For further details, including an extensive survey of incentives offered by nation states to transnationals, see UNCTAD (1996).
22. Not surprisingly, evidence on cases of transfer pricing is difficult to obtain. Nevertheless, Dicken (2003, p. 283) reports a U.S. study where more than half of forty foreign firms surveyed had paid virtually no taxes over a ten-year period, with an estimated $35 billion being lost to transfer pricing. Similarly, a study of 210 transnationals in the United Kingdom revealed that 83 percent had been involved in a transfer pricing dispute (ibid.).

References

Axelrod, Robert M. *The Evolution of Cooperation*. London: Penguin Books, 1984.
Bailey, David, George Harte, and Roger Sugden. *Transnationals and Governments: Recent Policies in Japan, France, Germany, the United States and Britain*. London: Routledge, 1994.
Bain, Joe S. *Barriers to New Competition*. Cambridge, Mass.: Harvard University Press, 1956.
Baran, Paul A., and Paul M. Sweezy. *Monopoly Capital*. New York: Monthly Review Press, 1966.
Baumol, William J., John C. Panzar, and Robert D. Willig. "Contestable Markets: An Uprising in the Theory of Industry Structure: Reply." *American Economic Review* 73 (June 1983): 491–496.
Becattini, Giacomo. "The Marshallian Industrial District as a Socioeconomic Notion." In *Industrial Districts and Inter-firm Co-operation*, ed. Frank Pyke, Giacomo Beccatini, and Werner Sengenberger, 37–51. Geneva: International Institute for Labour Studies, 1990.
Berle, Adolf A., and Gardiner C. Means. *The Modern Corporation and Private Property*. New York: Macmillan, 1932.
Berlin, Isaiah. *Four Essays on Liberty*. Oxford: Oxford University Press, 1969.
Blattner, Niklaus. "Domestic Competition and Foreign Trade: The Case of the Excess Capacity Barrier to Entry." *Zeitschrift für Nationalökonomie* 33 (Sept. 1973): 403–412.
Blomström Magnus, and Ari Kokko. "Sweden." In *Governments, Globalization and International Business*, ed. John H. Dunning. Oxford: Oxford University Press, 1997.
Branston, J. Robert, Keith Cowling, and Roger Sugden. "Corporate Governance and the Public Interest." *International Review of Applied Economics* 20 (2006): 189–212.

Brusco, Sebastiano. "The Emilian Model: Productive Decentralisation and Social Integration." *Cambridge Journal of Economics* 6 (June 1982): 167–184.
Claycombe, Richard J. "The Effects of Market Structure on Prices of Clothing and Household Furnishings." *International Journal of Industrial Organization* 28 (July 2000): 827–841.
Coase, Ronald H. "The Nature of the Firm." *Economica* 4 (Nov. 1937): 386–405.
Coffey, Dan, and Philip R. Tomlinson. "Globalisation, Vertical Relations and the J-Mode Firm." *Journal of Post Keynesian Economics* 26 (Fall 2003a): 117–144.
Coffey, Dan, and Philip R. Tomlinson. "Coordination and Hierarchy in the Japanese Firm: The Strategic Decision Making Approach vs. Aoki." In *Competition, Monopoly and Corporate Governance. Essays in Honour of Keith Cowling*, ed. Michael Waterson, 3–19. Cheltenham: Edward Elgar, 2003b.
Congleton, Roger D, Arye L. Hillman, and Kai A. Konrad, eds. *40 Years of Research on Rent Seeking*. Heidelberg: Springer, 2008.
Cook, Gary. "A Comparative Analysis of Vertical Integration in the UK Brewing and Petrol Industries." *Journal of Economic Studies* 24 (1997): 152–166.
Cowling, Keith. "Oligopoly, Distribution and the Rate of Profit." *European Economic Review* 15 (1981): 195–224.
Cowling, Keith. *Monopoly Capitalism*. London: Macmillan, 1982.
Cowling Keith, John Cable, Michael Kelly, and Tony McGuinness. *Advertising and Economic Behaviour*. London: Macmillan, 1975.
Cowling, Keith, and Dennis C. Mueller. "The Social Costs of Monopoly Power." *Economic Journal* 88 (Dec. 1978): 727–748.
Cowling, Keith, and Roger Sugden. *Beyond Capitalism, towards a New World Economic Order*. London: Pinter, 1994.
Cowling Keith, and Roger Sugden. "The Essence of the Modern Corporation: Markets, Strategic Decision-Making and the Theory of the Firm." *Manchester School* 66 (Jan. 1998): 59–86.
Cowling Keith, and Roger Sugden. "The Wealth of Localities, Regions and Nations: Developing Multinational Economies." *New Political Economy* 4 (Nov. 1999): 361–378.
Cowling Keith, and Philip R. Tomlinson. "The Japanese Crisis—A Case of Strategic Failure?" *Economic Journal* 110 (June 2000): F358–F381.
Cowling, Keith, and Philip R. Tomlinson. "Revisiting the Roots of Japan's Economic Stagnation: The Role of the Japanese Corporation." *International Review of Applied Economics* 16 (2002): 373–390.
Cowling, Keith, Fahmi Mohd Yusof, and Guy Vernon. "Declining Concentration in UK Manufacturing? A Problem of Measurement." *International Review of Applied Economics* 14 (2000): 45–54.
Cubbin, John S. *Market Structure and Performance: The Empirical Research*. London: Harwood Academic Publishers, 1988.
Daripa, Arup, and Sandeep Kapur. "Pricing on the Internet." *Oxford Review of Economic Policy* 17 (Summer 2001): 202–216.
Dicken Peter. *Global Shift: Transforming the World Economy*. London: Sage, 2003.
Dixit, Avinash, and Victor Norman. "Advertising and Welfare." *Bell Journal of Economics* 9 (Spring 1978): 1–17.
Dobson, Paul W., and Michael Waterson. "Countervailing Power and Consumer Prices." *Economic Journal* 107 (March 1997): 418–430.
Fellner, William J. *Competition among the Few*. New York: Knopf, 1949.
Financial Times. "Is Google Now a Monopoly?" *Financial Times*, February 26, 2010.

Galbraith, John K. *The New Industrial State*. London: Hamish Hamilton, 1967.
Geroski, Paul. "What Do We Know about Entry?" *International Journal of Industrial Organization* 13 (Dec. 1995): 421–440.
Glyn, Andrew, and Bob Sutcliffe. *British Capitalism, Workers and the Profit Squeeze*. Harmondsworth: Penguin, 1972.
Gordon, Myron J. "Monopoly Power in the United States Manufacturing Sector, 1899–1994." *Journal of Post Keynesian Economics* 20 (Spring 1998): 323–335.
Harberger, Arnold C. "Monopoly and Resource Allocation." *American Economic Review* 44 (May 1954): 77–87.
Hughes, Kirsty, and Christine Oughton. "Diversification, Multimarket Contact and Profitability." *Economica* 60 (Feb. 1993): 203–224.
Hymer, Stephen H. "The Multinational Corporation and the Law of Uneven Development." In *International Firms and Modern Imperialism*, ed. Hugo Radice, 38–50. New York: Penguin, 1975.
Jacquemin, Alexis, and Jacques-Francois Thisse. "Strategy of the Firm and Market Structure: An Application of Optimal Control Theory." In *Market Structure and Corporate Behaviour*, ed. Keith Cowling. London: Gray-Mills, 1972.
Jamison, Mark A. "Emerging Patterns in Global Telecommunications Alliances and Mergers." *Industrial and Corporate Change* 7 (Dec. 1998): 695–713.
Johnson, Chalmers. *MITI and the Japanese Miracle: The Growth of Industrial Policy 1925–1975*. Stanford, Calif.: Stanford University Press, 1982.
Johnston, John. *Statistical Cost Analysis*. New York: McGraw-Hill, 1960.
Just, Richard E., Darrell L. Hueth, and Andrew Schmitz. *Applied Welfare Economics*. Cheltenham: Edward Elgar, 2008.
Kalecki, Michal. *Essays in the Theory of Economic Fluctuations*. London: Allen and Unwin, 1938.
Kalecki, Michal. *Dynamics of the Capitalist Economy*. London: Cambridge University Press, 1971.
King, Mervyn A. "The United Kingdom Profits Crisis: Myth or Reality?" *Economic Journal* 85 (March 1975): 33–54.
Koutsoyiannis, A. *Non-Price Decisions: The Firm in a Modern Context*. London: Macmillan, 1982.
Lancaster, Kelvin. "Socially Optimal Product Differentiation." *American Economic Review* 65 (Sept. 1975): 567–585.
Modigliani, Franco. "New Developments on the Oligopoly Front." *Journal of Political Economy* 66 (June 1958): 215–232.
Monopolies Commission. *Man-Made Cellulosic Fibres*. London: U.K. Monopolies Commission, 1968.
Nelson, Philip B., and John C. Hilke. "Retail Featuring as a Strategic Entry or Mobility Barrier in Manufacturing." *International Journal of Industrial Organization* 9 (Dec. 1991): 533–544.
Pagoulatos, Emilio, and Robert Sorenson. "What Determines the Elasticity of Industry Demand?" *International Journal of Industrial Organization* 4 (Sept. 1986): 237–250.
Peoples, James, and Roger Sugden. "Divide and Rule by Transnational Corporations." In *The Nature of the Transnational Firm*, 2nd ed., ed. Christos N. Pitelis and Roger Sugden, 174–192. London: Routledge, 2000.
Piore, Michael J., and Charles F. Sabel. *The Second Industrial Divide*. New York: Basic Books, 1984.

Posner, Richard A. "The Social Costs of Monopoly and Regulation." *Journal of Political Economy* 83 (Aug. 1975): 807–827.
Pryor, Frederic L. "New Trends in US Industrial Concentration." *Review of Industrial Organisation* 18 (May 2001): 301–326.
Rothschild, Kurt W. *Power in Economics*. Houndmills: Penguin, 1971.
Rothschild, Kurt W. "The Absence of Power in Contemporary Economic Theory." *Journal of Socio-Economics* 31 (2002): 433–442.
Rothschild, Kurt W. "New Worlds—New Approaches. A Note on Future Research Strategies." *Kyklos* 58 (July 2005): 439–447.
Russell, Ellen, and Mathieu Dufour. *Rising Profit Shares, Falling Wage Shares*. Canadian Centre for Policy Alternatives, June 2007.
Scherer, F. M., Alan Beckenstein, Erich Kaufer, and R. Dennis Murphy. *The Economics of Multi-Plant Operation: An International Comparison Study*. Cambridge, Mass.: Harvard University Press, 1975.
Scherer, F. M., and David R. Ross. *Industrial Market Structure and Economic Performance*. Boston: Houghton and Mifflin, 1990.
Servan-Schreiber, Jean-Jacques. *The American Challenge*. London: Holiday House, 1967.
Simon, Herbert. *Models of Man*. New York: Wiley, 1957.
Simpson, John. "Geographic Markets in Hospital Mergers: A Case Study." Working Paper 237, Washington, D.C. Federal Trade Commission, February 2001.
Singh, Satwinder, Michael Utton, and Michael Waterson. "Strategic Behaviour of Incumbent Firms in the UK." *International Journal of Industrial Organization* 16 (March 1998): 229–251.
Smiley, Robert. "Empirical Evidence on Strategic Entry Deterrence." *International Journal of Industrial Organization* 6 (1988): 167–180.
Smith, Howard. "Entry and Exit in Grocery Retailing: Local Pre-Emption and Social Efficiency." Discussion Paper no. 7, Department of Economics, University of Oxford, March 2000.
Spence, A. Michael. "Entry, Capacity, Investment and Oligopolistic Pricing." *Bell Journal of Economics* 8 (Autumn 1977): 534–544.
Stigler, George J. "A Theory of Oligopoly." *Journal of Political Economy* 72 (Feb. 1964): 44–61.
Stiglitz, Joseph E. *Globalization and Its Discontents*. New York: Norton, 2002.
Stiglitz, Joseph E. *Making Globalization Work*. New York: Penguin, 2006.
Sugden, Roger, Robbin Te Velde, and James R. Wilson. "Economic Development Lite: Communication, Art and ICTs in a Globalised Economy." In *Knowledge in the Development of Economies: Institutional Choices under Globalisation*, ed. Silvia Sacchetti and Roger Sugden, 205–228. Cheltenham: Edward Elgar, 2009.
Swan, Peter L. "Market Structure and Technological Progress: The Influence of Monopoly on Product Innovation." *Quarterly Journal of Economics* 84 (Nov. 1970): 627–638.
Sylos-Labini, Paolo. *Oligopoly and Technical Progress*. Cambridge, Mass.: Harvard University Press, 1969.
Thomas, Louis A. "Incumbent Firms' Response to Entry: Price, Advertising and New Product Introduction." *International Journal of Industrial Organization* 17 (May 1999): 527–555.
Tullock, Gordon. "The Welfare Costs of Tariffs, Monopolies and Theft." *Western Economic Journal* 5 (June 1967): 224–232.
UNCTAD. *World Investment Report 1996: Investment, Trade and International Policy Arrangements*. New York: United Nations.

Vita, Michael G., and Seth Sacher. "The Competitive Effects of Not-for-Profit Hospital Mergers: A Case Study." Working Paper no. 226, Washington, D.C., Federal Trade Commission, May 1999.
Williamson, Oliver E. *The Economics of Discretionary Behavior: Managerial Objectives in a Theory of the Firm*. Englewood Cliffs, N.J.: Prentice Hall, 1964.
Williamson, Oliver E. "A Dynamic Theory of Interfirm Behavior." *Quarterly Journal of Economics* 79 (Nov. 1965): 579–607.
Williamson, Oliver E. *Corporate Control and Business Behavior*. Englewood Cliffs, N.J.: Prentice Hall, 1970.
Zeitlin, Maurice. "Corporate Ownership and Control: The Large Corporations and the Capitalist Class." *American Journal of Sociology* 79 (March 1974): 1073–1119.

CHAPTER 12

AGENCY PROBLEMS AND THE FATE OF CAPITALISM

RANDALL MORCK
AND
BERNARD YEUNG

Neoclassical economics presents "capitalism" as a system where multitudes of firms compete to offer customers the best prices. To many, especially outside North America and Britain, capitalism is a system where a handful of old-money families run the economy—often badly. The economists marvel at the others' credulity for conspiracy theories, while the others marvel at economists' naiveté about the "real world." Close inspection of corporate governance in different countries suggests that each side should take the other seriously. Capitalism has genuinely different forms in different countries, and these reflect fundamental differences in the distributions of corporate and political control.

Neoclassical economics readily allows that who controls a country's government matters, but traditionally takes firms as profit-maximizing black boxes and capital as a return-generating substance that Samuelson dubbed *shmoo.* Yet who controls firms and their capital matters (Berle and Means 1932). How microeconomics can incorporate this insight is the core issue of agency theory (Jensen and Meckling 1976).

Running a business requires scarce talent, and competition among potential leaders ideally assigns corporate control to the most able. Adam Smith (1759) posits that business success requires an empathic ability to predict potential customers' desires. Hayek (1941, chapter 25, p. 335) stresses the importance of exceptional foresight; Knight (1921, chapter 9, §3.9.7) stresses the rarity of rational decision-making ability; and Schumpeter (1912) sees uniquely creative innovators building new corporations that destroy old ones, and thereby earning the wrath of all who preferred the status quo.

Somewhat more cynically, and more in line with the recent corporate governance literature, Smith (1776, book 5, chapter 1, part 3, article 1) holds that corporate directors "seldom pretend to understand anything of the business of the company." Keynes (1936, chapter 12, §5) concurs with Smith, Hayek, Knight, and Schumpeter that "the social purpose of skilled investment is to defeat the dark forces of time and ignorance which envelop our future," although he despairs that this is beyond the ability of corporate executives, whose decisions he attributes to behavioral "animal spirits" (chapter 12, §7). Mueller (1992) thus advocates a broadly behavioral approach to modeling managerial decision making. Brandeis (1914) blasts the ethics of corporate tycoons running firms built with "other people's money," and Berle and Means (1932) describe a fundamental misalignment of their incentives.

Corporate governance, broadly defined, continues this discussion. Capital is not schmoo, for who controls businesses matters, as do the institutions that determine this, the interest groups that affect these institutions, and thus the interface between financial economics and political economy.

Although economic theory addresses all these issues, incentive misalignment attracts the most attention—perhaps because it highlights an internal contradiction within that theory. Neoclassical economics posits that individuals maximize utility and that firms maximize economic profits or, more precisely, the expected net present values (NPVs) of their capital investments—which, in turn, precisely equal the expected present values of economic profits. This presents problems because, as Grabowski and Mueller (1972) rightly note, firms are run by people. Which, then, is paramount: a CEO's utility or her firm's NPV?

Jensen and Meckling (1976), expanding earlier theories (Ross 1973) and reflecting previous empirical work rejecting pure value maximization (Baumol 1959; Grabowski and Mueller 1972; and others), provide the now standard resolution to this inconsistency. They assume utility maximization more fundamental, and their firms therefore do not maximize NPVs. The implicit sacrificed value they dub an *agency cost*. Specifically, they model outside investors—the firm's owners or *principals*, as in corporations law—buying shares in firms run by utility-maximizing insiders, whom corporations law declares to be their *agents*. Elaborating what is now standard terminology, they christen this divergence of interests a *principal agent problem*, now often abbreviated to *agency problem*. Corporate governance is the study of agency problems and the monitoring and control mechanisms that limit agency costs.

Neoclassical economics posits that price competition culls firms that do not maximize NPVs, and thus holds that agency problems ought to be brief and economically negligible (Demsetz and Villalonga 2001). However, the empirical literature increasingly confirms non–value-maximizing decisions to be common in corporate boardrooms and far too economically important to be abstracted away (e.g., Shleifer and Vishny 1997; Gompers et al. 2003; Bebchuk and Fried 2004; Bebchuk et al. 2009).

If firms do not maximize value, managerial utility maximization might cause them to effectively maximize something else. Baumol (1959) posits sales or growth maximization as best fitting the facts—at least in the United States. Recent work in behavioral finance suggests alternative objective functions for individuals (Shleifer 2000), and Mueller (1992) argues that such considerations should be incorporated into models of managerial behavior. Early work along these lines includes Stein (1989) and Scharfstein and Stein (1990), and Baker et al. (2004) review the area. Morck (2008) argues that a "loyalty reflex" demonstrated in Milgram's (1974) experiments might compromise directors' judgment and draws from variants of those experiments and the broader social psychology literature to evaluate governance reforms. Nonetheless, most work in the area presumes utility maximization by managers. This is perhaps justifiable, in that the critical issue is that neoclassical economics assigns people, including managers, and firms different objective functions.

Thus, Baumol (1959), Grabowski and Mueller (1972), Jensen (1986), and others argue that top executives attain higher utility from running larger firms, and thus invest in negative NPV projects merely to grow their firms. Jensen calls this sort of capital misallocation a *free cash flow agency problem*, defining *free cash flow* as the firm's cash flow (revenues minus operating costs) less the setup costs of all its positive NPV investments. A value-maximizing firm should pay its free cash flow out to its shareholders, rather than invest it in negative NPV projects, but Jensen presents evidence that free cash flow agency problems are a first-order determinant of overall agency costs. If this thesis is right, and the data suggest it is, microeconomic theory missed something very fundamental before the advent of agency theory.

Fortunately, this gap can be spanned with deeper economics (Jensen and Meckling 1976). Moral outrage about corporate misgovernance, in contrast, may be largely misdirected. Agency costs are often described as shareholder wealth *expropriation*. This is incorrect in an efficient market, where shareholders buy low because they rationally foresee extensive agency problems, costly monitoring and control mechanisms to limit agency problems, or a mixture of the two. Firms' founders thus absorb all agency costs by selling their shares at depressed initial public offering (IPO) prices; and the shares trade at fair value thereafter. Only outside shareholders who underestimate agency problems overpay and lose money on average, and this is expropriation unless caveat emptor applies.

The real social costs of agency problems lie deeper, in the inner workings of the economy. Inefficient resource allocation by firms costs money, as do the monitoring and control mechanisms that might limit those problems. Some level of agency costs is thus unavoidable. But both firms and economies can seek ways to reduce unavoidable agency costs.

All else equal, if corporate insiders more credibly precommit to maximize NPVs, investors pay more for shares. Higher share prices make outside capital readily available to firms that need it, permitting growth in firms with genuine business opportunities (Mueller 2006a). But less trusting outside investors and low share prices make outside capital scarce, and growth is restricted to firms with abundant earnings from existing operations (La Porta et al. 1997a, 1997b)—and these need not be the firms with the most farsighted, rational, or innovative leadership. Governments can curtail agency costs with institutions that better facilitate or require such commitments by corporate insiders. All else equal, success at this cuts costs of capital to entrants and incumbents alike—promoting competition, innovation, and efficient resource allocation. Corporate governance is therefore more fundamentally about how honest and able corporate insiders can most efficiently and credibly commit to limit agency costs and about how governments can lower their costs of doing so (Shleifer and Vishny 1997; Bebchuk and Weisbach 2010).

Finally, a handbook of capitalism survey of corporate governance must pay due honor to Marx. The internal contradiction at the heart of corporate governance is not unrelated to Marx's more famous contention that competition drives surplus value to zero, and that this dooms capitalism. Schumpeter (1942, p. 31) interprets surplus value as the present value of abnormal returns to capital, essentially the NPVs of finance textbooks, and argues correctly that competition indeed drives these to zero. This still disturbs the equanimity of an occasional MBA student, who learns in microeconomics how economic profits fall to zero under perfect competition, and then learns in corporate finance of the need for "positive NPV" projects—that is, investments with positive economic profits. A well-placed between-term or summer break obscures this discrepancy from all but the most insightful students; but its true resolution, due to Schumpeter (1912), is that investment in innovation can have positive economic profits for a time (Cable and Mueller 2008) and that successful innovators are exceptionally foresighted and coldly rational rarities. Corporate governance is thus most fundamentally about how to entrust the governance of businesses to people who are both able and willing to find the positive NPV projects that Schumpeter evokes to save capitalism from Marxist doom. Good corporate governance is therefore fundamentally about piloting firms through disequilibrium situations, where economic profits can be very large and positive or negative.

Ultimately, a free market economy creates social welfare by organizing the efficient division of labor (Smith 1776). Increased efficiency in corporate governance thus places corporations more reliably under the control of top executives with specialized skills, talents, or information necessary for leading their firm, organizing its core activities, developing its future capabilities, and mobilizing capital to financing its growth opportunism. But designing institutions that better align CEOs' personal utility maximization with value maximization also promises improved microeconomic efficiency. The normative goal of economic analysis in this context is trustworthy and well-qualified top corporate managers running firms that raise capital from rationally trusting investors. The positive goal of economic analysis in this area is enlightenment as to how top corporate insiders, firms, and investors actually behave and the economic consequences of this.

Agency Problems and the Wealth of Nations

The social purpose of the financial system is to entrust people's savings to firms governed by trustworthy people. Schumpeter's famous circular flow fails if savers do not trust financial institutions or financial markets and instead bury coins in their gardens. Financial economists (e.g., Mueller 2006a) argue that if savers can invest in bank accounts, bonds, and stocks knowing their money will be entrusted to genuine entrepreneurs who can capture genuine economic profits, the economy can mobilize its savers' capital to finance huge firms capturing vast economies of scale, daring technological innovators, and perceptive entrepreneurs who perceive previously unexploited profit opportunities.

Big Business, Trust, and Riches

Rosenberg and Birdzel (1986) argue that the joint stock company and other similar business organizational forms that let anonymous investors assemble huge pools of capital, and the institutional arrangements necessary to them, are fundamental to "how the West grew rich" and surpassed previously more advanced civilizations such as the Arab world, China, and India. The West developed institutions that let entrepreneurs assemble vast pools of capital from diverse investors, and the rest did not.

For large, publicly traded companies to be viable, savers must trust corporate insiders to govern efficiently. Insiders can make commitments to do so at the firm level by granting shareholders voting rights, nominating trustworthy directors, mandating independent board committees, voluntarily disclosing important information, adopting managerial incentive pay schemes, and the like. However, Rosenberg and Birdzel stress how country-level institutional developments are more important to the credibility of such commitments. Promises to honor shareholders appear incredible without predictable laws and regulations governing financial markets, efficient and dispassionate courts, honest civil servants, mandatory disclosure rules, responsible government, and the like.

With the discovery of sea routes around Africa to Asia and the New World, the spice, fur, tobacco, and slave trades promised high returns but required vast capital outlays beyond the capabilities of even the wealthiest merchants and aristocrats. The solution to this quandary, the joint stock company, was a seventeenth-century Dutch invention.[1]

Before the invention of the joint stock company, maritime trade was organized one ship at a time. At the end of each voyage, the ship and cargo were sold and the proceeds divided between the captain and crew, the provisioners, and the financiers with each party's dividend (in the arithmetic sense) prespecified in the contract. Financiers diversified the risk of loss at sea by buying shares in multiple voyages, rather than backing a single ship. Over time, these arrangements expanded to include several ships or all voyages for a fixed number of years.

The modern world's first joint stock company, the Dutch East India Company, or Vereenigde Oost-Indische Compagnie (VOC), was formed in 1602.[2] It was, according to the prominent investor Isaac le Maire (1558–1624), governed in a way "entirely absurd and impertinent" to the "displeasure and complaint of both the people in the street and the investors."[3] This displeasure arose because, to le Maire's fury, the VOC directors refused to dissolve the venture and instead used each voyages' profits to finance the next, paying dividends from the residual only. Moreover, they appeared intent on continuing this "absurd" practice indefinitely! Le Maire wanted his money out of the VOC because he felt its directors were running the company too laxly. They were building fine houses along Amsterdam's best canals, but letting others grab promising business opportunities in Asia.

On January 24 ,1609, in what (to our knowledge) is the first recorded corporate governance dispute, le Maire formally charged that the directors sought to "retain another's money for longer or use it ways other than the latter wishes" and petitioned for the liquidation of the VOC in accordance with standard business practice. The petition was denied, and investors who wanted out were forced to find another exit strategy. The only option left to them was selling the shares of the VOC they owned to other investors, for some merchants who had not participated in the initial voyage were indeed interested in earning dividends from a second round of voyages.

Because le Maire lost, a new business model arose—the professionally run, indefinitely long-lived, joint stock corporation with publicly traded shares. This innovation financed the successive waves of industrial revolution that created the modern world. But le Maire was also quite likely correct in arguing that the VOC directors were growing fat and indolent, living off the shareholders' hard-earned money. Today's top managers have moved on, graduating from fine canal houses to Learjets, and shareholders object just as vociferously. Today's top corporate managers, just as confidently, assure shareholders it's all actually in their best interests.

Ultimately, Dutch shareholders accepted the new model, and British organizers copied it, especially after the Glorious Revolution of 1688 brought Dutch courtiers and ideas to London. Vast pools of capital funded huge joint stock companies, like the British East India Company and the Hudson's Bay Company which, at their apogees, owned sizable fractions of India and Canada, respectively. Others organized settler colonies, slaving expeditions, and slave plantations. The model soon spread to France and across Europe.

Questionable business models, especially slaving and slave plantations, and later the opium trade in China, attracted opprobrium to joint stock companies. But so did a popular perception of rampant mismanagement. Writing more than half a century later, Smith (1776, book 5, chapter 1, part 3, article 1) despairs that

> The directors of such companies... being the managers rather of other people's money than of their own, it cannot well be expected that they should watch over it with the same anxious vigilance with which the partners in a private copartnery frequently watch over their own. Like the stewards of a rich man, they are apt to consider attention to small matters as not for their master's honour, and very

> easily give themselves a dispensation from having it. Negligence and profusion, therefore, must always prevail, more or less, in the management of the affairs of such a company.

Courts, legislatures, and regulators ever since have sought to achieve the vast pools of capital joint stock companies permit without the "negligence and profusion" Smith denounces. As noted, Rosenberg and Birdzell (1986) argue that Western countries first developed institutions, legal and informal, that brought this goal closer than ever before, and this is "how the West grew rich" and escaped the Malthusian trap that once bound every part of the world equally.

Subsequent research in corporate governance elaborates on this theme. Over the four centuries since the VOC first defied its shareholders, much has changed to better protect public shareholders in joint stock companies and similar structures—listed trusts, listed limited partnerships, widely held cooperatives, and the like—from errant or inept insiders. In some countries, more efficient hierarchies that better let honest and competent insiders credibly commit to good governance encouraged broader, deeper, and more efficient capital markets in a virtuous circle or expanding prosperity; in other countries, this feedback loop either fails to form or quickly collapses after occasionally materializing (La Porta et al. 1997b; Rajan and Zingales 2003), preserving de facto feudal institutions (Haber 2000; Acemoglu et al. 2001, 2002).

Differences in national institutions therefore merit the interest of corporate governance researchers—either as factors directly responsible for these differences or as instruments behind other factors that are responsible. However, before exploring these issues, we pause to consider how governance quality can be measured and modeled.

Who Governs Firms Matters

The literature on agency problems uses a range of models and notation that remains inconsistent. However, common themes are evident. Corporate insiders create wealth worth V from capital K, and the wealth created, $\Delta V = V - K$, is the NPV of the profits of their ventures. Agency problems arise because the insiders must provide the investors—the people who provided the capital—with a return r that is higher the greater the risk the investors perceive in the venture. Business ventures have intrinsic risk, but agency problems add to this risk if insiders might keep part of r, or run the firm to enhance their utility and leave insufficient funds to pay the return the investors expect. Perceiving these elevated risks, rational investors withhold capital unless the promised return is very high or measures are in place to make the actual payment of the return credible. Agency problems thus increase firms' costs of outside capital, and sufficiently serious agency problems preclude access to outside capital altogether (La Porta et al. 1997b).

The scope for agency problems depends on the benefits b corporate insiders pay themselves. Entrepreneurs contributing foresight, rationality, creativity, or other scarce talents the firm needs merit compensation b_E. Because this compensates them for their skill in creating value, it is theoretically paid entirely out of ΔV and leaves sufficient earnings to pay investors r. However, utility-maximizing insiders determine their own compensation, within the limits the country's regulations and the firm's contractual obligations permit.

The benefits insiders glean thus contain other terms. These private benefits of control come in two flavors. Some private benefits—social status and the sheer utility of power, for example—need not compromise the firm's ability to allocate resources optimally, though they can if their consumption induces unqualified insiders to retain control. Other private benefits—self-dealing, excess compensation, pet projects, pursuit of the good life at corporate expense, and so on—can allocate resources suboptimally from the perspectives of potential investors as well as society. The former we call intangible private benefits of control, denoted b_I, and the latter we call tangible private benefits of control, b_T.

Agency problems arise because, in general, b_E and b_T are indistinguishable until after the fact, and b_I may be largely unobservable. Monitoring and control mechanisms, whose cost we denote m, can curtail b_T, but generally curtail b_E and b_I, too. Thus, outside investors' return is reduced by insiders' tangible private benefits, b_T, and may be further reduced if incumbent insiders' enjoyment of intangible private benefits b_I induces them to hold onto corporate power when more qualified people might take charge. The economic importance of such entrenchment is evident in the positive stock price reaction that occur on announcements of the sudden deaths of top corporate insiders (Johnson et al. 1985; Etebari et al. 1987; Faccio and Parsley 2009).

The efficacy with which insiders have added to a firm's value can be assessed by estimating Tobin's average q ratio, $q = V/K$ (Tobin and Brainard 1976). If corporate insiders have, on average, added to a firm's value, $q > 1$. If they have, on average, destroyed value, $q < 1$. Because events beyond insiders' control can also create or destroy value, q is usually adjusted with industry benchmarks and for other factors like firm size or age. However, we can proceed without loss of generality by declaring that $q = 1 + NPV/K$, where K is the firm's total stock of capital and NPV is the total aggregated net present value of all the firm's operations.

Figure 12.1 shows mean firm-level estimates of q, by country, from the mid-1990s from La Porta et al. (2002), who go on to show higher average q ratios in countries whose governments offer outside investors stronger legal rights against corporate insiders. Buttressing this finding, Gompers et al. (2003) show that U.S. firms with stronger commitments to shareholder democracy in their corporate charters exhibit higher average q ratios; Bebchuk and Cohen (2005), Faleye (2007), and others show markedly depressed average q ratios in firms with staggered boards, that is, whose corporate charters grant directors three-year terms with a third facing reelection each year.

These limitations on shareholders' legal and democratic rights clearly cause depressed average q ratios, rather than the converse. When U.S. states pass legislation constricting shareholders' legal rights, the average share price of all firms incorporated in those states drops significantly (Ryngaert and Netter 1990; Jahera and Pugh

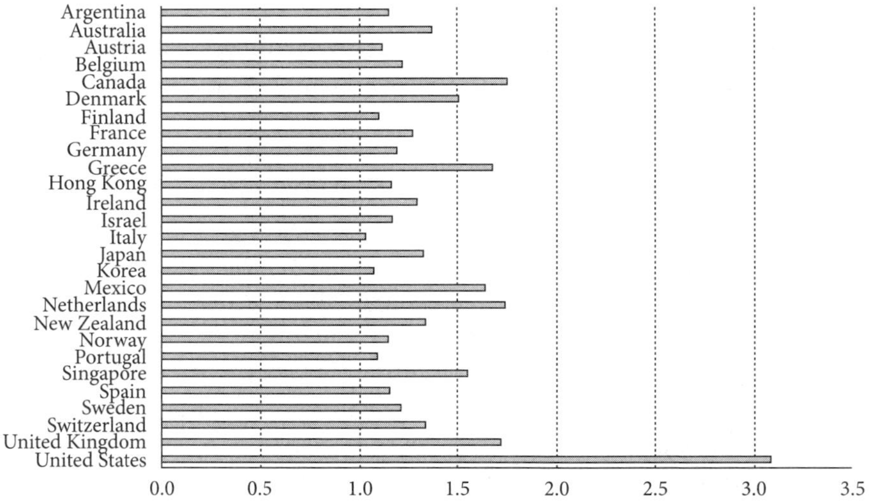

Figure 12.1. Mean Tobin's Average q Ratios around the World

Notes: The means of the Tobin's average q ratios of the twenty largest listed firms in each country are proposed as gauges of the overall quality of corporate governance in each country. Values above 100% indicate a preponderance of value creating investments by the country's corporations in the eyes of their public investors. Data are for the mid 1990s, and the estimates are constructed by La Porta et al. (2002).

1991), as do the prices of firms that modify their corporate charters to limit shareholder democracy (DeAngelo and Rice 1983; Jarrell and Poulsen 1987, 1988; Bhagat and Jefferis 1991; Datta and Iskandar-Datta 1996; Bebchuk et al. 2002), though see also Comment and Schwert (1995), who highlight how less democracy can create more value under the right management, and McWilliams and Sen (1997) and others, who highlight trade-offs between different dimensions of shareholder democracy.

An alternative approach Tobin's marginal q (Tobin 1969), designated here q', assesses the efficiency of corporate investment on the margin. This gauge of growth opportunities differs from Tobin's average q (Tobin and Brainard 1976), discussed above; for $q' = dV/dK$ is the marginal value the firm's management creates from a marginal unit of capital.[4] The (tax-adjusted) optimal value of q' is 1, for if $q' > 1$ the firm ought to expand and if $q' < 1$ it has overexpanded. Higher average $q = V/K$, in contrast, always signifies net value creation. Empirical work reveals directly estimated marginal q ratios to be closer to one (or its tax-adjusted optimum) in firms about which investors have more information (Durnev et al. 2004b) and in countries with common law legal systems that accord public shareholders stronger rights against insiders (Mueller 2005; Gugler et al. 2004a, 2007). Empirical studies using alternative measures of investment efficiency find similar cross-country results (Rajan and Zingales 1998; Wurgler 2000).

Yet another approach compares a firm's stock price after it announces a large investment relative to the price before so as to back out investors' estimate of the marginal q ratio of that investment (Morck et al. 1990). Increases in firms' R&D spending sharply elevate share prices (Chan et al. 1990; Chan et al. 2001), as do foreign acquisitions by R&D-intensive U.S. firms (Morck and Yeung 1992), consistent with innovation as a source of genuine economic profits (Schumpeter 1912; Grabowski and Mueller 1978). In contrast, corporate takeovers, among the largest capital investments firms undertake, more markedly depress the share prices of acquiring firms with more evident agency problems (Morck et al. 1990) and in countries whose legal systems offer public shareholders weaker legal recourse against insiders (Mueller and Yurtoglu 2007). The change in value of the target and bidder combined can be positive in some cases, but the mere fact that numerous acquirer value-destroying takeovers happen suggests that corporate insiders gain personal utility from ruling over larger business empires, regardless of their profitability (Morck et al. 1990; Mueller and Sirower 2003).

Determining the optimal protection of shareholders' rights is complicated by several interrelated considerations. First, shareholders entrust corporate governance to top insiders because those insiders possess exceptional foresight, rationality, or creativity. This means shareholders recognize that insiders are better qualified to govern the firm and that excessive shareholder power might interfere with this. Indeed, limits on shareholder democracy correlate with both unusually good and unusually poor corporate performance (Adams et al. 2005; Adams and Ferreira 2007), suggesting that democracy limits both extremes.

Governments can impose conditions on corporate charters, force firms to spend money making themselves transparent, and assign shareholders stronger rights in court. All such measures can limit corporate insiders' freedom to extract private benefits of control, but always at a cost. Just as more democratic charters can limit truly creative CEOs' freedom of action, transparency requirements entail auditing and compliance costs, and legal rights enable opportunistic and even extortionary lawsuits (Jensen and Meckling 1976).

Shareholder Value as an Imperfect Governance Meter

The agency literature tends to identify superior corporate governance with higher share prices. Normative chapters in economics and finance textbooks charge firms with maximizing NPVs, the expected discounted values of future profits. This makes sense, for outside investors almost always invest solely to grow their savings. Obviously, a sole proprietorship maximizing its owner's utility and financed solely with her savings entails no agency conflict, for owner and manager are one, though the textbooks describe this situation poorly. But capitalism prospers off specialized firms exploiting economies of scale, and this typically requires mobilizing very large pools of outside investors' capital. This justifies shareholder value as a corporate governance metric; however, conditions under which the metric can go askew merit note.

First, shareholders are not the only people with investments in a firm. However, the prices of firms' other securities—bonds, debentures, bank loans, and so on—fluctuate relatively little compared to stock prices. A firm's obligations to its other investors almost always have legal priority over those to its shareholders. Firms with cash flow shortfalls must cut or skip dividends first. Only if the shortfall is very large does a firm lay off employees or miss an interest payment, for the former triggers often costly labor laws and the latter triggers bankruptcy. Thus, any cash flow shortfalls initially hurt dividends, and hence shareholder wealth, before affecting any other securities. Likewise, any unexpected positive revisions in a firm's future cash flow estimates normally augment expected future payouts available to common shareholders, and thus raise the share price. Bondholders do not get higher interest payments whenever the firm has an unusually good year. Consequently, most of the variation in a firm's market value, and therefore in its average q ratio, is due to variation in shareholder value.

This is the fundamental reason why corporate governance must focus on shareholder value. Shareholders are not more important than the firm's other claimants, but their squawking amid plummeting share prices turns out to be a highly sensitive corporate misgovernance alarm system. If shareholders' anger can prevent or reverse misbegotten corporate policies, creditors and workers are protected.[5] Nonetheless, many countries charge top insiders with balancing shareholders' interests against those of all stakeholders—creditors, employees, retired employees, consumers, suppliers, the environment, the state, the community, and so on—seemingly to the detriment of overall wealth creation (Gugler et al. 2003) and quite probably to overall employment levels as well (Jensen and Meckling 1979; Faleye et al. 2006).

Second, stock prices can misrepresent the quality of corporate management. If the firm is perfectly transparent, public investors can estimate the cash flows each of its projects will generate in all future periods. But the public relies on public information, so shareholders might think brilliant entrepreneurs mad and depose them or laud truly mad corporate insiders as brilliant. The former misperception retards growth, and the latter destroys existing wealth.

This seemingly obvious point nonetheless causes much confusion. The Dutch court that upheld the VOC's right to life encapsulated this confusion in a mantra for disgruntled shareholders: "if you don't like the way the firm is run, sell your shares." If the firm was badly run when the shareholders bought their shares, and is no worse run now, this is reasonable advice. But selling out is no solution to unexpected misgovernance. In an efficient market, the shares of an unexpectedly mismanaged firm drop instantly and fetch too little too late to assuage disgruntled shareholders.

However, outside investors sometimes do misgauge the true value of a firm's ongoing investments. Firms are not perfectly transparent; their inner workings can be occluded by unavoidable information gathering and processing costs, or by deliberate obfuscations designed to conceal dubious management decisions. Taxes and other transaction costs further complicate the picture. The validity of the efficient markets hypothesis—the speed and accuracy with which all relevant new information accurately revises stock prices to reflect fundamental values—is therefore critical to the validity of shareholder value being a defensible metric of corporate governance. Tobin (1984) thus stresses the functional form of the efficient markets hypothesis as holding if financial markets are "efficient enough" to guide capital to its highest value uses with a tolerably low error rate. The extent to which financial market inefficiency biases corporate governance is one of the most understudied topics in current finance research (though see Wurgler 2000; Durnev et al. 2004a).

Third, bubbles and financial panics are especially troublesome deviations from market efficiency, and recent work in behavioral finance suggests that investors' perceptions can be distorted in more normal market conditions as well. All the stocks in an industry, or even in a country, can rise or fall because of altered terms of trade, consumer tastes, or government policies. Thus, the high Tobin's average *q* ratios of U.S. firms in figure 12.1 might reflect more sensible regulations, a low dollar, or an expanding stock market bubble in the mid-1990s. Some evidence suggests that firms' share prices relative to each other retain a relationship to their relative underlying fundamentals even as prices overall rise and fall with bubbles and panics (Samuelson 1998; Jung and Shiller 2005). These possible problems motivate measuring the quality of governance by firms' average *q* ratios relative to industry or country benchmarks (Morck et al. 1988).

Fourth, companies can go from seemingly robust financial health to probable bankruptcy quickly, depressing both their equity and debt valuations, and even putting employment and factor market contracts at risk. Once bankruptcy is in the cards, the values of debt and other contractual obligations fluctuate, too, and changes in shareholder valuation are no longer the whole picture. If only debt is affected, switching the focus from shareholder value to the firm's total market value is viable. If supplier and employment contracts are put at risk, these valuation decreases must also be weighed.

Fifth, political rent seeking can disconnect firms' NPVs, and therefore shareholder value, from genuine economic profits. In many countries, one of the highest NPV investment a firm can undertake is bribing public officials—either directly or, more often, indirectly via favors (Baumol 1990; Murphy et al. 1991)—to gain state-protected market power, subsidies, tax breaks, or regulatory favors. The importance of such favors becomes visible when corrupt governments change, as when the stocks of Indonesian firms favored by President Suharto collapsed on his overthrow (Fisman 2001). Is a firm whose share price soars because of the hugely profitable bribing of a politician a "well-governed" firm? Is a firm ill-governed if it refuses to bribe officials and therefore suffers regulatory disfavor that depresses its profits and share value? The answer to both is affirmative if shareholder value is the metric used. But this is misleading because corporate governance is fundamentally about allocating the economy's savings efficiently. Corruption can twist shareholder value badly out of alignment with efficient capital allocation.

Despite all of these caveats, shareholder value is the best corporate governance gauge available. Shareholders, like canaries in a mine, are especially sensitive to danger. Their squawking is a sometimes overly sensitive alarm system, and they occasionally doze through an approaching crisis. We therefore keep our eye on share prices but bear in mind the conditions under which this gauge can stick.

Constitutional Finance

Good corporate governance is difficult because of an underlying time inconsistency problem: before corporate insiders sell shares to outsiders, they promise value maximization so the shares fetch the highest possible price. After the shares are issued, the same insiders rationally appreciate the utility of policies other than shareholder value maximization. Good corporate governance thus entails a credible commitment against insiders maximizing their utility ex post. The problem resembles that of a government that must tie its own hands (Kydland and Prescott 1977), and thus the problem of designing an optimal constitution (Buchanan and Tullock 1962; Mueller 1996). The best tether is often unclear because the non–value-maximizing actions corporate insiders might take are often hard to anticipate—even for the insiders themselves.

This is most evident in the different attitudes toward good governance measures held by insiders of younger versus older firms. Younger firms' insiders, contemplating issuing new shares to public investors, logically want each share to fetch as high a price as possible, and so favor strong monitoring and control mechanisms, which are indeed more common in the charters of firms with more bountiful growth opportunities (Durnev and Kim 2005). But a mature or declining firm's share issuance days are in its distant past, and its insiders quite plausibly come to favor larger private benefits of control over a higher share price (Grabowski and Mueller 1975). Thus, a time inconsistency problem inevitably arises as a firm ages, despite the most earnest protestations of the young firm's insiders.

How countries deal with this time inconsistency matters, for this affects the pace of Schumpeter's creative destruction and thus the country's long-term economic growth (Shleifer and Wolfenzon 2002; Rajan and Zingales 2004; Morck et al. 2005; Mueller 2006a). This is readily illustrated by the venture capital cycle documented by Gompers and Lerner (1999), whereby innovative entrepreneurs build new firms, entrust them to professional managers, sell out, and use the proceeds to start another innovative venture. This cycle, or something analogous to it, appears important in the United States and other high-income economies but is altogether lacking in low-income economies (Morck et al. 2005). If professional managers cannot be trusted, the entrepreneur must stay in charge. She cannot cash out, nor can her children, nor can her children's children. Rather, they must take their pay in the form of private benefits. Such an economy is bereft of entrepreneurship and its capital assets are governed by heirs, who are rarely the beneficiaries of talent as well as wealth. To avoid this fate, capitalist economies need institutions that render professional corporate managers credibly trustworthy by constraining their scope for private benefits.

The corporate finance literature often follows Jensen and Meckling (1976) in referring to corporate insiders' generic non–value-maximizing behavior as "shirking"—relaxing to enjoy a philosopher's good life instead of striving to defeat Keynes's "dark forces" to unveil the future. This is historically valid, for in his complaint to the Dutch court, le Maire accused the VOC directors of neglecting the company to enjoy quiet lives of luxury in expensive Amsterdam canal houses. It is also empirically supported, for John et al. (2008) present evidence of personally risk-averse U.S. CEOs safeguarding their perks and pay by shunning risky projects that nonetheless likely had positive NPVs.

Yet other utility-maximizing CEOs might spend their investors' money to build ego-satisfying but ultimately financially unstable corporate empires (Jensen 1986), to pay themselves handsomely for running their firms poorly (Jensen and Murphy 1990), or on perks like executive jets (Yermack 2006). Utility-maximizing CEOs might restrict hiring to a favored gender or an ethnicity, or to ego-pleasing yes-men, even though this fills the firm with suboptimally qualified employees (Becker 1957). Politically or socially aware CEOs might even spend their investors' money lobbying for favored political agendas (Högfeldt 2005) or funding pet charities (Atkinson and Galaskiewicz 1988)—all with the best of utility-maximizing intentions.

The list of tangible and intangible private benefits of control insiders might extract, and the cost to share prices of these actions, is impossible to complete for it grows naturally with financial innovations like stock options, technological innovations like commuter helicopters, new tax loopholes, and so on. Credibly precommitting to avoid every conceivable item on this list is beyond the ability of even the finest contract lawyers. Credible commitments to good governance must thus be of a more general character: they must be open-ended promises to inform and empower shareholders.

Genuinely credible commitments may therefore require that public policy enforce governance standards. Empirical evidence suggests that public policy is typically more effective than measures taken by individual firms in reducing agency costs (Doidge et al. 2007). But arguments that regulations, such as the Sarbanes-Oxley Act in the United States, impose inefficiently large compliance costs on listed firms cannot be dismissed summarily (Romano 2005).

Obviously, the more credible the good governance measures with which the entrepreneur can bind the professional CEO who succeeds her, the higher the return to entrepreneurship. Public policies that enforce higher standards of corporate governance are thus defensible to encourage entrepreneurship. Because new firms often bring important productivity-enhancing technologies into play, this has dynamic efficiency consequences (Schumpeter 1912). Even without new technology, higher returns to the founders of new firms encourage entry and enhance competition.

This concern for long-term dynamic efficiency, rather than the ethical arguments about expropriation already shown to be of dubious validity, is the more defensible economic logic underlying corporate governance laws, regulations, and standards. These let corporate insiders tie themselves and their successors to the mast, so that public shareholders can rationally expect agency problems to be mitigated, and thus can be persuaded to pay more for corporate shares. Since Schumpeter (1912) argues that much economic growth arises through innovative entrepreneurs founding new firms, unnecessarily large agency costs could reduce social welfare quite substantially over the long run.

Different countries use different mixes of alternative mechanisms to encourage shareholder value maximization and discourage insiders from shirking or otherwise extracting private benefits. Given these, different firms can constrain their insiders in different ways by relying on some available mechanisms more than others. These mechanisms range along a spectrum from open-access governance, where shareholder democracy (with all its flaws) is paramount, to restricted access governance, where big business is entrusted to (hopefully enlightened) corporate despots.

Shareholder Democracy

The most basic such mechanism is shareholder democracy, as specified in law and by the firm's charter. A corporate charter is essentially a firm's constitution, specifying voting rights, constituencies, voting procedures, allocation rules for board seats, and the like. This reflects historical accident: joint stock companies arose before governments were ready for them and, in England and elsewhere, were formed under laws cribbed from those pertaining to municipal governments (Dunlavy 2007).

This made a certain sense, in that both towns and joint stock companies are the joint property of large numbers of strangers, whether landowners or shareholders. Thus, both are legal persons capable of owning corporate property and run by elected boards and CEOs within the constraints of bylaws and corporate charters that specify rules for electing boards and enacting bylaws. Some early corporate charters even imitated municipal elections in granting one vote per shareholder, rather than the modern standard of one vote per share (Dunlavy 2007).

Corporate charters and bylaws, like those of towns and cities, specifying voting rights, election rules, administrative organization, financial accountability, audit procedures, and the general freedom of action entrusted to the board and management. Some corporations can thus be substantially more democratic than others. Gompers et al. (2003) rank the strength of shareholder democracy in each of a large sample of U.S. firms in the 1990s and find that more democratic governance correlates significantly with higher shareholder valuations and superior financial performance.

Shareholders' ultimate trump card is the annual general shareholders meeting, at which the shareholders can vote out the board of directors if they don't like the way the company was run. A new board can then fire the old managers, hire new ones, and set the company on a new course more to the shareholders' liking. To stay in charge, the VOC's directors had to convince a majority of its shareholders that the strategy of staying in business perpetually made sense. They succeeded—in part because shareholders who disagreed sold out and others who agreed bought in.

How shareholder democracy works thus depends critically on the corporation's voting rules at that meeting (Bebchuk and Cohen 2005). Corporations experimented with remarkably variegated shareholder voting rules through the nineteenth century (Dunlavy 2007). One especially democratic model was one vote per shareholder, based on a direct analogy to municipal corporations (Maier 1993). Other early English trading companies, for example the Hudson's Bay Company's 1670 charter, pioneered one vote per share instead, and the latter model won out by the twentieth century.

The logic behind restricting large shareholders' relative power is that a firm's top managers can better act in all the shareholders' true interests if they are not controlled too heavily by any given shareholder—precisely the message in the VOC example. But an a priori equally plausible chain of reasoning holds powerful large shareholders improve the quality of corporate decision making because they have the sophistication, resources, and financial incentives to monitor the firm and intervene to correct wrong strategies (Shleifer and Vishny 1986). The latter logic might not justify super-voting shares for insiders, but it can justify one vote per share under appropriate convexity assumptions (Grossman and Hart 1988).

Other companies in the nineteenth century had sliding scales, where shareholders with larger stakes had fewer votes per share—so as not to marginalize smaller shareholders utterly, while still giving larger shareholders more say (Dunlavy 2007).[6] Related structures survive to the present in many countries in the form of voting caps, which restrict any shareholder from voting more than a certain fraction of a company's shares. For example, voting caps currently limit the power of large shareholders in all the major Canadian banks.

But these relics are oddities. In 1811, New York State mandated one vote per share (for manufacturing corporations), and other states followed suit. One vote per share became the standard for shareholder democracy by the early twentieth century. One vote per shareholder is now barely a historical footnote, and further reforms to let insiders' shares have superior voting pushed some firms and countries to antidemocratic extremes, which we explore shortly.

Even under one vote per shareholder, consulting all the shareholders for every business decision was impracticable—even more so in earlier centuries when transportation by horse or boat made quick meetings impossible. This forced dispersed shareholders to entrust important decisions to the board and top management.

Electing highly trustworthy directors was not always easy. For example, Charles II granted Rupert Palatyne, his cousin and a royalist civil war hero, a monopoly on the fur trade out of most of what is now Canada. Palatyne organized an IPO in 1670, and the Hudson's Bay Company's shareholders elected a board of elite courtiers. From 1685 to 1690, the company's share price soared as it paid large and increasing dividends, and then the whole board resigned. The new directors discovered the meteoric dividends were financed with asset sales, and the share price plummeted accordingly—well after the old directors safely sold all their shares at the peak. The law courts had no sympathy for the impoverished shareholders, for one of the old board's last decisions was to pay a "special dividend" in gold to the king.

Over the subsequent decades and centuries, directors' duties gelled around preventing such abuses. At common law, directors' fiduciary duty is to put aside their private interests, act for the shareholders, and treat all shareholders (even kings) equally. In most common law countries, these duties are fundamental legal principles.

However, the common law courts may trust shareholder democracy excessively. First, most small shareholders do not vote in firms' shareholder meetings. This because a typical small shareholder, perhaps owning only a few hundred or a few thousand dollars' worth of stock, must spend considerable time and money to become informed about the issues; these costs typically exceed the dollar gain governance improvements would create for her (Grossman and Hart 1980). Second, most shareholder votes resemble elections to the North Korea People's Congress more than to the New York City Council. The typical election has one candidate standing for each board position, and shareholders are offered the choice of voting for the candidate or withholding their votes. The CEO traditionally selected the candidates, though existing directors are now sometimes entrusted with selecting candidates instead.

Contested elections do occur, but rarely. A proxy challenge—a campaign to replace incumbent directors with a so-called dissident slate of candidates—is time-consuming and expensive (Dodd and Warner 1983; Brickley 1986; Pound 1988; DeAngelo and DeAngelo 1989; Bhagat and Jefferis 1991; Van Nuys 1993; Mulherin and Poulsen 1998; Romano 2003; Davis and Kim 2007). Dissidents must campaign with their own money, while insiders can use corporate funds; dissidents' access to shareholders' names and addresses can be constrained; and small shareholders may still not be motivated to investigate the issues and vote. Proxy contests are therefore rare and occur only where the costs of mismanagement are perceived to be great (Bebchuk and Hart 2001). This means only extremely large-scale shareholder value devastation is likely to result in insiders being turfed out.

Representative Shareholder Democracy

These and other limitations on direct shareholder democracy lead recent rounds of expert reports in Australia, Britain, Canada, and other common law countries to advocate more responsible representative democracy: more independent directors, independent "lead directors" or board chairs, and key committees composed of independent directors. The Sarbanes-Oxley reforms in the United States also mandate greater numbers and responsibilities for outsider directors.

The social psychology literature (Milgram 1974) shows that people tend to reflexively obey legitimate authority figures unless dissenting peers or alternate authority figures voice dissent, so these reforms are defensible as ways of limiting excessive director loyalty to CEOs and promoting critical thought (Morck 2008). Of course, endless debate over every decision is unhelpful, and an optimal amount of dissent ought to exist (Landier et al. 2009).

Consistent with such a role for independent directors, Weisbach (1988) finds subpar performance more likely to trigger CEO turnover in U.S. firms whose boards contain more independent directors. However, whether independent directors increase shareholder value is unclear. Although early work finds no correlation, more recent studies indicate a growing traction (Adams et al. 2010). This may reflect increasingly rigorous definitions of independence preventing CEOs selecting directors by combing through lists of their friends for people who meet the literal criteria for independence.

Defining "independence" for directors can be tricky. People drawn from the ranks of top management are clearly not outsiders; defying the CEO puts their jobs at risk. People with financial ties to the firm—its lawyers, accountants, marketing agencies, or suppliers—are also unlikely to defy the CEO, for they risk losing business. CEOs often invite other CEOs to serve as independent directors, raising the possibility of tit-for-tat (Axelrod 1984) mutual support networks insulating each other from genuine shareholder democracy.

Especially tight such networks of interlocking directorships are found in France, where the alumni of a few elite colleges fill most top government and business jobs (Kramarz and Thesmar 2006), often migrating from civil service to top business positions over their careers (Bertrand et al. 2006). Pistor (2011) details similarly tight networks interweaving the top echelons of the Communist Party into the boards of Chinese financial firms. Reputational concerns might keep even imperfectly independent directors focussed on shareholder value and firm performance (Fama 1980; Fama and Jensen 1983), and Kaplan and Reishus (1990) find senior U.S. executives whose firms cut their dividends only half as likely as their peers to be offered additional outside directorships. But loyalty to fellow network insiders might just as easily induce a defensive huddle (Hallock 1997; Haunschild and Beckman 1998).

The effectiveness of shareholder democracy depends critically on both corporations' charters and bylaws and on national standards. For example, U.S. companies can adopt "poison pills," rights offerings that massively dilute the stake of any unfriendly shareholder bent on acquiring enough stock to oust the board (Ryngaert 1988; Brickley et al. 1994), or amend their corporate charters to establish staggered boards (Bebchuk and Cohen 2005), which recast annual shareholder votes as electing only a third of the board every year for a three-year term. Bebchuk and Cohen find that these innovations, especially staggered boards, substantially depress shareholder value in U.S. firms. In contrast, British and Canadian courts found these innovations to violate directors' traditional common law duties to treat all shareholders equally and to act for shareholders. Staggered boards are disallowed in both countries; poison pills are banned in Britain and vulnerable to legal challenge after a brief stay in Canada.

Multiple Constituencies

Shareholder democracy plays a role in corporate governance in every country, but some restrict it more severely than others. A major recent trend is the shifting of directors' duties away from shareholders and toward more vaguely defined "stakeholders." These reforms are inspired by Germany and other Central and Northern European countries that long explicitly set directors a fiduciary duty not only to shareholders but also to stakeholders—employees, customers, suppliers, the environment, the people, the state, and so on. Different countries operationalize this differently.

A large listed German firm typically has a management board, or *Vorstand*, charged with week-to-week operational decisions, and a supervisory board, or *Aufsichtsrat*, charged with higher level strategic decisions. Half of the supervisory board members in large firms are elected by shareholders and the other half by employees, though the chair, an additional shareholder representative, can break ties. In addition, German companies have works councils (*Betriebsrat*), elected by employees and empowered to veto human resources decisions. Supervisory board members owe a general fiduciary duty to all stakeholders, though their constituencies presumably affect their priorities.

This system, established by Adolf Hitler to inspire boards with a duty to stakeholders—such as their *Volk*, *Reich*, and *Führer* (Fohlin 2005)—still inspires progressive reformers today. Several U.S. states, beginning with Massachusetts and Pennsylvania, now mandate a German-style fiduciary duty of directors toward all stakeholders, not just shareholders (Karpoff and Malatesta 1989). A recent Supreme Court decision (*Peoples v. Wise*) in Canada also shifts directors' duty, but to act in the interests of "the corporation," rather than those of "the shareholders, creditors, employees, or any other stakeholders." This engenders considerable confusion, for the "interests" of a fictitious legal person are not readily discernible, and the court provides no further guidance. Recent reforms in Britain also move that country's directors' duty toward a broader responsibility to stakeholders and a less exclusive duty to shareholders.

With stakeholder rights ascendant, shareholder democracy is necessarily weakened. CEOs and directors, citing their duties to other stakeholders, can instruct their firms' lawyers to fight shareholders seeking to oust them. Because almost any corporate policy can be defended as in the interests of some stakeholder, top insiders need only pick the stakeholders whose interests align with their own on an issue-by-issue basis to defend sequences of entirely self-interested decisions. Because Arrow (1964) shows that no simple rule aggregates the preferences of heterogeneous constituents, such cynically self-interested governance cannot objectively be judged socially worse than alternative decision rules.

Open-Access Corporate Governance

In politics, the electorate's ultimate power is to "throw the bums out" (Haber et al. 2008; North et al. 2009). Shareholders have a similar last line of defence: the corporate takeover. If insiders let the share price fall too far below its replacement cost[7] per share, they put their firm "on sale." Even if the dismayed shareholders cannot replace top management, they can sell their shares to a raider who, on acquiring undisputable control, can fire the board and bring in new management.

In the United States in the 1980s, serial raiders amassed huge fortunes buying up misgoverned firms whose share prices were severely depressed (Easterbrook and Fischel 1982; Jensen and Ruback 1983; Jarrell et al. 1988; Morck et al. 1989). After gaining control, the raider replaced management, imposed credible commitments to good governance, and sometimes broke up bloated firms into more manageable pieces (Berger and Ofek 1996). This done, the raiders sold the firms back into the open stock market, where they fetched far more than acquiring the mismanaged firm cost. This "market for corporate control" saw raiders specializing in fixing broken firms, much like specialists in gentrification buying broken-down houses, fixing them up, and selling them. Criticisms that raiders create no value because they build no new factories or office buildings miss this fundamental point.

A more considered criticism is that some raiders are worse managers than the ones they oust. Jensen (1986) argues that ego-driven CEOs sometimes use takeovers to build shaky corporate empires that they cannot manage, and a wealth of empirical evidence now supports this (Lang and Litzenberger 1989; Morck et al. 1990; Lang et al. 1991; Opler and Titman 1993; Nanda and Christie 1994). This is plausible, for much evidence suggests top corporate insiders gain more utility from running larger firms (Baumol 1959; Grabowski and Mueller 1972).

Another plausible criticism is that stock market bubbles can trigger nonsensical takeovers (Shleifer and Vishny 2003; Rhodes-Kropf and Viswanathan 2004; Rhodes-Kropf et al. 2005; Baker et al. 2007). Acquirers, whose own shares are boosted by a bubble in, say, high-tech stocks, can use their overvalued shares as a currency with which to buy other firms and can again amass huge corporate empires. Once the bubble bursts, former target shareholders left holding the acquirers' now greatly deflated stock may well feel short-changed (Moeller et al. 2005; Mueller and Yurtoglu 2007).

These problems call for better corporate governance of acquirer firms, not prohibitions of takeovers. Indeed, bad acquirers in the 1980s often became targets of more adept raiders (Mitchell and Lehn 1990). Mueller (chapter 15 in this volume) points out that while hostile takeovers can be an effective constraint on managerial excess, "the market for corporate control is not sufficiently effective to eliminate all wealth destroying mergers." In particular, many countries and U.S. states curtail their markets for corporate control in response to various mixtures of legitimate and illegitimate concerns.

Some countries resist this trend more than others. In Britain, the courts nullified a succession of devices CEOs tried to use to stop raiders, and a robust market for corporate control persists, preventing insiders from becoming too neglectful of shareholder value or they risk ouster by a raider (Cheffins 2009). Takeovers also continue to rein in any excessively utility-maximizing top managers of firms that lack defensive armaments in the United States, Canada, Australia, and elsewhere.

However, hostile takeovers, where a raider aggressively buys control with the avowed purpose of ousting underperforming top management, grew rare in the United States after the 1980s because potential target firms' top managers erected arrays of takeover defenses (Mikkelson and Partch 1997). As mentioned, the most important are poison pills, rights offerings that dilute raiders' stakes before they become large; staggered boards, which lock directors into three-year terms with a third standing for election each year and thus make a raider wait two years before replacing a majority of directors; and state takeover laws, which empower CEOs to litigate against takeover bids (DeAngelo and Rice 1983; Linn and McConnell 1983; Jarrell and Poulsen 1987; Mitchell and Netter 1989; McWilliams 1990; Bhagat and Jefferis 1991; Comment and Schwert 1995; Brunarski et al. 1997; Bebchuk et al. 2002; Cheng et al. 2005).

Takeovers still happen in the United States, but now require the consent of the incumbent management, who have the power to waive poison pills, fire staggered boards, and undo other takeover defenses. Underperforming managers now expect large golden parachutes, side payments for dismantling takeover defenses and stepping aside (Hartzell et al. 2004). Since the potential gains from fixing up broken corporations can be very large, even very big golden parachutes can still leave the control transaction viable. Only if the CEO gleans so much utility from remaining in control that no feasible golden parachute side payment can induce him to step aside does the market for corporate control fail. Because these negotiations are conducted behind the scenes, we have no reliable estimate of the full shadow cost of takeover defenses to the U.S. economy in terms of takeovers of underperforming corporations that did not happen.

Underperforming firms in other countries use different takeover defenses. In Japan, the *keiretsu* defense was long favored (Sheard 1991; Morck and Nakamura 2005). This entails a group of CEOs, who all fear ouster by raiders, greatly increasing their firms' treasury shares—shares that exist but have not been sold to any investor. The firms swap these shares with each other so that each ends up with of a majority of its shares held by other firms in the new keiretsu group. Each of thirty firms might end up with a 1 percent or 2 percent stake in every other firm in the group, and every firm in the group then ends up more than 50 percent owned by other firms in the group. At no cost, these firms are now all insulated from raiders, for the groups' CEOs pledge never to sell their shares in each others' firms. The keiretsu defense remains important in Japan, but shareholder pressure to sell interlocking shares has induced many firms to adopt poison pills in recent years.[8]

Dutch firms use a variety of oligarchic mechanisms that let insiders control seemingly widely held firms with no fear of shareholder rebellion (de Jong et al. 2001; de Jong and Röell 2005). Large seemingly widely held German firms are controlled by the country's big banks, which are empowered to vote small shareholders shares (Fohlin 2005), though perhaps with growing disquiet.

But most countries in continental Europe, Asia, and Latin America have no effective market for corporate control. This is because most listed companies have a controlling shareholder, usually a wealthy business family, who controls an effective majority of the votes in the shareholder meeting and thus essentially appoints the board (La Porta et al. 1999; Fogel 2006). As long as the CEO and other top managers please that shareholder, their positions are secure. In these countries, corporate governance is the realm of despots (Gugler et al. 2007).

Corporate Despots

Like the government of nations, corporate governance can provide very open access or restrict decision making to tiny elites of insiders (North et al. 2009). Entrusting governance to a controlling shareholder brings to the corporation the efficiency of the dictator (Blau 1957). As in politics, a brilliant and highly ethical despot can provide very good government (Johnson 1910). But several strands of empirical work converge to show that, again as in politics, despots of this ilk are exceedingly rare.

Enlightened Corporate Despots

If a firm's controlling large shareholder demands economic efficiency, top management has little choice but to forego maximizing their utility functions and maximize value (Shleifer and Vishny 1986). The individuals or institutions that can afford to hold large equity blocks in large corporations are typically either enormously wealthy families or institutional investors like pension funds, insurance companies, banks, government organs, and large charitable foundations. All are able to employ sophisticated financial analysts, accountants, and lawyers who can and do take action to make sure the firms their employer controls are run as their employer wants. Because large shareholders have large, multimillion-dollar investments in their firms, the benefits of better management often outweigh their costs of becoming informed and taking action. Large shareholders thus overcome the free-rider problem of Grossman and Hart (1980).

Institutional investors' effect on corporate governance appears to vary markedly across countries. British pension funds and insurance companies were empowered by postwar Labour governments to finance workers' retirements and are largely run by independent professional fund managers. Black and Coffee (1994) describe how the institutional investor whose portfolio is most heavily weighted in a problem firm is expected to take the lead in forcing changes, and how other institutional investors organize to back the lead institution. Cheffins (2009) also highlights the effectiveness of institutional investors lobbying against takeover defenses. Canadian and Australian institutional investors may be on the path toward similar roles.

American institutional investors are less independent, for most private sector workers' pension funds are managed by their employers (Bodie and Davis 2000; Woidtke 2002). Thus, General Motors, IBM, and Northwest Airlines each run pension funds for their employees. Corporate pension funds seem reluctant to vote against the incumbent top management of firms they own—perhaps hoping their pension funds will reciprocate should the need arise (Wahal 1996; Del Guercio and Hawkins 1999; Faccio and Lasfer 2000; Woidtke 2002). This leaves only government employees' pension funds and a few pension funds organized by occupation rather than employer, to act as genuine guardians of good governance. CalPERS, the California Public Employees Retirement System, and various pension funds for teachers and university professors denounce problematic governance and often vote against incumbents in proxy contests (Pound 1988). However, civil servants' pension funds can be stymied by other problems, such as political pressure to favor firms with strong government connections (Romano 1993a, 1993c, 1995), and can suffer governance problems of their own (Lakonishok et al. 1991).

But most controlling shareholders in most countries are tycoons or wealthy families (La Porta et al. 1999), for independent institutional investors up to the job of challenging corporate insiders are rare outside a handful of English-speaking countries (Turner and Dailey 1991). Top insiders who are also large shareholders might be less prone to agency problems than the top managers running the widely held firms featured earlier. This is because any drop in shareholder value due to the insider sacrificing value for utility costs him money, too—because he is also a shareholder. However, top insiders who are also large shareholders might be more prone to agency problems than the managers of widely held firms because the former cannot be ejected by shareholder votes or corporate raiders, whereas the latter can. Modest levels of managerial share ownership seem to mitigate agency problems, but higher levels that precipitate entrenchment appear to magnify agency problems (Morck et al. 1988; McConnell and Servaes 1990; Holderness et al. 1999; Mueller 2005).

The founders of great family business dynasties are necessarily highly talented business leaders, and that talent may more than make up for any problems associated with entrenchment. Indeed, powerful tycoons may do their countries great service by coordinating so-called Big Push industrialization (Murphy et al. 1989), a process that requires the coordinated capitalization of interdependent firms across many sectors of the economy. Rosenstein-Rodan (1943) argues that a modern economy is a complex web of interdependencies, with each firm implicitly relying on hosts of suppliers, customers, and complementary good producers in numerous other industries, and on their suppliers, customers, and complementary goods providers, and so on. This, he argues, means rapid industrialization must be run under central planning, for otherwise early movers are subject to hold-up problems, economy of scale mismatches, and problems due to missing industries or insufficient competition in early stage industries.

Morck and Nakamura (2007) argue that the large business groups tycoons assemble in rapidly industrializing countries may reflect Big Push growth in progress. The firms in such a group are usually arranged in a control pyramid, with the tycoon controlling an apex firm that controls other listed firms, each of which controls yet other listed firms, and so on—as illustrated in figure 12.2. Actual control pyramids also involve an apex firm, directly controlled by the family, controlling several listed firms, each of which controls several more listed firms, and so on, but are often complicated by cross-holdings, control blocks split between multiple parent firms, control by parent firms in more distant tiers, dual class stock, and numerous other factors. Thus, figure 12.3 illustrates an actual business group, that of Italy's Agnelli family.

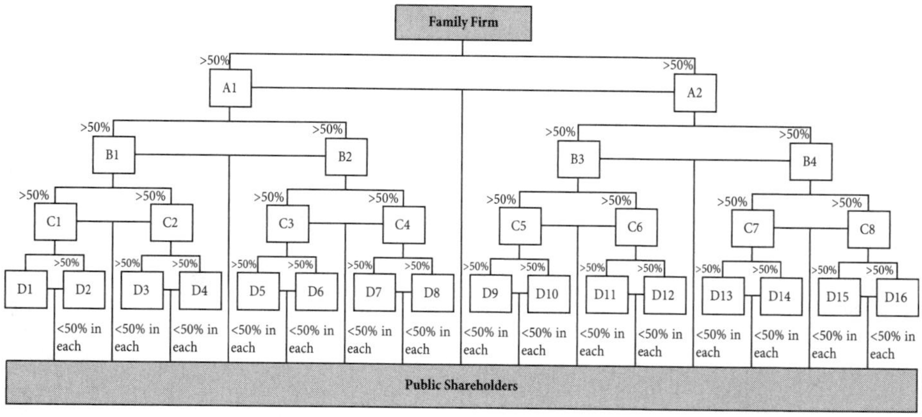

Figure 12.2. An Archetypical Pyramidal Business Group

Note: Each box represents a listed firm. Lines connect controlled firms to the firm that controls them or, at the apex of the structure, to the controlling family. Such structures let business families or tycoons magnify control over one firm into control over business groups containing vastly greater assets that, in some cases, amount to sizable fractions of national economies.

Source: Morck et al. (2005)

These structures can contain dozens and even hundreds of distinct firms, each drawing energetically on public equity capital but controlled through a dominant voting bloc held by the firm above it (Bebchuk et al. 2000). This structure lets the business group mobilize vast amounts of capital, yet preserves for the controlling shareholder of the apex firm an indisputable rule over every firm in the group. One person in command means the group member firms do not hold each other up, ventures in new industries can be established as firms in other sectors need them, and firms forced to operate at inefficient scales can be subsidized via intercorporate income shifting or tunneling (Johnson and et al. 2000).

Consistent with a big push coordination role, pyramidal groups in emerging economies tend to be extraordinarily widely diversified, with one firm in virtually every major sector (Khanna and Yafeh 2007). Business group member firms also tend to be more profitable, on average, than independent firms in emerging markets (Khanna and Palepu 2000a, 2000b; Khanna and Rivkin 2001; Khanna and Yafeh 2005), perhaps reflecting their central role in big push industrialization. Finally, some Indian business groups appear to take a leading role in setting up new firms in new industries (Khanna and Palepu 2005), and similar patterns are evident elsewhere (Almeida and Wolfenzon 2006).

However, the contribution of pyramidal business groups to rapid industrialization is evident only in Meiji Japan (Morck and Nakamura 2007). Further evidence from other countries is needed to assess the generality of this theory validating despotic corporate governance. Meanwhile, other potential benefits of a controlling shareholder in emerging market economies include reputational capital (Khanna and Palepu 2000b) and an ability to sidestep weak institutions and commonplace market failures by controlling firms on both sides of an otherwise risky transaction (Khanna and Yafeh 2005).

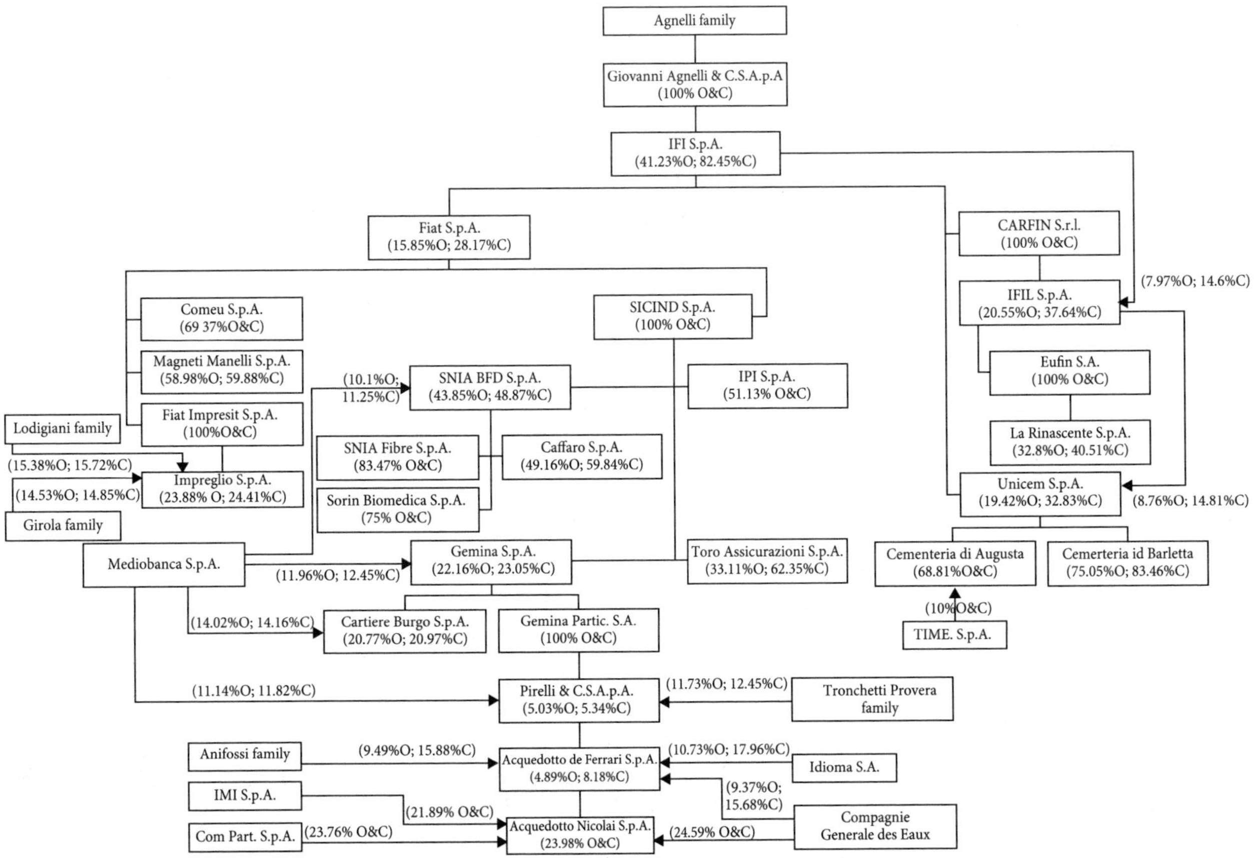

Figure 12.3. The Agnelli Pyramidal Business Group

Note: Each box is a separate firm, with lines indicating controlling equity blocks. Figures designated "O" are the family's actual ownership stake and those designated "C" are the fraction of votes the family controls in the annual general shareholder's meeting. The group is depicted as it was in the mid 1990s.

Source: Againin and Volpin (2005), Morck (2005).

Simple Despots

This benign view of despotic corporate governance may well be valid in some countries, or even in all countries at a certain stage of development where Big Push industrialization is needed. But there is ample empirical evidence that despotic corporate governance is often malign and can seriously retard living standards and institutional development.

First, intelligence need not run reliably in families, and brilliant tycoons, whose sweeping governance power is entirely appropriate, may leave their empires to sons and grandsons of decidedly less ability. Consistent with this, studies using data from developed economies find family control blocs in the hands of heirs correlating with depressed firm performance (Morck et al. 1988; Villalonga and Amit 2006). Event study evidence from successions in family firms confirms that control passing to an heir causes poor performance (Smith and Amoako-Adu 2005; Péréz-González 2006), as does careful instrumental variables estimation (Bennedsen et al. 2007). This appears to be a lesser problem in many developing economies (Khanna and Yafeh 2007)—perhaps because arranged marriages let business families breed for talent (Mehrotra et al. 2010), or perhaps because wealthy heirs can readily substitute connections for talent in more corrupt economies (Krueger 2002; Morck and Yeung 2004; Fogel 2006), or have unique (in their countries) access to good education and management training.

Second, business tycoons and families often control firms without actually owning many of their shares. They usually accomplish this by using dual class shares, pyramiding, or both. Regardless, this greatly expands the scope for agency problems and non–value-maximizing corporate governance.

Dual class shares are the rotten boroughs of corporate finance. A dual class equity structure means a firm has two kinds of shares: superior voting shares, owned by the insiders, their friends, and their relatives, give their owners 10, 100, or more votes per share; inferior voting shares, owned by outside investors, give their owners 1, or often even no votes per share. Examining U.S. dual class firms, Gompers et al. (2010) report that average q ratios fall sharply with the extent to which their insiders voting rights exceed their actual ownership stake. Other evidence, including event studies around the establishment of dual class structure and changes in the relative importance of different share classes, suggests that dual class equity causes depressed shareholder value (DeAngelo and DeAngelo 1985; Jarrell and Poulsen 1988; Smith and Amoako-Adu 1995; Amoako-Adu and Smith 2001; Nenova 2003).

Dual class shares long barred firms from graduating from the NASDAQ or AMEX to the NYSE, so up-and-coming U.S. firms tended to avoid them. However, dual class equity is more common in other countries such as Canada (Smith and Amoako-Adu 1995; Amoako-Adu and Smith 2001) and Sweden (Högfeldt 2005). A general trend toward unification of such equity structures is evidenced by the Israeli policy of 1989 that dual class firms unify their equity prior to issue additional shares (Hauser and Lauterbach 2004).

In many countries, super-voting shares and inferior-voting shares in the same company trade side by side on the same stock exchange. Zingales (1994) explains an 80 percent premium for super-voting shares on the Milan stock exchange as reflecting the extensive private benefits Italy's legal system permits controlling shareholders to extract. Nenova (2003) shows that superior voting rights command higher premiums in more corrupt economies, suggesting that more efficient and public shareholder-friendly legal and regulatory systems curtail private benefits of control.

Pyramiding lets a controlling shareholder leverage a modest fortune into control over firms worth vastly more. For example, a family might own 50 percent plus one share of Firm A, with small shareholders owning the remainder of its stock. Firm A might then own 50 percent plus one share of Firm B, again with small shareholders owning the remainder. The family can thus appoint Firm A's board, control of which lets the family also appoint Firm B's board. But the family has only 50 percent of a 50 percent stake in Firm B, and thus really only owns 25 percent of Firm B. To see this, consider what happens if Firm B's value drops $1 million. This causes Firm A's stock in Firm B to drop in value by $500,000, and this causes the family's wealth to drop by $250,000. This precisely replicates what would happen if the family owned a 25 percent stake in B directly.

Actual pyramids can involve much longer chains of firms controlling firms, and those reinforced with super-voting shares, golden shares, and the like can include links with far less than 50 percent control. For example, in the 1990s a branch of the Canadian Bronfman family directly controlled Broncorp, which controlled HIL with a 19.6 percent stake. HIL owned 97 percent of Edper Resources, which owned 60 percent of Brascan Holdings, which owned 5.1 percent (with effective control rights) of Brascan, which owned 49.9 percent of Braspower Holdings, which owned 49.3 percent of Great Lakes Power, which owned 100 percent of First Toronto Investments, which owned a 25 percent effective control block of Trilon Holdings, which owned 64.5 percent of Trilon Financial, which owned 41.4 percent of Gentra, which owned a controlling 31.9 percent of Imperial Windsor Group (Morck et al. 2000).

This gives rise to two sorts of potentially severe agency problems. First, if the family were to sacrifice $1 million of Imperial Windsor's assets to obtain a private benefit, this would reduce the value of Gentra by 31.9% × $1M = $399K, which would reduce the value of Trilon Financial by 41.4% × $399K = $165K. Multiplying ownership stakes all the way back shows the personal financial cost to the family would be $300, or 0.03 percent of the $1 million total cost of private benefit. If the family had no concern for public shareholders, a private benefit worth $301 would outweigh the $1 million loss for Imperial Windsor.[9] Because the family fully controls this firm by dint of controlling its parent, and its parent's parents all the way up through the control chain, they could do this if they chose.

Second, pyramiding can tempt a controlling shareholder to favor one firm in the pyramid over another. For example, a business deal between Imperial Windsor and HIL that caused the former to lose $1 million, costing the family $300, and the latter to gain $1 million, increasing the family's wealth by 19.6 percent of that amount, or $196,000. Because the family controls the boards of both, it could easily instruct both boards to approve the one-sided deal. Such transactions are variously called transfer pricing, income shifting, related party transactions, or tunneling and can involve the sale of goods, services, insurance, or financial assets at artificial prices that shift wealth from one firm to the other.

Tunneling is entirely legal in many countries and is considered a routine business practice. In many Western European countries, Latin America, and much of Asia the practice is either explicitly legal or essentially unregulated (Johnson et al. 2000). Other countries regulate related party transactions (Djankov et al. 2008). For example, Israel requires approval by one third of disinterested shareholders before group firms can proceed with substantial related party transactions. In Canada, large related party transactions must be disclosed and can require approval by the majority of disinterested shareholders in a vote. Empirical studies reject pervasive tunneling in Canada (Tian 2010) and Western Europe (Faccio and Lang 2002) but not in India (Bertrand et al. 2002), Korea (Bae et al. 2002), or other East Asian economies (Claessens et al. 2002, 2006).

Shares not part of the control blocks holding the structure together are sold to outside investors and are discounted appropriately for the agency problems expected in each firm. This differs across firms in the group, for it depends on the controlling family's likely propensity to use the firm to generate private benefits of control and on whether the firm is more likely to give or receive in tunneling.

Efficient Despotism

Top corporate insiders whom shareholders cannot fire are said to be *entrenched* (Stulz 1988). The tycoons and business families who control pyramidal business groups command control blocks in every firm in the pyramid, and so are entrenched. But so are the CEOs of widely held U.S. firms who rig their corporate charters with staggered boards or reincorporate their firms in states that curtail hostile takeovers.

A degree of entrenchment might not be inefficient. First, Almazan and Suarez (2003) argue that an efficient compensation contract for top managers might provide a degree of entrenchment because job security is a component of compensation along with salary, bonus, and options. Indeed, job security might be a desirable way of compensating CEOs when taking risks with very long-term payoffs maximizes share value. Second, if interpersonal utility comparisons are permitted, an entrenched insider might gain so much utility from controlling a great corporation that it outweighs the disutility her blunders inflict on others. Stulz (1988) models how she selects what fraction of her firm to sell to outside shareholders and what level of monitoring and control mechanisms to install so as to balance her marginal utility of wealth against the marginal utility she gains from control. In such a situation, altering the rules to let shareholders remove her would not be a Pareto improvement and could only be justified on distributional grounds. Finally, an exceptionally able and socially minded insider might deliver more efficient capital allocation, all else equal, if freed from constraints imposed by less insightful public shareholders.

Corporate Governance and Capitalism

The division of labor underlies capitalism's success: just as people specialize in specific trades, firms specialize in core business activities. Capitalism achieves economies of scale, despite specialization, by mobilizing vast pools of public savings to capitalize efficiently large efficiently specialized firms run by people with specialized abilities.

Capitalism thus entrusts top executives with huge amounts of "other people's money" and commands they be trustworthy agents that maximize the value of the pool of capital under their stewardship. That is, without regard for their own utility, they must identify and undertake ventures that earn genuinely positive economic profits exploiting new markets, technologies, business models, or other opportunities. Clearly, such expertise deserves compensation, but its appropriate magnitude and form are ill-understood at present. If the top managers are inefficiently selected or incentivized, and attend too much to their own utility rather than their investors' wealth, we have an agency problem.

Firm performance aggregates to economy performance, so how top corporate executives are selected and incentivized matters for productivity, jobs, and tax-financed public goods and services. One such public service is the evenhanded enforcement of cost-effective regulations to efficiently select and incentivize top executives so firms are credibly trustworthy, and their stock are viable investments. The voters of virtually all major democracies have elected governments that mandate standardized accounting information and criminal penalties for releasing false information. This imposes compliance costs on firms, reducing investors' returns, but helps reassure investors that the firm is run in a trustworthy way. Governments that get this trade-off right mobilize their savers' wealth efficiently and optimize their citizens' potential well-being.

Most major democracies reward unfaithful corporate insiders with fines or jail for a range of excessively self-interested behavior. However, the range varies across countries, as does the definition of good faith. A CEO loading corporate assets into a truck to be sold for personal gain violates the law almost everywhere. Insider trading is illegal in an increasing number of countries, though enforcement varies. In the United States, and a few other countries to a lesser extent, investors sue top corporate insiders for failing to run their firms well. Good faith in the United States and United Kingdom traditionally meant making reasonable decisions aimed at maximizing long-term shareholder value (Romano 1993b), but other countries define it otherwise. In Canada, top corporate officers and directors have a duty only to the legal person of the corporation, not to its shareholders or any other stakeholders (Lee 2005). In Germany, their duty is to balance the interests of shareholders against those of all others with a stake in the firm—creditors, workers, managers, communities, the environment, and so on (Fohlin 2005).

Over the past decades, U.S. corporate governance laws and regulations have grown progressively less interested in shareholder value (Bebchuk 2007). Courts in many U.S. states now require top managers to balance the interests of all stakeholders and let top managers protect themselves from shareholder democracy with poison pills, staggered boards, and other entrenchment devices. Some students of corporate governance see this arising from a yet deeper agency problem (Bebchuk and Cohen 2003; Bar-Gill et al. 2006).

In a democracy, the people entrust politicians and top civil servants with command over the capital assets of the government, rule-making authority, and police powers of enforcement to advance the public interest. In the framework of agency theory, these public sector managers are agents of the people, much as top corporate managers are agents of shareholders. Politicians and top civil servants also have utility functions, and are as prone to maximize them as anyone else (Krueger 1974). If public officials put personal utility ahead of the public interest, the public sector also has an agency problem.

Just as shareholders can sell to a raider, the voters can turn out errant leaders in elections and force civil service rationalizations in referendums. But just as corporate governance can, in reality, drift far from efficient value maximization; government can lose sight of the public interest. Indeed, the two sorts of agency problem may well reinforce each other: CEOs might use shareholders' money to support politicians who grant them greater leeway in using shareholders' money as they will, whereas politicians might use taxpayers' money to support inefficiently governed firms that open competition would otherwise destroy. Market failure begets government failure, which begets more market failure in an accelerating race to the bottom to drain away investor wealth and the public good (Morck et al. 2005).

As with corporate governance, different countries at different times use different institutions to check public officials' all too human self-interest. Again, as with corporate governance, different systems have different strengths and weaknesses, and the optimal system has yet to identify itself (Mueller 2006b). The genuine marvel is perhaps that capitalism and democracy both work as well as they do, given this shared internal contradiction. Their vitality suggests that economists may underestimate the strength and resilience of less appreciated checks on self interest—perhaps religion, self-worth, and ethics long constrained most agents' self-interest as effectively as Smith (1759) claims. Even more remarkably, such forces may well continue to gather force even now, amid the cynical sophistication of the twenty-first century (Mueller 2009).

The development of institutions surrounding corporate governance is nonetheless clearly incomplete, for most countries employ regulations that are both costly and largely ineffective (La Porta et al. 2006). This may well reflect lobbying by corporate insiders in mature firms, who benefit directly from the freedom to use their investors' money as they please, or by financial advisers, lawyers, accountants, and others who benefit indirectly from regulatory complexity and opacity.

In this sense, corporate governance is where political science was a century or two ago. Hereditary power entrusted to family dynasties remains the default form of corporate governance in most countries, and the limited shareholder democracy on offer often works poorly. Intelligent observers can, with straight faces, argue that despots serve some economies better than can democrats. Competition between governments for capital and skilled labor to tax may well induce continually stronger and more efficiently provided shareholder rights (Tiebout 1956; Buchanan 1965). But lobbying by powerful top corporate insiders might equally well induce a "race to the bottom" in corporate governance (Bebchuk and Ferrell 2000) among governments.

Here we see grounds for optimism. Institutions arose in other areas to promote social welfare at the expense of previously seemingly immovable elites. Democracy is more prevalent now than a century ago; courts in the industrial democracies are also arguably less tolerant of corruption in high places, and academia is more open to new ideas. In these is discernible a well-beaten path toward reform that corporate governance might also follow (Morck 2008). Thus, calls for boards to designate a lead independent director evoke political parallels in the "leader of the loyal opposition," whose duty of loyalty to democracy requires a continual criticism of government policies. Calls for more and stronger independent directors likewise seem bent on injecting more argument and dissent into boardrooms, rather like the constructive argument the adversary system evokes in common law courtrooms, which, somewhat inexplicably, appear to deliver better decisions in cases involving business disputes than do the inquisitorial proceedings in legal systems descended from the Napoleonic code (Gennaioli and Shleifer 2007). These efforts to induce dissent in corporate boardrooms are likely to be unpopular with some CEOs, just as discussants and referees were initially controversial in academia. But opposition politicians, counterarguments in court, and referees do seem to deliver better decisions, and so might corporate boardrooms subjected to more shareholder democracy and accountability.

NOTES

1. Subsequent paragraphs draw from Frentrop (2002).
2. The Dutch translates literally as *United East Indian Company*. The VOC had antecedents in Flanders, and probably elsewhere; businesses similar to joint stock companies likely existed in Roman times (Malmendier 2005).
3. Frentrop (2002, chapter 2) superbly documents the early corporate governance disputes of the VOC, and is the source for the following historical case studies.
4. Marginal q ratios are also called profitability indexes in capital budgeting textbooks, and average q ratios can be conceived of as profitability indexes for entire firms, rather than marginal projects. Much confusion arises in the literature because of the confounding of Tobin's marginal and average q ratios (Durnev et al. 2004; Gugler et al. 2004a, 2004b), for Hayashi (1982) shows extremely strong linearity assumptions are needed for q' to equal q, and Durnev et al. (2004) find them empirically uncorrelated

in U.S. data. The validity of both measures depends on the efficiency of financial markets—that is, on investors accurately assessing the value implications of all the firm's investment opportunities and its top managers' decisions. If irrational investors bias asset prices, *V* must be reinterpreted as an unobservable fundamental value that would prevail under full rationality and full information, and this is no simple task (Stein 1996). Also, a marginal *q* of 1 indicates only efficiency of capital allocation on the margin and does not indicate the complete exploitation of all value-maximizing inframarginal investment opportunities.

5. Of course, this early warning system can fail, and a corporate decision can be so awful as to adversely affect creditors, workers, or other stakeholders before shareholders can sound an alarm. The laws of most countries recognize that in such cases, top insiders' duty is expanded to encompass all affected stakeholders. Moreover, if shareholder value is already near zero, shareholders may favor high-risk gambles that might save the firm but are likely to leave creditors or other stakeholders worse off in a looming bankruptcy. In such cases, the legal systems of most countries shift insiders' duties toward creditors—now the likely residual claimant.
6. Alexander Hamilton (1790), as reported in Gales (1850, p. 2101) supported such a graduated voting scale in his proposal for the Bank of the United States, arguing that "A vote for each share renders a combination of a few principal stockholders, to monopolize the power and benefits of the bank, too easy. An equal vote to each stockholder, however great or small his interest in the institution, allows not that degree of weight to large stockholders which it is reasonable they should have, and which, perhaps, their security and that of the bank require."
7. Chapter 15 in this volume, "Mergers and the Market for Corporate Control," by D. Mueller, provides a more in-depth discussion of the issues discussed in this subsection.
8. See Andrew Morse and Sebastian Moffett, "Japan's Companies Gird for Attack—Fearing Takeovers, They Rebuild Walls—The Rise of Poison Pills," *Wall Street Journal*, April 30, 2008.
9. This example is illustrative only of the potential for agency problems. Daniels et al. (1995) find no evidence of governance problems in this business group during this period.

References

Acemoglu, Daron, Simon Johnson, and James Robinson. "The Colonial Origins of Comparative Development: An Empirical Investigation." *American Economic Review* 91 (Dec. 2001): 1369–1401.

Acemoglu, Daron, Simon Johnson, and James Robinson. "Reversal of Fortune: Geography and Institutions in the Making of the Modern World Income Distribution." *Quarterly Journal of Economics* 117 (Nov. 2002): 1231–1294.

Adams, Renee, Heitor Almeida, and Daniel Ferreira. "Powerful CEOs and Their Impact on Corporate Performance." *Review of Financial Studies* 18 (Winter 2005): 1403–1432.

Adams, Renee, and Daniel Ferreira. "A Theory of Friendly Boards." *Journal of Finance* 62 (Feb. 2007): 217–250.

Adams, Renee B., Benjamin E. Hermalin, and Michael S. Weisbach. "The Role of Boards of Directors in Corporate Governance: A Conceptual Framework and Survey." *Journal of Economic Literature* 48 (March 2010): 58–107.

Aganin, Alexander, and Paulo Volpin. "The History of Corporate Ownership in Italy." In *A History of Corporate Governance around the World: Family Business Groups to Professional Managers*, ed. Randall Morck, 325–361. Chicago: University of Chicago Press, 2005.

Almazan, Andres, and Javier Suarez. "Entrenchment and Severance Pay in Optimal Governance Structures." *Journal of Finance* 58 (April 2003): 519–547.

Almeida, Heitor, and Daniel Wolfenzon. "A Theory of Pyramidal Ownership and Family Business Groups." *Journal of Finance* 61 (Dec. 2006): 2637–2680.

Amoako-Adu, Ben, and Brian F. Smith. "Dual Class Firms: Capitalization, Ownership Structure and Recapitalization Back into Single Class." *Journal of Banking and Finance* 25 (June 2001): 1083–1111.

Arrow, Kenneth. *Social Choice and Individual Values*. New York: Wiley, 1964.

Atkinson, Lisa, and Joseph Galaskiewicz. "Stock Ownership and Company Contributions to Charity." *Administrative Science Quarterly* 33 (March 1988): 82–100.

Axelrod, Robert. *The Evolution of Cooperation*. New York: Basic Books, 1984.

Bae, Kee-Hong, Jun-Koo Kang, and Jin-Mo Kim. "Tunneling or Value Added? Evidence from Mergers by Korean Business Groups." *Journal of Finance* 57 (Dec. 2002): 2695–2740.

Baker, Malcolm, Joshua Coval, and Jeremy C. Stein. "Corporate Financing Decisions When Investors Take the Path of Least Resistance." *Journal of Financial Economics* 84 (May 2007): 266–298.

Baker, Malcolm, Richard S. Ruback, and Jeffrey Wurgler. "Behavioral Corporate Finance: A Survey." NBER Working Paper no. 10863, National Bureau of Economic Research, 2004.

Bar-Gill, Oren, Michal Barzuza, and Lucian A. Bebchuk. "The Market for Corporate Law." *Journal of Institutional and Theoretical Economics* 162 (March 2006): 134–160.

Baumol, William J. *Business Behavior, Value and Growth*. New York: Macmillan, 1959.

Baumol, William J. "Entrepreneurship: Productive, Unproductive, and Destructive." *Journal of Political Economy* 98 (Oct. 1990): 893–921.

Bebchuk, Lucian A. "The Myth of the Shareholder Franchise." *Virginia Law Review* 93 (May 2007): 675–732.

Bebchuk, Lucian A., John C. Coates IV, and Guhan Subramanian. "The Powerful Antitakeover Force of Staggered Boards: Further Findings and a Reply to Symposium Participants." *Stanford Law Review* 54 (May 2002): 887–951.

Bebchuk, Lucian A., and Alma Cohen. "Firms' Decisions Where to Incorporate." *Journal of Law and Economics* 46 (Oct. 2003): 383–425.

Bebchuk, Lucian A., and Alma Cohen. "The Costs of Entrenched Boards." *Journal of Financial Economics* 78 (Nov. 2005): 409–433.

Bebchuk, Lucian A., Alma Cohen, and Allen Ferrell. "What Matters in Corporate Governance?" *Review of Financial Studies* 22 (Feb. 2009): 783–827.

Bebchuk, Lucian A., and Allen Ferrell. "Federalism and Takeover Law: The Race to Protect Managers from Takeovers." NBER Working Paper no. 7232, National Bureau of Economic Research, 2000.

Bebchuk, Lucian, and Jesse Fried. *Pay without Performance: The Unfulfilled Promise of Executive Compensation*. Cambridge, Mass.: Harvard University Press, 2004.

Bebchuk, Lucian A., and Oliver Hart. "Takeover Bids vs. Proxy Fights in Contests for Corporate Control." NBER Working Paper no. 8633, National Bureau of Economic Research, 2001.

Bebchuk, Lucian A., Reinier Kraakman, and George Triantis. "Stock Pyramids, Cross-Ownership, and Dual Class Equity: The Mechanisms and Agency Costs of Separating

Control from Cash-Flow Rights." In *Concentrated Corporate Ownership*, NBER Conference Report Series, ed. Randall Morck, 295–315. Chicago: University of Chicago Press, 2000.
Bebchuk, Lucian A., and Michael S. Weisbach. "The State of Corporate Governance Research." *Review of Financial Studies* 23 (March 2010): 939–961.
Becker, Gary S. *The Economics of Discrimination*. Chicago: University of Chicago Press, 1957.
Bennedsen, Morten, Kaspar M. Nielsen, Francisco Pérez-González, and Daniel Wolfenzon. "Inside the Family Firm: The Role of Families in Succession Decisions and Performance." *Quarterly Journal of Economics* 122 (May 2007): 647–691.
Berger, Philip G., and Eli Ofek. "Bustup Takeovers of Value-Destroying Diversified Firms." *Journal of Finance* 51 (Sept. 1996): 1175–1200.
Berle, Adolf A., and Gardiner C. Means. *The Modern Corporation and Private Property*. New York: Commerce Clearing House, 1932.
Bertrand, Marianne, Francis Kramarz, Antoinette Schoar, and David Thesmar. "Politicians, Firms and the Political Business Cycle: Evidence from France." MIT Working Paper, Nov. 2006.
Bertrand, Marianne, Paras Mehta, and Sendhil Mullainathan. "Ferreting Out Tunneling: An Application to Indian Business Groups." *Quarterly Journal of Economics* 117 (Feb. 2002): 121–148.
Bhagat, Sanjai, and Richard Jefferis. "Voting Power in the Proxy Process: The Case of Antitakeover Charter Amendments." *Journal of Financial Economics* 30 (Nov. 1991): 193–225.
Black, Bernard S., and John C. Coffee Jr. "Hail Britannia?: Institutional Investor Behavior under Limited Regulation." *Michigan Law Review* 92 (June 1994): 1997–2087.
Blau, Julian. "The Existence of Social Welfare Functions." *Econometrica* 25 (April 1957): 302–313.
Bodie, Zvi, and E. Philip Davis. *The Foundations of Pension Finance*. Cheltenham: Edward Elgar, 2000.
Brandeis, Louis. *Other People's Money and How the Bankers Use It*. New York: Stokes, 1914.
Brickley, James A. "Interpreting Common Stock Returns around Proxy Statement Disclosures and Annual Shareholder Meetings." *Journal of Financial and Quantitative Analysis* 21 (Sept. 1986): 343–349.
Brickley, James A., Jeffrey L. Coles, and Rory L. Terry. "Outside Directors and the Adoption of Poison Pills." *Journal of Financial Economics* 35 (June 1994): 371–390.
Brunarski, Kelly R., Kenneth A. Borokhovich, and Robert Parrino. "CEO Contracting and Antitakeover Amendments." *Journal of Finance* 52 (Sept. 1997): 1495–1517.
Buchanan, James M. "An Economic Theory of Clubs." *Economica* 32 (Feb. 1965): 1–14.
Buchanan, James M., and Gordon Tullock. *The Calculus of Consent. Logical Foundations of Constitutional Democracy*. Ann Arbor: University of Michigan Press, 1962.
Cable, John R., and Dennis C. Mueller. "Testing for Persistence of Profits' Differences across Firms." *International Journal of the Economics of Business* 15 (July 2008): 201–228.
Chan, Louis K. C., Josef Lakonishok, and Theodore Sougiannis. "The Stock Market Valuation of Research and Development Expenditures." *Journal of Finance* 56 (Dec. 2001): 2431–2456.
Chan, Su Han, John D. Martin, and John W. Kensinger. "Corporate Research and Development Expenditures and Share Value." *Journal of Financial Economics* 26 (Aug. 1990): 255–276.

Cheffins, Brian. *Corporate Ownership and Control: British Business Transformed*. Oxford: Oxford University Press, 2009.
Cheng, Shijun, Venky Nagar, and Madhav V. Rajan. "Identifying Control Motives in Managerial Ownership: Evidence from Antitakeover Legislation." *Review of Financial Studies* 18 (Summer 2005): 637–672.
Claessens, Stijn, Simeon Djankov, Joseph P. H. Fan, and Larry H. P. Lang "Disentangling the Incentive and Entrenchment Effects of Large Shareholdings." *Journal of Finance* 57 (Dec. 2002): 2741–2771.
Claessens, Stijn, Joseph P. H. Fan, and Larry H. P. Lang. "The Benefits and Costs of Group Affiliation: Evidence from East Asia." *Emerging Markets Review* 7 (March 2006): 1–26.
Comment, Robert, and G. William Schwert. "Poison or Placebo? Evidence on the Deterrence and Wealth Effects of Modern Antitakeover Measures." *Journal of Financial Economics* 39 (Sept. 1995): 3–43.
Daniels, Ronald J., Randall Morck, and David Stangeland. "High Gear: A Case Study of the Hees-Edper Corporate Group." In *Corporate Decision-Making in Canada*, ed. Ronald J. Daniels and Randall Morck, 223–240. Calgary: University of Calgary Press, 1995.
Datta, Sudip, and Mai Iskandar-Datta. "Takeover Defenses and Wealth Effects on Securityholders: The Case of Poison Pill Adoptions." *Journal of Banking and Finance* 20 (Aug. 1996): 1231–1250.
Davis, Gerald F., and E. Han Kim. "Business Ties and Proxy Voting by Mutual Funds." *Journal of Financial Economics* 85 (Aug. 2007): 552–570.
DeAngelo, Harry, and Linda DeAngelo. "Managerial Ownership of Voting Rights: A Study of Public Corporations with Dual Classes of Common Stock." *Journal of Financial Economics* 14 (March 1985): 33–69.
DeAngelo, Harry, and Linda DeAngelo. "Proxy Contests and the Governance of Publicly Held Corporations." *Journal of Financial Economics* 23 (June 1989): 29–59.
DeAngelo, Harry, and Edward M. Rice. "Antitakeover Charter Amendments and Stockholder Wealth." *Journal of Financial Economics* 11 (April 1983): 329–359.
De Jong, Abe, Rezaul Kabir, Teye Marra, and Ailsa Röell. "Ownership and Control in The Netherlands." In *The Control of Corporate Europe*, ed. Fabrizio Barca and Marco Becht, 188–206. Oxford: Oxford University Press, 2001.
De Jong, Abe, and Ailsa Röell. "Financing and Control in the Netherlands: A Historical Perspective." In *A History of Corporate Governance around the World: Family Business Groups to Professional Managers*, ed. Randall Morck, 467–506. Chicago: University of Chicago Press, 2005.
Del Guercio, Diane, and Jennifer Hawkins. "The Motivation and Impact of Pension Fund Activism." *Journal of Financial Economics* 52 (June 1999): 293–340.
Demsetz, Harold, and Belén Villalonga. "Ownership Structure and Corporate Performance." *Journal of Corporate Finance* 7 (Sept. 2001): 209–233.
Djankov, Simeon, Rafael La Porta, Florencio Lopez-de-Silanes, and Andrei Shleifer. "The Law and Economics of Self-dealing." *Journal of Financial Economics* 88 (June 2008): 430–465.
Dodd, Peter, and Jerold B. Warner. "On Corporate Governance: A Study of Proxy Contests." *Journal of Financial Economics* 11 (April 1983): 401–438.
Doidge, Craig, G. Andrew Karolyi, and René M. Stulz. "Why Do Countries Matter So Much for Corporate Governance?" *Journal of Financial Economics* 86 (Oct. 2007): 1–39.
Dunlavy, Colleen. "From Citizens to Plutocrats: Nineteenth-Century Shareholder Voting Rights and Theories of the Corporation." In *Constructing Corporate America - History,*

Politics, Culture, ed. Kenneth Lipartito and David B. Sicilia, 66–93. Oxford: Oxford University Press, 2007.

Durnev, Art, and E. Han Kim. "To Steal or Not to Steal: Firm Attributes, Legal Environment, and Valuation." *Journal of Finance* 60 (2005): 1461–1493.

Durnev, Art, Kan Li, Randall Morck, and Bernard Yeung. "Capital Markets and Capital Allocation: Implications for Economies in Transition." *Economics of Transition* 12 (Dec. 2004a): 593–634.

Durnev, Art, Randall Morck, and Bernard Yeung. "Value-Enhancing Capital Budgeting and Firm-Specific Stock Return Variation." *Journal of Finance* 59 (Feb. 2004b): 65–105.

Easterbrook, Frank H., and Daniel R. Fischel. "Corporate Control Transactions." *Yale Law Journal* 91 (March 1982): 698–737.

Etebari, Ahmad, James O. Horrigan, and Jan L. Landwehr. "To Be or Not to Be—Reaction of Stock Returns to Sudden Deaths of Corporate Chief Executive Officers." *Journal of Business Finance & Accounting* 14 (June 1987): 255–278.

Faccio, Mara, and Larry H. P. Lang. "The Ultimate Ownership of Western European Corporations." *Journal of Financial Economics* 65 (Sept. 2002): 365–395.

Faccio, Mara, and M. Ameziane Lasfer. "Do Occupational Pension Funds Monitor Companies in Which They Hold Large Stakes?" *Journal of Corporate Finance* 6 (March 2000): 71–110.

Faccio, Mara, and David C. Parsley. "Sudden Deaths: Taking Stock of Geographic Ties." *Journal of Financial and Quantitative Analysis* 44 (June 2009): 683–718.

Faleye, Olubunmi. "Classified Boards, Firm Value, and Managerial Entrenchment." *Journal of Financial Economics* 83 (Feb. 2007): 501–529.

Faleye, Olubunmi, Vikas Mehrotra, and Randall Morck. "When Labor Has a Voice in Corporate Governance." *Journal of Financial and Quantitative Analysis* 41 (Sept. 2006): 489–510.

Fama, Eugene F. "Agency Problems and the Theory of the Firm." *Journal of Political Economy* 88 (April 1980): 288–307.

Fama, Eugene F., and Michael C. Jensen. "Separation of Ownership and Control." *Journal of Law and Economics* 26 (June 1983): 301–325.

Fisman, Raymond. "Estimating the Value of Political Connections." *American Economic Review* 91 (September 2001): 1095–1102.

Fogel, Kathy. "Oligarchic Family Control, Social Economic Outcomes, and the Quality of Government." *Journal of International Business Studies* 37 (Sept. 2006): 603–622.

Fohlin, Caroline. "The History of Corporate Ownership and Control in Germany." In *A History of Corporate Governance around the World: Family Business Groups to Professional Managers*, ed. Randall Morck, 223–277. Chicago: University of Chicago Press, 2005.

Frentrop, Paul Marie Louis. "Corporate Governance 1602–2002." Ph.D. diss., Universiteit van Tilburg, 2002.

Gennaioli, Nicola, and Andrei Shleifer. "The Evolution of Common Law." *Journal of Political Economy* 115 (Feb. 2007): 43–68.

Gompers, Paul, Joy Ishii, and Andrew Metrick. "Corporate Governance and Equity Prices." *Quarterly Journal of Economics* 118 (Feb. 2003): 107–155.

Gompers, Paul, Joy Ishii, and Andrew Metrick. "Extreme Governance: An Analysis of Dual-Class Firms in the United States." *Review of Financial Studies* 23 (March 2010): 1051–1088.

Gompers, Paul A., and Joshua Lerner. *The Venture Capital Cycle*. Cambridge, Mass.: MIT Press, 1999.

Grabowski, Henry G., and Dennis C. Mueller. "Managerial and Stockholder Welfare Models of Firm Expenditure." *Review of Economics and Statistics* 54 (Feb. 1972): 9–24.

Grabowski, Henry G., and Dennis C. Mueller. "Life-Cycle Effects on Corporate Returns on Retentions." *Review of Economics and Statistics* 57 (Nov. 1975): 400–409.

Grabowski, Henry G. and Dennis C. Mueller. "Industrial Research and Development, Intangible, Capital Stocks, and Firm Profit Rates." *Bell Journal of Economics* 9 (Autumn 1978): 328–343.

Grossman, Sanford J., and Oliver D. Hart. "Takeover Bids, the Free-Rider Problem, and the Theory of the Corporation." *Bell Journal of Economics* 11 (Spring 1980): 42–64.

Grossman, Sanford J., and Oliver D. Hart. "One Share–One Vote and the Market for Corporate Control." *Journal of Financial Economics* 20 (Jan.–March 1988): 175–202.

Gugler, Klaus, Dennis C. Mueller, and B. Burcin Yurtoglu. "The Impact of Corporate Governance on Investment Returns in Developed and Developing Countries." *Economic Journal* 113 (Nov. 2003): F511–F539.

Gugler, Klaus, Dennis C. Mueller, and B. Burcin Yurtoglu. "Corporate Governance and the Returns on Investment." *Journal of Law and Economics* 47 (Oct. 2004a): 589–633.

Gugler, Klaus, Dennis C. Mueller, and B. Burcin Yurtoglu. "Marginal q, Tobin's q, Cash Flow, and Investment." *Southern Economic Journal* 70 (Jan. 2004b): 512–531.

Gugler, Klaus, Dennis C. Mueller, and B. Burcin Yurtoglu. "Corporate Governance and the Determinants of Investment." *Journal of Institutional and Theoretical Economics* 163 (Dec. 2007): 598–626.

Haber, Stephen H. *Political Institutions and Economic Growth in Latin America: Essays in Policy, History, and Political Economy*. Stanford, Calif.: Hoover Institution Press, 2000.

Haber, Stephen H., Douglass C. North, and Barry R. Weingast. *Political Institutions and Financial Development*. Stanford, Calif.: Stanford University Press, 2008.

Hallock, Kevin F. "Reciprocally Interlocking Boards of Directors and Executive Compensation." *Journal of Financial and Quantitative Analysis* 32 (Sept. 1997): 331–344.

Hamilton, Alexander. "Report on a National Bank." *Comminications to the House of Representatives* (Dec. 14, 1790); as reported in Joseph Gales, *Debates and Proceedings in the Congress of the United States*, vol. 2, U.S. Congress, 1850.

Hartzell, Jay C., Eli Ofek, and David Yermack. "What's in It for Me? CEOs whose Firms Are Acquired." *Review of Financial Studies* 17 (Jan. 2004): 37–61.

Haunschild, Pamela R., and Christine M. Beckman. "When Do Interlocks Matter? Alternate Sources of Information and Interlock Influence." *Administrative Science Quarterly* 43 (Dec. 1998): 815–844.

Hauser, Shmuel, and Beni Lauterbach. "The Value of Voting Rights to Majority Shareholders: Evidence from Dual-Class Stock Unifications." *Review of Financial Studies* 17 (Oct. 2004): 1167–1184.

Hayashi, Fumio. "Tobin's Marginal q and Average q: A Neoclassical Interpretation." *Econometrica* 50 (Jan. 1982): 213–224.

Hayek, Friedrich A. *The Pure Theory of Capital*. Chicago, 1941.

Högfeldt, Peter. "The History and Politics of Corporate Ownership in Sweden." In *A History of Corporate Governance around the World: Family Business Groups to Professional Managers*, ed. Randall K. Morck, 62–85. Chicago: University of Chicago Press, 2005.

Holderness, Clifford G., Randall S. Kroszner, and Dennis P. Sheehan. "Were the Good Old Days that Good? Changes in Managerial Stock Ownership since the Great Depression." *Journal of Finance* 54 (April 1999): 435–469.

Jahera, John S. Jr., and William Pugh. "State Takeover Legislation: The Case of Delaware." *Journal of Law Economics & Organization* 7 (Fall 1991): 410–428.

Jarrell, Gregg A., James A. Brickley, and Jeffry M. Netter. "The Market for Corporate Control: The Empirical Evidence since 1980." *Journal of Economic Perspectives* 2 (Winter 1988): 49–68.
Jarrell, Gregg A., and Annette B. Poulsen. "Shark Repellents and Stock Prices: The Effects of Antitakeover Amendments since 1980." *Journal of Financial Economics* 19 (Sept. 1987): 127–168.
Jarrell, Gregg A., and Annette B. Poulsen. "Dual-Class Recapitalizations as Antitakeover Mechanisms: The Recent Evidence." *Journal of Financial Economics* 20 (Jan.–March 1988): 129–152.
Jensen, Michael C. "Agency Costs of Free Cash Flow, Corporate Finance, and Takeovers." *American Economic Review* 76 (May 1986): 323–329.
Jensen, Michael C., and William H. Meckling. "Theory of the Firm: Managerial Behavior, Agency Costs and Ownership Structure." *Journal of Financial Economics* 3 (Oct. 1976): 305–360.
Jensen, Michael C., and William H. Meckling. "Rights and Production Functions: An Application to Labor-Managed Firms and Codetermination." *Journal of Business* 52 (Oct. 1979): 469–506.
Jensen, Michael C., and Kevin J. Murphy. "Performance Pay and Top-Management Incentives." *Journal of Political Economy* 98 (April 1990): 225–264.
Jensen, Michael C., and Richard S. Ruback. "The Market for Corporate Control: The Scientific Evidence." *Journal of Financial Economics* 11 (April 1983): 5–50.
John, Kose, Lubomir Litov, and Bernard Yeung. "Corporate Governance and Risk-Taking." *Journal of Finance* 63 (Aug. 2008): 1679–1728.
Johnson, Arthur. H. *The Age of the Enlightened Despot, 1660–1789*. New York: Macmillan, 1910.
Johnson, Simon, Rafael La Porta, Florencio Lopez-de-Silanes, and Andrei Shleifer. "Tunneling." *American Economic Review* 90 (May 2000): 22–27.
Johnson, W. Bruce, Robert P. Magee, Nandu J. Nagarajan, and Harry A. Newman. "An Analysis of the Stock Price Reaction to Sudden Executive Deaths: Implications for the Managerial Labor Market." *Journal of Accounting & Economics* 7 (April 1985): 151–174.
Jung, Jeeman, and Robert J. Shiller. "Samuelson's Dictum and the Stock Market." *Economic Inquiry* 43 (April 2005): 221–228.
Kaplan, Steven N., and David Reishus. "Outside Directorships and Corporate Performance." *Journal of Financial Economics* 27 (October 1990): 389–410.
Karpoff, Jonathan M., and Paul H. Malatesta. "The Wealth Effects of Second-Generation State Takeover Legislation." *Journal of Financial Economics* 25 (Dec. 1989): 291–322.
Keynes, John Maynard. *The General Theory of Employment, Interest and Money*. New York: Harcourt, 1936.
Khanna, Tarun, and Krishna Palepu. "Emerging Market Business Groups, Foreign Intermediaries, and Corporate Governance." In *Concentrated Corporate Ownership*, ed. Randall K. Morck, 265–292. Chicago: University of Chicago Press, 2000a.
Khanna, Tarun, and Krishna Palepu. "Is Group Affiliation Profitable in Emerging Markets? An Analysis of Diversified Indian Business Groups." *Journal of Finance* 55 (April 2000b): 867–891.
Khanna, Tarun, and Krishna Palepu. "The Evolution of Concentrated Ownership in India: Broad Patterns and a History of the Indian Software Industry." In *A History of Corporate Governance around the World: Family Business Groups to Professional Managers*, ed. Randall K. Morck, 283–320. Chicago: University of Chicago Press, 2005.

Khanna, Tarun, and Jan W. Rivkin. "Estimating the Performance Effects of Business Groups in Emerging Markets." *Strategic Management Journal* 22 (Jan. 2001): 45–74.

Khanna, Tarun, and Yishay Yafeh. "Business Groups and Risk Sharing around the World." *Journal of Business* 78 (Jan. 2005): 301–340.

Khanna, Tarun, and Yishay Yafeh. "Business Groups in Emerging Markets: Paragons or Parasites?" *Journal of Economic Literature* 45 (June 2007): 331–372.

Knight, Frank H. 1965. *Risk, Uncertainty, and Profit*. Boston: Houghton Mifflin, 1921.

Kramarz, Francis, and David Thesmar. *Social Networks in the Boardroom*. CEPR Discussion Paper no. 5496, SSRN eLibrary, Feb. 2006.

Krueger, Anne O. "The Political Economy of the Rent-Seeking Society." *American Economic Review* 64 (June 1974): 291–303.

Krueger, Anne O. "Why Crony Capitalism Is Bad for Economic Growth." In *Crony Capitalism and Economic Growth in Latin America: Theory and Evidence*, ed. Stephen H. Haber, 1–23. Stanford, Calif.: Hoover Institution Press, 2002.

Kydland, Finn E., and Edward C. Prescott. "Rules Rather Than Discretion—The Inconsistency of Optimal Plans." *Journal of Political Economy* 85 (1977): 473–492.

Lakonishok, Josef, Andrei Shleifer, Richard Thaler, and Robert Vishny. "Window Dressing by Pension Fund Managers." *American Economic Review* 81 (May 1991): 227–231.

Landier, Augustin, David Sraer, and David Thesmar. "Optimal Dissent in Organizations." *Review of Economic Studies* 76 (2009): 761–794.

Lang, Larry H. P., and Robert H. Litzenberger. "Dividend Announcements: Cash Flow Signalling vs. Free Cash Flow Hypothesis?" *Journal of Financial Economics* 24 (Sept. 1989): 181–191.

Lang, Larry H. P., René M. Stulz, and Ralf A. Walkling. "A Test of the Free Cash Flow Hypothesis: The Case of Bidder Returns." *Journal of Financial Economics* 29 (Oct. 1991): 315–335.

La Porta, Rafael, Florencio Lopez-de-Silanes, and Andrei Shleifer. "Corporate Ownership around the World." *Journal of Finance* 54 (April 1999): 471–517.

La Porta, Rafael, Florencio Lopez-de-Silanes, and Andrei Shleifer. "What Works in Securities Laws?" *Journal of Finance* 61 (Feb. 2006): 1–32.

La Porta, Rafael, Florencio Lopez-de-Silanes, Andrei Shleifer, and Robert W. Vishny. "Trust in Large Organizations." *American Economic Review* 87 (May 1997a): 333–338.

La Porta, Rafael, Florencio Lopez-de-Silanes, Andrei Shleifer, and Robert W. Vishny. "Legal Determinants of External Finance." *Journal of Finance* 52 (July 1997b): 1131–1150.

La Porta, Rafael, Florencio Lopez-de-Silanes, Andrei Shleifer, and Robert W. Vishny. "Investor Protection and Corporate Valuation." *Journal of Finance* 57 (June 2002): 1147–1170.

Lee, Ian B. "*Peoples Department Stores v. Wise* and the 'Best Interests of the Corporation.'" *Canadian Business Law Journal* 41 (2005): 212–222.

Linn, Scott C., and John J. McConnell. "An Empirical Investigation of the Impact of 'Antitakeover' Amendments on Common Stock Prices." *Journal of Financial Economics* 11 (April 1983): 361–399.

Maier, Pauline. "The Revolutionary Origins of the American Corporation." *William and Mary Quarterly*, 3rd series, 50 (Jan. 1993): 51–84.

Malmendier, Ulrike. "Roman Shares." In *The Origins of Value. The Financial Innovations that Created Modern Capital Markets*, ed. William N. Goetzmann and K. Geert Rouwenhorst, 31–42. Oxford: Oxford University Press, 2005.

McConnell, John J., and Henri Servaes. "Additional Evidence on Equity Ownership and Corporate Value." *Journal of Financial Economics* 27 (Oct. 1990): 595–612.

McWilliams, Victoria B. "Managerial Share Ownership and the Stock Price Effects of Antitakeover Amendment Proposals." *Journal of Finance* 45 (Dec. 1990): 1627–1640.

McWilliams, Victoria B., and Nilanjan Sen. "Board Monitoring and Antitakeover Amendments." *Journal of Financial and Quantitative Analysis* 32 (Dec. 1997): 491–505.

Mehrotra, Vikas, Randall Morck, Jungwook Shim, and Yupana Wiwattanakantang. "Adoptive Expectations: Rising Sons in Japanese Family Firms." Paper presented at the National Bureau of Economic Research Corporate Finance Summer Institute, Cambridge, Mass., 2010.

Mikkelson, Wayne H., and M. Megan Partch. "The Decline of Takeovers and Disciplinary Managerial Turnover." *Journal of Financial Economics* 44 (May 1997): 205–228.

Milgram, Stanley. *Obedience to Authority: An Experimental View*. New York: Harper & Row, 1974.

Mitchell, Mark L., and Kenneth Lehn. "Do Bad Bidders Become Good Targets?" *Journal of Political Economy* 98 (April 1990): 372–398.

Mitchell, Mark L., and Jeffry M. Netter. "Triggering the 1987 Stock Market Crash: Antitakeover Provisions in the Proposed House Ways and Means Tax Bill?" *Journal of Financial Economics* 24 (Sept. 1989): 37–68.

Moeller, Sara B., Frederik P. Schlingemann, and René M. Stulz. "Wealth Destruction on a Massive Scale? A Study of Acquiring-Firm Returns in the Recent Merger Wave." *Journal of Finance* 60 (April 2005): 757–782.

Morck, Randall. "Behavioral Finance in Corporate Governance: Economics and Ethics of the Devil's Advocate." *Journal of Management and Governance* 12 (May 2008): 179–200.

Morck, Randall, and Masao Nakamura. "A Frog in a Well Knows Nothing of the Ocean: A History of Corporate Ownership in Japan." In *A History of Corporate Governance around the World: Family Business Groups to Professional Managers*, ed. Randall Morck, 367–459. Chicago: University of Chicago Press, 2005.

Morck, Randall, and Masao Nakamura. "Business Groups and the Big Push: Meiji Japan's Mass Privatization and Subsequent Growth." *Enterprise and Society* 8 (Sept. 2007): 543–601.

Morck, Randall, Andrei Shleifer, and Robert W. Vishny. "Management Ownership and Market Valuation: An Empirical Analysis." *Journal of Financial Economics* 20 (Jan.–March 1988): 293–315.

Morck, Randall, Andrei Shleifer, and Robert W. Vishny. "Alternative Mechanisms for Corporate Control." *American Economic Review* 79 (Sept. 1989): 842–852.

Morck, Randall, Andrei Shleifer, and Robert W. Vishny. "Do Managerial Objectives Drive Bad Acquisitions?" *Journal of Finance* 45 (March 1990): 31–48.

Morck, Randall, David Stangeland, and Bernard Yeung. "Inherited Wealth, Corporate Control, and Economic Growth: The Canadian Disease?" In *Concentrated Corporate Ownership*, ed. Randall K. Morck, 319–369. Chicago: University of Chicago Press, 2000.

Morck, Randall, Daniel Wolfenzon, and Bernard Yeung. "Corporate Governance, Economic Entrenchment, and Growth." *Journal of Economic Literature* 43 (Sept. 2005): 655–720.

Morck, Randall, and Bernard Yeung. "Internalization: An Event Study Test." *Journal of International Economics* 33 (Aug. 1992): 41–56.

Morck, Randall, and Bernard Yeung. "Family Control and the Rent-Seeking Society." *Entrepreneurship: Theory and Practice* 28 (June 2004): 491–509.

Mueller, Dennis C. "The Corporation and the Economist." *International Journal of Industrial Organization* 10 (June 1992): 147–170.

Mueller, Dennis C. *Constitutional Democracy*. Oxford: Oxford University Press, 1996.

Mueller, Dennis C. "The Economics and Politics of Corporate Governance in the European Union." ECGI Law Working Paper no. 37/2005. http://papers.ssrn.com/sol3/papers.cfm?abstract_id=730366##.

Mueller, Dennis C. "The Anglo-Saxon Approach to Corporate Governance and its Applicability to Emerging Markets." *Corporate Governance—An International Review* 14 (July 2006a): 207–219.

Mueller, Dennis C. "Corporate Governance and Economic Performance." *International Review of Applied Economics* 20 (Dec. 2006b): 623–643.

Mueller, Dennis C. *Reason, Religion, and Democracy*. New York: Cambridge University Press, 2009.

Mueller, Dennis C., and Mark Sirower. "The Causes of Mergers: Tests Based on the Gains to Acquiring Firms' Shareholders and the Size of Premia." *Managerial and Decision Economics* 24 (Aug. 2003): 373–391.

Mueller, Dennis C., and B. Burcin Yurtoglu. "Corporate Governance and the Returns to Acquiring firms' Shareholders: An International Comparison." *Managerial and Decision Economics* 28 (Dec. 2007): 879–896.

Mulherin, J. Harold, and Annette B. Poulsen. "Proxy Contests and Corporate Change: Implications for Shareholder Wealth." *Journal of Financial Economics* 47 (March 1998): 279–313.

Murphy, Kevin M., Andrei Shleifer, and Robert W. Vishny. "Industrialization and the Big Push." *Journal of Political Economy* 97 (Oct. 1989): 1003–1026.

Murphy, Kevin M., Andrei Shleifer, and Robert W. Vishny. "The Allocation of Talent: Implications for Growth." *Quarterly Journal of Economics* 106 (May 1991): 503–530.

Nanda, Vikram, and William Christie. "Free Cash Flow, Shareholder Value, and the Undistributed Profits Tax of 1936 and 1937." *Journal of Finance* 49 (Dec. 1994): 1727–1754.

Nenova, Tatiana. "The Value of Corporate Voting Rights and Control: A Cross-Country Analysis." *Journal of Financial Economics* 68 (June 2003): 325–351.

North, Douglass, John Wallis, and Barry Weingast. *Violence and Social Orders: A Conceptual Framework for Interpreting Recorded Human History*. Cambridge: Cambridge University Press, 2009.

Opler, Tim, and Sheridan Titman. "The Determinants of Leveraged Buyout Activity: Free Cash Flow vs. Financial Distress Costs." *Journal of Finance* 48 (Dec. 1993): 1985–1999.

Pérez-González, Francisco. "Inherited Control and Firm Performance." *American Economic Review* 96 (Dec. 2006): 1559–1588.

Pistor, Katharina. "The Governance of China's Finance." In *Capitalizing China*, ed. Randall Morck. Chicago: University of Chicago Press, 2011.

Pound, John. "Proxy Contests and the Efficiency of Shareholder Oversight." *Journal of Financial Economics* 20 (Jan.–March 1988): 237–265.

Rajan, Raghuram G., and Luigi Zingales. "Financial Dependence and Growth." *American Economic Review* 88 (June 1998): 559–586.

Rajan, Raghuram G., and Luigi Zingales. "The Great Reversals: The Politics of Financial Development in the Twentieth Century." *Journal of Financial Economics* 69 (July 2003): 5–50.

Rajan, Raghuram, and Luigi Zingales. *Saving Capitalism from the Capitalists: Unleashing the Power of Financial Markets to Create Wealth and Spread Opportunity*. Princeton, N.J.: Princeton University Press, 2004.

Rhodes-Kropf, Matthew, David T. Robinson, and S. Viswanathan. "Valuation Waves and Merger Activity: The Empirical Evidence." *Journal of Financial Economics* 77 (Sept. 2005): 561–603.
Rhodes-Kropf, Matthew, and S. Viswanathan. "Market Valuation and Merger Waves." *Journal of Finance* 59 (Dec. 2004): 2685–2718.
Romano, Roberta. "Public Pension Fund Activism in Corporate Governance Reconsidered." *Columbia Law Review* 93 (May 1993a): 795–853.
Romano, Roberta. *Foundations of Corporate Law*. New York: Foundations Press, 1993b.
Romano, Roberta. "Getting Politics out of Public Pension Funds and out of Corporate Board Rooms." *American Enterprise* 4 (Nov./Dec. 1993c): 42–49.
Romano, Roberta. "The Politics of Public Pension Funds." *Public Interest* 119 (Spring 1995): 42–53.
Romano, Roberta. "Does Confidential Proxy Voting Matter?" *Journal of Legal Studies* 32 (June 2003): 465–509.
Romano, Roberta. "The Sarbanes-Oxley Act and the Making of Quack Corporate Governance." *Yale Law Journal* 114 (May 2005): 1521–1611.
Rosenberg, Nathan, and L. E. Birdzell Jr. *How the West Grew Rich: The Economic Transformation of the Industrial World*. New York: Basic Books, 1986.
Rosenstein-Rodan, Paul. "Problems of Industrialisation of Eastern and South-Eastern Europe." *Economic Journal* 53 (June 1943): 202–211.
Ross, Stephen. "The Economic Theory of Agency: The Principal's Problem." *American Economic Review* 63 (May 1973): 134–139.
Ryngaert, Michael. "The Effect of Poison Pill Securities on Shareholder Wealth." *Journal of Financial Economics* 20 (Jan.–March 1988): 377–417.
Ryngaert, Michael, and Jeffry Netter. "Shareholder Wealth Effects of the 1986 Ohio Antitakeover Law Revisited—Its Real Effects." *Journal of Law, Economics & Organization* 6 (Spring 1990): 253–262.
Samuelson, Paul A. "Summing upon Business Cycles: Opening Address." In *Beyond Shocks: What Causes Business Cycles*, ed. Jeffrey C. Fuhrer and Scott Schuh. Boston: Federal Reserve Bank of Boston, 1998.
Scharfstein, David S., and Jeremy C. Stein. "Herd Behavior and Investment." *American Economic Review* 80 (June 1990): 465–479.
Schumpeter, Joseph A. *Theorie der Wirtschaftlichen Entwicklung*. Leipzig: Duncker & Humblot, 1912.
Schumpeter, Joseph A. *Capitalism, Socialism, Democracy*. New York: Harper and Row, 1942.
Sheard, Paul. "The Economics of Interlocking Shareholding in Japan." *Ricerche Economiche* 45 (1991): 421–448.
Shleifer, Andrei. *Inefficient Markets: An Introduction to Behavioral Finance*. Oxford: Oxford University Press, 2000.
Shleifer, Andrei, and Robert W. Vishny. "Large Shareholders and Corporate Control." *Journal of Political Economy* 94 (June 1986): 461–488.
Shleifer, Andrei, and Robert W. Vishny. "A Survey of Corporate Governance." *Journal of Finance* 52 (June 1997): 737–783.
Shleifer, Andrei, and Robert W. Vishny. "Stock Market Driven Acquisitions." *Journal of Financial Economics* 70 (Dec. 2003): 295–311.
Shleifer, Andrei, and Daniel Wolfenzon. "Investor Protection and Equity Markets." *Journal of Financial Economics* 66 (Oct. 2002): 3–27.
Smith, Adam. *The Theory of Moral Sentiments*. London: A. Millar, 1759.

Smith, Adam. *The Wealth of Nations*. 1776; New York: Random House, 1937.
Smith, Brian F., and Ben Amoako-Adu. "Relative Prices of Dual Class Shares." *Journal of Financial and Quantitative Analysis* 30 (June 1995): 223–239.
Smith, Brian F., and Ben Amoako-Adu. "Management Succession and Financial Performance in Family Controlled Firms." In *Governance and Ownership*, ed. Robert Watson, 27. Cheltenham: Edward Elgar, 2005.
Stein, Jeremy C. "Efficient Capital Markets, Inefficient Firms: A Model of Myopic Corporate Behavior." *Quarterly Journal of Economics* 104 (Nov. 1989): 655–669.
Stein, Jeremy C. "Rational Capital Budgeting in an Irrational World." *Journal of Business* 69 (Oct. 1996): 429–455.
Stulz, René M. "Managerial Control of Voting Rights: Financing Policies and the Market for Corporate Control." *Journal of Financial Economics* 20 (Jan.–March 1988): 25–54.
Tian, Gloria Y. "Pyramidal Groups and Firm Performance: Empirical Evidence from Canadian Corporations." *Corporate Ownership and Control* 7 (Spring 2010): 104–122.
Tiebout, Charles M. "A Pure Theory of Local Expenditures." *Journal of Political Economy* 64 (Oct. 1956): 416–424.
Tobin, James. "A General Equilibrium Approach to Monetary Theory." *Journal of Money, Credit and Banking* 1 (Feb. 1969): 15–29.
Tobin, James. "On the Efficiency of the Financial System." *Lloyd's Bank Review* 153 (1984): 1–15.
Tobin, James, and William Brainard. "Asset Markets and the Cost of Capital." In *Economic Progress, Private Values and Public Policy (Essays in Honor of William Fellner)*, ed. Richard R. Nelson and Béla A. Balassa, 235–262. Amsterdam: North-Holland, 1976.
Turner, John, and Lorna Dailey. *Pension Policy: An International Perspective*. Washington, D.C.: U.S. Dept. of Labor, 1991.
Van Nuys, Karen. "Corporate Governance through the Proxy Process: Evidence from the 1989 Honeywell Proxy Solicitation." *Journal of Financial Economics* 34 (Aug. 1993): 101–132.
Villalonga, Belen, and Raphael Amit. "How Do Family Ownership, Control and Management Affect Firm Value?" *Journal of Financial Economics* 80 (May 2006): 385–417.
Wahal, Sunil. "Pension Fund Activism and Firm Performance." *Journal of Financial and Quantitative Analysis* 31 (March 1996): 1–23.
Weisbach, Michael S. "Outside Directors and CEO Turnover." *Journal of Financial Economics* 20 (Jan.–March 1988): 431–460.
Woidtke, Tracie. "Agents Watching Agents? Evidence from Pension Fund Ownership and Firm Value." *Journal of Financial Economics* 63 (Jan. 2002): 99–131.
Wurgler, Jeffrey. "Financial Markets and the Allocation of Capital." *Journal of Financial Economics* 58 (1–2) (2000): 187–214.
Yermack, David. "Flights of Fancy: Corporate Jets, CEO Perquisites, and Inferior Shareholder Returns." *Journal of Financial Economics* 80 (April 2006): 211–242.
Zingales, Luigi. "The Value of the Voting Right: A Study of the Milan Stock Exchange Experience." *Review of Financial Studies* 7 (Jan. 1994): 125–148.Figure CaptionsFigure 12.1. Mean Tobin's Average q Ratios around the World

CHAPTER 13

EXECUTIVE COMPENSATION: GOVERNANCE AND THE FINANCIAL CRISIS

MARTIN J. CONYON

THE 2008 financial and economic crisis catapulted executive compensation into the spotlight. Interest in CEO pay is unprecedented. Regulators, politicians, the public, the media, and some academics have frequently been highly critical of executive pay practices—especially at banks and financial institutions.[1] Authorities in the United States and around the world are seeking ways to improve the system of executive compensation and associated corporate governance arrangements. In the United States, the 2010 Dodd-Frank Act was the outcome of the financial regulatory reforms of President Barack Obama's administration. It creates new rules for executive compensation and corporate governance. The goal of this chapter is to provide an overview of executive compensation practices and give some guidance on the reasons why pay has increased. In addition, the chapter considers executive compensation issues in the light of the financial crisis.

At least three factors are driving the unprecedented recent interest in CEO pay. First, even as the economic recession deepened, Wall Street bankers appeared to be making even higher compensation. In 2009 Merrill Lynch allocated $3.6 billion in bonuses to its employees, and at American International Group (AIG) $218 million was paid in bonuses to employees of its financial services division. The public was outraged, especially as many of these firms were relying on taxpayer dollars for their continued survival. Second, many CEOs do receive very large amounts of money, and the dollar amounts can attract significant attention. The median CEO in the S&P 500 earned about $8 million in 2008. Annual growth rates in CEO pay can often exceed 10 percent. Critics also contend that CEO compensation is not sufficiently tied to the performance of their firms. Worse still, CEOs often receive high pay when company performance goes down, creating the impression that they are "rewarded for failure." Third, U.S. CEOs earn significantly more than the typical American employee. In 1993, CEO pay was approximately 100 times higher than median household income. By 2006 it was more than 200 times higher (Kaplan, 2008). Growing income equality has sparked considerable interest in executive compensation.

There are two broad and essentially competing perspectives on executive compensation. The first is "optimal contracting" theory. According to this perspective, markets ultimately determine executive compensation. CEO pay arrangements, although not always perfect, reflect the (marginal) costs and benefits of arm's-length bargaining between boards and CEOs. Executive pay contracts provide efficient incentives for dealing with agency costs (Core and Guay, 2010a; Holmstrom, 1979). Agency theory is at the heart of the optimal contracting approach and is the standard economic approach to understanding executive pay (Murphy, 1999). The second perspective is the "managerial power" theory. It claims that executive pay arrangements are not the outcome of arm's-length contracting. CEO pay arrangements are fundamentally flawed, and managerial excess is widespread. This view sees executive compensation as part of the corporate governance problem, rather than the solution to it (e.g., Bebchuk and Fried, 2004). According to this approach, CEOs have significant power over pay-setting institutions (such as boards of directors, remuneration committees, and pay consultants) and use this power to influence pay arrangements in their favor.

This chapter provides a broad discussion of executive compensation and incentives, investigating whether outcomes are consistent with economic theory. The rest of this chapter is organized as follows. The next section discusses various economic approaches to executive pay. Then I investigate factors that have been driving the growth in CEO compensation. I provide a commentary on executive compensation and the recent financial crisis. A final section offers some concluding remarks.

Setting Executive Pay

The goal of a well-designed compensation contract is to align the interests of the CEO and the firm's owners (Murphy, 1999). The firm needs to attract, retain, and motivate talented executives. In theory, shareholders set pay. In practice, the board of directors sets pay, ostensibly acting faithfully on behalf of the company shareholders. If the board fails in its fiduciary duties of care and loyalty to the principal, this can lead to poorly designed compensation contacts. Indeed, much of criticism of executive pay focuses on alleged board ineffectiveness in the face of too powerful CEOs. If boards fail, then excess pay and too lax incentives may result (Bebchuk and Fried, 2004, 2005).

The economics of executive compensation is generally motivated by principal agent considerations (Holmstrom, 1979). A risk-neutral owner and rational self-interested utility-maximizing CEO is assumed. There is an asymmetry of information between the owner of the firm (the principal) and the CEO (the agent) who makes decisions on behalf the owner.[2] This gives rise to a moral hazard problem, namely, that the actions or care taken by the CEO are not perfectly observable, at zero or low cost, to the owner. The CEO can opportunistically pursue his[3] own interest at the expense of shareholders because he is better informed about his own actions. Practically, moral hazards come in many forms. First, the CEO can enjoy the quiet life by picking easy-to-manage tasks. A risk-averse CEO may avoid undertaking risky projects with positive net present values, especially if the ex post outcomes of such projects turn out to be poor and lead to termination. Second, the CEO may engage in self-interested empire building. One mechanism to achieve this is via mergers and acquisitions. Mueller's review (chapter 15 in this volume) concludes that on average mergers do not increase efficiency, but instead ultimately destroy wealth for the acquiring firm's shareholders. Given that salaries are often strongly linked to firm size, CEOs have incentives to engage in mergers, even mergers that may not be in the owners' interests. Third, the CEO may make excessive or unwarranted use of company perks that may not be beneficial for shareholders. This may include excessive use of corporate aircraft, financial services, or club memberships. In the extreme, moral hazard also includes intentional misappropriation of shareholder funds, including fraud and theft. Corporate accounting scandals such as Enron, or the Ponzi scheme perpetrated by former investment banker Bernard Madoff are (unfortunately) prime examples of unethical behaviors.

One solution to the myriad potential moral hazards is for the firm's owners to design a contract that makes management rewards contingent on performance. In this context, the CEO chooses the correct (i.e., optimal) action (focuses on increasing firm performance) because it is in his best interests to do so (for example, it leads to greater individual wealth). Others are less sanguine about the current state of affairs. Morck and Yeung (chapter 12 in this volume) state that the "institutions surrounding corporate governance is clearly incomplete, for most countries employ regulations that are both costly and largely ineffective." However, they point to examples from the political science literature that are optimistic that institutional reforms of corporate governance mechanisms will arise and lead to better outcomes in advanced capitalist economies.

Agency theory, then, provides the underlying logic for "pay-for-performance" plans in organizations (Murphy, 1999). Theory predicts that executive pay contracts include instruments such as stock options, accounting earnings, and individual performance metrics that provide a valuable signal of the executive's effort. This is the optimal contracting approach to executive pay. Two points are worth noting. First, the agency model predicts that second-best contracts reduce opportunistic behavior. The use of compensation such as stock options motivates CEO effort to increase stock prices. Second, agency costs are not completely eliminated. Instead, the firm evaluates the incremental benefits and costs of designing, implementing, and verifying the contract. Exogenous changes in the firm's environment (e.g., regulation, change in technologies) can alter the marginal costs and benefits that the board faces, leading to potentially better contract design (Core and Guay, 2010a). In addition, the optimal contract may change over time. Improvements in board governance arrangements (e.g., the addition of high-quality independent directors) may lead to reoptimization of contracts by the boards and hence to different patterns of executive compensation and incentives.

A popular alternative view is that CEOs set pay in their own (rather than shareholder) interests. It has been termed the managerial power view (or sometimes "skimming" hypothesis) and contrasts with optimal contracting theory (Bebchuk and Fried, 2004; Bertrand, 2009). It argues that bargaining between corporate boards and CEOs is not arm's length and executive pay is excessive. The resulting pay contracts are not in shareholders' interests. How might this come about? One version of the theory is that CEOs exercise significant power and influence over the board and use this to lobby for high pay levels. The excess pay constitutes an economic rent, which is an amount greater than that required for the CEO to provide labor services to the firm. There are limits or constraints on how high CEO pay can be. Too much compensation can ultimately damage an executive's reputation or cause embarrassment (e.g., via adverse media exposure or annual shareholder meetings). Bebchuk and Fried (2004) call this phenomenon "outrage costs." The "outrage" matters because ultimately it can impose market penalties on CEOs (such as devaluation of a manager's reputation) as well as social costs. They argue that market constraints and the social costs coming from excessively favorable pay arrangements are not sufficient in preventing significant and widespread deviations from optimal contracting.

Executive Compensation Structures

Executive compensation typically contains four broad elements: an annual salary, an annual bonus, equity compensation in the form of stock options and restricted stock, and other benefits in the forms of retirement pay and perks (Murphy, 1999). In the United States, changes in disclosure requirements in 1992 led to significantly enhanced information about salaries, options, and bonuses reported in proxy statements. Disclosure was enhanced in other countries too. In the United Kingdom, the Cadbury Report in 1992 ushered in a new era of governance leading to greater pay disclosure from 1995 onward. In continental Europe and parts of Asia, disclosure of executive compensation is less complete, but progress is being made. The core structure of the Cadbury Report (or similar recommendation) is increasingly being adopted in many countries, and transparency of executive pay is getting better.

A central component of CEO pay is the base salary. CEO salaries are determined annually and are not mechanically related to firm performance, such as stock returns. Two points about salaries are worth emphasizing. First, CEO salaries are strongly correlated with firm size. Research suggests that an increase in firm size of 50 percent can increase CEO pay by approximately 20 percent. The elasticity of executive pay to firm size is often estimated in the range of about 0.2 to 0.4 (Murphy, 1999). It is regularly interpreted as the economic returns to managerial talent, as larger firms require better managers to run them. However, it also implies that CEOs have incentives to increase firm size, even if this is not in the interests of owners. For example, CEOs might engage in merger and acquisition activities even if these are not profitable (see chapter 15). Second, firms set CEO salaries by benchmarking to other similar CEOs using survey data and professional advice from pay consultants. Consultants label salaries at or above the median as "competitive" and those less than the median as "below market." This can lead to unintended (but nevertheless predictable) consequences. First, salaries might ratchet upward as firms avoid the uncompetitive (below median) part of the executive pay distribution. Second, if a self-interested CEO can exert inappropriate influence over the board's compensation committee, the consultants, or the choice of peer firms, then CEO salaries can be driven up beyond what is optimal for shareholders.

CEOs also receive annual incentives—a bonus that is generally paid in cash. The performance measure triggering the bonus is usually an internal company accounting variable, such as budgeted earnings. External or market-based performance measures such as stock returns or share price returns relative to the market are rarely used in driving bonus pay—internal accounting measures are predominant (Murphy, 1999). The expected payment (i.e., the typical payoff schedule) for CEO bonuses is nonlinear. Below some threshold performance level the CEO receives nothing, above this trigger there is a pay-for-performance zone where increases in performance translate into higher pay, and then at some upper performance level bonus payments are capped.[4] Two important points are worth emphasizing. First, a central problem with this type of payoff schedule is that it may encourage strategic behavior by the executive. Those who design the plan do not intend this gaming, but it is predictable if the CEO is rational. For example, executives have few incentives to increase effort beyond the pay cap. This encourages the CEO to focus on activities that postpone revenue recognition (e.g., inventories) or accelerate cost recognition (e.g., write downs or R&D expenditures). For performance levels significantly below the minimum level that triggers the bonus, the plan participants might engage in "big-bath" accounting because the probability of achieving the minimum performance standard is unlikely. Second, the CEO may lobby for a softer performance target or more easily obtainable performance metric. The main point is that the typical CEO bonus plan, found in many companies, can easily lead to unintended but nevertheless predictable CEO behavior, such as strategic manipulation of the plan or gaming.

A major element of executive compensation is stock options and other forms of equity compensation such as restricted stock (Core et al., 2003; Murphy, 2009).

Stock options are the right but not the obligation to purchase a share in the firm at some prespecified price at some date in the future. Restricted stocks are shares given to an executive (or cash equivalents) contingent on some restriction being met. For example, the recipient may have to meet a financial performance target, or there might be a time restriction before the options vest. The use of stock options, as a central form of executive compensation, expanded greatly in the 1990s. Research shows that perhaps up to 50 percent of a CEO's total pay came in the form of options by the late 1990s (Murphy, 1999). Stock options became increasingly common in parts of Europe, too, especially the United Kingdom (Conyon and Murphy, 2000). Stock options were a less popular compensation instrument in continental Europe and do not appear to have had as long a history as in the United States.

Stock options are usually valued as the economic cost to the firm of granting an option to an employee. This is the opportunity cost to the firm that is forgone by not selling the call option in the open market. The expected value can be obtained by using the Black and Scholes (1973) model, including dividend payments by Merton (1973). The price of a European call option on a dividend paying stock is $c = Se^{-qt}N(d_1) - Xe^{-rt}N(d_2)$, where $d_1 = (\ln(S/X) + (r - q + \sigma^2/2)t)/\sigma\sqrt{t}$, $d_2 = d_1 - \sigma\sqrt{t}$, and S is the stock price, X the exercise price, t the maturity term, r the risk-free interest rate, q the dividend yield, and σ the volatility of returns. $N(.)$ is the cumulative probability distribution function for a standardized normal variable (Black and Scholes, 1973). Given some reasonable values for the input variables (i.e., the risk-free rate, dividend yield, stock volatility), a call option on a stock whose current face value (i.e., price) is $100 has an expected value of about $13.5.[5] The price of a stock option granted to an executive is generally about 30 percent to 50 percent of the face value of the stock,[6] and the value of all options granted to the CEO in a given period is simply the sum of the excepted value of each option grant. Stock options given to executives are normally granted "at the money," such that the exercise price is set equal to the stock price. In addition, options might have a three-year period before they vest (i.e., when ownership is transferred to the executive). Once vested, the typical exercise window is usually between three and ten years, at which time the option contract matures. Because options can be granted annually, the executive can build up a considerable stash of stock options over time.

Two features about stock option pay should be emphasized. First, many assumptions underlying the Black-Scholes model are unlikely to hold in practice, meaning the recipient of the option will place a different value on it compared to the firm. Executives are typically risk-averse, undiversified, and prevented from trading their options or, indeed, hedging their risk by selling short company stock. In consequence, they will place a lower value on the stock option compared to the Black-Scholes cost to the company. Second, the difference in valuations between the firm and the option recipient can be thought of as a premium that the firm must pay employees to accept the risky option versus cash compensation. Firms will want to make sure that the resulting increase in executive and firm performance from using options covers the premium. In this sense, stock options are an expensive way to reward executives compared to simply providing cash to the executive. However, the use of options is warranted if they generate sufficient extra effort or performance by the executive. There is currently little field, experimental, or other empirical evidence on precisely how executives attach value to their stock options. An exception is Lambert and Larcker (2001), who find that employees often do not value options in accordance with the standard Black-Scholes model. In addition, they hold unrealistic expectations about what will happen to the future stock price. More research in this area is required. If options are expected to really motivate CEOs and align their interests to owners, then presumably executives must attach significant value to them. If not, the legitimacy of options as a motivational tool is questionable. Despite these limitations Black-Scholes pricing strategies are routinely used by firms as a way of arriving at the expected value of an option.

The Growth in Executive Pay

Many studies have demonstrated that U.S. CEO pay increased dramatically from the late 1980s and early 1990s (Core and Guay, 2010a; Kaplan, 2008; Conyon, 2006; Murphy, 1999; Hall and Liebman, 1998). Many studies focus on the United States partly because of the availability of a relatively long time series of high-quality data, and because U.S. executives are thought highly paid compared to their European counterparts. Total CEO compensation is usually measured as salary, bonus, long-term incentive payouts, the value of stock options granted during the year (valued on the date of the grant using the Black-Scholes method), and other cash payments (including signing bonuses, benefits, tax reimbursements, and above-market earnings on restricted stocks). This is a flow measure of executive pay, capturing compensation received by the executive in a given year. However, pay is different from CEO *wealth* held in the firm, which also includes the value of stock and options that have been granted in previous periods. Making the distinction between CEO firm wealth and pay in providing the executive with incentives is critical (Core and Guay, 2010a).

Empirical evidence on CEO pay is provided in figure 13.1 for the constituents of the S&P 500. It shows that average and median CEO pay increased significantly over time. Median pay is below average reflecting an important characteristic of the CEO pay distribution—CEO pay is positively skewed and has a long right tail. This means that most CEOs earn relatively low compensation, and a few in the right tail receive excessively generous rewards. The notion that all CEOs receive stratospheric sums is inaccurate. CEO pay increased significantly over the period 1992 to 2008. Median pay increased about threefold. Notice, however, that average pay fell from about 2000, reflecting market declines and the dot-com crash.

Subsequently pay has increased. One important reason that CEO compensation increased at this time was the willingness of firms to grant stock options (Murphy, 1999). Table 13.1 contains data and evidence produced by Core and Guay (2010a). They show that median CEO pay in the S&P 500 firms increased

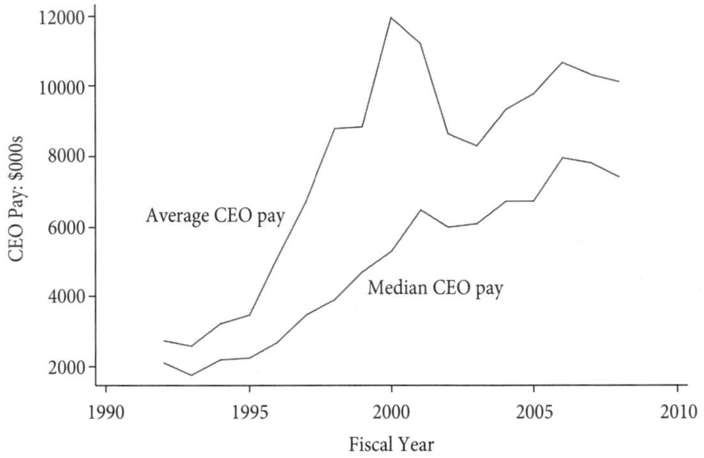

Figure 13.1. CEO Pay in S&P 500 Firms between 1992 and 2008

Notes: The data source – Standard & Poor's ExecuComp Database. Total CEO compensation is measured as salary, bonus, long-term incentive payouts, the value of stock options granted during the year (valued on the date of the grant using the Black-Scholes method), and other cash payments (including signing bonuses, benefits, tax reimbursements, and above-market earnings on restricted stocks). ExecuComp data item TDC1 is used.

from approximately $2 million in 1993 to about $7.7 million in 2008, and the annual rate of growth in pay was approximately 9.4 percent. Total annual pay is calculated as the sum of salary, bonus, the value of stock and option grants, and other pay in the year. Core and Guay further show that the growth in CEO pay (9.4 percent) is positively correlated with growth in firm market values over the period 1993 to 2008 (10.1 percent) and that CEO pay as a fraction of firm market value has remained approximately constant over time. This is consistent with Gabaix and Landier (2008), who predict that CEO pay is explained by the growth in firm size.

The exceptional growth in CEO pay since the mid-1980s can be gauged by looking at historical data. Long time-series data on CEO pay are rare and difficult to collect. The study by Frydman and Saks (2010) is an exception. They analyze long-run trends in U.S. executive compensation using hand-collected panel data from 1936 to 2005. They assembled information for all available years for the largest fifty companies in 1940, 1960, and 1990, a period covering most of the twentieth century. Striking conclusions emerge from the study. First, Frydman and Saks (2010) find the median value of real executive compensation was remarkably flat from around the late 1940s until the mid-1970s. This finding is surprising, and likely different to what many would have conjectured. It suggests the correlation between executive pay and firm growth was actually pretty weak at this time. Second, the authors show that the very large increases in CEO pay, sometimes in excess of 10 percent per annum, occurred since the mid-1970s. Dramatic pay increased occurred from the 1980s onward. Prior to this, modest growth of about 1 percent per annum was the

Table 13.1. Median CEO Pay, Portfolio Value, and Incentives for the CEOs of U.S. S&P 500 Firms from 1993 to 2008

Year	Total Annual Pay ($millions)	Beginning-of-Year Portfolio Value ($millions)	Beginning-of-Year Incentives "Stock Equivalent Value" ($millions)	Annual Pay/ Beginning-of-Year Incentives (%)
All years	5.2	27.1	40.2	14.5
1993	2.0	7.7	11.4	20.3
1994	2.4	10.2	14.7	18.0
1995	2.7	10.6	15.6	19.2
1996	3.0	12.8	19.0	17.0
1997	3.8	17.5	26.7	16.4
1998	4.2	24.0	34.9	12.9
1999	5.3	26.9	40.7	16.0
2000	6.3	35.5	50.2	15.8
2001	6.8	39.3	55.3	13.2
2002	6.4	35.1	53.2	13.9
2003	6.6	31.6	46.9	15.4
2004	7.0	38.5	58.7	13.2
2005	7.2	45.0	68.0	11.0
2006	8.2	45.8	74.2	12.0
2007	8.6	48.5	78.7	11.6
2008	7.6	43.0	66.0	11.7
Growth	9.4%	12.2%	12.4%	−3.6

Notes: Core and Guay (2010a, p. 7) state: "The data are S&P 500 CEO compensation data from 1993 to 2008. Values are not inflation-adjusted. Total Annual Pay is median CEO salary, bonus, stock and option grants, and other pay for the year shown. Beginning-of-Year Portfolio Value is the median total value of stock plus the value of exercisable and unexercisable options held by the CEO at the beginning of the year shown. To compute the value and incentives of the CEOs' option portfolio, we use the method developed by Core and Guay (2002) with a modification that assumes times-to-exercise equal to 70% of the stated times-to-maturity. Beginning-of-Year Incentives is an estimate of the change in the beginning-of-year value of CEO stock and option holdings for a 100% change in stock price. Annual Pay/ Beginning-of-Year Incentives is the median ratio of Annual Pay to Beginning-of-Year Incentives."
Source: Core and Guay (2010a), table 1, p. 7. Columns 3 to 6 of their paper are extracted and reported here.

norm. A key takeaway from Frydman and Saks (2010) is that the growth in executive pay is, in the wider historical context, a phenomenon of the past thirty years or so. As such it presents numerous challenges. A convincing explanation of CEO pay needs to explain both the short-run and long-run pattern in CEO pay, as well as the patterns in the cross-section distribution of executive compensation.

CEO Financial Incentives: Paying for Performance

The pay-for-performance issue is central to the economics of executive pay. Critics of compensation arrangements frequently contend that CEO pay is not sufficiently linked to firm performance, implying the interests of executives and shareholders are not well aligned. Jensen and Murphy (1990) lamented this fact. In their influential article they showed that U.S. CEOs were paid like bureaucrats. The problem, they argued, was that executives received most of their compensation in the form of salaries and cash pay, and hardly any in the form of corporate equity, such as stock options and restricted stock. The implication was that executives had few financial incentives to focus on wealth creation, and instead could enjoy the quiet life, or even built leviathan empires since salaries were paid to the size (not performance) of the firm. Since the 1990s, however, the U.S. executive pay landscape has changed radically. CEO pay is inexorably and mechanically linked to stock price performance by the use of options and other share-based payments. As noted, the value of a stock option varies positively with the share price, creating an automatic link between the value to the CEO and share price performance. However, as some commentators strongly argue, the trend to use more options has created its own set of problems, such as encouraging risky and nonoptimal behavior by executives (Bebchuk and Fried, 2004).

It is useful to distinguish between CEO pay and CEO incentives. *CEO pay* is the amount of remuneration received in a given period of time in exchange for labor services. This includes salaries, bonuses received, the value of option grants, and other share-based compensation granted during the reporting or accounting period. In contrast, *CEO financial incentives* are driven in large part by the accumulated wealth the CEO has in the firm. The incentives from firm wealth may be defined as the incremental change in total CEO wealth brought about by an incremental change in performance (Murphy, 1999). This captures the link between pay and performance. In consequence, CEO wealth is made up not only of the grants of options this year but also the value of all of the equity-based compensation held by the CEO in the firm, usually accumulated over time (Core and Guay, 2010a; Murphy, 1999).

Pay-for-performance can be calculated in a number of ways. The implicit link between cash compensation and performance may be calculated using regression methods (see Murphy, 1999). More generally, financial economists define it as the change in the value of the CEO's portfolio of assets held in the firm for a given change in performance (Murphy, 1999). Core and Guay (1999) measure incentives as the dollar change in the value of the CEO wealth from a 1 percent change in the stock price. Incentives are the dollar change in executive portfolio wealth arising from a 1 percent increase in shareholder wealth, written as: 1% × (share price) × (the number of shares held) + 1% × (share price) × (option delta) × (the number of options held).[7] An alternative measure found in the literature and used by Jensen and Murphy (1990) calculates incentives as the dollar change in CEO wealth from a $1,000 change in firm wealth, summarized as: (fraction of shares held) × $1,000 + (option delta) × (fraction of options held). It varies between $0 (no incentives) to $1,000 (the CEO receives all the increase in generated firm wealth). This measure views incentives as being driven by fractional ownership of the firm. Both measures have appeared in the economics, finance and accounting literature (Conyon and He, 2004; Conyon and Murphy, 2000; Core and Guay, 2010a; Gao, 2010; Murphy, 1999,).

Jensen and Murphy's (1990) original research showed that CEO wealth increased only $3.25 for every $1,000 change in shareholder wealth, suggesting that CEOs had only weak incentives to promote shareholder value. An important reason for the lack of incentives in the original Jensen-Murphy data was the relative low level of equity ownership by CEOs. Hall and Liebman (1998) extended the analysis by Jensen and Murphy, asking whether CEOs were really paid like bureaucrats. Their hand-collected data showed that since about the mid-1980s stock options had become a critical feature of CEO pay. The hypothesis that CEO pay was not linked to performance was overturned. Importantly, they showed a strong positive correlation between CEO compensation and firm performance, arising almost entirely by changes in the value of CEO holdings of stock and stock options. In addition, they demonstrated that both the level of CEO compensation and the sensitivity of compensation to firm performance increased dramatically since 1980, largely because of increases in stock option grants.

Core et al. (2005) also show that CEO pay, the value of equity holdings, and incentives all increased significantly between 1993 and 2003. Importantly, because of the very large holdings of options and stock, CEOs experience significant changes in wealth when the stock price changes. Again, most CEO incentives arise from the portfolio holding of options and stock, not from the correlation between current pay and firm performance. They show that if the stock price declined by 20 percent, then the value of the typical CEO's wealth in the form of stock and options would actually fall by a greater amount than the typical CEO's whole annual pay in that year. Core et al. (2005, p. 1174) conclude: "the assertion that US CEOs receive 'pay without performance' is clearly inconsistent with the evidence."

Recently, Core and Guay (2010a) have examined the provision of CEO incentives within a wealth-based contracting framework. They argue that there are both benefits *and* costs of imposing performance-based economic incentives on CEOs and senior managers. The implication is that agency problems will arise not only if CEOs have too few incentives but also if they have too many. A central idea in their study is that performance-based incentives should be determined in the context of the CEO's overall personal wealth, including that owned both inside and outside the firm. CEOs with different levels of outside wealth will have potentially very different levels of incentives. Consider the case where a firm requires the CEO to own $10 million of the firm's equity. This will give rise to a different set of incentives for an executive who has $100 million in wealth outside the firm compared to one with $10 million. The implication is that the actual incentives faced by two different executives, each with the same level of equity ownership inside the firm, can be very different depending on their individual levels of outside wealth.[8]

Core and Guay (2010a) calculate incentives for CEOs from 1993 to 2008. These are reproduced (along with CEO pay figures) in table 13.1. It shows the beginning-of-year market value of the median CEO's stock and option portfolio. In addition, the incentives arising from this portfolio are also given. Core and Guay (2010a) express these incentives as the "stock equivalent value," using their methodology in Core and Guay (2002) and then converting to stock equivalents. The conversion of options to their stock equivalent is necessary "because $1 of options provides greater incentives to increase stock price than does $1 of stock (options provide more incentives because they are effectively a leveraged position in firm stock)" (Core and Guay, 2010a, p. 6). The ratio of CEO pay to stock equivalent incentives is given in the last column. The following thought experiment helps for understanding the role of incentives. In 2000 the median CEO has incentives of $50.2 million. If the stock price fell by 20 percent, then CEO's incentives would fall by $10.4 million (i.e., minus 20 percent times $50.2). This figure is much greater than the median CEO's total compensation for that year, $6.3 million. Similar effects can be calculated for different years. The final column shows the ratio CEO annual pay to beginning-of-year incentives. It can be interpreted as the necessary negative stock return that reduces CEO beginning-of-year wealth incentive to the same level of annual pay.

Core and Guay (2010a) also find strong evidence that CEO pay is correlated to performance. For 1999 to 2004 they sort the S&P 500 firms into ranked deciles based on the stock return performance of the firms. They find that stock returns in the lowest decile are −44.7 percent and returns in the top decile are 68.8%. As many critics contend, changes in annual CEO pay are only weakly related to stock market performance. In the lowest ranked decile, despite stock returns of −44.7 percent, CEO pay falls by only −13.7 percent. In the top decile, despite returns of 68.8 percent, annual CEO pay increases by 19.7 percent. However, this misses the central point that wealth and equity incentives drive the pay for performance relation. In the bottom decile (firms with stock returns of −44.7 percent), CEOs see losses of $32 million on their beginning-of-year wealth incentives. In the top decile (firms with stock returns of 68.8 percent), CEOs enjoy gains of $31.4 million on their beginning-of-year wealth incentives. The authors conclude that stock price changes can cause large changes in the CEOs portfolio and wealth even though changes in annual compensation might be fairly small.

In addition, Kaplan and Rauh (2010) find strong evidence that wealth and portfolio factors are important in linking CEO pay to performance. For 1999 to 2004 they sort the set of U.S. S&P 1500 firms into five size groups. For each group they sorted CEOs into five subgroups based on how much the CEO had realized in terms of pay and option gains. They then investigated how each of these groups (within each size band) performed relative to the industry over the past three years. They, too, find that actual compensation was highly related to performance. Firms in the top quintile of pay were also in the top quintile of stock performance relative to peers. Firms in the bottom quintile of pay were the worst performance firms relative to the market. They conclude that CEO pay is linked to performance, driven in large part by the use of stock options and equity compensation.

Explaining Executive Pay Outcomes

The empirical evidence suggests that CEO pay has increased significantly, in the United States and elsewhere.[9] Not only has the level of compensation increased, the structure of CEO pay has changed, too. Equity compensation, in the form of options and restricted stock, has become much more prevalent. As already noted, significant changes in the pattern of executive pay appeared to happen around the middle of the 1980s. What explains these changes? One reason may have been the increased acceptance by shareholders of equity-based compensation, especially since the publication of Jensen and Murphy's (1990) much cited research on the lack of incentives for U.S. firms. Since then, boards and compensation committees became much more willing to take advantage of option pay that led to large payoffs to executives.

As noted earlier, there are two main theories explaining executive pay. "Optimal contracting" theory explains executive pay as the outcome of market forces and contracting costs. Boards set pay in the context of significant contracting and information costs as well as the market for CEO talent. Pay outcomes, although not always perfect or first-best, are optimal when balanced against information asymmetries and contracting costs (Core and Guay, 2010a; Kaplan, 2008). The second theory is the "managerial power" model. CEOs exercise power and influence over compliant boards and weak owners. They use their power for self-enrichment at the expense of owners, and the resulting pay contracts turn out to be suboptimal. Boards, for various reasons, are unable to resist or are too friendly with the CEO, and in consequence the CEO receives overly generous compensation that is not in the interests of shareholders (Bebchuk and Fried, 2004; Bertrand, 2009).

There is empirical evidence supporting both theories. At present it is too early to conclude that one theory is ultimately correct. The goal of ongoing research, adhering to the scientific method, is to design reproducible experiments or tests that effectively discriminate between competing hypotheses and hence ultimately the broad theories. There are two significant research challenges. First, the data are inherently nonrandom, and double-blind randomized trials are typically not possible. This leads to major difficulties in trying to identify causal effects in pay studies. In consequence, many empirical analyses are observational or correlation studies. Second, it is difficult to design clean tests that effectively differentiate between the optimal contracting and managerial power approaches. For example, empirical evidence that appears to favor one of the theories can be reinterpreted in such a way as to support the other. This can happen due to selection effects or if explanatory variables are endogenous.

CEO Pay and the Board of Directors

Managerial power models of executive pay generally claim that compensation arrangements are too generous (Bebchuk and Fried, 2004). CEO power leads to levels of pay above the arm's-length negotiated optimal contracting level. Corporate boards are relatively weak compared to the CEO. Executive pay does not increase indefinitely because of "outrage" costs or other binding constraints. However, CEO power and influence is sufficiently widespread that deviation from market forces and optimal contracting are common. There are many potential tests of the managerial power hypothesis, and a challenge for research is to design tests that rule out the competing efficiency (optimal contracting) explanation.

One test of the managerial power hypothesis is that weak boards lead to high CEO pay (Bebchuk and Weisbach, 2010). What constitutes a weak board? The literature typically designates a board as poorly constituted if it is too large, and therefore it is difficult for directors to oppose the CEO, or if the CEO has appointed the outside directors, who are beholden to the CEO for their jobs. In addition, boards may be called weak when directors serve on too many other boards, making them too busy to be effective monitors; or if the CEO is also chair of the board, since conflicts of interest arise. Alternatively, the board may be too friendly with the CEO, coming from the same social or friendship groups, and therefore pay insufficient attention to their fiduciary duties to shareholders. When boardroom governance is poor, excess pay as an agency cost is expected. Empirical evidence using cross-section data often support the claim that agency costs are greater when boards are poorly constituted. The evidence shows that in a cross-section, poorly designed board structures are associated with greater excess pay (Core et al., 1999).

However, there is an important challenge to the hypotheses that weak boards lead to excess pay: the time-series data do not fully support it. Boards have become much more independent over time, measured by the absence of affiliated directors at the same time pay has increased. An affiliated director is a person who is an employee of the company or in some other material way is linked or affiliated to the firm. The most prevalent reasons are providing professional services or being a recent former employee. The fraction of affiliated directors on company boards has been declining over time—the implication being that the quality of board governance has increased. The time-series data, then, are at odds with managerial power (rent-extraction) hypothesis. It predicts as governance quality goes up CEO pay should go down. However, CEO pay and board quality have both increased over time in the United States. This suggests one should look elsewhere for the growth in CEO pay in the United States.

An essential feature of the executive pay-setting process is the compensation committee (Baker et al., 1988). Ineffective pay committees give the CEO an opportunity to promote his interests at the expense of shareholder welfare. Studies find little evidence that compensation committees are ineffective. Conyon and Peck (1998) investigate the relation between board control, the compensation committee, and executive pay, using panel data on the 100 largest U.K. firms between 1991 and 1994. The quality of governance increases over time. In 1991, 78 percent of firms have a compensation committee, increasing to 99 percent in 1994. The proportion of independent directors on the committee increases from 87 percent in 1991 to 91 percent in 1994. The study shows that CEO pay is greater in firms with compensation committees or those with a greater fraction of outsiders on the committee.

However, they find the link between pay and performance is greater in firms with a greater proportion of outside directors on the compensation committee. Daily et al. (1998) study 200 *Fortune* 500 companies in 1992. They find no relationship between CEO pay and the proportion of affiliated directors on the compensation committee. Other studies from the United States and the United Kingdom have also failed to find that compensation committees result in excess CEO pay or poorly designed compensation contracts (Anderson and Bizjac, 2003; Bender, 2003; Conyon and He, 2004; Gregory-Smith, 2009).

Compensation Consultants and CEO Pay

Compensation consultants are firms or individuals who advise the board of directors about executive pay practices. Critics contend that consultants lead to excessive CEO pay and poorly designed contracts (Bebchuk and Fried, 2004; Waxman, 2007).[10] They argue that consultants are not sufficiently independent and suffer from conflicts of interest because they sell other services to their clients and are thus wary of provoking the CEO for fear of jeopardizing this other business. An alternative (optimal contracting) perspective is that compensation consultants are experts who provide valuable information and data to busy boards of directors. Their presence ameliorates opportunistic behavior by CEOs and leads to well-structured optimal compensation contracts. Do pay consultants promote the best interests of the firm's owners, or do they simply enrich entrenched CEOs?

The available empirical evidence shows that consultants have only a limited effect on CEO pay and incentives. Consultants do not appear to be the primary driver of the recent growth in executive pay. Murphy and Sandino (2010) find evidence in both the United States and Canada that CEO pay is greater in companies where the consultant provides other services. In addition, they find that pay is higher in Canadian firms when the fees paid to consultants for other services are large relative to the fees for executive compensation services. This evidence suggests that greater agency costs lead to higher compensation. However, they unexpectedly find that CEO pay is higher in U.S. firms where the consultant works for the independent board rather than for management. In another study, Cadman, Carter, and Hillegeist (2010) investigate compensation consultants' potential cross-selling incentives using 755 firms from the S&P 1500 for 2006. Conditional on the firm retaining a consultant, Cadman et al. (2010, p. 263) are "unable to find widespread evidence of higher levels of pay or lower pay-performance sensitivities for clients of consultants with potentially greater conflicts of interest." They conclude there is little evidence that potential conflicts of interest between the firm and its consultant are a primary driver of excessive CEO pay. Conyon, Peck, and Sadler (2009) also perform a comparative study of the relation between CEO pay and consultants using British and American data for 2006. They find that CEO pay is generally greater in firms that use compensation consultants, which is consistent with the managerial power theory of executive pay. They also show that the amount of equity used in the CEO compensation package, such as stock options, is greater in firms that use consultants. This is consistent with alignment of manager and shareholder interests and the optimal contracting theory of pay. Finally, there is little evidence that using consultants with potential conflicts of interest, such as supplying other business to client firms, leads to greater CEO pay or the adverse design of pay contracts. The evidence is consistent with Cadman et al. (2010).

Option Plans and Relative Performance

Another proposed test of the managerial power hypothesis is the lack of relative performance in U.S. CEO compensation contracts. Stock option contracts reward CEOs based on absolute, not relative performance. Simple agency models predict that the market component of firm performance should be removed from the CEO's compensation package because the CEO's actions do not influence the market, incentives are not improved, and the pay contract is riskier. By indexing stock options to the market, contract efficiency is improved—and only rewards the CEO for outperforming peers. Bebchuk and Fried (2004) argue that because option contracts lack explicit relative performance conditions, executives enjoy windfall gains as market value increases. In short, CEOs are rewarded for "luck," not their performance or skill. The typical U.S. stock option plan does not explicitly filter out general stock price increases that are attributable to market or industry trends and are therefore unconnected to the executive's own performance. This means that in rising markets, the value of a CEO's options increases even if firm performance is worse than the market.

Using indexed options would be one way to explicitly introduce relative performance evaluation into the pay contract and provide incentives at lower cost. However, the nearly universal use of fixed price options, where the option exercise price is usually set equal to the stock price at grant, does not necessarily reflect managerial power. First, U.S. accounting treatment of options in the 1990s meant that indexed options would attract an accounting charge and need to be expensed. Thus, faced with a decision to use an indexed option that would increase firm costs versus using a standard fixed price option, which attracts no charge, firms choose the latter. This choice is not necessarily because of managerial power but because of an accounting anomaly. The perceived cost to the board made options seem lower than their economic cost (Murphy, 2002).

Bebchuk and Fried (2004) argued the accounting explanation for lack of relative performance (or reduced-windfall options) is incomplete, because, among other reasons, management lobbied against expensing options and did not exert effort to get nonexpensing for indexed options. Second, in the United Kingdom, stock options and other long-term equity incentive plans generally have performance triggers. These performance measures are growth in earnings per share, or stock returns relative to a market index. Of course, one might question if the performance measures are sufficiently demanding, and so on, for CEOs. However, the differences between the United Kingdom and the United States suggest that regulatory differences might be an important explanation for the different styles of equity pay.

Not only is explicit market indexing in compensation contracts rare in the United States, studies also find that there is little evidence of relative performance evaluation in the estimated relationship between pay and performance (Gibbons and Murphy, 1990). A test of relative performance in CEO contracts is a negative correlation between CEO pay at a focal firm and industry performance, after controlling for firm performance. The data do not generally support this hypothesis. The lack of a negative correlation between CEO pay and market performance, however, may not necessarily imply managerial power. For instance, more complicated agency models suggest the value of a CEO's human capital changes with market fortunes. If so, CEO compensation also moves in the same direction as the market.

CEO Perks

In addition to salaries, restricted stock, stock options, and so on, executives also receive benefits in the form of perks. These can include the use of corporate aircraft, country clubs, and financial planning advice from the firm. Boards are therefore responsible for setting perks and pensions—as well as the level of cash pay, stock options, and other equity pay. Although compensation in publicly trade firms is now highly visible, critics contend that "backdoor pay" or "stealth pay" in the form of perks and pensions are prevalent. More recently changes in disclosure rules in the United States and the United Kingdom mean that investors can observe deferred payments in more detail than was previously the case. A central question is whether such payments represent compensation by the back door, or whether they form part of an optimal compensation strategy that aligns the interests of managers to owners.

Rajan and Wulf (2006) investigated whether perks represent managerial excess. They use proprietary data on a number of company perks. They conclude that firms offer perks in situations where they are most likely to facilitate managerial productivity. That is, perks are used to enhance owner welfare. In consequence, the authors conclude that perks do not represent managerial excess, but instead form part of the complex contracting between the CEO and the board. In contrast, Yermack (2006) investigated CEO use of corporate jets disclosed by firms in their annual reports. His main finding is that when the use of aircraft is disclosed publicly to shareholders, there is a drop in stock price of about 1 percent. The negative impact on asset values implies that executive perks destroy firm value. Interestingly, Yermack (2006) does not find that the perk consumption is related to CEO ownership stake in the firm or CEO salaries. The optimal provision of pension and perquisite arrangements in firms promises to be an important topic for future research.

Market-Based Explanations

One important explanation for changes in executive compensation is the shifts in the demand and supply for managerial talent. As in all labor markets, for a given supply of talent, an increase in the demand for skilled CEOs increases CEO compensation. Himmelberg and Hubbard (2000) argue that the supply of highly skilled CEOs who are capable of running large, complex firms is relatively inelastic. Economic shocks to aggregate demand increase both the value of the firm as well as the marginal value of the CEO's labor services to the firm. They show that in equilibrium, such shocks lead to greater executive compensation. Some argue that the labor market for executives is in reality thinly traded, and that CEOs of firms all know one another or sit on each other's boards. This is a fruitful line for future research. However, it might be noted that the available number of CEO job positions at leading companies seems far fewer than the number of individuals who aspire to occupy those posts.[11]

Gabaix and Landier (2008) build an economic model of CEO pay determination. CEOs have different talents and are then competitively matched to firms. In equilibrium, the model predicts that CEO pay is determined by the size of the firm. The theoretical model explains the level of CEO pay across firms and over time. Dispersion in CEO talent can lead to large differences in compensation outcomes. The model is tested using U.S. data. They show that firm size has increased significantly in recent decades and conclude that the "size of large firms explains many of the patterns in CEO pay, across firms, over time, and between countries." They find that the sixfold increase of U.S. CEO pay between 1980 and 2003 can be fully attributed to the sixfold increase in market capitalization of large companies during that period. In consequence, their model and empirical evidence points to economic and market factors driving CEO pay, rather than the rent-seeking power of CEOs.

Murphy and Zábojnik (2004) explain CEO pay based on changes in the relative importance of general and specific managerial capital. General managerial capital (such as knowledge of finance, accounting, or management of human capital) is valuable and transferable across companies, whereas specific managerial capital skills (such as knowledge of firm suppliers or clients, etc.) are only valuable within the organization. The firm decides whether to fill a CEO vacancy by choosing an incumbent or external candidate. A firm that hires outside managers forgoes a CEO with valuable firm-specific skills. However, it selects from a larger pool of managers, allowing better matching of managers to firms. Firms will increasingly appoint external CEO candidates as general managerial capital becomes increasingly valuable relative to firm-specific managerial capital. Labor market competition for talent, especially for CEOs with general transferable skills, then determines CEO pay. Murphy and Zábojnik (2004) argue that general managerial skills have become more important in the modern firm, driving up pay. Empirically, they show external CEO hires as a percentage of all CEO appointments increased from 15 percent in the 1970s to 27 percent during the 1990s. In addition, external appointments to the CEO position receive a compensation premium—and this premium has increased during the 1990s.

Kaplan and Rauh (2010) also ague that market forces are primarily responsible for changes in executive compensation arrangements. Such pressures determine not only CEO pay but also the compensation received by other talented individuals in society. They compare the pay of CEO at publicly traded U.S. firms to other similarly well-qualified individuals. If people in the "control group" have done as well as the "treatment" group of publicly traded firms, then by this test CEO pay is not excessive. Kaplan and Rauh (2010) conclude that the pay of talented groups such as hedge fund mangers have done better than CEOs at publicly traded firms. Kaplan (2008, p. 12) similarly remarks: "while CEOs earn a great deal, they are not unique. Other groups with similar backgrounds and talents— particularly hedge fund, venture capital, and private equity investors; investment bankers; and lawyers have done at least as well over the last 10 or 15 years. The increase in pay at the top appears to be systemic."

Conyon, Core, and Guay (2011) provide a market-based explanation for changes in CEO pay. They contrast the United States to the United Kingdom to test the excess pay hypothesis. They choose the United Kingdom because it shares common governance and capital market features with the United States but (at least until recently) has been less prone to claims that executive pay is excessive. The authors find that median U.S. CEO pay in 2003, defined as the sum of salary, bonus, grant date value of restricted stock and options, and benefits and other compensation, is approximately 40 percent greater than for U.K. CEOs. However, they argue that CEOs who hold greater risky pay in the form of equity are likely to demand a risk premium in the form of greater pay. They demonstrate that U.S. CEOs bear substantially greater equity risk than U.K. CEOs. Their findings bear out evidence contained in Conyon and Murphy (2000). In addition, Conyon et al. (2011) make risk adjustments to observed total pay, based on assumptions about CEO risk aversion and outside wealth owned, to reflect the differences in equity incentives held by CEOs in the two countries. They then document that there is little evidence that U.S. CEOs' risk-adjusted pay is significantly greater than that of U.K. CEOs. In a related study, Fernandes et al. (2009) also find that the U.S. CEO pay premium falls significantly if one controls for relative risk aversion. Their analysis is based on compensation practices in fourteen countries where there is sufficient mandated pay disclosure. Overall, they conclude that a large part of the observed U.S. pay premium reflects compensating differentials for the higher risk of U.S. pay packages.

Executive Compensation and the Financial Crisis

The catastrophic meltdown of capital markets in 2008, and the economic global recession that followed, fueled intense debate about the role of executive compensation at major financial institutions.[12] The compensation arrangements at banks were blamed for igniting the worst economic downturn since the Great Depression of the 1930s. Critics of CEO pay asserted that compensation arrangements at many financial institutions encouraged individuals to take actions that were too risky, or worse, that bankers were effectively rewarded for the failure of their firms (Bebchuk and Spamann, 2010). Others argue that pay practices in the financial sector were not a major contributing factor to the financial and economic crisis.

Since the 2008 financial crisis there has been major corporate governance legislation in the form of the Dodd-Frank Act (2010). The Dodd-Frank Act significantly increases transparency in relation to executive compensation in the United States and requires further accountability via a regular shareholder vote on executive compensation. In addition, a blue-ribbon commission, the Financial Crisis Inquiry Commission (http://www.fcic.gov) investigated the causes of the financial and economic crisis. It attributed part of the blame for the crisis to compensation practices at financial institutions, which encouraged inappropriate risk taking. At the time of this writing, the precise causes of the financial crises remain a hotly debated issue. The role played by compensation contracts during the financial crisis, especially incentive arrangements at leading banks, remains a topic for continued research. A discussion of the issues, and emerging empirical evidence, is provided in Conyon et al. (2010).[13]

Outrage over Executive Compensation and the Financial Crisis

Public outrage at executive pay increased from 2008 in the wake of the financial crisis. There are at least three reasons for this. First, bankers received lavish bonuses at around the same time their firms required substantial government bailouts. Second, there was a suspicion that compensation systems in place at banks, together with bank corporate culture, created perverse incentives for excessive risk taking that led to the financial crisis. Third, there was outrage at the way the financial crisis detrimentally affected those on Main Street compared to Wall Street. Rising unemployment, falling wages, and deteriorating output on Main Street immediately followed from the 2008 macroeconomic shock. But for many observers it seemed that bankers on Wall Street were immune to the harsh new economic realities. Ailing banks continued in business, aided by government and taxpayer funding, because they were deemed "too big to fail." The continued high levels of CEO pay made it seem as if it was just business as usual.

The history of compensation at financial institutions during the financial crisis is yet to be written, but firms such as Merrill Lynch and AIG will figure prominently. These two institutions triggered considerable outrage over banker pay. In December 2009, just before the completion of the merger with Bank of America, Merrill Lynch distributed about $3.6 billion in bonuses to its 36,000 employees. The top 4 employees received a combined total of $121 million; the top 14 individuals received a combined total $249 million, and the top 140 received a collective amount of $858 million (Cuomo, 2009). The use of taxpayer bailout money from the federal Troubled Assets Relief Program (TARP) to rescue the banks caused immense public outrage and scandal. Likewise, controversy and outrage was fuelled from the

AIG bonus payments. AIG disclosed it was allocating approximately $218 million in bonus payments to employees of its financial services division. It had received colossal amounts of bailout money ($170 billion) and had posted massive financial losses ($61.7 billion). In addition, further payments to AIG employees were widely anticipated.

The public's outrage spurred regulators' appetites to rein in executive compensation via legislation. Conyon et al. (2010) document that seven bills were introduced in the House of Representatives and Senate aimed specifically at bonuses paid by AIG and other bailed-out firms using TARP funds. Government action and the regulation of bank pay also appeared as a favorable option among the general public. An *Economist* newspaper/YouGov poll in 2009 asked: "Are you in favor of allowing the government to set the salaries of top executives at banks and financial institutions that receive assistance from the federal government?" It found 57.8 percent favored intervention and only 23.5 percent opposed such measures; the remainder were unsure.[14] Further evidence of public and policy maker outrage over lavish compensation arrangements (especially at banks) from about 2008 onward can be easily found in mainstream media outlets.

Bank Executive Compensation and Performance

Compensation patterns at banks are undoubtedly controversial. Untangling the relation between bank pay, firm performance, and the financial crisis is difficult—and it is especially challenging to identify causal effects. Pay is high in banks and the crisis had something to do with banks, but these facts do not imply that bank pay *caused* the financial crisis. To what extent was CEO pay and other compensation arrangements at financial institutions a contributory factor in the 2008 financial crisis? Were CEOs unduly rewarded as their firms failed?

The claim that CEO pay was instrumental in triggering a financial crisis can be framed in a number of ways (Bebchuk and Spamann, 2010; Fahlenbrach and Stulz, 2011). One hypothesis is that CEOs focus excessively on the short-term rather than long-term organizational performance. Another is that stock options and other forms of equity pay promoted excessive risk taking, inconsistent with shareholder interests. Another theme is that the capital structure at banks contained too much financial leverage, encouraging conflicts between debt- and equity-holders and promoting excessive risk taking. Ultimately, the relation between pay arrangements at banks and other financial institutions and the depth of the financial crisis are a matter for empirical scrutiny and evidence. A few nascent studies have begun this task by comparing bank to nonbank pay structures and by analyzing compensation contracts before, during, and since the financial collapse of 2008. It is important to emphasize that the evidence is only beginning to emerge, so any conclusions at this stage must remain tentative.

Bebchuk and Spamann (2010) argue that executive compensation arrangements at banks are poorly designed and contend that the regulation of banks' executive pay should be a central feature of future financial regulation. Moreover, they assert that this approach can complement and strengthen traditional types of financial regulation. Their main argument is that the capital structure at banks leads to economic distortions and risky behavior by executives: "Equity-based awards, coupled with the capital structure of banks, tie executives' compensation to a highly levered bet on the value of banks' assets. Because bank executives expect to share in any gains that might flow to common shareholders, but are insulated from losses that the realization of risks could impose on preferred shareholders, bondholders, depositors, and taxpayers, executives have incentives to give insufficient weight to the downside of risky strategies" (Bebchuk and Spamann, 2010, p. 1). They claim that evidence from the extant economics and finance literature supports their arguments. However, other emerging research has so far been unable to show a robust causal link between the structure of bank executive compensation and the financial crisis.

Cai, Cherny, and Milbourn (2010) study risk-taking incentives in executive compensation contracts and compare banks to nonbanks. They argue that standard agency model give rise to a conflict of interest between debt- and equity-holders. Contracts are designed to be optimal from the shareholders' point of view and focus managers' attention stock prices and earnings by using stock options, restricted stock, earnings bonuses, and so on. Managers may take actions that are good for shareholders, but not necessarily so for debtholders such as banks, bondholders, and depositors. They argue there is more reliance on debt and leverage in banking and so a greater bias toward excessive risk taking. They conclude that the standard executive pay structure "in banking and finance before the financial crisis reveals some potentially problematic practices." These practices may have encouraged "short-termism" and "excessive risk taking." The theoretical arguments are analogous to the Jensen and Meckling (1976) agency cost of debt problem. Although conceptually plausible, it is also important to address why the debt-versus-equity issue became more problematic around 2007, as opposed to some other time.

In a recent study Bhagat and Bolton (2011) analyzed executive pay arrangements in the fourteen largest U.S. financial institutions from 2000 to 2008. They focused on the buy and sell decisions of executives of their own bank's shares. Their empirical analysis finds that CEOs are about thirty times more likely to be involved in a sell transaction compared to a buy transaction. They suggest that CEOs believed their stock was over- rather than undervalued—and this may have lead to excessive risk taking. Recently, Bell and Reenen (2010) documented the relation between bankers' pay and income inequality in the United Kingdom. They show that observed increases in U.K. wage inequality is correlated to the increases in bank bonuses.

Fahlenbrach and Stulz (2011) investigate a sample of ninety-five U.S. banks in 2006 and follow them through to December 2008. Of the original ninety-five institutions in 2006, seventy-seven remain in the sample; twelve merged and eight were delisted. The authors perform numerous tests and ultimately reject the hypothesis that compensation arrangements at U.S. banks were fundamentally flawed. They find evidence of a negative relation between measures of CEO incentives at the end of 2006 and long-term performance of banks, measured as the buy-and-hold returns between July 2007 and December 2008.[15] Their evidence shows that CEOs with incentives that are better aligned to shareholders actually performed worse in the crisis. Similarly, Cheng, Hong, and Scheinkman (2009) find that executives with better incentives have higher CAPM betas, have higher return volatilities, and are more likely to be in the tails of performance, with high precrisis performance and low performance during the crash. In Europe, Bechmann and Raaballe (2009) analyzed CEO pay and performance in a sample of Danish banks. They find that CEOs with more incentive-based compensation, and therefore much more to lose from poor performance, fared significantly worse than other banks during the crisis. This evidence, then, points to a negative correlation between incentive compensation structures and performance during the crisis: banks that performed worst in the crisis are those with better ex ante executive financial incentives.

Fahlenbrach and Stulz (2011) interpret their results as meaning that CEOs took decisions they felt would be profitable for shareholders ex ante, but ultimately these turned out to perform badly ex post. To support this conjecture, they argue that if CEOs had advance knowledge that their decisions were not in the best interests of shareholders, then they would have taken actions to insulate their personal wealth from adverse stock price movements. For example, they would have sold their shares or engaged in other hedging activities. However, the authors find no evidence of unusual share selling or other hedging activity by bank executives in advance of the crisis. Furthermore, the value of the median CEO's 2006 aggregate stock and option holdings is significant: more than eight times the value of his 2006 total compensation. CEO ownership, in the form of shares and vested unexercised options, is very important in banks. Modest declines in asset values can easily outweigh the CEO's annual pay. The amount of CEO wealth at risk prior to the financial crisis makes it seem less likely that rational CEOs knew of an impending financial crash or knowingly engaged in too-risky behavior. To do so would put in jeopardy considerable personal wealth.[16] In the authors' study, on average, CEOs in their sample lost $30 million in stock and option value, and the median CEO lost over $5 million. Ultimately, Fahlenbrach and Stulz (2011) reject the claim that bank CEOs were to blame for the crisis. Adams (2009) compared financial and nonfinancial firms from 1996 to 2007. She found that corporate governance arrangements in financial firms are on average no worse compared to nonfinancial firms. Controlling for the size of the firm, she documents that both the level of CEO pay and the fraction of equity-based CEO pay is actually lower in banks, even in 2007 at the start of the crisis. Also, she documents that banks receiving bailout money had more independent boards of directors compared to nonbailout banks. In addition, Adams (2010) cautions that employing the same governance standards advanced in nonfinancial firms to banks is unlikely to improve the governance of banks.

Murphy (2009) also examined CEO pay in U.S. financial institutions during the recent crisis. He also documents that bank CEO pay and wealth are adversely affected as the crisis unfolds, especially relative to other firms. He studies thirty-six companies receiving TARP funding from the U.S. government. He finds that average CEO bonuses fell significantly by 84.3 percent from over $2.3 million in 2007 to only $363,082 in 2008 for banks in receipt of TARP funds. In contrast, CEO bonuses in twenty-three financial services firms *not* receiving TARP funds fell by only 13 percent. CEO bonuses fell even less in a control group of nonfinancial firms. The evidence shows that the financial shock of 2008 had a large negative impact on the compensation received by CEOs. In addition, wealth from holding stock and options in their firms fell dramatically for CEOs of financial firms receiving TARP funds. Murphy (2009) finds that the average intrinsic value of in the money options fell by about 95 percent from $8,694,980 in 2007 to $428,880 in 2008 for CEOs of firms receiving TARP funds. In contrast, the intrinsic value of options decline by about 65 percent for CEOs of non-TARP financial firms, from $21,909,390 to $7,550,710. A similar pattern emerges for restricted stock. The value of restricted stock for CEOs of firms in receipt of TARP funds falls by about 80 percent between 2007 and 2008, whereas the value of restricted stock in firms not in receipt of TARP funds falls by about 43 percent. Murphy (2009, p. 6) concludes: "Given the penalties for poor performance inherent in both cash and equity incentive plans, there is nothing inherent in the current structure of compensation in financial service firms that lead to obvious incentives to take excessive risks." Core and Guay (2010b) also conduct a comparative analysis of CEO pay and incentives in the financial services industry relative to a matched sample of nonfinancial firms over the period 1993 to 2008. They find that trends in median total CEO pay for banks and nonfinancial firms are fairly highly correlated and find few persistent differences in CEO pay levels across the two groups of firms. Indeed, comparing the wealth incentives between banks and nonbanks, they find evidence that points to the bank sector having *fewer* performance and risk-taking incentives compared to nonbanks. Erkens, Hung, and Matos (2010) investigate the relation between corporate governance and firm performance from 2007 to 2008 using data on 296 financial firms from 30 countries. They found that firms with more independent boards and higher institutional ownership had worse stock returns during the crisis, attributed to the fact that firms with higher institutional ownership took more precrisis risk, leading to larger shareholder losses. In addition, the firms with more independent boards raised more equity capital during the crisis. This led to a wealth transfer from existing shareholders to debtholders. The authors conclude that their "findings cast doubt on whether regulatory changes that increase shareholder activism and monitoring by outside directors will be effective in reducing the consequences of future economic crises."

Conyon et al. (2010) provide further evidence on bank compensation, this time investigating both the United States and Europe for 2006 and 2008. Table 13.2 is based on their report. In Europe they find that median CEO bonuses declined by about 84 percent in banks compared to about 6 percent in nonbanks, between 2006 and 2008. In the United States, median CEO bonuses fell by about 97 percent in banks and only about 26 percent in nonbanks.[17] A similar pattern emerges for CEO wealth between 2006 and 2008. In Europe, median CEO wealth declined

Table 13.2. Comparison of 2006 and 2008 Bonuses and Year-End Wealth for CEOs of Banking and Nonbanking Firms.

	Europe		United States	
	Banks	Nonbanks	Banks	Nonbanks
Median bonuses (€000s)				
Number of CEOs	48	844	120	1306
2006	592.0	228.5	488.4	555.9
2008	96.3	214.5	14.5	409.1
Difference	−495.7	−14.0	−473.9	−146.8
	(−83.7%)	(−6.1%)	(−97%)	(−26.4%)
Median wealth (€000s)				
Number of CEOs	42	708	120	1301
2006	10,632.9	3,981.6	23,062.0	11,710.6
2008	5,757.6	2,258.4	5,653.1	5,233.3
Difference	−4,875.4	−1,723.2	−17,408.9	−6,477.3
	(−45.9%)	(−43.3%)	(−75.5%)	(−55.3%)

Notes: Derived from Conyon et al. (2010), table 4.4. CEO Wealth is the fiscal year-end value of the CEO's stock and restricted stock, plus the year-end intrinsic value of stock options. Data described in Conyon et al. (2010). The European data are from BoardEx and the U.S. data (including Black-Scholes values) are calculated based on year-end option holdings. "Bonuses include payouts from both annual and longer-term (non-equity-based) incentive plans. Monetary amounts are in 2008-constant Euros; US dollar-denominated data are converted to Euros using the 2008 year-end exchange rate (€1 = $1.3919)." Conyon et al. (2010).

by about 46 percent in banks compared to about 43 percent in nonbanks. In the United States, CEO wealth fell by about 75 percent in banks and approximately 55 percent in nonbanks. Conyon et al. (2010, p. 110) remark: "Overall, the results for both European and American banking CEOs are inconsistent with the idea that banking executives faced rewards for success but no real penalties for failure." The evidence is consistent with the hypothesis that bank CEOs with better ex ante incentives, namely, those aligning their interests with shareholders, faced significant penalties for poor performance, ex post.

The current empirical evidence suggests that compensation and incentives do not appear especially unusual in banks and financial institutions compared to nonbanks. Indeed, CEOs of banks suffered significant negative wealth effects following the financial crisis, along with executives at nonfinancial institutions. In addition, the current evidence suggests that incentive structures at banks did not lead to excessive risk taking by CEOs. If bank CEO incentives did not cause the financial crisis, what did? Conyon et al. (2010) speculate on myriad other potential candidate explanations including "social policies on home ownership, loose monetary policies, 'Too Big to Fail' guarantees, and poorly implemented financial innovations such as exotic mortgages, securitization, and collateralized debt obligations." Allen, Babus, and Carletti (2009) review the financial crisis, providing both theory and evidence. Incentive compensation as a cause of crises is conspicuously absent from their review. The authors state: "The first explanation of banking crises is that they are a panic. The second is that they are part of the business cycle." In addition, the financial crisis was characterized by severe liquidity problems in interbank markets and problems of contagion. Undoubtedly, the causes of the crises will be debated for years to come.

The Financial Crisis Inquiry Commission, 2011

The scale of the financial crisis prompted official enquiries into its causes and consequence. The remit of the U.S. Financial Crisis Inquiry Commission (FCIC, 2011) was to "examine the causes of the current financial and economic crisis in the United States" (FCIC, 2011, p. xi). The commission concluded that the "financial crisis was avoidable," noting that the crisis was promulgated by the actions, inactions, and mistakes of individuals in the financial system that failed to properly manage risk. The report is over 600 pages long, and contains 22 chapters and supporting material. There were ten members of the commission. It is noteworthy that six voted to accept the commission's report and four members dissented. The disagreement was serious enough for dissenting statements and reports to be issued. This suggests that it is very difficult to obtain unanimous or even consensus agreement about the primary causes of the crisis.

In the area of corporate governance, the FCIC asserted that "dramatic failures of corporate governance and risk management at many systemically important financial institutions were a key cause of this crisis." The commission was critical of the compensation practices, asserting that these led to perverse incentives and excessively risky behavior:

> The Compensation systems—designed in an environment of cheap money, intense competition, and light regulation—too often rewarded the quick deal, the short-term gain—without proper consideration of long-term consequences. Often, those systems encouraged the big bet—where the payoff on the upside could be huge and the downside limited. This was the case up and down the line—from the corporate boardroom to the mortgage broker on the street. (FCIC, 2011, p. xix)

The commission's conclusions were based largely on observing the levels and properties of the compensation systems in place at many financial institutions, along with interviews with key individuals. First, the commission documented that compensation in financial institutions began to outstrip pay in nonfinancial institutions from about 1980 onward, and the gap between them steadily increased up to 2008. As noted, Cai et al. (2010) also document that executive pay in the financial sector was greater than in nonfinancials, and the equity pay (such as options) was more prevalent. Second, the commission was critical of stock options and other performance-based compensation systems: "Stock options had potentially unlimited upside, while the downside was simply to receive nothing if the stock didn't rise to the predetermined price." Other pay mechanisms, such as tying compensation to earnings also provided (unintended) incentives for executives to focus on the short term. The commission says that these pay structures created incentives to increase risk and leverage to achieve higher returns and profits. However, the report asserts that problems with such pay structures were systemic and those involved were unable to change the underlying reward model. The commission's report cites Sandy Weill, former Citigroup CEO, as saying "I think if you look at the results of what happened on Wall Street, it became 'Well, this one's doing it, so how can I not do it, if I don't do it, then the people are going to leave my place and go some place else.'" Risk management "became less of an important function in a broad base of companies, I would guess" (FCIC, 2011, pp. 63–64).

The FCIC is wide-ranging and documents many potential causes. Accordingly, it is difficult to apportion precisely how much weight to give the problems caused by executive and banker compensation in contributing to the crisis. Moreover, in dissenting statements, four of the ten commissioners disagreed with significant aspects of the commission's analysis. Hennessey, Holtz-Eakin, and Thomas (2011, pp. 413–439) ascribed the major causes of the crisis to ten separate factors. These include a credit bubble, a housing bubble, nontraditional mortgages, credit rating and securitization, financial institutions correlated risk, leverage and liquidity risk, risks of contagion, common macroeconomic shocks, a severe financial shock, and the financial shock causing an associated economic crisis in the real economy. These authors do not see compensation arrangements as a prime cause of the crisis.

Dodd-Frank Act, 2010

In the wake of the financial crisis, President Obama signed into law the Dodd-Frank Wall Street Reform and Consumer Protection Act, also known as the Dodd-Frank Act, on July 21, 2010.[18] The act extends regulation in the financial and nonfinancial sectors. It has important sections relating to corporate governance, accountability, and executive compensation (Title IX, Subtitle E). The act is very detailed and runs over 800 pages.

The Dodd-Frank Act requires a regular shareholder vote on executive compensation at least once every three years (Section 951). The goal is to make executive compensation practices more accountable to shareholders. The Dodd-Frank Act requires enhanced transparency. Compensation committees must be independent, and the act outlines rules relating to the governance of external advisers, such as compensation consultants. Section 952 requires the members of the compensation committee to be independent, which takes into account factors such as the source of compensation received by the member of the board of directors, including any consulting, advisory, or other compensatory fee paid to the member of the board of directors. In addition, independence is assessed by whether a member of the board of directors is affiliated with the issuer, a subsidiary, or an affiliate of a subsidiary of the issuer. The goal is to improve the context of executive pay setting.

Section 953 of Dodd-Frank deals with enhanced compensation disclosure. The following new information is required to be disclosed by firms. First is the median of the annual total compensation of all employees of the firm, except the CEO. Second is the annual total compensation of the CEO, and third is the ratio of the amount employee compensation to the amount received by the CEO. These new information disclosure rules will give shareholders, investors, and policy makers more information about the distribution of pay within the firm. In addition, Dodd-Frank makes provision for the recovery of erroneously awarded compensation (Section 954), more disclosure regarding any employee or director hedging activity (Section 954), and enhanced compensation structure reporting (Section 956). This includes prohibiting incentive pay arrangements that encourage inappropriate risk taking by covered financial institutions. In summary, the Dodd-Frank Act significantly upgrades disclosure on executive compensation and empowers shareholders.

Conclusions

Executive compensation is a controversial subject attracting significant attention from the media, policy makers, and academics. For many years, commentators have highlighted the high levels of pay, asking whether CEOs were paid too much. There are two, essentially competing views about CEO pay. The managerial power view contends that CEOs are able to set their own pay in ways that lead to significant deviations from what is optimal from shareholder and society welfare. The alternative optimal contracting theory argues that CEO pay arrangements, though not always perfect, are determined by market forces. Pay is the outcome of the costs and benefits of contracting and arm's-length bargaining between boards and CEOs.

This chapter reviewed some contemporary themes in the economics of executive compensation. I considered the evolution of executive pay—CEO pay is made up of salaries, bonuses, stock options, restricted stock, and other benefits, such as pensions and perks. CEO pay has increased significantly over the past thirty or so years. The increase in pay from the 1980s onward in the United States was largely driven by the increased use of stock options. During this time, compensation contracts morphed and CEOs began holding more of their firm's common equity, or call options, on those securities. The level of pay is not the only factor to consider: the structure of compensation matters, too. Since the mid-1980s equity compensation became an increasingly important factor in CEO compensation contracts, leading to much more significant pay for performance. Historically, the issue for investors was the lack of pay-for-performance in executive pay contracts. The classic academic statement of this is Jensen and Murphy's (1990) study showing how little CEO pay varied with firm performance (value) in the United States. The use of stock options and other equity pay plans rectified this state of affairs.

Another section summarized some of the (many) reasons for the changes in CEO compensation. These included managerial power explanations and optimal contracting or market-based explanations. Attention was given to the importance of the pay-setting process, including the board of directors, compensation committees, and compensation consultants.

Set against the recent financial crisis, I consider the governance of executive pay at banks. The causes of the financial and economic crisis are many. Several commentators pointed to executive compensation contracts as the source of excessive risk taking. The nascent empirical evidence for this conjecture is mixed, and other causes centering on housing bubbles, monetary policy, credit policies, and financial market contagion are also important to consider.

Undoubtedly, the issue of executive compensation will remain at the forefront of corporate governance debates for the foreseeable future. The recent financial crisis has reignited interest in executive pay regulation, enhanced disclosure rules, and legislation on a scale not anticipated only a few years ago. The issue of executive pay is also likely to become more global. Criticism of executive pay in several European counties has increased, and proposals for legislation and regulation of CEO pay are openly advocated. Future research designed to provide a better understanding the operation of executive labor market, and especially how CEO compensation allocates scarce talent, is critical.

NOTES

1. *The Economist* magazine sponsored a debate with the following proposition: "This house believes that on the whole, senior executives are worth what they are paid." The result was that 78 percent were against the motion. http://www.economist.com/debate/debates/archive/page:2 (October 2009). Popular opinion, at least according *The Economist*'s survey, is highly dissatisfied with executive pay outcomes.
2. See the seminal contribution of Mirrlees (1976). Holmstrom (1982) and Laffont and Martimort (1982) describe contributions to agency theory. Further theory and evidence on the risk-incentive trade-off is provided in Prendergast (2002).
3. There are, in fact, very few women CEOs (Bertrand, 2009; Bertrand and Hallock, 2001).
4. A little more formally, the bonus, B, can be written as $B = 0$ if $0 < P < P^{min}$, $B = a + bP$ if $P^{min} < P < P^{max}$, and $B = B^{max}$ if $P > P^{max}$, where B is the bonus payment, P is a typically an accounting performance variable, and the superscripts *max* and *min*

are, respectively, the maximum and minimum. The constant term *a* is the minimum bonus and *b* is the incentive parameter. A bonus planner can modify incentives and CEO behavior by adjusting each of these. A higher base bonus is represented by increasing *a* or greater pay-for-performance by increasing *b*.

5. In this example, suppose $S = X = \$50$, stock volatility is 30 percent, the annual risk-free interest rate is 3.0%, the option maturity term is set at 7 years, and the stock's dividend yield is 2.5 percent. Inserting this information into the modified Black-Scholes pricing formula gives a value of $13.46.
6. To see this, if one holds constant all the input variables in the pricing equation and changes *S* and *X* (always setting $S = X$ because the option is granted at the money), then the ratio of the Black-Scholes estimate to the face value (*S*) is constant. The values of the other variables correspond to terms that might be found in an option contract given to an executive.
7. The option delta (or hedge ratio) is the derivative of Black-Scholes call option value with respect to the asset price. It can be thought of as a weight, varying between zero and one, reflecting the likelihood that the stock option will end up in the money.
8. This also raises other challenges. A complete picture of executive incentives would require full information of CEO wealth. But the benefits of providing this information publicly to investors, say, in the proxy statements, need to be set against the costs in terms of the CEOs' legitimate rights to privacy in financial matters.
9. This section draws on Conyon (2006).
10. Crystal (1991, p. 9) remarks: "Executive compensation in the United States did not go out of control simply through some random process; it went out of control because of the actions—or inactions—of a number of parties. The first culprits in what will be a litany of culprits are compensation consultants."
11. For example, business schools are populated with MBA students with goals of competing for such positions.
12. This section draws on my joint research with Kevin Murphy, Nuno Fernandes, Miguel Ferreira, and Pedro Matos; see Conyon et al. (2010).
13. New evidence in this area is beginning to become available. Important sources of information on the financial crisis, especially in relation to corporate governance, include the Social Science Research Network (http://www.ssrn.com) and the European Corporate Governance Institute (http://www.ecgi.org/wp/index.php).
14. Results varied by political preferences. About 75 percent of Democrats were in favor of government action on bank pay, compared to 37 percent of Republicans in favor. Source: http://media.economist.com/images/pdf/Toplines20091030.pdf.
15. A similar negative correlation is documented between measures of accounting performance and incentives. Incentives are defined as the dollar change in the value of the CEO's equity portfolio for a percentage change in the stock price; or alternatively as the percentage ownership of shares and options.
16. Fahlenbrach and Stulz (2011) also investigate whether alternative measures of incentives are correlated with inferior long-term performance. They find no relation between financial performance and CEO equity risk, or between bank performance and the ratio of bonuses to cash compensation. Equity risk was measured in two ways: (1) as the dollar change in the value of the CEOs equity portfolio for a percentage change in the volatility of the option, and (2) the percentage change in equity values for a percentage change in the stock price volatility. The authors also find no difference in their general pattern of empirical results between firms receiving funding from TARP and other non-TARP firms.

17. A similar pattern emerges for the averages, too. In Europe, average CEO bonuses fell about 30 percent in banks and 16 percent in nonbanks, whereas in the United States, average bonuses fell by about 70 percent in banks and 15 percent in nonbanks.
18. Dodd-Frank Wall Street Reform and Consumer Protection Act, Pub.L. No. 111-203, 124 Stat. 1376 (2010).

References

Adams, Renee B. "Governance and the Financial Crisis." Finance Working Paper no. 248/2009, ECGI, 2009.

Adams, Renee B. "Corporate Governance: Governance of Banking Institutions." In *Corporate Governance: A Synthesis of Theory, Research and Practice*, ed. Kent Baker and Ronald Anderson, 451–467. Hoboken, N.J.: Wiley, 2010.

Allen, Franklin, Ana Babus, and Elena Carletti. "Financial Crises: Theory and Evidence." *Annual Review of Financial Economics* 1 (Oct. 2009): 97–116.

Anderson, Ronald C., and John M. Bizjak. "An Empirical Examination of the Role of the CEO and the Compensation Committee in Structuring Executive Pay." *Journal of Banking and Finance* 27 (July 2003): 1323–1348.

Baker, George P., Kevin J. Murphy, and Michael C. Jensen. "Compensation and Incentives: Practice vs. Theory." *Journal of Finance* 43 (July 1988): 593–616.

Bebchuk, Lucian A., and Jesse M. Fried. *Pay without Performance: The Unfulfilled Promise of Executive Remuneration*. Cambridge, Mass.: Harvard University Press, 2004.

Bebchuk, Lucian A., and Jesse M. Fried. "Pay without Performance: Overview of the Issues." (*Journal of Corporation Law* 30 (2005): 647–673.

Bebchuk, Lucian A., and Holger Spamann. "Regulating Bankers' Pay." *Georgetown Law Journal* (Jan. 2010): 247–287.

Bebchuk, Lucian A., and Michael S. Weisbach. "The State of Corporate Governance Research." *Review of Financial Studies* 23 (March 2010): 939–961.

Bechmann, Ken L., and Johannes Raaballe. "Bad Corporate Governance and Powerful CEOs in Banks: Poor Performance, Excessive Risk-Taking, and a Misuse of Incentive-Based Compensation." Working Paper, Copenhagen Business School and University of Aarhus, 2009.

Bell, Brian, and John Van Reenen. "Bankers Pay and Extreme Wage Inequality in the UK." Center for Economic Performance Discussion Paper, London, April 2010.

Bender, Ruth. "How Executive Directors' Remuneration Is Determined in Two FTSE 350 Utilities." *Corporate Governance: An International Review* 11 (July 2003): 206–217.

Bertrand, Marianne. "CEOs." *Annual Review of Economics* 1 (Sept. 2009): 121–150.

Bertrand, Marianne, and Kevin F. Hallock. "The Gender Gap in Top Corporate Jobs." *Industrial and Labor Relations Review* 55 (Oct. 2001): 3–21.

Bhagat, Sanjai, and Brian Bolton. "Bank Executive Compensation and Capital Requirements Reform." Working Paper, University of Colorado, 2011.

Black, Fischer, and Myron Scholes. "The Pricing of Options and Corporate Liabilities." *Journal of Political Economy* 81 (May–June 1973): 637–654.

Cadman, Brian, Mary Ellen Carter, and Stephen Hillegeist. "The Incentives of Compensation Consultants and CEO Pay." *Journal of Accounting and Economics* 49 (April 2010): 263–280.

Cai, Jian, Kent Cherny, and Todd Milbourn. *Compensation and Risk Incentives in Banking and Finance*. Economic Commentary, Federal Reserve Bank of Cleveland, Sept. 2010. http://www.clevelandfed.org/research/commentary/2010/2010-13.cfm.

Cheng, Ing-Haw, Harrison Hong, and Jose Scheinkman. "Yesterday's Heroes: Compensation and Creative Risk-Taking." Working Paper, Princeton University, 2009. http://papers.ssrn.com/sol3/papers.cfm?abstract_id=1502762.

Conyon, Martin J. "Executive Compensation and Incentives." *Academy of Management Perspectives* 20 (2006): 25–44.

Conyon, Martin J., John E. Core, and Wayne R. Guay. "Are US CEOs Paid More than UK CEOS? Inferences from Risk-Adjusted Pay." *Review of Financial Studies* 24 (Feb. 2011): 402–438.

Conyon, Martin, J., Nuno Fernandes, Miguel A. Ferreira, Pedro Matos, Kevin J. Murphy. *The Executive Compensation Controversy: A Transatlantic Analysis*. Presentation at "Productivity, Profits and Pay," Fondazione Rodolfo DeBenedetti, May 2010. http://www.frdb.org/scheda.php?id=1&doc_pk=11042.

Conyon, Martin J., and Lerong He. "Compensation Committees and CEO Compensation Incentives in U.S. Entrepreneurial Firms." *Journal of Management Accounting Research* 16 (2004): 35–56.

Conyon, Martin J., and Kevin J. Murphy. "The Prince and the Pauper? CEO Pay in the US and UK." *Economic Journal* 110 (Nov. 2000): F640–F671.

Conyon, Martin J., and Simon Peck. "Board Control, Remuneration Committees, and Top Management Compensation." *Academy of Management Journal* 41 (April 1998):146–157.

Conyon, Martin J., Simon I. Peck, and Graham V. Sadler. "Compensation Consultants and Executive Pay: Evidence from the United States and the United Kingdom." *Academy of Management Perspectives* 23 (2009): 43–55.

Core, John E., and Wayne R. Guay. "The Use of Equity Grants to Manage Optimal Equity Incentives." *Journal of Accounting and Economics* 28 (Dec. 1999): 151–184.

Core, John E., and Wayne R. Guay. "Estimating the Value of Employee Stock Option Portfolios and Their Sensitivities to Price and Volatility." *Journal of Accounting Research* 40 (June 2002): 613–630.

Core, John E., and Wayne R. Guay. "Is CEO Pay Too High and Are Incentives Too Low? A Wealth-Based Contracting Framework." *Academy of Management Perspectives* 24 (Feb. 2010a): 5–19.

Core, John E., and Wayne R. Guay. "Is There a Case for Regulating Executive Pay in the Financial Services Industry?" Working Paper, Wharton School, Jan. 2010b. http://ssrn.com/abstract=1544104.

Core, John E., Wayne R. Guay, and David F. Larcker. "Executive Equity Compensation and Incentives: A Survey." *Federal Reserve Bank of New York Economic Policy Review* 9 (April 2003): 27–44.

Core, John E., Wayne R. Guay, and Randall S. Thomas. "Is U.S. CEO Compensation Inefficient Pay without Performance?" *Michigan Law Review* 103 (May 2005): 1142–1185.

Core, John E., Robert W. Holthausen, and David F. Larcker. "Corporate Governance, Chief Executive Officer Compensation, and Firm Performance." *Journal of Financial Economics* 51 (March 1999): 371–406.

Crystal, Graef S. "Why CEO Compensation Is So High?" *California Management Review* 34 (1991): 9–29.

Cuomo, Andrew M. *No Rhyme or Reason: The "Heads I Win, Tails You Lose" Bank Bonus Culture*. State of New York, 2009. http://www.ag.ny.gov/media_center/2009/july/pdfs/Bonus%20Report%20Final%207.30.09.pdf.

Daily, Catherine M., Jonathan L. Johnson, Alan E. Ellstrand, and Dan R. Dalton. "Compensation Committee Composition as a Determinant of CEO Compensation." *Academy of Management Journal* 41 (April 1998): 209–220.

Erkens, David, Mingyi Hung, and Pedro P. Matos. "Corporate Governance in the 2007–2008 Financial Crisis: Evidence from Financial Institutions Worldwide," Finance Working Paper no. 249/2009, ECGI, Sept. 2010. http://ssrn.com/abstract=1397685.
Fahlenbrach, Rüdiger, and René M. Stulz. "Bank CEO Incentives and the Credit Crisis." *Journal of Financial Economics* 99 (Jan. 2011): 11–26.
FCIC. The Financial Crisis Inquiry Commission Report. 2011. http://www.fcic.gov/report.
Fernandes, Nuno G., Migueal A. Ferreira, Pedro P. Matos, and Kevin J. Murphy. *The Pay Divide: (Why) Are U.S. Top Executives Paid More?* Finance Working Paper no. 255/2009, ECGI, 2009. http://ssrn.com/abstract=1341639.
Frydman, Carola, and Raven E. Saks. "Executive Compensation: A New View from a Long-Term Perspective, 1936–2005." *Review of Financial Studies* 23 (May 2010): 2099–2138.
Gabaix, Xavier, and Augustin Landier. "Why Has CEO Pay Increased so Much?" *Quarterly Journal of Economics* 123 (Feb. 2008): 49–100.
Gao, Huasheng. "Optimal Compensation Contracts When Managers Can Hedge." *Journal of Financial Economics* 97 (Aug. 2010): 218–238.
Gibbons, Robert, and Kevin J. Murphy. "Relative Performance Evaluation for Chief Executive Officers." *Industrial and Labor Relations Review* 43 (Feb. 1990): 30–51.
Gregory-Smith, Ian. "Chief Executive Pay and Non-Executive Director Independence in the UK: Optimal Contracting vs. Rent Extraction." Nottingham University Business School Research Paper no. 2009-02, 2009. http://ssrn.com/abstract=1345926.
Hall, Brian J., and Jeffrey B. Liebman. "Are CEOs Really Paid Like Bureaucrats?" *Quarterly Journal of Economics* 113 (Aug. 1998): 653–691.
Hennessey, Keith, Douglas Holtz-Eakin, and Bill Thomas. The Financial Crisis Inquiry Report (FCIC) Dissenting Report. http://www.fcic.gov/report.
Himmelberg, Charles P., and R. Glenn Hubbard. "Incentive Pay and the Market for CEOs: An Analysis of Pay-for-Performance Sensitivity." Working Paper, Columbia University, March 2000.
Holmstrom, Bengt. "Moral Hazard and Observability." *Bell Journal of Economics* 10 (Spring 1979): 74–91.
Holmstrom, Bengt. "Moral Hazard in Teams." *Bell Journal of Economics* 13 (Autumn 1982): 324–340.
Jensen, Michael C., and William H. Meckling. "Theory of the Firm: Managerial Behavior, Agency Costs, and Ownership Structure." *Journal of Financial Economics* 3 (1976): 305–360.
Jensen, Michael C, and Kevin J. Murphy. "Performance Pay and Top-Management Incentives." *Journal of Political Economy* 98 (April 1990): 225–264.
Kaplan, Steven N. "Are U.S. CEOs Overpaid?" *Academy of Management Perspectives* 22 (May 2008): 5–20.
Kaplan, Steven N., and Joshua Rauh. "Wall Street and Main Street: What Contributes to the Rise in the Highest Incomes?" *Review of Financial Studies* 23 (March 2010): 1004–1050.
Laffont, Jean-Jacques, and David Martimort. *The Theory of Incentives: The Principal-Agent Model.* Princeton, N.J.: Princeton University Press, 2002.
Lambert, Richard, and David Larcker. "How Employees Value (Often Incorrectly) Their Stock Options." Knowledge@Wharton, 2001. http://knowledge.wharton.upenn.edu/article.cfm?articleid=363.
Merton, Robert C. "Theory of Rational Option Pricing." *Bell Journal of Economics and Management Science* 4 (Spring 1973): 141–183.
Mirrlees, James A. "The Optimal Structure of Incentives and Authority within an Organization." *Bell Journal of Economics* 7 (Spring 1976): 105–131.

Murphy, Kevin J. "Executive Compensation." In *Handbook of Labor Economics*, vol. 3, ed. Orley Ashenfelter and David Card, 2485–2563. Amsterdam: North-Holland, 1999.

Murphy, Kevin J. "Explaining Executive Compensation: Managerial Power versus the Perceived Cost of Stock Options." *University of Chicago Law Review* 69 (Summer 2002): 847–869.

Murphy, Kevin J. "Compensation Structure and Systemic Risk." Marshall School of Business Working Paper no. FBE 34-09, June 2009. http://ssrn.com/abstract=1461944.

Murphy, Kevin J., and Tatiana Sandino. "Executive Pay and 'Independent' Compensation Consultants." *Journal of Accounting and Economics* 49 (April 2010): 247–262.

Murphy, Kevin J., and Ján Zábojnik. "CEO Pay and Appointments: A Market-Based Explanation for Recent Trends." *American Economic Review* 94 (May 2004): 192–196.

Prendergast, Canice. "The Tenuous Trade-off between Risk and Incentives." *Journal of Political Economy* 110 (Oct. 2002): 1071–1102.

Rajan, Raghuram G., and Julie Wulf. "Are Perks Purely Managerial Excess?" *Journal of Financial Economics* 79 (Jan. 2006): 1–33.

Waxman, Henry. "Executive Pay: Conflicts of Interest among Compensation Consultants." Washington, D.C.: U.S. House of Representatives, Committee on Oversight and Government Reform Majority Staff, 2007.

Yermack, David. "Flights of Fancy: Corporate Jets, CEO Perquisites, and Inferior Shareholder Returns." *Journal of Financial Economics* 80 (April 2006): 211–242.

CHAPTER 14

BUBBLES IN ASSET PRICES

BURTON G. MALKIEL

THE severe worldwide recession of 2008–2009 has focused attention on the role of asset-price bubbles in exacerbating economic instability in capitalist economies. The boom in house prices in the United States from 2000 through 2006 is a case in point. According to the Case-Shiller twenty-city index, the inflation-adjusted price of a median-sized house in the United States doubled over the period 2000–2006. House prices rose far more than the underlying fundamental drivers of home prices, such as family income and rents. The bursting of the bubble was followed by a sharp rise in foreclosures and massive declines in the value of mortgage-backed securities and a variety of derivatives tied to these securities. The collapse of these prices led to the weakening, and in some cases collapse, of major financial institutions around the world and contributed to one of the most serious recessions in the United States in the entire post–World War II period.

The housing bubble is the most recent example of the asset-price bubbles that have often afflicted capitalist economies. Sharp increases in asset prices have frequently led to crashes and subsequent sharp declines in economic activity. Many economists have argued, controversially, that central banks should adjust their policy instruments to account not only for their forecasts of future inflation and the gap between actual and potential output but for asset prices as well.[1]

This chapter addresses three topics. First, I describe what economists mean when they use the term "bubble," and I contrast the behavioral finance view of asset pricing with the efficient market paradigm in an attempt to understand why bubbles might persist and why they may not be arbitraged away.

Second, I review some major historical examples of asset-price bubbles as well as the (minority) view that they may not have been bubbles at all. I also examine the corresponding changes in real economic activity that have followed the bursting of such bubbles.

Finally, I examine the most hotly debated aspect of any discussion of asset-price bubbles: what, if anything, should policy makers do about them? Should they react to sharp increases in asset prices that they deem to be unrelated to "fundamentals"? Should they take the view that they know more than the market does? Should they recognize that asset-price bubbles are a periodic flaw of capitalism and conduct their policies so as to temper any developing excesses? Or should they focus solely on their primary targets of inflation and real economic activity? In my discussion I pay particular attention to bubbles that are associated with sharp increases in credit and leverage.

The Efficient Market Hypothesis

Throughout most of the second half of the twentieth century, the efficient market hypothesis (EMH) was broadly accepted by financial economists. Indeed, during the 1970s, Michael Jensen (1978) called the EMH "the best established empirical fact in economics." Though the hypothesis was never fully accepted by practicing security analysts, even professional portfolio managers recognized how difficult it was to outperform the broad stock market indexes. As a result, the investment strategy of indexing—simply buying and holding all the stocks in the entire market in proportion to their capitalization weighting—became increasingly popular, especially among institutional portfolio managers.

According to the EMH, when information arises about an individual stock or about the stock market as a whole, investors act on that information without delay, causing the price of each stock to adjust so that it reflects completely all that is known about its future prospects. Thus, one stock is likely to be just as good a buy as another (adjusted for risk), and it will be pointless to attempt to buy "undervalued" stocks or sell "overvalued" ones in forming an actively managed equity portfolio that will outperform the market on a risk-adjusted basis.

Similarly, any information that is contained in the past history of stock prices will be fully reflected in current prices. In an efficient market, no arbitrage opportunities are possible. Although some investors may not be informed about the news and other investors may not behave rationally, the EMH holds that there are a sufficient number of well-financed, rational, profit-seeking traders in the market to ensure that no profitable arbitrage opportunities remain unexploited. Stock prices will change when new information arises, but the generation of true "news" is unpredictable. Hence, stock price changes will be unpredictable and will develop over time, much like a random walk. Moreover, stock prices at any time will reflect the best possible estimates regarding the future prospects of each company. Hence, stock markets will give correct signals to capital markets to guide the efficient allocation of capital.

The EMH does not assert that the current tableau of stock prices will prove to have been correct when viewed in hindsight. Stock markets can and do make mistakes. Even in efficient markets, we must recognize that today's stock price can only be estimated by calculating the discounted present value of all cash flows expected in the future. Such flows can only be estimated with considerable imprecision. Thus, many believers in market efficiency may not accept the proposition that bubbles can exist, even when subsequent events demonstrate quite clearly that market prices turned out to be "incorrect" or "mispriced" by a substantial margin.

The Role of Financial Markets in Capitalist Economies

Efficiently priced financial markets are essential for the smooth functioning of capitalist economies. Firms need permanent financing for their long-run real investment needs. Most providers of capital funds have financial investment horizons that are considerably shorter. Individuals make financial investments for limited time periods, expecting to use the funds for large future expenditures or to provide resources during retirement. Similarly, institutions tend to have limited investment horizons. For example, pension funds face a set of firm payment obligations at specific dates in the future. Securities markets can satisfy the objectives of both the users and providers of financial capital by what William Baumol (1965) has called "an act of magic." When firms issue either long-term bonds or permanent equity capital, these securities trade in the capital markets and provide liquidity for the buyers. Thus, common stocks can provide permanent capital for businesses while at the same time providing financial investment instruments that can be converted into cash on short notice. By imparting a measure of liquidity to claims against long-term investments, markets can lower the cost to the firm of acquiring capital funds. If stock markets are not functioning efficiently, however, they will be neither an effective medium for financial investment nor an attractive source of capital.

The financial markets also play an essential role in allocating a nation's capital resources among competing uses. The efficiency of these markets thus influences the efficiency and growth potential of the economy itself. But stock markets must provide accurate signals to firms and potential investors. The market will be an efficient allocator only if stocks are valued properly as the present value of the expected future earnings of companies, as determined by the investment opportunities available to them.

Stock prices should be more favorable for well-run firms with very attractive real investment opportunities, making it easier for them to raise equity capital. Alternatively, firms that have been poorly run should be punished by the stock market. This will facilitate the development of a market for corporate control. If the stock market correctly disciplines the firms that are inefficient and unprofitable, opportunities will arise for more competent managers to make a tender offer for the firm at its low stock price and take over its assets and operations. Such corporate takeovers can benefit the new management and also lead to a more optimal allocation of the economy's resources. In sum, efficiently priced stocks are critical if markets are to be effective resource allocators. The existence of bubbles, on the other hand, interferes with the ability of the capital markets to help ensure an efficient allocation of an economy's resources.

Bubbles in Asset Prices

An asset-price bubble—if one exists—represents a mispricing of asset values relative to prices that would be consistent with the existence of efficient markets. Bubbles are typically associated with substantial and long-lasting divergences of asset prices from valuations that would be determined from the rational expectation of the present value of the cash flows from the asset(s). Bubbles are therefore associated with some form of irrationality.

There are discussions in the literature of so-called rational bubbles that result from the possibility that expectations of rising prices can be self-fulfilling.[2] But such bubbles require the unrealistic assumption that there is no upper limit to the size of the bubble. In contrast, the bubbles considered here rest on the possibility of heterogeneous beliefs and the existence of market participants who can be considered behavioral traders. The insights of behavioral finance are therefore helpful in informing our understanding of how these bubbles might arise and how they propagate.

Bubbles often start with some exogenous factor that can be interpreted rationally as presenting large future prospects for profit. In England in the early 1700s, it was the formation of the promising new corporation the South Sea Company and the rise of its stock price. The wave of new companies that followed was expected to provide profitable investment outlets for individual savings. In the United States during the late 1990s, it was the promise of the Internet, which was expected to revolutionize the way consumers obtained information and purchased goods and services. The generation of sharply rising asset prices that followed, however, seemed to have more to do with the behavioral biases emphasized by scholars such as Shiller (2000, 2003).

Tversky and Kahneman (1981) argued that people forming subjective judgments have a tendency to disregard base probabilities and make judgments solely in terms of observed similarities to familiar patterns. Thus, investors may expect past price increases to continue even if they know from past experience that all skyrocketing stock markets eventually succumb to the laws of gravity. Investors also tend to enjoy the self-esteem that comes from having invested early in some "new era" phenomenon, and they are overconfident of their ability to predict the future.

Shiller (2000) emphasized the role of "feedback loops" in the propagation of bubbles. Price increases for an asset lead to greater investor enthusiasm, which then leads to increased demand for the asset, and therefore to further price increases. The very observation of past price increases alters the subjective judgment of investors and reinforces their belief that the price increases will continue. The news media play a prominent role in increasing the optimism of investors. The media are, in Shiller's view, "generators of attention cascades." One news story begets another, and the price increases themselves (whether of common stocks or single-family houses) appear to justify the superficially plausible story that started the rise in the price of the asset(s). According to Shiller, bubbles are inherently a social phenomenon. A feedback mechanism generates continuing rises in prices and an interaction back to the conventional wisdom that started the process. The bubble itself becomes the main topic of social conversation, and stories abound about certain individuals who have become wealthy from the price increases. As the economic historian Charles Kindleberger has stated, "There is nothing so disturbing to one's well-being and judgment as to see a friend get rich."[3]

The question naturally arises why the arbitrage mechanism of the EMH doesn't prick the bubble as it continues to inflate. Enormous profit opportunities were certainly achievable during the Internet bubble for speculators who correctly judged that the prices of many technology stocks were too high. But the kind of arbitrage that would have been necessary was sometimes difficult to effect and, in any event, was very risky. There appear to be considerable "limits to arbitrage."[4] For example, in one celebrated case during the Internet bubble, the market price of Palm Inc. (makers of the PalmPilot) stock (which was 95 percent owned by the company 3Com) implied a total capitalization considerably greater than that of its parent, suggesting that the rest of 3Com's business had a negative value. But the arbitrage (sell Palm stock short and buy 3Com stock) could not be achieved because it was impossible to borrow Palm stock to accomplish the short sale.

Arbitrage is also risky; one can never be sure when the bubble will burst. The mantra of hedge fund managers (the natural arbitragers) in the United States was "markets can remain irrational much longer than we can remain solvent." Moreover, some arbitragers may recognize that a bubble exists but are unable to synchronize their strategies to take advantage of it.[5] They might prefer to ride the bubble for as long as possible. Indeed, one empirical study by Brunnermeier and Nagel (2004) found that rather than shorting Internet stocks, hedge funds were actually buying them during the late 1990s. Hedge funds were embarking on a strategy of anticipating that the momentum of the price increases would continue and thus were contributing to the mispricing rather than trading against it.

Some Putative Bubbles

Here I describe a sample of some of the classic bubbles that are generally believed to illustrate the occasional irrationality of the speculative markets that are an integral part of capitalist market systems.

The Tulip Bulb Craze

The classic historical bubble had nothing to do with common stocks or real estate; it was a speculative mania involving tulip bulbs.[6] Although tulip bulbs had been popular in Holland for years, the frenzy erupted when some bulbs became infected with a nonfatal virus that produced rather bizarre contrasting colored stripes. The Dutch valued these infected bulbs highly, and the more bizarre the bulb, the greater the price it fetched in the market. As prices rose, people began to view tulip bulbs as sound investments, and prices rose even further, inducing more investors to enter the market. Charles Mackay (1841), who chronicled the events in *Extraordinary Popular Delusions and the Madness of Crowds*, noted that the ordinary industry of the country was dropped in favor of speculation in tulip bulbs: "Nobles, citizens, farmers, mechanics, seamen, footmen, maid-servants, even chimney sweeps and old clothes women dabbled in tulips." The feedback mechanism was in full swing. Everyone imagined that the passion for tulips would last forever and that buyers from all over the world would come to Holland and pay whatever prices were asked for them.

At the height of the bubble, in early 1637, a single rare bulb sold for an amount equivalent to the price of a nobleman's castle. Eventually, as happens in all speculative crazes, prices got so high that some people decided they would be prudent and sell their bulbs. Soon others followed suit. The process continued in a negative feedback loop; bulb deflation grew at an increasingly rapid pace, and in no time at all, panic reigned. Most bulbs became almost worthless, selling for no more than the price of a common onion. According to Mackay, the episode was followed by a severe decline in economic activity from which it took many years to recover.

The popular account of the bubble is not without controversy, however. The economist Peter Garber (1990, 2000) has suggested that tulip bulb pricing in seventeenth-century Holland was far more rational than was commonly believed. The *Semper augustus*, for example, was a particularly rare and beautiful bulb and, as Garber reveals, was valued greatly even in the years before the tulip mania. Moreover, Garber's research indicates that rare individual bulbs commanded high prices even after the general collapse of bulb prices, albeit at levels that were only a fraction of their peak prices. But Garber can find no rational explanation for such phenomena as a twentyfold increase in tulip bulb prices during January 1637, followed by an even larger decline in prices in February.

The South Sea Bubble

The next example took place in England three-quarters of a century later. Established in 1711, the South Sea Company helped restore faith in the government's credit worthiness by purchasing £10 million of government bonds. As a reward, the company was given a monopoly over all trade to the South Seas. There was great enthusiasm over the profits that might be made from trade with the New World, especially after the war between England and Spain ended. As word spread among investors about the fortunes to be made, the stock of the South Sea Company soared almost tenfold. The speculative craze was in full bloom.

Though the bubble started with one particular stock, it quickly spread to other enterprises. Investors looked for other new ventures where they could get in on the ground floor. Just as speculators today search for the next Google, in England in the 1700s they looked for the next South Sea Company. Promoters obliged by organizing and bringing to the market a flood of new issues to meet the insatiable craving for investment.

As the days passed, new financing proposals ranged from ingenious to absurd—from importing a large number of jackasses from Spain to a new offering of a machine gun company that promised to revolutionize the art of war. The machines could discharge both round bullets (to be used against Christians) and square ones (to be used against infidels). The prize, however, must surely go to the promoter who started "a company for carrying on the undertaking of great advantage, but nobody to know what it is."

As in all speculative manias, eventually the bubble popped, and investors suffered massive losses in most of the new issues of the period (see figure 14.1). Big

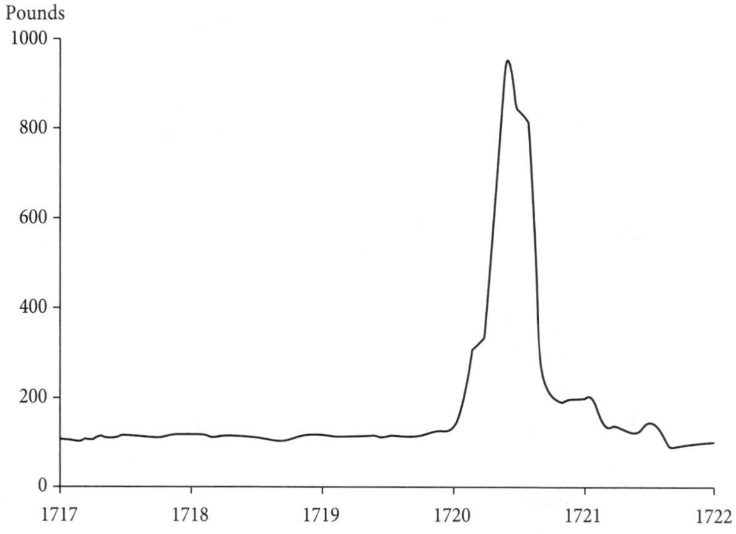

Figure 14.1. British South Sea Company Stock Price, 1717–1722
Source: Larry Neal, The Rise of Financial Capitalism (Cambridge University Press, 1990).

losers in the South Sea Bubble included Isaac Newton, who exclaimed, "I can calculate the motions of heavenly bodies, but not the madness of people."

The U.S. Stock Market Bubble and Crash, 1928–1932

Turning to more modern markets, the great bull market in the United States that collapsed in 1929 is generally regarded as one of the biggest stock market bubbles of all time. Beginning in 1928, stock market speculation became a national pastime. From early March 1928 through early September 1929, the market's percentage increase equaled that of the entire period from 1923 through early 1928. The price increases for the major industrial corporations sometimes reached 10 or 15 percent per day. A future of endless prosperity was taken for granted. The speculative spirit was at least as widespread as in the previous crazes and was certainly unrivaled in its intensity. More important, stock market speculation was central to the culture. John Brooks, in *Once in Golconda* (1991),[7] recounted the remarks of a British correspondent newly arrived in New York: "You could talk about Prohibition, or Hemingway, or air conditioning, or music, or horses, but in the end you had to talk about the stock market, and that was when the conversation became serious."

Unfortunately, there were hundreds of smiling operators only too glad to help keep the speculative spirit alive. Manipulation on the stock exchange set a new record for unscrupulousness. On September 3, 1929, the market averages reached a peak that was not surpassed for a quarter of a century. The "endless chain of prosperity" was soon to break. General business activity had already turned down months before. Prices drifted for the next day, and on the following day, September 5, the market suffered a sharp decline known as the "Babson Break," named in honor of Roger Babson, a financial adviser from Wellesley, Massachusetts. At a financial luncheon that day, Babson repeated his prediction that sooner or later "a crash is coming." At 2 P.M., when Babson's words were quoted on the Dow Jones news tape, the market went into a nosedive. It was a prophetic episode, and after the Babson Break, the possibility of a crash, which was entirely unthinkable a month before, suddenly became a common subject for discussion. Just as the amplification feedback loop made the bubble grow, the downward feedback loop was equally powerful.

Confidence faltered. September had many more bad days than good ones. At times the market fell sharply. Bankers and government officials assured the country that there was no cause for concern. Professor Irving Fisher of Yale, one of the leading economists of the time, offered his soon-to-be immortal opinion that stocks had reached what looked like a "permanently high plateau."

By Monday, October 21, the stage was set for a classic stock market break. The declines in stock prices had led to calls for more collateral from margin customers, who had purchased stocks with borrowed money. Unable or unwilling to meet the calls, these customers were forced to sell their holdings. This depressed prices and led to more margin calls and finally to a self-sustaining selling wave.

The volume of sales on the exchange soared to a new record on October 21, and prices declined sharply. The indomitable Fisher dismissed the decline as a "shaking out of the lunatic fringe that attempts to speculate on margin." He went on to say that prices of stocks during the boom had not caught up with their real value and would go higher. Among other things, the professor believed that the market had not yet reflected the beneficent effects of Prohibition, which had made the U.S. worker "more productive and dependable."

On October 24, later called Black Thursday, the market volume more than doubled its record earlier in the week, and many stocks dropped forty or fifty points (as much as 25 percent) during a couple of hours. The next day, President Herbert Hoover offered his famous diagnosis: "The fundamental business of the country...is on a sound and prosperous basis."

Tuesday, October 29, 1929, was among the most catastrophic days in the history of the New York Stock Exchange. Only October 19 and 20, 1987, rivaled in intensity the panic on the exchange. Compared with its high price one month earlier, even blue-chip General Electric had lost 60 percent of its value. By the time the decline ended in 1932, GE had lost 98 percent of its market value. The stock market crash was followed by the most devastating depression in the history of the country.

But the view that the stock market boom of the late 1920s was a bubble is not universally shared. Harold Bierman Jr., for example, in his book *The Great Myths of 1929* (1991), has suggested that without perfect foresight, stocks were not obviously overpriced in 1929, because it appeared that the economy would continue to prosper. After all, very intelligent people, such as Irving Fisher and John Maynard Keynes, believed that stocks were reasonably priced. Bierman argues that the extreme optimism undergirding the stock market might even have been justified had it not been for inappropriate monetary policies. The crash itself, in his view, was precipitated by the Federal Reserve Board's policy of raising interest rates to punish speculators. There are at least grains of truth in Bierman's arguments, and economists today often blame the severity of the 1930s depression on the Federal Reserve for allowing the money supply to decline sharply. Nevertheless, history teaches us that very sharp increases in stock prices are seldom followed by gradual return to relative price stability. Even if prosperity had continued into the 1930s, stock prices could never have sustained their advance of the late 1920s.

My own view is that the anomalous behavior of closed-end investment company shares provides clinching evidence of wide-scale stock market irrationality during the 1920s. The "fundamental" value of these closed-end funds consists of the market value of the securities they hold. In most periods since 1930, these funds have sold at discounts of about 20 percent from their asset values. From January to August 1929, however, the typical closed-end fund sold at a premium over net asset value of 50 percent. Moreover, the premiums for some of the best known funds, such as Goldman Sachs Trading and Tri-Continental, sold at up to two and a half times the value of their underlying assets. Clearly, irrational speculative enthusiasm drove the prices of these funds far above the value at which their individual security holdings could be purchased.

The Japanese Real Estate and Stock Market Bubble of the 1980s

In Japan during the 1980s, all asset prices rose rapidly. The Nikkei stock market index soared close to the 40,000 level, having risen almost 500 percent for the decade. At their peak in December 1989, Japanese stocks had a total market value of about $4 trillion, almost 1.5 times the value of all U.S. equities and close to 45 percent of the world's equity market capitalization.[8] Japanese stocks sold at more than 60 times earnings, almost 5 times book value, and more than 200 times dividends. In contrast, U.S. stocks sold at about fifteen times earnings, and London equities sold at twelve times earnings. The high prices of Japanese stocks were even more dramatic in a company-by-company comparison. The value of NTT, Japan's telephone giant, which was privatized during the boom, exceeded the value of AT&T, IBM, Exxon, General Electric, and General Motors put together. Dai Ichi Kangyo Bank sold at 56 times earning, whereas an equivalent U.S. bank, Citicorp, sold at 5.6 times earnings.

The boom in real estate prices was even more dramatic. From 1955 to 1990, the value of Japanese real estate increased more than seventy-five times. By 1990, the total value of all Japanese property was estimated at nearly $20 trillion—equal to more than 20 percent of the entire world's wealth and about double the total value of the world's stock markets. Although the United States was five times bigger than Japan in terms of physical acreage, Japan's property in 1990 was appraised to be worth five times as much as all U.S. property. Theoretically, the Japanese could have bought all the property in the United States by selling off metropolitan Tokyo. Just selling the Imperial Palace and its grounds at their appraised value would have raised enough cash to buy all of California.

As in the previous bubbles we have considered, the inflation of prices was a social phenomenon. Playing the stock market became a national preoccupation. It is said that in Britain there is a betting shop (or turf accountant) on every corner. In Japan, there was a stockbroker on every corner. The stock market was an integral part of the Japanese culture.

Figure 14.2 shows how the bubble represented a change in valuation metrics (illustrated by the price to book value ratios), rather than price increases generated by the fundamental growth in the value of the assets (or earnings) of Japanese corporations.

I consider shortly the issue of what response, if any, the monetary authorities should take if they recognize that a bubble is inflating. The experience of Japan is therefore relevant. The Japanese monetary authorities did believe that a dangerous bubble existed, and they decided to take deliberate action. The Bank of Japan judged that easy credit and a borrowing frenzy were underwriting an unsustainable rise in land and stock prices. So the central bank restricted credit and engineered a rise in interest rates. The hope was that further rises in property prices would be choked off and the stock market might be eased downward.

Interest rates, which had already been going up during 1989, rose sharply in 1990. But the stock market was not eased down; instead, it collapsed. It is not easy to let the air out of a bubble gradually. The fall was almost as extreme as the U.S. stock market crash of 1929 to 1932. The Nikkei stock market index reached a high of almost 40,000 on the last trading day of the 1980s. By mid-August 1992, the index had declined to 14,309, a drop of about 63 percent. In contrast, the Dow Jones Industrial Average fell 66 percent from December 1929 to its low in the summer of 1932 (although the decline was over 80 percent from the September 1929 level). As figure 14.2 shows, the decline reflected a return of price to book value relationships to those that were typical in the early 1980s.

The collapse of the bubble in Japan had profound effects on the financial system and the Japanese economy. Japanese commercial banks, life insurance companies, and even nonfinancial corporations had large stock and real estate holdings. The bursting of the bubble weakened the entire financial system and was followed by a severe recession that lasted into the next century.

The Internet Bubble

The biggest stock market bubble of all time burst in March 2000. During the next two and a half years, over $7 trillion of market value evaporated. Most bubbles have been associated with some new technology or with some new business opportunity (as when profitable new trade opportunities sparked the South Sea bubble). The Internet was associated with both: it represented a new technology, and it offered

Figure 14.2. The Japanese Stock Market Bubble. Japanese Stock Prices Relative to Book Values, 1980–2000

Source: Morgan Stanley Research and author's estimates.

new business opportunities that promised to revolutionize the way we live. The promise of the Internet generated both one of the largest creations and the largest destructions of wealth of all time.

There was such fascination with the Internet that companies that changed their names to include some Web orientation (such as .com or .net) doubled in price overnight. One new offering, VA Linux, rose over 730 percent from its issue price in its first day of trading. (By 2002, the stock traded at less than a dollar a share.) Investors were willing to throw their money at almost anything that claimed an Internet link. The volume of new issues during the period was unprecedented. As was the case at the time of the South Sea bubble, many companies that received financing were absurd. These ranged from a company called Digiscents (that offered a computer peripheral that would make websites smell) to ezboard.com, which produced Internet pages called toilet paper to help people "get the poop" on the Internet community. All became dot-com disasters.[9]

As in other bubbles, the media contributed to the sense of excitement. Across the world, health clubs, airports, bars, and restaurants were permanently tuned into financial news channels. While the bubble undoubtedly encouraged a large number of useful new technology start-ups, it also encouraged considerable misallocation of resources. Most of the new companies were not viable, even those that were engaged in considerable overinvestment. Enough long-distance fiber optic cable was laid to circle the Earth 1,500 times. About $1 trillion was poured into telecom investments during the bubble. The dot-com bust also led to a recession in economic activity, albeit one that was relatively short and mild.

The Great Real Estate and Leverage Bubble of 2007

The last bubble I consider is the recent real estate and leverage bubble that originated in the United States. The bubble was associated with a fundamental change in the way the U.S. banking system operated.

Under the old system, which might be called the originate-and-hold system of banking, banking institutions would make mortgage loans to individual homeowners and then keep those loans as assets on their books. During the 2000s, that system changed to what might be called an originate-and-distribute system of making mortgage loans (as well as other kinds of loans). Banks would continue to originate mortgage loans but would hold them for only a brief period of time, after which they would be sold to an investment banking institution, which would package the mortgages into mortgage-backed securities. The mortgage-backed securities would be sliced into various "tranches." The first (or senior) tranches would have first claims on principal and interest payments and the lower tranches would have only residual claims. Through this system, by a kind of alchemy, the investment banks would produce very highly rated securities on the senior tranches, even though the underlying mortgages might be of relatively low quality (so-called subprime mortgage loans). The system led to a deterioration in lending standards. If the originating institution was only holding the mortgage for a few days, the lending officers were far less careful to ensure the creditworthiness of the borrower of the mortgage debt instrument over the long term. As originators, banks were joined by other lenders, especially mortgage-finance companies.

At the same time that the private sector had devised ways to securitize mortgages, and thus bring a tremendous amount of new capital into the industry, the federal government was contributing as well. Government-sponsored enterprises (GSEs) such as the Federal National Mortgage Association (Fannie Mae) and the Federal Home Loan Mortgage Corporation (Freddie Mac) also securitized home loans and encouraged originators to make credit available to borrowers with less than perfect credit. Since the bonds of the GSEs had implicit government backing, they could continue to sell their mortgage-backed debt at relatively low interest rates.

The result of all of these changes was to make vast additional sums of money available for the purchase of housing. In addition, homeowners who already had first mortgages were encouraged to increase the size of their mortgages or take out second mortgages on their houses, thus increasing the amount of debt carried by consumers. It was said that consumers in the United States used their homes as an ATM. The investment banks and commercial banks themselves decided to eat their own cooking, holding considerable amounts of mortgaged-backed securities they had underwritten and increasing their leverage ratios. Investment banks, life insurance companies, and even commercial banks tended to carry a far lower equity cushion than in previous years with a correspondingly large increase in debt. Moreover, a substantial share of the debt was short-term rather than long-term, subjecting these institutions to the possibility that they would be unable to roll over their indebtedness during a time of crisis.

The lowered lending standards and the vast increase in the amount of funds available for mortgages led to an enormous bubble in the prices of single-family houses. As figure 14.3, based on the Case-Shiller home price index, indicates, the inflation-adjusted price of a typical single-family home was approximately the same in 1999 as it was in 1899. Between 2000 and 2006, however, inflation-adjusted home prices doubled.[10]

When the bubble burst, house prices began to plummet. By the middle of 2009, house prices had declined by over a third from their peak. As prices declined and many homeowners found that their houses were worth less than the amount of the money owed on their mortgage, defaults began to increase, and some homeowners simply returned the keys to their houses to the lenders and stopped servicing their loans. As defaults increased, the value of the vast amounts of mortgage-backed securities declined precipitously. Because these securities were held by highly leveraged institutions (which were holding long-term assets and financing themselves with short-term liabilities), a major panic ensued. With the exception of the U.S. Treasury securities market, all credit markets froze up and institutions became unable to roll over their short-term indebtedness. Only because of the provision of credit by the U.S. central bank was a collapse of the financial system averted. These mortgage-backed securities were sold throughout the world, thus weakening banking systems not only in the United States but in Europe, Asia, and Australia as well.

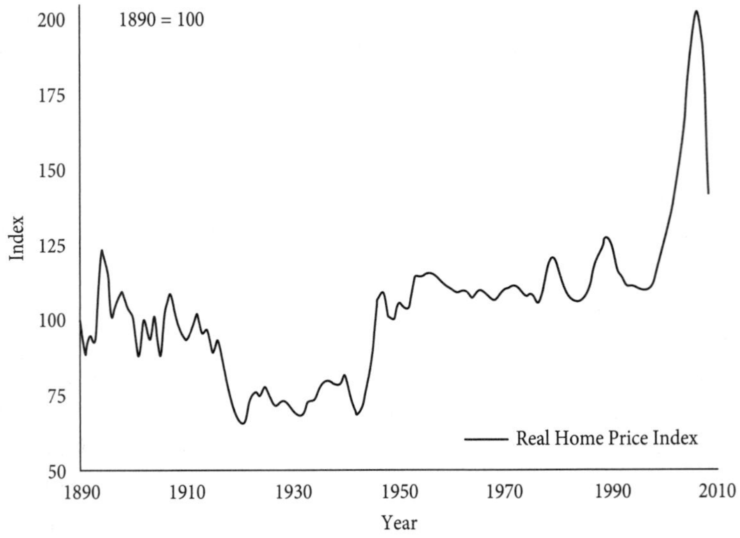

Figure 14.3. The Housing Bubble in the United States
Source: Case-Shiller Home Price Index

A severe worldwide recession followed, and unemployment rates soared, especially in the United States.

Bubbles and Economic Activity

This survey of historical bubbles makes clear that the bursting of bubbles has invariably been followed by severe disruptions in real economic activity. The fallout from asset-price bubbles has not been confined to speculators. Bubbles are particularly dangerous when they are associated with a credit boom and widespread increases in leverage for both consumers and financial institutions.

The experience of the United States during the early 2000s provides a dramatic illustration. Increased demand for housing raised home prices, which in turn encouraged further mortgage lending, which led to further price increases in a continuing positive feedback loop. The cycle of increased leverage involved loosening credit standards and even further increases in leverage. At the end of the process, individuals and institutions alike became dangerously vulnerable.

When the bubble bursts, the feedback loop goes into reverse. Prices decline, and individuals find not only that their wealth has declined but that in many cases their mortgage indebtedness exceeds the value of their houses. Loans then go sour, and consumers reduce their spending. Overly exposed financial institutions begin a deleveraging process. The attendant tightening of credit weakens economic activity further, and the outcome of the negative feedback loop is a severe recession. Credit boom bubbles are the ones that pose the greatest danger to real economic activity.

SHOULD THE MONETARY AUTHORITIES ATTEMPT TO DEFLATE ASSET BUBBLES?

The history of asset-price bubbles informs us that destabilizing influences in an economy arising from asset-price bubbles can occur with little or no general price inflation. For example, wage and price pressures were absent in the United States during the 1920s and were only moderate in Japan during the 1980s. In both cases, however, the collapse of the bubble ushered in a decade or more of stagnating economic performance. Periodic asset bubbles are one of the costs of capitalism. The natural question that arises is whether bubbles in financial markets and the subsequent dislocations in the real economy can be reduced if central bankers react in advance to prevent asset-price bubbles from inflating.

The answer of former Federal Reserve Chairman Alan Greenspan was that central bankers should not react to asset-price bubbles themselves but should be prepared to take vigorous action to offset the economic dislocations that might follow. The question considered here is whether a more symmetric reaction is called for. Rather than simply addressing the hangover, would it be better to avoid the drunkenness in the first place?

The answer of Cecchetti et al. (2000) is definitely yes. They believe that a central bank concerned about stabilizing inflation around a specific target level will achieve superior performance by adjusting its policy instruments, not only in response to forecasts of future inflation and the output gap but to asset prices as well. Financial cycles brought about in part by asset-price movements can and do create real economic imbalances. One way to consider asset prices explicitly is suggested by Lansing (2008). He recommends using the Taylor (1999) framework that explains the conduct of central bank policy. An augmented Taylor rule would have monetary policy react not only to anticipations of inflation and the output gap but to asset prices as well. He would explicitly include stock market variables to guide monetary policy.

Similar views have been offered by Borio and Lowe (2002) and by Bordo and Olivier (2002). They stress that asset-price bubbles tend to be associated with overly high investment and a buildup of debt. Moreover, appreciating asset values raise the value of the collateral that facilitates the accumulation of debt. Therefore, balance sheets may look unrealistically healthy as the appreciated asset values offset the buildup of debt. But when the bubble bursts, the consequence will be a deterioration of net worth and financial distress.

Asset-price bubbles then create distortions in both investment and consumption and ultimately have substantial effects on real output and inflation. The central bank then is advised to raise interest rates when asset prices rise above what are considered "warranted" levels and lower rates when asset prices fall below those levels. By this kind of augmented "leaning against the wind," the central bank might be able to reduce the probability of bubbles arising in the first place and contribute to greater economic stability. To be sure, asset price misalignments are difficult to measure, but so are central bank forecasts of inflation and the output gap. According to this view, there are clearly times when egregious misalignments exist.[11] Examples would be the Japanese stock and land prices in 1989, the height of the NASDAQ market in late 1999 and early 2000, and the U.S. real estate market in 2006.

Arguments against Having the Central Bank React to Perceived Bubbles in Asset Prices

For all the possible arguments in favor of asking the monetary authorities to take preemptive actions against bubbles, there are powerful arguments to suggest a very cautious approach. The major problem is that bubbles are not easy to identify in advance. Indeed, as the survey of bubbles indicated, it is not even certain that they can be identified ex post. Even some of the most famous bubbles, such as the tulip bulb craze and the 1928–1929 U.S. stock market, can be explained by fundamentally justified expectations in the view of some analysts. The extreme difficulty of identifying asset-price bubbles should make monetary policy makers hesitant to take preemptive actions.

But wasn't the technology/Internet stock market bubble easy to identify as it was inflating? Robert Shiller published his book *Irrational Exuberance* in early 2000, just at the peak of the market. True, but the same models that identified a bubble in early 2000 also identified a vastly "overpriced" stock market in 1992, when low dividend yields and high price-earnings multiples suggested that long-run equity returns would be close to zero in the United States.[12] In fact, from 1992 through 2004, annual stock market returns were over 11 percent, well above their historical average. In December 1996, those same models predicted *negative* long-run equity returns, leading Greenspan (1996) to wonder whether the stock market was "irrationally exuberant."[13] From the date of the chairman's speech through December 2009, the stock market returned nearly 7 percent a year, even after withstanding two sharp bear markets. Only in retrospect do we know that it was during 1999 and early 2000 when stock prices were "too high."

Randall Kroszner (2003) also questions our ability to identify incipient bubbles. He shows that the boom in stock prices that peaked in March 2000 looked very similar to a number of stock price patterns in the past. Some of those previous rising stock markets continued to go up even after their initial advance. Kroszner also points out that a historical pattern of flat prices could be followed by a devastating loss in value. He recounts that the Argentine peso was pegged to the dollar from 1997 to 2002, and therefore its chart pattern was perfectly flat. After January 2002, the peg was removed, and the peso depreciated sharply to move the price of the currency close to a value that the market assessed to be fundamentally warranted. In this case, a sharp change in the asset price can represent a restoration toward a more appropriate value, rather than the adjustment from a bubble. Thus, identifying asset-price bubbles from their time series behavior as suggested by Kindleberger (1978) is simply not possible.

It is also difficult for the central bank to distinguish rising asset prices that result from technology shocks from those due to financial shocks. There is a big difference between the collapse of asset prices resulting from a change in economic fundamentals and a crash in prices resulting from a bubble and the negative feedback mechanism. The difficulty then in identifying asset-price bubbles ex ante should make central bankers extremely cautious about taking preemptive actions. This point has been vigorously argued by Kohn (2006, 2008).

Even if the monetary authorities could identify bubbles, there is a question of how soon preemptive action could be taken. By the time that asset prices rise so much that they appear unduly elevated, other data may already be signaling that monetary policy should be tightened sharply. Given the lags in the operation of monetary policy, it may be highly unlikely that the effects of the action take place in time. Indeed, policy actions reacting to perceived asset-price bubbles could increase the volatility of asset prices rather than reducing them.

It is also important to keep in mind that monetary policy is a very blunt instrument. It cannot be made to operate on the particular asset prices that may be misaligned. Again, the 1999–2000 technology/Internet bubble is instructive to examine. During this period, it was only the high technology stocks that experience proved were overpriced. So-called value stocks, those with low price-earnings multiples and price-to-book value multiples, were, in fact, quite reasonably priced. After the bubble burst, value stocks produced satisfactory positive rates of return, even while many high-technology stocks lost 80 or 90 percent of their value. Finally, it is virtually impossible to let the air out of a bubble gradually, as the experience of Japan in the 1990s illustrates. It is easy to imagine circumstances where a monetary authority that tried to prick incipient bubbles might well do more harm than good.

The work of Stock and Watson (2001) makes clear that it is extremely difficult to link current asset prices with future inflation. Even when a relationship is found in a particular sample, that relationship often breaks down in more realistic out-of-sample forecasting tests. Finally, the work of Bernanke and Gertler (2001) shows a number of simulation results indicating that central banks should not respond to movements in asset prices. Bernanke and Gertler argue that reacting to stock prices *instead* of reacting to expectations of inflation and the output gap results in inferior economic performance. Their conclusion is that the changes in asset prices should affect monetary policy *only* to the extent that they affect the central bank's forecasts of inflation.

Selective Central Bank Policies

If broad monetary measures are considered inappropriate instruments to restrain asset-price bubbles, are there selective measures that could usefully be implemented?

For example, could margin requirements, the minimum equity that must be put up to finance stock market purchases, be raised when stock prices appear to be approaching bubble levels? Or could transaction taxes on short-term trading be imposed to restrain speculative purchases?

Clearly, the first problem with such approaches is the aforementioned difficulty in recognizing that a bubble, in fact, exists. But in addition, there is scant evidence that margin requirements can be altered so as to successfully manipulate stock prices. Research by Schwert (1989) and Hsieh and Miller (1990) suggests that there is no reliable evidence that altering margin requirements is an effective instrument to influence stock prices. The Federal Reserve in the United States has consistently expressed skepticism about the effectiveness of changes in margin requirements as instruments to control stock-price bubbles.

Another selective policy that is sometimes suggested is to impose some form of "Tobin tax," that is, some tax on short-term speculative stock market transactions. Supporters of such a tax argue that it could reduce the volatility of stock prices. But such a tax could reduce liquidity, and in some cases, increase volatility. Moreover, in an environment of global capital markets, writers such as Frankel (1996) have questioned how well a reliable enforcement mechanism can be imposed. Such a selective policy might cause more problems than it would solve.

Conclusion

I have argued that asset-price bubbles do, in fact, exist. They are a periodic flaw of capitalist systems. I have suggested, however, that they are virtually impossible to identify ex ante. Therefore, monetary authorities are unlikely to have informational advantages over market participants, and an attempt by the monetary authorities to prick incipient bubbles is likely to do more harm than good. It is my view, then, that changes in asset prices should affect monetary policy only to the extent that they affect the central bank's forecast for inflation and the output gap.

It is important to understand, however, that some asset-price bubbles are particularly dangerous. Bubbles are likely to be costly if they are associated with high leverage, which was certainly the case in the housing price bubble in the United States during the early 2000s. During that episode, both individuals and institutions became dangerously overleveraged. Moreover, the institutions that took on an inordinate amount of debt were, in many cases, "too big to fail," and thus they caused systemic risks to the entire financial system. These kinds of bubbles should surely be of concern to the central bank because, ultimately, they engender economic instability. Housing and finance are central to the U.S. economic system. Moreover, the financial innovations that securitized mortgages and other loans into a complex set of collateralized securities led to very heavy financial losses, not only for U.S. financial institutions but for financial institutions throughout the world. Very large increases in debt that create risks for the financial system are clearly matters that fall within the traditional concerns of monetary policy.

In my view, preemptive action was required in this particular case. But the failure was less one of monetary policy in general and more one of adequate regulation. Financial institutions, which pose systemic risks to the economy, were allowed to take on leverage ratios far beyond those that were warranted. The failure then was not in letting a bubble inflate but in inadequate regulation that allowed both financial institutions and individual home buyers to take on undue risk. We need to rethink the way capital requirements are administered, and we may need to supplement them with minimum liquidity standards. Similarly, there was a failure to monitor the lending standards that allowed many individual homeowners to take on exceptional risk as their consumption expenditures surged. The solution is one of better regulation, not of having the central bank attempt to influence asset prices themselves.

Monetary policy, therefore, should not react directly to asset price developments, but should clearly take into consideration all the consequences of these developments for inflation, aggregate demand, and the fragility of the entire financial system. Asset prices and their effects on the balance sheets of individuals and institutions may well give the central bank incremental information about the macroeconomic goals of monetary policy. On that proposition, I believe, most analysts would agree.

Acknowledgment

The author is indebted to Alan Blinder and Dennis Mueller for extremely helpful comments and to the Center for Economic Policy Studies for financial support.

Notes

1. See, for example, Cecchetti et al. (2000).
2. See, for example, Blanchard and Watson (1982) and Blanchard (1979).
3. See Kindleberger (1978).
4. See, for example, Shleifer and Vishny (1992) and DeLong et al. (1990).
5. See Abreu and Brunnermeier (2003).
6. The following description of historical bubbles follows the discussion of bubbles in my book, *A Random Walk down Wall Street* (2011).
7. Golconda, now in ruins, was a city in India. According to legend, everyone who passed through it became rich.
8. The Japanese system of cross-ownership undoubtedly makes the total capitalization of the market unrealistically high. To the extent that company A owns half the stock of company B and vice versa, there will be considerable double counting. Moreover, the capitalization of the stock market also reflected the inflated value of the real estate holdings of Japanese companies.

9. It is important to note that even when a new industry is wildly successful, most individual companies are likely to fail. It was true of the automobile and computer industries in the United States. Similarly, most Internet service companies failed.
10. Although the Case-Shiller index may have exaggerated the volatility of house prices, other data provide estimates that are qualitatively the same.
11. Of course, by the time such misalignments can be recognized, it may be too late to do anything useful to ameliorate the situation.
12. See Shiller (2003) and Campbell and Shiller (1988, 1998).
13. See Greenspan (1996).**Figure 14.3. The Housing Bubble in the United States**

References

Abreu, Dilip, and Markus K. Brunnermeier. "Bubbles and Crashes." *Econometrica* 71 (Jan. 2003): 173–204.

Bernanke, Ben S., and Mark Gertler. "Should Central Banks Respond to Movements in Asset Prices?" *American Economic Review* 91 (May 2001): 253–257.

Baumol, William A. *The Stock Market and Economic Efficiency.* New York: Fordham University Press, 1965.

Bierman, Harold Jr. *The Great Myths of 1929 and the Lessons to be Learned.* New York: Greenwood Press, 1991.

Blanchard, Olivier. "Speculative Bubbles, Crashes, and Rational Expectations." *Economic Letters* 3 (Jan. 1979): 387–389.

Blanchard, Olivier, and Mark Watson. "Bubbles, Rational Expectations and Financial Markets." In *Crisis in the Economic and Financial Structure*, ed. Paul Wachtel, 295–316. Lanham, Md.: Lexington Books, 1982.

Bordo, Michael D., and Jeanne Olivier. "Boom-Busts in Asset Prices, Economic Instability, and Monetary Policy." NBER Working Paper no. 8966, Cambridge, Mass., National Bureau of Economic Research, May 2002.

Borio, Claudio, and Phillip Lowe. "Asset Prices, Financial and Monetary Stability: Exploring the Nexus." Bank for International Settlements Working Paper 114, 2002. http://www.bis.org/publ/work114.htm.

Brooks, John. *Once in Golconda: A True Drama of Wall Street 1920–1938.* New York: Wiley, 1991.

Brunnermeier, Markus K., and Stefan Nagel. "Hedge Funds and the Technology Bubble." *Journal of Finance* 59 (Oct. 2004): 2013–2040.

Campbell, John Y., and Robert J. Shiller. "Stock Prices, Earnings, and Expected Dividends." *Journal of Finance* 43 (July 1988): 661–676.

Campbell, John Y., and Robert J. Shiller. "Valuation Ratios and the Long-Run Stock Market Outlook." *Journal of Portfolio Management* 25 (Fall 1998): 11–26.

Cecchetti, Stephen, Hans Genberg, John Lipsky, and Sushil Wadhwani. "Asset Prices and Central Bank Policy." *Geneva Report on the World Economy* 2. CEPR and ICMB, July 2000.

DeLong, J. Bradford, Andrei Shleifer, Lawrence Summers, and Robert J. Waldmann. "Noise Trader Risk in Financial Markets." *Journal of Political Economy* 98 (Aug. 1990): 703–738.

Frankel, Jeffrey A. "How Well Do Markets Work: Might a Tobin Tax Help?" In *The Tobin Tax: Coping with Financial Volatility*, ed. Mahbub ul Haq, Inge Kaul, and Isabelle Grunberg, 41–82. New York: Oxford University Press, 1996.

Garber, Peter M. "Famous First Bubbles." *Journal of Economic Perspectives* 4 (Spring 1990): 35–53.
Garber, Peter. *Famous First Bubbles: The Fundamentals of Early Manias.* Cambridge, Mass.: MIT Press, 2000.
Greenspan, Alan. "The Challenge of Central Banking in a Democratic Society." Annual Dinner and Francis Boyer Lecture of the American Enterprise Institute for Public Policy Research. Washington, D.C., Dec. 1996.
Hsieh, David A., and Merton H. Miller. "Margin Regulation and Stock Market Volatility." *Journal of Finance* 45 (March 1990): 3–29.
Jensen, Michael C. "Some Anomalous Evidence Regarding Market Efficiency." *Journal of Financial Economics* 6 (June/Sept. 1978): 95–101.
Kindleberger, Charles P. *Manias, Panics, and Crashes: A History of Financial Crises.* New York: Basic Books, 1978.
Kohn, Donald L. "Monetary Policy and Asset Prices." Speech delivered at "Monetary Policy: A Journey from Theory to Practice," European Central Bank Colloquium held in honor of Otmar Issing., Frankfurt, Germany, March 16, 2006.
Kohn, Donald L. "Monetary Policy and Asset Prices Revisited." Speech at the Cato Institute's Twenty-Sixth Annual Monetary Policy Conference. Washington, D.C., November 19, 2008.
Kroszner, Randall S. "Asset Price Bubbles, Information, and Public Policy." In *Asset Price Bubbles: The Implications for Monetary, Regulatory, and International Policies*, ed. William C. Hunter, George G. Kaufman, and Michael Pomerleano, 3–13. Cambridge, Mass.: MIT Press, 2003.
Lansing, Kenneth J. "Monetary Policy and Asset Prices." *FRBSF Economic Letter* 34 (Oct. 31, 2008).
Mackay, Charles. *Extraordinary Popular Delusions and the Madness of Crowds.* New York: Harmony, 1841.
Malkiel, Burton G. *A Random Walk down Wall Street.* Rev. ed. New York: Norton, 2011.
Neal, Larry. *The Rise of Financial Capitalism: International Capital Markets and the Age of Reason.* Cambridge: Cambridge University Press, 1990.
Schwert, Willliam G. "Business Cycles, Financial Crises and Stock Volatility." NBER Working Paper 2957, Cambridge, Mass., National Bureau of Economic Research, May 1989.
Shiller, Robert J. *Irrational Exuberance.* Princeton, N.J.: Princeton University Press, 2000.
Shiller, Robert J. "From Efficient Markets Theory to Behavioral Finance." *Journal of Economic Perspectives* 17 (Winter 2003): 83–104.
Shleifer, Andrei, and Robert Vishny. "Liquidation Values and Debt Capacity—A Market Equilibrium Approach." *Journal of Finance* 47 (Sept. 1992): 1343–1366.
Stock, James H., and Mark W. Watson. *Forecasting Output and Inflation: The Role of Asset Prices.* Harvard University and Princeton University, manuscript, 2001.
Taylor, John B. "A Historical Analysis of Monetary Policy Rules." In *Monetary Policy Rules*, ed. J. B. Taylor, 319–341. Chicago: University of Chicago Press, 1999.
Tversky, Amos, and Daniel Kahneman. "The Framing of Decisions and the Psychology of Choice." *Science* 211 (Jan. 1981): 453–458.

CHAPTER 15

MERGERS AND THE MARKET FOR CORPORATE CONTROL

DENNIS C. MUELLER

MERGERS have long been an enigma for economists. Despite their prominence in capitalist countries and the immense literature about them, economists remain divided as to their causes and consequences. Indeed, mergers resemble the elephant with economists playing the roles of the blind men who try to determine the characteristics of the beast they are examining. Each comes up with a different theory of what the beast is.

One set of theories treats mergers as just another form of investment and uses investment theory to explain and predict mergers.[1] A second set views mergers in the context of Coase's theory of the firm and regards them as efficiency-enhancing solutions to market failures.[2] Perhaps the most venerable hypothesis about why mergers occur sees them as attempts to eliminate competition and increase market power.[3] These three sets of theories can all be characterized as *neoclassical* in that they assume that managers are maximizing profits and thus that mergers increase profits. A fourth set of theories can be described as *behavioral* because they posit other goals for managers, like empire building, or hypothesize that managers are gripped by irrational impulses out of hubris.[4] These theories do not imply that mergers increase profits, but that they are likely to destroy shareholder wealth. The behavioral theories presume that managers have sufficient freedom from shareholder control to make decisions that destroy shareholder wealth, and thus subsume the existence of a principal–agent (PA) relationship between managers and shareholders. A fifth theory of mergers, perhaps better named hostile takeovers, sees takeovers as solutions to managerial failures. Poorly managed companies get taken over and their managers replaced.[5]

Examples of mergers that fit into each of these five categories can be found. One of the important conclusions to draw from the literature is that no single theory explains all mergers. It is nevertheless useful to examine the evidence to see which theories receive the most empirical support. If mergers are simply normal investments of a different form, or if they increase efficiency, then they tend to improve the functioning of capitalism and need not concern policy makers. If the preponderance of mergers reduce competition, then they should be a concern for competition policy authorities. If managerial motives lead to mergers that destroy wealth, again they should be a concern to society, but not necessarily for competition policy. If, on the other hand, the market for corporate control adequately constrains managerial excesses, mergers should be left to transpire without the intervention of the state. The evidence reviewed in this chapter indicates that takeovers can be an effective constraint on managers, but the market for corporate control is not sufficiently effective to eliminate all wealth-destroying mergers. Moreover, in many countries, like France and Germany, it barely operates at all.

I begin by reviewing some stylized facts. These facts pose some puzzling questions that must be answered, if we are to understand the role mergers play in capitalist systems. I then turn to the evidence of their effects on profitability, efficiency, and shareholder wealth. This evidence is used to resolve some of the questions raised by the stylized facts about mergers.

Stylized Facts and Riddles about Mergers

Mergers Come in Waves

Figure 15.1 plots the number of mergers taking place in the United States since the end of the nineteenth century and the aggregate Standard and Poor's price/earnings (P/E) ratio. The merger series has been deflated by the U.S. population to adjust for the country's growth from the end of the nineteenth century to the beginning of the twenty-first. Two facts stand out: mergers have tended to come in waves, and these waves have coincided with increases in share prices relative to earnings. A similar pattern has been observed for the United Kingdom.[6] Any general theory of merger activity must account for this time-series pattern of mergers.

The wave pattern of mergers is difficult to reconcile with some theories of mergers. Why should market failures requiring mergers increase dramatically as share prices rise, and disappear when a stock market boom ends? If anything, one would expect the pressure to increase efficiency to be greatest during recessions, when competition is stiff and share prices are low. Why should market power increases be especially attractive during stock market booms? Many of the

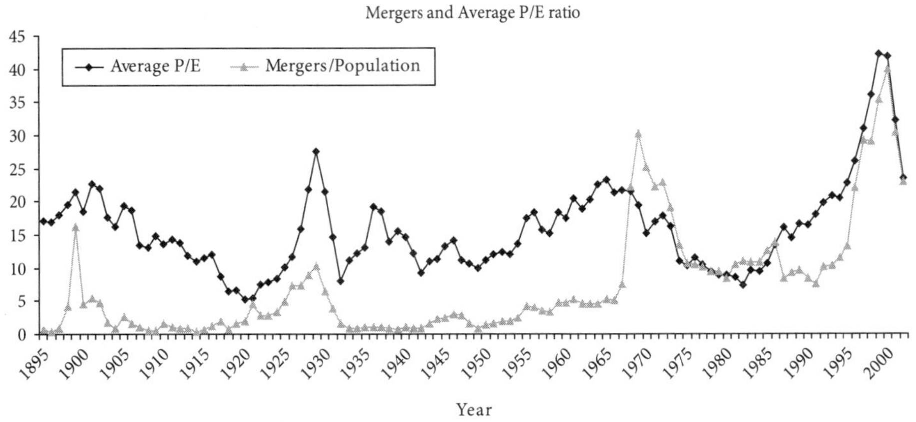

Figure 15.1. Mergers and Average P/E Ratio

Sources: Mergers: 1895–1920 from Nelson (1959); 1921–67 from FTC; 1968–2002 from M&A. P/E ratios: Homepage of Robert Shiller: http://aida.econ.yale.edu/~shiller/data.htm. Population: Statistical Abstract of United States (several years).

hypotheses put forward to explain mergers have not been formulated as explanations of merger waves and are not easily reconcilable with them. A handful of hypotheses do attempt to account for merger waves. These are examined later.

Profitability

Stylized fact two is that mergers on average do not tend to increase the profits of the merging firms, and more often reduce them. This evidence is reviewed elsewhere. This observation poses an obvious challenge to those theories that assume mergers take place to increase profits. Either managers are not attempting to maximize profits, or they are not very good at doing it.

Shareholder Returns

The only clear winners from mergers are the targets' shareholders. Premiums for targets' shares average 20–30 percent in normal times, and rise to 50–100 percent during merger booms. Acquirers' shareholders experience little or no gain when mergers are announced, on the other hand, and often large losses in the years that follow. As with the results regarding profitability, this pattern seems to imply that managers of acquiring companies are either not trying to maximize shareholder wealth or do a poor job of it. This literature is reviewed later. I now attempt to unravel some of these riddles.

The Profitability of Mergers

One of the most difficult problems when assessing the effects of mergers on some measure of performance like profits is to determine the counterfactual. What would have happened to the profits of two merging firms if they had not merged? Some studies simply assume that profits would have remained unchanged, and compare postmerger profits to premerger profits. This methodology is likely to produce biased results, however, if economic conditions change and the merging companies' profits would have changed with them. A better approach, therefore, is to define a control group and assume that the merging companies' profits would have changed in the same way as the control group's profits changed. Table 15.1 summarizes the findings of studies, which have used this approach. Typical choices for control groups are companies in the same industry or the industry itself. Premerger profits are generally from one to three years before the mergers, postmerger profits from three to five years afterward. Part A of table 15.1 lists the studies that found a statistically significant increase in profits relative to the control group. Part B contains studies that found little or no difference between the merging companies' changes in profits and those of the control group. The symbol ≥ 0 indicates either that profits were statistically significantly higher for merging firms than for the control group but only modestly so, or that they were only higher in some of the tests. Studies reporting significantly worse profit performance for merging companies appear in part C.

The bulk of the studies find little or no improvement in profits for merging companies relative to their control groups. I could find only four studies that reported significant improvements—three for the United States and one looking at bank mergers in Germany. Three studies, including two of the largest investigations of mergers to date (Meeks, 1977, for the United Kingdom and Ravenscraft and Scherer, 1987, for the United States), observed significant declines in relative profitability for merging companies. The studies cited in table 15.1 underscore the first stylized fact and raise the question of whether managers consistently overestimate the effects of mergers on profits, or undertake them for other reasons.

The Effects of Mergers on Efficiency

The Effects of Mergers on Sales

If mergers reduce costs and thereby prices, they should increase sales, assuming that firms operate in the elastic portions of their demand schedules. An indirect way to see if mergers improve efficiency, therefore, is to examine their effects on sales. Two approaches have been followed. One adopts essentially the same methodology described for profit studies—each merging firm is matched to a similar nonmerging company (same industry, perhaps similar size), and the changes in sales for the merging and matched nonmerging companies are compared. The second approach uses the sales of the merging companies' industries as the control group. This can be done by substituting industry sales for control company sales

Table 15.1 The Effects of Mergers on Profitability

Country	Authors	Time Period	Merger Sample	Control Group	Profitability Measure	Profit Change Relative to Control Group
			Part A			
United States	Healy, Palepu and Ruback, 1992	1979–84	50 largest mergers	base industries	before-tax-cash-flow/assets	>0
	Akhavein et al., 1997	1981–89	69 large bank mergers	all large banks	profit efficiency function	>0
	Andrade, Mitchell and Stafford, 2001	1973–98	≈ 2000 mergers	base industries	cash flow/sales	>0
Germany	Koetter, 2008	1994–2005	1517 bank mergers	non-merging banks	profits before taxes	>0
			Part B-1			
United States	Conn, 1976	1964–70	28 firms acquired by 4 conglomerates	base industries acquired firm	after-tax profit/total assets	≤0
	Mueller, 1980b	1962–72	247 manufacturing mergers	base industries; merging firms, size and industry matched firms	before-tax profit/assets	≤0
			280 manufacturing firms	companies in 551 making no acquisitions	after-tax profit/assets	≥0
	Mueller, 1986	1950–72	merger activity 551 manufacturing firms		after-tax profit/total assets	≤0

	Rhoades, 1987	1968–78	413 acquired banks	3600 non-acquired banks	after-tax profit/assets	≈0
	Gugler et al., 2003	1981–98	889–1272 domestic and cross border mergers	base industries	profits before taxes	≥0
United Kingdom	Singh, 1971	1955–60	77 horizontal mergers	none	before-tax profit/assets	≈0
					after-tax profit/assets	≈0
	Cosh, Hughes and Singh, 1980	1967–70	225 manufacturing mergers	size and industry matched firms	after-tax profit/assets	≥0
					before-tax profit/assets	≥0
	Kumar, 1985	1967–74	241 mergers	base industries	after-tax profit/assets	≤0
	Cosh, Hughes, Kumar and Singh, 1985	1972–76	66 mergers	base industries	after-tax profit/assets	≈0
	Gugler et al., 2003	1981–98	181–297 domestic and cross border mergers	base industries	profits before taxes	≥0
Part B-2						
Australia	McDougall and Round, 1986	1970–81	88 takeovers	size and industry matched firms	before-tax profit/assets	≈0
					after-tax profit/assets	
Australia, New Zealand, Canada	Gugler et al., 2003	1981–98	66–101 domestic and cross border mergers	base industries	profits before taxes	≈0

(Cintinued)

Table 15.1 (Continued)

Country	Authors	Time Period	Merger Sample	Control Group	Profitability Measure	Profit Change Relative to Control Group
Belgium	Kumps and Wtterwulghe, 1980	1962–74	21 mergers	size and industry matched non-merging firms	after-tax profit/assets	≈0
Canada	Baldwin, 1995	1970–79	1575 acquired plants	nonacquired plants in same industry	value-added per worker/ shipments	≥0
France	Jenny and Weber, 1980	1962–75	40 mergers	size and industry matched non-merging firms	after-tax profit/asset	≈0
Germany	Cable, Palfrey and Runge, 1980	1964–74	50 mergers	size and industry matched non-merging firms	after-tax profit/assets	≈0
Sweden	Ryden and Edberg, 1980	1962–76	26 mergers	size and industry matched non-merging firms	after-tax profit/assets	≈0
				base industry		≤0
Continental Europe	Gugler et al., 2003	1981–98	87–102 domestic and cross border mergers	base industries	profits before taxes	≥0
Japan	Odagiri and Hase, 1989	1980–87	46 mergers	size and industry matched non-merging firms	profits before taxes	≥0 ≤0

			Part B-3			
Japan	Gugler et al., 2003	1981–98	15–19 domestic and cross border mergers	base industries	profits before taxes	≤0
	Yeh and Hoshino, 2002	1970–94	86 mergers	base industries	profits before taxes	≤0
	Yoshida, 2007 Odagiri, 2008[a]	1991–2002	53 mergers	base industries	profits	≤0
			Part C			
United States	Ravenscraft and Scherer, 1987	1950–77	5966 acquired manufacturing companies	base industry (line of business)	before-tax profit/total assets	<0
United Kingdom	Meeks, 1977	1950–71	1000 + mergers	base industries	after-tax profit/assets	<0
	Dickerson et al., 1997	1948–77	2941 mergers of listed companies	non-merging listed companies	profits before taxes	<0
The Netherlands	Peer, 1980	1962–73	31 mergers	size and industry matched non-merging firms	after-tax profit/assets	<0

a Results from unpublished thesis of Kenzi Yoshida as reported in Odagiri (2008).

in the calculations or simply by looking at changes in market shares after mergers. The results from several studies are summarized in table 15.2.

I have found no studies in which merging companies have been able to achieve significantly larger market shares or more rapid growth than their industries or control group companies. The studies divide roughly equally into those finding no significant difference between merging firms' sales growth and that of the control groups (part A), and those finding significantly worse postmerger sales performance (part B). Moreover, most of the relative declines in sales reported in part B of table 15.2 are quite dramatic. In my study of 209 mergers using five-digit Federal Trade Commission data on market shares, I found that nonmerging companies retained on average 85 percent of their 1950 market shares up through 1972. In contrast, companies acquired during this twenty-three-year period retained on average only 15 percent of their 1950 market shares (Mueller, 1986). Sales of U.S. companies that merged between 1981 and 1998 were roughly 25 percent lower after four years than predicted if they had grown at the same rates as the median firms in their industries.[7] Similarly large relative declines in sales were observed for the United Kingdom, Australia, New Zealand, Canada, and continental Europe.[8] Studies of the impacts of mergers on sales and market shares over the past thirty years offer no evidence that mergers have on average increased efficiency.

Other Evidence of the Effects of Mergers on Efficiency

Other evidence of the effects of mergers paints a less gloomy picture. A handful of studies have estimated cost functions for specific industries to determine the impact of mergers on efficiency. Mergers in the United States between hospitals, railroads, and paper manufacturers have been found to reduce costs.[9] On the other hand, Sung and Gort (2006) found no evidence that mergers in telecommunications significantly reduced costs.

Studies using U.S. Census data have recorded increases in plant productivity following ownership changes.[10] Baldwin (1995, pp. 246–253) reports similar results for Canada for plants acquired through spin-offs and horizontal mergers. The U.S. findings also include spin-offs, which are almost always the undoing of previous mergers. If the original mergers led to a decline in efficiency, the subsequent spin-offs and productivity increases might simply be undoing the damage of the earlier mergers. Sung and Gort (2006) observed no increases in productivity following mergers in telecommunications in the United States. Yeh and Hoshino (2002) recorded significant declines in productivity following mergers in Japan. On the other hand, Sourafel et al. (2006) estimate significant increases in productivity in technology importing industries following acquisitions by U.S. and European multinationals.

Baldwin's findings are a bit puzzling. The productivity of plants acquired through horizontal mergers increases, while their sales fall (see table 15.2). This combination suggests that the increase in productivity might have been due to laying off workers. Sales fell but employment fell even more. Gugler and Yurtoglu

Table 15.2 The Effects of Mergers on Sales and Market Share

Country	Authors	Time Period	Merger Sample	Control Group	Sales Measure	Sales Change Relative to Control Group
			Part A			
United States	Goldberg, 1973		44 mergers of advertising intensive companies	base industries	market share	≈0
	Rhoades, 1987	1968–78	413 acquired banks	3600 non-acquired banks	market share	≈0
Belgium	Kumps and Wtterwulghe, 1980	1962–74	21 mergers	size and industry matched non-merging firms	sales growth	≈0
Canada	Baldwin, 1995	1970–79	acquired plants in unrelated industries	nonacquired plants in same industries	market share	≈0
France	Jenny and Weber, 1980	1962–75	40 mergers	size and industry matched non-merging firms	sales growth	≈0
Germany	Cable, Palfrey and Runge, 1980	1964–74	50 mergers	size and industry matched non-merging firms	sales growth	≈0
Sweden	Ryden and Edberg, 1980	1962–76	26 mergers	size and industry matched non-merging firms	sales growth	≈0
United Kingdom	Cosh, Hughes and Singh, 1980	1967–70	225 manufacturing mergers	size and industry matched firms	sales growth	≈0
					before-tax profit/ assets	≥0
Japan	Odagiri and Hase, 1989	1980–87	46 mergers	size and industry matched non-merging firms	sales growth	≤0

(Continued)

Table 15.2 (Continued)

Country	Authors	Time Period	Merger Sample	Control Group	Sales Measure	Sales Change Relative to Control Group
	Odagiri and Hase, 1989	1980–87	243 mergers	base industries	sales growth	≤ 0
	Gugler et al., 2003	1981–98	15–19 domestic and cross border mergers	base industries	sales growth	≈ 0
			Part B			
United States	Mueller, 1986	1950–72	209 manufacturing mergers	base industries	market share	<0
	Simon, Mokhtari and Simon, 1996	1947–85	33 mergers of advertising agencies	base industries	sales growth	<0
	Gugler et al., 2003	1981–98	889–1272 domestic and cross border mergers	base industries	sales growth	<0
Australia, New Zealand, Canada	Gugler et al., 2003	1981–98	66–101 domestic and cross border mergers	base industries	sales growth	<0
Canada	Baldwin, 1995	1970–79	acquired plants in related industries	nonacquired plants in same industries	market share	<0
The Netherlands	Peer, 1980	1962–73	31 mergers	size and industry matched non-merging firms	sales growth	<0
United Kingdom	Gugler et al. 2003	1981–98	181–297 domestic and cross border mergers	base industries	sales growth	<0
Continental Europe	Gugler et al., 2003	1981–98	87–102 domestic and cross border mergers	base industries	sales growth	<0
Japan	Yeh and Hoshino, 2002	1970–94	86 mergers	base industries	sales growth	<0

(2004) report significant reductions in employment following mergers in continental Europe, although not in the United States. Odagiri (2008) also reports that mergers in Japan between 1991 and 2002 were followed by increases in productivity but reductions in profits (table 15.1). Finally, mention should be made of two studies of the pharmaceutical industry that find "little evidence that [mergers] increased long-term R&D performance or outcomes."[11] Although these studies of the effects of mergers on costs and productivity are more favorable with respect to mergers' effects on efficiency, by no means are they consistent enough to overturn the findings related to profits and sales.

Discussion

Mergers take place for many reasons, and when assessing their impact it is important to determine which mergers support which hypotheses. If mergers increase market power, prices should rise, profits should rise, and sales should fall as a result of the increase in price. If mergers increase efficiency, prices should fall, profits rise, and sales will also rise because of the fall in price. Conversely, if efficiency declines, both profits and sales will fall. In their study of mergers from around the world, Gugler et al. (2003) found that roughly 30 percent of mergers fit the pattern expected if market power increases, with similar percentages indicating either efficiency increases or efficiency declines. The remaining small fraction of mergers fell into the somewhat puzzling category of sales increases and profit declines. Thus, a majority of mergers were followed by profit increases relative to their industries, although the differences were generally insignificant (table 15.1). If we assume that market power increases are welfare reducing, then a majority of mergers also reduces social welfare by either increasing market power or reducing efficiency.

The Effects of Mergers on Shareholders' Returns

The Stylized Facts

Event studies estimate the effects of mergers by calculating the market's reaction to a merger announcement over a particular time interval (window). Other factors that might affect share prices are accounted for by estimating an abnormal return equal to the difference between the returns of a merging firm over the window of observation and the returns on some control group. Many studies have used the market portfolio as the control group, but some have used a merging company's industry, and more recently control groups have been selected with similar sized companies and similar market to book ratios.

A second approach estimates the following equation for some benchmark period,

$$R_{it} = \alpha_i + \beta_i R_{mt} + \mu_{it}, \tag{15.1}$$

where R_{it} is the return on a share of firm i in t, and R_{mt} is the return on the market portfolio.

The estimates of α_i and β_i are then used to predict R_{it} during the event period. If a benchmark period is chosen in which the returns for firm i were relatively high, the estimated α_i will be high, and the merging firm i will have to earn a higher return over the event window to produce a positive abnormal return for the merger event.

To induce the managers and shareholders to sell their firm, a potential acquirer must offer a premium for their shares. These premiums result in an immediate large abnormal return for a target's shareholders—on the order of 20–30 percent in normal times, rising to over 50 percent at the peaks of merger waves, as the demand for willing targets outstrips the supply. Thus, the pattern of abnormal returns to target shareholders consists of a sharp rise in returns around the merger announcement, and perhaps further rises if additional bids are forthcoming. Within six months or so, the target is absorbed and the event window closes, revealing a significant gain to target shareholders.

Many early event studies estimated abnormal returns for acquirers over long periods both before and after the merger announcements. A representative pattern appears in figure 15.2, constructed from Asquith (1983). Asquith's null hypothesis was that the acquiring companies' shares would have performed as those of firms in the market portfolio with comparable betas. Acquiring firms begin to earn positive abnormal returns roughly two years prior to the merger announcements. These

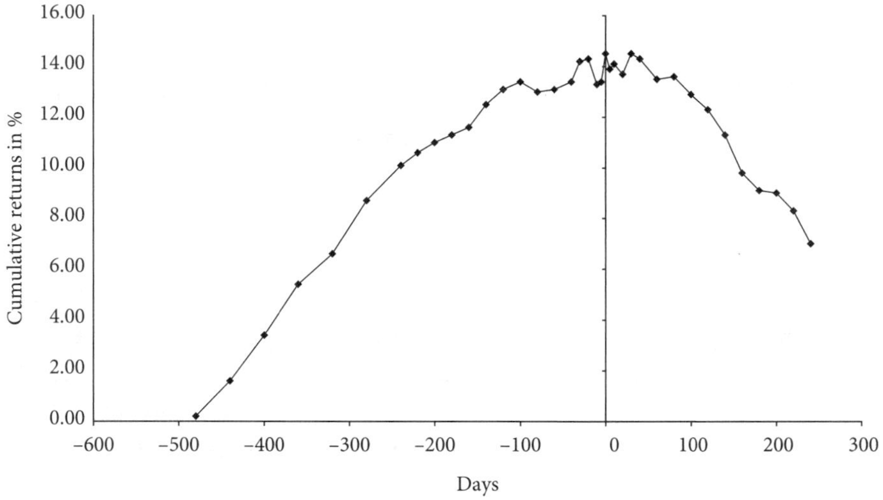

Figure 15.2. Cumulative Residuals for Successful Bidding Firms

Source: Asquith, 1983

cumulate to 14.3 percent of the acquirers' market values by the day before the merger announcement. On that day, day 0, bidders earn an average return of 0.2 percent. Points to the right of day 0 represent observations following the consummation of the mergers. Thus, a gap of variable length averaging roughly six months occurs following day 0. Starting at the time that the mergers are completed, acquirers' abnormal returns become negative and fall a cumulative 7.0 percent. Thus, over about one year following the mergers, the acquirers' shareholders lost roughly half of the substantial gains that they experienced over the two years leading up to them.

What are we to make of this pattern of returns? The biggest gains for the acquirers come *before* the mergers are announced. The two years rise in acquirers' abnormal returns is too far in advance of the mergers to have been *caused* by them. If causality is involved, it must be that large abnormal returns for some companies lead them to make acquisitions, a hypothesis I return to later. The market treats the announcements themselves with indifference. As Mandelker (1974, p. 321) put it, "for the shareholders of acquiring firms, 'news' of an acquisition may not be worthwhile news." Indeed, the significant drop in returns following the consummation of the mergers suggests that news of them should be a signal to sell.

The pattern in figure 15.2 is typical of studies that have calculated abnormal returns over long pre- and postannouncement windows.[12] Abnormal returns for acquirers reported by Dodd and Ruback (1977), for example, rise continuously over more than forty months *prior* to the merger announcements reaching a cumulative value of 11.7 percent, and fall continuously for most of the thirty months following the announcements (cumulative loss 5.9 percent).[13] Moreover, their postmerger residuals were calculated using equation 15.1 for a benchmark period *after* the merger announcements. Given that the acquirers' share prices performed poorly after the mergers, this choice of benchmark produces smaller declines in abnormal returns than would have been obtained using a premerger benchmark. The difference can be large. Using a benchmark period of from thirty-six to three months before the announcement month, Magenheim and Mueller (1988) calculated cumulative losses to acquirers of a significant 11.3 percent over the first twelve months after the announcements. Using a postannouncement benchmark, the losses were an insignificant 3.2 percent. Thus, studies that have estimated the effects of mergers using postmerger benchmarks have *underestimated the change* in performance that occurred at the announcements.

The most reasonable interpretation of the pattern of abnormal returns in figure 15.1 and similar patterns in other studies is that (1) long intervals of positive abnormal returns may lead some companies to undertake acquisitions, (2) merger announcements tend to result in little or no change in returns for acquirers, and (3) with time, as the market learns more about the mergers, it reevaluates downward its judgment of them. Some early studies did conclude from such patterns that mergers had been wealth-destroying.[14] Most, however, tended to ignore the postmerger declines or dismissed them as "puzzling."[15] All early studies ignored the premerger run-ups in returns. Thus, after an exhaustive survey of the early event study literature, Jensen and Ruback (1983, p. 47) were able to conclude that

> the evidence seems to indicate that corporate takeovers generate positive gains, that target firm shareholders benefit, and that bidding firm shareholders do not lose. Moreover, the gains created by corporate takeovers do not appear to come from the creation of market power. Finally, it is difficult to find managerial actions related to corporate control that harm shareholders.

Mergers with Efficient Capital Markets

A justification for ignoring the postmerger losses to acquirers' shareholders is provided by efficient capital market theory. At the announcement, the market makes an unbiased prediction of the effects of the merger on future share prices of firms, and thus all of the effects of the mergers can be estimated before they even occur. Many of the event studies that appeared after 1983 invoked the efficient market assumption and calculated abnormal returns over very short windows around announcements. Bhagat et al. (1990), for example, estimated abnormal returns for a seven-day window centered on the announcement, Maquieira et al. (1998) used a five-day window, and Doukas (1995) used a two-day window.[16] Such short windows often produce small and insignificant returns. Thus, much of the more recent literature has agreed with Jensen and Ruback that mergers generate wealth, because acquirers do not lose when the mergers are announced and targets gain.

Even if we ignore the postmerger losses to acquirers, there is something awkward about the persistent findings of negligible returns to acquirers at merger announcements. Mergers are a very risky investment. Mueller and Sirower (2003) estimated mean abnormal returns to acquirers in large mergers of −$50.7 million after two years, about 2 percent of the acquirers' premerger market values. The standard deviation around this mean was $1,892 million, however, thirty-seven times the mean loss. If managers of the acquirers are trying to maximize the wealth of their shareholders, why do they continually undertake such highly risky investments with near zero returns? Some hypotheses are discussed next.

Mergers When Capital Markets Are Not Efficient

Although many scholars chose to rely on the efficient capital market assumption to avoid estimating acquirers' returns over long postmerger windows, not all did. Of particular interest is the article by Agrawal, Jaffe, and Mandelker (1992) (AJM). They estimated returns over five-year postannouncement periods using the market portfolio with adjustments for size as their control group (see table 15.3). Negative cumulative abnormal returns were estimated over the whole time period, 1955–1987, and for every subperiod except the 1970s. This decade was one of depressed share prices. AJM's results suggest that not only is merger activity correlated with stock prices—higher stock prices correlate with more mergers—but that the *returns* from mergers may be correlated with aggregate stock price movements. We discuss theories making this prediction next.

Estimates of returns by Loderer and Martin (1992) and Higson and Elliott (1998) were also sensitive to the time period. Estimating returns over different windows

Table 15.3. Merger Returns over Five-Year Postannouncement Periods

Time Period	Sample Size	Postmerger Abnormal Returns
1955–87	765 mergers	−10.3% (sig. 5% or better)
1955–59	51 mergers	−23.2% (sig. 5% or better)
1960–69	299 mergers	−15.1% (sig. 5% or better)
1970–79	247 mergers	+ 4.1% (insignificant)
1980–87	168 mergers	−19.4% (sig. 5% or better)

Source: Agrawal, Jaffe, and Mandelker (1992).

between 1966 and 1986, Loderer and Martin obtained only one significant estimate of a postannouncement abnormal return—a −61.2 percent return for 261 mergers between 1966 and 1969.[17] These were the years of the third great merger wave and coincided with a stock market boom. Thus, this finding also implies that booming stock markets are associated with negative long-run returns to acquirers.

Higson and Elliott found that U.K. mergers between 1975 and 1980 and again between 1985 and 1990 were followed by significant wealth losses to acquirers. Mergers between 1981 and 1984, on the other hand, were followed by significant *positive* abnormal returns. Gregory (1997) estimated a significant −12.5 percent abnormal return for U.K. acquirers between 1984 and 1992. Putting these two studies together, we see that U.K. mergers have been followed by negative abnormal returns to acquirers for every time period between 1975 and 1992, except for 1981–1984, a period of stagnant stock market prices.

Finally, mention must be made of the study of Rau and Vermaelen (1998). They estimated significant postannouncement returns of −4 percent for 2,823 acquirers, and significant positive returns for 316 tender offers (time period 1980–1991). Theirs is one of several studies that have reported significantly different findings for tender offers and friendly mergers. These findings support the market for corporate control hypothesis.

The Market for Corporate Control Hypothesis

Robin Marris (1964) developed a model of the firm in which managers maximized the growth of their firm rather than profits. Managers were so motivated because their salaries were more closely related to the size and growth of their companies than to profitability, and because they were assumed to enjoy "psychic rewards" from managing large, growing companies. Marris postulated that managers were constrained in their pursuit of growth by the threat of a hostile takeover should their share price fall too low. Henry Manne (1965) put forward a similar argument about the role of takeovers and coined the phrase "market for corporate control."

Much of the literature that finds that acquirers' shareholders do not benefit from mergers has rationalized this observation using the market for corporate control hypothesis (MCCH). Company T has a market value of less than its potential maximum, because its managers pursue growth or some other objective that conflicts with shareholder wealth maximization, or simply because they are incompetent. Company B's managers recognize that a gain could be made by buying T at its current market price and replacing its managers. Because any company that bought T could secure this gain, a bidding war arises and the premium that must be paid for T rises to such a level that *all* of the gains from replacing T's managers go to its shareholders.

Although this explanation for why acquirers do not gain from mergers seems consistent with the MCCH, it still raises the question of why the managers of B get involved or stay in a bidding war that eats up all of the potential gains from acquiring T, if they are trying to increase the wealth of their own shareholders. Under this interpretation of the MCCH, managers emerge as good Samaritans who remove incompetent or non–wealth-maximizing managers but turn over all of the gains from this action to the target's shareholders.

A possible way out of this conundrum arises if we do not assume that *all* mergers fit the MCCH, but only those that take on a hostile nature. Hostile takeovers typically take the form of tender offers, and the results of Rau and Vermaelen that tender offers have positive returns following mergers, while friendly mergers exhibit negative returns, is consistent with this interpretation. Magenheim and Mueller (1988) also found significantly higher postmerger returns for acquirers in tender offers than for friendly mergers.

Tender offers must be funded with cash; friendly mergers can be financed by exchanging shares or a combination of shares and cash. The findings of Loughran and Vijh (1997) that cash financed mergers had an insignificant 18.5% return for acquirers over a five-year postannouncement window, while stock-only and stock-plus-cash–financed acquisitions had significant negative returns of −24.2% is thus also consistent with the hypotheses that hostile takeovers and tender offers have different motivations than friendly mergers and thus different effects on acquiring shareholders' returns. I now discuss different hypothesis about what these motivations are and attempt to explain the different findings about the effects of mergers and their wave patterns.

Hypotheses about Merger Waves

The Managerial Discretion Hypothesis

The idea that the leaders of firms engage in "empire building" has been around for a long time. In his treatise on economic development, first published in 1911,

Schumpeter (1934, p. 93) placed "the dream... to found a private kingdom" at the head of his list of entrepreneurial goals. Marris (1964) first posited that managers maximize growth and not profits in part because of a close correlation between managerial compensation and the size of the company. He surveyed considerable evidence in support of this hypothesis. Mergers are the fastest way to grow and are thus attractive investments for any manager pursuing growth. Recent research finds that large acquisitions are followed by large increases in compensation for CEOs, and this relationship holds in the case of banks even when the bidder's stock price falls after the merger.[18] What is more, pay increases following corporate expansions are not reversed following corporate downsizings.[19]

The market for corporate control is most likely to constrain managers in their pursuit of growth, if the capital market is efficient. Company B bids 150 for company T, whose prebid market value is 100. The efficient capital market recognizes that the merger will not generate additional profits, and B's market value immediately falls by the full amount of its overbid, fifty, perhaps making it itself an attractive takeover target.

Although the efficient capital market assumption is often invoked, its plausibility is called into question during stock market booms and deep recessions. The Standard & Poor's aggregate P/E topped forty during the stock market boom of the late 1990s, almost three times its long-run average. To reconcile such P/Es with an efficient capital market, the capital market must be assuming that corporate earnings will grow at unprecedented rates indefinitely. When analyzing the great crash of 1929, Galbraith (1961, p. 8) observed that an "indispensable element of fact" during stock market bubbles is that individuals "build a world of speculative make-believe. This is a world inhabited not by people who have to be persuaded to believe but by people who want an excuse to believe." These excuses to believe take the form of "theories" as to why share prices should rise to unprecedented levels, why the economy has entered a "new era" (Shiller, 2000, chapter 5). Prominent among these are "theories" about wealth increases from mergers. Shiller (2000, p. 101) quotes a *New York Times* editorial from April 1901, which prophesied that the U.S. Steel merger would avoid "much economic waste" and effect "various economies coincident to consolidation." Similar benefits were predicted from railroad mergers. Such optimism caused U.S. Steel's share price to soar from the $38 it was floated at in 1901 to $55. By 1903 it had plunged to $9 (*Economist*, 1991, p. 11).

In a survey of the early literature, Markham (1955, p. 162) attributed the first great merger wave to the overoptimism that gripped the market.

> The literature provides convincing evidence that the abnormally large volume of mergers formed in 1897–1900 stemmed from a wave of frenzied speculation in asset values. Several students of the early merger movement agree that the excessive demand for securities was an impelling force in the mass promotion of mergers after 1896.

Overoptimism also fueled the merger wave of the late 1960s. The distinguishing feature of this wave was the large number of diversification mergers by the so-called conglomerates.[20] The managers of the leading conglomerates, men like Charles Bluhdorn of Gulf & Western and Harold Geneen of ITT, came to be regarded as corporate geniuses who could create synergies by combining companies in unrelated industries. Optimism about the conglomerates' merger strategies drove up their P/E ratios and gave rise to "P/E magic."[21] A conglomerate with a P/E ratio of 30, say, would buy a slow-growing company with a P/E of 10. The market's optimism about the merger would lead it to reevaluate the target's growth potential upward and apply the ratio of 30 to its earnings. Instantaneously, the target had a value as part of the conglomerate equal to three times its premerger market value. The collapse of the conglomerates' share prices when the 1960s stock market boom ended revealed that they were not able to produce the continued growth in earnings that would justify a P/E of 30. The belief in P/E magic, which fueled the merger wave of the 1960s, resembles the kind of Ponzi scheme that Shiller (2000, pp. 64–66) claims is a part of all stock market bubbles.[22]

The optimism that characterizes stock market booms makes them an ideal time to announce mergers that are unlikely to increase profits and shareholder wealth. A news conference is held, various synergies and economies of scale and scope are proclaimed, and a merger, which in normal times would be met with skepticism by the market and a decline in the bidder's share price, now produces no change or even an increase. Thus, wealth-destroying mergers of the type that empire-building managers undertake increase in frequency during stock market booms.

The Hubris Hypothesis

Under the managerial discretion theory, mergers can destroy the wealth of acquirers' shareholders, because the mergers may not generate any synergies and the bidder must offer a premium for the target's shares, and perhaps because of transaction and other costs associated with the acquisition. Roll (1986, 1988) offered an alternative explanation for why acquiring companies' shareholders suffer losses. Roll assumed, as in the MCCH, that bidding for a target occurs, and the bidding process is characterized by the "winner's curse." The company whose management has the highest expectations of the target's profit potential wins the bidding but on average pays more than the target's true profit potential justifies.

Although the winner's curse can explain why acquiring companies' shareholders lose from mergers, it does not explain why managers, who seek to maximize the wealth of their shareholders, participate in a game when the "winner" usually loses. Roll solved this riddle by suggesting that the managers suffer from hubris. Each manager knows that the *average* acquirer loses, but believes that he or she is better at spotting value than the average acquirer. Roll did not offer this hypothesis as an explanation for merger waves, but it is reasonable to assume that the kind of hubris that underlies the hypothesis is more prevalent during stock market booms. Indeed, managerial hubris is merely another manifestation of the kind of overoptimism that prevails during these booms.

The Overvaluation Hypotheses

Shleifer and Vishny (2003) (SV) have offered yet another explanation for merger waves coinciding with stock market booms. They assume that some firms become overvalued during stock market booms, and their managers realize this. Managers attempt to protect their shareholders from the fall in share price that will come once the market corrects its mistaken overvaluation by trading the overvalued shares for real assets through the acquisition of another firm. The acquired firm's managers are willing to accept the buyer's overvalued shares, because they wish to cash in their stakes in their company at attractive terms. The general overoptimism prevailing in the market ensures that the merger announcement is not immediately greeted with a dramatic fall in the bidder's share price. SV's theory explains why merger waves coincide with stock market booms—more firms are overvalued during a boom—and why acquirers' shareholders suffer wealth losses over long windows following the mergers.

SV abandon the efficient capital market assumption and explain merger waves as a result of differences in the evaluations of a company's shares—its managers know their true value, the market overestimates their value. Gort (1969) also offered an explanation for merger waves that relied on differences in evaluations of a company's worth. Mergers occurred when outsiders placed a higher value on a company's assets than its own shareholders did. Such divergences in opinions about the worth of companies were assumed to increase during stock market booms when share prices were changing rapidly. More recently, Rhodes-Kropf and Viswanathan (2004) have hypothesized that merger waves occur because the managers of target firms are more prone to make evaluation errors during stock market booms and mistakenly accept the overvalued shares of a bidder. All of these theories have in common that some group—the market, the bidders' managers, the targets' managers—make systematic errors in valuing the shares of particular companies during stock market booms, and thus implicitly rely in part on the psychology of stock market booms already discussed.

The next two theories attempt to explain merger waves while retaining the assumption of capital market efficiency.

The q-Theory of Mergers

Jovanovic and Rousseau (2002) extend the q-theory of investment to mergers. They liken mergers to purchasing used plant and equipment and argue that the gap between potential acquirers' and targets' q's increases during a stock market boom, leading managers to favor purchasing assets in the form of other firms rather than as capital equipment. The q-theory of investment assumes that a $q > 1$ indicates that a company can profitably expand its existing capital stock, and thus can only be used to explain horizontal mergers. To use the theory to explain all sorts of mergers, one must assume that a high q implies that the market believes that a firm is well managed and can expand in any direction.

The Industry Shocks Theory of Mergers

Harford (2005) has proposed a "neoclassical explanation of merger waves" as a direct alternative to SV's behavioral theory of mergers (p. 530).

> Merger waves occur in response to specific industry shocks that require large scale reallocation of assets. However, these shocks are not enough on their own. There must be sufficient capital liquidity to accommodate the asset reallocation. The increase in capital liquidity and reduction in financing constraints that is correlated with high asset values must be present for the shock to propagate a wave....
>
> Thus, the explanation for merger waves is intuitive: merger waves require both an economic motivation for transactions and relatively low transaction costs to generate a large volume of transactions.

Harford provides empirical support for his neoclassical theory by showing that the 1990s merger wave was accompanied by clusters of mergers in several industries, and a fall in borrowing costs as measured by the federal funds rate.

Discussion

The different theories of merger waves reveal fundamental differences in the assumptions scholars make when analyzing the merger phenomenon—differences that reappear in several other chapters in this volume and color the views of different observers as to how capitalism and markets work and their benefits and costs. If the market for corporate control is sufficiently efficient to induce managers to maximize their shareholders' wealth, as the neoclassical theories assume, then merger waves will generate wealth by reallocating assets to their most profitable uses. Firms with talented managers, as evidenced by the high *q*'s of their firms, will be the bidders, firms with less talented managers will be the targets. Alternatively, mergers may be wealth-enhancing responses to industry shocks. If the discipline of the market for corporate control is less stringent, however, agency problems may exist, and managers will have the discretion to undertake mergers that provide private benefits to themselves but harm their shareholders.

In addition to differences in assumptions about the motivations of managers, the neoclassical and behavioral theories of merger waves differ over whether the capital market is efficient. Harford explicitly assumes it is, Jovanovic and Rousseau implicitly do so by assuming that Tobin's *q*'s correctly identify well-managed companies. All of the behavioral theories relax the assumption of capital market efficiency in one way or another by assuming that certain actors in mergers make systematic mistakes.

Whether or not the capital market is efficient is crucial for mustering up evidence for or against the different theories. If it is efficient, the wealth effects of mergers are revealed when they are announced. The many studies that find that targets' shareholders gain and bidders' shareholders do not lose over short windows around announcements can be taken as evidence that acquisitions generate wealth. The presumption of capital market efficiency allows the researcher to dismiss the long and dramatic declines in acquiring shareholders' wealth following mergers, which many have observed, as econometric aberrations.[23] The assumption of capital market efficiency allows one to treat the wealth created at merger announcements—all or mostly accruing to target shareholders—as unbiased estimates of the future wealth that the mergers will generate.

More is at stake with respect to the assumption of capital market efficiency, however, than just the determination of which theory of merger waves receives the most support. If the capital market is not efficient in the strong sense assumed in event studies of mergers, then the whole event study approach is called into question. Share price movements before announcements, at announcements, and afterward could all be biased estimates of firm values and changes in these values. Nothing can be concluded from the hundreds of merger event studies that have been published if the capital market is not efficient.

This difficulty is nicely illustrated in Franks and Harris (1989). When they use estimates from the market model (equation 15.1) estimated over a pre-event period, they obtain a cumulative return to acquirers over the two years following the announcements of −12.6 percent. Acquirers' shares performed significantly worse after the mergers than before. When Franks and Harris estimated post-merger returns using the capital asset pricing model,, thereby ignoring the strong performance of the acquirers prior to the mergers, they obtained *positive* returns of 4.6 percent. They concluded this was the true effect of the mergers on the acquiring shareholders. They dismissed the −12.6 percent returns, arguing in part that "bidders time mergers to take advantage of recent abnormal returns in their own stock prices... positive [pre-merger] αs, if unsustainable, would introduce a negative drift in abnormal returns, which could be interpreted as 'too' high a control return rather than poor performance by bidders" (p. 246, note omitted). They did not discuss, however, why the acquirers in their sample outperformed the market portfolio by almost 1 percent a month for a period of five years before the mergers, and why this extraordinarily good performance happened to come to an end at the time when the companies announced their acquisitions, thus justifying a change in benchmark.

Several studies have reported significant negative abnormal returns for targets prior to being taken over.[24] The usual explanation for this invokes the MCCH—the targets were badly managed and the takeovers occurred to replace their managers. But perhaps their shares were merely *undervalued* prior to the takeovers, just as the acquirers' shares might have been overvalued. The premiums paid may then not have reflected the creation of wealth through the replacement of bad managers or other synergies, but merely the return of the targets' market values to their unbiased levels just as, following Franks and Harris, the decline in returns to the acquirers was merely a return to normalcy. Once we allow for the possibility that some shares can be substantially overvalued, we must assume that some can be substantially undervalued. If shares can be overvalued for periods of up to five years, they can conceivably also be overvalued over a few days surrounding merger announcements—especially when these announcements are made during stock market booms, when optimism in the market is at its peak. Unless we can remove the market's systematic over- or undervaluation of share prices at each point in time, the event study approach becomes utterly useless.

Why the Neoclassical Theories Cannot Explain Merger Waves

Although the sustained losses to acquirers' shareholders over long periods following mergers observed in many studies are perhaps the strongest evidence against the neoclassical theories of mergers, there are other characteristics of merger waves that undermine the neoclassical theories, which I briefly review.

The Market for Corporate Control Hypothesis

The negligible gains to acquirers' shareholders at merger announcements could be taken as support for the MCCH, if we assume an efficient capital market and that all of the gains from the mergers are associated with the replacement of the targets' managers and accrue to the targets' shareholders, because of a bidding war among potential acquirers. Many event studies have interpreted their results in this way.

Because most managers do not want to lose their jobs, hostile takeovers usually take the form of tender offers for the target's shares. Table 15.4 reports the numbers of mergers of listed companies taking the form of tender offers (TOs) and friendly mergers (FMs) from 1981 through 2002 in the United States. Any merger that is not a TO takes place as a result of an agreement between the managements of the two merging companies and is called a friendly merger. Only 9 percent of all mergers over this twenty-two-year period were tender offers. The fraction of TOs rose to around 20 percent or more during the so-called hostile takeover wave of the second half of the 1980s. During this period, some giant companies were acquired through hostile takeovers. Typically their managers were removed, and the companies were often broken up. Indeed, many of the hostile takeovers undid inefficient corporate structures created during the conglomerate merger wave of the 1960s.

Managers of large companies responded to the increase in hostile merger activity of the 1980s in two ways. First, they adopted policies to increase shareholder wealth—poorly performing divisions were sold or spun off, cash flows were diverted from investment and acquisitions to share repurchases, the pursuit of "shareholder value" and return to "core competencies" became the mantras of the day. The second managerial response was to go to state legislatures and demand new laws to protect them from hostile takeovers. The legislatures readily complied.[25] Thus, by 1992 TOs had declined to a mere 3 percent of all mergers.

Table 15.4. Number of Acquirers and Targets in Friendly Mergers (FM) and Tender Offers (TO) and Mean Tobin's q's

				Acquirers			Targets		
Year	FM	TO	%TO	FM	TO	FM	FM	TO	TO
				MVit–1/Kit–1	MVit–1/Kit–1	MVit–1/Kit–1	Mit/Kit–1	MVit–1/Kit–1	Mit/Kit–1
1981	205	14	6.39	1.275	0.664	1.011	0.756	1.066	0.787
1982	311	23	6.89	1.216	0.906	0.846	0.829	0.758	0.711
1983	486	23	4.52	1.377	0.781	1.052	1.018	0.797	0.804
1984	478	29	5.72	1.411	0.921	1.218	1.097	1.073	0.897
1985	166	41	19.81	1.154	0.902	1.085	1.465	1.075	1.754
1986	156	56	26.42	1.245	1.001	1.234	1.654	1.232	1.815
1987	177	47	20.98	1.380	1.118	1.204	1.564	1.140	1.662
1988	181	60	24.90	1.298	1.316	1.384	2.048	1.046	1.757
1989	273	55	16.77	1.327	0.998	1.306	1.588	1.266	2.008
1990	318	26	7.56	1.532	1.356	1.341	1.435	1.253	1.694
1991	346	19	5.21	1.459	1.282	1.397	1.857	1.274	2.144
1992	513	16	3.02	1.873	2.034	1.343	2.123	1.133	1.720
1993	607	25	3.96	1.681	1.557	1.384	2.096	1.706	2.548
1994	726	33	4.35	1.644	1.732	1.238	2.060	1.259	2.556
1995	817	57	6.52	1.623	1.570	1.147	2.292	1.503	2.951
1996	960	55	5.42	1.803	1.581	1.490	2.819	1.200	2.525
1997	1001	73	6.80	1.902	1.652	1.213	2.295	1.057	2.340
1998	599	72	10.73	2.004	1.732	1.590	3.095	1.274	2.602

(Continued)

Table 15.4. (Continued)

Year	FM	TO	%TO	Acquirers		Targets			
				FM	TO	FM	FM	TO	TO
				MVit–1/Kit–1	MVit–1/Kit–1	MVit–1/Kit–1	Mit/Kit–1	MVit–1/Kit–1	Mit/Kit–1
1999	588	63	9.68	2.218	1.860	1.687	3.109	1.498	2.216
2000	550	63	10.28	2.708	1.646	2.012	2.340	1.886	2.076
2001	453	47	9.40	1.962	2.416	1.490	2.281	1.091	1.865
2002	339	37	9.84	1.705	2.006	0.862	1.000	1.017	1.468
Total	10250	934	9.11	1.742	1.489	1.298	1.976	1.118	1.854
Wave (1995–2000)	4515	383	7.82	1.988	1.683	1.433	2.611	1.358	2.471
Nonwave	5735	551	8.35	1.548	1.347	1.216	1.589	1.117	1.618

Note: MVi_{t-1} = market value of the firm in year $t-1$. K_{it-1} = total assets of the firm in year $t-1$. M_{it} = deal value: amount paid for target in year t. Wave years are 1995–2000; nonwave years are 1981–1994 and 2001–2002.

Tender offers differ dramatically from friendly mergers in both the manner in which they are consummated and their effects on acquirers' shareholders. As noted, FMs tend to be followed by losses to acquirers over long windows, whereas TOs have been followed by either smaller losses or gains.[26] These differences underscore the point that mergers are not all alike, and no single theory can explain all mergers. The results regarding TOs in the United States are broadly consistent with the proposition that this form of merger increases shareholder wealth and fits the MCCH. At the same time, the data in table 15.4 reveal that the MCCH does not offer an explanation for merger waves. Although TOs increased in number during the wave of the late 1990s, they never became more than 10 percent of total merger activity. Other theories must account for the remaining 90 percent.

The *q*-Theory of Mergers

Jovanovic and Rousseau (2002) claim that merger waves occur because high *q* firms find it more profitable to expand by buying other companies than by buying used plant and equipment. Table 15.4 present the average *q*'s of acquirers in FMs and TOs from 1981 through 2002. Acquirers' *q*'s during the late 1990s wave are roughly double their values in the early 1980s. The table also presents the average amounts paid for the targets (the deal values, D_{it}) divided by the book value of their capital stocks at the end of the previous year (K_{it-1}), which is a kind of Tobin's *q* for the targets using the actual amount paid for them rather than some earlier market value. They rise to well over 2 for targets in TOs and over 3 for targets in FMs. Given that a *q* for new plant and equipment is by definition 1, table 15.4 indicates that the purchase of other companies *could not* have been a cheaper way for high *q* firms to expand than by simply buying plant and equipment.

The Industry Shocks Hypothesis

Under the industry shocks hypothesis, merger waves occur when a set of simultaneous shocks to several industries coincides with a decline in borrowing costs. Although Harford (2005) presents evidence of concurrent merger waves in several industries during the 1990s aggregate wave, Gärtner and Halbheer (2009) failed to identify such a concurrence. Thus, the evidence regarding this part of the hypothesis seems to be ambiguous.

If falling borrowing costs drive merger waves, we should observe an expansion of the use of debt during merger waves. Table 15.5 reports the sources of finance for mergers between 1986 and 2002. Debt finance (the largest portion of "other") actually fell during the wave years, 1995–2000, whereas equity-financed mergers expanded by 50 percent. This part of the industry shocks hypothesis also is unsupported.

Harford (2005) lists a variety of shocks as causes for industry waves during the 1990s. The pattern observed in figure 15.1 and the dramatic expansion of the use of equity to finance mergers visible in table 15.5 suggests that a common "shock" to all industries may explain the 1990s wave—the overall rise in share prices. The fact

Table 15.5. Sources of Finance for Acquisitions: Total Amounts of Assets Financed by the Various Sources

Year	Equity	Cash	Other
1986	14.54	78.06	7.45
1987	22.18	73.38	4.73
1988	16.57	78.7	5.12
1989	18.25	74.89	7.09
1990	16.85	76.36	6.96
1991	22.33	68.79	9.3
1992	25.69	63.88	10.81
1993	14.62	73.97	10.21
1994	22.23	68.17	9.64
1995	29.88	63.63	7.04
1996	31.00	62.89	6.57
1997	27.97	65.55	7.00
1998	30.45	63.19	6.85
1999	35.33	59.49	5.72
2000	35.86	60.00	4.53
2001	29.52	63.96	7.21
2002	18.40	74.28	7.77
Nonwave	20.11	72.22	7.85
Wave (1995–2000)	31.75	62.46	6.29
All years	24.22	68.77	7.30

Source: Thompson Financial Securities database as reported in Gugler et al. (2012, forthcoming).

that all merger waves have been accompanied by stock market booms suggests that some combination of the behavioral theories, which emphasize the psychology of stock markets, offers the best explanation for merger waves.

Conclusions

I began this chapter by observing that considerable disagreement exists over the causes and consequences of mergers. This disagreement stems in part from differences in the presumptions various scholars make when studying mergers. One group sees "the market for corporate control" as just another market for assets; like all markets, it is assumed to achieve efficient allocations. Well-managed companies take over poorly managed companies, and economies of scale and scope are achieved through the intelligent combining of different companies.

Other scholars emphasize important differences between the market for corporate control and other markets. For one, the buyers in this market are typically managers of large firms who are, due to the principal agent problem in large firms, effectively buying companies with other people's money. Second, both the ability of a buyer to finance an acquisition and the price it must pay for the other firm may depend on the stock market's valuations of the two companies. If the stock market is prone to periods of overoptimism or pessimism, both buyers and sellers of assets in the market for corporate control may be mispriced, and this mispricing may affect the efficiency with which the market allocates assets. Thus, one's views about the role mergers play in the capitalist process, as one's views about capitalism in general, will depend on the assumptions one makes about how the two processes work. If principal agent problems are unimportant in large companies, and the capital market is efficient, the market for corporate control will contribute to increasing economic efficiency like most other markets. If one or both of these conditions do not hold, mergers may destroy wealth as well as create it.

The evidence reviewed in this chapter does not support the proposition that mergers improve allocative efficiency on average. The fact that acquirers' shareholders gain little if any from mergers in the short run and often suffer huge losses in the long run, belies the assumption that acquirers' managers are trying to maximize their shareholders' wealth. The fact that merger activity increases greatly during stock market booms, when optimism in the market is at its peak, suggests that this optimism fuels the undertaking of wealth-destroying mergers.

In trying to make sense of the historical patterns of merger activity and the diverse findings with respect to their effects, one should keep in mind that no one theory explains all mergers. *Some* mergers do increase efficiency; some—particularly hostile takeovers—do result in the removal of bad managers; and some even result in increases in market power for the merging companies. Opportunities to merge falling into these categories presumably arise all the time, and regardless of whether they are maximizing profits, or growth, or pursuing some other goal, managers will take advantage of them. Thus, it is reasonable to assume that some mergers at every point in time are occurring for the reasons posited by the various neoclassical theories of mergers. During a stock market upswing, other opportunities for mergers arise, however. The optimism in the market allows empire-building managers to undertake wealth-destroying mergers without seeing their share prices fall dramatically; it feeds the hubris of managers, leading them into bidding wars for companies that result in losses for their shareholders; and it allows managers to finance mergers that promise no synergies with their overvalued shares. Thus, during stock market booms mergers take place that would not be undertaken during normal times or in depressed markets. These additional mergers tend to be wealth-destroying or at least lead to losses for the acquirers' shareholders.

These losses are great enough to offset the gains from the mergers that do increase efficiency or market power, so that the average merger is found to result in little or no increase in profits, sales, and other measures of performance. Moreover, the wealth destruction can be quite large. Mueller and Yurtolglu (2007) estimated wealth losses to acquirers' shareholders after three years for acquisitions in the 1990s of 19 percent. Moeller et al. (2005) estimated a wealth loss to acquirers for mergers during the merger wave of 1998–2001 of 12 percent compared to a 1.6 percent loss in nonwave years. The wealth destruction during the wave amounted to some $240 billion.

Public policy with respect to mergers has been confined almost exclusively to preventing mergers that increase market power. This has been a mistake. Wealth-destroying mergers result in much bigger social welfare losses than market power–increasing mergers. When efficiency declines as a result of a merger, producers and consumers both lose, whereas only consumers lose when market power increases. Policies that would eliminate wealth-destroying mergers and improve the efficiency of the market for corporate control are the same as those that would improve the performance of capitalism more generally—reduce principal agent problems in large companies and eliminate speculative bubbles in stock markets. Easier said then done.

NOTES

1. Bittlingmayer (1996), Ebard and Schaller (2002), and Jovanovic and Rousseau (2002).
2. Coase (1937), Weston (1970), and Williamson (1970).
3. Stigler (1950) is the classic reference. For a recent theoretical analysis, see Nocke and White (2007).
4. Mueller (1969) and Roll (1986).
5. Marris (1964) and Manne (1965).
6. Hannah and Kay (1977), Gugler, Mueller, and Weichselbaumer (2012), Gugler et al. (2012, forthcoming).
7. Gugler et al. (2003).
8. Ibid.
9. Connor et al. (1998), Pesendorfer (2003), and Bitzan and Wilson (2007).
10. Lichtenberg and Siegel (1987) and McGucken and Nguyen (1995).
11. Quote is from Grabowski and Kyle (2008). Ornaghi (2009) reaches a similar conclusion.
12. See discussion and references in Mueller (2003).
13. My calculations are based on data reported by Dodd and Ruback (1977).
14. For example, Malatesta (1983).
15. Asquith (1983).
16. For an exhaustive survey, see Mueller (2003).
17. The −61.2 percent figure is the negative and significant daily estimate of Loderer and Martin multiplied by 1,250, the length of their postmerger window, to produce a long-run estimate. It seems too large in absolute value, however.
18. See Bliss and Rosen (2001) and Harford and Li (2007).

19. See, Bebchuk and Grinstein (2005).
20. I attempted to explain the conglomerate merger wave of the late 1960s using the managerial discretion hypothesis (Mueller, 1969).
21. P/E magic was much discussed in the popular press and also made its way into the academic literature; Mead (1969) and Lintner (1971).
22. See also Malkiel's contribution to this volume (chapter 14).
23. Fama and French (1993), for example, criticized the use of the capital asset pricing model and market model to estimate gains to acquirers, because these models fail to account for the systematic effects of firm size and book-to-market ratios on company returns. They speculated that the acquirers' negative postmerger returns would disappear once these characteristics were accounted for. See also Franks and Harris (1989) and Franks et al. (1991).
24. Mandelker (1974), Ellert (1976), Smiley (1976), Langetieg (1978), Asquith (1983), and Malatesta (1983).
25. See Roe (1993).
26. For example, Magenheim and Mueller (1988) and Rau and Vermaelen (1998).

References

Agrawal, Anup, Jeffrey F. Jaffe, and Gershon N. Mandelker. "The Post-Merger Performance of Acquiring Firms: A Re-Examination of an Anomaly." *Journal of Finance* 47 (Sept. 1992): 1605–1621.

Akhavein, Jalal D., Allen N. Berger, and David B. Humphrey. "The Effects of Megamergers on Efficiency and Prices: Evidence from a Bank Profit Function." *Review of Industrial Organization* 12 (Feb. 1997): 95–139.

Andrade, Gregor, Mark Mitchell, and Erik Stafford. "New Evidence and Perspectives on Mergers." *Journal of Economic Perspectives* 15 (Spring 2001): 103–120.

Asquith, Paul. "Merger Bids, Uncertainty, and Stockholder Returns." *Journal of Financial Economics* 11 (April 1983): 51–83.

Baldwin, John R. *The Dynamics of Industrial Competition*. Cambridge: Cambridge University Press, 1995.

Bebchuk, Lucian, and Yaniv Grinstein. "The Growth of Executive Pay." *Oxford Review of Economic Policy* 21 (Summer 2005): 283–303.

Bhagat, Sanjai, Andrei Shleifer, and Robert W. Vishny. "Hostile Takeovers in the 1980s: The Return to Corporate Specialization." *Brookings Papers on Economic Activity, Microeconomics* (1990): 1–84.

Bittlingmayer, George. "Mergers as a Form of Investment." *Kyklos* 49 (1996): 127–153.

Bitzan, John D., and Wesley W. Wilson. "Industry Costs and Consolidation: Efficiency Gains and Mergers in the U.S. Railroad Industry." *Review of Industrial Organization* 30 (March 2007): 81–105.

Bliss, Richard T., and Richard J. Rosen. "CEO Compensation and Bank Mergers." *Journal of Financial Economics* 61 (July 2001): 107–138.

Cable, J. R., J. P. R. Palfrey, and J. W. Runge. 1980. "Federal Republic of Germany, 1964–1974." In *The Determinants and Effects of Mergers: An International Comparison*, ed. D. C. Mueller, 99–132. Cambridge, Mass.: Oelgeschlager, Gunn, and Hain, 1980.

Coase, Ronald H. "The Nature of the Firm." *Economica* 4 (Nov. 1937): 386–405. Reprinted in *Readings in Price Theory*, Homewood, Ill.: Irwin, 1952, pp. 331–351.

Conn, Robert L. "The Failing Firm/Industry Doctrines in Conglomerate Mergers." *Journal of Industrial Economics* 24 (March 1976): 181–187.
Connor, Robert A., Roger D. Feldman, and Bryan E. Dowd. "The Effects of Market Concentration and Horizontal Mergers on Hospital Costs and Prices." *International Journal of Economics and Business* 5 (July 1998): 159–180.
Cosh, Andrew D., Alan Hughes, M. S. Kumar, and Ajit Singh. *Institutional Investment Company Performance and Mergers: Empirical Evidence for the UK.* London: Office of Fair Trading, 1985.
Cosh, Andrew, Alan Hughes, and Ajit Singh. "The Causes and Effects of Takeovers in the United Kingdom: An Empirical Investigation for the Late 1960s at the Microeconomic Level." In *The Determinants and Effects of Mergers: An International Comparison,* ed. D. C. Mueller, 227–270. Cambridge, Mass.: Oelgeschlager, Gunn, and Hain, 1980.
Dickerson, Andrew P., Heather D. Gibson, and Euclid Tsakalotos. "The Impact of Acquistions on Company Performance: Evidence from a Large Panel of UK Firms." *Oxford Economic Papers* 49 (July 1997): 344–361.
Dodd, Peter, and Richard Ruback. "Tender Offers and Stockholder Returns: An Empirical Analysis." *Journal of Financial Economics* 5 (Dec. 1977): 351–374.
Doukas, John. 1995. "Overinvestment, Tobin's q and Gains from Foreign Acquisitions." *Journal of Banking and Finance* 19 (Oct. 1995): 1185–1303.
Ebard, Brian, and Huntley Schaller. "Acquisitions and Investment." *Economica* 69 (Aug. 2002): 357–370.
Economist. "From Morgan's Nose to Milken's Wig: In America Takeovers Never Die" (International Finance Survey by J.P. Morgan, Michael Milken). *Economist,* April 27, 1991, p. 11.
Ellert, James C. "Mergers, Antitrust Law Enforcement and Stockholder Returns." *Journal of Finance* 31 (May 1976): 715–732.
Fama, Eugene F., and Kenneth R. French. "Common Risk Factors in the Returns on Stocks and Bonds." *Journal of Financial Economics* 33 (Feb. 1993): 3–56.
Franks, Julian R., and Robert S. Harris. "Shareholder Wealth Effects of Corporate Takeovers." *Journal of Financial Economics* 23 (Aug. 1989): 225–249.
Franks, Julian, Robert Harris, and Sheridan Titman. "The Postmerger Share-Price Performance of Acquiring Firms." *Journal of Financial Economics* 29 (March 1991): 81–96.
Galbraith, John Kenneth. *The Great Crash 1929.* New York: Pelican, 1961.
Gärtner, Dennis L., and Daniel Halbheer. "Are There Waves in Merger Activity after All?" *International Journal of Industrial Organization* 27 (2009): 708–718.
Goldberg, Lawrence G. "The Effect of Conglomerate Mergers on Competition." *Journal of Law and Economics* 16 (April 1973): 137–158.
Gort, Michael. "An Economic Disturbance Theory of Mergers." *Quarterly Journal of Economics* 83 (Nov. 1969): 624–642.
Grabowski, Henry, and Margaret Kyle. "Mergers and Alliances in Pharmaceuticals: Effects on Innovation and R&D Productivity." In *The Economics of Corporate Governance and Mergers,* ed. Klaus Gugler and B. Burcin Yurtoglu, 262–287. Cheltenham: Edward Elgar, 2008.
Gregory, Alan. "An Examination of the Long Run Performance of UK Acquiring Firms." *Journal of Business Finance and Accounting* 25 (Sept. 1997): 971–1002.
Gugler, Klaus, Dennis C. Mueller, and Michael Weichselbaumer. "The Determinants of Merger Waves: An International Perspective." *International Journal of Industrial Organization* 30 (Jan. 2012): 1-15.

Gugler, Klaus, Dennis C. Mueller, Michael Weichselbaumer, and B. Burcin Yurtoglu. "Market Optimism and Merger Waves." *Managerial and Decision Economics* (2012) forthcoming.
Gugler, Klaus, Dennis C. Mueller, B. Burcin Yurtoglu, and Christine Zulehner. "The Effects of Mergers: An International Comparison." *International Journal of Industrial Organization* 21 (May 2003): 625–653.
Gugler, Klaus, and B. Burcin Yurtoglu. "The Effects of Mergers on Company Employment in the USA and Europe." *International Journal of Industrial Organization* 22 (April 2004): 481–502.
Hannah, Leslie, and John A. Kay. *Concentration in Modern Industry*. London: Macmillan, 1977.
Harford, Jarrad. "What Drives Merger Waves?" *Journal of Financial Economics* 77 (Sept. 2005): 529–560.
Harford, Jarrad, and Kai Li. "Decoupling CEO Wealth and Firm Performance: The Case of Acquiring CEOs." *Journal of Finance* 62 (April 2007): 917–949.
Healy Paul M., Krishna G. Palepu, and Richard S. Ruback. "Does Corporate Performance Improve after Mergers?" *Journal of Financial Economics* 31 (April 1992): 135–175.
Higson, Chris, and Jamie Elliott. "Post-Takeover Returns: The UK Evidence." *Journal of Empirical Finance* 5 (Jan. 1998): 27–46.
Jenny, Frédéric, and André-Paul Weber. "France, 1962–1972." In *The Determinants and Effects of Mergers: An International Comparison,* ed. D. C. Mueller, 133–162. Cambridge, Mass.: Oelgeschlager, Gunn, and Hain, 1980.
Jensen, Michael C., and Richard S. Ruback. "The Market for Corporate Control." *Journal of Financial Economics* 11 (April 1983): 5–50.
Jovanovic, Boyan, and Peter L. Rousseau. "The Q-Theory of Mergers." *American Economic Review* 92 (May 2002): 198–204.
Koetter, Michael. "An Assessment of Bank Mergers Success in Germany." *German Economic Review* 9 (May 2008): 232–264.
Kumar, M. S. "Growth, Acquisition Activity and Firm Size: Evidence from the United Kingdom." *Journal of Industrial Economics* 33 (March 1985): 327–338.
Kumps, Anne-Marie, and Robert Wtterwulghe. "Belgium, 1962–1974." In *The Determinants and Effects of Mergers: An International Comparison,* ed. D. C. Mueller, 67–97. Cambridge, Mass.: Oelgeschlager, Gunn, and Hain, 1980.
Langetieg, Terence C. "An Application of a Three-Factor Performance Index to Measure Stockholders Gains from Merger." *Journal of Financial Economics* 6 (Dec. 1978): 365–383.
Lichtenberg, Frank R., and Donald Siegel. "Productivity and Changes in Ownership of Manufacturing Plants." *Brookings Papers on Economic Activity* 3 (1987): 643–673.
Lintner, John. "Expectations, Mergers and Equilibrium in Purely Competitive Securities Markets." *American Economic Review* 61 (May 1971): 101–111.
Loderer, Claudio, and Kenneth Martin. "Postacquisition Performance of Acquiring Firms." *Financial Management* 21 (Autumn 1992): 69–91.
Loughran, Tim, and Anand M. Vijh. "Do Long-Term Shareholders Benefit from Corporate Acquisitions?" *Journal of Finance* 52 (Dec. 1997): 1765–1790.
Magenheim, Ellen, and Dennis C. Mueller. "Are Acquiring-Firm Shareholders Better Off after an Acquisition?" In *Knights, Raiders and Targets*, ed. John Coffee, Louis Lowenstein, and Susan Rose-Ackerman, 171–193. Oxford: Oxford University Press, 1988.
Malatesta, Paul H. "The Wealth Effect of Merger Activity and the Objective Functions of Merging Firms." *Journal of Financial Economics* 11 (April 1983): 155–181.
Mandelker, Gershon. "Risk and Return: The Case of Merging Firms." *Journal of Financial Economics* 1 (Dec. 1974): 303–335.

Manne, Henry G. "Mergers and the Market for Corporate Control." *Journal of Political Economy* 73 (April 1965): 110–120.
Maquieira, Carlos P., William P. Megginson, and Lance Nail. "Wealth Creation versus Wealth Redistribution in Pure Stock-for-Stock Mergers." *Journal of Financial Economics* 48 (April 1998): 3–33.
Markham, Jesse W. "Survey of the Evidence and Findings on Mergers." In *Business Concentration and Price Policy*, National Bureau of Economic Research, 141–182. New York: NBER, 1955.
Marris, Robin. *The Economic Theory of Managerial Capitalism*. Glencoe, Ill.: Free Press, 1964.
McDougall, Fred M., and David K. Round. *The Determinants and Effects of Corporate Takeovers in Australia, 1970–1981*. Victoria: Australian Institute of Management, 1986.
McGuckin, Robert H., and Sang V. Nguyen. "On the Productivity and Plant Ownership Change: New Evidence from the Longitudinal Research Database." *Rand Journal of Economics* 26 (Summer 1995): 257–276.
Mead, Walter J. "Instantaneous Merger Profit as a Conglomerate Merger Motive." *Economic Inquiry* 7 (Dec. 1969): 295–306.
Meeks, Geoffrey. *Disappointing Marriage: A Study of the Gains from Merger*. Cambridge: Cambridge University Press, 1977.
Moeller, Sara B., Frederik P. Schlingemann, and René M. Stulz. "Wealth Destruction on a Massive Scale? A Study of Acquiring-Firm Returns in the Recent Merger Wave." *Journal of Finance* 60 (April 2005): 757–782.
Mueller, Dennis C. "A Theory of Conglomerate Mergers." *Quarterly Journal of Economics* 83 (Nov. 1969): 643–659.
Mueller, Dennis C.. "The United States, 1962–1972." In *The Determinants and Effects of Mergers: An International Comparison,* ed. D. C. Mueller, 271–298. Cambridge, Mass.: Oelgeschlager, Gunn, and Hain, 1980.
Mueller, Dennis C. *Profits in the Long Run*. Cambridge: Cambridge University Press, 1986.
Mueller, Dennis C. "The Finance Literature on Mergers: A Critical Survey." In *Competition, Monopoly and Corporate Governance, Essays in Honour of Keith Cowling*, ed. M. Waterson, 161–205. Cheltenham: Edward Elgar, 2003.
Mueller, Dennis C., and Mark Sirower. "The Causes of Mergers: Tests Based on the Gains to Acquiring Firms' Shareholders and the Size of Premia." *Managerial and Decision Economics* 24 (Aug. 2003): 373–391.
Mueller, Dennis C., and B. Burcin Yurtoglu. "Corporate Governance and the Returns to Acquiring Firms' Shareholders: An International Comparison." *Managerial and Decision Economics* 28 (Dec. 2007): 879–896.
Nocke, Volker, and Lucy White. "Do Vertical Mergers Facilitate Upstream Collusion?" *American Economic Review* 97 (Sept. 2007): 1321–1339.
Odagiri, Hiroyuki. "Mergers and Efficiency: Theory, Empirical Evidence, and Competition Policy in Japan." In *The Economics of Corporate Governance and Mergers*, ed. Klaus Gugler and B. Burcin Yurtoglu, 203–225. Cheltenham: Edward Elgar, 2008.
Odagiri, Hiroyuki, and Tatsuo Hase. "Are Mergers and Acquisitions Going to Be Popular in Japan Too? An Empirical Study." *International Journal of Industrial Organization* 7 (March 1989): 49–72.
Ornaghi, Carmine. "Mergers and Innovation in Big Pharma." *International Journal of Industrial Organization* 27 (Jan. 2009): 70–79.

Peer, Henk. "The Netherlands, 1962–1973." In *The Determinants and Effects of Mergers: An International Comparison*, ed. D. C. Mueller, 163–191. Cambridge, Mass.: Oelgeschlager, Gunn, and Hain, 1980.

Pesendorfer, Martin. "Horizontal Mergers in the Paper Industry." *Rand Journal of Economics* 34 (Autumn 2003): 495–515.

Rau, P. Raghavendra, and Theo Vermaelen. "Glamour, Value and the Post-acquisition Performance of Acquiring Firms." *Journal of Financial Economics* 49 (Aug. 1998): 223–253.

Ravenscraft, David J., and F. M. Scherer. *Mergers, Sell-Offs, and Economic Efficiency*. Washington, D.C.: Brookings Institution, 1987.

Rhoades, Stephen A. "The Operating Performances of Acquired Firms in Banking." In *Issues after a Century of Federal Competition Policy*, ed. R. L. Wills, J. A. Caswell, and J. D. Culbertson, 277–292. Lexington, Mass.: Lexington Books, 1987.

Rhodes-Kropf, Matthew, and S. Viswanathan. "Market Valuation and Merger Waves." *Journal of Finance* 59 (Dec. 2004): 2685–2718.

Roe, Mark J. "Takeover Politics."In *The Deal Decade*, ed. M. B. Blair, 321–353. Washington, D.C.: Brookings Institution, 1993.

Roll, Richard. "The Hubris Hypothesis of Corporate Takeovers." *Journal of Business* 59 (1986): 197–216.

Roll, Richard. "Empirical Evidence on Takeover Activity and Shareholder Wealth." In *Knights, Riders and Targets: The Impact of the Hostile Takeover*, ed. John C. Coffee Jr., Louis Lowenstein, and Susan Rose-Ackerman, 241–252. Oxford: Oxford University Press, 1988.

Rydén, Bengt, and Jan-Olof Edberg. "Large Mergers in Sweden, 1962–1976." In *The Determinants and Effects of Mergers: An International Comparison*, ed. D. C. Mueller, 193–226. Cambridge, Mass.: Oelgeschlager, Gunn, and Hain, 1980.

Schumpeter, Joseph A. *The Theory of Economic Development*. Cambridge, Mass.: Harvard University Press, 1934.

Shiller, Robert J. *Irrational Exuberance*. Princeton, N.J.: Princeton University Press, 2000.

Shleifer, Andrei, and Robert W. Vishny. "Stock Market Driven Acquisitions." *Journal of Financial Economics* 70 (Dec. 2003): 295–311.

Simon, Julian L., Manoucheher Mokhtari, Daniel H. Simon. "Are Mergers Beneficial or Detrimental? Evidence from Advertising Agencies." *International Journal of the Economics of Business* 3 (Feb. 1996): 69–82.

Singh, Ajit. *Take-Overs: Their Relevance to the Stock Market and the Theory of the Firm*. Cambridge: Cambridge University Press, 1971.

Smiley, Robert. "Tender Offers, Transactions Costs and the Theory of the Firm." *Review of Economics and Statistics* 58 (Feb. 1976): 22–32.

Sourafel, Girma, Steve Thompson, and Peter W. Wright. "International Acquisitions, Domestic Competition and Firm Performance." *International Journal of the Economics of Business* 13 (Nov. 2006): 335–349.

Stigler, George J. "Monopoly and Oligopoly by Merger." *American Economic Review* 40 (May 1950): 23–34. Reprinted in *Readings in Industrial Organization and Public Policy*, ed. R. B. Heflebower, and G. W. Stocking, 69–80. Homewood, Ill.: Irwin, 1958.

Sung, Nakil, and Michael Gort. "Mergers, Capital Gains, and Productivity: Evidence from U.S. Telecommunications Mergers." *Contemporary Economic Policy* 24 (July 2006): 382–394.

Weston, J. Fred. "The Nature and Significance of Conglomerate Firms." *St. John's Law Review* 44, special edition (Spring 1970): 66–80.

Williamson, Oliver E. *Corporate Control and Business Behavior: An Inquiry into the Effects of Organization Form on Enterprise Behavior*. Englewood Cliffs, N.J.: Prentice Hall, 1970.

Yeh, Tsung-ming, and Yasuo Hoshino. "Productivity and Operating Performance of Japanese Merging Firms: Keiretsu-Related and Independent Mergers." *Japan and the World Economy* 14 (Aug. 2002): 347–366.

Yoshida, Kenji. "Kigyo gappei ni okeru kigyo bunka to performance" ("Corporate Culture and Performance in Mergers"). Bachelor's thesis, Department of Economics, Hitotsubashi University, 2007.

PART V

CAPITALISM AND THE STATE: DIFFERENT APPROACHES

CHAPTER 16

DISPERSED OWNERSHIP: THE THEORIES, THE EVIDENCE, AND THE ENDURING TENSION BETWEEN "LUMPERS" AND "SPLITTERS"

JOHN C. COFFEE JR.

FROM a global perspective, the most salient fact about corporate governance is its seemingly binary character. At least at first glance, the world divides neatly into two categories: (1) "concentrated ownership" systems, and (2) "dispersed ownership" systems, with the former being far more common. In the former system, a controlling shareholder, a family group, or a small number of blockholders holds either majority or de facto control and places their representatives on the controlled firm's board of directors.[1] In the latter system, there is instead a "separation of ownership and control," with neither the directors nor the senior executives typically holding significant blocks of the company's stock and with share ownership instead being dispersed among many institutional and retail shareholders.[2] Defining elements of this latter system also include (1) an independent board, whose members will typically have no business relationships with the corporation; and (2) relative investor passivity, at least to the extent that highly diversified institutional investors do not seek to actively manage the business or participate in most managerial decisions.

Much hangs on this difference in the structure of share ownership, as the nature of the agency costs faced by shareholders depends on ownership structure. In the dispersed ownership structure, managers have broad discretion, can act opportunistically, and need to be monitored and constrained by an independent board. In the concentrated ownership structure, the focus of monitoring shifts from the manager to the controlling shareholder.[3] Moreover, the prospect of a truly independent board is less likely when ownership is concentrated, and thus alternative protections that do not depend on board oversight must be found.

Commentators commonly refer to the dispersed ownership structure as the "Anglo-Saxon model" of corporate governance, because only in two Anglo-Saxon countries—the United States and the United Kingdom—does the structure of share ownership appear to conform relatively closely to the foregoing profile of "dispersed ownership" systems.[4] Elsewhere, concentrated ownership tends to predominate (with a few countries falling between these two poles and with Canada actually having evolved to dispersed ownership only to regress back in the direction of family-controlled concentrated ownership[5]).

Still, this binary perspective oversimplifies. Although the contrast between dispersed and concentrated ownership as divergent systems of corporate governance is basically accurate, this dichotomy can mislead in at least two respects.

First, the implicit message of Anglo-American exceptionalism is highly questionable. The assumption that something about the common heritage of the Anglo-Saxon countries—their common law, politics, cultural heritage, or whatever—explains their unique convergence on a dispersed ownership system of corporate governance simply does not hold up under closer analysis. After all, Australia and Canada have origins at least as Anglo-Saxon as the United States, probably deriving their law to an even greater degree from British sources, but in these countries concentrated ownership is more common than dispersed ownership. Curiously, the nation with the next highest level of dispersed ownership to the United States and the United Kingdom is probably Japan, hardly an Anglo-Saxon country, but one where a former network of cross-ownership among firms in the same corporate group has become increasingly attenuated, resulting in a high level of ownership dispersion.[6]

Second, an even more fundamental problem with attempts to attribute dispersed ownership to a particular set of legal or political circumstances is that companies with dispersed ownership are present in virtually all developed economies.[7] Although concentrated ownership clearly predominates in most of the world, individual firms with broadly dispersed ownership can be identified in all major securities markets. Thus, although some commentators argue that dispersed ownership survives only in the presence of strong legal protection for minority shareholders,[8] the actual data they present undercut this claim. Specifically, LaPorta, Lopez-de-Silanes, and Schleifer find that even in countries with "poor" shareholder protection, "widely held" large firms still constitute 27 percent of the large firms in their sample (La Porta et al. 1999). Even when one shifts one's focus from large firms to "medium-sized firms," the global percentage of "widely held" firms among "medium-sized firms" falls only to 24 percent, and, most surprisingly, in countries with "poor" shareholder protection, such "widely held" firms still account for 13 percent of all "medium sized" firms (La Porta et al. 1999, p. 497). In short, the difference is relative, not absolute. Even if firms with dispersed ownership are a modest minority in many countries, such firms persist in nearly all markets, regardless of the prevailing legal rules.

In turn, this fact that a minority of dispersed ownership firms coexists with a majority of concentrated ownership firms in most securities markets confounds attempts to explain dispersed ownership as a function of any single variable. Apparently, dispersed ownership can survive even in an inhospitable legal climate. More generally, dispersed ownership appears to be neither the winner nor loser in a Darwinian evolution toward the most competitive business form, because both kinds of ownership seem to be persisting at relatively stable levels. Ultimately, there may some day come an "end to history" with one system dominating the other, but for the present the contest remains undecided.

Predictably, the sharp dichotomy between dispersed ownership and concentrated ownership systems has attracted the attention of theorists who have sought to explain contemporary patterns of share ownership by identifying an underlying cause or variable that explains the evolution towards dispersed ownership in some countries and its relative absence elsewhere. "Lumpers," rather than "splitters," in this article's terminology,[9] these theorists—some stressing law, some emphasizing politics—share a strong assumption of path dependency: namely, that business firms necessarily evolved in one direction because other alternative trajectories were foreclosed.

This chapter disagrees, arguing instead that the evidence is more consistent with a simpler alternative explanation: dispersed ownership resulted less from inexorable forces and more from private ordering. Neither legal nor political conditions mandated or prevented the appearance of dispersed ownership. Rather, entrepreneurs, investment bankers, and investors—all seeking to maximize value—sometimes saw reasons why selling control into the public market would maximize value for them. But when and why? That is this chapter's focus. It argues that law played less of a role than specialized intermediaries—investment banks, securities exchanges, and other agents—who found it to be in their self-interest to foster dispersed ownership and who compensated for weak legal protections. Initially, relying on reputational capital, self-regulatory institutions, and contractual mechanisms, entrepreneurs found ways to assure investors that they would not be exploited if they invested in their companies as minority shareholders. This resulted in a localized dispersion of ownership with control remaining with the founder/entrepreneur. Private ordering, not mandatory legal rules, facilitated this process of trust formation. Later, partly as the result of exogenous changes involving the tax and antitrust laws in the United States and United Kingdom, founders (or their heirs) did pass control to public shareholders. Again, investment bankers and stock exchanges facilitated this transition. Only once this passage occurred and dispersed ownership had taken root in a jurisdiction did a new political constituency of minority shareholders coalesce (usually following a stock market crash) to demand legislation, enhanced legal protections, and improved disclosure.

Under this view, law followed the market and did not create the preconditions that explain the market's evolution toward dispersed ownership. From this perspective, some level of dispersed ownership would arise in all markets (as we observe), but whether it predominated would depend largely on whether the firm's founders believed they could maximize their profits by selling control in the public market.

Put differently, the choice that most needs explanation is why the founders of a firm would decide to sell control into the public market, rather than either retaining control or selling it at a premium to a new incoming controlling shareholder. Of course, at an abstract level, the answer has to be that entrepreneurs anticipated a higher premium from a sale of their controlling blocks into the public market, rather than to a new controlling shareholders. But why did such sales seems more attractive in those jurisdictions (chiefly the United States and the United Kingdom) that eventually became characterized as dispersed ownership countries? Here, even a partial answer requires that attention be given to other legal developments, including the antitrust laws in the United States and the tax laws in the United Kingdom, that encouraged or necessitated such sales.

Ultimately an adequate explanation of the passage of control from controlling families to public shareholders compels us to face an added complexity: public investors will not rationally pay a premium for control unless they can retain that control in their hands. The key issue, then, is the sustainability of control in public hands. If control can be divested from public shareholders by a new control seeker who conducts a secret "creeping" acquisition in a dispersed ownership market and pays little or no premium, then the public shareholders made a strategic misjudgment in earlier paying a premium for a controlling interest that they could not retain. Over time, they will learn not to repeat this mistake, and so control, even if briefly dispersed, will predictably reconcentrate.

Indeed, this pattern of short-lived dispersed ownership is apparent in recent corporate history. When Russia and Eastern Europe privatized in the 1990s through mass privatizations, dispersed ownership proved to be a very transient phenomenon—precisely because it could not be protected and preserved in the hands of public shareholders.[10] This experience frames the key question: what was different in the U.S. and U.K. histories that enable dispersed ownership to persist? How were public shareholders able to retain control? In truth, the early U.S. experience resembled that of Russia and Eastern Europe in the 1990s.[11] But as will be seen, private ordering and strong intermediaries mitigated the level of predatory opportunism in both the United States and the United Kingdom—and in the absence of strong legal protections for minority shareholders.

Against this backdrop, later sections of this chapter examine the emergence of dispersed ownership in the United States and the United Kingdom. It finds roughly the same sequence of events (although occurring at different points in time) under which legal reforms followed and did not precede the rise of dispersed ownership. In overview, the evidence shows that:

1. dispersed ownership arose at markedly different times in these two countries (much earlier in the United States than in the United Kingdom);
2. it evolved in a markedly different fashion (with dispersed ownership preceding the appearance of institutional investors in the United States and following their rise in the United Kingdom);
3. in the United States, investment bankers and the New York Stock Exchange had strong incentives to encourage control sales into the public markets and played a critical role in protecting the maintenance of control in public hands;
4. although legal rules did play some role in encouraging the transition to dispersed ownership, these legal rules had little to do with shareholder protection. Instead, in the United States, an unprecedented merger wave at the end of the nineteenth century, which may have been induced in part by the passage of the Sherman Antitrust Act of 1890, hastened the transition toward dispersed ownership. Correspondingly, in the United Kingdom, tax changes, enacted during and after World War II, penalized controlling shareholders and induced them to sell to institutional investors (who were relatively immune from these same tax disincentives).

The United States and the United Kingdom thus present distinctly different stories, but they share at least one common denominator: in neither country was this evolution toward dispersed ownership significantly influenced by the prior existence of strong legal rules that protected minority investors. If anything, legal rules in both countries were more part of the problem than part of the answer. Instead, intermediaries—investment banks, stock exchanges, and institutional investors—engaged in extensive private ordering to facilitate the rise of dispersed ownership. Also in both countries, legal rules protecting public shareholders were eventually adopted, but only after the transition to dispersed ownership had first taken hold.

What common characteristics can be found in the U.S. and U.K. experiences? This chapter concludes that in both, law followed the market with the result that legal changes came after, not before, the transition to dispersed ownership, as a new constituency of public shareholders lobbied for legislative change. It also hypothesizes that the absence of a strong central government intent on managing economic development distinguishes both the U.S. and U.K. experiences from that of continental Europe; in essence, the laissez-faire policies of these governments toward issues of corporate governance gave a greater role to private ordering.

I then turn to a final problem: why does the "Anglo-Saxon" system of dispersed ownership persist? Why do institutional investors today not assert themselves and assume control, rather than maintain a basically passive, hands-off approach that leads them to intervene only when the incumbent management appears to have become dysfunctional? Even if there were once political and/or legal constraints in the United States that prevented such institutional control of large public corporations, those constraints have recently eroded with the rise of hedge funds and private equity firms. Today, retail share ownership has declined to roughly 25 percent of the stock in U.S. public corporations,[12] whereas institutions hold the majority. Hence, past barriers to institutional control no longer appear formidable.

This chapter answers the question of why institutions do not typically seek control with a provocative assertion: institutional investors do not really want control. The logistical demands on any institutional investor who sought to manage actively a large portfolio of companies through collective decision making by multiple institutions are unacceptably costly. As a result, institutional investors implicitly recognize a basic "liquidity/control" trade-off that leads them to avoid active involvement in managerial decision making, except under special circumstances.[13] In particular, two factors that are neither "legal" nor "political" in nature constrain institutional investors from exercising control: (1) the cost differential between a low-cost policy of indexed diversification and a more activist, but high-cost, policy of attempting to monitor corporate managements over a broad portfolio of investments; and (2) the collective action problems that institutional investors face in funding interventions in corporate governance. How these latter costs are to be allocated and how free riders are to be taxed pose difficult problems, in both design and enforcement. In combination, these factors have led most institutional investors (in both the United States and the United Kingdom) to prefer liquidity to control. It can, of course, be debated whether this preference will continue under all future market conditions and regulatory structures, but the fact that this preference has now persisted in the United States and the United Kingdom for at least several decades suggests that it is likely to endure—at least absent major changes in the market and regulatory environment.

Theories of Share Ownership Structure

When Adolf Berle and Gardiner Means (1932) announced their discovery that ownership and control had separated, scholars assumed that they knew what explained this development: family-controlled companies could not finance the growth and investment that industrialization necessitated. Dispersed ownership, it was assumed, followed from the enormous capital needs of an industrialized economy undergoing rapid technological development. Only much later did the weakness in this argument become apparent when mounting evidence in the late twentieth century began to show that German and Japanese companies were competing successfully with American corporations in basic industries, notwithstanding the fact that they operated within a concentrated ownership framework.

This recognition posed a puzzle for academics: if dispersed ownership was not inevitable, what then explained the phenomenon of dispersed ownership? The initial academic response was Mark Roe's political theory of corporate governance, most fully articulated in his book *Strong Managers, Weak Owners* (1994), which argued that dispersed ownership was the product (at least in the United States) of a strong populist distrust of concentrated financial power. Still, as later discussed, this theory faced major problems. Most notably, it could not explain the United Kingdom, which also had dispersed ownership but no similar history of resistance to large financial institutions or of regulatory policies that discouraged financial institutions from taking collective action to influence board decisions. Yet as discussed later, in the United Kingdom as well as the United States, institutional investors have remained largely passive.

Meanwhile, during the 1990s, the Soviet Union crumbled, and wholesale privatizations of formerly state-owned firms occurred across Eastern Europe and Russia. In the wake of rapid and often poorly designed privatizations, fraud became endemic, and ownership that was initially widely dispersed through voucher privatizations swiftly reconcentrated into the hands of a few controlling shareholders. Frustrated by the fraud and predatory behavior they had witnessed at close hand, the academics who had helped design and orchestrate Russian privatization developed a second, alternative theory to explain dispersed ownership. Dispersed ownership, they explained, was the product of strong legal rules that protected minority shareholders from exploitation by controlling shareholders. Although this theory had an empirical foundation, replete with elaborate regressions, it was the product of a particular historical moment that may have led its authors to overemphasize the role of law.

Each of these theories is examined in more detail.

The Law Matters Thesis

In the wake of the privatizations in Russia and Eastern Europe in the 1990s, dispersed ownership proved to be a transient phenomenon. Tunneling and other predatory practices, often involving egregious self-dealing, depleted the assets and revenues of privatized firms, allowing managers and controlling shareholders to exploit minority shareholders.[14] This experience understandably led academics who had worked on privatization to reach a seemingly logical conclusion: dispersed ownership could persist only in those countries with laws that effectively protected minority shareholders from unfair self-dealing and other forms of overreaching by dominant shareholders. If the law protected minority shareholders, they reasoned, then controlling shareholders would have less ability to exploit the private benefits of control. In turn, as the private benefits of control that could be expropriated by controlling shareholders declined, the incentive to assemble control blocks would in turn decline, and existing blocks might be liquidated, thus enabling dispersed ownership to develop (or persist).

Starting from this premise that ownership concentration is a consequence of weak legal protection of minority shareholders, four financial economists—La Porta,

Lopez-de-Silanes, Shleifer, and Vishny (commonly referred to as LLS&V)—developed an extraordinarily influential (but equally controversial) model of how to measure the strength of the legal protections accorded minority shareholders. They constructed a six-element "anti-director rights" index to rate the strength of legal protections accorded minority shareholders. Using this index, they found a statistically significant correlation between the "quality" of corporate law, as rated by their index, and the degree of shareholder dispersion.[15] In later work, largely this same group of authors moved beyond their initial anti-director rights index and constructed other indices to measure either the specific protections accorded shareholders against self-dealing[16] or the adequacy of the country's securities laws.[17] These later indices focused more on enforcement (both public and private); again, the authors found statistically significant correlations between their indices measuring the strength of enforcement and various measures of stock market development.[18]

LLS&V's findings have elicited a legion of critics. First, there have been penetrating methodological critiques of their work. Some have reported that LLS&V's coding was inaccurate and inconsistent and in particular that errors associated with their coding of their shareholder rights indices accounted for the strength of their results.[19] Others have criticized the highly selective quality of their indices, arguing that the few variables chosen did not serve as accurate proxies for the underlying system's legal rules (Armour et al. 2002). In later work, the principal LLS&V authors have acknowledged the legitimacy of these criticisms.[20]

A second problem has been the direction of causality. Even if LLS&V's anti-director rights were in fact correlated with greater dispersed ownership, did this mean that they had produced dispersed ownership? Or could these legal rights have been instead the product of dispersed ownership, as a broad coalition of public shareholders, once formed, came to demand legislative protection that produced the legal rules picked up in LLS&V's anti-director index.[21] Although LLS&V never examined the historical origins of the legal variables on their anti-director index, others have and found that several are of fairly recent origin, having been adopted well after dispersed ownership became the dominant structure in the United States and the United Kingdom.[22] In short, law may well have followed economics, with the development of dispersed ownership causing a shift in legal rules in those countries where it became prevalent.

In response to this problem of endogeneity, LLS&V shifted their focus. Instead of measuring the "quality of law" by tabulating the existing or nonexistence of specific legal rights, they later moved to a more generalized hypothesis: namely, that the quality of legal institutions varied systematically with the "origin" of a country's legal system. Here, they divided the world's legal systems into basically four categories: (1) Anglo-American common law systems, (2) French civil law systems, (3) German civil law systems, and (4) Scandinavian civil law systems. This shift appears to have been an effort to deal with the direction of causality, because these legal families predated the Industrial Revolution and the spread of the corporate form. Given this clear timing difference, it could not be plausibly argued that either the structure of share ownership or the level of economic development had caused or influenced a country's legal origins. Legal origins were thus a truly independent variable.

Still, even if they had thus resolved the problem of causation to their own satisfaction, the attempt to use legal origins to explain economic development created even greater controversy. LLS&V reported that countries whose legal origins derived from the civil law systems (and, worst of all, French civil law systems) exhibited the lowest protections for minority shareholders; in turn, lower shareholder protection correlated with high levels of concentrated share ownership. Conversely, higher quality corporate, securities, and bankruptcy laws were found to be associated with common law systems. Because these latter jurisdictions provided higher levels of protection for minority shareholders, it was no surprise to LLS&V that firms incorporated in those jurisdictions exhibited more dispersed share ownership, paid out greater dividends, and generally had higher share prices than those incorporated in civil law jurisdictions.

Nonetheless, this revised legal origins approach was equally fraught with methodological peril. LLS&V's division of all legal systems with four categories—common law, French, German, and Scandinavian—may have worked for Europe, but outside of Europe the appropriate classification of the legal systems of countries in Asia, Africa, Latin America, and even Eastern Europe remains highly debatable.[23] For example, although LLS&V deemed China and Japan to be countries of German legal origin, China's corporation law actually derives from Taiwan, France, and Japan as well. In the case of Japan, although Japan borrowed much German civil law at the end of the nineteenth century, its corporate and securities law were taken nearly intact from the United States after World War II. Latin America is even more ambiguous, as its law was borrowed from Spanish sources that were, at most, only briefly influenced by France prior to South America's wars of independence.[24] Indeed, the strength of LLS&V's correlation between the quality of the common law and the superior economic development in countries with common law legal systems depends heavily on the ambiguous status of Latin America.[25] Yet however we classify Latin America in terms of its legal origins, the possibility looms large that its relatively poor economic development may be the product of unrelated factors (poor economic endowments, a weak political tradition, a history of military dictatorship, etc.) that had little if anything to do with specific legal rules.[26]

A final problem is that there is evidence that some "civil law" countries did develop strong securities markets, but later reversed policies and discouraged their further growth and development.[27] This suggests that politics could trump law and that political attitudes could change abruptly. To sum up: even if the United Kingdom and the United States developed stronger securities markets, the debate remains open as to whether this development was the product of politics, law, or more general factors in their social structure. Precisely because both countries were decentralized and adopted common laissez-faire positions toward economic planning and corporate development, their governmental inaction may have fostered private lawmaking and robust self-regulatory institutions (such as stock exchanges).[28]

The Politics Matters Thesis

In 1994, Mark Roe announced a thesis that was provocative, iconoclastic, and path-breaking: the structure of shareholder ownership in the United States was determined not by economic efficiency, but by political constraints. Because the United States historically disfavored concentrated financial power, the bank-centered system of financial control of public corporations that had arisen in Europe and Japan could not develop in the United States, and so shareholder ownership stayed dispersed, rather than concentrated. The book was widely and deservedly heralded, in large part because it seemed to show that political factors could and did trump economic efficiency. In retrospect, however, his specific thesis seems much influenced by the then seeming superiority of Japanese and German corporate governance.[29] Within a few years of his statement of this thesis, Japanese and German corporate governance faded in their seeming efficiency. But Roe's thesis persisted in its popularity because it focused scholars on the political factors that might determine economic structure (and thus encouraged scores of political science graduate students to explore a range of possibilities).

Nonetheless, original as his thesis was, it faces some basic problems. First, the most obvious indications that the U.S. political system disfavored concentrated financial power came after the advent of the separation of ownership and control.[30] Second, simpler explanations are possible for the underdeveloped size of U.S. financial institutions. Early in his book, Roe focuses on the fragmentation of banking power in the United States, but this fragmentation does not really require a political theory to explain it. As he emphasizes, by 1900, the National Banking Act had already been interpreted to preclude multistate banking.[31] Arguably, this could have been because of a political distaste for concentrated financial power. Or, it could more simply be attributed to the fact that banks in each state wanted to evade competition from larger, out-of-state rivals. Inherently, the U.S. federal system had guaranteed state banks a local oligopoly—unless federal law permitted national banks to leapfrog over state boundaries. Banks in smaller jurisdictions naturally feared that larger banks in New York or other major cities would compete business and clients away from them if interstate banking were facilitated.

Thus, that state banks resisted legislation giving national banks such multistate banking powers is hardly surprising. From Roe's perspective, the restrictions placed on interstate banking can be viewed as an expression of hostility toward concentrated financial power, but the simpler interpretation is that local banks united to lobby for the preservation of the economic rents a fragmented federal system gave them. To use a humble analogy, if one were mugged in a city alley, this could be viewed as a political act that expressed the egalitarian values (or at least the Robin Hood–like politics) of the assailant. But the simpler view is just that the mugger wanted your money. Thus, if one accepts Occam's razor and believes that the simpler hypothesis should be preferred, the Roe theory seems overly complicated. That is, a federal structure alone can explain fragmented banking power and may have precluded an efficient consolidation of financial firms—all without any need for resort to a political theory such as Roe offered.

A good case can also be made that as of 1900, the largest, most powerful financial institutions in the United States did not want the combined ownership and control of industrial America. Rather than owning industrial companies, J.P. Morgan, the dominant financial institution of the era, found it more profitable (as described later) to serve these companies and their shareholders as their financial adviser and underwriter. During this period it was able to exercise a degree of control without any ownership by quietly serving on the boards of these firms, and it profited greatly in doing so. But it (and similar firms) refused to grow into European-style universal banks; for example, they refused to hold large blocks of securities or to accept bank deposits from all but special clients.[32] Such investments carried risks, and taking retail deposits required a large staff. Over time, the banks that took retail deposits superceded Morgan and its peers in size and scale, but J.P. Morgan and its fellow aristocrats opted for a leaner business model and may have profited more handsomely from their decision. Conversely, those financial institutions that wanted to expand found it possible to escape the restrictions on multistate banking by forming separate securities affiliates, which several operated on a coast-to-coast basis.[33] The case has not been dispositively made that the restrictions on concentrated financial power were truly binding and could not be evaded.

From a global perspective, the major limitation of the Roe political thesis is that it works only for the United States. If it was more efficient for large financial institutions to monitor and control industrial corporations (as they did in Germany and Japan), why didn't the United Kingdom evolve in this direction? None of the populist resentment of financial concentration stressed by Roe applied to the United Kingdom, which had a very different political history than the United States. Yet as will be seen, by the last quarter of the twentieth century, after following a very different trajectory, the United Kingdom's corporate ownership structure looked very much like that of the United States.

To explain the persistence of dispersed and concentrated ownership in different countries, Roe later moved to a more general political theory: because left-leaning countries favor employees over shareholders, he argued, concentrated ownership persists primarily in such social democratic countries as a means of enabling controlling shareholders to resist confiscation of their wealth by managers seeking to play owners off against employees.[34] If dispersed ownership were to develop instead, managers would use their greater discretion under such an ownership system to favor the interests of employees over shareholders. Put differently, the inevitable conflicts between managers and shareholders (plus governmental pressure) would lead managers to subordinate shareholder interests to employee interests in these countries. But controlling shareholders could intervene to stop such behavior.

Plausible as this more generalized political theory may be, it seems counterfactual as applied to the United Kingdom. As Cheffins has convincingly shown, dispersed ownership developed in the United Kingdom during the extended reign of Labour governments after World War II.[35] Under Roe's theory, the leftward drift of the United Kingdom during this period should have made controlling shareholders struggle mightily to preserve concentrated ownership. But they did not. Instead, it was precisely at this time that concentrated ownership in the United Kingdom exited—with a whimper, not a bang. Indeed, Cheffins (2008, p. 51) concludes that "left-wing politics" may have accelerated the divorce of ownership and control in the United Kingdom because the threat of nationalization caused controlling shareholders to liquidate their blocks.

In any event, Britain at no point restricted commercial banks with a Glass-Steagall Act; nor did it chill institutional investors in their ability to communicate with regard to proxy solicitations or takeovers (as the United States once did aggressively and still does to a degree). Yet even without these restrictions, British financial institutions did not develop into German or Japanese universal banks; nor did they behave as activist monitors. At most, their level of activism was only marginally higher than that of U.S. institutions.[36] The conclusion seems inescapable that law has been less of a restraining force than Roe has hypothesized.

The point here is not to claim that Roe's political theory is invalid or that LLS&V were misguided in searching for the variables that distinguished countries with strong securities markets from those with weak ones. But broad brush strokes do not explain the evolution of dispersed ownership, and the convergence of the United States and the United Kingdom in share ownership requires a fuller understanding of both the business models of the principal intermediaries who guided this process and the special environments in which self-regulation, not mandatory law, played a major role.

The Spread of Dispersed Ownership in the United States

Dispersed ownership arrived in the United States during the first quarter of the twentieth century, but the developments that paved its way began in the last quarter of the nineteenth century. By that point, large industrial empires had formed in the United States in a variety of capital-intensive industries: chiefly railroads, steel, mining industries, chemicals, and oil. Founder/entrepreneurs—men such as Carnegie, Vanderbilt, Rockefeller, and the DuPonts—controlled these empires, and in the normal course of events, succession problems would inevitably have arisen on the deaths of these founders. In Europe, control would typically stay within the family, or in few cases would be sold at a premium to an incoming controlling shareholder. But control was seldom sold to the public. One can attempt to explain this difference by saying that Europe lacked an "equity culture" in which investors were ready to invest in shares, but that response only begs the deeper question: why did such a culture not develop? The greater obstacle, as noted earlier, was that control could not be successfully held by the public—at least with sufficient confidence to justify the payment of a substantial premium. Sooner or later, a new control seeker would surreptitiously assemble a control block and either squeeze out the public shareholders at a low price or leave them holding an illiquid security, while the new controlling shareholder extracted high private benefits of control. Events did not work out this way in the United States, and the reasons for its different evolution fall under essentially three headings.

The Role of Investment Bankers as Guardians

Commodore Cornelius Vanderbilt, then the richest man in America and the founder of the New York Central Railroad, died in 1877. He left a clearly unsuitable heir, William Henry Vanderbilt, who the commodore had considered a "dunce" and exiled to farm on Staten Island, never training him in the business.[37] William Henry Vanderbilt, who received 87 percent of the stock in the New York Central under his father's will, was not only untrained but, on assuming control, he quickly exacerbated a preexisting political controversy between the railroad and the New York State legislature. In 1879, the New York State Assembly held hearings to investigate preferential rates that the New York Central was giving to some oil refiners. Public hostility toward the Vanderbilts was already growing, and it intensified exponentially in the wake of William Henry Vanderbilt's clumsy testimony at these hearings and his infamous remark at this time: "The public be damned."[38] New York State appeared to be on the brink of imposing punitive taxes on the railroad, in large part because of public animosity toward the Vanderbilts and their unrivaled wealth.

Strategists for the Vanderbilts and the New York Central decided that the best way to protect their firm was to have William sell a large block of his holdings (some 250,000 shares) so that he would become only a minority shareholder and thus reduce the Vanderbilt association with the railroad. But such a sale was no small order and was in fact unprecedented. The problem was not only that public investors might be reluctant to buy but that knowledge of this impending sale (and thus of the overhanging excess supply of New York Central stock) might cause its stock price to nosedive.

The sensitive assignment of conducting the sale of the Vanderbilt control block in the New York Central was given to J.P. Morgan, largely because of its Anglo-American structure. Junius Morgan—the father of J. Pierpont Morgan and founder of the firm—had made the family's fortune selling railroad bonds to British investors, and he still ran the London office. Not only did he have the trust of his British clients, he could quietly sell New York Central stock to them without the scale of the massive distribution becoming apparent in the railroad's home market in New York, where full disclosure would have caused its stock price to plummet.

But even sales to Morgan's long-standing loyal British customers were not enough. To pull off this syndication, Morgan had to strike a truce with some of Vanderbilt's foes, including his archenemy, Jay Gould, who bought a large

20,000-share block in the offering.[39] Gould and Vanderbilt had long operated competing lines and had bitterly battled for control of the Erie Railroad, sometimes engaging in intense price wars. Could these bitter rivals coexist in peace? Or would Gould use his initial stake to mount a control fight, now that the ineffectual William Henry Vanderbilt held only a minority stake?

Although such an eventual control fight was a plausible scenario, it never materialized. Instead, it was precluded when J. Pierpont Morgan asserted himself. Demanding a board seat to represent "the London interest,"[40] he skillfully used that seat and proxies from his British bondholder clients to take de facto control of the New York Central board. In so doing, he realized multiple objectives: (1) he held off opportunistic control seekers (such as Gould and other robber barons of the era) who could not assemble a control position in the face of his opposition; (2) he served as an effective fiduciary and guardian for his distant British clients, thereby maintaining their loyalty and future business; (3) he was able to negotiate and maintain a truce between adversaries in an industry regularly characterized by ruinous competition (of the kind that economists applaud but shareholders dread); and (4) he used his pivotal position to earn fees for serving the New York Central as its principal underwriter and adviser, performing whatever services might be needed.[41]

The episode assured J. Pierpont Morgan's reputation for industrial statesmanship. Not only did he protect his overseas clients, but once on the board, he could guide an industry and steer it clear of "ruinous" price competition—thereby benefiting all shareholders in the industry (at the expense of consumers, of course). His success was emulated, as the industry learned that investment banker control could be good for everyone (except consumers). Over time, the use of investment bankers as directors to share sensitive information among competitors and to mitigate unnecessary competition became increasingly common, until Congress in the Progressive Era sought to end this practice in the Clayton Act, which barred interlocking directors—a move that was largely aimed at the perceived role of investment bankers as the engineers of pricing collusion.

Unique only in scale, the New York Central episode was far from an isolated incident. Earlier, J. Pierpont Morgan had gone on the board in other railroad battles to protect his British client/shareholders,[42] and his father, Junius, had organized a "defense committee" to protect the firm's British clients from the trepidations of Jay Gould in one of the many battles over the Erie Railroad.[43] Rival investment banking firms appear to have also organized small shareholders to resist raids by robber barons intent on seizing control.[44] Although J.P. Morgan had an unrivaled relationship with British investors, other prominent investment bankers had corresponding relationships with other constituencies of European clients: Auguste Belmont had a long-standing relationship with the House of Rothschild and its largely French investors, and Joseph Seligman and Kuhn, Loeb each represented groups of German investors.[45]

Historically, American investment banks grew up in the middle of the nineteenth century to finance the construction of railroads across the North American continent. Because the United States was then a capital-importing nation and because the amount of capital required to build railroads across a continent was vastly greater than that required to build railroads between British or European cities, these investment banks had succeeded only to the extent they could gain the confidence of European investors. Because the railroad industry was often dominated by robber barons and other seeming buccaneers and because railroads often became overleveraged and entered bankruptcy, the maintenance of these relationships with distant European clients required American investment bankers also to serve these clients as guardians during the bankruptcy and reorganization process. Although not unprofitable, this role prepared these bankers to similarly serve their clientele when the focus shifted from selling bonds to selling stock. Once again, their natural mission was to protect their European clients from well-known financial predators (of whom the names Jay Gould, Jim Fisk, Russell Sage, and Daniel Drew stood out). Moreover, because their predominant business continued to be marketing railroad bonds to European investors, the investment banks had strong incentives in their role as corporate directors to forgo any opportunistic or self-seeking conduct that might tarnish their reputations. J. Pierpont Morgan appears to have been particularly meticulous in this regard.

This pattern of directors serving on boards to protect dispersed shareholders quickly generalized, and by the turn of the twenthieth century investment bankers, often several from the same firm, were on the boards of most major corporations, particularly banks, to protect both dispersed shareholders and management from perceived threats to control.[46] But the investment banks held small (if any) stakes in the corporations they so served.

Here, a central difference emerges between the American and European contexts: U.S. investment banks remained agents and did not seek to take over industrial empires as the founders of those empires died off. Why not? Conceivably, they might have bought control of these firms with financing from their European clients. But such a strategy faced a variety of obstacles. First, it might have placed them in conflict with their European clients. Those clients wanted a safe stream of dividends and a liquid stock. Had J.P. Morgan sought, for example, to take the New York Central "private" (although that term was not yet known), the buyout group would probably have had to accept additional risk by increasing the firm's leverage and surrendering the liquidity that the New York Central enjoyed as a New York Stock Exchange–listed security. This additional risk might have been unattractive to a clientele looking more for a safe dividend return. Equally important, a large-scale buyout transaction was probably then beyond the capacity of most American investment banks. In 1879, the Vanderbilt stake in the New York Central was estimated to be worth roughly $100 million.[47] Yet according to his biographer, J. Pierpont Morgan's annual salary in the early 1870s was only $75,000 a year—princely on a relative scale, but hardly suggesting that his firm could then consummate a major acquisition.[48] In short, U.S. investment banks were not then capitalized on the scale of the House of Rothschild or a major European universal bank.

Taking a firm "private" might also mean the end of a variety of lucrative fees the investment bank received from a public corporation. J.P. Morgan typically served its public corporate clients in a variety of roles: underwriter, disbursing agent, and merger adviser. Put simply, serving dispersed shareholders paid well.

Finally, as well understood as the idea of "going private" is today, it would have been far harder to conceive at that time because of the organizational challenges involved. J. Pierpont Morgan and his contemporaries were bond salesmen who knew little about running a railroad. In contrast, Vanderbilt was seen as a master of efficiency who had broad vision, understood the business, cut costs, and maintained a constant stream of dividends to his stockholders.[49] Today, private equity firms know that they can buy the managerial talent to run an acquired business, but that insight was probably beyond the capacity of men experienced only at selling bonds to investors.

For all these reasons, American investment banks performed as agents, rather than principals, loyally representing both their domestic and European investors. On behalf of these shareholders (and managements), they sought to negotiate industrial peace and restrain competition by helping industries maintain collusive pricing. Later, during the Progressive Era, reformers became convinced that the primary function of investment bankers serving as directors was to police cartels.[50] Certainly, investment bankers were well positioned to know the plans and strategies of rival firms and wished to curry favor with all sides. In fairness, it must also be remembered that price fixing was not clearly illegal before 1890 (with the passage of the Sherman Antitrust Act in that year). In any event, the investment banker's fiduciary loyalty ran to its investors, not to the public. For the investment banker, the rise of dispersed ownership meant increased fees from equity underwritings, increasing trading opportunities, and a variety of advisory roles.

That investment bankers as directors added value—by protecting public shareholders and possibly by restraining competition within industries—is not simply a logical inference. Strong empirical evidence supports this claim. DeLong has found that in 1911–1912, the presence of a partner at J.P. Morgan on a corporation's board of directors added approximately 30 percent to that firm's common stock equity value and about 15 percent to the total market value of the firm.[51] Exactly why the presence of a Morgan partner resulted in such a significant market premium has been debated. DeLong theorized that these firms could better replace inferior managers; other financial economists have argued that it gave such a firm better access to external finance.[52] Both hypotheses could be valid, but an alternative and simpler hypothesis may also be true: the 30 percent premium may partly reflect the reduced agency costs that a public corporation with a J.P. Morgan partner faced because it was less exposed to a coercive raid by a Gould or a similar predatory control seeker. In short, the Morgan partners of 1910–1911 might have been doing precisely what J. Pierpont Morgan did for much of his career: protecting their shareholder clients from predatory control seekers, who might either manipulate the stock price or seek to acquire control without paying a control premium.

Undoubtedly, investment bankers on corporate boards faced conflicts of interest, and often they may have been more loyal to the interests of management than to those of the public shareholders. At times, investment bankers may have aligned with management. At other times, controlling shareholders used them so that they could sell their majority interest, thereby obtaining the benefits of diversification, while still relying on their investment bankers on the corporate board to protect their de facto control.[53] In short, by playing a guardian-like role, investment bankers could accomplish multiple (and occasionally conflicting) objectives, sometimes protecting dispersed shareholders from external attack by the robber barons of this era, sometimes serving the interests of founders who wanted to remain influential while disposing of their majority block, and sometimes fostering relationships with the new cadre of professional managers (while also assisting all of the above in policing price fixing and similar agreements that ensured peace in the industry). Despite these multiple goals, the precondition to any sale of control to the public at an attractive premium was that the public shareholders believed they would be able to retain control for the long run. In this sense, the role of the investment banker was indispensable to the rise of dispersed ownership in the United States.

The Great Merger Boom of the 1890s

The United States experienced its first great merger boom between 1890 and 1902. By some accounts, as much as half of U.S. manufacturing capacity was involved in mergers during this period.[54] Often, these mergers involved most of the firms in an industry, and not infrequently they united firms that already had been loosely connected through trusts, loose price-fixing agreements, or holding company devices. The 1901 creation of U.S. Steel well illustrates this pattern. Negotiated by J.P. Morgan and Andrew Carnegie, it united a host of firms, accounting for the majority of the steel-making capacity in the United States.[55] Although intended to realize economies of scale, it also appears to have been the product of the growing potential for competition between Carnegie's firm and smaller firms in the steel pipe and tube business that were sponsored by J.P. Morgan.[56] The result was America's first corporation with a capitalization of over $1 billion (at a time when the capitalization of all manufacturing companies in the United States just reached $9 billion) (Chernow 1990, pp. 82–83).

What drove these mergers? A popular, if much debated, view is that this merger wave was a response to the passage of the Sherman Antitrust Act in 1890. That act outlawed price fixing but did not prohibit mergers among competitors. Hence, if it was unlawful to fix prices across firms, but lawful to merger competitors into a single firm, the latter route became the preferred technique by which to avoid "ruinous competition" and achieve economic rents after 1890.

Although this theory has its critics,[57] there is little doubt that this merger wave (whatever its cause) played a major role in the rise of dispersed ownership at the close of the nineteenth century.[58] Some of the best known mergers during this period—for example, the formation of Standard Oil and U.S. Steel—combined the majority of the firms in the industry into a single entity. Inherently, such industry-wide mergers diluted the controlling shareholders at individual firms and created dispersed ownership. At the same time, because these new combined entities were usually oligopolies, their enhanced market power explains why controlling shareholders would happily sell out in such transactions: they could receive a higher premium in a merger transaction because oligopolies create value for shareholders. Revealingly, Andrew Carnegie sold his company in the U.S. Steel transaction for bonds and took no stock in U.S. Steel.[59] Clearly, he thought he was selling at the top of the market and at a value beyond what any incoming controlling shareholder would pay him.

Skeptics doubt that antitrust law played a critical role in causing the merger wave of the 1890s, and they instead attribute that wave to the technological revolution caused by the growth of railroads.[60] Railroads vastly increased the size of the market for manufactured goods and enabled manufacturers to profit from economies of scale. Improved communications—first the telegraph and later the telephone—also opened new and enlarged markets. Still, significant capital investments were necessary to introduce these economies of scale, and competition produced overinvestment and excess capacity. Alfred Chandler (1977) has observed that intense pressures developed within U.S. industry to escape from competition, which pressures were "particularly strong in the new capital and energy-intensive industries where several entrepreneurs had simultaneously adopted new technologies of production" (p. 72). In response, business leaders sought ways to reduce uncertainty and ensure high rates of return by reducing competition. Economists of this era even developed theories of "ruinous competition" to justify cartels and similar practices.[61] Although price-fixing agreements were used, cartels prove unstable and tended to break down; in contrast, mergers produced a permanent consolidation that inherently reduced competition and ensured higher returns.

Ultimately, for our purposes, it is not necessary to choose between these overlapping theories of what caused this merger wave. Both explanations stress reasons why entrepreneurs turned to mergers, and investment bankers naturally rushed to facilitate this new trend, thereby generating very high fee income. Historically, merger waves have been accompanied by stock market booms, and the 1895–1904 merger wave was no exception (see chapter 15 in this volume). For example, U.S. Steel's shares soared from $38 when it was floated in 1901 to $55, but then plunged to s9 by 1903 (chapter 15). Whether merger waves create stock market bubbles or vice versa, the financial community saw mergers as driving stock market appreciation. Indeed, these transactions offered high premiums because they promised oligopolistic market power. In so doing, mergers diluted blockholders and facilitated dispersed ownership.

The merger wave of the 1890s had its corollaries in England and Europe, but it was more pronounced in the United States, because in the United States (1) the technological revolution ushered in by transcontinental railroads had generated the greatest potential for improved economies of scale and enlarged markets; (2) the problems of overinvestment and excess capacity had repeatedly frustrated industry leaders in the United States; and (3) cartels remained legal in much of Europe, thus reducing the incentive to merge. Also, even if new technologies created potentially enlarged markets in Europe, these new markets intersected with national boundaries, where tariffs and legal issues restricted the full realization of the potential economies of scale. Hence, although mergers and industrial concentration increased throughout the industrialized world during this period, the rate of increased concentration was greatest in the United States. With greater concentration through mergers came greater dispersed ownership. Once again, the historical evidence explains the rise of dispersed ownership without resort to legal rules protecting minority shareholders.

Self-Regulation and the Role of the New York Stock Exchange

Stock exchanges are natural allies of dispersed ownership. Because they profit from increased trading, they do better when the structure of share ownership involves many small shareholders who constantly make portfolio revision decisions and trade as a result. In contrast, controlling shareholders infrequently trade and inherently deprive the market of liquidity.

Stock exchanges developed in the United States and the United Kingdom well before the Industrial Revolution (principally to trade debt securities), but they grew exponentially in the wake of that revolution. Although stock exchanges existed in Europe, they encountered resistance there from the large banks who regarded them as competitors, and they actually shrank in size as the twentieth century dawned.[62] During the late nineteenth and early twentieth centuries, the more centralized governance regimes in France and Germany were acutely conscious of the need to develop defense industries and sought to plan their economic development around this goal. They realized they could better manage and direct economic development through a close partnership between the Ministry of Finance and the largest banks. In contrast, stock exchanges could not be as easily coordinated or controlled and were unpredictable in terms of how they allocated capital.

Because the political economies of the United States and the United Kingdom were much more decentralized, these same issues of economic planning never arose. Indeed, in this era the United States did not even have a central bank, and its banking structure was highly fragmented as the result of a federal system that kept banks confined within a single state. Hence, in the absence of natural rivals or an activist state, stock exchanges grew more rapidly in these countries (particularly in the United States) and faced less resistance. But the stock exchanges in these two countries developed in different directions, and this helps explain the later arrival of dispersed ownership in the United Kingdom than in the United States.

Unlike the London Stock Exchange (LSE), the New York Stock Exchange (NYSE) faced stiff competition throughout the late nineteenth century from other stock exchanges (indeed, more companies were listed on the Boston Stock Exchange as of 1900[63]). In response, the NYSE sought to develop its brand as a high-quality exchange that listed only "safe," low-risk companies.[64] Economic reasons underlay the different behavior of the two exchanges: the NYSE was a closed exchange, which did not admit new members; instead, outgoing members sold their seats to incoming members. In contrast, the LSE was an open exchange, always ready to admit new brokers and list virtually any security that would trade.[65] This difference created a stronger desire on the part of the NYSE to increase the value of its seats by enhancing its reputational capital.

Also, the NYSE employed fixed brokerage commissions, which naturally gave it a higher cost structure. Other exchanges could trade securities at lower cost, and this particularly made the NYSE an uneconomic venue on which to trade lower-priced securities. Arguably, the NYSE made a virtue of this necessity by marketing itself as a selective exchange that would not list low-priced "penny" stocks. Clearly, there was a quality differential between the securities listed on the NYSE versus those listed on its rivals. The NYSE's high listing standards also protected it from the danger that the failure of a high-risk company could cause the failure of a broker that dealt heavily in its stock—the latter failure would have broad repercussions because a broker's failure would cause its liabilities to fall on all NYSE members.[66]

Given these differences in organizational structure, it logically followed that the NYSE took a more activist approach to listing standards and issues of corporate governance than the LSE. In frequently rejecting listings and insisting on an adequate earnings track record before listing an issuer, the NYSE was distinguishing itself from its competitors and marketing itself as the guardian of public shareholders. This guardian role manifested itself in two concrete ways: (1) the NYSE, beginning in 1900, insisted that its listed companies publish annual audited financial statements, and (2) it protected shareholder voting rights by resisting attempts by issuers to deviate from the norm of "one share, one vote."[67] These steps were taken by a private body as a matter of self-regulation, not mandatory law, but the result was to attract public shareholders to invest in NYSE stocks as safer and better monitored.

The point here is not that the NYSE was altruistic or public regarding, but that it pioneered dispersed ownership by engendering public confidence (which others later exploited). Although the NYSE was younger and smaller than the LSE, many of the companies that listed on it became widely held shortly after 1900. As of 1913, the Pennsylvania Railroad had 86,804 shareholders; AT&T had 53,737 shareholders; and U.S. Steel, organized only in 1901, had 44,398 common shareholders and 77,420 persons holding its preferred stock.[68] This degree of shareholder dispersion was measurably ahead of similar companies in the United Kingdom, and few of these three companies had any clear controlling shareholder.

A distinctive feature of the spread of dispersed ownership in the United States was that retail shareholders, not institutional investors, were induced to buy the blocks sold by controlling shareholders. Of course, neither pension funds nor mutual funds existed to any significant degree at this point, and the major investment banks and merchant banks of this era largely avoided investments in speculative securities.[69] Thus, individual shareholders had to be convinced that equity securities were more than speculative gambles. In part, the NYSE prepared the way for this transition by steadily communicating that its listed securities were sound and safe investments.

Well before 1900, the NYSE had come to view itself as the guardian of the financial quality of the issuers listed on it. To be sure, its selective listing standards were for self-interested reasons,[70] but they still contrasted sharply with the LSE, which was basically prepared to list any company that could be traded. Identifying its interests with those of public shareholders, in 1900 the NYSE began to require newly listing companies to publish audited financial information, and some financial historians date the advent of modern financial reporting from this moment.[71]

The Full Flowering of Dispersed Ownership: 1900–1930

The year 1900 supplies a useful reference point. Based on data he compiled on share ownership at forty large companies as of 1900, Herman (1981, p. 67) concludes that "the separation of ownership and control was already well advanced by the turn of the century." Specifically, he finds that only five of these forty companies (or 12.5 percent) had a majority shareholder (ibid.); these five were all industrial corporations, as railroads and utilities had already fully achieved dispersed ownership and uniformly lacked majority shareholders.

Thereafter, the pace quickened. Cheffins and Bank (2009) use data compiled by the National Civic Federation, which followed seventy-five large U.S. corporations from 1901 to 1913. This roughly contemporaneous survey found that the aggregate number of shareholders in these firms rose from 141,000 in 1901 to 415,000 in 1913. Similarly, Warshow (1924) followed the growth in shareholders in a different sample of sixty-eight firms from 1900 to 1923. Between 1900 and 1913, he found that the number of shareholders had at least doubled in thirty-one of these firms and that the aggregate number of shareholders in all rose from 342,000 to 769,000 (Warshow 1924, pp. 21–25).

During the 1920s, the rate of growth accelerated. One measure of this growth is the number of companies listed on U.S. stock exchanges, which rose from 682 in 1900 to 970 in 1915 and, finally, to 2,659 in 1930. By one estimate, the number of individuals owning stock in listed companies rose from 500,000 in 1900 to 2 million in 1920 to 10 million by 1930.[72]

Driving this growth was, of course, a stock market bubble that inflated and exploded at the end of the 1920s. Behind that bubble were again investment banks, but this time it was a different type of investment bank. Mass marketing and retail advertising were distinctively American inventions. Not surprisingly, some American underwriters proved to be as adept (or as irresponsible) at marketing equity securities as other retailers were at selling cars, tobacco, soft drinks, or gasoline to the American public. During the 1920s, National City Bank, under its flamboyant CEO, Charles Mitchell, became the largest U.S. underwriter of securities, surpassing J.P. Morgan largely by applying mass marketing techniques to the sale of equity securities. Chernow describes Mitchell as bringing "a carnival tone to securities marketing" and turning his brokers into "garrulous hucksters" (1990, p. 304).

These retail-oriented banks (which, unlike Morgan, did seek retail deposits and thereby gained greater underwriting and distributional capacity) were clearly in a different business from "wholesale" firms, such as J.P. Morgan and Kuhn, Loeb, but their style was distinctively American. During the 1920s, several major banks (including Chase) incorporated separate securities affiliates so as to be able to outflank limits on interstate banking, and this enabled them to operate a brokerage business from coast to coast (Chernow 1990, p. 304). By the end of the 1920s, the number of securities dealers in the United States had risen from 250 at the beginning of World War I to 6,500 by 1929 (Chernow 1990, p. 303). By 1929, in a nation of 120 million, some 1.5 to 3 million U.S. citizens regularly played the stock market (ibid.). These new marketing techniques ultimately resulted in a record bubble and the stock market crash of 1929, but by then dispersed ownership had become an accomplished fact.

The Rise of Dispersed Ownership in the United Kingdom

Brian Cheffins has recently marshaled evidence showing that dispersed ownership came later to the United Kingdom than to the United States, probably arriving in fully developed form only after 1970.[73] Some of the reasons for this delay have already been surveyed; the factors that accelerated the appearance of dispersed ownership in the United States were simply not present (at least to the same extent) in the United Kingdom. The 1890s merger boom was only faintly felt in the United Kingdom (possibly because British antitrust law was also much less developed); as a result, there was less dilution of U.K. controlling shareholders. Because the shareholders of the LSE (who were different from its brokers or seat holders) profited from selling new seats, the LSE had less interest in maximizing instead the value of existing seats. Desiring to trade any security that could be traded, the LSE was less selective about listings, did not impose corporate governance-related listing standards, and did not seek to present itself as a proactive guardian of public shareholders (as the NYSE did). Investment bankers in the United Kingdom neither needed to raise capital across the Atlantic nor confronted adversaries quite as predatory as the American robber barons of the late nineteenth century; hence, they were also less motivated to undertake a guardian role. Finally, the enormous and growing American middle class was convinced by retail-oriented underwriters to buy equity securities in the 1920s, while nothing similar occurred in the United Kingdom (possibly because of greater class stratification and wealth inequalities).

That dispersed ownership came to the United Kingdom does not seem to have been the result of any distinctive legal rules or judicial concern for the rights of minority shareholders. British academics agree that "from a legal perspective, the United Kingdom was not a protective jurisdiction for minority shareholders during the first half of the twentieth century."[74] In particular, the judiciary largely maintained a hands-off approach, and certain legal remedies, such as the appraisal remedy and the derivative action, were significantly less available than in the United States.[75] Exculpatory provisions in corporate charters were common and enforceable, thereby undercutting the duty of loyalty,[76] and shareholder ratification could waive most alleged breaches of a legal duty.[77] Although U.S. legal remedies may have been marginally stronger in this period, the fairest generalization is that courts in both countries were reluctant to become involved in the internal affairs of a business corporation. Legal protections for minority shareholders and the quality of disclosure improved in both countries after World War II, but this development followed, and did not precede, the separation of ownership and control.

From this perspective, the United Kingdom's experience seems inconsistent with the hypotheses of both LLS&V and Roe. Most obviously, the United Kingdom did not provide the legal protections for minority shareholders that LLS&V view as the precondition to dispersed ownership. Nor was the United Kingdom characterized by a populist distrust of concentrated financial power or by a federal system that fragmented financial institutions. Hence, under Roe's reasoning, large financial institutions should have controlled most British corporations—but clearly such concentrated financial power did not arise until well after World War II.

Although not all commentators agree,[78] dispersed ownership appears to have developed at a slower pace in the United Kingdom. Initially, it spread within local communities (as in the United States), as companies sold shares to investors in the vicinity of their headquarters. Studying the shareholder records of twenty-six companies incorporated around 1900, Franks, Mayer, and Rossi found that, as of 1910, 56 percent of the common shareholders lived within six miles of the corporation's headquarters.[79] The New England textile mills had a similar experience, and both examples suggest that entrepreneurs can market their shares locally to investors who know them. To this extent, as Franks, Mayer, and Rossi argue, trust is probably more important than legal protections in encouraging investment (2008, pp. 31–32), and trust was founded on personal relationships, which kept ownership local. Still, even if shares were being sold to local investors, control remained with the founders and their families; little, if any, evidence suggests that powerful financial institutions assembled significant stakes in these companies.

Moving forward to 1920, Franks, Mayer, and Rossi used a random cross-section of fifty-three companies quoted on the LSE and found that the largest shareholder held 20.8 percent of the shares; furthermore, in only 43 percent of these companies did the largest shareholder own less than 10 percent.[80] Such evidence shows the glass to be half full: noncontrolling public shareholders owned the majority of the stock, but control was likely still in the hands of a small insider group. This pattern continued between the two world wars. In a well-known study, Florence compiled a data set, as of 1936, of eighty-two manufacturing and commercial companies and found that 59 percent of these companies had a "dominant ownership interest," 32 percent were "marginal," and only 9 percent had no dominant shareholder or shareholder group (Florence 1953, pp. 187–190, 194). In short, although these companies generally had a substantial number of shareholders, there was still no separation of ownership and control.

Three studies have focused on ownership concentration as of approximately 1950. One surveyed the one hundred largest U.K. manufacturers (as of 1970) and found that (as of 1950), a thin majority (fifty out of ninety-two) was still under family control (Channon 1973). Franks, Mayer, and Rossi examined fifty-five listed companies, and found that 49 percent of these firms could be considered to be "widely held," based on the criterion that no single shareholder held 10 percent of the stock.[81] This was marginally up from 43 percent in their survey for companies as of 1920, but the largest shareholder in 1950 held only 15 percent (down from their 20.8 percent figure for the largest shareholder in their 1920 survey) (Franks et al. 2008). Finally, a follow-up study by Florence (1961) examined ninety-eight "very large" manufacturing and commercial companies as of 1951 and found 41 percent of them had a dominant shareholder, 42 percent were marginal, and 17 percent had no dominant shareholder. Thus, based on Florence's data, between 1936 and 1951, the percentage of U.K. firms in which control and ownership had indisputably separated had nearly doubled—from 9 percent to 17 percent. This was change, but the Berle-Means model was still very far from well established.

Commentators have generally opined that "family capitalism" in the United Kingdom declined during the 1950s and 1960s.[82] Channon finds that of the 100 largest British manufacturing companies, only 30 percent still had "family control" as of 1970 (1973, p. 75). Still, large ownership blocks remained common. Leech and Leahy, using data from the 1983–1985 period, surveyed 470 U.K.-listed companies and found 34 percent had a shareholder owning at least 20 percent and 61 percent had a shareholder owning 10 percent or more (Leech and Leahy 1991, pp. 1421–1423, 1435). Only with the 1990s does a study by La Porta et al. find that large ownership blocks had largely disappeared, at least among the largest U.K. companies. Surveying the 20 largest UK publicly quoted companies, they find that none had a 20 percent blockholder and only two had a 10 percent blockholder (La Porta et al. 1999, pp. 474, 492–493). Other, more recent studies, employing much larger samples, have replicated this result, finding in common that the vast majority of U.K.-listed companies lacked a shareholder owing a 25 percent block.[83] In the absence of such a large shareholder, ownership does appear to have at last become separated from control.

This does not mean, however, that evolution of dispersed ownership in the United Kingdom followed the American pattern. One difference stands out: in the United States, the appearance of broadly dispersed ownership preceded the rise of the institutional investor, but in the United Kingdom, it clearly followed their rise and was dependent on it. That is, U.S. public corporations had become widely held during the first quarter of the twentieth century—well before the rise of institutional investors, which came largely after World War II in both countries (with the United Kingdom again lagging marginally behind the United States). Thus, in the United States, the transition went through three stages: from family control to broadly dispersed retail ownership to its current form of dispersed institutional ownership. In the United Kingdom, that middle step appears to have been largely omitted, with the transition instead being directly from family control to institutional ownership. This is an important simplification because it clarifies who were the sellers and who were the buyers, enabling us to focus on what caused them to transact.

In overview, three different forces converged to produce a delayed separation of ownership and control in the United Kingdom: (1) the rise of institutional investors; (2) an active merger market, which included the liberal use of hostile takeovers; and (3) tax laws that pressured controlling shareholders to sell control and that invited institutional investors to buy it.

The Growth of Institutional Ownership

As of the early 1930s, individual investors held over 80 percent of the securities traded on the LSE, and even as of 1957, individuals still held 66 percent of the shares of public companies in the United Kingdom.[84] But within a dozen more years, this percentage fell to less than a majority.[85] By 1991, pension funds and insurance companies together held 51 percent of the shares of U.K. public companies, up sharply from 9 percent in 1957 and 33 percent in 1975.[86] Unit trusts and investment trusts—collective investment vehicles resembling the American mutual fund—held a much smaller percentage of shares, probably never exceeding 8 percent prior to 2000.[87] In the early 1980s, the lines crossed for individuals and pension funds, with individual ownership falling from 66 percent in 1957 to around 20 percent in the early 1990s, while pension funds rose from under 5 percent in 1957 to a peak of over 30 percent around 1993.[88] The mathematically inescapable fact about the structure of share ownership in the United Kingdom is that institutions were persistent buyers and individuals persistent sellers from at least 1957 to at least the early 1990s.[89]

What explains this pattern? No comprehensive description will be attempted of why one group was consistently optimistic and the other consistently pessimistic over so long a period. The answer probably lies more in the fact that institutional investors (most notably insurance companies and pension funds) had limited alternatives to equity securities to fund their own future obligations. That individual investors sought exit over this long a period can be explained by multiple factors: (1) a general stagnation in the British economic outlook from 1957 through the early 1990s; (2) an increasingly regulatory stance taken by U.K. corporate law (which may have reduced the private benefits of control for controlling shareholders and so encouraged them to sell[90]); (3) a merger boom that offered attractive premia; and, most of all, (4) changing tax considerations that forced controlling shareholders to liquidate their blocks. This desire for exit was accommodated by the rise of institutional investors in the United Kingdom. But the appearance and growth of U.K. pension funds seems an exogenous fact, attributable to the Labour government's egalitarian agenda and not explainable in terms of any desire to influence corporate governance.

The British Merger Movement

Franks, Mayer, and Rossi measured changes in ownership structure on a decade-by-decade basis for a sample of sixty companies throughout the twentieth century (forty of which companies were incorporated around 1900 and the other twenty around 1960) (2008, pp. 24–29). They conclude that the "overwhelming use to which equity issuances were put," both in the first and second half of the twentieth century in the United Kingdom, was to fund mergers and acquisitions.[91] To the extent that incumbent blockholders were thereby diluted, mergers may have been the primary cause of dispersed ownership. Similarly, Florence followed some thirty "very large" firms that he classified as "owner-controlled" as of 1951 and finds that twenty-five of these thirty companies experienced major changes in ownership structure between 1951 and 1980, generally as the result of merger activity.[92] During this brief period, each of these twenty-five companies eliminated two-tier capitalization voting structures that gave founder/insiders greater voting rights.

Although prior to the middle of the twentieth century mergers had been relatively uncommon events in the case of firms listed on the LSE, some 43 percent of publicly listed commercial and industrial companies in the United Kingdom were taken over between 1957 and 1969.[93] In substance, the United Kingdom experienced a merger wave in this era that was functionally equivalent to the U.S. merger wave of the 1890s. The leading difference was that many of these acquisitions were made by conglomerates and do not appear to have been attempts to organize oligopolies or increase market share. Sometimes, the acquirer already had dispersed ownership, and sometimes it had a controlling shareholder group. Either way, repetitive mergers produced an acquisition-driven dilution of ownership. In addition, as the Florence data noted earlier indicate, an acquirer that wished to make acquisitions using its stock as currency needed to eliminate those features (such as unequal voting rights or nonvoting classes) that made its stock an unattractive currency. Hence, control blocks weakened in a variety of ways.

The Role of Tax Law

Cheffins's careful analysis of the rise of dispersed ownership in the United Kingdom places tax incentives at center stage. Tax considerations (1) induced blockholders to liquidate their blocks, and (2) encouraged institutional investors, who enjoyed relative tax immunity, to buy.

On the sell side, high corporate tax rates, and particularly an excess corporate profit tax imposed on the eve of World War II, eclipsed corporate profits (Cheffins 2008, pp. 321–328). An especially punitive feature of the post–World War II tax system was a provision that denied "director-controlled" companies the ability to deduct remuneration paid to employee directors (ibid., pp. 322–323). Individual income tax rates also soared up to a maximum taxable rate of 95 percent for taxable income over £20,000 (ibid., p. 823). The combination of high tax rates and the denial of a deduction for remuneration paid to insiders serving on the board essentially eliminated managerial employment as an attractive private benefit of corporate control (ibid., p. 324). British tax law was also dividend-unfriendly, as such investment income was subjected to a special surcharge (ibid., p. 325).

Estate taxation probably provided the principal motive for blockholders to exit. Following World War II, the Labour government raised death duties across the board, with the 50 percent rate beginning at estates exceeding £100,000 and with the maximum rate being 80 percent (ibid., pp. 326–327). To avoid such confiscatory taxation, tax planners urged controlling shareholders to sell their control blocks prior to death and make inter vivos transfers. In this process, family businesses usually sold their control blocks and then placed the cash proceeds of these sales into long-term trusts (ibid., pp. 327–328).

On the buy side, pensions and insurance received relatively favorable tax treatment, thus creating a stronger market for these products (ibid., pp. 346–347). Probably as a result, the total financial assets of pension funds grew thirty-two times between 1952 and 1979, and by the 1970s, pension funds accounted for approximately one-third of all personal savings in the United Kingdom (ibid., p. 348). As money flooded into pension funds, there was little practical alternative for money managers but to invest in equity shares. Insurance companies also increased their allocation of assets to equities from 10 percent in 1946 to 16 percent by 1956 and to 21 percent by the early 1960s (ibid., p. 350). Exchange controls, initially introduced in 1947, greatly limited the ability of U.K. institutional investors to invest in foreign equities (ibid., pp. 352–353). As a result, U.K. capital was "trapped" in domestic equities (which did at least outperform fixed-income securities during this period). These exchange controls were largely abolished in 1979, but by then dispersed ownership had largely arrived.

A Comparison of the U.S. and the U.K. Experiences

The first conclusion is the simplest: exogenous factors largely explain the rise of dispersed ownership in the United States and the United Kingdom. In the United States, the merger wave of the 1890s provides the factor that best explains the timing of this transition. In the United Kingdom, tax considerations similarly supply the primary explanation for the break-up of family ownership. High income and estate taxes, partly necessitated by World War II and partly the product of a Labour government intent on achieving a more egalitarian distribution of wealth, forced blockholders to exit, and the tax-induced flood of money into pension funds and insurance products created a new class of buyers. Corporate and securities law played little role in inducing this transition. Arguably, but for the U.S. merger wave and the changes in the U.K. tax laws, dispersed ownership might have remained only a minority pattern and not the principal form of ownership in both countries.

More must be said, however. In explaining the appearance of the Berle-Means corporation in the United Kingdom, Cheffins disagrees with Franks et al.[94] Cheffins places the British tax laws at stage center in his account, whereas Franks and colleagues give greater emphasis to the creation of trust and the impact of mergers. Who is right? At least in part, their disagreement may stem from their focus on different developments. In overview, the separation of ownership and control needs to be broken into two stages: (1) the appearance of substantial dispersed ownership among minority shareholders, and (2) the eventual break-up of the control blocks that still dominated these firms as of the foregoing stage. In the United Kingdom, the appearance of firms with large and numerous minority owners came well before the dilution of controlling blockholders, while in the United States much less of a time lag separated the two stages. Although the U.K. tax laws may explain the dilution of controlling blockholders, they cannot explain earlier broad dissemination of stock into public hands. Retail investors did not buy stock because controlling shareholders faced tax problems. Here, Franks et al. properly emphasize the role of mergers and the creation of trust (2008, pp. 31–34). Trust is an ineffable quality and is usually based on personal knowledge. As a result, few entrepreneurs could hope to establish sufficient personal contacts to generate trust on the part of a broad class of minority shareholders, and ownership was therefore likely to stay local (as Franks et al. find that it did in the United Kingdom until well into the twentieth century).

This finding should not be a surprise. A strong bias in favor of domestic securities on the part of international money managers has been well established in the economic literature, and even domestic money managers exhibit a strong preference for firms locally headquartered near their offices.[95] Whether one explains this investor preference in terms of trust or asymmetric information, the fact remains that investors tend to prefer geographically proximate investments. As a result, for ownership to disperse beyond a localized region, professional intermediaries may play a necessary role to build trust (or reduce informational asymmetries) beyond the geographic region in which the entrepreneur is personally known. The U.S. experience illustrates how underwriters could develop trust on a transatlantic basis and serve as bonding agents to elicit foreign shareholder investment. This process was probably more visible in the United States because the United States was a capital-importing nation until after World War I, and greater efforts were needed to attract foreign capital. To the European investor, the nineteenth-century railroad wars between rival American robber barons resembled the Wild West. Before the United States could successfully present itself as an attractive venue for European investors, special bonding measures were necessary. The House of Morgan initiated and perfected this process by placing its directors on corporate boards. Although U.S. law did little to ease the anxieties of foreign investors, U.S. intermediaries—both investment bankers and the NYSE—filled this void.

In the transition to the next stage, in which control blocks are diluted, an active merger market in both countries (peaking at different times) appears to have hastened the transition to dispersed ownership by offering sellers a higher premium than they could expect to receive ordinarily from buyers in the secondary market. Because the U.S. merger wave of the 1890s essentially offered stockholders enhanced market power, it inherently promised them the equivalent of a control premium. Also, firms that did not join in the formation of such industry-wide oligopolies faced the risk of being excluded and thereby made worse off. Thus, there was an element of coercion in the break-up of U.S. blocks during this merger wave, just as the British tax laws later supplied an even clearer degree of coercion to induce control dilution.

British heightened merger activity in the 1950s and 1960s cannot be as easily explained. The conglomerate merger movement of this era no longer appears to have had a strong foundation in economic efficiency. Still, controlling shareholders of acquired firms already had tax-motivated reasons to sell and thus may have welcomed merger transactions at lower premiums than they otherwise would have demanded. The only practical alternative for blockholders seeking to avoid estate taxes was to sell into the secondary market on the LSE, where prices were also arguably inflated by the strong, but similarly tax-induced demand for securities on the part of pension funds and insurance companies.

Nowhere in this story do the legal rules protecting minority shareholders play an important role. The most important protection accorded to U.K. minority shareholders during this period—that is, the elimination of unequal voting rights—was the product not of mandatory law but of voluntary action by acquiring firms to enable them to use their shares as merger currency.

Viewed through the prism of Roe's political theory, the dispersion of share ownership and the death of "family capitalism" in the United Kingdom did have a political cause (i.e., high tax rates and death duties that were imposed by a Socialist government seeking to redistribute wealth), but this impact on share ownership seems not to have been foreseen. For those on the Left, the break-up of family capitalism was an unintended but probably serendipitous, result.

In the United States and the United Kingdom, private ordering and self-regulation played decisive roles. In the United States, the House of Morgan and the NYSE developed bonding devices that made equity investments in the United States attractive to foreign investors. In the United Kingdom, institutional investors quickly filled the void left by controlling shareholders and lobbied for practices (such as the Takeover Code) that significantly reduced the private benefits of control. In this light, the centrality of private ordering and industry "best practices" may give a continuing relevance to the work of LLS&V. Their efforts to prove the superiority of the common law to the civil law have encountered nearly unanimous skepticism from legal scholars. But in their later reinterpretations, they have suggested that the specific elements of the common law that they find correlated with strong capital markets may be only proxies for deeper differences between the governance regimes of "common law" economies and "civil law" economies. Those deeper differences may include the greater receptivity (or at least tolerance) for private ordering and self-regulation. Capital markets began to develop in the United Kingdom and later in the United States during the eighteenth century (and arose even earlier in the Netherlands). All three countries were pluralistic and relatively decentralized societies in which political and economic power were separated. In contrast, France and Germany were far more centralized states in which the governments sought to plan and channel economic growth and investment.[96] As a result, in the United States and the United Kingdom, private ordering was given greater room in which to function, and this gave rise to self-regulatory institutions (such as the NYSE and LSE). These self-regulatory bodies were flexible and able to adapt relatively quickly to new circumstances. Viewed in this light, in the turn-of-the-century United States, J. Pierpont Morgan may have been the ultimate self-regulatory authority, relied on by the markets to quell panics and by industries to establish a collusive peace and order.

To sum up, in the United States and the United Kingdom, intermediaries and self-regulatory bodies played necessary and critical roles, both in establishing the institutional mechanisms necessary for creating trust and in regulating markets. They were able to do so because the political and legal environment gave them greater space in which to operate and did not directly control or supervise them. In this sense, LLS&V were correct to search for the fundamental differences in social and economic structures of different societies, and the decentralized political and economic structure within the United States and the United Kingdom may have been the critical variable that explains their convergence.

The Persistence of Passivity: Why Don't Institutional Investors Reunite Ownership and Control?

As retail share ownership has declined and institutional ownership has concentrated, the separation of ownership and control could end, as institutional investors reunite the two in the United States and the United Kingdom. By the early 1990s, the twenty-five largest institutional investors in a U.K. public company had come to hold roughly one-half of its stock, and in the United States the corresponding figure would have been a roughly one-third ownership.[97] In principle, coalition formation is feasible in both countries, if somewhat easier in the United Kingdom. In reality, the degree of concentration may be even higher, both because pension funds typically delegate decisions to an even more limited number of professional fund managers and because many (and possibly most) institutional investors rely on a limited number of professional proxy advisers with regard to voting decisions.[98] Finally, proactive hedge funds have appeared whose basic business model involves searching for opportunities to participate in corporate governance—apparently in the belief that by challenging management ("rattling the cage" in the vernacular), they can raise the stock price. Thus, numerous commentators have suggested that institutional investors could (or should) end the separation of ownership and control.[99]

Nonetheless, this pattern of concentrated institutional ownership has been in place for over two decades, and the basic tendency of institutional investors to remain passive has not changed dramatically.[100] What explains the persistence of passivity? Two basic answers can be given.

The Costs of Coalition Formation

Coalition formation among institutional owners is simpler and easier in the United Kingdom, both because share ownership is more concentrated and because the typical institutional investor owns a larger stake in the equity market. As of the early 1990s, Prudential Corporation, the largest British insurer and also the largest British shareholder, owned some 3.5 percent of the British stock market.[101] Many other institutional investors owned slightly smaller amounts in the 1 to 2 percent range, whereas the largest U.S. institutional investor then owned or managed less than 1.5 percent of the larger U.S. equity market.[102] Prudential estimated as of this time that it held some 900 U.K. stocks and held a 5 percent or greater stock in "probably 200 companies."[103] But it would seldom exceed a 10 percent stake.[104] Hence, even for the largest institution in a concentrated market, it is a safe estimate that assembling a majority voting block would require it to gain the support of probably more than twenty additional institutions.[105]

Of course, this is costly, both in terms of out-of-pocket costs (such as legal fees) and diverted executive time. But there are at least three additional complications associated with coalition formation.

The "Race to the Exit" Scenario

Institutional investors in the United Kingdom have reported that attempts at coalition formation could backfire if those approached learn that a leading investor is dissatisfied. Because the implicit message is thus that a major investor is unhappy with management (and may therefore sell its stock unless changes are implemented), other investors face a dilemma: if the large (and usually "overweighted") investor organizing the coalition fails in achieving its purpose, it will likely reduce its holdings and drive down the stock price.[106] For the institutions so approached by it, the choice is whether to join the coalition or "race for the exit" and sell before the news becomes public. Moreover, because the process of organizing the coalition and then challenging management would take a number of months, it may be obvious that adverse publicity and a war of contending press releases will follow, during which the corporate management's competence and/or integrity will be challenged. Because of this fear of an early rush to the exit, some institutions reported that they would be careful in terms of the institutional investors they contacted to join a prospective coalition, thereby reducing the field of eligible coalition candidates.

This problem is probably less severe in the United States where the holdings of the institutional investor seeking to organize the coalition will typically be smaller (and probably under 5 percent). In short, the more concentrated the institutional market, the greater the fear of a race to the exit.

The Passivity of the "Underweighted"

The normal expectation in the United Kingdom is that the institutional investor who organizes a coalition of investors to negotiate with management will be "overweighted"—that is, it will own a higher percentage of the company's stock than its overall share of the U.K. market (Black and Coffee 1994, pp. 2048, 2063). Sometimes, such an "overweighted" investor has even been assigned the role of lead organizer by U.K. authorities.[107] Although it is not surprising that an investor with a large stake will be more motivated to challenge management than a small investor, the point here is subtler. One institution holding 1.0 percent of the U.K. market might be "overweighted" in a particular stock and own 2 percent; another investor might also own 2 percent and yet be "underweighted" because it owned 2.5 percent of the U.K. equity market. Only the first investor is perceived to be willing to take on the costs and effort of coalition formation.

Why? Because institutions are locked in a competition for investors' funds, which turns largely on their relative performance, none want to help its competitors. Yet an underweighted firm essentially does that when it bears expenses to change management or policies at a corporation in its portfolio; the result is to benefit its overweighted rivals in that firm more than itself. Thus, lacking any means of taxing other shareholders, underweighted institutions tend to remain passive; they may vote with a coalition but not contribute to the costs of collective action (Black and Coffee 1994, p. 2064). This likely passivity of "underweighted" institutions means again that only a limited number of institutions can be expected to lead or fund organized shareholder resistance.

The "Free Rider" Problem

Even when an institutional investor is willing to vote with an activist coalition of fellow shareholders, it does not follow that it will contribute to their common defense on a pro rata basis. In a well-known episode in the early 1990s, institutional investors organized and removed the board of Tace PLC (Black and Coffee 1994, pp. 2042–2043). This revolt was led by Norwich Union, an insurance company that held a 5 percent block in Tace and whose chief financial officer then chaired the Institutional Shareholders' Committee. Although the institutions succeeded in ousting the founder and CEO of Tace, who held a 23 percent block, the victory was arguably a Pyrrhic one, because Norwich Union was forced to split a substantial legal bill with one other shareholder, as all the other institutions in the group declined to contribute (ibid., pp. 2043–2044). Because Tace was a relatively small corporation, it is uncertain that this same coalition of investors would have been able to undertake a more costly campaign against a larger company.

More important, if other coalition members cannot be induced to contribute, then those organizing the coalition will rationally invest funds only if they believe that collective action will produce an expected benefit to the corporation or to its share price that, when divided by their percentage of stock ownership, equals their costs. That is, for a 5 percent shareholder to expend $1 million in costs, it would have to anticipate $20 million in gains to the corporation or its aggregate stock price.[108] This is a mathematics that will deter most activists most of the time.

The Liquidity/Control Trade-off

The foregoing problems of coalition formation are mitigated if institutional investors hold larger stakes. Roe and others have argued that institutions would take such larger equity positions but for regulatory constraints that deter them. There is possibly some truth to this argument in the United States, where a variety of regulatory provisions did discourage institutions from holding large blocks.[109] Although similar restrictive rules are not in force in the United Kingdom, the same pattern persists.

The simple truth is that institutional investors are generally unwilling to sacrifice liquidity.[110] Thus, even in the absence of legal restrictions in the United Kingdom, Prudential and other institutional investors reported themselves to be extremely "cautious" about exceeding the 10 percent level in any stock for fear of losing liquidity.[111] Small institutions may also fear a loss of diversification if they hold very large blocks, but the fear of illiquidity is common to most all institutional investors. Yet if institutions feel compelled to hold less than 10 percent to preserve liquidity, the task of coalition formation is made more difficult—particularly when no mechanism exists to enforce pro rata cost sharing among coalition members.

To generalize, investors that want liquidity must surrender control.[112] As a result, a basic control/liquidity trade-off arises. A few institutions (most notably, hedge funds) may be able to accept relative illiquidity and so are more able to participate in control, but others (such as mutual funds) find the need for liquidity to be paramount and so remain generally aloof from control and corporate governance disputes.

Although liquidity is the primary concern, other factors also constrain institutional activism. As noted earlier, a large indexed institution may own the securities of 900 or more corporations.[113] Neither pension funds nor mutual funds have the in-house logistical capacity to monitor such portfolios in detail. To be sure, they can use professional money managers and can rely on proxy advisers with regard to voting issues. But mutual funds in particular need to economize on their costs to remain competitive, and this further constrains their monitoring capacity. To the extent that they rely on outside consultants, they are likely to receive advice and voting instructions based on rules of thumb or industry best practices, and not an in-depth, specific evaluation of a company's management. In any event, in interviews, institutional investors regularly stress that they are stock traders and portfolio managers, not management consultants.[114]

The claim here is not that institutional investors will never intervene (clearly, they have). Some (such as hedge funds) may be more proactive because they have accepted illiquidity and a lack of diversification as part of their business model. But such institutions will not be broadly marketed to most investors and so will not predominate. As a result, institutional passivity seems likely to remain an enduring characteristic of dispersed ownership systems.

To be sure, their level of passivity is not fixed and can be influenced by legal rules. The rise of hedge funds and recent regulatory reforms in the United States (most notably, "access to the proxy" statement[115]) may result in more challenges to incumbent managements. But these are differences of degree, not of kind.

In short, a reunification of ownership and control appears unlikely as long as dispersed ownership persists as the dominant structure of share ownership in a jurisdiction. This does not mean that dispersed ownership cannot be superceded. Canada supplies an example of a jurisdiction that has gone from a dominant system of concentrated family ownership to dispersed ownership and then back to family ownership—all within half a century.[116] But for the foreseeable future, dispersed institutional owners seem likely to remain more distant and aloof from management decision making than traditional controlling shareholders.

Conclusion

Inherently, scholarship involves a continuing debate between lumpers and splitters. Academic glory normally goes to the lumpers, who generate grand theories by operating at a high level of abstraction. Yet eventually the tide turns as too much inconsistent evidence surfaces. The recent literature on global corporate governance has been a heyday for lumpers, with provocative meta-theories advanced by a number of incisive theorists, most notably Roe and LLS&V. But gradually the splitters begin to reassert themselves, dissecting and dismantling overbroad generalizations. That process is now well under way. Across a variety of jurisdictions, splitters are finding that strong legal rules protecting minority shareholders were not a precondition for dispersed ownership to arise. Instead, intermediaries could and did structure private ordering mechanisms that protected minority shareholders.

This conclusion should not surprise. Studies of contemporary emerging markets also find that, particularly in countries with weak legal protections, firms with higher corporate governance and transparency rankings are valued higher in the stock market (Durney and Kim 2005). To be sure, not all firms will seek to bond themselves in this fashion (because the private benefits of control may often be more valuable). Thus, the availability of such bonding mechanisms do not alone induce the widespread break-up of control blocks. Rather, the fuller history of dispersed ownership must recognize the role of historical contingencies (merger waves in the United States and tax laws in the United Kingdom). Nonetheless, the fact the United States and the United Kingdom converged on a similar pattern of share ownership was because of neither their common law roots nor similar political histories. The most that can be argued is that both countries encouraged and accepted private ordering and self-regulation.

By no means do these conclusions imply that there is little role for theory. Similarities between the political economies of the United States and the United Kingdom—most notably their decentralized governance, their separation of political and economic power, and their preference for private ordering—do stand out and may have played a significant role in the rise of dispersed ownership. Further modeling is thus needed of the relationship between political economies and financial markets. Finally, because firms with dispersed ownership are known in all markets, their ubiquity seems to imply that private ordering can create enduring, stable firms in which ownership and control are separated in virtually any legal or political environment. To be sure, such mechanisms are used only sporadically. But precisely because entrepreneurs only sometimes seek to maximize share value through such arrangements, their use (and non-use) is the phenomenon (not mandatory legal rules) that most merits future study.

Notes

1. Marco Becht and Colin Mayer found that, as of 2001, in the majority of European companies a single voting block held a majority of the voting shares, whereas in the United States and the United Kingdom, the corresponding figure was less than 3 percent. See Becht and Mayer (2001).
2. This is, of course, a one-sentence summary of the Berle and Means thesis, which announced that a "separation of ownership and control" had left professional managers running U.S. public corporations. See Berle and Means (1932). Debate still continues as to the accuracy of this thesis, with some maintaining that the separation is less complete or prevalent than those authors claimed. For a thorough review of this debate and a guarded reaffirmation of the Berle-Means thesis, see Cheffins and Bank (2009). It is, of course, undeniable that many U.S. and U.K. firms do have controlling shareholders.
3. For an overview of these differences in agency costs, see Coffee (2005). How closely the United States and the United Kingdom conform to the Berle-Means or Anglo-American model remains open to debate. See Cheffins and Bank (2009).
4. Debates have long continued over the relative superiority of the Anglo-Saxon model versus European or concentrated ownership models of corporate governance. For a review of the empirical evidence, see Gugler, Mueller, and Yurtoglu (2004). For a strong assertion of the superiority of the European model over the Anglo-Saxon model, see Albert (1993, pp. 160–190).
5. See Morck et al. (2005).
6. Japan has recently experienced "steep declines in cross-shareholding and stable shareholding," and the shareholdings of Japanese commercial banks in Japanese public corporations fell from 16 percent in 1992 to 6 percent in 2004. See Milhaupt

(2005, pp. 2184–2185). Offsetting this decline has been an increase in the ownership in Japanese corporations held by foreign investors, most of whom are activist institutional investors. Ibid., pp. 2185–2186.

7. See LaPorta et al. (1999), surveying shareholder ownership structure in the twenty-seven most developed countries. Using a definition of control under which a 20 percent shareholder is deemed to hold control, they find only two countries (Argentina and Mexico) among the twenty-seven surveyed in which none of the twenty largest corporations in that jurisdiction was "widely held." Ibid., p. 492 (table II, panel A). Using the lower threshold of 10 percent to define control, they find that three more countries join this short list (Belgium, Portugal, and Sweden). Ibid., p. 493 (table II, panel B). Otherwise, twenty-two out of these largest economies had some "widely held" public corporations among their twenty largest companies (ranked by market capitalization).
8. This is the essential position taken by LaPorta, Lopez-de-Silanes, and Shleifer.
9. In academic parlance, *lumpers* are those who seek broad gestalt-like patterns and emphasize similarities, rather than differences. *Splitters* tend, in turn, to both focus on differences and emphasize institutional detail. Lumpers may also be thought of as meta-level theorists who operate at a high level of generality and abstraction, whereas splitters tend to function at a lower level of altitude and concentrate on specific legal or institutional detail. Splitters accuse lumpers of overgeneralization, and lumpers retort that splitters focus on differences without distinctions. No suggestion is intended that one is usually right and the other usually wrong. The dialogue between the two sides is essential.
10. See generally Johnson et al. (2000), giving examples from Eastern Europe and Russian privatization, and Coffee (1999), also describing examples of tunneling.
11. *Tunneling* is a new word, developed by economists to characterize egregious self-dealing that loots an enterprise. But it could have been easily applied to the Erie Railroad in the nineteenth century, when it became known as the "Scarlet Lady of Wall Street" because of rampant self-dealing by insiders. See Gordon (1988).
12. See Choper et al. (2008, p. 15), showing share ownership breakdown in the United States.
13. See Coffee (1991), developing concept of liquidity/control trade-off.
14. See Johnson et al. (2000) and Coffee (1999).
15. See La Porta et al. (1997, 1998).
16. See Djankov et al. (2008).
17. See La Porta et al. (2006).
18. However, in Djankov et al. (2008), only ex post private enforcement showed any statistically significant correlation with ownership dispersion. This led the authors to conclude that private enforcement worked, while public enforcement appeared not to. This conclusion has attracted much (deserved) criticism. See Jackson and Roe (2009), concluding that public enforcement is at least as effective as private enforcement.
19. See Spamann (2006, 2008) and Cools (2005).
20. See Djankov et al. (2008).
21. For this view, see Coffee (2001).
22. For example, see Cheffins (2008, pp. 358–359), noting that the high level at which prospectus disclosure regulation in the United Kingdom was rated by LLS&V was the result only of a 1986 legislative change, which formalized certain preexisting stock exchange rules. In short, the dating was arbitrary.
23. For an overview of these problems, see Siems (2007).

24. The Napoleonic influence of French law on Latin America seems to have been short-lived, whereas the influence of U.S. law may have had a far longer duration. See Dam (2006), pp. 42–45.
25. Ibid., arguing that low economic growth in Latin America explains the difference between the economic performance of common law and French civil law countries and doubting that Latin America should be classified as of French civil law origin.
26. For the views that geography and colonial endowments better explain variations in postcolonial economic growth, see Diamond (1997) and Acemoglu et al. (2001), pp. 1372–1373.
27. See Rajan and Zingales (2003), pp. 14–17. This shift away from financial development could have been motivated by the desires of commercial banks to slow the development of rival institutions, or because finance ministries wanted greater control over the allocation of capital and to spur defense-related industries.
28. For a fuller development of this argument, see Coffee (2001), pp. 59–64.
29. A year earlier, Roe had focused on the advantages of German and Japanese corporate governance. See Roe (1993).
30. Roe recognizes this timing problem, but much of his book is still focused on the restrictive laws regulating banking, mutual funds, pension funds, insurers, and takeovers that were adopted during the New Deal or afterward. The Glass-Steagall Act, separating commercial and investment banking, was enacted in 1933. The Investment Company Act of 1940 regulated mutual funds and effectively required them to be highly diversified. In Roe's view, this precluded most mutual funds from holding large blocks. See Roe (1994), pp. 104–105. Roe analyzes the regulation of takeovers and proxy solicitations and similarly views provisions in the Securities Exchange Act of 1934 (and the Williams Act, which was largely added in 1970 to the Securities Exchange Act) as intended to protect managers from shareholder control. Ibid., pp. 151–168. All this may well be evidence of hostility to financial concentration, but it comes well after the separation of ownership and control.
31. See Roe (1994), pp. 54–55.
32. As a wholesale and privately held bank, J.P. Morgan had neither public customers nor public shareholders. It would only accept deposits from the large corporations it served. See Chernow (1990), 256. It first sold stock to the public in 1942. In opting to remain private, it allowed itself to be superceded in size by those banks that did take retail deposits. Ibid., p. 304. But this was its voluntary decision, not the result of legal rules.
33. Ibid., p. 304, discussing major banks, including Chase Bank, that used securities affiliates to conduct a national securities distribution business in the 1920s.
34. See Roe (2003) and Roe (2000), pp. 552–560, 577–578.
35. See Cheffins (2008), pp. 47–51. As he notes, "Britain had a left-wing government all but three years between 1945 and the election of Margaret Thatcher's Conservatives in 1979." Id. at 49.
36. For a detailed examination as of the mid-1990s, see Black and Coffee (1994), contrasting behavior of institutional investors in corporate governance and finding real, but marginal differences.
37. For a fuller description of the two Vanderbilts, see Chernow (1990), pp. 42–43.
38. Ibid. The full quotation (often wrongly ascribed to the commodore) was: "The public be damned. I am working for my stockholders." Although this claim of loyalty to shareholders may be a more defensible position, it was a public relations nightmare that immediately elicited a hostile press reaction.

39. Ibid., p. 43. Several other robber barons of this era also bought very large blocks.
40. Ibid., p. 44.
41. J.P. Morgan earned an unprecedented $3 million commission for handling this underwriting. See Chernow (1990), p. 44. In addition, the New York Central appointed it its fiscal agent to disburse its dividends to its British shareholders. Ibid. Lucrative fees were available at a variety of junctures, if one controlled the swing votes.
42. In 1869, in a smaller but more violent confrontation, Morgan hired a small army to confront Jay Gould and Jim Fisk (and the latter's army of Bowery thugs) in a shareholder battle for control of the Albany and Susquehanna Railroad, which climaxed in a pitched battle at the annual shareholders' meeting in upstate New York. Morgan's side won both the physical and legal battle, and he went on the board to protect his British clients. See Chernow (1990), pp. 30–32.
43. Ibid., p. 44; see also Gordon (1988).
44. For example, in the late 1880s, Kidder Peabody and Barings took control of the nearly insolvent Santa Fe Railroad, placing three Kidder Peabody partners on its board and implementing a complex voting trust to thwart a takeover attempt by Jay Gould. See Carosso (1970).
45. With respect to the Belmont–Rothschild connection, see Chernow (1990), p. 40; with respect to Seligman's relationship to German investors, see ibid., p. 30; with respect to Kuhn Loeb's relationship to investors in France and Germany, see ibid., p. 90.
46. For example, at one point shortly after the turn of the twentieth century, J.P. Morgan held twenty-three directorships in just thirteen banks, and First National City, which worked closely with J.P. Morgan, held fourteen directorships in other banks and a total of thirty-two directorships at financial institutions. See Ramirez (1995), p. 665. By the time of the Pecora hearings in the wake of the 1929 stock market crash, Pecora was able to present charts at these hearings showing J.P. Morgan directors holding 126 directorships at 89 companies. See Chernow (1990), p. 366.
47. Chernow (1990), p. 42.
48. Ibid., p. 32. When, a few years before the Vanderbilt offering, the Morgans formed a partnership with the then larger Drexel firm, J.P. Morgan's capital in the firm was listed at only $350,000. Chernow (1990), p. 34. Even if this did not represent all his capital, it does suggest that his firm was not capable of financing a major takeover on its own at that time.
49. See Adams (1965).
50. This was also a recurrent theme in the Pecora hearings in 1934, and it led to legislative restrictions on mutual funds, which are barred from making certain concentrated investments in controlled firms "engaging in the same or similar trades or businesses." See Roe (1994), p. 115, explaining that as late as 1942, Congress feared that mutual funds would appoint directors to police cartels across an entire industry.
51. See DeLong (1991).
52. See Ramirez (1995).
53. When the Guggenheim family sold their controlling block in American Smelting and Refining Company in 1908, they did so based on the assurances of their advisers that they could still retain de facto control through their investment bankers on the board. See Becht and DeLong (2007), pp. 616–617.
54. See Bittlingmayer (1985).

55. See Chernow (1990), pp. 83–84.
56. Ibid. Carnegie's firm was beginning to move beyond producing crude steel to making finished steel products (such as pipe). This implied both economies of scale and disruptive competition.
57. See Smythe (2005), arguing that the trend toward increased concentration preceded the Sherman Antritrust Act and largely provoked it.
58. For the fullest statement of this theme, see Cheffins (2003).
59. See Chernow (1990), p. 84.
60. See Smythe (2005), pp. 144–145.
61. For an overview of these justifications, see Smythe (2005), pp. 136–137.
62. See Rajan and Zingales (2003).
63. Prior to 1900, the Boston Stock Exchange was the principal market for industrial securities. See Carosso (1970), p. 44. It had gained this role by listing New England textile mills, whose shares were largely distributed to investors in its community.
64. For a fuller discussion of the NYSE's strategy and the organizational differences between the NYSE and the LSE, see Coffee (2001), pp. 34–40.
65. Between 1850 and 1905, the number of brokers admitted to the LSE rose from 864 to 5,567, whereas the seats on the NYSE stayed constant. Ibid., pp. 34–35. As of 1900, the LSE listed 3,631 different issuers of securities, and the NYSE listed only 1157. Ibid., p. 36. This difference was largely the product of the NYSE's decision to reject most listing applications.
66. Ibid., p. 36.
67. Ibid., pp. 37–39.
68. See Michie (1987), pp. 222–223.
69. J.P. Morgan remained primarily a wholesale bond house and generally (but not always) avoided investments in speculative securities. See Chernow (1990), p. 305. J. Pierpont Morgan appears to have abided by his father's iron rule to avoid speculative securities. Ibid., p. 84.
70. The NYSE also feared that listing risky stocks would produce predictable insolvencies among its members when such a listed company failed. See Coffee (2001), pp. 36–37. Indeed, the U.S. financial markets had witnessed several such panics in the late nineteenth century.
71. See Hawkins (1986), pp. 166–167.
72. See Baskin and Miranti (1997), p. 190. This and other estimates are assessed at greater length in Cheffins and Bank (2009), pp. 15–16.
73. See Cheffins (2008), pp. 12–15.
74. See Cheffins (2001), p. 469. Cheffins adds: "Neither companies legislation nor relevant common law principles afforded much explicit protection to minority shareholders." Ibid. See also Franks et al. (2008), pp. 11–18, arguing that formal investor protections only emerged in the second half of the twentieth century.
75. Cheffins observes that "derivative actions were relatively uncommon and undeveloped since the judiciary was reluctant to give minority shareholders standing to sue on a company's behalf." Cheffins (2001), p. 470. Under *Foss v. Harbottle*, 2 Hare 461 (1843), at least as that decision came to be interpreted by later cases, a derivative action could not be brought in the United Kingdom as long as the alleged misconduct was capable of ratification by an independent majority of the shareholders. This is a more restrictive position than U.S. law took.
76. Cheffins (2001), p. 470; see also Franks et al. (2008), p. 14, discussing leading cases.
77. See Cheffins (2001), p. 470; Franks et al. (2008), p. 14.

78. Leslie Hannah has strongly dissented from the conventional view and challenged what he terms "the erroneous belief that America led in divorcing ownership from control." See Hannah (2007), p. 423. His principal focus is on the ownership of railroads, utilities, and industrial companies in the United States, Britain, France, and Germany at the turn of the twentieth century. He concludes that as of 1900, the United States lagged behind these other countries, largely because it had fewer companies with listed equity securities. Although Hannah has shown that U.K. banks and railroads did have dispersed ownership as of 1900, his claim that share ownership in the United Kingdom was already more dispersed as of 1900 than in the United States seems dubious. His critics have responded that he undercounted U.S. equities by counting only NYSE-listed firms. See Cheffins and Bank (2009), pp. 6–8. As noted earlier, the NYSE was extremely selective in accepting listings, and many public companies traded on other exchanges or on an over-the-counter basis. In any event, the studies by Herman and Warshow show broadly dispersed ownership in the numerous U.S. companies by 1913.
79. See Franks et al. (2008), pp. 33–34. They further report that the median distance between shareholders' addresses and the corporate headquarters was 15.4 miles (p. 33).
80. Ibid., pp. 19–20; see also Cheffins (2008), pp. 12–14. In addition, Cheffins notes that the ten largest shareholders in this sample appear to have owned collectively on average some 43 percent of the stock (2008, p. 297). This suggests that a fairly compact and cohesive insider group held control.
81. Franks et al. (2008), p. 20; see also Cheffins (2008), p. 13.
82. See Cheffins (2008), p. 14 (citing sources); see also Wilson (1995), pp. 190–191.
83. Goergen and Renneboog found that 85 percent of the companies in their random sample of 250 listed companies lacked a 25 percent blockholder. See Goergen and Renneboog (2001), pp. 259, 264. They found that on average the largest block was 15 percent. Faccio and Lang examined 1,953 publicly traded U.K. companies and found that in 63 percent no shareholder controlled a 20 percent block. See Faccio and Lang (2002), p. 379. Van der Elst found that 68 percent of the companies in his sample of 1,333 publicly traded U.K. companies lacked a 25 percent blockholder. See Van der Elst (2005), pp. 3, 41–42.
84. See Cheffins (2008),p. 344.
85. Ibid.
86. Ibid., p. 345. The holdings of pension funds peaked at just over 30 percent around 1993 and then declined. Insurance rose more gradually from around 10 percent in 1957 to over 20 percent by the end of the 1990s and then also declined. Ibid., p. 88 (figure I).
87. Ibid., p. 89 (figure V).
88. Ibid., p. 88 (figure I).
89. This is clearly shown by Cheffins (2008), figure I (p. 88). Institutional investors did not simply buy in the secondary market; they also subscribed heavily in primary offerings, but this distinction changes nothing and had only a reinforcing impact.
90. Cheffins argues that post–World War II changes in British corporate law and stock exchange regulations may have encouraged controlling shareholders to sell and institutional investors to buy. See Cheffins (2008), pp. 356–360. The major amendments to the British Companies Act were in 1948, 1967, and 1981. However, Cheffins finds that the 1948 act did not fundamentally change "the legal position of corporate insiders and minority shareholders" (p. 328). The LSE's listing rules were also extensively revised in 1986 (pp. 357–358).

91. Franks et al. (2008), p. 26. Cheffins, however, is skeptical of this conclusion, given the small sample size and extreme longevity of this sample. See Cheffins (2008), p. 17.
92. Florence (1961), appendix A; for an analysis of these data, see Cheffins (2008), pp. 307–310.
93. See Kuehn (1975), pp. 9, 153. For related studies of the impact of mergers on the structure of share ownership, see Cheffins (2008), pp. 309–310.
94. In particular, Cheffins discounts Franks et al.'s arguments about the need for trust and deems the concept of trust "ultimately unhelpful." See Cheffins (2008), p. 41.
95. See Coval and Moskowitz (1999).
96. I have elaborated on these differences at length elsewhere. See Coffee (2001), pp. 59–64. In particular (as Roe has emphasized), the United States lacked a true central bank from the administration of Andrew Jackson to that of Woodrow Wilson. Inherently, this precluded any effort at centralized economic planning and left greater space for private ordering.
97. See Cheffins (2008), p. 371.
98. RiskMetrics Group, which acquired Institutional Shareholder Services in 2007, is the best known of these firms and dominates the industry. Some controversy surrounds these proxy advisers because of their alleged conflicts of interest. See Vo (2008).
99. Probably the first author to make this point was Adolf Berle, himself. See Berle (1959), pp. 56–59, 75.
100. For a similar assessment, see Cheffins (2008), pp. 370–375.
101. See Black and Coffee (1994), p. 2011.
102. Ibid.
103. Ibid. The interviews with all the U.K. institutions discussed in this article were conducted by this author.
104. Ibid. It then held stakes of up to 14 percent.
105. This estimate assumes that the original proponent held nearly 10 percent and needed to obtain an additional 40 percent.
106. Black and Coffee (1994), pp. 2061–2062. Other investors might also believe that the investor seeking to form this coalition had material adverse information that it was not willing to share. Id. at 2062.
107. Ibid., p. 2043 (noting that Bank of England suggested that Norwich Union lead a shareholder battle as the most "overweighted" institutional investor).
108. It is possible that some institutions may believe there is a general deterrent benefit from curbing managerial excesses that can benefit them, even if they do not directly recover their costs. Even if valid in theory, this view is not widely shared.
109. The clearest example is Section 16(b) of the Securities Exchange Act of 1934, which denies any shareholder the ability to profit on a gain made (or a loss averted) on a purchase and sale (or sale and purchase) transactions that are within six months if the shareholder owns more than 10 percent of the publicly held company. This mandatory six-month holding period creates illiquidity and forces most U.S. institutions to keep their ownership below the 10 percent level.
110. For the fuller development of this argument, see Coffee (1991).
111. See Black and Coffee (1994), p. 2011.
112. In the United States, there are many legal restrictions (Section 16(b) of the Securities Exchange Act, insider trading rules, and the Williams Act) that backstop this generalization. Roe has covered these provisions at length. See Roe (1994),

pp. 151–168. But even in the United Kingdom, where the same legal restrictions are largely lacking, a control block is inherently illiquid, thereby forcing the same choice.

113. This was the figure given by Prudential, and some U.S. institutions are both larger and more indexed. See Black and Coffee (1994), p. 2011.
114. For such comments by institutional investors, see Black and Coffee (1994), pp. 2047–2048.
115. For a discussion of this and related proposals, which would allow institutions to economize greatly on the costs of a proxy contest, see Brown (2008).
116. See Morck et al. (2005).

References

Acemoglu, Daron, Simon Johnson, and James A. Robinson. "The Colonial Origins of Comparative Development: An Empirical Investigation." *American Economic Review* 91 (Dec. 2001): 1369–1401.

Adams, Charles Francis Jr. "A Chapter of Erie." In *The Railroads: The Nation's First Big Business*, ed. Alfred D. Chandler Jr., 74–79. New York: Harcourt, Brace and World, 1965.

Albert, Michel. *Capitalism vs. Capitalism*. London: Whurr Publishers, 1993.

Armour, John, Brian R. Cheffins, and David A. Skeel Jr. "Corporate Ownership Structure and the Evolution of Bankruptcy Law: Lessons from the U.K." *Vanderbilt Law Review* 55 (Nov. 2002): 1699–1785.

Baskin, Jonathan B., and Paul Miranti Jr. *A History of Corporate Finance*. Cambridge: Cambridge University Press, 1997.

Becht, Marco, and J. Bradford DeLong. "Why Have There Been so Little Block Holdings in America?" In *A History of Corporate Governance around the World: Family Business Groups to Professional Managers*, ed. Randall K. Morck, 613–617. Chicago: University of Chicago Press, 2007.

Becht, Marco, and Colin Mayer. "Introduction." In *The Control of Corporate Europe*, ed. Fabrizo Barco and Marco Becht. 1–45. New York: Oxford University Press, 2001.

Berle, Adolf A. Jr. *Power without Property: A New Development in American Political Economy*. New York: Harcourt, Brace, 1959.

Berle, Adolf A. Jr., and Gardiner C. Means. *The Modern Corporation and Private Property*. New Brunswick, N.J.: Transaction Publishers, 1932.

Bittlingmayer, George. "Did Antitrust Policy Cause the Great Merger Wave?" *Journal of Law and Economics* 28 (April 1985): 77–118.

Black, Bernard, and John C. Coffee Jr. "Hail Brittania?: Institutional Investor Behavior under Limited Regulation." *Michigan Law Review* 92 (June 1994): 1997–2087.

Brown, J. Robert Jr. "The SEC, Corporate Governance and Shareholder Access to the Board Room." *Utah Law Review* 2008 (4): 1339–1393.

Carosso, Vincent P. *Investment Banking in America*. Cambridge, Mass.: Harvard University Press, 1970.

Chandler, Alfred D. Jr. *The Visible Hand: The Managerial Revolution in American Business*. Cambridge, Mass.: Harvard University Press, 1977.

Channon, Derek F. *The Strategy and Structure of Business Enterprise*. Cambridge, Mass.: Harvard Business School Press, 1973.

Cheffins, Brian R. "Does Law Matter? The Separation of Ownership and Control in the United Kingdom." *Journal of Legal Studies* 30 (June 2001): 459–484.
Cheffins, Brian R. "Merger and Corporate Ownership Structure: The United States and Germany at the Turn of the 20th Century." *American Journal of Comparative Law* 51 (Summer 2003): 473–503.
Cheffins, Brian R. *Corporate Ownership and Control: British Business Transformed*. New York: Oxford University Press, 2008.
Cheffins, Brian R., and Steven Bank, "Is Berle and Means Really a Myth?" ECGI Law Working Paper no. 121, 2009. http://ssrn.com/abstract=1352605.
Chernow, Ron. *The House of Morgan: An American Banking Dynasty and the Rise of Modern Finance*. New York: Grove Press, 1990.
Choper, Jesse, John Coffee, and Ronald Gilson. *Cases and Materials on Corporations*, 7th ed. New York: Aspen Publishers, 2008.
Coffee, John C. Jr. "Liquidity versus Control: The Institutional Investor as Corporate Monitor." *Columbia Law Review* 91 (Nov. 1991): 1277–1368.
Coffee, John C. Jr. "Privatization and Corporate Governance: The Lessons from Securities Market Failure." *Journal of Corporate Law* 25 (Winter 1999): 1–39.
Coffee, John C. Jr. "The Rise of Dispersed Ownership: The Role of Law and the State in the Separation of Ownership and Control." *Yale Law Journal* 111 (Oct. 2001): 1–82.
Coffee, John C. Jr. "A Theory of Corporate Scandals: Why the U.S. and Europe Differ." *Oxford Review of Economic Policy* 21 (Summer 2005): 198–211.
Cools, Sofie. "The Real Difference in Corporate Law between the United States and Continental Europe: Distribution of Powers." *Delaware Journal of Corporate Law* 30 (2005): 697–766.
Coval, Joshua D., and Tobias J. Moskowitz. "Home Bias at Home: Local Equity Preference in Domestic Portfolios." *Journal of Finance* 54 (Dec. 1999): 2045–2073.
Dam, Kenneth. *The Law-Growth Nexus: The Rule of Law and Economic Development*. Washington, D.C.: Brookings Institute, 2006.
DeLong, J. Bradford. "Did J.P. Morgan's Men Add Value?: An Economist's Perspective on Financial Capitalism." In *Inside the Business Enterprise: Historical Perspectives on the Use of Information*, ed. Peter Temin, 205–236. Chicago: University of Chicago Press, 1991.
Diamond, Jared. *Guns, Germs and Steel: The Fates of Human Societies*. New York: Norton, 1997.
Djankov, Simeon, Rafael La Porta, Florencio Lopez-de-Silanes, and Andrei Shleifer. "The Law and Economics of Self-Dealing." *Journal of Financial Economics* 88 (June 2008): 430–465.
Durney, Art, and E. Han Kim. "To Steal or Not to Steal: Firm Attributes, Legal Environment and Valuation." *Journal of Finance* 50 (June 2005): 1461–1493.
Faccio, Mata, and Larry H. P. Lang. "The Ultimate Ownership of Western European Corporations." *Journal of Financial Economics* 65 (Sept. 2002): 365–395.
Florence, P. Sargant. *The Logic of British and American Industry: A Realistic Analysis of Economic Structure and Government*. Chapel Hill: University of North Carolina Press, 1953.
Florence, P. Sargant. *Ownership, Control and Success of Large Companies: An Analysis of English Industrial Structure and Policy 1936–1951*. London: Sweet and Maxwell, 1961.
Franks, Julian, Colin Mayer, and Stefan Rossi. *Ownership: Evolution and Regulation*. ECGI Finance Working Paper no. 09/2003. Rev. June 30, 2008. http://ssrn.com/abstract=354381.

Goergen, Marc, and Luc Renneboog. "Strong Managers and Passive Institutional Investment in the U.K." In *The Control of Corporate Europe*, ed. Fabrizo Barco and Marco Becht, 259–264. New York: Oxford University Press, 2001.

Gordon, John Steele. *The Scarlet Woman of Wall Street*. New York: Grove/Atlantic, 1988.

Gugler, Klaus, Dennis C. Mueller, and B. Burcin Yurtoglu. "Corporate Governance and the Returns on Investment." *Journal of Law and Economics* 47 (Oct. 2004): 589–633.

Hannah, Leslie. "The 'Divorce' of Ownership from Control from 1900 Onwards: Re-Calibrating Imagined Global Trends." *Business History* 49 (July 2007): 404–438.

Hawkins, David F. "The Development of Modern Financial Reporting Practices among American Manufacturing Companies." In *Managing Big Business*, ed. Richard Tedlow and Richard John Jr. Cambridge, Mass.: Harvard Business School Press, 1986.

Herman, Edward S. *Corporate Control, Corporate Power*. Cambridge: Cambridge University Press, 1981.

Jackson, Howell E., and Mark J. Roe. *Public and Private Enforcement of Securities Laws: Resource-Based Evidence*. Harvard Public Law Working Paper no. 08–28. Rev. July 22, 2009. http://ssrn.com/abstract=1000086.

Johnson, Simon, Rafael La Porta, Florencio Lopez-de-Silanes, Andrei Shleifer, and Robert Vishny. "Tunneling." *American Economic Review* 90 (May 2000): 22–27.

Kuehn, Douglas. *Takeovers and the Theory of the Firm*. London: Macmillan, 1975.

La Porta, Rafael, Florencio Lopez-de-Silanes, and Andrei Shleifer. "Corporate Ownership around the World." *Journal of Finance* 54 (April 1999): 471–517.

La Porta, Rafael, Florencio Lopez-de-Silanes, and Andrei Shleifer. "What Works in Securities Laws?" *Journal of Finance* 61 (Feb. 2006): 1–32.

La Porta, Rafael, Florencio Lopez-de-Silanes, Andrei Shleifer, and Robert W. Vishny. "Legal Determinants of External Finance." *Journal of Finance* 52 (July 1997): 1131–1150.

La Porta, Rafael, Florencio Lopez-de-Silanes, Andrei Shleifer, and Robert W. Vishny. "Law and Finance." *Journal of Political Economy* 106 (Dec. 1998): 1113–1155.

Leech, Dennis, and John Leahy. "Ownership Structure, Control Type and Classifications and the Performance of Large British Companies." *Economic Journal* 101 (Nov. 1991): 1418–1437.

Michie, Ranald C. *The London and New York Stock Exchanges: 1850–1914*. London: Allen and Unwin, 1987.

Milhaupt, Curtis. "In the Shadow of Delaware: The Rise of Hostile Takeovers in Japan." *Columbia Law Review* 105 (Nov. 2005): 2171–2216.

Morck, Randall K., Michael Perry, Gloria Y. Tian, and Bernard Yeung. "The Rise and Fall of the Widely Held Firm: A History of Corporate Ownership in Canada." In *A History of Corporate Governance around The World*, ed. Randall K. Morck, 65–148. Chicago: University of Chicago Press, 2005.

Rajan, Raghuram G., and Luigi Zingales. "The Great Reversals: The Politics of Financial Development in the Twentieth Century." *Journal of Financial Economics* 69 (July 2003): 5–50.

Ramirez, Carlos. "Did J.P. Morgan's Men Add Liquidity?: Corporate Investment, Cash Flow, and Financial Structure at the Turn of the Twentieth Century." *Journal of Finance* 50 (June 1995): 661–578.

Roe, Mark J. "Some Differences in Corporate Structure in Germany, Japan and the United States." *Yale Law Journal* 102 (June 1993): 1927–2003.

Roe, Mark J. *Strong Managers, Weak Owners: The Political Roots of American Corporate Finance*. Princeton, N.J.: Princeton University Press, 1994.

Roe, Mark J. "Political Preconditions to Separating Ownership from Corporate Control." *Stanford Law Review* 53 (Dec. 2000): 539–606.
Roe, Mark J. *Political Preconditions of Corporate Governance*. Cambridge: Cambridge University Press, 2003.
Siems, Mathias. "Reconciling Law and Finance and Comparative Law." *McGill Law Journal* 52 (Spring 2007): 55–81.
Smythe, Donald J. "The Supreme Court and the Trusts: Antitrust and the Foundations of Modern American Business Regulation from Knight to Swift." *University of California Davis Law Review* 39 (Nov. 2005): 85–148.
Spamann, Holger. *On the Insignificance and/or Endogeneity of LaPorta et. al's "Anti-Director Rights Index" under Consistent Coding*. ECGI Law Working Paper no. 67/2006. Rev. June 2, 2006. http://papers.ssrn.com/sol3/papers.cfm?abstract_id=894301.
Spamann, Holger. "*Law and Finance*" *Revisited*. Harvard Law School John M. Olio Center Discussion Paper no. 12, 2008. Rev. Jul. 30, 2009. http://papers.ssrn.com/sol3/papers.cfm?abstract_id=1095526.
Van der Elst, Christopher. "The Equity Markets, Ownership Structures and Control: Towards an International Harmonization." In *Capital Markets and Company Law*, ed. Klaus J. Hopt and Eddy Wymeersch, 3–45. Oxford: Oxford University Press, 2005.
Vo, Thuy-Nga T. "Rating Management Behavior and Ethics: A Proposal to Upgrade Corporate Governance Rating Criteria." *Journal of Corporation Law* 34 (2008): 1–41.
Warshow, H. T. "The Distribution of Corporate Ownership in the United States." *Quarterly Review of Economics* 39 (1924): 15–35.
Wilson, John F. *British Business History, 1720–1944*. Manchester: Manchester University Press, 1995.

CHAPTER 17

THE EAST ASIAN (MOSTLY JAPANESE) MODEL OF CAPITALISM

HIROYUKI ODAGIRI

Is there an East Asian model of capitalism? My first instinct is to say no, because free enterprises and market competition are at the heart of East Asian economies as much as that of U.S. and European economies. Also true, however, is that many differences exist between Asian economies and U.S. or European economies and, for that matter, within Asian economies themselves.

Granovetter (1985, p. 482) proclaimed, using the word *embeddedness,* that "the behavior and institutions to be analyzed are so constrained by ongoing social relations that to construe them as independent is a grievous misunderstanding." The way a nation's capitalism is organized and behaves is embedded in its social relations and historical background and, accordingly, differs across countries and across development stages. To discuss capitalism as a universal regime is a gross simplification and may lead one to misunderstand other countries' economic systems. Of course, there are a number of principles that apply to any market economy just as our economics textbooks teach. Yet the way such principles are implemented and affect the economy is bound to be country-specific.

There is therefore an Asian model of capitalism, as there are a U.S. model, a British model, a German model, and so on. Moreover, as Asia is a vast area with 60 percent of world population residing there, there is too wide a variety of capitalisms to be discussed in a single chapter. The East Asian model is distinctly different from the South Asian models, such as the Indian model. It is also different from that in mainland China, as the country was under central planning until recently and still is under a communist political regime. We thus concentrate our discussion on East Asia, mainly Japan, with occasional references to Korea and Taiwan. By no means, therefore, do I pretend this chapter to be a detailed discussion of the East Asian model in general, not to mention the whole Asian model. Rather, my purpose is to contrast it with the textbook version of capitalism, which in most cases is based on an Anglo-American model, and illustrate that the latter is hardly universal. In fact, the latter can be a minority model.

But what is "capitalism"? As the readers should find throughout this handbook, this is not an easy question, and the answer differs across authors. My own cursory look at several books and dictionaries gave me such diverse perspectives as private ownership of capital, employment of labor, pursuit of profits, free enterprise system, and market society. In the following, I discuss the East Asian model from four perspectives that I believe must be at the center of any such discussion. They are business groups, corporate ownership and management, interfirm relationships, and laissez-faire versus industrial policy. The following sections discuss these questions in turn.

Business Groups and Main Banks

Literature on the Japanese business system and industrial organization, particularly those written by foreign authors, tends to start with the discussion of big conglomerates, *zaibatsu* (and looser zaibatsu-based groups after World War II), and the main bank system (e.g., Caves and Uekusa, 1976; Flath, 2000). These are in fact important characteristics of the Japanese system. Yet two questions need be raised. First, are they really peculiar to Japan? Is it not actually the case that they are observed, probably with varying degrees, in other countries as well? Second, are they as simple and stable as the authors tend to assume? Zaibatsu, in fact, are diverse in their origins, ownership structures, and business compositions.

Modernization and industrialization of Japan started in the mid-nineteenth century when the country opened up for international relationships and trade in 1854. The Meiji Restoration of 1867 abolished a feudal system controlled by the Tokugawa clan (as shogun) and started a modern government. Two of the so-called big four zaibatsu, Mitsui and Sumitomo, started earlier, in the seventeenth century, as innovators at the time in, respectively, the draper and copper refining businesses. They prospered owing to continuous organizational innovation in management structure, labor management, and accounting systems. Even to them, the revolutionary political and social changes at the time of restoration gave extreme hardship. Many equally big merchants and financiers failed. It was only because of the shrewd business acumen of the nonfamily managers that the two survived.

The other two of the big four, Mitsubishi and Yasuda, began around the time of the restoration. Mitsubishi inherited ships owned by a feudal lord and began a shipping business, whereas Yasuda had no such connection but nevertheless succeeded in a financial business. Thus, the historical background of the four zaibatsu is diverse. They all expanded further by purchasing government-built mines and plants at low prices. Most of these government businesses, it should be noted, were poorly managed and had huge deficits. The market values of these businesses must have been zero or even negative (though Japan was yet to have a stock market), and therefore the purchase of government assets was very risky and, at the time, did not promise profits (Odagiri and Goto, 1996). This fact implies that the usual argument that zaibatsu gained a base for growth through government-subsidized sales of its business is misleading, to say the least.

The four are also different in business compositions—Yasuda's core business was banking and other financial services; Mitsui, trade and banking; Mitsubishi, shipping and shipbuilding; and Sumitomo, mining and refinery. Mitsui and Sumitomo were managed mostly by nonowner managers, whereas Mitsubishi and Yasuda were managed by the founders and their heirs. They were similar in that the group firms were essentially controlled by the holding companies, even if some of them were partly public and owned by outside investors. The holding companies were privately owned by founding families.

The big four were not the only zaibatsu. There were so-called industrial zaibatsu, like Kawasaki, Asano, and Furukawa, which started as industrial firms and diversified. There were also new zaibatsu, like Nihon Sangyo (a.k.a. Nissan, meaning "Japan industries") and Nihon Chisso Hiryo (a.k.a. Nitchitsu, meaning "Japan nitrogenous fertilizer"), which were founded in later periods (around the time of World War I) and expanded rapidly. By the time of World War II, Nissan, in particular, was nearly as big as the big four. They also had holding companies as the headquarters but, unlike the big four, the holding companies were public and so were most of the member firms. Besides, they did not have financial business.

Therefore, there are large differences among zaibatsu groups. Common among them is that the founders were innovators in their own ways, they expanded owing to continued innovation and good management even if the connection with politicians (in the case of big four) or the military (in the case of new zaibatsu) helped, and by World War II, they were diversified and organized as groups of firms with holding companies at the top. These characteristics, many readers will notice, are common among the leading firms of most countries. Even in the United States, companies like DuPont are similar except that they used multidivisional structures rather than holding-company structures (Chandler, 1962).

Of course, such big family-controlled business groups account for a large proportion of economic activity in Korea and Taiwan. In Taiwan, their business origins are diverse, ranging from construction and commerce to textiles and plastics. Gradually, they diversified into many industries, for instance, electric appliances. Still, they tended to be biased toward traditional sectors and service sectors, partly because state-led firms, such as spinoffs from government research institutes, played a significant role in semiconductors and other high-tech sectors (Amsden and Chu, 2003).

In Korea, there are business groups called *chaebols* that are similar to zaibatsu. Until recently, they were family-controlled and had holding companies. The relationship with the government was stronger in Korea than in Japan because to foster recovery from the damages created by the Korean War, and promote industrial development, the Korean government gave preferential treatment to chaebols (Amsden, 1989). Another difference is that, owing to the nationalization of banks in the early period, chaebols did not have banks. However, after a series of government deregulations during the 1980s, many chaebols started nonbank financial businesses and expanded them (Lee et al., 2002). In the past decade, they were forced to reorganize by the government to deal with the financial crisis, as well as by the strengthened competition law.

In Japan, such reorganization took place in a drastic fashion after World War II, by the order of the occupation force. The holding companies of zaibatsu were forced to liquidate, with their shares confiscated by the government (the shares were then gradually resold to the public), and the high-rank managers of zaibatsu and other major firms were purged, with the consequence that both ownership and personnel ties among group members were eliminated. These members subsequently formed looser and voluntary coalitions called *kigyo-shudan* (literally, "business groups") or, by some foreign authors, horizontal *keiretsu*. Even though minority cross-shareholding is commonly observed among group members, they are equal partners and the participation is voluntary. The main advantages of being within a group were information sharing and better opportunities for joint ventures and alliances (Odagiri, 1992). Under changing environment and increasing cross-group mergers, as typified by the merger of former Mitsui Bank and Sumitomo Bank, in-group coherence has weakened, particularly after 1990 when the so-called bubble collapsed.

How should we evaluate the presence of such business groups (zaibatsu, kigyo-shudan, chaebols, etc.) in the context of "capitalism"? One of the chief features (if not the feature) of capitalism is the ownership of firms by shareholders, that is, capitalists. In a business group structure, the member firms are wholly or partly owned by their parents whether or not these are pure holding companies (meaning that their only business is to own and control subsidiaries). These parent companies may be owned in turn by their parents, resulting in a pyramidal structure. Such a business group structure, consisting of a group of firms, some of them in diversified fields, in a pyramidal structure is actually known to exist in many countries around the world (La Porta et al., 1999; Khanna and Yafeh, 2007). An exception is the United States, in which conglomerates and multidivisional forms are more common because of the tax system that makes pyramidal business structures unfavorable (Morck et al., 2005).

The difference between business groups and conglomerates is that in conglomerates all divisions and subsidiaries are wholly owned by the headquarters, whereas in business groups it is common that some of the subsidiaries are public, that is, listed on stock markets, and owned by independent investors. Because the top holding company maintains controlling shares of the listed subsidiaries, concerns have been expressed about the possible exploitation of the interests of minority shareholders by the holding companies and, ultimately, their owners, which are often families. This phenomenon has been called tunneling. However, as the investors possess an option of investing in nongroup firms, they will not invest in listed subsidiaries if the shareholders' returns to these subsidiary companies are lower than the market rate. That is, in the stock market, the share prices must be determined so that the shareholder rate of return is common between group subsidiaries and independent firms. For this reason, the argument of tunneling is dubious, and it need not hurt the shareholders' interest (Khanna and Yafeh, 2007).

However, if big business groups are dominant in an economy, the concentration of control in the hands of a few wealthy families or elite managers may cause agency problems or slow economic growth by deterring other firms' entry and innovation. This concern was raised by Morck et al. (2005), who called it economic entrenchment. In Japan's case, however, many entrepreneurs, including those who later established new zaibatsu themselves, entered into markets despite the dominance of zaibatsu during the pre–World War II period (Odagiri and Goto, 1996). A comparative study of nine Asian countries, including Japan and Korea, found no significant effect of group affiliation on Tobin's q, and actually, group affiliation was found beneficial for slower-growing firms in Japan and for older firms in other Asian countries (Claessens et al., 2006), casting doubt on the proposition that groups are earning monopolistic profits in new or growing industries.

There is also an argument that the group structure reduces transaction costs, particularly in an environment in which markets are underdeveloped and property rights and legal contracts are obscure, because of in-group identity and information exchange (Granovetter, 2005). The group structure may also facilitate an easier in-group transfer of human and financial capital. The net effect of business groups, whether or not they are peculiar to East Asia, is unclear.

Another feature of postwar Japan is the system of main banks, that is, those banks that organize loan syndicates for firms in need of a large amount of finance and then monitor these firms. A main bank has an informational advantage because it is involved in most of the firm's financial transactions, such as the receipt of sales revenue, payment to suppliers, and deposit of salaries to employees' accounts. In the case of the firm's financial distress, the main bank will play a major role in rescue operation (Sheard, 1994). For instance, the main bank is likely to dispatch directors at senior levels on such an occasion (Saito and Odagiri, 2008).

The main bank system started around 1940, immediately before World War II (Teranishi, 1994; Okuno-Fujiwara and Okazaki, 1999). Under increasing military influence, the government increased its regulations on business activities to secure a steady supply of munitions. One such regulation was to place a cap on dividends companies pay to shareholders. This made stock investment unattractive, thereby making it difficult for firms to finance through the stock market. They relied on bank loans instead. To deal with increased loan demand, banks started to form loan syndicates with one of them acting as the coordinator, namely, the main bank. Soon, the government started to designate a main bank for every munitions producer.

The system continued after the war. Throughout the high-growth period until around 1970, investment was active, and so was demand for bank loans. Again, main banks coordinated bank loans, supported by lending from the Bank of Japan. The result was both high debt ratios of firms and the continued influence of main banks. The merits and demerits of the main bank system have been discussed by many (Aoki and Patrick, 1994; Weinstein and Yafeh, 1998), with the proponents stressing that main banks have stronger incentive and capability for monitoring and the advocates stressing that main banks are more risk-averse and discourage firms' risky but promising investments. By contrast, Hoshi et al. (1991) argued that main banks reduced liquidity constraints of firms, thereby fostering investment.

The importance of main banks have gradually diminished, however, owing to lessened investment opportunities, firms' wish to reduce debt ratios, the availability of other financial sources, and the shift of industrial composition from heavy manufacturing industries (for which main banks tended to have a high stake) to nonmanufacturing sectors. The proportion of loans by large banks to main firms (i.e., firms with main bank relationship) in their total loans decreased from 42 percent in 1970 to 10 percent in 1990 (Hanazaki and Horiuchi, 2000). Instead banks increased loans to real estate, which became the source of nonperforming loans that caused the postbubble financial difficulties of the 1990s.

In Korea, banks were government-owned or government-controlled during the 1960s and 1970s, through which the government provided funds to support investment in target industries, many such investments being made by chaebols. These banks were privatized in the early 1980s with chaebol ownership to the private banks limited to 8 percent. Many chaebols, however, set up nonbank financial institutions, taking advantage of the financial deregulation that took place around the same time. These financial institutions expanded rapidly, displacing commercial banks as a major source of funds for chaebols. Further deregulation in the 1990s allowed chaebols to extend their financial businesses further, to include life insurance and investment trust companies. Lee et al. (2002) argue that overinvestment made possible through their financial expansion contributed to the financial crisis of 1997 and the collapse of a number of chaebols.

Thus, increased financial availability and careless lending by banks that lost their main firms (in Japan) or by chaebol-affiliated nonbank financial institutions (in Korea) seem to have caused financial crises in these countries. Lee et al. suggest that, given that chaebols had already achieved controlling financial power, financial liberalization in haste has done more harm than benefit. It is possible that the main bank system (in Japan) and the government-controlled banks (in Korea) contributed in providing finances to growing industries during their high-growth periods. However, the transition to a mature and internationally open economy necessitated financial liberalization, and the financial crises in these countries may have been unavoidable. It is extremely difficult to evaluate the contributions of and the distortions caused by the loan policies during the growth era of these countries and of the subsequent financial liberalization. After all, even the United States, a country with a supposedly freer and more competitive financial sector, failed to avoid the financial crisis caused by, most prominently, subprime loans.

Corporate Governance and Management

According to Claessens et al. (2000), Japanese firms are the most "widely held" among firms of nine East Asian countries, whereas Korean firms are one of the most "family controlled"; see table 17.1.

Perhaps these international differences should not be overemphasized, because they may be due to differences in development stages. Before the postwar zaibatsu breakup, most zaibatsu firms would have been classified as family-controlled, even though there also were many independent firms. For Korea, note that the figures in table 17.1 were collected from 1996 data, that is, before the financial crisis. This crisis, together with the demise of the founders and the rise of professional managers, significantly changed the structure of some of the chaebols. Six of the top twenty chaebols in 1997 collapsed, including Daewoo and Kia. The biggest, Hyundai, broke up into Hyundai Motors, Hyundai Heavy Industries, and others. A few of them shrank by selling some of their businesses. Therefore, one can conjecture that the proportion of family control in table 17.1 for Korea must now be smaller. Still, as table 17.2 shows, the proportion of internal ownership remains high among the chaebols that survived the financial crisis, the most representative being Samsung, now the biggest chaebol.

From this ownership viewpoint, the thesis by Berle and Means (1932) of diffused ownership and separation of ownership from control seems to fit Japan well. That is, as La Porta et al. stated in a survey of corporate ownership around the world, "the Japanese model of ownership seems to be closer to that in other countries with good shareholder protection, like the United States or the United Kingdom, than it is to the continental European model" (La Porta et al., 1999, p. 497). What differs from the United States and the United Kingdom is that, in Japan, banks are allowed to own the shares of nonfinancial firms provided that a bank's holding of a company's share does not exceed 5 percent. Among all the shares traded in the stock markets in Japan, the proportion held by financial institutions (including pension funds managed by trust banks, mutual funds, and insurance companies) reached 46 percent in 1989 but then declined to 27 percent in 2008. City banks and regional banks, which play the role of main banks to many companies, had a 16.4 percent share in 1989 but only a 3.6 percent share in 2008.[1] This share decrease was mostly offset by the holdings by foreigners (including foreign companies), which increased from 4 percent to 24 percent during the same period. Thus, in this regard, too, Japan has become more akin to the Anglo-American model.

Table 17.1. Control of Publicly Traded Companies in East Asia, 1996

Country	Number of Corporations	Widely Held	Family	State	Widely Held Financial	Widely Held Corporation
10% cutoff						
Hong Kong	330	0.6	64.7	3.7	7.1	23.9
Indonesia	178	0.6	68.6	10.2	3.8	16.8
Japan	1,240	42.0	13.1	1.1	38.5	5.3
Korea	345	14.3	67.9	5.1	3.5	9.2
Malaysia	238	1.0	57.5	18.2	12.1	11.2
Philippines	120	1.7	42.1	3.6	16.8	35.9
Singapore	221	1.4	52.0	23.6	10.8	12.2
Taiwan	141	2.9	65.6	3.0	10.4	18.1
Thailand	167	2.2	56.5	7.5	12.8	21.1
20% cutoff						
Hong Kong	330	7.0	66.7	1.4	5.2	19.8
Indonesia	178	5.1	71.5	8.2	2.0	13.2
Japan	1,240	79.8	9.7	0.8	6.5	3.2
Korea	345	43.2	48.4	1.6	0.7	6.1
Malaysia	238	10.3	67.2	13.4	2.3	6.7
Philippines	120	19.2	44.6	2.1	7.5	26.7
Singapore	221	5.4	55.4	23.5	4.1	11.5
Taiwan	141	26.2	48.2	2.8	5.3	17.4
Thailand	167	6.6	61.6	8.0	8.6	15.3

Note: "For example, suppose that a family owns 11% of the stock of publicly traded Firm A, which in turn has 21% of the stock of Firm B. The same family owns 25% of Firm C, which in turn owns 7% of Firm B. Looking at control rights, we would say that the family controls 18% of Firm B, or the sum of the weakest links in the chains of voting rights" (Claessens et al., 2000, p. 91). In "10% cutoff," if a family owns 10% or more of the control right of a company, it is classified as family-controlled. Similarly for "20% cutoff." If there is no single owner with the respective threshold control rights or more, the firm is classified as widely held.
Source: Claessens et al. (2000), table 6 (by permission of the publisher).

Another difference concerns the composition of the board of directors. On average among 1,153 listed nonfinancial firms (excluding subsidiaries) in Japan in 1990, a firm had 16.3 directors, of which 3.1 were out-bred in the sense that they joined the firm from outside (Saito and Odagiri, 2008). These out-bred directors included those who joined the firm in mid-career and then were promoted to become directors; therefore, it is a wider concept than outside directors or external directors, as these usually refer to nonexecutive part-time directors who have their

Table 17.2. Percentage of Internal Ownership of Zaibatsu in Korea

	1995	2000	2005
Hyundai	60.4	43.2	20.3
Samsung	49.3	44.5	52.6
LG	39.7	43.1	40.3
SK	51.2	57.2	51.3

Note: "Internal ownership" refers to the ownership by founders, their families, and subsidiaries.
Source: Ko (2009), table 4–2, compiled from the data of Korean Fair Trade Commission.

main positions outside of the firm. In fact, 81 percent of the out-bred directors were full-timers. Therefore, the number of outside directors, if present at all, was at most one in most firms, a marked difference from Anglo-American firms, in which outside directors tend to constitute the majority of the board. As discussed in the previous section, main banks may dispatch directors to failing firms. In these cases, they usually become full-time executive members of these firms, sometimes assuming the presidency or vice presidency, quitting their original positions at the bank; therefore, they are not outside directors in the usual sense.

Put differently, most directors were in-bred, having worked with the firm for many years, typically since graduating from universities, and promoted to the directorship. They therefore tended to have strong identity with the employees at large. This tendency is strengthened by the fact that most employees stay with the firm for their entire working career. The term "lifetime commitment" or "lifetime employment," publicized by Abegglen (1958) and others, is not entirely correct because discharges can actually take place (if disguised as voluntary exit with favored severance pay package), and compulsory retirement at the age of sixty is common. Still, it is true that in most large firms, management makes great efforts to maintain employment, and most workers stay with the same firms. That is, lifetime employment is not always a reality but is considered to be, say, a social norm by many, at least to a greater extent than in Western societies (Odagiri, 1992).

Based on these three features of the Japanese firm—diffused ownership, the board consisting mainly of internally promoted executives, and a long-term firm-employee relationship—two hypotheses have been put forward to explain the behavioral mode.

The first argues that the managerial growth theory, pioneered by Marris (1964, 1998), applies better to Japanese firms than to U.S. or U.K. firms because, first, shareholder control is weaker and the threat of hostile takeover is weaker; second, management is more sympathetic to employees' interests; and third, employees' lifetime utility depends on the chances of promotion, which are greater in an expanding organization (Odagiri, 1992). Therefore, the firm tends to pursue a growth rate beyond the shareholder welfare-maximizing level. Odagiri (1981) even argued that this growth pursuit by the management of representative firms explains the postwar rapid growth of the Japanese economy, using an equilibrium model of economic growth that proves that when firms invest in research and development, the management's choice of a higher firm growth rate results in a faster technical progress rate and a higher macroeconomic growth rate.

The second hypothesis tries to analyze the behavior of Japanese firms in terms of bargaining between shareholders and employees. The management is assumed to play the role of a referee between these two parties (Aoki, 1984). If the employees' utility depends not only on wages but also on the rate of growth of the firm for the reason already discussed, a Nash equilibrium in the bargaining game again results in a firm growth rate higher than that which maximizes shareholder welfare (Odagiri, 1982). This result owes to the fact that employees accept a lower wage rate as a concession to a higher growth rate. In consequence, both shareholders and employees are better off in this equilibrium than in the traditional equilibrium where the management, as an agent of shareholders, maximizes the value of the firm given the wage rate. The latter solution, in this sense, creates "internal dynamic inefficiency" (Aoki, 1984, p. 112).

How, then, can one reconcile the growth orientation predicted in these theories with Japan's reality since 1990: during 1990–2007 its GDP grew at the annual rate of 1.3 percent only. One explanation can be the reduced opportunity for technological catch-up. Both during the prewar era and the postwar high-growth era, Japan raised the technological level rapidly through technology importation and learning (Odagiri and Goto, 1996). However, as Japan had mostly caught up with the technological level of the West by the 1980s, it became harder to raise productivity. Another explanation can be the shift of production to overseas, most notably China and Southeast Asian countries. The third explanation can be the change in corporate governance.

In 2006, a new law, the Companies Act, came into effect in Japan. One important change was the addition of a stock company structure called a "company with committees," in addition to the existing structure that is now called a "company with board of auditors." If a company adopts the former structure, it has to have a nominating committee, an audit committee, and a compensation committee. Each committee has to be composed of three or more members, all of which must be also members of the board of directors. Importantly, the majority of each of these committees must be outside directors (as defined more or less in the sense already given). This structure, called the U.S.-type structure in Japan, requires therefore that the nomination and the determination of compensation of the directors have to be made by committees of which the majority are outsiders. In this regard, it is, theoretically, a big break from the traditional Japanese governance system. In reality, however, the impact has been limited, partly because most firms still use the "company with board of auditors" structure (with exceptions including Sony, Hitachi, and Eisai at the time of this writing) and partly because, as is often the case in the United States as well, the outside directors tend to be selected by the incumbent management among those friendly to them.

Other changes that occurred since 1990 include several hostile takeovers and the bankruptcy of a few big firms, which gave many workers a sense that their jobs may not last a lifetime. Job mobility, as a result, has steadily increased, even if the rate is still much smaller than in the United States or United Kingdom. These changes may have caused convergence, to a certain extent, of the Japanese management system to the Anglo-American system.

In contrast to the management-controlled characteristics of Japanese firms, Korean firms tend to be family-controlled, as discussed earlier. The advantages and disadvantages of family control and business groups have been discussed widely (Khanna and Yafeh, 2007). The major advantage is the ease of making risky but promising investment decisions under asymmetric information (i.e., ordinary investors lacking information on the details of proposed investment projects and their expected returns) and the ease of financing through in-group financial institutions. These conditions, however, can turn into disadvantages if managers invest in too risky projects, motivated by the desire to build empires. Another often-discussed disadvantage is the use of miscellaneous tactics to enrich majority shareholders (i.e., families) at the cost of minority shareholders, that is, tunneling or entrenchment. As discussed already, the presence of such tunneling has not been confirmed.

It is likely that the tendency to overinvest by the founding families of chaebols made the rapid development of Korea possible until the mid-1990s. Also possible is that the same tendency triggered, together with international conditions, the financial crisis of 1997 and the demise of several chaebols. One apparent change in recent years is the rise of professional managers to high-rank positions, together with the retirement, death, or even arrest of some of the founders and their families (Chang, 2006; Ko, 2009). Thus, even if family ownership remains significant, a likely scenario is that the professional and internally promoted nonfamily managers will become involved in strategic decisions more and more. In this regard, Korea's model in coming years may become more akin to the Japanese model of managerial capitalism.

The Supplier System

Long-term relationships are also common in the exchange of goods and services, the most apparent being the procurement of materials and components in the automobile, electrical equipment, and other industries.

In a textbook description of capitalism, interfirm and intrafirm relationships are distinct, respectively called market transactions and hierarchical structure. Thus Williamson started *Markets and Hierarchies* by saying "this book is concerned with the organization of economic activity within and between markets and hierarchies. Whereas market transactions involve exchange between autonomous economic entities... hierarchical transactions are ones for which a single administrative entity spans both sides of the transaction, some form of subordination prevails, and, typically, consolidated ownership obtains" (Williamson, 1975, xi).

In market transactions, buyers and sellers only meet at the market place with an arm's length between them. Buyers maximize their utility by buying from the cheapest supplier given quality, and sellers maximize their profits by selling as much as possible at market prices. If this arm's-length transaction does not work for whatever reason—say, for fear of being held up after making a relation-specific investment—the transaction costs become so high that the buyer and seller should integrate and use hierarchical authority to minimize cost.

In real life, however, many transactions take place somewhere between the polar cases of arm's-length and intrafirm transactions. This fact was noted even before Williamson by the British author Richardson, who said,

> we must not imagine that reality exhibits a sharp line of distinction; what confronts us is a continuum passing from transactions, such as those on organised commodity markets, where the co-operative element is minimal, through intermediate areas in which there are linkages of traditional connection and goodwill, and finally to those complex and inter-locking clusters, groups and alliances which represent co-operation fully and formally developed. (Richardson, 1972, p. 887)

That is, in any real economy, "intermediate areas" between market transactions and intrafirm transactions are present and prevalent. Yet significant international differences are there and, in my opinion, the intermediate areas are broader and more diverse in East Asian economies than in the United Kingdom or United States. In other words, the boundary of the firm in reality is not that clear in any country and is even blurrier in Japan and other East Asian countries than elsewhere.

In a survey by Japan's Fair Trade Commission (JFTC, 1987), all except two of the eighty-nine large nonfinancial companies replied that all or most of their non-investment purchases (materials, fuel, etc.) had been made on a continuous basis over the previous five years. Such long-term relationships may have been caused by a cultural factor. Yamagishi et al. (1994, 1998) argue in a U.S.-Japan comparative study that perhaps contrary to the received view, the level of general trust is higher in the United States than in Japan and that, to deal with social uncertainty under weaker general trust, the Japanese tend to form stable and committed relationships. Cultural influences aside, in Japanese supplier–assembler relations, considerable efforts are being made to maintain and enhance long-term relationships. Toyota, for example, organizes supplier associations to promote information exchange and run consulting divisions to help suppliers solve operational problems (Dyer and Nobeoka, 2000). Visits by the assembler's engineers and other staff to suppliers are common. Such a hands-on approach by Japanese assemblers was taken by surprise when they invested in the United Kingdom and started using U.K. suppliers. According to one such supplier, "the Japanese tend to camp out on your doorstep.

We've got English firms that we see once or twice a year... it's nothing for the Japanese to turn up two, three or four times a day."[2]

As a consequence of such efforts, the suppliers' trust in assemblers is higher in Japan than in the United States or even Korea (Dyer and Chu, 2003).[3] Sako (1991, 1992) provides similar evidence from her survey. She asked about the following hypothetical case to the suppliers: "When you are negotiating a new order, the customer talks about other favourable offers he is getting, implying that if you don't put the price down, he will switch to sourcing from your competitors instead of from you. By this time you have become quite dependent on this customer for business, and agree to lower the price. Subsequently, you discover that the story of other offers was entirely fictitious" (Sako, 1992, p. 247). Significantly more Japanese suppliers considered such a case unacceptable than British suppliers, saying, "I would not deal with anyone who did that." Significantly more Japanese suppliers also agreed that they hardly ever encounter such behavior from their customers.

The presence of such trust goes hand in hand with long-term relationships, because continuous and frequent contact cultivates an air of mutual trust, and the anticipation of long-term relationships makes cheating less desirable as the theory of repeated games predicts (Kreps, 1990). With complexity, uncertainty, and bounded rationality, it is prohibitively costly, if possible at all, to write a contract that depicts a whole set of actions to be taken under various possible future states. Asymmetric information is inevitable in many cases with, for instance, assemblers having better knowledge of demand conditions. If either side of the transaction is afraid of the other's opportunistic behavior taking advantage of information asymmetry, the relationship cannot last and opportunities for gaining from collaboration would be lost. To be true, as transaction cost economics predicts, vertical integration is one way to deal with this difficulty. That is, under uncertainty, the use of authority created with an employment contract is advantageous over a market transaction that uses a sales contract (Simon, 1951). However, vertical integration also has disadvantages, such as weakened motivation for efficiency improvement due to reduced threat of competition, and agency problems caused by, for instance, the employee acting to enhance his own utility rather than the firm's.

The use of long-term supplier–assembler relationships in Japan is an intermediate organizational form, in the manner suggested by Richardson. Such relationships have been also called keiretsu relationships or subcontracting relationships. The use of these words can mislead, however. *Keiretsu* has been more often used to indicate business groups discussed earlier and, to distinguish the two, foreign observers tend to use the phrase "horizontal keiretsu" to indicate business groups and "vertical keiretsu" to indicate pyramidal structures (Lincoln and Gerlach, 2004). However, the common Japanese word for horizontal keiretsu is *kigyo shudan*, which should be translated as nothing but business groups. Vertical keiretsu is used more to mean a group of firms consisting of an unambiguous leader firm and the firms subordinate to it, either because of share ownership or technological and business dependence. An example is the Hitachi group, with Hitachi at the top and more than a thousand subsidiaries and affiliates with major or minor ownership by

Hitachi. In the supplier–assembler relationship, some suppliers may be the members of such a vertical keiretsu of the assembler; however, many are independent. The word *subcontracting* is also inappropriate because it refers to the case where the subcontractors do the work according to specifications and orders given by the subcontracting firm, sometimes using the capital assets and even shop space of the latter. By contrast, in many of the actual supplier–assembler relations, the suppliers develop and design the material and components. For instance, a major supplier to not just Toyota but also all other Japanese automakers is Denso, one of the biggest auto component makers in the world with its own strong technological capability.

As already discussed, within the Japanese supplier–assembler relationship, knowledge sharing and technical assistance are frequent. The relationship tends to persist from one product model to another. Mutual trust is valued. Still, competitive threat is also there. For one thing, a multivendor policy is commonly adopted so that the assembler can compare price and quality among suppliers including potential ones. For another, the assembler makes a detailed evaluation of the supplier's performance and treats the supplier accordingly (Asanuma, 1985, 1989). How much effort has the supplier made to increase efficiency and improve quality? How reliable and stable has quality been? How accurate and in-time has the delivery been? How many proposals has the supplier made to improve the product and improve the group performance as a whole? These are all evaluated by the assembler. If the performance is considered substandard, then the supplier may have to accept a lower margin in the next round of supply or, at worst, may not be able to get further orders. By contrast, if the performance is evaluated highly, the supplier may be awarded with higher margins or a wider range of products to supply in the next round. When the supplier improves efficiency, they will be able to capture a large part of the fruit even if the improvement was made with the assembler's assistance. In return, they will be asked to share knowledge with other suppliers. The contrast of this practice of Toyota's with that of General Motors is obvious, where PICOS is GM's team of consultants. According to one U.S. supplier executive, "We don't want to have a PICOS team poking around our plant. They will just find the 'low hanging fruit'—the stuff that's relatively easy to see and fix. We all have things in our plants that we know need to be fixed. They'll just come in, see it, and ask for a price decrease" (Dyer and Nobeoka, 2000, p. 359).

In textbook capitalism, competition occurs through "exit." But as Hirschman (1970, 1987) argued, "voice" also plays an important role in fixing deficiencies and improving relationships. That is, if the assembler is dissatisfied with the supplier's performance, it may exit, that is, stop purchasing from the supplier and switch to another. Or it may express its dissatisfaction to the supplier, propose an alternative, give managerial and technical assistance, and warn them before exercising an exit option. Such use of voice, together with the threat of exit, seems to be at work in the Japanese supplier–assembler relationship.

This relationship, it is noted, has not been a constant feature of the Japanese system. Rather, it has been the product of historical necessity and has been evolving over time. When Nissan started large-scale production (though minuscule by today's standard) in 1935 and Toyota followed suit in 1937, there was no parts supplier of sufficient skill around except the suppliers to Ford and General Motors, which had plants in Japan at the time and dominated the Japanese market. Nissan and Toyota were both too small and weak to produce all the necessary components. Partly they procured from the suppliers to Ford and GM, but they also had to approach local blacksmiths and other firms and assist them in producing necessary parts. This was the origin of the supplier system. Subsequently, both because of changing economic conditions and government policies to promote small and medium firms, and because of the assemblers' strategy to foster suppliers' capability to deal with increasing market demand, the supplier system evolved (Nishiguchi, 1994).

The supplier system, therefore, is not free from the surrounding conditions, and its development is subject to path dependency. Accordingly, it differs across countries and, within a country, across industries. In the shipbuilding industry, like in the automobile industry, few sufficiently capable suppliers were available when Japan started building large, modern iron-made vessels in the early twentieth century. This makes a clear contrast to the United Kingdom, the world leader at the time. As the United Kingdom developed its shipbuilding industry, parts suppliers also grew based on the accumulated craft technologies; thus, the shipbuilders could procure from them on a more or less arm's-length basis. In Japan, such suppliers were absent. However, there was an important difference from the automobile industry. Both Nissan and Toyota, at the time, were new enterprises and lacked sufficient resources to produce components internally. By contrast, the largest shipbuilder at the time in Japan was Mitsubishi Shipbuilding (now Mitsubishi Heavy Industries) and had reasonable financial resources. Besides, they were dependent on the orders from the navy, and the government was eager to support domestic shipbuilders. For these reasons, Mitsubishi could develop a large part of components internally, together with procurement from outside, and the extent of vertical integration was higher than in the automobile industry. Gradually, Mitsubishi spun off some of the component divisions, including an electric parts division that became Mitsubishi Electric. These spin-off companies constituted an important part of Mitsubishi zaibatsu.

Again, therefore, we emphasize that capitalism is embedded (to use Granovetter's word) in economic and social as well as historical conditions. The Japanese system of capitalism is thus different from the U.S. or U.K. system.

So is the Korean system. In a U.S.-Japan-Korea comparative study of suppliers to automakers, Dyer and Chu (2003) found that supplier trust in Korea is lower than in Japan and about the same as in the United States. Also in Korea, the transaction cost per dollar of sales is highest among the three countries, and supplier information sharing is lower than in Japan. These are the suppliers to three Korean assemblers: Hyundai, Daewoo, and Kia. Hyundai first prospered as a building contractor and expanded into shipbuilding and then automobiles. Daewoo started as a trading company and then expanded into construction, finance, machinery, and so forth, before buying an auto manufacturer in financial trouble to enter into automobile production. Unlike these two, Kia was in manufacturing from the beginning. It started by making bicycle parts and then upgraded to bicycle assembling, motorcycles, and then cars.[4] Thus, with Kia aside, these firms, like Mitsubishi Shipbuilding, could depend on financial resources earned from other businesses. The three also benefited from low-interest loans, subsidies, and other policies that the government made to promote the automobile industry. Also, at one time or another, all three licensed technologies or had joint ventures with American or Japanese automakers. These differences perhaps created the Korean supplier system which, unlike in Japan, did not nurture trusting relationships between suppliers and assemblers.

Neither did Taiwan, in which arm's-length transaction appears to be a norm in such assembling industries as the bicycle and IT industries. The reason for the lack of long-term relationships is apparently different from that in Korea. In Taiwan, "technology generation mainly involved some organ of the government, whether in relation to a supplier or a parts supplier" (Amsden and Chu, 2003, p. 92) and this fact made it difficult for a particular supplier and a particular assembler to establish an intimate and exclusive relationship. In addition, with the economy being more open than in Japan and Korea, Taiwanese assemblers could procure components from foreign, mostly U.S. and Japanese suppliers with advanced and reliable technology. Again, this Japan-Korea-Taiwan comparison should illustrate how much a country's economic organizational form is embedded in social, political, and international surroundings.

Industrial Policy

Another fiction of textbook capitalism is the assumption of a laissez-faire economy in which markets work without government intervention. The fact is that government does play significant roles in any economy, in providing public goods, education services, and infrastructure; establishing laws and the judicial system; issuing money and making (or at least trying to make) macroeconomic management; and regulating business activities for environmental protection, health, safety, and other reasons. That is, in any country, the economy is a mixed economy as discussed by Nelson in this volume.

Besides these reasons, the government tries to influence industrial structure by promoting certain industries, supporting domestic firms competing against foreign firms, or helping declining industries reduce excess capacity. Such policy, now widely called industrial policy, is often indistinguishable from other policies that also affect industries. An example is competition policy. Even though the aim of competition policy is to maintain competition by means of competition laws (Anti-Monopoly Law in Japan, Monopoly Regulation and Fair Trade Act in Korea, and Fair Trade Law in Taiwan) and let market forces determine the industrial structure, it inevitably influences the structure by, for instance, regulating mergers and cooperative behavior, including standard setting and patent pools, and prohibiting entry-preventing monopolistic behavior. Another example is science and technology policies, together with the country's regime of intellectual property rights. Some of such policies are primarily made to deal with the public goods nature of technological knowledge or as a part of education policy, most relevantly, university education. Some are made as a part of military activity, since many inventions have come out of military research, for instance, to develop more effective weapons and faster tanks, submarines, and aircrafts. In addition, all the countries have recognized the importance of raising innovative capability to promote industries and hence have actively engaged in technology policies for this purpose.

Basically, there are two categories of industrial policy: one is to promote entry into an infant and expanding market, and the other is to adjust capacity to deal with declining demand or with factor conditions that are lessening the country's comparative advantage. In the Japanese case, the majority of the policies were those for promotion until around 1970 and then, following the oil crisis, a number of adjustment policies were also made. In Korea, promotion policies were dominant until the financial crisis of the late 1990s and then, to deal with the crisis, several adjustment policies were put in place. In Taiwan, the government policies were mostly made to raise the technology capabilities of industries and promote new industries. Thus, prevalent among these countries during their catch-up phases were policies for promotion, and these policies have been extensively discussed among foreign observers.

The principal theoretical justification for promotion policies is the infant industry theory (Negishi, 1968). An industry is said to be infant if entry is costly so that initially the profit is negative, but in the future, the profit is expected to turn positive. For instance, if in the beginning the domestic firm is technologically inferior to foreign firms importing to the country, it will have to bear a loss to sell at a competitive price against imports. However, once the firm enters, it can accumulate technological capabilities through R&D efforts and learning by doing. Accordingly, in the future, the firm is expected to be able to compete effectively against foreign firms and earn positive profits.

If the future positive profits more than outweigh the initial loss so that the present value is positive, the firm will find it in their interest to enter into the industry; hence, there is no need for policy support. However, there are two cases that call for a policy to promote the entry of a domestic firm. First, the financial market may be incomplete, so that the firm will not be able to sustain itself during the initial loss-making period. Such incompleteness may occur because of underdeveloped financial institutions or information asymmetry between the firm (which can predict future profits) and financial institutions (which do not have such information). Second, even if the present value of profits is negative, the present value of total surplus (the sum of profits and consumer surplus) can be positive.[5] Such a case takes place when the entry causes the future price to decrease, thereby increasing consumer surplus. Entry can cause intensified competition, resulting in a lower price. Or the entrant may achieve technological progress, decreasing the cost or developing new or better products. In either case, the consumer gains a higher surplus, and thus, the protection of an infant industry may be justified theoretically.

Japan, Korea, and Taiwan and, for that matter, almost all developing countries have, at one time or another, adopted policies to protect and promote infant industries. These policies, in short, have been the major part of industrial policies. The tools commonly used for this purpose are of two types. The first is a policy to secure demand for domestic firms, and the other is a policy to shift the cost curve downward so that the firm can compete against foreign, more advanced rivals. Among the demand-supporting measures are import restriction and the control of inward direct investment, that is, protection against imports and against local production by multinationals. Preferential procurement by the government and military has also been used in many countries. Among the cost-reducing measures are subsidies, low-interest loans, tax concessions, and other financial assistance. These policies were taken partly to overcome an entry barrier raised by the need for sunk investment. As the contestable market theory teaches, sunk costs create entry barriers because these costs have already been paid by the incumbents and cannot be recovered, whereas the entrants have yet to pay them (Baumol et al., 1982). Therefore, assisting the entrants in covering sunk costs can be welfare-improving by encouraging entry and promoting competition. This argument obviously applies not just in developing countries but in any country generally.

An argument particularly applicable to developing countries is the need for catch-up. In many industries, the technological capabilities of developing countries are insufficient compared to advanced countries and, to narrow the technological gap, they have to catch up. For this purpose, they learn the technologies of more advanced countries through various channels, including movement of people, such as immigration, studying abroad, and hiring foreign experts; open-source information, such as books, journals, and patent documents; imported machines and components; and spillover from local subsidiaries of multinationals (Odagiri et al., 2010). The government can aid domestic firms in their catch-up efforts by sending students abroad, disseminating information, assisting domestic firms in buying imported machines, and investing in R&D. However, just buying advanced foreign machines does not immediately raise the technological capability of the domestic firm. For sure, the imported machine will raise productivity; however, to really learn the technology embodied in the machine, the firm may need to accumulate experience and make further investment to improve the machine or the entire process around the machine. Such learning by using takes time, and in the meantime, the firm may not be able to support itself. Thus, governmental financial support can help the firm survive and eventually succeed in catching up. Once having succeeded in catch-up, consumers would benefit from a lower price, better quality, or broader choice, fulfilling the above-mentioned conditions for the support of infant industry.

In many countries, some of these policies were taken irrespective of industries, for instance, by lowering duties on all imported machines, providing low-interest loans to all qualifying firms, and giving tax credits to R&D expenditures. Some policies were applied to select industries only, called "targeting." In the East Asian countries, electric appliances, computers, automobiles, and their components were commonly chosen as the target industries. In the early period, protection against imports and direct investment was a popular tool; in later years, such a protection policy became more difficult to implement owing to World Trade Organization agreements and complaints from advanced countries. Hence, subsidies and tax concession came to be used more commonly in later years.

It is not the purpose of this chapter to give a full description of post–World War II industrial policies in Japan, Korea, and Taiwan. Many studies are available for this purpose: see, for instance, Johnson (1982), Komiya et al. (1988), Fransman (1990), and Odagiri and Goto (1996) for Japan; Amsden (1989) for Korea; and Wade (1990) and Amsden and Chu (2003) for Taiwan. For broader East Asian countries, reports by the World Bank (1993, 2003) are well known. Not all authors agree on whether the industrial policies have played the intended roles. These policies necessarily distort resource allocations. That is, giving low-interest loans and adopting differential taxes and duties changes relative prices, thereby favoring some sectors at the expense of others. Targeting policies have the same effect more directly. Protection policy not only protects infant domestic firms from international competition but also protects them from market competition in general, possibly allowing a firm to indulge in inefficient management rather than making necessary investment for catch-up and innovation. In consequence, even though one may argue that, internationally compared, Japan, Korea, and Taiwan had relatively successful industrial policies (or, at least, less harmful policies), whether they really contributed to growth is still under debate. An argument may be made that the private sector in these countries had sufficient capabilities and entrepreneurship so that the industries would have developed with or without industrial policies. There were even cases in which the industry seems to have grown despite industrial policies, like the case of the Japanese Ministry of International Trade and Industry (MITI) trying to consolidate the automobile industry into two groups (i.e., Toyota and Nissan) in the early 1960s and Honda entering into car production, ignoring MITI's strong opposition (Odagiri and Goto, 1996).

It is therefore too simplistic to argue that industrial policies were always useful or that East Asian countries developed owing to industrial policies. Some policies were probably useful, but some were not. Whether the government has a comparative advantage over the business sector in predicting the future course of economic development may also be questioned. If based on a mistaken future forecast (like MITI's worry at the time that the Japanese automobile industry would collapse once trade and capital are liberalized), the government policy may turn out ineffective or even harmful.

With this caution in mind, I say that industrial policies have been prevalent in East Asian countries (as in many other countries worldwide), and some are likely to have contributed to industrial growth. These industries might not have developed under the laissez-faire economy as posited in textbook capitalism. The process of development and evolution is, indeed, so complex that one cannot fully understand it with the textbook price theory and economic growth theory alone. What is needed is a detailed and case-by-case understanding of how industries really evolved and accumulated capabilities, and how government policies as well as legal systems influenced them.

Summary and Conclusion

In this chapter, I discussed the East Asian model of capitalism, mostly the Japanese one, with occasional references to the Korean and Taiwanese models. As its salient features, I raised four aspects—business groups and main banks, corporate governance and management, the supplier system, and industrial policy. I emphasize again that these features are actually observed not just in East Asian countries but almost everywhere, particularly in many developing countries as well as continental European countries. In other words, the textbook version of capitalism—characterized by an atomistic structure of industries composed of independent firms, capitalists as owners and managers of firms, arm's-length transactions in which firms always compete on prices, and laissez-faire markets without government intervention—is far from reality not just in the countries discussed here but, to a varying degree, in every country including the United States and United Kingdom.

Having said that, I acknowledge that East Asian economies have a few distinctive features. First, business groups were dominant in pre–World War II Japan, and postwar Korea and Taiwan. These groups, however, should not be taken as a static presence because they evolved in important ways. Without exception, they were started by Schumpeterian entrepreneurs who innovated and took risks. Gradually, they diversified and expanded, sometimes taking advantages of their connection to the government, politicians, and the military. Competition was not absent and, as in the case of the financial crisis in Korea, some went bankrupt. Even if (a big if) their raison d'être become unclear, it is hard to break up existing groups. Despite the effort of the Korean government at the time of financial crisis, some chaebols have increased their power. In Japan, zaibatsu breakups could be made only with the extraordinary power that the occupation army had after Japan's defeat in World War II (and the group relationships being replaced by loose relationships with main banks). Still, even in Korea and Taiwan, the founders have gradually disappeared with the consequence of family control getting loose and professional managers gaining more power. Thus, one may speculate that the business group structure has been making an evolutionary change, if not a revolutionary change, toward a more competitive structure.

Second, such a change leads to the question of corporate governance—who really controls the firm? It was suggested that in Japan particularly until around 1990, shareholder control was limited and internally promoted management tended to be sympathetic to the employees, which resulted in the pursuit of growth. This tendency was reinforced by the fact that employees tended to feel attached to the firm, with long-term company–employee relationships being the norm (though not always reality) in big Japanese firms. More recently, with strengthened shareholder rights and increased labor mobility, the management's goal may have shifted toward more value pursuit than growth pursuit, and one may speculate that this shift, together with increased uncertainty, contributed to the stagnation in the last couple of decades.

Third, long-term relationships are also prevalent in supplier–assembler relations. Between markets, where allocation is made with arm's-length transactions, and hierarchy, where allocation is made with internal control, there are intermediate forms in which firms interact on a long-term basis and the exercise of voice is more frequent and more effective than that of exit. Still, competition is strict and those failing to respond to the trading partner's trust or those failing to improve (kaizen) are punished. Of course, the long-term relationship may prove to be a handicap when a swift and radical change is in need; yet more often than not, it was a device with which opportunistic behavior was suppressed and transaction costs were saved.

Fourth and last, it was argued that another myth of textbook capitalism is laissez-faire. Actually, all countries have mixed economies, with the government playing significant roles in many aspects. Often the government consciously adopted policies to promote targeted industries, that is, industrial policies. The main justification for such industrial policies is the infant industry theory. Virtually every country has adopted industrial policies at one time or another. Perhaps the experience of Japan, Korea, and Taiwan is particularly well publicized owing to its conspicuous success in promoting such industries as electrical equipment, electrical components including semiconductors, PCs, shipbuilding, and automobiles. In these countries, technological catch-up to the then frontier countries was more successful than in other regions of the world, owing to investment and learning. How much government policies contributed to this process of catch-up is difficult to say and apparently varies widely across industries, periods, and countries.

The purpose of this chapter was not to give a full description of the East Asian model of capitalism. Rather, it was to show that the textbook description of capitalism is a gross simplification and nowhere present in reality. The way capitalism is structured, the way it works, and the way it solves economic problems are very much embedded in the social relations and historical background. An economy is nowhere static: it evolves over time in a path-dependent fashion (Nelson and Winter, 1982). The consequence is that every country has its model of capitalism. The Japanese model, the Korean model, and the Taiwanese model—these are just a few of such models.

NOTES

1. Data source: Tokyo Stock Exchange, http://www.tse.or.jp/english/market/data/shareownership/english2008.pdf, accessed in December 2009.
2. BBC film documentary, *Chopsticks, Bulldozers and Newcastle Brown* (1987), cited in Oliver and Wilkinson (1988, p. 70).
3. Note that the "trust" here refers to the suppliers' trust in assemblers, that is, trust within supplier–assembler relations, and not the "general trust" mentioned by Yamagishi in the previous paragraph.
4. After the financial crisis of the late 1990s, Daewoo was acquired by General Motors and Kia by Hyundai.
5. Note that a country's total surplus is the sum of consumer surplus and the profits of domestic firms; that is, it does not include the profits of foreign firms, because the foreign firms are supposedly owned by foreigners (this assumption is likely satisfied in developing countries, but not in developed countries where the investors tend to invest worldwide, particularly in recent years).

REFERENCES

Abegglen, James C. *The Japanese Factory*. Glencoe, Ill.: Free Press, 1958.

Amsden, Alice H. *Asia's Next Giant*. Oxford: Oxford University Press, 1989.

Amsden, Alice H., and Wan-wen Chu. *Beyond Late Development*. Cambridge, Mass.: MIT Press, 2003.

Aoki, Masahiko. *Corporative Game Theory of the Firm*. Oxford: Oxford University Press, 1984.

Aoki, Masahiko, and Hugh Patrick, eds. *The Japanese Main Bank System*. Oxford: Oxford University Press, 1994.

Asanuma, Banri. "The Organization of Parts Purchases in the Japanese Automotive Industry." *Japanese Economic Studies* 13 (Summer 1985): 32–53.

Asanuma, Banri. "Manufacturer-Supplier Relationships in Japan and the Concept of Relation-Specific Skills." *Journal of the Japanese and International Economies* 3 (March 1989): 1–30.

Baumol, William J., John C. Panzar, and Robert D. Willig. *Contestable Markets and the Theory of Industry Structure*. New York: Harcourt Brace Jovanovich, 1982.

Berle, Adolf A. Jr., and Gardiner C. Means. *The Modern Corporation and Private Property*. New York: Macmillan, 1932.

Caves, Richard E., and Masu Uekusa. *Industrial Organization in Japan*. Washington, D.C.: Brookings Institution, 1976.

Chandler, Alfred D. Jr. *Strategy and Structure*. Cambridge, Mass.: MIT Press, 1962.

Chang, Sea-Jin. "Korean Business Groups: The Financial Crisis and the Restructuring of Chaebols." In *Business Groups in East Asia*, ed. Sea-Jin Chang, 52–69. Oxford: Oxford University Press, 2006.

Claessens, Stijn, Simeon Djankov, and Larry H. P. Lang. "The Separation of Ownership and Control in East Asian Corporation." *Journal of Financial Economics* 58 (2000): 81–112.

Claessens, Stijn, Joseph P. H. Fan, and Larry H. P. Lang. "The Benefits and Costs of Group Affiliation: Evidence from East Asia." *Emerging Markets Review* 7 (March 2006): 1–26.

Dyer, Jeffrey H., and Wujin Chu, "The Role of Trustworthiness in Reducing Transaction Costs and Improving Performance: Empirical Evidence from the United States, Japan, and Korea." *Organization Science* 14 (Jan.–Feb. 2003): 57–68.

Dyer, Jeffrey H., and Kentaro Nobeoka. "Creating and Managing a High-Performance Knowledge-Sharing Network: The Toyota Case." *Strategic Management Journal* 21 (March 2000): 345–367.

Flath, David. *The Japanese Economy*. Oxford: Oxford University Press, 2000.

Fransman, Martin. *The Market and Beyond*. Cambridge: Cambridge University Press, 1990.

Granovetter, Mark. "Economic Action and Social Structure: The Problem of Embeddedness." *American Journal of Sociology* 91 (Nov. 1985): 481–510.

Granovetter, Mark. "Business Groups and Social Organization." in *The Handbook of Economic Sociology*, 2nd ed., ed. Neil J. Smelser and Richard Swedberg, 429–450. Princeton, N.J.: Princeton University Press, 2005.

Hanazaki, Masaharu, and Akiyoshi Horiuchi. "Is Japan's Financial System Efficient?" *Oxford Review of Economic Policy* 16 (Summer 2000): 61–73.

Hirschman, Albert O. *Exit, Voice, and Loyalty*. Cambridge, Mass.: Harvard University Press, 1970.

Hirschman, Albert O. "Exit and Voice." In *The New Palgrave: A Dictionary of Economics* ii, ed. John Eatwell, Murray Milgate, and Peter K. Newman, 219–224. London: Macmillan, 1987.

Hoshi, Takeo, Anil Kashyap, and David Scharfstein. "Corporate Structure, Liquidity, and Investment: Evidence from Japanese Industrial Groups." *Quarterly Journal of Economics* 106 (Feb. 1991): 33–60.

Japan Fair Trade Commission. "Waga Kuni Kigyo no Keizokuteki Torihiki no Jittai ni Tsuite" [On the Continuous Trading of Japanese Firms]. Unpublished report, 1987.

Johnson, Chalmers. *MITI and the Japanese Miracle*. Stanford, Calif.: Stanford University Press, 1982.

Khanna, Tarun, and Yishay Yafeh. "Business Groups in Emerging Markets: Paragons or Parasites?" *Journal of Economic Literature* 45 (June 2007): 331–372.

Ko, Yong Soo. *Kankoku no Kigyo Kinyu Kaikaku* [Corporate and Financial Reform of Korea]. Tokyo: Tokyo Keizai, 2009.

Komiya, Ryutaro, Masahiro Okuno, and Kotaro Suzumura, eds. *Industrial Policy of Japan*. New York: Academic Press, 1988.

Kreps, David M. "Corporate Culture and Economic Theory." In *Perspectives on Positive Political Economy*, ed. James E. Alt and Kenneth A. Shepsle, 90–143. Cambridge: Cambridge University Press, 1990.

La Porta, Rafael, Florencio Lopez-de-Silanes, and Andrei Shleifer. "Corporate Ownership around the World." *Journal of Finance* 54 (April 1999): 471–517.

Lee, Chung H., Keun Lee, and Kangkook Lee. "Chaebols, Financial Liberalization and Economic Crisis: Transformation of Quasi-Internal Organization in Korea." *Asian Economic Journal* 16 (March 2002): 17–35.

Lincoln, James R., and Michael L. Gerlach. *Japan's Network Economy*. Cambridge: Cambridge University Press, 2004.

Marris, Robin L. *The Economic Theory of "Managerial" Capitalism*. London: Macmillan, 1964.

Marris, Robin L. *Managerial Capitalism in Retrospect*. Houndmills: Macmillan, 1998.

Morck, Randall, Daniel Wolfenzon, and Bernard Yeung, "Corporate Governance, Economic Entrenchment and Growth." *Journal of Economic Literature* 43 (Sept. 2005): 655–720.

Negishi, Takashi. "Protection of the Infant Industry and Dynamic Internal Economics." *Economic Record* 44 (March 1968): 56–67.
Nelson, Richard R., and Sidney G. Winter. *An Evolutionary Theory of Economic Change*. Cambridge, Mass.: Harvard University Press, 1982.
Nishiguchi, Toshiaki. *Strategic Industrial Sourcing*. Oxford: Oxford University Press, 1994.
Odagiri, Hiroyuki. *The Theory of Growth in a Corporate Economy*. Cambridge: Cambridge University Press, 1981.
Odagiri, Hiroyuki. "Internal Promotion, Intrafirm Wage Structure, and Corporate Growth." *Economic Studies Quarterly* 33 (1982): 193–210.
Odagiri, Hiroyuki. *Growth through Competition, Competition through Growth*. Oxford: Oxford University Press, 1992.
Odagiri, Hiroyuki, and Akira Goto. *Technology and Industrial Development in Japan*. Oxford: Oxford University Press, 1996.
Odagiri, Hiroyuki, Akira Goto, Atsushi Sunami, and Richard R. Nelson, eds. *Intellectual Property Rights, Development, and Catch-Up*. Oxford: Oxford University Press, 2010.
Okuno-Fujiwara, Masahiro, and Tetsuji Okazaki. *The Japanese Economic System and its Historical Origins*. Translated by Susan Herbert. Oxford: Oxford University Press, 1999.
Oliver, Nick, and Barry Wilkinson. *The Japanization of British Industry*. Oxford: Basil Blackwell, 1988.
Richardson, G. B. "The Organisation of Industry." *Economic Journal* 82 (Sept. 1972): 883–896.
Saito, Takuji, and Hiroyuki Odagiri. "Intraboard Heterogeneity and the Role of Bank-Dispatched Directors in Japanese Firms: An Empirical Study." *Pacific Basin Financial Journal* 16 (Nov. 2008): 572–590.
Sako, Mari. "The Role of 'Trust' in Japanese Buyer-Supplier Relationships." *Ricerche Economiche* 45 (1991): 449–474.
Sako, Mari. *Prices, Quality and Trust*. Cambridge: Cambridge University Press, 1992.
Sheard, Paul. "Main Banks and the Governance of Financial Distress." In *The Japanese Main Bank System*, ed. Masahiko Aoki and Patrick Hugh, 188–230. Oxford: Oxford University Press, 1994.
Simon, Herbert A. "A Formal Theory of the Employment Relationship." *Econometrica* 19 (July 1951): 293–305.
Teranishi, Juro. "Loan Syndication in War-Time Japan and the Origins of the Main Bank System." In *The Japanese Main Bank System*, ed. Masahiko Aoki and Patrick Hugh, 51–88. Oxford: Oxford University Press, 1994.
Wade, Robert. *Governing the Market*. Princeton, N.J.: Princeton University Press, 1990.
Weinstein, David E., and Yishay Yafeh. "On the Costs of a Bank-Centered Financial System: Evidence from the Changing Main Bank Relations in Japan." *Journal of Finance* 53 (April 1998): 635–672.
Williamson, Oliver E. *Markets and Hierarchies*. New York: Free Press, 1975.
World Bank. *The East Asian Miracle*. Oxford: Oxford University Press, 1993.
World Bank. *Innovative East Asia*. Oxford: Oxford University Press, 2003.
Yamagishi, Toshio, and Midori Yamagishi. "Trust and Commitment in the United States and Japan." *Motivation and Emotion* 18 (June 1994), 129–166.
Yamagishi, Toshio, Karen S. Cook, and Motoki Watabe. "Uncertainty, Trust, and Commitment Formation in the United States and Japan." *American Journal of Sociology* 104 (July 1998): 165–194.

PART VI

WHITHER CAPITALISM?

CHAPTER 18

REFOUNDING CAPITALISM

EDMUND S. PHELPS

The response to the financial crisis of 1929 and the ensuing slump was the enactment of rather broad regulatory legislation. In the United States, laws were passed to reduce the vulnerability of investors, lenders, banks, companies, and workers to unanticipated swings in financial markets. The response to the recent crisis and slump—by some governments at any rate—has been intervention of a different sort. In Europe and the United States too, new legislation has been directed more at social cohesion than at structural reform. Bills before the U.S. Congress, for example, would supplement the ailing capitalist system with new programs for health care, climate control, and energy conservation rather than rebuild the system.

Yet the malfunctions of the system—the bizarre speculative excesses in the housing market, the heedless risks taken in the financial sector, the preference to "insure" against default risks rather than evaluate them, the bankers' turn away from financing business investment, and the fixation of CEOs on meeting quarterly earnings targets rather than making long-term investments—reveal a perverse financial sector and a dysfunctional business sector, which are not well treated by new welfarist initiatives and new national causes, however worthy they may be. In the felicitous term of French President Nicolas Sarkozy, the need is to "refound" *capitalist systems* in ways that will make them function well again. Nowhere is this need more acute than in the United States, where the perversion and deterioration of capitalist mechanisms appear to have left the economy with less dynamism as well as less business activity. The need is profound in Europe, where capitalist mechanisms have long been hamstrung by Italian corporatism, French statism, German socialism, Scandinavian welfarism, and the rest.

Over the past decade, I have maintained that countries would still benefit from the innovative activity of original thinkers, visionary entrepreneurs, canny investors, pioneering managers, and devoted employees that—starting in the nineteenth century and in some countries ending in the twentieth—drew an ever-widening share of people in an ever-growing number of nations into engaging jobs, exciting explorations, and remarkable commercial advances. I try to explain, leaving for the last section the issues of instability and their resolution.

What Is Capitalism?

Any concept of a capitalist economy must include private wealth owning. Yet that private wealth must extend to ownership of all or most of the economy's business capital—not merely cars, homes, and debts of the state and state enterprises, as under market socialism. It is also necessary that private owners of businesses be accorded control over where to invest—not just along the narrow lines assented to by managers, guilds, or unions, as in corporatism, or as dictated by the state or oligarchs. To this day there survives an image of capitalism as a game in which each generation's players make their moves in hopes of riches and then leave the field to take stock of the wealth they won or lost. But these wealth-centered features are insufficient to capture the character of capitalism in the modern age, particularly the importance of the experience of participating in it.

Modern economies—of which several well-functioning capitalist economies are thus far the sole historical specimens—started to sprout up only in the nineteenth century. With the development of company law, corporate finance, investment banking, and patent law, the way was opened for a process of innovation: the conception of novel commercial ideas, the selection by financiers of some of these ideas for development, the realization by entrepreneurs of the envisioned products or methods, and the adoption or rejection by managers or consumers of some of the new products reaching the market. The propensity of such a system to innovate depends very much on a multiplicity of idea-men, entrepreneurs, financiers, marketers, and end users—consumers and managers. It helps to have diversity in their business backgrounds, education, strategic vision, and talents. It is not surprising, therefore, that significant indigenous innovation, since it began early in the nineteenth century, has been driven mainly by the private sector; private ownership has been typical, whether or not required in every case. Laissez-faire—a free market of low taxes, tariffs, and regulation—is not required; so much freedom would badly undermine capitalism's functioning. In the recent episode, we have seen again that capitalist systems require well-chosen regulations.

Note that a new commercial idea in a country may be an application of an invention or discovery made by scientists outside the economy or an innovation made by a business in another economy. That was Josef Schumpeter's early view of how commercial ideas came to a country.[1] Or the new idea might come from within the nation's economy: an original idea inspired by the observations and imagination of producers, employees, managers, or consumers—people "on the spot." This was the view of Friedrich Hayek[2] and most experts today.[3] If innovation were mere Schumpeterian application or imitation, a socialist system could approximate the results of a capitalist system.[4]

What Is the Distinctive Merit of a Well-Functioning Capitalism?

For many, capitalism's main merits are the wealth accumulation it fosters and the "individual freedom" it helps protect. Referring to capitalism in his Inaugural Address, President Barack Obama said that "its power to generate wealth and expand freedom is unmatched" (Obama 2009). For me, that does not capture the value of a well-functioning capitalism. In fact, it largely misses the value.

Regarding wealth, it may be that the challenge of making money, perhaps getting rich, in one's young or middle years is absorbing and fun: as Friedrich Nietzsche and Frank Knight suggested, trying to make a fortune is like participating in a sport. Yet social observers are right to question whether people find significant satisfaction from increased relative wealth beyond a certain point.[5] After you have won the game, what point is there in winning by a bigger point spread? Many entrepreneurs speak of the wealth received as a by-product of what they sought to do or achieve, rather than as the goal. In any case, an increase in some people's relative wealth means a decrease in some others' relative wealth. There is no reason for the government of a society to promote that sort of sport. The value of nationwide advances in wealth may be on more solid ground. It is better to have more wealth in a city or nation where most others have more wealth, too: possibilities of a richer and more rewarding life result.

The fault in this view is that the relatively capitalist countries are not distinguished by their high levels of wealth. The somewhat more socialist economies and more corporatist economies of Western Europe reach wealth levels exceeding the levels in the capitalist economies. The reasons are familiar. One of the major drivers of wealth, the propensity to save, is higher in Luxembourg, Switzerland, Belgium, France, and Germany than in the United States, the United Kingdom, and Canada—despite the security offered by Continental welfare systems.

The other driver of private wealth, namely, the level of productivity, is also equal if not greater in the former group of countries than in the latter group. A proposed explanation is that although the capitalist exemplars may be at or close to the "technical frontier," thanks to their "lead" in cutting-edge innovation, they "waste" much of their output potential in false steps, in the costly processes of marketing, and in overinvestment caused by the winner-take-all competition of costly

R&D projects.[6] Furthermore, the top-down techno-nationalist projects that some relatively corporatist nations have substituted for discoveries bubbling up naturally from the business sector may do well on that score thanks to the resources saved by avoiding "wasteful competition" for new products involving parallel development work and marketing efforts. One has to conclude that "generation of wealth" is not special to capitalism. Corporatist economies are quite good at that.

As for freedom, some have argued that a capitalist economy—far more than a socialist or a corporatist one—helps buttress people's political freedoms and some of their personal freedoms against the tyrannies of the state, communities, and the culture. Owners of a firm in a capitalist economy would feel it in their pocketbook if employees were hired or fired on the basis of their beliefs rather than the firm's profits.[7] Yet the evidence is mixed: some of the relatively socialist and corporatist economies of Western Europe appear to be pretty tolerant of deviance from the mainstream.

A merit of a well-functioning capitalism (again, I do not mean free-market policy: low tax rates, etc.) is the economic freedoms it offers entrepreneurs, managers, employees, and consumers—freedoms that socialist, corporatist, and statist systems do not provide. It is worth noting that some "personal" freedoms are also economic. If you have a deep need, say, to be a dancer or to restore mid-1930s films, capitalism is likely to be the system for you. I came away with the impression that Milton Friedman valued these economic freedoms (and other freedoms) for their own sake, though other readers may interpret him differently.

Friedman's work, however, does clearly value the "freedom to choose" as a means to income.[8] He suggests that incomes will be higher when participants are free to move over a wide range of regions, occupations, and industries and when individuals and enterprises are free to collect micro-data on which to make decisions. But as noted earlier, the thesis that well-functioning capitalist economies are better at producing income and wealth than more corporatist systems (and socialist ones) is in doubt: the best corporatist economies tend to exhibit comparable productivity. In a different vein, Amartya Sen has been emphasizing the value of economic systems that provide participants with an expansion of their "capabilities."[9]

The work of Hayek from his *Road to Serfdom* onward is suggestive of another kind of value in some economic freedoms.[10] In any real-life economy (not theoretical models in which everything in the present and the future is known), actors may sense or conjecture opportunities or dangers about which there is little or no public knowledge while the individual has significant *private knowledge* about possible benefits or costs as well as *imagination* and *personal experience*. Individuals' freedom *to act* (or not act) on their unique knowledge, intuition, and judgment may be indispensable to their sense of self-worth and self-reliance. Furthermore, people's exercise of their creativity, such as conceiving an innovative activity that is developed by an entrepreneur, may well be essential for their sense of autonomy and self-expression. Similarly people actively choosing a course that appears to them to be most rewarding, such as taking on a project that presents the challenges for which they are best suited, may be equally essential for their sense of autonomy and self-expression.

In this view, it would be *inadequate* to gauge the value of freedom by its contribution to income, consumption, investment, and even to the pragmatists' "expansion of talents" and "capabilities." The freedom to act on this basis—to take charge of one's own heading, to make one's own mistakes and grow stronger in the process—is a primary good in itself, one of huge importance. Is there evidence of greater economic freedoms in capitalist economies than in the more socialist or corporatist economies?[11] My research using survey data supports the widespread impression that in the relatively capitalist economies, people in ordinary jobs have freedoms that they value—more so than workers in the relatively socialist or corporatist economies. In the former economies more than in the latter, workers say they want jobs offering chances to take initiative and responsibility (which reveals that they know that such jobs are available), while acknowledging also the value of teamwork—thus the need both to give and take orders (Phelps 2006). Relatedly, earning one's way in the impersonal world of business—supporting oneself—is, for most people, necessary for what John Rawls (1971) called self-respect.

I would make a further point in the same context and in a somewhat similar vein that Hayek left unsaid. As a long line of Western humanists and philosophers from Bergson, James, and Nietzsche back to Cervantes and Cellini have propounded, in a world in which we know little about the effects of what is untried, one's freedom to experiment, explore, act on impulse, and test ideas offer another category of benefits: "self-actualization" and "self-discovery." In my recent papers, I have been arguing that most people (if not all) find such satisfactions from taking part in the innovation process of a capitalist economy: from examining untried ways of producing something, conceiving and developing an innovative product or method, and pioneering the adoption of a new product or method.[12]

From the latter perspective, the dynamism of a well-functioning capitalism has a fundamental merit. Ordinary people, if they are to find intellectual growth and an engaging life, have to look outside the home: these things can be found only at work, if anywhere. For these rewards to be available for large numbers of people, the economy must be modern. As a practical matter, that requires that it be based predominantly on a well-functioning capitalist system. Thanks to the grassroots, bottom-up processes of innovation, capitalism at its best can deliver—far more broadly than Soviet communism, Eastern European socialism, and Western European corporatism can—chances for the mental stimulation, problem solving, exploration, and discovery required for a life of engagement and personal growth.[13]

Can Dynamism Justify Capitalism?

Could it be that the value of a well-functioning capitalism in providing participants with opportunities to act on their own knowledge, intuition, and judgment, and in providing opportunities to be engaged and to flourish serves to justify that capitalism?

It is clear how that might be argued: if a well-functioning capitalist system offers a broad swath of society chances for a life of initiative and discovery, while the other systems deprive people of that experience, then imposing the latter systems on society would be terribly unjust. The answer would appear to be yes. I argue as follows.

Dynamic innovation transforms the workplace (in the firms developing an innovation and also in the firms competing against them). The challenges that arise in developing a new idea and in its acceptance in the marketplace provide the workforce with high levels of mental stimulation, problem solving, and thus employee engagement and personal growth. An individual working alone cannot easily create the continual arrival of new challenges; it "takes a village," or even a whole society.

The notion that people need problem solving and intellectual development is an old one. Aristotle wrote of the "development of talents"; in the Renaissance, Cellini celebrated his achievements and Cervantes admired vitality and challenge. In 1892, Alfred Marshall observed that the job is in the worker's thoughts for most of the day. Gunnar Myrdal wrote in 1932 that the time would soon come when people would be more satisfied by working than by consuming. This view, sometimes called vitalism, became strongly associated with the pragmatist school of philosophy, perhaps most famously with Abraham Maslow's concept of "self-actualization."

All of these writers were pointing out the importance of a person's emerging sense of mastery and the experience of adventure. The American application of this Western ethic—Aristotle plus Cervantes—is the thesis that self-realization and self-discovery can come from the involvement and challenge offered by the business sphere of a modern economy. Americans cannot go tilting at windmills, but they can take on the ever-fresh challenges of a business career. For most people, there is nowhere else from which such challenges can arise.

I should also mention a "derived" benefit of the capitalist model that flows from the effects of dynamism on productivity. A more innovative economy tends to devote more resources to investments of all kinds—to investing in new employees and new customers as well as new office and factory space. Although this may come about through a shift of resources from the consumer goods sector, it also comes from the recruitment of new participants into the labor force. Employees who are thus engaged—employees who do not need to work for pressing financial reasons, but are drawn to work for its intrinsic satisfactions—are less likely to quit, reducing the "natural" unemployment rate. Thus, dynamism tends to bring a pervasive prosperity to an economy in addition to higher levels of productivity caused by product innovation—as well as higher levels of self-realization. Of course, even the healthiest economy may suffer slumps.

A plausible objection is that even a well-functioning capitalist system would not be just if it failed to strive for the largest possible *inclusion* of the productive population in that system. We can accept that such a system is not fully just, thus unjust. I certainly agree. But that does not imply that dynamism is not and cannot be just until a just level of inclusion is sought and achieved. Moreover, it is not capitalism that stands in the way of inclusion; it is the failure to legislate wage subsidies and inadequate desegregation of neighborhoods and schools.

Taking Instability and Crisis into Account

When President Sarkozy spoke of a "refounding" of capitalism, I wondered whether he had in mind what might be termed a capitalist reformation analogous to the Protestant Reformation of the 1500s. There is the appearance of a parallel between the Church's creation in medieval times of lucrative indulgences, which national governments did nothing to stop, and the banking industry's sale in recent years of overvalued packages of mortgages, called collateralized debt obligations (CDOs), which governments did nothing to stop. But the banks held such CDOs on their own account, in addition to selling them to naive buyers. The moral shortcoming in the banks, it appears, was that the leaders did not have the moral strength to protest the rise of leverage and the deterioration in the quality of the securitized assets to which they gave their seal of approval. With varying discomfort, the CEOs seem to have felt too weak to try to call a halt to further expansion of credit—to "get off the merry-go-round," in the famous words of Charles Prince, former CEO of Citigroup.

I feel that in combating this aspect of the financial sector's problem, the first line of defense ought to be laws and regulations. Altruism is a valuable resource, but we do not want to risk wreaking havoc by appealing to it in a comprehensive way at all levels of life. There must be social responsibility at critical points, but we cannot afford to overuse this resource lest we find ourselves with too little of it left when we need it most.

How does the element of instability in capitalist systems affect the argument for continuing with capitalism? One's first reaction, especially if one has high appreciation for capitalism, might be to say that the big swings to which capitalist systems are inherently prone should not stay society's hand in creating and maintaining a system that is so essential to engaging work and personal growth. The instability experienced diminishes our satisfaction as participants in the economy, but it does *not* diminish our thirst for the good life.

On reflection, there are valid points in favor of regulation aimed at reducing vulnerability to severe fluctuation. First of all, the good life is not a binary variable: you have it or you don't. A capitalist system dogged by frequent crises and fears of crisis may levy a toll not only on people's comforts and sense of security but also on the generation of innovation itself. So there may be a gain in the degree of dynamism to be obtained by fortifying the financial system against speculative crises. The second point I would make involves another dimension: no human system can be expected to innovate at all times, just as no composer would be expected to constantly be in the heat of creation. It is possible, then, that a financial system that is more robust in the face of speculative movements will exhibit dynamism a greater proportion of the time. So, in principle, creating a financial sector that is less vulnerable to speculative shifts might not be harmful to dynamism.

It is worth noting that unemployment is viewed with far more anxiety and far more fear by politicians in the United States than it is in Continental Europe—no matter that there is unemployment compensation in the United States as well as Europe. The reason may be partly that in an economy with as much dynamism as ours, there really is no "compensation" for unemployment. Employment has become a good in itself. The paradox is that the greater the dynamism of an economy, the more anxiety there is over the prospect of unemployment. If so, another paradox is that many Americans call for an end to dynamism in the interest of job security—as if their own job would remain as engaging and rewarding as ever. But this enters the realm of speculation.

Indeed, most economists discussing the need for financial reform appear to believe that better alignment of "incentives" and serious regulatory restraints on ruinous competition for profits, though aimed at "economic efficiency" and perhaps increased returns to shareowners, will cost the economy nothing in innovation and employment. But this sort of theorizing, though well intentioned and even useful in exposing the perils of excessive gearing of pay to crude measures of performance, is itself dangerous in leaving the impression that after reforming bonuses, asset markets will no longer be susceptible to huge asset price swings that are driven only by "speculative excesses" (to use Spiethoff's convenient shorthand).

Unambiguously Good Reforms

Are there reforms that address speculative swings while causing little or no damage to economic dynamism and inclusion? There are ways of fortifying the financial sector against the speculative fever of investors and entrepreneurs in the business sector without obstructing the speculative investment waves that are emblematic of a healthy capitalism. One suggestion, which comes from my colleague Richard Robb, calls for a small tax on the short-term indebtedeness of financial companies such as banks. So much of the banks' problems arose from excessive short-term borrowing of little or no social utility. Let us tax that to force banks to finance their lending with long-term borrowing instead. There are also ways of tempering the speculative swings themselves without suppressing the spirit of capitalism. A suggestion from my longtime collaborator Roman Frydman calls for the introduction of a band around the index of housing prices, a band around the main index of stock market prices, and so forth. When the index rises or falls outside the band, the government will increase margin requirements, short-selling requirements, and various other costs so as to dampen—but not outlaw—speculation on a further move of the asset price index.

Are there reforms that would address the decline in the past decade of economic dynamism while causing little or no increase in instability? I have been moving toward a proposal to establish new banks of a new kind. It is not uncommon to see financial entities in a country that are dedicated to residential construction, agriculture, or exports, and so forth. This is curious and disturbing because little or no economic dynamism comes from our stock of housing as against, say, our stores of clothing and from producing for export rather than home use. There is no awareness among the general public and its legislatures that most of the economic dynamism inherent in the structure of a country's economy comes from the innovative inclinations of the ordinary people making their careers in the business sector! To right the balance, I suggest that every country's government establish a corps of banks that are dedicated to lending to or investing in companies in the business sector, particularly for investment projects of an innovative character. This is not really "new." I like to remind audiences that Germany, with its famous Deutsche Bank, had just such a financial institution serving its business sector during its brilliant economic development in the 1890s, when the bank backed the new electrical engineering industries.

Are there reforms that would address the still insufficient levels of economic inclusion without stifling dynamism? Here I recall the sort of program that has been adopted to a degree in France, the Netherlands, and most recently Singapore: subsidies to companies for their ongoing employment of low-wage workers. (Mention might be made also of Italy's *Cassa integrazione* and Germany's *Kurzarbeit.*) Notwithstanding these breakthroughs, the United States as yet still has no program of general subsidies for low-wage employment. And the outlays of this kind in Europe are still under 2 percent of the GDP.

Yet there is the looming threat that the public, in its understandable desire to keep fluctuations within tighter limits, will push regulations affecting incentives and competition to a point where a trade-off begins: where further regulatory tightening weakens or narrows some of the sources of dynamism. Europeans, in vilifying all hedge funds, all private equity, and all short selling, are making it more difficult to increase dynamism in their economies—while failing to get at the real sources of excessive swings. We must hope that the Europeans will come to see that they are aiming their wrath at the wrong targets.

This chapter is a revised version of a presentation at the symposium "New World, New Capitalism," cochaired by French President Nicolas Sarkozy and former U.K. Prime Minister Tony Blair, Paris, January 8–9, 2009. The presentation was in a way directed to them.

Notes

1. See Schumpeter (1912). His main thesis was that developing a new idea into a new product at an economical price required the skills of a savvy entrepreneur.
2. The earliest example is Hayek (1935). See also Hayek (1978).
3. It is the view of Alfred Chandler, Peter Drucker, Richard Nelson, Sidney Winter, Giovanni Dosi, Roman Frydman and Andrzej Rapaczynski, Virginia Postrel, Amar Bhide, and my view, too.
4. In the United States, the greater part of medical progress comes from practice, not from science. See Nelson (2008).
5. I am thinking of attitude surveys and commentaries by Bruno Frey, Richard Layard, and Andrew Oswald, to name just those that immediately come to mind.

6. Historically, some corporatist economies have sought to substitute a top-down "scientism" for the discoveries bubbling up naturally from the business sector. Of course, the techno-nationalist projects undertaken in corporatist economies may produce some productivity gains. Yet the selection among these projects and the development decisions along the way are not immune to missteps. Techno-nationalism is prone to flaws of its own, such as a tendency to the grandiose and overengineering. So it is doubtful that industrial research policy can be credited for the good productivity levels exhibited in some corporatist economies.
7. See, for example, Wallich (1960). Somewhere, Wallich is quoted as writing that "power is the great enemy of freedom."
8. Friedman (1962) and Friedman and Friedman (1980).
9. Sen (1992, 1999). The critique of both communism and capitalism by John Dewey was that neither system was good at allowing workers to develop their talents. The classic work is *Experience and Education* (1938).
10. See Hayek (1944). See also the commentary in Sen (2004).
11. Jeffrey D. Sachs says no in his "Response to Easterly on Hayek," (2006). He notes that the Heritage Foundation/Wall Street Journal Index of Economic Freedom ranks Finland, Sweden, and Denmark as "free economies," with Denmark ranked ahead of the United States—and this in spite of their high rates of taxation, which counts heavily in the Heritage index. This is undeniably interesting, because those three countries are widely regarded as pretty corporatist as well as somewhat socialist. However, the Heritage indicators of "freedom" largely differ from the individual freedoms in the workplace, financial markets, and product markets that I am clearly referring to.
12. See Phelps (2007), and papers of mine going back at least to 2003.
13. My argument can be sampled in my paper for a 2003 Baumol conference and my June 2006 speech at Sciences Po as well as the Venice paper (2006) and Nobel Prize Lecture already cited.

References

Dewey, John. *Experience and Education*. New York: Simon and Schuster, 1938.

Friedman, Milton. *Capitalism and Freedom*. Chicago: University of Chicago Press, 1962.

Friedman, Milton, and Rose Friedman. *Free to Choose*. New York: Harcourt, 1980.

Hayek, Friedrich von. *Collectivist Economic Planning*. London: Routledge, 1935.

Hayek, Friedrich von. *The Road to Serfdom*. London: Routledge, 1944.

Hayek, Friedrich von. "Competition as a Discovery Procedure." In *New Studies in Philosophy, Politics, Economics, and the History of Ideas*, ed. Friedrich Hayek, 179–190. Chicago: University of Chicago Press, 1978.

Nelson, Richard R. "How Medical Know-How Progresses." Working Paper no. 23, Center on Capitalism and Society, 2008.

Obama, Barack. Inaugural Address. January 20, 2009. http://www.nytimes.com/2009/01/20/us/politics/20text-obama.html.

Phelps, Edmund. "Capitalism vs. Corporatism." Critical Review (January 11, 2010). Lecture given at the June 2006 Celebration of Honorary Doctorates, Sciences Po, Paris.

Phelps, Edmund S. "Economic Culture and Economic Performance: What Light Is Shed on the Continent's Problem?" 3rd Annual Conference of the Center on Capitalism and Society, Venice, July 2006.

Phelps, Edmund. "The Economic Performance of Nations: Prosperity Depends on Dynamism, Dynamism on Institutions." Conference on Entrepreneurship, Innovation and the Growth Mechanism of the Free-Market Economies. In *Entrepreneurship, Innovation, and the Growth Mechanism of Free Enterprise Economies*, ed. Eytan Sheshinski, Robert J. Strom, and William J. Baumol, 342–356. Princeton, N.J.: Princeton University Press, 2007.

Phelps, Edmund S. Nobel Prize Lecture, "Macroeconomics for a Modern Economy." Stockholm, Nobel Foundation, 2007.

Rawls, John. *A Theory of Justice*. Cambridge, Mass.: Harvard University Press, 1971.

Sachs, Jeffrey D. "Response to Easterly on Hayek." *Greg Mankiw's Blog*, November 27, 2006. http://gregmankiw.blogspot.com/2006/11/sachs-on-hayek-and-easterly.

Schumpeter, Joseph. *Theorie der wirtschaftlichen Entwicklung*. Leipzig: Duncker & Humblot, 1912.

Sen, Amartya. *Inequality Reexamined*. New York: Norton, 1992.

Sen, Amartya. *Commodities and Capabilities*. New York: Oxford University Press, 1999.

Sen, Amartya. "An Insight into the Purpose of Prosperity." *Financial Times*, September 20, 2004.

Wallich, Henry C. *The Cost of Freedom*. New York: Harper, 1960.

Name Index

Subject Index